THE BANKRUPTCY ISSUES HANDBOOK

HARVEY J. WILLIAMSON, Esq.

ARGYLE PUBLISHING COMPANY
Glenwood Springs, Colorado
(www.argylepub.com)

Other law books published by Argyle Publishing Company:

The Attorney's Handbook on Consumer Bankruptcy and Chapter 13

The Wills, Trusts, and Estate Planning Handbook

The Attorney's Handbook on Small Business Reorganization Under Chapter 11

Handbook on The Law of Small Business Enterprises

Sixth Edition, 2013

ISBN 13: 978-1-880730-61-4

ISBN 10: 1-880730-61-8

Published and Distributed by

ARGYLE PUBLISHING COMPANY, INC.

P.O. Box 925
Glenwood Springs, Colorado 81602
(Telephone: 1-800-955-4569)
(Email: info@argylepub.com)
(Website: www.argylepub.com)

Printed in the United States of America

CONTENTS

CHAPTER TWO

CHAPTER 7 BANKRUPTCY ISSUES

CHAPTER THREE

CHAPTER 13 BANKRUPTCY ISSUES

INTRODUCTION

The **Bankruptcy Issues Handbook** is designed to assist attorneys and other legal professionals in analyzing and dealing with important issues in Chapter 7 consumer bankruptcy cases and Chapter 13 cases. This handbook is intended to complement the Attorney's Handbook on Consumer Bankruptcy and Chapter 13, which has been in publication since 1977. This handbook provides in-depth coverage and analysis for many of the issues discussed in the Attorney's Handbook on Consumer Bankruptcy and Chapter 13.

This handbook contains 24 articles, each dealing with a distinct Chapter 7 or Chapter 13 issue. Each article consists of an in-depth analysis and discussion of a particular bankruptcy issue and is followed by a bibliography containing citations to other articles and annotations on the issues dealt with in the article.

Chapter One of this handbook contains 18 articles dealing with general bankruptcy issues. The articles in this chapter deal with bankruptcy issues that may arise in either Chapter 7 cases or Chapter 13 cases. Most of the issues discussed in this chapter, however, arise more often in Chapter 7 cases than in Chapter 13 cases. Many of these articles, for example, deal with the dischargeability of debts, an issue which, while relevant in Chapter 13 cases, is normally of more importance in Chapter 7 cases. Chapter Two contains three articles dealing with issues that are exclusively Chapter 7 in scope. Chapter Three contains three articles dealing with issues that arise in Chapter 13 cases.

The author has attempted to support each significant legal proposition with a citation of authority, either case law or statutory. However, readers are cautioned to check each case for restrictions and nuances. Some opinions discussed in this annotation may be restricted by court rule as to publication and citation in briefs. A number of jurisdictions may have rules, regulations, constitutional provisions, or legislative enactments directly bearing upon this subject. These provisions are discussed herein only to the extent and in the form that they are reflected in the court opinions that fall within the scope of this annotation. The reader is consequently advised to consult the appropriate statutory or regulatory compilations to ascertain the current status of all statutes discussed herein.

The order in which the articles appear in any chapter of this handbook is not significant. In using this handbook, the reader may either look for the desired subject in the table of contents or use the subject index in the back of the book. The paragraph notes appearing on each page of text should quickly guide the reader to the relevant material.

In writing this handbook the author has attempted to address the issues that most often arise in Chapter 7 consumer bankruptcy cases and Chapter 13 cases. If the reader feels that one or more important issues have been omitted, the author would appreciate being advised so that these issues may be addressed in future editions of this handbook.

CHAPTER ONE

GENERAL BANKRUPTCY ISSUES

The articles in this chapter deal with issues that arise under the provisions of Chapters 1, 3 or 5 of the Bankruptcy Code and are therefore relevant to cases filed under any chapter of the Bankruptcy Code. Accordingly, the articles in this chapter are applicable to both Chapter 7 and Chapter 13 cases unless a provision to the contrary appears in a particular discussion.

1.01 Under what circumstances is a person precluded from filing a bankruptcy case because he or she has been a debtor in another bankruptcy case within the preceding 180 days?

Text of statute. Section 109(g) of the Bankruptcy Code (11 U.S.C. § 109(g)) provides as follows:

109. Who may be a debtor

(g) Notwithstanding any other provision of this section, no individual or family farmer may be a debtor under this title who has been a debtor in a case pending under this title at any time in the preceding 180 days if -

§109(g), text of

(1) the case was dismissed by the court for willful failure of the debtor to abide by orders of the court, or to appear before the court in proper prosecution of the case; or

(2) the debtor requested and obtained the voluntary dismissal of the case following the filing of a request for relief from the automatic stay provided by section 362 of this title.

Introduction. The purpose of Section 109(g) is to prevent debtors from abusing the bankruptcy process through repetitive bankruptcy filings. The intent of Congress in enacting Section 109(g) was to give creditors at least 180 days of relief from the automatic stay between bankruptcy filings. See Tooke v. Sunshing Trust Mortgage Trust No. 86-225.

§109(g), purpose of

§ 109(g), legislative history

Section 109(g) provides that an individual or family farmer is not eligible to file a bankruptcy case under any chapter of the Bankruptcy Code if he or she has been a debtor in another bankruptcy case within the preceding 180 days that was dismissed by the court either (1) for willful misconduct by the debtor or (2) upon the request of the debtor after the filing by a creditor of a request for relief from the automatic stay.

§109(g), essential provisions of

To be ineligible to file a bankruptcy case under Section 109(g), the following conditions must exist:

§109(g), conditions for ineligibilty under

(1) The person filing the case must be either an individual or a family farmer. Other entities are not precluded from filing by Section 109(g).

(2) The person filing the case must have been a debtor in a prior bankruptcy case (under any chapter of the Bankruptcy Code) that was dismissed within the last 180 days. Cases that were dismissed more than 180 days ago are not covered by Section 109(g) and do not render a person ineligible to file a subsequent bankruptcy case, regardless of how or for what reason they were dismissed.

(3) The debtor›s previous bankruptcy case must have been dismissed either because of willful misconduct by the debtor or voluntarily by the debtor after the filing of a motion for relief from the stay by a creditor. Dismissals for other reasons are not covered by Section 109(g) and do not prevent the filing of another bankruptcy case within the next 180 days.

§109(g), applicability, chapter 7 cases, chapter 13 cases

As indicated above, Section 109(g) applies to cases filed under any chapter of the Bankruptcy Code, both as to the case being filed and the prior case. For example, a person who has a Chapter 7 case dismissed for a covered reason is not eligible to file a case under any chapter of the Bankruptcy Code, including a Chapter 13 case or another Chapter 7 case, for 180 days after the dismissal of the Chapter 7 case. Similarly, a person who has a Chapter 13 case dismissed for a covered reason is not eligible to file a bankruptcy case under any chapter of the Bankruptcy Code, including a Chapter 7 case or another Chapter 13 case, for 180 days after the dismissal.

§109(g), duty of debtor›s attorney to inquire

An attorney representing a debtor who has recently had a bankruptcy case dismissed should inquire as to the cause and circumstances of the dismissal of the prior case because sanctions may be imposed against the attorney under Bankruptcy Rule 9011 if a case is filed in obvious or flagrant violation of Section 109(g). Attorneys have a duty to search the court's available electronic records. In In re Oliver, 323 B.R. 769 (Bankr. M. D. Ala. 2005) sanctions were imposed on an attorney under Bankruptcy Rule 9011 for filing a petition in violation of an injunction which was disclosed by readily-available online records. See also In re Deville, 280 B.R. 483 (B.A.P. 9th 2002) (fining lawyer $23,597 for vexatious, bad faith, serial filings). Also, the debtor may have been enjoined by the court in dismissed case from filing another bankruptcy case for a specified period. See page 8, infra, for further reading on the issue of the extent to which a debtor may be enjoined from filing another bankruptcy case in the future.

Ineligibility because of willful misconduct in prior case. Section 109(g)(1) provides that an individual or family farmer is not eligible to file a bankruptcy case if he or she has been a debtor in another bankruptcy case during the preceding 180 days if the other bankruptcy case was dismissed by the court for willful failure of the debtor to abide by orders of the court, or to appear before the court in proper prosecution of the case. Despite the appearance of a comma after the word court in Section 109(g)(1), the words "willful failure" apply to both failure to abide by orders of the court and failure to appear before the court. This means that to be covered by Section 109(g)(1), a failure by the debtor to appear before the court in the proper prosecution of the case must be willful. See In re Fulton, 52 B.R. 627 (Bankr. D. Utah, 1985); In re Allen, 79 B.R. 757 (WD TN, 1987). Therefore, willful misconduct by the debtor for purposes of Section 109(g)(1) may consist of either a willful failure by the debtor to abide by orders of the court or a willful failure by the debtor to appear before the court in the proper prosecution of the case.

willful misconduct under §109(g)(1), what constitutes

Willful misconduct for purposes of Section 109(g)(1) is intentional, knowing, and voluntary misconduct, as opposed to conduct that is accidental or beyond the debtor's control. A willful failure to do a required act requires intentionally disregard or plain indifference. See In re Campbell, 266 B.R. 709 (WD AR, 2001). Whether the debtor's actions in the prior case were willful within the meaning of Section 109(g)(1) is a factual issue to be resolved by the court in the subsequent case. See Tolbert v. Fink, 255 B.R. 214 (B.A.P. 8th Cir., 2000). In In re Wen Hua Xu, 386 B.R. 451 (Bankr. S. D. N.Y. 2008), willful failure to do a required act required a showing that the person's actions were deliberate and intentional, rather than accidental or beyond the debtor's control. See also In re McIver, 78 B.R. 439 (SC, 1987).

willful misconduct, what constitutes

In determining whether a debtor has willfully failed to abide by orders of the court for purposes of Section 109(g)(1), most courts consider the totality of the debtor's conduct in the prior bankruptcy case or cases and the effect of such conduct on creditors. In other words, most courts attempt to determine whether the debtor is abusing the bankruptcy process to the detriment of creditors.

failure to abide by orders of court, general rule

In In re Patel, 48 B.R. 418 (MD AL, 1985), the debtor had demonstrated a willful failure to abide by orders of the court by failing to make the required payments under a confirmed Chapter 13 plan where the debtor had also previously filed a Chapter 7 case followed by two Chapter 13 cases and that creditors had been forced to wait years for payment while the debtor's net worth had increased by over $40,000. See also In re Krattiger, 52 B.R. 383 (WD WI, 1985), (holding the debtor's failure to file a financial statement by a date set in a prior court order constituted a willful failure to abide by orders of the court for purposes of Section 109(g) in a Chapter 11 case where the debtor had perpetrated numerous other delays in attempts to stall). A failure by the debtor in the prior case to make the preconfirmation payments required by a local standing order was also a willful failure by the debtor to abide an order of the court for purposes of Section 109(g)(1). See In re Nix, 217 B.R. 237 (WD TN, 1998).

failure to abide by orders of court, what constitutes

failure to abide by orders of court, what constitutes

On the other hand, if it does not appear to the court that the debtor was attempting to delay proceedings in the previous case to the detriment of creditors, a failure by the debtor to obey an order of the court in the previous case is less likely to be found to have been willful. For example, in In re Hollis, 150 B.R. 145 (MD, 1993), the failure of a Chapter 13 debtor in the previous case to make a $300 deposit required by the local rules, which were implemented by an order of the bankruptcy court, did not constitute a willful failure by the debtor to abide by orders of the court where there was no evidence that the failure to make the deposit was willful or that the debtor was attempting to delay the proceeding to the detriment of creditors.

failure to abide by orders of court, what constitues

In In re Morris, 49 B.R. 123 (WD KY, 1985), the debtor's second Chapter 13 case should not be dismissed under Section 109(g)(1) where the debtor's first Chapter 13 case was dismissed on the grounds that the debtor failed to make the payments required under a confirmed plan. The court found that the dismissal of the first case did not result from the debtor's willful failure to abide by orders of the court because of the existence of factors that were beyond the debtor's control. The court stated that for the filing of a subsequent case to be barred by Section 109(g)(1), the dismissal of the prior case must result from a willful act, which the court defined as a deliberate, intentional, knowing and purposeful act without justification or excuse. The court further stated that factors beyond the control of the debtor, such as unemployment or illness, do not constitute the degree of willfulness required under Section 109(g)(1).

failure to abide by orders of court, what constitutes

In In re Dodge, 86 B.R. 535 (SD OH, 1988), the failure of the debtor in the previous Chapter 13 case to attend the meeting of creditors or make the required payments did not, standing alone, constitute a willful failure to abide by orders of the court for purposes of Section 109(g)(1). See also In re Glover, 53 B.R. 14 (OR, 1985); In re Howard, 134 B.R. 225 (ED KY, 1991); In re Quinones, 73 B.R. 333 (PR, 1987); In re Chmura, 63 B.R. 12 (NJ, 1986), (holding a dismissal under Section 109(g)(1) was improper where it was uncontroverted that the debtors' were unable to make the Chapter 13 payments in the previous case because of serious health and financial problems). See also, In re Zahniser, 58 B.R. 530 (CO, 1986), (holding the dismissal of a Chapter 11 case on the grounds that there was no reasonable probability of a successful rehabilitation of the debtor and that there would be a continuing diminution of the estate, without more, was not a dismissal for willful failure to abide by orders of the court for purposes of Section 109(g)(1)). See also In re Olson, 102 B.R. 147 (CD IL, 1989) (involving the dismissal of a prior Chapter 11 case).

failure to appear before court, what constitutes

What acts constitute a willful failure of the debtor to appear before the court in the proper prosecution of the case for purposes of Section 109(g)(1)? Again, the acts of a debtor are seldom considered in a vacuum. The entire conduct of the debtor during the previous case or cases is usually considered in determining whether the debtor willfully failed to appear before the court. For example, in In re Nelkovski, 46 B.R. 542 (ND IL, 1985), the mere failure to make payments under a Chapter 13 plan or to appear at the meeting of creditors or a court hearing in the previous case was insufficient to sustain a finding of willful failure to appear before, or abide by, orders of the court. Repeated failures in this regard, together with a failure to file plans in previous cases with no showing of changed circumstances in the present case constitutes the degree of willfulness warranting dismissal under Section 109(g)(1).

In In re Fulton, 52 B.R. 627 (UT, 1985), the court found that the term "appear before the court" in Section 109(g)(1) includes appearance at the meeting of creditors even though the court is precluded by statute from attending the meeting and that a failure by the debtor to attend such a meeting may constitute a violation of Section 109(g)(1). However, the court stated that a failure by the debtor to attend such a meeting does not automatically result in a dismissal under Section 109(g)(1) and found under the facts of that case that the dismissal was not for willful misconduct because the debtor had negligently written down the wrong date for the meeting and had failed to attend the meeting for that reason. Similarly, in In re Allen, 79 B.R. 757 (WD TN, 1987), the court held that the debtor's failure to appear at the meeting of creditors in the previous case did not constitute a willful failure to appear before the court because the failure to appear was caused by the debtor's hospitalization. In In re Lewis, 67 B.R. 274 (ED TN, 1986), the court found that the debtor's failure to appear at the meeting of creditors in his previous Chapter 13 case was not willful because his mail had been intercepted and he had not received notice of the meeting.

failure to appear before court, meeting creditors, cases

In In re Arena, 81 B.R. 851 (ED PA, 1988), the court found that the debtor's failure to attend the dismissal hearing in the prior case did not, without more, constitute a willful failure to appear before the court in proper prosecution of the case for purposes of Section 109(g)(1). Similarly, in In re Glover, 53 B.R. 14 (OR, 1985), the failure of the debtor in the previous Chapter 13 case to oppose the trustee's motion to dismiss did not constitute a willful failure to appear before the court in proper prosecution of the case for purposes of Section 109(g)(1). See also In re Gamble, 72 B.R. 75 (ID, 1987).

failure to appear before court, cases not finding

However, in In re Correa, 58 B.R. 88 (ND IL, 1986), the court found the debtor's failure in the previous case to attend three meetings of creditors, coupled with a failure to produce financial information and disclose foreclosure proceedings, was a willful failure by the debtor to appear before the court in proper prosecution of the case for purposes of Section 109(g)(1), where the debtor's excuse for not attending the meetings was the habitual use of cocaine. A debtor's unexplained failure to attend a Section 341 meeting of creditors may be found to constitute a willful failure to appear before the court in proper prosecution of the case for purposes of Section 109(g)(1). See Montgomery v. Ryan, 37 F.3d 413 (8th Cir., 1994); In re Glenn, 288 B.R. 516 (ED Tenn, 2002).

failure to appear before court, cases so finding

The court in In re Wen Hua Xu, 386 B.R. 451 (SD NY, 2008) found the debtor's conduct to be "willful" under Section 109(g)(1) where the debtor failed to attend multiple 11 U.S.C. § § 341 meetings, failed to disclose certain assets and personal business interests on his schedules and to the Chapter 7 trustee. The court ruled that the debtor's lack of any credible explanation for these actions was clearly indicative of a willful failure to abide by court orders.

failure to attend creditor meeting or schedule assets

voluntary dismissal after request for relief from stay, effect of

Ineligibility because of voluntary dismissal after request for relief from stay. Section 109(g)(2) provides that an individual or family farmer is ineligible to file a bankruptcy case if he or she has been a debtor in another bankruptcy during the preceding 180 days if the debtor requested and obtained the voluntary dismissal of the other bankruptcy case after the filing by a creditor of a request for relief from the automatic stay. An individual is not eligible to file a bankruptcy case if his or her (or their) prior bankruptcy case was dismissed within 180 days prior to the date of filing of the present case and was voluntarily dismissed by the debtor after the filing of a request for relief from the automatic stay. See, e.g., In re Tooke, 133 B.R. 661 (MD FL, 1991); In re Denson, 56 B.R. 543 (ND AL, 1986); and In re Vanfossen, 258 B.R. 814 (ND AL, 2001).

§109(g),(2), requirements of, when applicable

The purpose of Section 109(g)(2) is to address the situation in which a debtor files a bankruptcy case in order to stay an existing or pending foreclosure and then voluntarily dismisses the case after the foreclosing creditor seeks relief from the automatic stay and subsequently files another bankruptcy case before the creditor completes its foreclosure and thereby continually frustrates the creditor's foreclosure attempts. See In re Patton, 49 B.R. 587 (MD GA, 1985); Rowe v. Ocwen Fed. Bank & Trust, 220 B.R. 591 (ED Tex., 1997).

§109(g),(2), requirements of, when applicable

In Eason v. Steltzer, 166 B.R. 793 (ED NY, 1994), the court held that Section 109(g)(2) applies only to debtors who have both requested and obtained voluntary dismissal of the prior case after the filing by a creditor of a request for relief from the stay. The court ruled that a debtor who had requested dismissal of the previous case prior to the filing of the creditor's request for relief from the stay was not barred by Section 109(g)(2) from refiling the case within 180 days, even though the previous case was actually dismissed after the filing of the request for relief from the stay. The creditor's request for relief from the stay must be filed prior to the filing of the debtor's request for dismissal in order for the second case to be barred by Section 109(g)(2). See In re Ransom, 60 B.R. 19 (ED PA, 1986); In re Hicks, 138 B.R. 505 (MD, 1992); but see In re Jarboe, 177 B.R. 242 (MD, 1995) (holding the filing of the debtor's second case was barred by Section 109(g)(2) even though the creditor's request for relief from the stay in the first case was not pending when the debtor filed his dismissal request where the request for relief from the stay was filed under a misapprehension of facts).

§109(g),(2), applicability when request for relief is withdrawn

In In re Santana, 110 B.R. 819 (WD MI, 1990), 109(g)(2) did not prevent the debtor from refiling a Chapter 13 case five days after the voluntary dismissal of the debtor's previous Chapter 13 case where the request for relief from the stay in the first case had been withdrawn by the creditor prior to dismissal, where the creditor seeking dismissal of the second case had not filed a request for relief from the stay in the first case, and where there was no evidence that either case was filed on the eve of foreclosure.

Section 109(g)(2) applies only where the prior bankruptcy was voluntarily dismissed by the debtor. See, e.g., In re Tune, 361 B.R. 466 (ED NC, 2007). If the prior case was dismissed at the request of a creditor or the trustee, Section 109(g)(2) does not bar a refiling of the case. See In re Marlatt, 116 B.R. 703 (NE, 1990). Further, the failure of the debtor in the prior case to oppose a motion to dismiss filed by another party does not constitute requesting and obtaining dismissal of the case for purposes of Section 109(g)(2). See In re Gamble, 72 B.R. 75 (ID, 1987); In re Nelkovski, 46 B.R. 542 (ND IL, 1985); In re Riekena, 456 B.R. 365 (Bankr. C. D. Ill. 2011 (holding 180 day bar on refiling is not dependent upon whether debtor's voluntary dismissal of prior case is motivated by motion for relief from stay).

§109(g),(2), requirement of voluntary dismissal

Most courts that have ruled on the issue have held that the application of Section 109(g)(2) is discretionary with the court and that the motives of both the debtor and the objecting creditor in the subsequent case should be examined before ruling on whether the subsequent case is barred by Section 109(g)(2). See In re Luna, 122 B.R. 575 (B.A.P. 9th Cir., 1991), where the court ruled that the application of Section 109(g)(2) is discretionary and that the bankruptcy court did not abuse its discretion by refusing to dismiss the debtor's second Chapter 13 case that was filed soon after the debtor voluntarily dismissed the first case due to a dispute with a mortgagee who subsequently proceeded with a foreclosure in violation of the stay imposed in the second case. See also In re Duncan, 182 B.R. 156 (Bankr. W. D. Va. 1995).

§109(g)(2). motives of parties, direction of court

Because the purpose of Section 109(g)(2) is to prevent debtors from using successive applications of the automatic stay to frustrate the foreclosure efforts of secured creditors, some courts in the exercise of their discretion have refused to dismiss a case under Section 109(g)(2) if the creditor seeking dismissal of the case was not damaged by the dismissal and refiling of the case. For example, several courts have ruled that if the creditor seeking dismissal of the second case did not file a request for relief from the stay in the first case, the filing of the second case is not barred by Section 109(g)(2) because the creditor seeking dismissal of the second case was not damaged by the dismissal and refiling of the case. See In re Santana, 110 B.R. 819 (WD MI, 1990); Tooke v. Sunshine Trust, 149 B.R. 687 (SD FL, 1992); In re Copman, 161 B.R. 821 (ED MO, 1993) (holding that for Section 109(g)(2) to be applicable there must be a causal connection between the dismissal of the prior case and the request for relief from the stay in that case; the filing of the second case was not precluded by Section 109(g)(2) because, even though a request for relief from the stay had been filed prior to the debtor's request for dismissal in the prior case, the dismissal was for reasons that were not related to the request for relief from the stay, which request had been complied with by the debtor in the prior case). See also In re Cline, 474 B.R. 789 (B.A.P. 6th Cir. 2012) (upholding 2 year ban on debtor's filing of bankruptcy case after 4th case in 3 years).

§109(g)(2), creditor requirements, necessity of casual connection

§109(g)(2), mandatory application of cases holding

Several courts have ruled that the application of Section 109(g)(2) is mandatory, and not discretionary, and must be applied regardless of the intent or motive of either the debtor or the objecting creditor. See In re Keziah, 46 B.R. 551 (WD NC, 1985); In re Rives, 260 B.R. 470 (ED MO, 2001); Chryler Fin. Corp. v. Dickerson, 209 B.R. 703 (WD TN, 1997); In re Andersson, 209 B.R. 76 (B.A.P. 6th Cir., 1997); Su Ming Kuo v. Walton, 167 B.R. 677 (MD FL, 1994) (stating the applicability of Section 109(g)(2) is mandatory and that the debtor's motives in dismissing the prior case are irrelevant, as is the outcome of the request for relief from stay in the prior case, and that the eligibility requirements of Section 109(g)(2) are not subject to the discretion of the court and that neither the purpose nor the intent of the debtor in the prior case is relevant in considering the validity of the subsequent case under Section 109(g)(2)). However, other courts have held that there must be a causal connection in the prior case between the creditor's motion for relief from the stay and the subsequent dismissal of the case by the debtor. See, e.g., In re Sole, 233 B.R. 347 (ED VA, 1998); In re Bates, 243 B.R. 466 (ND AL, 1999).

order of dismissal in prior case, effect of generally

Effect of order of dismissal in prior case. If the court in dismissing the prior case specifically found that the debtor had willfully failed to abide by orders of court or had willfully failed to appear before the court in proper prosecution of the case, this finding is binding on the court in the subsequent case if a request to dismiss the subsequent case under Section 109(g)(2) is filed. See In re Hildreth, 165 B.R. 429 (ND OH, 1994); In re Bono, 70 B.R. 339 (ED NY, 1987). By the same reasoning, if the court in the first case found that the debtor had not willfully failed to abide by the orders of the court and had not willfully failed to appear in the case, such a finding would also be binding on the court in the second case. If the prior case was dismissed without prejudice, Section 109(g) is not applicable and does not prevent the debtor from refiling the case within 180 days. See In re Felts, 60 B.R. 736 (WD KY, 1986); c.f. In re Tomlin, 105 F.3d 933, 939 (4th Cir. 1997).

order of dismissal in, prior case, effect of injunction

The court in dismissing a bankruptcy case also has the authority under Sections 109(g) and 105(a) to enjoin the debtor from refiling the case. See In re Jolly, 143 B.R. 383 (ED VA, 1992); In re King, 126 B.R. 777 (ND IL, 1991). However, if the order enjoining the debtor from refiling the case for 180 days is issued without notice to the debtor, the order is void and does not bar the debtor from refiling within that period. See In re Surace, 52 B.R. 868 (CD CA, 1985). Several courts have limited a bankruptcy court's authority to enjoin future bankruptcy filings to the 180 day period set forth in Section 109(g). See In re Cooper, 153 B.R. 898 (CO, 1993), In re Standfield, 152 B.R. 528 (ND IL, 1993), and In re Jolly, 143 B.R. 383 (ED VA, 1993). In In re Frieouf, 938 F.2d 1099 (10th Cir., 1991), the bankruptcy court's denial of all access to the bankruptcy court for more than 180 days was beyond the court's authority under 11 U.S.C. § 349. Further, 11 U.S.C. § 105(a) could not be utilized to enjoin future filings for more than 180 days because such an injunction encroaches upon Fifth Amendment due process and equal protection guarantees. Other courts, however, have held that a bankruptcy court has the power under 11 U.S.C. § § 105 to prohibit the filing of another bankruptcy case for more than 180 days. See In re Casse, 198 F.3d 327 (2d Cir., 1999).

Likewise, In re Legree, 285 B.R. 615 (ED PA, 2002), the court noted that all circuits except the Tenth Circuit have found that both district courts and bankruptcy courts have the statutory authority under Sections 105(c) and 349(a) to sanction serial filers by prohibiting them from filing for periods longer than the 180 days specified in Section 109(g).

order of dismissal in prior case, length of injunction

If, as is usually the case, the order of dismissal in the prior case is silent as to the Section 109(g) issues, the court in the subsequent case is free to make its own findings on these issues. Several courts have held that the failure of the court in the prior case to find that the debtor willfully failed either to abide by the orders of the court or to appear before the court in the proper prosecution of the case does not prevent the court in the subsequent case from ruling on these issues. See In re Zahniser, 58 B.R. 530 (CO, 1986); In re Marlatt, 116 B.R. 703 (NE, 1990) (both cases holding that the case may be refiled within 180 days if the court in the prior case made no finding of willful misconduct by the debtor); Montgomery v. Ryan, 37 F.3d 413 (8th Cir., 1994) (holding the court in the subsequent case could find that the prior case was dismissed because of willful misconduct by the debtor even if the order of dismissal in the prior case did not contain such a finding.

order of dismissal in prior case, effect of when silent on §109(g),(2), issues

Burden of proving debtor ineligibility. In the absence of an order of the court in the prior case, the party seeking dismissal of the subsequent case has the burden of proving that the debtor's conduct in the prior case satisfied at least one of the causes of ineligibility listed in Section 109(g). See In re Arena, 81 B.R. 851 (ED PA, 1988); In re Ristich, 57 B.R. 568 (ND IL, 1986) (holding if the record in the prior case fails to establish evidence of willful misconduct by the debtor, the subsequent case should not be dismissed under Section 109(g)); see also, In re Key, 58 B.R. 59 (ED PA, 1986) (holding where the court held that it is incumbent upon the moving party in the subsequent case to introduce evidence in support of its allegations that the debtor voluntarily dismissed the prior case following a request for relief from the stay). In in re Key, the court stated that although the required information may be contained in the clerk's files, it is the duty of the moving party to present that information to the court.

§109(g),(2), issues, burden of proof

In Montgomery v. Ryan, 37 F.3d 413 (8th Cir., 1994), the court held that once the objecting creditor established that the debtor failed to attend the meeting of creditors in the prior case, the burden was on the debtor to explain his failure to attend the meeting and if the debtor presented no evidence on the issue, the court in the subsequent case could find that the prior case was dismissed because of the debtor's willful misconduct. Even though the issue was raised in the creditor's motion to dismiss, when the Section 109(g) issue of willful misconduct was properly raised by the creditor, the burden of proof shifts to the debtor to establish that his misconduct was not willful.

willful misconduct, when burden of proof on debtor

case filed in violation of §109(g),(2), effect of automatic stay

If a bankruptcy case is found to have been filed in violation of Section 109(g), the automatic stay issued in the case was a nullity from the outset and had no effect on a sheriff's sale held after the filing of the case. See Miller v. First Federal S & L Assn., 143 B.R. 815 (WD PA, 1992) (holding that a debtor who files a subsequent bankruptcy case in violation of Section 109(g) has no standing to obtain any relief from the subsequent filing, including the relief provided by the automatic stay). Also, an ex parte lifting of the automatic stay by the bankruptcy judge in a case filed in violation of Section 109(g) is not an abuse of discretion. See In re Smith, 58 B.R. 603 (WD PA, 1986).

Bibliography. For further reading on the issues discussed in this article, see the annotations and articles listed below.

Annotations: AmJur Bankruptcy, § 39.

Articles:

17 Bankr. Dev. J. 331, Abusive Filings: Can Courts Stop the Abuse Within the Confines of the Bankrupcty Code?

Must courts apply Section 109(g)(2) when debtors intend no abuse in an early dismissal of their case? Comment. 7 Bankruptcy Dev. J. 103, 1990.

New law and an increase in consumer bankruptcies have changed bankruptcy practice - and contributed to some abuses. 6 Ca. Law. 10, November 1986.

Chapter 20 cases: An appropriate debtor tool. 4 J. Bankruptcy L. & Pract. 53, 1994.

Bankruptcy Rule 9011, Sanctions in Chapter 13 Proceedings, 199 ALR Fed. 21 (2005).

1.02 To what extent are debts that were or could have been listed in a prior bankruptcy case dischargeable in a subsequent bankruptcy case?

Text of statutes. Sections 349(a), 523(a)(10), and 523(b) of the Bankruptcy Code (11 U.S.C. § 349(a), 523(a)(10), 523(b)) are applicable to the subject discussed in this article. These statutes provide as follows:

349. Effect of dismissal

(a) Unless the court, for cause, orders otherwise, the dismissal of a case under this title does not bar the discharge, in a later case under this title, of debts that were dischargeable in the case dismissed; nor does the dismissal of a case under this title prejudice the debtor with regard to the filing of a subsequent petition under this title, except as provided in section 109(g) of this title. §349, text of

523. Exceptions to discharge

(a) A discharge under section 727, 1141, 1228(a), 1228(b), or 1328(b) of this title does not discharge an individual debtor from any debt -

. . . .

(10) that was or could have been listed or scheduled by the debtor in a prior case concerning the debtor under this title or under the Bankruptcy Act in which the debtor waived discharge, or was denied a discharge under section 727(a)(2), (3), (4), (5), (6), or (7) of this title, or under section 14c(1), (2), (3), (4), (6), or (7) of such Act; §523(a)(10), text of

. . . .

(b) Notwithstanding subsection (a) of this section, a debt that was excepted from discharge under subsection (a)(1), (a)(3), or (a)(8) of this section, under section 17a(1), 17a(3), or 17a(5) of the Bankruptcy Act, under section 439A of the Higher Education Act of 1965, or under section 733(g) of the Public Health Service Act in a prior case concerning the debtor under this title, or under the Bankruptcy Act, is dischargeable in a case under this title unless, by the terms of subsection (a) of this section, such debt is not dischargeable in the case under this title. §523(b), text of

Introduction. It is not uncommon for a Chapter 7 or Chapter 13 debtor to have filed a prior bankruptcy case that was dismissed or wherein the debtor failed to obtain the discharge of one or more of his or her debts. The general issue addressed in this section is the extent to which debts that were or could have been listed by the debtor in a prior bankruptcy case wherein the debts were not discharged, are dischargeable in a subsequent bankruptcy case filed by the same debtor. general issue discussed in section

legislative history of §349, (a), 523 (a)(10), & 523(b)

Section 349(a) was originally enacted in the Bankruptcy Reform Act of 1978. In 1984 the second phrase of the statute beginning with "nor does the dismissal..." was added. In 1994 "section 109(f)" in the second phrase was changed to "section 109(g)." Section 523(a)(10) was originally enacted as Section 523(a)(9) in the Bankruptcy Reform Act of 1978. It has remained unchanged since its enactment except that in 1986 its designation was changed from Section 523(a)(9) to Section 523(a)(10). Section 523(b) was also enacted in the Bankruptcy Reform Act of 1978 and has remained unchanged since its enactment.

§349(a) essential provisions

Section 349(a) essentially provides that the dismissal of a prior bankruptcy case does not affect the dischargeability of debts listed in a subsequent bankruptcy case unless the court in the prior case, for cause, orders otherwise. This normally means that debts listed in a prior bankruptcy case may be discharged in a subsequent case unless the prior case was dismissed with prejudice or unless the court in the prior case specifically precluded the discharge of a specified debt in a subsequent case.

§523(a)(10), essential provisions

Section 523(a)(10) provides, in essence, that if the debtor in a prior bankruptcy case waived his or her discharge or was denied a Chapter 7 discharge for any reason other than having been granted a discharge within the previous 8 years, the debtor may not discharge the debts listed in the prior case in a subsequently-filed Chapter 7 case or in a subsequently-filed Chapter 13 case in which the debtor receives a Section 1328(b) discharge, which is an uncompleted plan or best efforts discharge. Because the Section 523(a)(10) exception to discharge is not applicable to Chapter 13 completed-plan discharges granted under Section 1328(a), debts that were or could have been listed in a prior bankruptcy case are dischargeable in a subsequently-filed Chapter 13 case in which the debtor receives a Section 1328(a) discharge, even if the debtor waived or was denied a discharge in the prior case.

§523(b), essential provisions

Section 523(b) provides for an exception to the general rule precluding redeterminations of dischargeability in subsequent bankruptcy cases. Section 523(b) provides, in essence, that a debt that was excepted from discharge in a prior bankruptcy case because the debt was a nondischargeable tax debt, because the debt was not duly scheduled, or because the debt was a nondischargeable student loan, may be discharged in a subsequent bankruptcy case if the debt is otherwise dischargeable in the subsequent case. All other debts that were excepted from discharge in a prior bankruptcy case, it should be noted, are nondischargeable in a subsequent bankruptcy case under the doctrines of res judicata and collateral estoppel.

Construed together, Sections 349(a), 523(a)(10), and 523(b) establish the following general rules governing the dischargeability in a subsequent bankruptcy case of debts that were listed but not discharged in a prior bankruptcy case.

compiled effect of §349(a), 523(a)(10) & 523(b), general rules

(1) If the prior case was dismissed without prejudice and if the debtor neither received, waived, nor was denied a discharge in the prior case, all debts listed in the prior case may be discharged in a subsequent case if they are otherwise dischargeable in the subsequent case.

(2) If the prior case was dismissed with prejudice, the debts listed in the prior case may not be discharged in a subsequent case under any circumstances.

(3) If the court in the prior case either ordered that one or more specified debts shall be nondischargeable in subsequent cases or dismissed the case with prejudice as to one or more specified debts, the specified debts are nondischargeable in a subsequent case. The other debts listed in the prior case are dischargeable in the subsequent case if they are otherwise dischargeable in the subsequent case, provided that the debtor neither received, waived, nor was denied a discharge in the prior case.

(4) If the debtor waived a discharge in the prior case, the debts that were or could have been listed in the prior case are nondischargeable in a subsequent case under any Chapter, except in a subsequent Chapter 13 case in which the debtor receives a Section 1328(a) completed plan discharge.

(5) If the debtor was denied a Chapter 7 discharge in the prior case on any of the grounds listed in 11 U.S.C. § 727(a)(2)-(7), the debts that were or could have been listed in the prior case are nondischargeable in a subsequent case under any Chapter except in a subsequent Chapter 13 case in which the debtor receives a Section 1328(a) completed plan discharge.

(6) Debts that were excepted from discharge in a prior case are nondischargeable in a subsequent case except that a debt that was excepted from discharge in a prior case because the debt was a nondischargeable tax debt, because the debt was not duly scheduled, or because the debt was a nondischargeable student loan is dischargeable in a subsequent case if it is otherwise dischargeable in that case.

The eligibility of a particular debt for discharge in a bankruptcy case should not be confused with the eligibility of the debtor to receive a discharge in the case. A debtor who has received a Chapter 7 or Chapter 11 discharge in a case filed within the previous 8 years is not eligible to receive a Chapter 7 discharge. See 11 U.S.C. § 727(a)(8). A debtor who has received a Chapter 13 or Chapter 12 discharge in a case filed within the previous six years is also not eligible to receive a Chapter 7 discharge unless the total amount of the debtor's payments under the plan in the prior case equaled at least 100 percent of the allowed unsecured claims in the case or 70 percent of such claims and constituted the debtor's best effort under a plan that was proposed in good faith. See 11 U.S.C. § 727(a)(9). These discharge eligibility requirements are not applicable to Chapter 13 cases.

eligibility of debtor for discharge

dismissal of prior case without discharge, general rule

Dischargeability of debt when prior case was dismissed without granting discharge. If a debtor wishes to discharge in a subsequently-filed case one or more debts that were listed in a previous bankruptcy case that was dismissed prior to the granting, waiver or denial of a discharge, the dischargeability of the debts in the subsequent case is determined by the terms of the order dismissing the prior case. Section 349(a) of the Bankruptcy Code provides, in essence, that the dismissal of a prior bankruptcy case does not bar the discharge in a subsequent case of debts that were dischargeable in the prior case unless the court in the prior case, for cause, orders otherwise.

dismissal of prior case with predjudice, effect of

dismissal of prior case without predjudice, effect of

It is clear that the dismissal of a bankruptcy case with prejudice bars the discharge in a later bankruptcy case of the debts listed in the dismissed case. See Leavitt v. Soto, 209 B.R. 935 (B.A.P. 9th Cir., 1997); In re Smith, 133 B.R. 467 (ND IN, 1991); In re Earl, 140 B.R. 728 (ND IN, 1992). It is equally clear that the dismissal of a bankruptcy case without prejudice does not bar the discharge in a later bankruptcy case of the debts listed in the dismissed case. See In re Pettey, 288 B.R. 14 (MA, 2003); In re Nash, 765 F.2d 1410 (9th Cir., 1985); Hall v. Vance, 887 F.2d 1041 (10th Cir., 1989). If the debtor wishes to discharge debts that were listed in a prior bankruptcy case, it is obviously important to ascertain whether the dismissal of the prior bankruptcy case was with or without prejudice.

dismissal with predjudice, requirement of order

Because dismissal with prejudice is a drastic remedy and may only be entered for cause, an order of dismissal must clearly specify that the dismissal is with prejudice if it is to be given that effect in a subsequent case. If an order of dismissal is silent as to whether the dismissal is with or without prejudice, the dismissal is deemed to be without prejudice. See In re Ray, 46 B.R. 424 (SD GA, 1984); In re Consolidated Equity Properties, Inc., 136 B.R. 261 (NV, 1991); In re Samora, 117 B.R. 660 (NM, 1990). Note, however, that "with prejudice" does not have a single "universally accepted" meaning. See In re Ellsworth, 455 B.R. 904 (B.A.P. 9th Cir. 2011).

dismissal with predjudice, types of

Instead of dismissing a case with general prejudice, a bankruptcy court for cause may, under Section 349(a), limit the prejudicial effect of the dismissal by either dismissing the case with prejudice as to one or more specified debts, enjoining the debtor from discharging in a subsequent case one or more specified debts that were listed in the dismissed case, or otherwise permanently disqualifying one or more debts or classes of debts listed in the dismissed case from discharge. See In re Frieouf, 938 F.2d 1099 (10th Cir., 1991), In re Cooper, 153 B.R. 898 (CO, 1993), and In re Mickler, 324 B.R. 613 (WD KY, 2006).

dismissal with prejudice, requirement of cause

Section 349(a) requires that cause be found to exist in order to dismiss a bankruptcy case with prejudice or otherwise bar the discharge in a later case of a debt listed in the dismissed case. In other words, a bankruptcy case may be dismissed with prejudice only for cause and not at the whim of a bankruptcy judge. Dismissal with prejudice is a severe sanction to which bankruptcy courts should resort only infrequently, and is a drastic sanction which may affect substantial rights of the debtor and should be used only in extreme situations.. Hall v. Vance, 887 F.2d 1041 (10th Cir., 1989); In re Martin-Trigona, 35 B.R. 596 (SD NY, 1983).

Cause for dismissal with prejudice is often found to exist in cases that have been filed in bad faith by the debtor. See In re Smith, 53 CBC2d 907 (UT, 2004) (5 Chapter 13 plans with no payments made under any); In re Latovljevic, 343 B.R. 817 (ND WV, 2006) (6 cases in 4 years); In re Penny, 243 B.R. 720 (WD AR, 2000) (5 Chapter 13 petitions filed); In re Jolly, 143 B.R. 383 (ED VA, 1992) (7 bankruptcy cases filed by debtor in past 3 years); In re Gros, 173 B.R. 774 (MD FL, 1994) (5 bankruptcy cases filed by debtor in 2 years); In re Standfield, 152 B.R. 528 (ND IL, 1993) (Chapter 13 case and plan filed in bad faith); In re Penz, 121 B.R. 602 (ED OK, 1990). In addition, cause for dismissal with prejudice is often found to exist in cases that are dismissed because of the failure of the debtor to appear before the court or obey orders of the court. See In re Rusher, 283 B.R. 544 (WD MO, 2002); In re Ladd, 82 B.R. 476 (ND IN, 1988); In re Maurice, 167 B.R. 114 (ND IL, 1994). Cause for dismissal with prejudice may also exist in Chapter 13 cases that are dismissed for bad faith in failing to file a plan or failing to comply with the requirements of a confirmed plan. See In re Petro, 18 B.R. 566 (ED PA, 1982); In re Martin-Trigona, 35 B.R. 596 (SD NY, 1983); In re Hundley, 103 B.R. 768 (ED VA, 1989); In re Doniff, 133 B.R. 351 (ED VA, 1991). See also In re Norton, 319 B.R. 671 (UT, 2005) (dismissal with prejudice was granted when debtor had filed 9 pro-se Chapter 13 cases in the previous 8 years, never filed statements or schedules, never attended 341 meetings, and never made a plan payment).

cause for dismissal with prejudice, what constitutes

Cause for dismissal with prejudice must be significant. Trivial causes, while they may constitute grounds for dismissal for cause, do not constitute sufficient cause for dismissal with prejudice. In Hall v. Vance, 887 F.2d 1041 (10th Cir., 1989), dismissal with prejudice was too harsh a remedy in a case where the Chapter 11 debtors, who were appearing pro se, were 3 days late in filing objections to proofs of claim, 1 day late in filing their plan, and substantially, but not prejudicially, late in filing their monthly reports.

cause for dismissal with prejudice, what constitutes

In In re Conley, 105 B.R. 116 (SD FL, 1989), cause for dismissal with prejudice did not exist in a Chapter 13 case that was voluntarily dismissed with the consent and stipulation of the debtor's sole creditor. In In re Moses, 171 B.R. 789 (ED MI, 1994), cause for dismissal with prejudice did not exist in a Chapter 7 case where the debtor failed to respond to questions regarding foreign assets and invoked and then waived her Fifth Amendment privilege against self-incrimination, but was not in contempt of any court order, did not fail to disclose assets, and did not unreasonably delay the case.

cause for dismissal with prejudice, what constitutes

Dischargeability of debt when discharge was waived or denied in prior case. If a debtor wishes to discharge in a subsequently-filed case one or more debts that were or could have been listed in previous bankruptcy case wherein the debtor either waived his or her discharge or was denied a Chapter 7 discharge, the dischargeability of the debts in the subsequent case is governed by the provisions of Section 523(a)(10) of the Bankruptcy Code. Debts that were or could have been listed in a prior Chapter 11, 12, or 13 case wherein the debtor was denied a discharge are not covered by Section 523(a)(10) and are therefore dischargeable in a subsequent bankruptcy case, while debts that were or could have been listed in a prior Chapter 11, 12, or 13 case wherein the debtor waived his or her discharge are covered by Section 523(a)(10) and are therefore nondischargeable in a subsequent bankruptcy case. It is important, therefore, to determine whether the debtor's discharge in a prior Chapter 11, 12, or 13 case was denied or waived.

§523(a) (10), applicability of

§523(a)(10), essential provisions of

Section 523(a)(10) provides that a Chapter 7 discharge and a Chapter 13 discharge under Section 1328(b) (i.e., an uncompleted plan or best effort discharge) does not discharge a debtor from a debt that was or could have been listed by the debtor in a prior bankruptcy case under any chapter wherein the debtor waived his or her discharge or in a prior Chapter 7 case wherein the debtor was denied a discharge on any ground other than having received a discharge in a case filed within the previous 8 years. Debts that were or could have been listed in a prior bankruptcy case under any chapter are dischargeable in a subsequent Chapter 13 case wherein the debtor receives a Section 1328(a) completed-plan discharge regardless of whether the debtor waived or was denied a discharge in the prior case.

revocation of discharge in prior case, effect of under §523(a)(10)

Even though Section 523(a)(10) contains the words "was denied a discharge" and does not refer to a revocation of discharge, debts listed in a previous Chapter 7 case wherein the debtor's discharge was revoked under the provisions of 11 U.S.C. § 727(d) may not be dischargeable in a subsequent Chapter 7 case. See In re Klapp, 706 F.2d 998 (9th Cir., 1983) (holding that for purposes of Section 523(a)(10), a revocation of discharge must be treated the same as a denial of discharge based on the same grounds or conduct).

denial of discharge in prior case, what constitutes

For a debt listed in a prior case to be nondischargeable in a subsequent case because the debtor was denied a discharge in the prior case, it must be clearly established that the debtor was in fact denied a Chapter 7 discharge under a covered provision of Section 523(a)(10) in the prior case. The fact that the prior case was dismissed does not necessarily mean that the debtor was denied a discharge in the prior case for purposes of Section 523(a)(10). For a debt to be nondischargeable under Section 523(a)(10) in the subsequent case, it must be shown that the debtor was denied a Chapter 7 discharge in the prior case in an order to that effect entered by the bankruptcy judge. Also, a denial of discharge should not be confused with the exception of a debt from discharge. The exception from discharge (i.e., the nondischargeability) of one or more debts in a prior case does not constitute the denial of a discharge in a prior case for purposes of Section 523(a)(10). Debts that were excepted from discharge in a prior case are dealt with in Section 523(b) and are discussed below in this section.

dismissal with prejudice, requirement of cause

In In re Hickman, 448 B.R. 769 (Bankr. C. D. Ill. 2011), although the debtor's previous Chapter 7 case was dismissed and the debtor's discharge was denied because the debtor failed to comply with a statutorily mandated audit, the debts listed in the prior case were not nondischargeable under Section 523(a)(10). See also In re Samora, 117 B.R. 660 (NM, 1990). A creditor seeking the nondischargeability of a debt under Section 523(a)(10) also may have the burden of proving both that the debt was or could have been listed in the prior case and that the debtor waived or was denied a discharge in the prior case. See McIntosh v. Webb, 157 B.R. 614 (ND OH, 1993).

The reaffirmation of a debt by the debtor in a prior case does not bar the discharge of that debt in a subsequent case. The reaffirmation of a debt does not constitute a waiver or denial of discharge with respect to the reaffirmed debt for purposes of Section 523(a)(10). See, e.g., In re Lones, 50 B.R. 801 (WD KY, 1985).

reaffirmation of debt, effect of

Dischargeability of debt that was excepted from discharge in prior case. If a debtor wishes to discharge in a subsequent bankruptcy case a debt that was excepted from discharge in a prior case, the dischargeability of the debt in the subsequent case is governed by the provisions of Section 523(b) of the Bankruptcy Code and by the common law doctrines of collateral estoppel and res judicata.

dischargability of excepted debt, rules governing

The general rule is that a debt that was excepted from discharge in a prior bankruptcy case is also nondischargeable in a subsequent case under the doctrines of collateral estoppel and res judicata unless otherwise provided in the Bankruptcy Code. See In re Matter of Swate, 99 F.3d 1282 (5th Cir. 1996); Royal American Oil & Gas Co. v. Szafranski, 147 B.R. 976 (ND OK, 1992). An exception to the general rule precluding redeterminations of dischargeability in subsequent bankruptcy cases is set forth in Section 523(b) of the Bankruptcy Code, which provides that if a debt was excepted from discharge in a prior bankruptcy case under Section 523(a)(1), Section 523(a)(3), or Section 523(a)(8), the debt may be discharged in a subsequent bankruptcy case if the debt is otherwise dischargeable in the subsequent case. Note that a debt that was not discharged in the prior case because it was not listed in the debtor's schedules may be discharged in a subsequent case because the issue of the dischargeability of the debt was not judicially determined in the prior case. See In re Moretti, 278 B.R. 300 (RI, 2002).

debt not discharged in prior case, general rules

Sections 523(a)(1), (3) and (8) deal respectively with the dischargeability of tax debts, unscheduled debts, and student loan debts. Therefore, Section 523(b), in essence, provides that if a tax debt, a debt that was not listed in the prior case, or a student loan debt was excepted from discharge in the prior case, the debt is dischargeable in a subsequent bankruptcy case provided that it is not otherwise nondischargeable in the subsequent case. Any other debts that were excepted from discharge in a prior case under any other subsection of Section 523(a) are nondischargeable in a subsequent case regardless of any change in the debtor's circumstances or standing in the subsequent case. See Royal American Oil & Gas Co. v. Szafranski, 147 B.R. 976 (ND OK, 1992).

§523(b), essential provisions of

§523(b), operation of, example

The operation of Section 523(b) can best be explained by an example. Section 523(a)(8) provides that debts for student loans are nondischargeable unless the loan first became due more than 7 years prior to the date the bankruptcy case was filed or unless the nondischarge of the debt will impose an undue hardship on the debtor. If in a prior case a student loan debt was found to be nondischargeable because it first became due less than 7 years prior to the date the case was filed and that the nondischarge of the debt would not impose an undue hardship on the debtor, the debt would be dischargeable in a subsequent bankruptcy case if the debtor could establish either that the loan first became due more than 7 years prior to the date of filing of the subsequent case or that the nondischarge of the debt would now impose an undue hardship on the debtor. However, if in the subsequent case the debtor could not establish either of these conditions of dischargeability, the debt would again be nondischargeable.

Bibliography. For further reading on the issues discussed in this article, see the annotations and articles listed below.

Annotations: None available.

Articles: None available.

1.03 To what extent is a debtor protected from discrimination by Section 525 of the Bankruptcy Code and what are a debtor's remedies for violations of Section 525?

Text of statute. Section 525 of the Bankruptcy Code (11 U.S.C. § 525) provides as follows:

525. Protection against discriminatory treatment

(a) Except as provided in the Perishable Agricultural Commodities Act, 1930, the Packers and Stockyards Act, 1921, and section 1 of the Act entitled "An Act making appropriations for the Department of Agriculture for the fiscal year ending June 30, 1944, and for other purposes," approved July 12, 1943, a governmental unit may not deny, revoke, suspend, or refuse to renew a license, permit, charter, franchise, or other similar grant to, condition such a grant to, discriminate with respect to such a grant against, deny employment to, terminate the employment of, or discriminate with respect to employment against, a person that is or has been a debtor under this title or a bankrupt or a debtor under the Bankruptcy Act, or another person with whom such bankrupt or debtor has been associated, solely because such bankrupt or debtor is or has been a debtor under this title or a bankrupt or debtor under the Bankruptcy Act, has been insolvent before the commencement of the case under this title, or during the case but before the debtor is granted or denied a discharge, or has not paid a debt that is dischargeable in the case under this title or that was discharged under the Bankruptcy Act. section 525(a), text of

(b) No private employer may terminate the employment of, or discriminate with respect to employment against, an individual who is or has been a debtor under this title, a debtor or bankrupt under the Bankruptcy Act, or an individual associated with such debtor or bankrupt, solely because such debtor or bankrupt -

(1) is or has been a debtor under this title or a debtor or bankrupt under the Bankruptcy Act; section 525(b), text of

(2) has been insolvent before the commencement of a case under this title or during the case but before the grant or denial of a discharge; or

(3) has not paid a debt that is dischargeable in a case under this title or that was discharged under the Bankruptcy Act.

(c)(1) A governmental unit that operates a student grant or loan program and a person engaged in a business that includes the making of loans guaranteed or insured under a student loan program may not deny a student grant, loan, loan guarantee, or loan insurance to a person that is or has been a debtor under this title or a bankrupt or debtor under the Bankruptcy Act, or another person with whom the debtor or bankrupt has been associated, because the debtor or bankrupt is or has been a debtor under this title or a bankrupt or debtor under the Bankruptcy Act, has been insolvent before the commencement of a case under this title or during the pendency of the case but before the debtor is granted or denied a discharge, or has not paid a debt that is dischargeable in the case under this title or that was discharged under the Bankruptcy Act. section 525(c), text of

(2) In this section, "student loan program" means any program operated under titleIV of the Higher Education Act of 1965 or a similar program operated under State or local law.

Bankruptcy Code, fresh start objective

Introduction. The core objective of the Bankruptcy Code is to provide a "fresh start" for bankruptcy debtors. It is also designed to provide equitable treatment to creditors. See, e.g., In re Westby, 473 B.R. 392 (Bankr. D. Kan. 2012). The drafters of the Code realized that a serious obstacle to a fresh start for many debtors is the stigma associated with bankruptcy. This stigma is especially damaging to a debtor if it is possessed and acted upon by persons in a position to discriminate against the debtor with respect to matters of financial importance, such as employment and the issuance of governmental licenses, permits and grants. To assist debtors in overcoming these obstacles to a fresh start, a section dealing with debtor discrimination (Section 525) was included in the Bankruptcy Code of 1978.

§525, legislative history of

As originally enacted in 1978, Section 525 dealt only with debtor discrimination by governmental units with respect to employment and the granting of licenses, permits, and similar grants. These provisions are contained in Section 525(a) of the present Bankruptcy Code. When it became apparent that the protection accorded debtors by Section 525(a), while important, was insufficient for many debtors and when the courts refused to extend the provisions of Section 525(a) to private employer discrimination, Congress enacted Section 525(b) in 1984. Section 525(b) prohibits debtor discrimination by private employers with respect to employment. Finally, when the courts failed to extend Section 525 to cover the granting and insuring of student loans, Congress in 1994 enacted Section 525(c) dealing with debtor discrimination with respect to the making and insuring of student loans.

§525,BAPCPA amendments to

The 2005 amendments to section 525(c) added the word "student" at the end of the second line in paragraph (c)(1) above and the eliminated of the words "part B, D, or E of" prior to "title IV" in the first line in paragraph (2) above. These amendments broadened the scope of prohibited student loan discrimination by making the antidiscrimination provisions of section 525(c) applicable to student loans made under any part of title IV of the Higher Education Act of 1965. Prior to the BAPCPA amendments only loans made under parts B, D or E of the Act were subject to the antidiscrimination provisions of this subsection. The Higher Education Act of 1965 was Public Law 89-329 and it is codified in Title 20 of the U.S. Code.

§525, types of discrimination prohibited by

In its present form, Section 525 prohibits three basic forms of discrimination against bankruptcy debtors: (1) discrimination by governmental units with respect to employment and with respect to the granting of licenses, permits, franchises and similar grants; (2) discrimination by private employers with respect to employment; and (3) discrimination with respect to the making or insuring of student loans. It should be understood that the discrimination protection provided by Section 525 is applicable to debtors under any chapter of the Bankruptcy Code. Therefore, a chapter 7 debtor, a chapter 13 debtor, a chapter 12 debtor, or a chapter 11 debtor may invoke the provisions of Section 525. Each form of discrimination is discussed separately below.

Governmental discrimination prohibited by Section 525(a). Section 525(a) provides that a governmental unit may not deny, revoke, suspend, refuse to renew, condition, or otherwise discriminate with respect to the granting of a license, permit, charter, franchise, or similar grant to, and may not deny employment to, terminate the employment of, or otherwise discriminate with respect to the employment of, a person who is or has been a debtor in a bankruptcy case or to another person with whom the debtor has been associated, solely because the debtor has filed a bankruptcy case, has not paid a dischargeable debt, or has been insolvent before or during a bankruptcy case. See 11 U.S.C. § 525(a).

§525(a), provisions of

Note that the forms of discrimination listed in Section 525(a) are not exclusive and that it has been held that a governmental unit may not discriminate against an individual debtor so as to frustrate the "fresh start" objective of the Bankruptcy Code. See In re Elsinore Shore Associates, 66 B.R. 708 (NJ, 1986).

§525(a), prohibited forms of discrimination

For background purposes at least, it should be understood that governmental discrimination against bankruptcy debtors was prohibited to some extent prior to the enactment of Section 525(a) in 1978. In the case of Perez v. Campbell, 402 U.S. 637, 91 S.Ct. 1704 (1971), the Supreme Court held that one of the purposes of the bankruptcy laws was to give debtors a fresh start after their bankruptcy discharge and that state laws that frustrated or circumvented the effect of a bankruptcy discharge issued under federal law were invalid as applied to bankruptcy debtors under the supremacy clause of the U.S. Constitution even if the primary purpose of the state law was not to frustrate or circumvent a bankruptcy discharge. Specifically, the court held invalid the provisions of the Arizona motor vehicle financial responsibility law that permitted the state to suspend a person's drivers license if the person failed to pay a judgment arising from an automobile accident even if the judgment was discharged in bankruptcy. The state financial responsibility law was held invalid as applied to the debtor because it was in conflict with provisions and intent of the federal bankruptcy laws. It was in this case law environment that Section 525(a) was enacted in 1978.

Perez v. Campbell, holding of

Section 525(a) prohibits discrimination or other governmental action that occurs solely because the debtor has filed a bankruptcy case, has failed to pay a dischargeable debt, or has been insolvent prior to or during a bankruptcy case. Section 525(a) does not prohibit governmental units from considering other criteria with respect to bankruptcy debtors, including a debtor's future financial prospects, as long as the same criteria are considered and applied to all persons. In essence, Section 525(a) prohibits governmental units from treating bankruptcy debtors differently from everyone else.

§525(a), the "soley because" requirement, effect of

§525(a), governmental acts prohibited by

Section 525(a) has been used to prohibit state motor vehicle departments from denying driver's licenses to debtors because of unpaid fines or judgments that are dischargeable in bankruptcy. Section 525(a) has also been used to prevent the denial of contractor licenses, real estate licenses, and liquor licenses to bankruptcy debtors. It has also been used to prevent colleges from withholding grades or transcripts from debtors who have unpaid student loans that are dischargeable in bankruptcy. Section 525(a) has also been used to prevent housing authorities from evicting tenants because of unpaid rent that is dischargeable in bankruptcy. Each significant category of debtor discrimination covered by Section 525(a) is discussed separately below.

governmental unit, what constitutes

Entities to which Section 525(a) is applicable. As indicated above, Section 525(a) prohibits debtor discrimination by governmental units. A governmental unit is defined in 11 U.S.C. § 101(27) to include the United States, a state or commonwealth, a district, territory, municipality or foreign state, a department, agency or instrumentality of any of the foregoing entities, or any other foreign or domestic government. Other entities may also be "governmental units." For example, a public housing authority may be a governmental unit in certain circumstances. See Stoltz v. Brattleboro Housing Authority, 259 B.R. 255 (VT, 2001). The Oklahoma Horse Racing Commission was a governmental unit in In re Will Rogers Jockey & Polo Club, Inc., 111 B.R. 948 (ND OK, 1990). The New Jersey Casino Control Commission was a governmental unit in In re Elsinore Shore Associates, 66 B.R. 708 (NJ, 1986). A city water board was a governmental unit in In re Heard, 84 B.R. 454 (WD TX, 1987), although Section 525(a) was found not to be applicable to its deposit requirements because utility deposits were intended to be dealt with exclusively in 11 U.S.C. § 366. In Green v. Yang, 29 B.R. 682 (SD OH, 1983) a creditor of a real estate broker debtor was a vicarious agent of the state for purposes of licensing real estate brokers.

governmental unit, what does not constitute

The definition of governmental unit, while broad, is not all encompassing and several government-related entities have been found not to be governmental units. For example, an educational association involved in accrediting colleges was found not to be a governmental unit in In re Nasson College, 80 B.R. 600 (ME, 1988). A privately owned company that participated in a federally regulated public housing program was held not to be a government unit in In re Lutz, 82 B.R. 699 (MD PA, 1988). A residential landlord who participated in a federally-subsidized housing program was found not to be a governmental unit in In re Liggins, 145 B.R. 227 (ED VA, 1992). But see In re Oksentowicz, 314 B.R. 638 (ED MI, 2004) (landlord that provided subsidized low income senior housing subject to a contract with HUD was determined to be a governmental unit under 525(a)). A state employees' credit union was not to be a governmental unit in Brown v. Penn. State Employees Credit Union, 851 F.2d 81 (3d Cir., 1988). See also In re Uplinger, 67 Collier Bankr. Cas. 2d 266 (Bankr. E. D. Va. 2012) (holding government contractor not a governmental unit).

Note that Section 525(a) prevents governmental discrimination against "a person" that is or has been a bankruptcy debtor. A "person" is defined in 11 U.S.C. § 101(41) to include an individual, a partnership and a corporation. This means the provisions of Section 525(a) are applicable to and may be invoked by a debtor under chapter 7, 11, 12, or 13 of the Bankruptcy Code, regardless of whether the debtor is an individual, a partnership, or a corporation. Section 525(a) also protects persons who have been associated with a bankruptcy debtor. In In re Dembek, 64 B.R. 745 (ND OH, 1986) it Section 525(a) prohibited a school district from attempting to collect tuition that was discharged in the debtor's bankruptcy case from a minor child of the debtor.

§525(a), persons protected from discrimination by

Of course it is the debtor's burden to prove that the governmental unit acted in a discriminatory manner. That is, the debtor must prove that the governmental action complained of occurred solely because the debtor either (1) filed a bankruptcy case, (2) failed to pay a dischargeable debt, or (3) was insolvent prior to or during a bankruptcy case. A debtor who fails to prove that the governmental action complained of occurred solely because of one of these three reasons is not protected by Section 525(a). See In re Helms, 46 B.R. 150 (ED MO, 1985).

§525(a), violations of burden of proof

As indicated above, to be in violation of Section 525(a) the governmental action complained of must be found by the court to have occurred "solely because" of either the filing of the debtor's bankruptcy case, a failure by the debtor to pay a dischargeable debt, or the debtor's insolvency. See White v. Kentuckiana Livestock Mkt., Inc., 397 F.3d 420 (6th Cir., 2005). If other significant reasons exist to justify the governmental action complained of and that the governmental unit relied, in part at least, on these other reasons in taking the action complained of, then the action is likely to be found not to be a violation of Section 525(a). See In re Exquisito Services, Inc., 823 F.2d 151 (5th Cir., 1987). In In re McKibben, 233 B.R. 378 (ED TX, 1999), the totality of the circumstances indicated that the County Appraisal District had released the debtor because of his bankruptcy filing where it was shown the debtor had never received less than a satisfactory job rating and the board members had expressed concern about his bankruptcy filing.

§525(a), the "solely because" requirement, general aspects

In In re Professional Sales Corp., 56 B.R. 753 (ND IL, 1985) the EPA's termination of the debtor's permit after the filing of the debtor's bankruptcy case was not a violation of Section 525(a) because the termination was based on four grounds, three of which had nothing to do with the debtor's bankruptcy. In In re Lutz, 82 B.R. 699 (MD PA, 1988) Section 525(a) did not require a government agency to continue contractual relations with a Chapter 13 debtor where prepetition defaults under the contract by the debtor gave the agency a legal right to terminate the contract. In In re National Cattle Congress, 179 B.R. 588 (ND IA, 1995) the revocation of the debtor's dog racing license by a state agency on the grounds that the debtor failed to demonstrate financial responsibility was not a violation of Section 525(a) because it was based on the debtor's overall financial condition and not solely on the debtor's bankruptcy or insolvency.

"solely because" requirement of §525(a), effect of

"solely because" requirement, burden of proof

Thus, the burden is higher than under other discrimination statutes. Unless it is obvious that the governmental action complained of occurred solely because of the debtor's bankruptcy, the burden of proving that the action complained of occurred solely because of the debtor's bankruptcy rests with the debtor. In In re Rose, 23 B.R. 662 (CT, 1982) while Section 525(a) prohibited a state housing finance authority from refusing to make a loan to a bankruptcy debtor solely because of the debtor's bankruptcy, the debtor had not borne the burden of proving that he was denied a loan solely because of the filing of his bankruptcy case, the nonpayment of a dischargeable debt, or his insolvency.

driver's license discrimination because of discharged debt

Prohibited discrimination as to driver's licenses. A state motor vehicle department violates section 525(a) if it suspends, denies, or revokes a debtor's driver's license solely because the debtor has failed to pay a motor vehicle related judgment that is dischargeable in bankruptcy. See Henry v. Heyison, 4 B.R. 437 (ED PA, 1980) (holding that to satisfy Section 525(a) the state must treat a person with a discharged debt in the same manner as it treats a person who never had a debt and not in the same manner as it treats a person who has a debt that has not been paid); see also In re Layfield, 12 B.R. 846 (ND AL, 1981); In re Duffey, 13 B.R. 785 (SD OH, 1981); In re Briner, 10 B.R. 850 (CO, 1981); Perkinson v. Woody, 419 N.E. 2d 1306 (IN, 1981); In re Taylor, 27 B.R. 83 (SD FL, 1983); In re Brown, 244 B.R. 62 (NJ, 2000).

driver's license discrimination, prohibited types of

The denial, suspension or revocation of a debtor's driver's license because of the nonpayment of a fine or other debt that is dischargeable in bankruptcy is also a violation of Section 525(a). In In re Young, 10 B.R. 17 (SD CA, 1980), the suspension of the debtor's driver's license because of the nonpayment of a criminal fine was a violation of Section 525(a) in a chapter 13 case where such a fine is dischargeable, but would not be a violation of Section 525(a) in a chapter 7 case where such a fine is nondischargeable. The suspension of a debtor's driver's license because the debtor failed to pay a dischargeable traffic fine was a violation of Section 525(a) in Smith v. Penn. Dept. of Transportation, 66 B.R. 244 (ED PA, 1986). The suspension or denial of a debtor's driver's license because of the nonpayment of fees or charges assessed by the state motor vehicle department has been held to be a violation of Section 525(a). See In re Bill, 90 B.R. 651 (NJ, 1988), and In re Christensen, 95 B.R. 886 (NJ, 1988).

driver's license discrimination, permitted acts

On the other hand, when the state motor vehicle laws are not designed to coerce the payment of a dischargeable judgment, fine, or debt and impose the same requirements on both debtors and nondebtors, the enforcement of such laws is not a violation of Section 525(a). See In re Kimsey, 263 B.R. 244 (ED AR, 2001). In Duffey v. Dollison, 734 F.2d 265 (6th Cir., 1984), the denial of a driver's license to a debtor for failing to comply with a state motor vehicle financial responsibility law requiring proof of future financial responsibility of persons who fail to satisfy a motor vehicle related judgment did not violate Section 525(a), at least when the financial responsibility requirement was imposed prior to the filing of the bankruptcy case. See In re Holder, 40 B.R. 847 (ED WI, 1984), for a similar ruling. In In re Norton, 867 F.2d 313 (6th Cir., 1989), it was held that the imposition by the state of a $65 license restoration fee on a bankruptcy debtor was not a violation of Section 525(a) because a similar fee was required of all uninsured persons who settled claims resulting from automobile accidents. Section 525 does not prohibit a state from denying or revoking a driver's license based upon a determination that granting the license would jeopardize the public safety. See Matter of Bradley, 989 F.2d 802 (5th Cir., 1993).

Prohibited discrimination as to other licenses and grants. Section 525(a) also prohibits a governmental unit from revoking or suspending a debtor's real estate, insurance, gambling or other license solely because of the debtor's bankruptcy or failure to pay a dischargeable debt. In F.C.C. v. NextWave Pers. Communications, Inc., 537 U.S. 293, 123 S.Ct. 832 (2003), the Supreme Court held that Section 525(a) prohibited the F.C.C. from revoking the debtor's spectrum licenses solely because of the debtor's failure to make timely payments owed to the F.C.C. for the purchase of the licenses. In In re Harris, 85 B.R. 858 (CO, 1988) Section 525(a) prohibited the state real estate commission from revoking an agent's real estate license solely because the agent failed to pay a real estate related debt that was discharged in the agent's bankruptcy case. See also In re Fasse, 40 B.R. 198 (CO, 1984). In In re William Tell II, Inc., 38 B.R. 327 (ND IL, 1983), the state liquor control commission violated Section 525(a) when it revoked the debtor's liquor license because the debtor failed to pay certain taxes that were dischargeable in bankruptcy. See also In re Maley, 9 B.R. 832 (WD NY, 1981); In re Mason, 18 B.R. 817 (WD TN, 1982); In re Elsinore Shore Associates, 66 B.R. 708 (NJ, 1986).

real estate license, denial of as violation of §525

liquor license, denial of as violation of §525

The revocation of an agent's insurance license by the state insurance commissioner solely because of the nonpayment of a dischargeable insurance-related debt constitutes a violation of Section 525(a). See In re Bradley, 989 F.2d 802 (5th Cir., 1993); Jacobs v. Oklahoma, 149 B.R. 983 (ND OK, 1993). The denial by the county of a contractor's license to a debtor because the debtor had filed bankruptcy was a violation of Section 525(a). In re Lambillotte, 25 B.R. 392 (MD FL, 1982).

other license denials as violations of §525

The refusal by a governmental unit to approve a developer's plat because the developer had failed to file a certificate showing that certain taxes which had been discharged in the developer's bankruptcy case had been paid was also a violation of Section 525(a) in In re General Development Corp., 163 B.R. 216 (SD FL, 1994). In In re Son-Shine Grading, Inc., 27 B.R. 693 (ED NC, 1983) the state department of transportation violated Section 525(a) when it refused to permit the debtor to bid on state contracts because the debtor had filed bankruptcy. Section 525(a) has been held to prohibit the state from denying a person admission to the bar solely because the person has filed bankruptcy, although the filing of a bankruptcy case may be considered along with other factors in determining the person's financial judgment for purposes of admission to the bar. See In re Application of Taylor, 647 P. 2d 462 (Or. 1982). In In re Borowski, 216 B.R. 922 (ED MI, 1998) an attorney discipline board violated Section 525(a) when it ordered an attorney to repay, as a condition of continuing to practice law, a malpractice award that was discharged by the attorney in a Chapter 7 case. In Berkelhammer v. Novella, 279 B.R. 660 (SD NY, 2002), a physician debtor was entitled to an injunction under Section 525(a) in order to prevent his removal from the state's list of Medicaid-eligible physicians.

contractor discrimination as violation of §525(a)

professional discrimination as violation of §525(a)

governmental acts not in violation of §525

On the other hand, a governmental unit may impose fees and taxes on a defaulting contractor who is a bankruptcy debtor if imposed by the governmental unit on all defaulting contractors. See In re Rees, 61 B.R. 114 (UT, 1986). Section 525(a) also does not prevent the state from denying or revoking an agent's real estate license based upon a determination that the public safety would be jeopardized by the granting or continuance of the license, even if the nonpayment of a discharged debt was considered, along with other factors, in the making of such a determination. See In re Bradley, 989 F.2d 802 (5th Cir., 1993).

§525(a), dischargeable debt requirement

Note that Section 525(a) only prohibits governmental discrimination with respect to dischargeable debts and not with respect to nondischargeable debts. Therefore, debtor discrimination by a governmental unit based on the nonpayment of a nondischargeable debt is not prohibited by Section 525(a). See In re Bradley, 989 F.2d 802 (5th Cir., 1993); In re Walker, 74 B.R. 311 (WD VA, 1987).

§525(a), applicability to student loans

Section 525(c), which is discussed separately below, specifically prohibits debtor discrimination with respect to the making and insuring of student loans. However, Section 525(a) has been held to prohibit other forms of discrimination with respect to dischargeable student loans. Under the present Bankruptcy Code most student loans are nondischargeable in both chapter 7 and chapter 13 cases and Section 525(a) does not prohibit discrimination with respect to these nondischargeable debts. However, prior to 1992 student loans were dischargeable in chapter 13 cases and most of the reported cases dealing with student loan discrimination arose prior to 1992. See article 1.06 of this handbook for a discussion on the dischargeability of student loans.

student loan discrimination, general aspects

Several reported cases have held that it is a violation of Section 525(a) for a public university or college to refuse to release transcripts or grades to a student because the student has not paid a dischargeable student loan. See In re Reese, 38 B.R. 681 (ND GA, 1984), In re Heath, 3 B.R. 351 (ND IL, 1980), Lee v. Board of Higher Education, 1 B.R. 781 (SD NY, 1979), and In re Howren, 10 B.R. 303 (KS, 1980). One court has held that it is a violation of Section 525(a) and of the fresh start policy of the Bankruptcy Code as expressed by the Supreme Court in Perez v. Campbell, supra, for a state college to withhold a student's transcripts because of the nonpayment of a student loan even if the loan is presently nondischargeable. See In re Johnson, 28 B.R. 406 (WD PA, 1982). Other courts, however, have held that it is not a violation of Section 525(a) for a state college or university to withhold transcripts or grades from a student because of the nonpayment of a student loan that is presently nondischargeable. See In re Richardson, 27 B.R. 560 (ED PA, 1982), and Johnson v. Edinboro State College, 728 F.2d 163 (3d Cir., 1984).

Prohibited discrimination as to public housing. Several reported cases have held that the eviction of a tenant by a public housing authority because the tenant had failed to pay rent or other charges that were discharged in the tenant's bankruptcy case is a violation of Section 525(a). See In re Couture, 225 B.R. 58 (VT, 1998); In re Curry, 148 B.R. 966 (SD FL, 1992); Gibbs v. Housing Authority of New Haven, 76 B.R. 257 (CT, 1987); In re Szymecki, 87 B.R. 14 (WD PA, 1988); In re Rose, 23 B.R. 662 (CT, 1982). The policy is that the eviction of a debtor for nonpayment of prepetition rent that is dischargeable in bankruptcy amounts to an attempt by the public housing authority to coerce the payment of a discharged debt in violation of Section 525(a) and violates the fresh start policy of the Bankruptcy Code. In addition to evictions, the denial of a rental application due to negative entries on a credit report from dischargeable debts and a bankruptcy filing has been held to be a violation of §525(a). See In re Oksentowicz, 314 B.R. 638 (ED MI, 2004).

public housing discrimination, what constitutes

On the other hand, Section 525(a) was not violated in cases where the debtor›s lease was terminated by the public housing authority in accordance with regulations prior to the filing of the debtor›s bankruptcy case for other reasons. See In re Ward, 2012 WL 2920123 (Bankr. S. D. Fla. 2012); In re Valentin, 309 B.R. 715 (ED PA, 2004); Robinson v. Chicago Housing Authority, 169 B.R. 171 (ND IL, 1994); Housing Authority v. Caldwell, 174 B.R. 650 (ND GA, 1994); and In re Smith, 259 B.R. 901 (B.A.P. 8th Cir., 2001) (holding Section 525(a) did not prohibit the Public Housing Authority from terminating the debtor's subsidized housing benefits where the debtor had failed to report income as required by contract).

public housing discrimination, what does not constitute

Because the making of loans is not an activity described in Section 525(a), several courts have ruled that discrimination lending is not prohibited by Section 525(a). In Watts v. Penn. Housing Finance Co., 876 F.2d 1090 (3d Cir., 1989), a state agency that provides foreclosure prevention loans to homeowners in financial difficulty was found not to be in violation of Section 525(a) by exercising its policy of suspending loan payments to debtors during the pendency of their bankruptcy proceedings, when the debtors were protected from foreclosure by the automatic stay, even though the suspension of loan payments by the agency often resulted in late charges and other expenses being assessed against the debtors. In Toth v. Mich. State Housing Dev. Authority, 136 F.3d 477 (6th Cir., 1998), a policy of denying low-income home improvement loans to bankruptcy debtors for a 3 year period following their bankruptcy discharge was not a violation of Section 525(a) because the making of loans is not an activity covered by Section 525(a). See also Bentley v. Glickman, 234 B.R. 12 (ND NY, 1999).

making loans as activity not prohibited by section 525(a)

employment discrimination, prohibition of by §525(a)

Prohibited discrimination as to governmental employment. Section 525(a) explicitly prohibits governmental units from discriminating against bankruptcy debtors with respect to employment. In In re Latchaw, 24 B.R. 457 (ND OH, 1982) a governmental agency's policy of disciplining or terminating employees whose wages were subjected to Chapter 13 wage deductions was a violation of Section 525(a). In In re Applegate, 64 B.R. 448 (ED VA, 1986) the Army was prohibited by Section 525(a) from discriminating against a military debtor with respect to such matters as assignments, promotions and pay benefits solely because the debtor had filed bankruptcy. However, the court stated that the Army could refuse to transfer a bankruptcy debtor to a sensitive position because of financial irresponsibility.

prohibited employment discrimination, what constitutes

To be a violation of Section 525(a), a debtor must prove that the employment offense was committed by the governmental unit solely because of the debtor's bankruptcy. If other reasons exist to justify the termination of the debtor's employment or the failure to promote the debtor, Section 525(a) has not been violated. See, e.g., Shaw v. Housing Authority, 158 B.R. 400 (WD LA, 1993); In re Anderson, 84 B.R. 426 (ED VA, 1988). The "solely because" requirement of Section 525(a) is discussed below.

§525(a) violation, injunctive and declaratory remedies

Debtors' remedies for Section 525(a) violations. A debtor who establishes a violation of Section 525(a) by a governmental unit is entitled to injunctive and declaratory relief. See 11 U.S.C. § 105(a). The most common type of relief granted in Section 525(a) proceeding is an injunction barring further discriminatory action by the governmental unit or an order directing the governmental unit to issue the requested license or grant. An order of reinstatement may also be an appropriate remedy.

§525(a) violation, allowability of damage awards for under prior law

Prior to the enactment of the Bankruptcy Reform Act of 1994 a debtor could not be awarded damages against a governmental unit for a Section 525(a) violation because of the sovereign immunity provisions of 11 U.S.C. § 106. See In re Saunders, 105 B.R. 781 (ED PA, 1989) (holding that unless the governmental unit files a proof of claim, an award of damages could not be awarded against it in a Section 525(a) proceeding because of the provisions of 11 U.S.C. § 106.

However, 11 U.S.C. § 106(a) was amended in 1994 to specifically provide for a waiver of sovereign immunity in Section 525 proceedings. See 11 U.S.C. § 106(a). The following language from the Congressional Report on the Bankruptcy Reform Act of 1994 reflects the intent of Congress with respect to the amendment to 11 U.S.C. § 106:

§525(a) violation, allowability of damage awards for under current law

This amendment expressly provides for a waiver of sovereign immunity by governmental units with respect to monetary recoveries as well as declaratory and injunctive relief. It is the Committee's intent to make section 106 conform to the Congressional intent of the Bankruptcy Reform Act of 1978 waiving the sovereign immunity of the States and the Federal Government in this regard. Of course the entire Bankruptcy Code is applicable to governmental units where sovereign immunity is not or cannot be asserted. As suggested by the Supreme Court, section 106(a)(1) specifically lists those sections of title 11 with respect to which sovereign immunity is abrogated. This allows the assertion of bankruptcy causes of action, but specifically excludes causes of action belonging to the debtor that become property of the estate under section 541. The bankruptcy and appellate courts will have jurisdiction to apply the specified sections to any kind of governmental unit as provided in section 106(a)(2). The bankruptcy court may issue any kind of legal or equitable order, process, or judgment against a governmental unit authorized by these sections or the rules, but may not enter an award for punitive damages. Furthermore, in awarding fees or costs under the Bankruptcy Code or under the Bankruptcy Rules, the award is subject to the hourly rate limitations contained in section 2412(d)(2)(a), title 28, United States Code, and these limitations are applicable to all governmental units, not just the Federal Government. Section 106(a)(4) permits an order, process, or judgment to be enforced against a governmental unit in accordance with appropriate nonbankruptcy law. Thus, an order against a governmental unit will not be enforceable by attachment or seizure of government assets, but will be subject to collection in the same manner and subject to the same nonbankruptcy law procedures as other judgments that are enforceable against governmental units. Of course, the court retains ample authority to enforce nonmonetary orders and judgments. Nothing in this section is intended to create substantive claims for relief or causes of action not otherwise existing under title 11, the Bankruptcy Rules, or nonbankruptcy law. (See Congressional report on House Bill No. 5116, Oct. 3, 1994.)

11 U.S.C. § 106 amendment, legislative report

sovereign immunity of state, waiver of by Section 106, validity of

Despite the explicit language of Section 106(a), several courts have held that it contains an unconstitutional attempt to waive a state's 11th Amendment sovereign immunity rights. See In re Sacred Heart Hospital, 133 F.3d 237 (3d Cir., 1998); In re Fernandez, 123 F.3d 241 (5th Cir., 1997) (modified in 130 F.3d 1138); In re Creative Goldsmiths, 119 F.3d 1140 (4th Cir., 1997). These cases are premised on Seminole Tribe v. Florida, 517 U.S. 44, 116 S. Ct. 1114 (1996), which is discussed in Article 1.15, infra. However, in In re Hood, 319 F.3d 755 (6th Cir., 2003), the court stated that Section 106(a) contains an unmistakably clear waiver of sovereign immunity and held that the state, as the holder of a student loan, was not immune from suit in a bankruptcy court. Section 106(b), which provides that a state waives its sovereign immunity by filing a proof of claim on a matter that arose out of the same transaction as the debtor's claim, has been held constitutional in several cases. See In re Straight, 143 F.3d 1387 (10th Cir., 1997); In re Charter Oaks Assocs., 203 B.R. 17 (CT, 1996); In re Lazar, 200 B.R. 358 (CD CA, 1996); In re Platter, 140 F.3d 676 (7th Cir., 1998).

§525(b), provisions of

Private employer discrimination prohibited by Section 525(b). Section 525(b) of the Bankruptcy Code provides that a private employer may not terminate or otherwise discriminate against an individual who is or has been a debtor in a bankruptcy case, or with respect to an individual associated with such a debtor, solely because the debtor has filed a bankruptcy case, has not paid a dischargeable debt, or has been insolvent prior to or during a bankruptcy case. See 11 U.S.C. § 525(b).

§525(b), key issues under

The key issues raised by the cases interpreting Section 525(b) are: (1) Who is protected by the statute? (2) When is an employer's conduct covered by the statute? (3) What types of employer conduct are prohibited by the statute? and (4) What are the appropriate remedies for a violation of the statute? Each of these issues is discussed separately below.

persons protected by §525(b)

Section 525(b) protects individual debtors and individuals associated with individual debtors. It covers and protects individual debtors under any chapter of the Bankruptcy Code and individuals who are associated with individual debtors. For example, Section 525 protects the minor child of a debtor from discrimination. In re Dembek, 64 B.R. 745 (ND OH, 1986). On the other hand, it does not protect and may not be invoked by corporate debtors. See In re Madison International, P.C., 77 B.R. 678 (ED WI, 1987).

For the discriminatory acts of a private employer to be covered by Section 525(b), an "employment relationship" must exist between the debtor and the employer at the time of the acts. See Myers v. TooJay's Management Corp., 640 F.3d 1278, 1287 (11th Cir. 2011) (upholding verdict that employment relationship existed where prospective employee was at restaurant for 2 days of "on the job" evaluation and "employment offer" was withdrawn); In re McNeely, 82 B.R. 628 (SD GA, 1987); In re Madison Madison International, P.C., supra, (holding an employment relationship did not exist in a situation where the parties were in the course of negotiating the terms of the debtor's employment when the discriminatory conduct occurred). However, in In re Hopkins, 81 B.R. 491 (WD AR, 1987) an employment relationship existed in a case where, although the debtor had not yet begun employment, she had been accepted for employment when the discriminatory conduct occurred. But see Cord v. Skinner Nurseries, Inc., 18 FLW Fed. B20 (MD FL, 2004) (holding an offer of employment which has been accepted by the employee does not create an "employment relationship," but instead only creates an unperformed executory contract).

discriminatory employer conduct, when covered by §525(b)

An "employment relationship" in the context of Section 525(b) is clearly broader than "employment" as that term in commonly used. In In re Mc Neeley, 82 B.R. 628 (SD GA, 1987) an employment relationship existed under circumstances where under state law the debtor would clearly have been an independent contractor. In that case a lumber company with whom the debtor had been transacting business refused to give the debtor his promised quota of contract work after the debtor failed to pay a dischargeable debt owed to a third party and the court found the lumber company's conduct to be a violation of Section 525(b). An "employment relationship" was not found in Kepple v. Miller, 572 SE 2d 687 (GA App 2002), where a real estate agent whose debts to her real estate company were discharged in her Chapter 7 case was thereafter terminated. The court found that the relationship was one of an independent contractor and not an employer-employee where the company did not control the time, manner, or method of her work.

employment relationship, what constitutes under §525(b)

In several cases the courts have found an "employment relationship" to exist between the debtor and a credit union affiliated with the debtor's employer. In those cases the cancellation of the debtor's credit union membership rights following the filing of a bankruptcy case by the debtor was found to be a violation of Section 525(b). The term "discriminate with respect to employment" may even include entities such as credit unions that are affiliated with employers. See In re Patterson, 967 F.2d 505 (11th Cir., 1992); In re Callender, 99 B.R. 378 (SD OH, 1989); and In re Brown, 95 B.R. 35 (ED VA, 1989).

credit union discrimination, when prohibited by §525(b)

credit union discrimination, when not prohibited by §525(b)

However, this is the exeception rather than the rule. See, e.g., In re Briggs, 143 B.R. 438 (ED MI, 1992 (holding Section 525(b) was not applicable to credit union discrimination against the debtor because an employment relationship did not exist between the debtor and the credit union); see also, In re Henry, 129 B.R. 75 (ED VA, 1991); In re Bobbitt, 174 B.R. 548 (ND CA, 1993) (holding Section 525(b) was not applicable to a credit union that was not affiliated with the debtor's employer). In In re Spaulding, 116 B.R. 567 (SD OH, 1990) the closing of a customer's bank account by the bank following the filing of a bankruptcy by the customer was not prohibited by Section 525(b) because an employment relationship did not exist between the bank and the customer. Similarly, the refusal of an insurance company to renew an insurance policy because the insured had filed a bankruptcy case was held to be outside the scope of Section 525(b) because of the lack of an employment relationship between the debtor and the insurance company. See In re Diamond & Gold Connection, Inc., 54 B.R. 917 (MA, 1985).

bank & insurance company discrimination

discriminatory conduct under §525(b), general aspects

Once an employment relationship has been established, the next issue is whether the conduct complained of is prohibited under Section 525(b). Section 525(b) prohibits the termination or discrimination against an individual solely because he or she is or has been a debtor in a bankruptcy case, has been insolvent prior to or during a bankruptcy case, or has not paid a dischargeable debt. To be prohibited by Section 525(b), an employer's conduct must be (1) discriminatory with respect to some aspect of the debtor's employment and (2) committed solely because of the debtor's bankruptcy case, insolvency, or failure to pay a dischargeable debt.

prohibited discrimination under §525(b), what constitutes

Section 525(b) clearly prohibits discrimination with respect to any aspect of a debtor's employment and is not limited to the termination of employment. Section 525(b) prohibits discrimination by an employer with respect to promotions and advancements. See In re Hopkins, 81 B.R. 491 (WD AR, 1987). The involuntary transfer of a bank employee from the position of teller to a noncontact position in accounting violated Section 525(b) even though the pay scale and advancement opportunities were the same in both positions. See In re Hicks, 65 B.R. 980 (WD AR, 1986). A refusal by a lumber company to give a logger his quota of logging work after the logger failed to pay a dischargeable debt violated Section 525(b) even though the logger's contract was not formally terminated by the lumber company. See In re Mc Neely, 82 B.R. 628 (SD GA, 1987).

prohibited employer conduct, what constitutes

The denial of an employee's right to obtain advances against commissions because the employee had filed bankruptcy violates Section 525(b). See In re Vaughter, 109 B.R. 229 (WD TX, 1989). A denial of credit union services to an employee because the employee had filed bankruptcy was prohibited by Section 525(b) in In re Callender, 99 B.R. 378 (SD OH, 1989), although the employer's conduct in that case was found not to be a violation of Section 525(b) on other grounds.

Section 525(b) prohibits a private employer may not discriminate with respect to the employment of an individual "solely because" the individual has filed a bankruptcy case, failed to pay a dischargeable debt, or been insolvent. In many cases the most difficult aspect of establishing a violation of Section 525(b) by a private employer is proving that the discriminatory conduct was committed solely because of the debtor's bankruptcy. In order to be a violation of Section 525(b) the filing of the debtor's bankruptcy case (or the debtor's insolvency or failure to pay a dischargeable debt) must be the sole and only significant reason for the employer's discriminatory conduct. Laracuente v. Chase Manhattan Bank, 891 F.2d 17 (1st Cir., 1989). In Laracuente, the court held that if other reasons exist that would justify the employer's conduct, the conduct is not a violation of Section 525(b) even if the filing of the bankruptcy case played a significant role in the employer's discriminatory conduct. In that case the court found that a violation of Section 525(b) had not occurred where the debtor's employment was terminated 18 months after the filing of his bankruptcy case and where it was established that the employer bank had previously been investigating the debtor for making loans to family members and other forbidden conduct. In the absence of a clearly-expressed legislative intention to the contrary, the clear language of the statute ("solely because" without qualifiers) should be followed literally. For similar rulings denying the debtor relief under Section 525(b) because grounds for the debtor's dismissal other than the filing of a bankruptcy case had been established by the employer, see In re Comeaux, 915 F.2d 1264 (9th Cir., 1990); In re Callender, 99 B.R. 378 (SD OH, 1989); In re Tinker, 99 B.R. 957 (WD MO, 1989); Stockhouse v. Hines Motor Supply, Inc., 75 B.R. 83 (WY, 1987).

§525(b), the "solely because" requirement, majority rule

A few lower courts have ruled that the "solely because" language in Section 525(b) should not be literally construed because a literal interpretation would render Section 525(b) meaningless by making it almost impossible for employees to prove that their bankruptcy was the sole reason for the employers' discriminatory conduct. Instead, these courts impose a "but for" test regarding the discriminatory conduct whereunder the test would be whether the conduct complained of would have occurred "but for" the filing of the bankruptcy case. In other words, an employee's bankruptcy would have to be a substantial, but not necessarily the only, significant reason for the employer's discriminatory conduct. See Bell v. Sanford-Corbitt-Bruker, Inc., 2 BNA 1ER Cas. 914, CCH Bkcy. L. Rptr. 72114 (SD GA, 1987); In re Tinker, 99 B.R. 957 (WD MO, 1989). In any event, the "but for" test described above in this paragraph was expressly rejected by the court in Laracuente v. Chase Manhattan Bank, supra.

§525(b), the "solely because" requirement, another interpretation

Even when a literal interpretation of the "solely because" requirement in Section 525(b) is used, if the circumstances so warrant the court may disregard as frivolous or unsubstantiated an employer's alleged other reasons for its discriminatory conduct and find the conduct to be a violation of Section 525(b). A court is most likely to rule in this manner when the termination of employment or other discriminatory conduct occurs soon after the filing of the debtor's bankruptcy case and when the other alleged reasons for the discriminatory conduct are first raised by the employer after the filing of the bankruptcy case.

§525(b), violation of by employer, when most likely to be found

§525(b) violation, facts warranting

For example, a bank's decision to suspend and then terminate a probationary employee violated Section 525(b) where the bank suspended the employee after learning that the employee had several unpaid debts and then terminated the employee after the filing of his bankruptcy case and where no other job-related reason for the termination was established by the employer bank. In re Sweeney, 113 B.R. 359 (ND OH, 1990). The bank's right to terminate probationary employees as set forth in its personnel manual and the bank's asserted right to obtain a satisfactory credit check as a condition of initial and continuing employment were superseded by the provisions of Section 525(b).

§525(b) violation, cases holding

Additinoally, in In re Hicks, 65 B.R. 980 (WD AR, 1986), the transfer of a long-time bank employee from her position as a teller to a noncontact position in accounting immediately after the filing of her bankruptcy case was found to have been solely because of the filing of the bankruptcy case despite the bank's unsubstantiated assertion that the bank's customer relations would be damaged by leaving the employee in the position of teller after the filing of her bankruptcy case. In In re Hopkins, 66 B.R. 828 (WD AR, 1986), the termination of a bank employee after the filing of a chapter 13 bankruptcy case was solely because of the filing of the bankruptcy case where there was no evidence of poor job performance or misconduct by the employee and where the reason for the transfer was the bank president's fear of a public outrage because of the debtor's continued employment at the bank after the filing of the bankruptcy case.

§525(b) violation, prima facie case

In In re Mc Neely, 82 B.R. 628 (SD GA, 1987), the court found that the denial of further timber quotas to a chapter 11 logger by a timber company was solely because the logger had refused to pay a dischargeable debt owed to a third-party. In this case the discriminatory conduct occurred immediately after the filing of the debtor's reorganization plan that called for the nonpayment of the debt in question and the court found that the timber company's unsupported assertion that the logger's quotas were denied the logger because his equipment needed repair was insufficient to overcome the logger's prima facie case of covered discrimination.

prefiling discrimination as a violation of §525(b)

The majority of jurisdictions hold that the discriminatory conduct must have occurred prior to the filing of an employee's bankruptcy case, See In re Davis, 380 F. App.'x 843 (11th Cir. 2010) (holding termination "a few days" prior to bankruptcy not covered); In re Kanouse, 53 F.3d 1286 (11th Cir. 1995); In re Majewski, 310 F.3d 653 (9th Cir. 2002); but see In In re Tinker, 99 B.R. 957 (WD MO, 1989) (holding the debtor's employment was terminated five days prior to the filing of her bankruptcy case and the court held, before denying relief to the debtor on other grounds, that the existence of the words "insolvency before the commencement of a case" in Section 525(b); In re Mayo, 322 B.R. 712 (Bankr. D. Vt. 2005). However, in Kanouse v. Gunster, Yoakley & Stewart, P.A., 153 B.R. 81 (SD FL, 1993) Section 525(b) was not applicable to discriminatory conduct that occurred 209 days prior to the filing of the employee's bankruptcy case, even though the employee had threatened to file bankruptcy prior to the discriminatory conduct.

Of course, the offensive conduct must be discriminatory in order to be a violation of Section 525(b). If the policy or conduct complained of is found by the court to have been applicable to all employees and not just to employees who have filed bankruptcy, there is no violation of Section 525(b). See Browning v. Tennsco Corp., 176 B.R. 805 (MD TN, 1995) (holding employer did not violate Section 525(b) when it assessed demerits against a chapter 7 debtor for missing work to attend her bankruptcy hearing when it was shown that demerits were assessed to all employees who miss work to attend legal proceedings).

§525(b) violation, requirement of discriminatory conduct

Debtors' remedies for Section 525(b) violations. Once a violation of Section 525(b) is established, the debtor may be entitled to one or more of the following remedies: (1) an order of reinstatement, (2) an order enjoining the employer further from discriminatory conduct against the debtor, and (3) monetary damages for lost income and other damages. The type of remedy or remedies available to a debtor depends on the facts and circumstances of the case.

§525(b) violations, debtor's remedies

Certain remedies are not available for Section 525(b) violations. A contempt citation against the offending employer was held not to be an appropriate remedy for a Section 525(b) violation in In re Hopkins, 66 B.R. 828 (WD AR, 1986). Also, punitive damages may not be recovered against an employer under Section 525(b). See Bell v. Sanford-Corbitt-Bruker, Inc., 2 BNA 1 ER Cas. 914, CCH Bkcy. L. Rptr. 72114 (SD GA, 1987). Most courts have held that attorneys' fees may not be awarded for a Section 525(b) violation. There is contrary authority on this issue, however, discussed below in this section.

§525(b) violations, inappropriate remedies

If an employee was terminated or involuntarily transferred in violation of Section 525(b), the bankruptcy court has the authority under 11 U.S.C. § 105(a) to order the employer to reinstate the employee to the position that he or she would have held had the discriminatory conduct not occurred. See In re Hicks, 65 B.R. 980 (WD AR, 1986); In re Hopkins, 81 B.R. 491 (WD AR, 1987). However, if reinstatement is inequitable or inappropriate under the circumstances, it will not be ordered by the court. See In re Sweeney, 113 B.R. 359 (ND OH, 1990) (holding the reinstatement would be inequitable and inadvisable under the circumstances because the debtor had worked only briefly in a probationary position prior to being terminated and had not maintained the required special skills since his termination).

§525(b) violation, remedy, order of reinstatement

An order enjoining the debtor's employer from further discriminatory conduct against the debtor is also an appropriate remedy under the proper circumstances. See In re Vaughter, 109 B.R. 229 (WD TX, 1989) (issuing a permanent injunction against the debtor's employer from prohibiting the debtor from participating in a program whereby employees were given advances against commissions).

§525(b) violation, remedy, injunction

§525(b) violation, remedy, monetary damages

Monetary judgments against the debtor's employer for damages for the pay or income lost by the debtor have been awarded in several cases. In In re Hopkins, 81 B.R. 491 (WD AR, 1987) the court, in addition to an order of reinstatement, awarded the debtor damages against her employer in the amount of $13,824.50 for back pay. The award included compensation for lost wages, including lost salary increases and bonuses, and a deduction for income earned by the debtor in other jobs during the period between the time of her termination and the effective date of the order of reinstatement (which was the date of the court's order denying a rehearing on the matter).

§525(b) violation, remedy, monetary damages

In In re Sweeney, 113 B.R. 359 (ND OH, 1990), the court awarded $84,592 in back pay for the period between the date of the wrongful termination and the date of the judgment. The award included the debtor's lost salary, including raises which the debtor would have received had the discrimination not occurred, plus the pension and other fringe benefits that the debtor would have received, less the amount earned by the debtor in other employment during the period in question. The court applied the general principles of federal job discrimination law (42 U.S.C. § 2000e et seq.) in determining the relief to which the debtor was entitled for the Section 525(b) violation.

§525(b) violation, types of damages awarded for

In In re Mc Neeley, 82 B.R. 628 (SD GA, 1987) the court awarded a logger whose contract had been terminated in violation of Section 525(b) $5,000 for lost profits. In Bell v. Sanford-Corbitt-Bruker, Inc., supra, the court awarded the debtor damages in the amount of $5,500 for lost wages and an additional $5,000 for emotional distress suffered by the debtor as a result of the employer's discriminatory conduct. In In re Vaughter, 109 B.R. 229 (WD TX, 1989) the court found that the employer's discriminatory conduct had not damaged the debtor monetarily but awarded the debtor nominal damages in the amount of $500.

§525(b) damage awards, when property of estate

Note also that awards to debtors for Section 525(b) violations are usually for conduct that occurrs after the filing of the bankruptcy case. This means that the award is the property of the debtor and not property of the bankruptcy estate, at least in a chapter 7 case. See 11 U.S.C. § 541(a). In a chapter 13 case the award, if received before the case is closed or converted, is property of the estate and the court may order that all or a portion of the award be distributed to creditors. See 11 U.S.C. § 1306; In re Tabor, 46 B.R. 677 (SD OH, 1985).

§525(b) violations, recovery of debtor's attorney's fees

Most courts have refused to permit the recovery of attorneys' fees incurred as a result of a Section 525(b) violation. See, e.g., In re Simms-Wilson, 434 B.R. 452 (Bankr. S. D. Tex. 2010). Some courts have held that attorneys' fees are not allowable because there is no specific statutory authorization for their allowance in a Section 525(b) proceeding. See In re Sweeney, 113 B.R. 359 (ND OH, 1990); In re Hicks, 65 B.R. 980 (WD AR, 1986); In re Hopkins, 81 B.R. 491 (WD AR, 1987) (refusing to allow an award for attorneys' fees because evidence had not been presented as to their amount); but see In re Vaughter, 109 B.R. 229 (WD TX, 1989) (ordering the employer to pay the debtor's attorneys' fees in the amount of $750).

Student loan discrimination prohibited by Section 525(c). 11 U.S.C. § 525(c) prohibits a governmental unit that operates a student loan or grant program, or a person engaged in a business that includes the making of loans guaranteed or insured under a student loan program, from denying a grant, loan, loan guarantee, or loan insurance to a person that is or has been a debtor in a bankruptcy case, or to an associated person, because the debtor has filed a bankruptcy case, has been insolvent prior to the filing of a bankruptcy case, or has not paid a debt that is dischargeable in a bankruptcy case. Note that the "solely because" requirement that appears in Sections 525(a) and 525(b) does not appear in Section 525(c). See also In Taylor v. U.S., 263 B.R. 139 (ND AL, 2001) (holding that even though Section 525(c) prohibits lenders from denying student loans solely because of bankruptcy, the statute does not prevent lenders from taking bankruptcy into consideration in the granting of student loans).

prohibited student loan discrimination under §525(c), general provisions

Section 525(c), effect of

However, where a lender's denial is based on other considerations, there is no violation of 525(c). See In re Moss, 470 B.R. 505 (Bankr. E. D. Wis. 2012)(holding no violation occurred where denial was based on debtor's default on prepetition loan, and where debtor proposed to pay only 1% of loan, but noting that holding may have been different if confirmed plan required 100% payment).

Section 525(c) is not applicable to private educational institutions. See In re Walker, 336 B.R. 534 (MD FL, 2005) (dismissing a claim of discrimination under 11 U.S.C. § § 525(c) against a private university alleging that the university refused to release the debtor's transcripts postpetition for non-payment of tuition, but acknowledging that it violated 11 U.S.C. § § 362(c)(6)). See also In re Jackson, FLW Fed. B. (MD FL, 2005).

§ 525(c), application to private universities

The Congressional Report on the Bankruptcy Reform Act of 1994 (House Bill No. 5116, Oct. 3, 1994) is still relevant after the BAPCPA amendments to section 525(c). It provides as follows with respect to Section 525(c):

> "This section clarifies the antidiscrimination provisions of the Bankruptcy Code to ensure that applicants for student loans or grants are not denied those benefits due to a prior bankruptcy. The section overrules In re Goldrick, 771 F.2d 28 (2d Cir. 1985), which gave an unduly narrow interpretation to Code section 525. Like section 525 itself, this section is not meant to limit in any way other situations in which discrimination should be prohibited. Under this section, as under section 525 generally, a debtor should not be treated differently based solely on the fact that the debtor once owned a student loan which was not paid because it was discharged; the debtor should be treated the same as if the prior student loan had never existed."

§525(c), Congressional report on

Bibliography. For further reading on the issues discussed in this article, see the annotations and articles listed below.

Annotations:

Validity of Section 106(a) of Bankruptcy Code Providing Waiver of Governmental Immunity in Title 11 Proceedings. 190 ALR Fed. 453.

Validity, construction, and application of statutes, regulations, or policies allowing denial of student loans, student loan guarantees, or educational services to debtors who have had student loans scheduled in bankruptcy. 107 ALR Fed 192.

Protection of debtor from acts of discrimination by private entity under §525(b) of Bankruptcy Code of 1978 (11 USC §525(b)). 105 ALR Fed 555.

Protection of debtor from acts of discrimination by governmental units under §525 of Bankruptcy Code of 1978 (11 USS §525). 68 ALR Fed 137.

Failure to pay creditors as affecting applicant›s moral character for purposes of admission to the bar. 4 ALR 4th 436.

Validity of motor vehicle financial responsibility act. 35 ALR2d 1011.

Articles:

Bankruptcy-based discrimination. 66 Am Bankr. L.J. 387, Fall, 1992.

Private Parties and Bankruptcy-Based Discrimination. 62 Ind. L.J. 159, 1987.

Anti-discrimination under the Bankruptcy laws. 60 Am. Bankr. L.J. 185 (1986).

Private College May Withhold Transcripts From Students Whose Educational Loans were Discharged. 22 How. L.J. 155, 1979.

Cause of Action Against Governmental Unit to Establish Violation of § 525(a) of Bankruptcy Code Prohibiting Discriminatory Treatment Respecting License or Similar, 25 COA 565

Withholding Transcripts for Non-Payment of Education Debts: Before and After Bankruptcy, 15 Willamette L. Rev 563, 1979.

Walking the Tightrope: Servicemembers, Bankruptcy and Debtor Protection. 7 J. Bankruptcy L. & Practice, 257, March/April 1998.

1.04 To what extent is a debtor's right to utility service protected by Section 366 of the Bankruptcy Code?

Text of Statute. Section 366 of the Bankruptcy Code (11 U.S.C. § 366) provides as follows:

366. Utility service

(a) Except as provided in subsections (b) and (c) of this section, a utility may not alter, refuse, or discontinue service to, or discriminate against, the trustee or the debtor solely on the basis of the commencement of a case under this title or that a debt owed by the debtor to such utility for service rendered before the order for relief was not paid when due. §366, text of

(b) Such utility may alter, refuse, or discontinue service if neither the trustee nor the debtor, within 20 days after the date of the order for relief, furnishes adequate assurance of payment, in the form of a deposit or other security, for service after such date. On request of a party in interest and after notice and a hearing, the court may order reasonable modification of the amount of the deposit or other security necessary to provide adequate assurance of payment.

(c)(1)(A) For purposes of this subsection, the term "assurance of payment" means –

(i) a cash deposit;

(ii) a letter of credit;

(iii) a certificate of deposit;

(iv) a surety bond;

(v) a prepayment of utility consumption; or

(vi) another form of security that is mutually agreed on between the utility and the debtor or the trustee.

(B) For purposes of this subsection an administrative expense priority shall not constitute an assurance of payment.

(2) Subject to paragraphs (3) and (4), with respect to a case filed under chapter 11, a utility referred to in subsection (a) may alter, refuse, or discontinue utility service, if during the 30-day period beginning on the date of the filing of the petition, the utility does not receive from the debtor or the trustee adequate assurance of payment for utility service that is satisfactory to the utility.

(3)(A) On request of a party in interest and after notice and a hearing, the court may order modification of the amount of an assurance of payment under paragraph (2).

(B) In making a determination under this paragraph whether an assurance of payment is adequate, the court may not consider –

(i) the absence of security before the date of the filing of the petition;

(ii) the payment by the debtor of charges for utility service in a timely manner before the date of the filing of the petition; or

(iii) the availability of an administrative expense priority.

(4) Notwithstanding any other provision of law, with respect to a case subject to this subsection, a utility may recover or set off against a security deposit provided to the utility by the debtor before the date of the filing of the petition without notice or order of the court.

Introduction. Section 366 was enacted by Congress in the Bankruptcy Reform Act of 1978 and has not been materially amended since its enactment. In enacting Section 366 Congress recognized (1) the importance of utility services to most bankruptcy debtors, (2) the monopolistic position held by most utility providers, and (3) the fact that many utility providers used their leverage as the only utility provider available to coerce debtors into paying dischargeable utility service debts as a condition of obtaining post-bankruptcy utility service. The purpose of Section 366 is to protect bankruptcy debtors from discrimination by utility providers, while providing utility providers with adequate assurance of payment for services to be provided in the future. See In re Kentech Corp., 36 B.R. 552 (ND KY, 1983).

§366, intent of Congress in enacting

§366(a), general provisions of

Section 366(a) prohibits a utility from discontinuing or refusing utility service to, and from otherwise discriminating against, a bankruptcy debtor solely because the debtor has filed a bankruptcy case or has not paid a pre-bankruptcy debt for utility service. Section 366(b) carves a narrow exception to the nondiscriminatory provisions of Section 366(a) whereunder a utility may discontinue or refuse service to a debtor after the 20 day period following the date of the order for relief, unless the debtor furnishes a deposit or other adequate assurance of payment for future service. The date of the order for relief refers to the date that the bankruptcy petition was originally filed, and not the date of conversion if the case is ultimately converted. See In re Allen, 69 B.R. 867 (ED PA, 1987).

In most cases, then, Section 366 prohibits a utility from discontinuing or refusing service to any bankruptcy debtor during the first 20 days after the filing of the case and prohibits the discontinuance or refusal of utility service after the expiration of the 20 day period to any debtor who furnishes a deposit or other adequate assurance of payment for future services. A utility may discontinue or refuse utility service after the 20 day period to a debtor who neither furnishes adequate assurance of payment nor requests a hearing on that issue during the 20 day period after the filing of the case. See In re Stagecoach Enterprises, Inc., 1 B.R. 732 (MD FL, 1979), In re Hanratty, 907 F.2d 1418 (3d Cir., 1990), and In re Santa Clara Circuits West, Inc., 27 B.R. 680 (UT, 1982).

§366, general prohibitions and requirements

It is important to understand the relationship between Section 366 and the debtor's duty to assume or reject executory contracts, especially in Chapter 13 cases. An agreement to provide utility service is an executory contract. 11 U.S.C. § 365(d)(2) requires a Chapter 13 debtor to assume or reject all executory contracts of the debtor within a specified period. If a Chapter 13 debtor is indebted to a utility, the utility may not use 11 U.S.C. § 365(d)(2) to require payment of a prepetition utility service debt as a condition of providing postpetition utility service. Congress intended that contracts for utility services be governed by Section 366 and not by Section 365(d)(2). See In re M. Miller, Ltd., 13 B.R. 5 (MD PA, 1980); In re Gehrke, 57 B.R. 97 (OR, 1985); In re Monroe Well Service, Inc., 83 B.R. 317 (ED PA, 1988). However, a debtor or trustee who rejects a utility contract under 11 U.S.C. § 365 is not entitled to the protections of Section 366. See In re Kentech Corp., 36 B.R. 552 (WD KY, 1983).

executory utility contract, effect of §366 on

Note that the automatic stay issued under 11 U.S.C. § 362(a) upon the filing of a bankruptcy case does not prevent a utility from seeking adequate assurance of payment for postpetition service or from collecting debts from the debtor for postpetition utility services. See Hennen v. Dayton Power & Light Co., 17 B.R. 720 (SD OH, 1982), Lloyd v. Champaign Tel. Co., 52 B.R. 653 (SD OH, 1985); In re Deiter, 33 B.R. 547 (WD WI, 1983); In re Santa Clara Circuits West, Inc., 27 B.R. 680 (UT, 1982). Refusal by a utility to provide utility service to the debtor is not a violation of the automatic stay. See In re Matthews, 24 B.R. 545 (ED PA, 1982); Johnson v. Philadelphia Electric Co., 80 B.R. 30 (ED PA, 1987).

automatic stay, effect of on utility

In In re Lucre, Inc. 333 B.R. 151 (WD MI, 2005), the court considered the effect of the new BAPCPA subsection (c) on a chapter 11 case. The court stated that it has no discretion to continue the automatic stay against a utility company simply because the utility did not respond to the debtors' multiple offers of adequate assurance. The In re Lucre case stands for the position that an offer of adequate assurance only binds the utility to continue service for the 21st through the 30th days following the filing of the petition.

§366(c), effect of section

The applicability of Section 366. The prohibitions imposed by Section 366 apply to a "utility." The term "utility" clearly includes public providers of electrical, gas, telephone, water and sewer services. The term clearly covers more than public utility providers and has generally been interpreted to include end suppliers of utilities including landlords, condominium associations, and other entities responsible for supplying utilities to debtors. See In re Moorefield, 218 B.R. 795 (MD NC, 1997) (a cable television company held not to be a "utility" under Section 366); In re Randolf Towers Cooperative, Inc., 458 B.R. 1 (Bankr. D. C. 2011) (holding a bank is not a "utility").

utility, what constitutes

private utility providers, applicability of §366

In In re Good Time Charlie's, Ltd., 25 B.R. 226 (ED PA, 1982), the court noted that the term used in Section 366 was "utility" rather than "public utility," which indicated that entities other than public utilities were intended to be covered. The court also noted that the legislative history of Section 366 indicated that its intention was to cover utility providers that have a special position with respect to the debtor such that the debtor cannot easily obtain comparable service from another utility. In that case the court held that the owner of a shopping mall in which the debtor operated its business who provided electrical service to all tenants in the mall was a utility for purposes of Section 366.

non-traditional utility providers, applicability of §366

In In re Hobbs, 20 B.R. 488 (ED PA, 1982), a condominium association that supplied electrical service to individual condominium owners was a utility for purposes of Section 366 because as a practical matter electrical service was not available to condominium owners from any other source. In In re Northwest Recreational Activities, Inc., 8 B.R. 7 (ND GA, 1980), the county department of revenue was a utility because it supplied water and sewer services to the debtor. In In re Gehrke, 57 B.R. 97 (OR, 1985) an electric cooperative association was a utility because it had a practical monopoly on the supply of electricity in the debtor's area. However, in In re Coachlight Dinner Theatre, Inc., 8 B.R. 657 (SD NY, 1981) a radio station that refused to carry the debtor's advertising was not a utility for purposes of Section 366.

§366, the "solely because" requirement, construction of

Section 366(a) prohibits a utility from discontinuing or refusing service to a debtor "solely because" of the debtor's bankruptcy or the nonpayment of a prepetition debt for utility service. Therefore, if other reasons for the discontinuance or refusal of service to the debtor are established by the utility, relief under Section 366 may not be available to the debtor. See In re Whittaker, 882 F.2d 791 (3d Cir., 1989) (holding the "solely because" provision in Section 366 should not be construed too narrowly and that once the debtor establishes that his or her utility service was terminated because of nonpayment of a prepetition debt the burden shifts to the utility to establish an alternative reason for the termination); In re Jones, 369 B.R. 745 (B.A.P. 1st Cir. 2007) (holding utility may refuse to furnish service for failure to pay post-petition bills).

§366, protection, effect of equipment tampering by debtor

In In re Webb, 38 B.R. 541 (ED PA, 1984) the court held that the protections of Section 366 were not available to the debtor where the debtor's gas service had been terminated because the utility's equipment had been tampered with on the debtor's premises. See also In re Morris, 66 B.R. 28 (ED MI, 1986); Memphis Light, Gas & Water Div. v. Farley, 135 B.R. 292 (WD TN, 1991). However, Section 366 is available to the debtor in these situation only where the utility affirmatively establishes that the debtor either performed or authorized the illegal tampering. See In re Broadnax, 37 B.R. 909 (ED PA, 1984); In re Webb, 38 B.R. 541 (ED PA, 1984).

A debtor must have some type of contractual relationship with the utility in order to be entitled to protection under Section 366. In In re Matthews, 24 B.R. 545 (ED PA, 1982), the debtor was not entitled to relief under Section 366 where the debtor shared a residence with another person in whose name the utility account was maintained and where there was no contractual relationship between the debtor and the utility. However, in In re Lanford, 10 B.R. 129 (MN, 1981), the debtor was entitled to relief under Section 366 in a case where the debtor and another person at the same residence maintained separate telephone accounts and where the telephone company has discontinued the debtor's telephone service because the other person's bill had not been paid.

§366 protection, requirement of utility contract

Restoration of utility service after prefiling termination. It frequently happens that a debtor's utility service has been discontinued by the utility for nonpayment of utility bills prior to the filing of the debtor's bankruptcy case. Section 366 entitles a debtor to a restoration of service upon the filing of the bankruptcy case, although it may be necessary for the debtor to comply with the "new customer" deposit requirements of the utility. See In re Tarrant, 190 B.R. 704 (SD GA, 1995) (holding Section 366 places an affirmative duty on utility companies to reinstate previously terminated service upon notice that the customer has filed bankruptcy).

prefiling utility cutoff, restoration requirement

In In re Whittaker, 882 F.2d 791 (3d Cir., 1989) a utility that terminated service prior to the filing of the debtor's Chapter 7 bankruptcy case was required by Section 366 to restore service to the debtor within 20 days after notice of the bankruptcy filing because the utility did not customarily require deposits from new residential customers the debtor was not required to make a deposit to be entitled to a restoration of services.

restoration of terminated service, time and deposit requirements

In In re Kiriluk, 76 B.R. 979 (ED PA, 1987) a utility company that has discontinued service to a debtor prior to the filing of the debtor's bankruptcy case is not required by Section 366 to restore service after the filing of the case without adequate assurance of future payment, but where the utility does not require security deposits from new customers it must restore service upon notice of the filing of the case without obtaining such assurance unless it seeks court approval to do otherwise.

prefiling service cutoff, restoration requirements

In In re Good Time Charlie's, Ltd., 25 B.R. 226 (ED PA, 1982), the court noted that the inclusion of the word "refuse" in Section 366 along with the words "alter" and "discontinue" compelled the court to conclude that a prefiling discontinuance of service was covered by Section 366 and that the utility must promptly restore service after the filing.

restoring prefiling service cutoff, requirement of

post-filing service cutoff, restoration requirements

Protection from postfiling termination of utility service. If a utility discontinues service to a debtor during the 20 day period following the filing of the bankruptcy case, the utility is clearly in violation of Section 366. If a utility discontinues service to a debtor after the 20 day period because of the nonpayment of a debt for prepetition services, the utility is also in violation of Section 366. However, if a utility discontinues service to a debtor after the 20 day period because of the nonpayment of a debt for postpetition services, the utility is not in violation of Section 366.

post-filing service cutoff, applicability of §366

In Begley v. Philadelphia Electric Co., 760 F.2d 46 (3d Cir., 1985) the court stated Section 366 is no longer applicable and the matter is governed by state law if, after the establishment and deposit of an adequate assurance amount, the debtor defaults on subsequent payments. The utility must comply with all applicable provisions of the state termination process if it wishes to terminate service to the debtor. In such a situation, the utility's remedy is to terminate services pursuant to state law rather than seeking an increase in the adequate assurance amount under Section 366. In Jones v. Boston Gas Co., 369 B.R. 745 (B.A.P. 1st Cir. 2007), a utility provider was allowed to terminate a Chapter 13 debtor's gas service without first obtaining relief from the automatic stay based upon the debtor's failure to pay for post-petition service. See also Saint Torrance v. Cincinnati Gas & Elec. Co., 58 CBC2d 817 (B.A.P. 6th Cir., 2007).

§366(b), general provisions of & duty of utility

Adequate assurance of payment for future service. Section 366(b) provides that a utility may alter, refuse, or discontinue service to a bankruptcy debtor if the debtor fails to furnish adequate assurance of payment for future service within 20 days after the date of the order for relief (which is the date the case is filed in most voluntary cases). Section 366(b) also provides that the court, after notice and a hearing, may modify the amount of the deposit or other security necessary to provide adequate assurance of payments for future service. See In re Stagecoach Enterprises, Inc., 1 B.R. 732 (MD FL, 1979). In In re Syroco, Inc., 374 B.R. 60 (BC DC Puerto Rico, 2007), the court ruled that a utility's failure to reply or object to a debtor's proposed cash deposit as adequate assurance was considered an acceptance of such proposed deposit under Section 366(c)(2).

adequate assurance of payment, what constitutes

The term "adequate assurance of payment" for future services does not mean an absolute guarantee of payment for future services by the debtor. Rather, the term is generally construed to mean that the utility should not be subjected to an unreasonable risk of nonpayment for future services provided to the debtor. See In re Caldor, 199 B.R. 1 (SD NY, 1996); In re Santa Clara Circuits West, Inc., 27 B.R. 680 (UT, 1982); Hennen v. Dayton Power & Light Co., 17 B.R. 720 (SD OH, 1982); In re George C. Frye Co., 7 B.R. 856 (ME, 1980).

cash deposit from debtor, necessity of

What constitutes adequate assurance of payment for future services rests in the sound discretion of the trial court, based on the facts and circumstances of each case. See In re Adelphia Bus. Solutions, Inc., 280 B.R. 63 (SD NY, 2002), and In re Marion Steel Co., 35 B.R. 188 (ND OH, 1983). In most Chapter 7 and Chapter 13 cases, the adequate assurance issues are whether the utility is entitled to a cash deposit from the debtor and if so, the amount and terms of the cash deposit.

Section 366(b) provides that adequate assurance of payment may be in the form of a deposit or "other security." Therefore, if the debtor is not in default on his or her utility bill at the time the case is filed and has a good payment record with the utility, the debtor's payment history constitutes adequate assurance of payment for future service and a cash deposit is not required. See Puget Sound Energy v. Pacific Gas & Elect. Co., 271 B.R. 626 (ND CA, 2002). Such a ruling is most likely to be entered if the utility does not require cash deposits from other customers. In In re Coury, 22 B.R. 766 (WD PA, 1982) a utility was not entitled to a deposit as adequate assurance of payment where it was shown that the debtor was not in default to the utility at the time the case was filed and that the state utility commission regulations provided that deposits were not required of customers with good credit or payment records. The court concluded that the utility could not require more of a debtor than it could of a new customer under the regulations.

debtor's payment history as adequate assurance of payment

In In re Demp, 22 B.R. 331 (ED PA, 1982) a utility was not entitled to a cash security deposit from a debtor who had a history of prompt and complete payment and was current on her account at the time of filing. The utility was afforded adequate assurance of payment for future services by the debtor's payment history coupled with postpetition remedies available to the utility in the event of a default by the debtor. See also In re Seinbach, 303 B.R. 634 (AZ, 2003); In re Shirey, 25 B.R. 247 (ED PA, 1982); In re Hobbs, 20 B.R. 488 (ED PA, 1982). However, in In re Hanratty, 907 F.2d 1418 (3d Cir., 1990), it was not necessary for a utility to require cash deposits from nondebtors in order to seek a deposit from bankruptcy debtors after the 20 day period.

necessity of cash deposit, cases on

When a utility is entitled to a deposit for adequate assurance of payment, the bankruptcy court has the authority to modify the amount requested by the utility and to permit the debtor to pay the deposit in installments. In re Bedford Town Condominium, 427 B.R. 380 (Bankr. D. Md. 2010) (permitting a $90,000 deposit to be paid in $3,333 monthly installments). In In re Cunha, 1 B.R. 330 (ED VA, 1979) the court, in a case where the debtor's utility bills varied from $42 to $167 per month, where the state utility commission regulations permitted a maximum deposit of 2 month's usage charges and permitted customers to pay deposits in three monthly installments, and where the utility had demanded a deposit of $280 while the debtor had offered a deposit of $75, held that the debtor must make a deposit of $150 payable in three monthly installments in order to provide adequate assurance of payment. The court further ordered that one-half of the $150 deposit be refunded with interest in one year and that the balance of the deposit be refunded by the utility as it would refund the deposit of any of its customers in the ordinary course of business. In In re Allen-Main Assocs. Ltd., 223 B.R. 59 (B.A.P. 2d Cir., 1998), a public utility could require a residential customer who was delinquent prior to filing bankruptcy to make a security deposit in an amount equal to the sum of the two highest monthly statements, without late charges, during the previous 12 months, in the absence of extraordinary circumstances. See also In re Steinbach, 303 B.R. 634 (AZ, 2003) (ruling that creditor utilities in a chapter 13 case were entitled to one month's average estimated bill as adequate assurance).

deposit by debtor, amount of, how determined

amount of deposit, effect of bad payment record

In In re Houdashell, 7 B.R. 901 (WD MO, 1981) a security deposit of twice the debtor's highest monthly bill during the preceding 12 months was necessary for adequate assurance of payment in a case where the debtor was deeply indebted to the utility and had a history of irregular and less than full monthly payments and where the state utility commission permitted such a deposit for individuals with delinquent payment records. In In re Smith, Richardson & Conroy, Inc., 50 B.R. 5 (SD FL, 1985) a Chapter 11 debtor's offer to prepay its utility bill was not adequate assurance of payment even though the debtor was not in default to the utility when the bankruptcy case was filed. In In re Coleman, 52 B.R. 1 (SD OH, 1985) the court held that the debtor's prebankruptcy security deposit with the utility did not constitute adequate assurance of payment for future service.

state utility regulations, effect of on §366

Effect of state law on Section 366. Many states have public utility commission regulations and other laws that govern both the right of a utility to discontinue or refuse service to a customer and the right of a utility to require a deposit from a customer. Generally, state statutes or regulations that limit the bankruptcy court's authority under Section 366 are preempted by Section 366. However, state statutes and regulations that create rights in utility users and which do not limit the authority of the bankruptcy court are not preempted by Section 366 and are often relied upon or followed by bankruptcy courts in Section 366 proceedings. See In re Steinbach, 303 B.R. 634 (AZ, 2003).

authority of court under §366, effect of state utility regulations

In Hennen v. Dayton Power & Light Co., 17 B.R. 720 (SD OH, 1982) the federal policy of safeguarding utility service to bankruptcy debtors who provide adequate assurance of payment to utility providers was preemptive of any state prerogative on the question and that the determination of what constituted adequate assurance of payment was a federal question upon which state law was evidentiary only and not binding on the court. In In re Lloyd v. Champaign Tel. Co., 52 B.R. 653 (SD OH, 1985) the determination of what constitutes adequate assurance of payment is within the province of the bankruptcy court, which was not bound by state regulations or policies promulgated on state regulations. See also In re Coury, 22 B.R. 766 (WD PA, 1982); In re Northwest Recreational Activities, Inc., 8 B.R. 7 (ND GA, 1980).

§366, effect of state laws that protect utility customers

The primary purpose of Section 366 is to protect debtors from unfair discrimination by utility providers. Therefore, state laws and regulations that are designed to protect the rights of utility customers are usually upheld by bankruptcy courts as not being preempted by Section 366. In Begley v. Philadelphia Electric Co., 760 F.2d 46 (3d Cir., 1985) a state regulation which required that utility customers be given an opportunity to amortize arrearages prior to service termination was not preempted by Section 366, at least with respect to utility obligations incurred by the debtor after the filing of the bankruptcy case. See also, In re Coury, 22 B.R. 766 (WD PA, 1982) (holding state regulations requiring notice and personal contact with a customer prior to the termination of service were not preempted by Section 366).

Debtor's remedies for violations of Section 366. The debtor's remedy in a Section 366 proceeding is usually injunctive or declaratory in nature. If the utility willfully and knowingly violates Section 366, the debtor may also seek a contempt citation. If the debtor is damaged by a utility shutoff in violation of Section 366, the debtor may be entitled to an award of damages against the offending utility. §366, debtor's remedies, summary of

The bankruptcy court clearly has the authority under 11 U.S.C. § 105 to stay the termination of utility service to the debtor during the 20 day period provided for in Section 366. See In re Marion Steel Co., 35 B.R. 188 (ND OH, 1983). In In re Hobbs, 20 B.R. 488 (ED PA, 1982) the court enjoined the utility from terminating the debtors' service as long as the debtors continued to pay their postpetition utility bills where it was shown that the utility had sent notices stating that service would be discontinued if all debts were not paid. §366, injunctive power's of court under

The bankruptcy court, in its discretion, may also stay the termination of utility service to a debtor after the expiration of the 20 day period provided for in Section 366 if a hearing on the debtor's motion to modify the deposit or other adequate assurance of future payment demanded by the utility has been requested. See In re Stagecoach Enterprises, Inc., 1 B.R. 732 (MD FL, 1979); In re Robmac, Inc., 8 B.R. 1 (ND GA, 1979). §366, stay of utility termination pending hearing

If a utility refuses to agree to continue service to the debtor pending a ruling on the issue of adequate assurance of future payment, the debtor may seek an extension of the 20 day period provided for in Section 366. See In re George C. Frye Co., 7 B.R. 856 (ME, 1980). However, if the debtor during the 20 day period has neither provided adequate assurance of future payment nor filed a Section 366 motion for continuation of service, the utility has the right to unilaterally discontinue utility service to the debtor. See In re Kentech Corp., 36 B.R. 552 (WD KY, 1983); In re Dandi-Line Plants, Inc., 27 B.R. 868 (ND AL, 1983). See also In re Lucre, 333 B.R. 151 (WD MI, 2005) (holding the utility is not under an affirmative duty to respond to a chapter 11 debtor's offers of adequate assurance). 20 day period, duties of debtor during

If a utility has discontinued service to a debtor in violation of Section 366, either prior to or after the filing of a bankruptcy case, the court clearly has the authority under 11 U.S.C. § 105, 28 U.S.C. § 1481, 1651, and Bankruptcy Rule 7065 to order reinstatement of the service. See In re Marion Steel Co., 35 B.R. 188 (ND OH, 1983); In re Stagecoach Enterprises, Inc., 1 B.R. 732 (MD FL, 1979). A debtor is also entitled to injunctive relief requiring a utility to comply with state regulatory requirements before terminating the debtor's service. See Begley v. Philadelphia Electric Co., 760 F.2d 46 (3d Cir., 1985). order of reinstatement, entitlement of debtor to

While a utility that willfully and knowingly terminates a debtor's utility service in flagrant violation of Section 366 may be held in contempt of court, there is no reported case to that effect. In In re Whittaker, 882 F.2d 791 (3d Cir., 1989) the court held that a utility's violation of Section 366 by refusing to restore electric service upon the debtor's request after the filing of a Chapter 7 case was not contemptuous because Section 366 is not an automatic injunction or court order and because the utility could not have known the incorrectness of its policy because of the unsettled status of the law on the subject. contempt citation against utility, when appropriate

utility cutoff, damage award for

A bankruptcy court also has the authority under 11 U.S.C. § 105 to award damages to a debtor who has been damaged by a utility termination or refusal in violation of Section 366. See In re Whittaker, 882 F.2d 791 (3d Cir., 1989) (holding a Chapter 7 debtor who was denied utility service for five days in violation of Section 366 was entitled to nominal damages of $20 but could not recover attorney's fees).

Bibliography. For further reading on the issues discussed in this article, see the annotations and articles listed below.

Annotations:

Debtor's protection under 11 U.S.C. § §366 against utility service cutoff. 83 ALR Fed. 207.

Right of public utility to deny service at one address because of failure to pay for past service rendered at another. 73 ALR 3d 1292.

Liability of telephone company to subscriber for failure or interruption of service. 67 ALR 3d 76.

Liability of electric power or light company to patron for interruption, failure, or inadequacy of power. 4 ALR 3d 594.

Articles:

Adequate assurance of payment for utilities under 11 USC §366(b): the need for a legislative solution. 4 J. Bankr. L. & Prac. 79, November/December, 1994.

Adequate assurance of payment under Section 366 of the Bankruptcy Code: A term for interpretive flexibility or judicial confusion. 20 Akron L. Rev., Spring, 1987.

Note, Bankruptcy Code section 366; Balancing a Utility›s Right to Terminate Against a Debtor›s Fresh Start-Begley v. Philadelphia Electric Co. (1985, 3d Cir. PA) 760 F.2d 46. 59 Temple L. Q. 1011, Fall, 1986.

Providing adequate assurance for utilities under section 366. 9 Bankr Dev J 199, 1992. Dobbs; Anderson. Bankruptcy Law Changes Will Affect Business Cases Too: The Bankruptcy Abuse Prevention and Consumer Protection Act of 2005. 11 Ga. Bar J. 32, October 2005.

1.05 To what extent may a debtor avoid liens on exempt property under Section 522(f) of the Bankruptcy Code?

Text of statute. Section 522(f) of the Bankruptcy Code (11 U.S.C. § 522(f)) provides as follows:

522. Exemptions

(f)(1) Notwithstanding any waiver of exemptions but subject to paragraph (3), the debtor may avoid the fixing of a lien on an interest of the debtor in property to the extent that such lien impairs an exemption to which the debtor would have been entitled under subsection (b) of this section, if such lien is - §522(f)(1)(A), text of

(A) a judicial lien, other than a judicial lien that secures a debt of a kind that is specified in section 523(a)(5); or

(B) a nonpossessory, nonpurchase-money security interest in any - §522(f)(1)(B), text of

(i) household furnishings, household goods, wearing apparel, appliances, books, animals, crops, musical instruments, or jewelry that are held primarily for the personal, family, or household use of the debtor or a dependent of the debtor;

(ii) implements, professional books, or tools, of the trade of the debtor or the trade of a dependent of the debtor; or

(iii) professionally prescribed health aids for the debtor or a dependent of the debtor.

(2)(A) For the purposes of this subsection, a lien shall be considered to impair an exemption to the extent that the sum of - §522(f)(2), text of

(i) the lien,

(ii) all other liens on the property; and

(iii) the amount of the exemption that the debtor could claim if there were no liens on the property;

exceeds the value that the debtor's interest in the property would have in the absence of any liens.

(B) In the case of a property subject to more than 1 lien, a lien that has been avoided shall not be considered in making the calculation under subparagraph (A) with respect to other liens.

(C) This paragraph shall not apply with respect to a judgment arising out of a mortgage foreclosure.

(3) In a case in which State law that is applicable to the debtor –

(A) permits a person to voluntarily waive a right to claim exemptions under subsection (d) or prohibits a debtor from claiming exemptions under subsection (d); and §522(f)(3), text of

(B) either permits the debtor to claim exemptions under State law without limitation in amount, except to the extent that the debtor has permitted the fixing of a consensual lien on any property or prohibits avoidance of a consensual lien on property otherwise eligible to be claimed as exempt property;

the debtor may not avoid the fixing of a lien on an interest of the debtor or a dependent of the debtor in property if the lien is a nonpossessory, nonpurchase-money security interest in implements, professional books, or tools of the trade of the debtor or a dependent of the debtor or farm animals or crops of the debtor or a dependent of the debtor to the extent the value of such implements, professional books, tools of the trade, animals, and crops exceeds $5,850.

§522(f)(4), text of

(4)(A) Subject to subparagraph (B), for purposes of paragraph (1)(B), the term "household goods" means-
(i) clothing;
(ii) furniture;
(iii) appliances;
(iv) 1 radio;
(v) 1 television;
(vi) 1 VCR;
(vii) linens;
(viii) china;
(ix) crockery;
(x) kitchenware;
(xi) educational materials and educational equipment primarily for the use of minor dependent children of the debtor;
(xii) medical equipment and supplies;
(xiii) furniture exclusively for the use of minor children, or elderly or disabled dependents of the debtor;
(xiv) personal effects (including the toys and hobby equipment of minor dependent children and wedding rings) of the debtor and the dependents of the debtor; and
(xv) 1 personal computer and related equipment.
(B) The term "household goods" does not include –
(i) works of art (unless by or of the debtor, or any relative of the debtor);
(ii) electronic entertainment equipment with a fair market value of more than $550 in the aggregate (except 1 television, 1 radio, and 1 VCR);
(iii) items acquired as antiques with a fair market value of more than $550 in the aggregate;
(iv) jewelry with a fair market value of more than $550 in the aggregate (except wedding rings); and
(v) a computer (except as otherwise provided for in this section), motor vehicle (including a tractor or lawn tractor), boat, or a motorized recreational device, conveyance, vehicle, watercraft, or aircraft.

§522(f), complexity of

Introduction. To the unfamiliar Section 522(f) is one of the most complex and difficult to understand sections of the Bankruptcy Code, especially since the addition of subsections (2) and (3) in 1994. The basic lien-avoidance provisions of Section 522(f), which are complex to begin with, appear to be laced with exceptions, qualifiers and provisos. All is not as it appears, however, and, while Section 522(f) is far from simple, with a little patience and guidance it can be understood by an attorney with a general understanding of bankruptcy law. Once understood, Section 522(f) can be used to assist debtors in obtaining the "fresh start" to which they are entitled under the Bankruptcy Code by enabling them to avoid liens securing dischargeable debts that would otherwise survive the bankruptcy case and encumber their post-bankruptcy property.

§522(f)(1)(A), general description of

Section 522(f) in its present form contains four paragraphs. The first paragraph is the operative paragraph of Section 522(f). It contains two subparagraphs. Subparagraph (A) (i.e., Section 522(f)(1)(A)) provides that a debtor may avoid judicial liens against his or her exempt property to the extent that the lien impairs an exemption of the debtor, except that judicial liens securing debts of a kind specified in section 523(a)(5) may not be avoided.

A section 523(a)(5) debt, as that section was amended by the BAPCPA, is a domestic support obligation. A domestic support obligation (a DSO) is defined in section 101(14A) of the Bankruptcy Code as follows: domestic support obligation, definition of

> (14A) The term "domestic support obligation" means a debt that accrues before, on, or after the date of the order for relief in a case under this title, including interest that accrues on that debt as provided under applicable nonbankruptcy law notwithstanding any other provision of this title, that is –
>
> (A) owed to or recoverable by –
>
> (i) a spouse, former spouse, or child of the debtor or such child's parent, legal guardian, or responsible relative; or
>
> (ii) a governmental unit;
>
> (B) in the nature of alimony, maintenance, or support (including assistance provided by a governmental unit) of such spouse, former spouse, or child of the debtor or such child's parent, without regard to whether such debt is expressly so designated;
>
> (C) established or subject to establishment before, on, or after the date of the order for relief in a case under this title, by reason of applicable provisions of –
>
> (i) a separation agreement, divorce decree, or property settlement agreement;
>
> (ii) an order of a court of record; or
>
> (iii) a determination made in accordance with applicable nonbankruptcy law by a governmental unit; and
>
> (D) not assigned to a nongovernmental entity, unless that obligation is assigned voluntarily by the spouse, former spouse, child of the debtor, or such child's parent, legal guardian, or responsible relative for the purpose of collecting the debt.

Subparagraph (B) (i.e., Section 522(f)(1)(B)) provides i that a debtor may avoid nonpossessory, nonpurchase money security interests in certain types of personal property to the extent that the security interest impairs an exemption of the debtor. Avoiding liens or security interests under subparagraphs (A) and (B) are discussed separately and at length below. §522(f)(1)(B), general description of

Paragraph (2) of Section 522(f) deals with the definition of the term "impairs an exemption." This paragraph contains three subparagraphs. Subparagraph (A) (i.e., Section 522(f)(2)(A)) defines the term "impairs an exemption" for purposes of Section 522(f). Subparagraph (B) contains a rule of construction that is applicable when a debtor avoids more than one lien against the same property. Subparagraph (C) provides that the definition of impairment set forth in subparagraph (A) is not applicable to mortgage foreclosure judgment liens. Paragraph (3) of Section 522(f) (i.e., §522(f)(2) & (3), general description of

Section 522(f)(3)) contains a $5,850 contingent lien avoidance limitation that is applicable only in certain specified situations. Section 522(f)(4) was added to the Bankruptcy Code by the BAPCPA. The new section 522(f)(4) works in conjunction with section 522(f)(1)(B) to define the term "household goods" found in section 522(f)(1)(B)(i). Subsection 522(f)(4) contains a codified definition of the term "household goods" for purposes of avoiding security interests in exempt personal property under section 522(f)(1)(B). This definition replaces the many bankruptcy cases that have attempted to define the term "household goods." The definition of "household goods" provided in subsection 522(f)(4) appears to be more restrictive than the definitions found in most of the reported cases. §522(f)(4), general description of

§522(f)(1)(A), purposes of

Like many statutes, Section 522(f) is easier to understand if the purposes for which it was enacted are understood. The purpose of Section 522(f)(1)(A), which is the provision in Section 522(f) dealing with the avoidance of judicial liens on exempt property, is to assist the debtor in obtaining a fresh start after bankruptcy by enabling the debtor to avoid the liens of creditors with dischargeable claims who have "beaten the debtor to the courthouse" and obtained judicial liens against exempt property that the debtor intends to retain after bankruptcy. See In re Scannell, 453 B.R. 36 (Bankr. D. N.H. 2011); In re Thompson, 867 F.2d 416 (7th Cir. 1989). If the debtor does not avoid these judicial liens they will survive the bankruptcy case and enable the creditor to in effect collect its claim from the debtor after bankruptcy by foreclosing on its lien even though the claim upon which the lien was based was discharged in the bankruptcy case. The intent of Section 522(f)(1)(A) is to permit debtors to avoid these liens. See House of Representatives Report No. 95-595, at pg. 126.

§522(f)(1)(B), purposes of

The purpose of Section 522(f)(1)(B), which is the provision in Section 522(f) dealing with the avoidance of security interests in certain types of exempt personal property, is to assist the debtor in his or her post-bankruptcy fresh start by permitting the debtor to avoid nonpurchase money related liens of creditors against personal property that is exempt to the debtor and that is of a type that is likely to be of considerable fresh-start value to the debtor and of little monetary value to a creditor. Another purpose of Section 522(f)(1)(B) is to prevent creditors with liens on this type of property from coercing debtors into reaffirming dischargeable debts that are secured by liens on this type of property. See House of Representatives Report No. 95-595, pg. 126 et seq.; In re Wetzel, 46 B.R. 254 (WD VA, 1984).

§522(f), legislative history of

A brief account of the legislative history of Section 522(f) may also assist the reader in understanding its provisions in their present form. Section 522(f) was first enacted in the Bankruptcy Reform Act of 1978. As originally enacted, Section 522(f) simply provided that a debtor could avoid (i.e., set aside, extinguish) judicial liens against any type of exempt property and nonpossessory, nonpurchase-money liens against the types of personal property listed above in Section 522(f)(1)(B), to the extent that either type of lien impaired an exemption to which the debtor was entitled. In construing Section 522(f) in its original form, the courts had difficulty construing the term "to the extent that such lien impairs an exemption of the debtor." The constructions given this term by various courts are described below in this section in connection with the impairment of exemption requirement in Section 522(f)(1)(A). The result was that Section 522(f) was not construed and applied uniformly throughout the country.

§522(f)(2)(A), purpose and effective date of

In an attempt to cure the interpretation problem, the Bankruptcy Reform Act of 1994 contained an amendment defining the term "impairs an exemption" for purposes of Section 522(f). This definition, which is set forth in Section 522(f)(2)(A), contains a simple arithmetic test for determining when a lien impairs an exemption of the debtor. This definition is also discussed below in this section in connection with the impairment of exemption requirement in Section 522(f)(1)(A).

The Bankruptcy Reform Act of 1994 also contained an amendment to Section 522(f) dealing with judicial liens securing debts for alimony, maintenance or support. This amendment, which was set forth in Section 522(f)(1)(A), provided that judicial liens securing debts owed by the debtor for alimony, maintenance or support could not be avoided under Section 522(f). This provision is discussed at length below in this section in connection with the DSO exclusion in Section 522(f)(1)(A).

§522(f)(1)(A), nonavoidable divorce liens

The final amendment to Section 522(f) in the Bankruptcy Reform Act of 1994 added a contingent $5,000 limitation to a debtor's right to avoid nonpossessory, nonpurchase money liens against certain types of exempt property. This limitation is set forth in Section 522(f)(3) and applies only in cases where the debtor claims exemptions under a state law that either permits an unlimited exemption in a specified type of property or prohibits the avoidance of liens against that type of property. This limitation is discussed below in this section in connection with the $5,000 contingent limitation requirement in Section 522(f)(1)(B). The $5,000 amount is readjusted every three years. See 11 U.S.C. § 104.

§522(f)(3) $5,475 limitation, when applicable

The BAPCPA amended section 522(f)(1)(A) to be read in conjunction with the 11 U.S.C. § 101(14A) definition of "domestic support obligation." The amendment to section 522(f)(1)(A) by the BAPCPA broadened the judicial lien avoidance exclusion for family law liens because the exclusion now includes postbankruptcy accruals on DSOs and most assigned DSOs. Under the BAPCPA amendment, judicial liens securing DSOs that have been assigned to or are owned or recoverable by government units are excluded from avoidance as are DSOs that have been voluntarily assigned to nongovernmental entities for purposes of collection. In essence, then, a judicial lien securing a DSO is avoidable under the amended section 522(f) only if the DSO has either been assigned to a nongovernmental entity for a purpose other than collection or involuntarily assigned to a nongovernmental entity. As under prior law, debts that are in the nature of property settlement debts are not covered by the exclusion and judicial liens securing such debts may be avoided under section 522(f)(1)(A). The BAPCPA also added section 522(f)(4), thus codifying the new definition of "household goods".

§522(f), BAPCPA amendments to

The general aspects of lien avoidance under Section 522(f). Section 522(f) is most often used in Chapter 7 cases. However, Section 522(f) is applicable to individual debtors under any chapter of the Bankruptcy Code and it is clear that Chapter 13 debtors may use Section 522(f) to avoid liens. See In re Bland, 793 F.2d 1172 (11th Cir., 1986), where the court held that a Chapter 13 debtor may avoid a nonpossessory, nonpurchase money security interest in household goods and furniture and, once the lien has been avoided and the property is no longer encumbered, may exempt the property. Section 522(f) may be used by debtors in Chapter 13 cases. See, e.e.g, In re Cohen, 305 B.R. 886 (B.A.P. 9th Cir., 2004); In re Vann, 166 B.R. 167 (KS, 1994); In re Hoffman, 96 B.R. 46 (WD PA, 1988); In re Evaul, 152 B.R. 31 (WD NY, 1993). In Tower Loan of Mississippi, Inc. v. Maddox, 15 F.3d 1347 (5th Cir., 1994) a Chapter 13 trustee had standing to seek lien avoidance under Section 522(f). A Chapter 12 debtor may also avoid liens under Section 522(f). See, e.g., In re Dykstra, 80 B.R. 128 (ND IA, 1987); In re Simmons, 86 B.R. 160 (SD IA, 1988). Section 522(f) may be used by the debtor in a Chapter 13 or 12 case to transform a secured creditor into an unsecured creditor for purposes of dealing with the creditor under the plan.

§522(f) applicab chapter chapte

§522(f) applicability, types of debtors

Because of the impairment of exemption requirement in Section 522(f), it is only applicable to, and may only be used by, persons with exempt property. This means that it is applicable only to individual or joint debtors. Section 522(f) is not applicable to, and may not be used by, corporate or other nonindividual debtors under any chapter of the Bankruptcy Code.

§522(f) applicability, time limitations

Section 522(f) contains no time constraints on its applicability. Therefore, a debtor may avoid a lien at any time during a pending case. See In re Skakalski, 67 B.R. 448 (WD PA, 1986); In re Newsome, 60 B.R. 169 (ED VA, 1986). Further, a debtor may reopen a closed bankruptcy case under 11 U.S.C. § 350(b) for the purpose of avoiding a lien under Section 522(f). See In re Chabot, 992 F.2d 891 (9th Cir., 1993) and In re Levy, 256 B.R. 563 (NJ, 2000).

§522(f) proceeding, reopening case for

In Mc Donald v. Home State Bank & Trust Co., 161 B.R. 697 (KS, 1993), the court stated that Section 350(b) of the Bankruptcy Code, when read in conjunction with Section 522(f), contemplates that debtors may be allowed to reopen their bankruptcy cases in order to file Section 522(f) motions unless equitable considerations dictate otherwise. The court further stated that in deciding whether to allow a debtor to reopen a case for this purpose, the court should consider the reasons for the debtor's delay, the prejudice to creditors that may result from the reopening of the case at that time, and other equitable considerations. In that case the court held that a local rule requiring the filing of Section 522(f) motions by a date fixed at 5 days prior to the date initially set for the debtor's discharge runs counter to the intention of Sections 350(b) and 522(f) and therefore did not prevent the debtor from reopening a closed case for the purpose of avoiding a lien under Section 522(f).

ding, for

In In re Quackenbos, 71 B.R. 693 (ED PA, 1987), a debtor's right to reopen a bankruptcy case for the purpose of avoiding a lien under Section 522(f) was subject to the doctrine of laches whereunder a debtor may lose the right to avoid a lien due to undue delay in initiating the proceeding if a creditor was unfairly prejudiced by the delay. This case held that unfair prejudice occurs only when there has been a change in position by reason of the delay that is injurious to the rights of a creditor or a third party. A delay by the debtor in initiating a lien avoidance proceeding until after the deadline set for the filing of complaints objecting to the debtor's discharge was not unfairly prejudicial to creditors. See also In re Sheckard, 394 B.R. 56 (ED PA, 2008); In re Jacobs, 154 B.R. 359 (SD FL, 1992); and In e Trevino, 78 B.R. 29 (MD PA, 1987) (permitting debtor, in the absence of fraud or bad faith by the btor or unfair prejudice to creditors, to reopen a bankruptcy case for the purpose of avoiding a lien ler Section 522(f) long after the case had been closed); In re Ricks, 62 B.R. 681 (SD CA, 1986) ding in the absence of prejudicial delay by the debtor, the court must reopen a case and permit ebtor to seek lien avoidance under Section 522(f)); In re Barlett, 326 B.R. 436 (ND IN, 2005) g Fed. R. Bankr. P. 1009 prevented the debtors from reopening their case under 11 U.S.C. § cause the debtor's ability to amend exemptions ended when the case was closed).

lity to 7 cases, 13 cases

If a creditor has incurred expenses by reason of the debtor›s delay in seeking lien avoidance under Section 522(f), a possible remedy is for the court to require the debtor to reimburse the creditor for its expenses as a condition of permitting lien avoidance under Section 522(f). In In re Dodge, 138 B.R. 602 (ED CA, 1992), the court, in the exercise of its equitable powers, required the debtor, as a condition of reopening the bankruptcy case for the purpose of avoiding a judgment lien under Section 522(f), to pay $1,000 to a judgment creditor who had incurred legal expenses in a state action foreclosing on its lien which were caused by the debtor›s delay in seeking lien avoidance in the bankruptcy court.

§522(f) proceeding, condition for permitting

Although there is some authority to the contrary, the predominant weight of authority is that a lien avoidance proceeding under Section 522(f) may be initiated by the filing of a motion under Bankruptcy Rule 9014 rather than the filing of a complaint initiating an adversary proceeding under Part VII of the Bankruptcy Rules. A Section 522(f) proceeding is a contested matter requiring only the filing of a motion by the debtor under Bankruptcy Rule 9014. See, e.g., In re Citrone, 159 B.R. 144 (SD NY, 1993); In re Patterson, 64 B.R. 120 (WD WI, 1986); In re Gomez, 140 B.R. 796 (CO, 1992); In re Newell, 71 B.R. 672 (MD GA, 1987); Mc Donald v. Home State Bank & Trust Co., 161 B.R. 697 (KS, 1993). The use of a motion to initiate a Section 522(f) proceeding was also approved without comment by the Supreme Court in Farrey v. Sanderfoot, 500 U.S. 291, 111 S. Ct. 1825 (1991). A Section 522(f) proceeding may also be initiated by the filing of an adversarial complaint, if desired. See Bankruptcy Rule 7001; In re Trevino, 78 B.R. 29 (MD PA, 1987); In re Shorts, 63 B.R. 2 (DC, 1985).

§522(f) proceeding, initiation of procedure

The burden of proof as to all issues in a Section 522(f) proceeding is on the debtor. See In re Indvik, 118 B.R. 993 (ND IA, 1990); In re Larson, 260 B.R. 174 (CO, 2001). However, on the issue of the entitlement of the debtor to an exemption, Bankruptcy Rule 4003(c) provides that the party objecting to the exemptions claimed by the debtor has the burden of timely proving that the exemptions were not properly claimed. This rule is applicable to Section 522(f) proceedings. See, e.g., Campbell v. Stewart, 313 B.R. 313 (B.A.P. 10th Cir., 2004); In re Magnus, 84 B.R. 976 (Ed PA, 1988); In re Thompson, 263 B.R. 134 (WD OK, 2001); In re Cilek, 115 B.R. 974 (WD WI, 1990). However, the debtor has the initial burden of claiming the exemptions and establishing the amount or value thereof. See In re Russell, 60 B.R. 190 (MD FL, 1986); In re Indvik, 118 B.R. 993 (ND IA, 1990).

§522(f) proceeding, burden of proof

In a lien avoidance proceeding under Section 522(f) it is often necessary to establish the value of the property to which the lien is attached. Also, for purposes of lien avoidance under Section 522(f), property must be valued as of the date the bankruptcy case was filed rather than the date the lien avoidance proceeding was initiated or the date of the hearing. See In re Finn, 151 B.R. 25 (ND NY, 1992); In re Salanoa, 263 B.R. 120 (SD CA, 2001). It has also been held that the estimated costs of sale of the property should not be deducted from the value of the exempt property in a Section 522(f) proceeding because it is the value that the exemption right yields to the debtor that must be determined and not the value realizable by a creditor upon execution. See In re Anderson, 68 B.R. 313 (WD PA, 1986).

§522(f) proceeding, valuation of property

§522(f)(1)(A), purposes of

Avoiding judicial liens under Section 522(f)(1)(A). Section 522(f)(1)(A) provides that a debtor may avoid a judicial lien that has attached to exempt property of the debtor to the extent that the lien impairs the debtor's exemption, except that judicial liens securing debts for DSOs may not be avoided. As indicated above, the general purpose of Section 522(f)(1)(A) is to assist debtors in obtaining a "fresh start" after bankruptcy by allowing them to avoid the liens of creditors who beat them to the courthouse and obtained judicial liens against their exempt property prior to the filing of their bankruptcy case.

To avoid a judicial lien under Section 522(f)(1)(A), a debtor must satisfy the requirements listed below with respect to the lien, the property subject to the lien (i.e., the secured property), and the debt secured by the lien:

judicial liens, avoidance of, requirements

(1) The interest sought to be avoided must be a "judicial lien," as that term is defined in the Bankruptcy Code.

(2) The debtor must have an interest in the secured property.

(3) The debtor must claim a valid exemption with respect to the secured property.

(4) The lien must impair an exemption of the debtor in the secured property.

(5) The debt secured by the lien must not be a debt for a DSO.

(6) The court-imposed requirement in most districts that the debt secured by the lien must be a dischargeable debt.

A debtor must satisfy all of the above-listed requirements in order to avoid a judicial lien under Section 522(f)(1)(A). Each of these requirements is discussed separately below.

§522(f)(1)(A), designation of prior to 1994 amendments

Prior to the 1994 amendments to Section 522(f) subparagraph (A) of paragraph (f)(1) did not exist and the judicial lien avoidance provisions were set forth in Section 522(f)(1) instead of Section 522(f)(1)(A). Therefore, all cases prior to 1995 refer to Section 522(f)(1) when discussing the avoidance of judicial liens.

lien, what constitutes

The "judicial lien" requirement for lien avoidance. A "lien" is defined in the Bankruptcy Code to mean a charge against or an interest in property to secure the payment of a debt or the performance of an obligation. See 11 U.S.C. § 101(37). As used in the Bankruptcy Code, the word "lien" is all encompassing and includes virtually any charge or interest against property, whether created by a statute, the common law, judicial process, or an agreement. See In re Michigan Avenue Nat. Bank, 2 B.R. 171 (ND IL, 1980). Not every agreement or court order creates a lien. For example, a foreclosure decree does not convert a consensual lien to an avoidable judicial lien. In re Ruck, 451 B.R. 128 (Bankr. D. Kan. 2011). Likewise a decree of specific performance of a real estate contract entered against the debtor in a state court did not create a lien in In re Pribonic, 70 B.R. 596 (WD PA, 1987).

As indicated above, a lien may be created by a statute (a statutory lien), by an agreement (a consensual or contractual lien), under the common law (a common-law lien), or by judicial process (a judicial lien). Only judicial liens may be avoided under Section 522(f)(1)(A). Other types of liens are not avoidable by the debtor under this section. In addition, judicial liens securing debts for DSOs are not avoidable by the debtor under Section 522(f)(1)(A), unless the debt has been assigned. The reader should be aware that liens of any type may be avoidable by the debtor under Sections 506(d) and 522(h) of the Bankruptcy Code. See Arts. 1.17 and 1.18, infra.

liens, types of, avoidability under §522(f)(1)(A)

A "judicial lien" is defined in the Bankruptcy Code to mean a lien obtained by judgment, levy, sequestration, or other legal or equitable process or proceeding. See 11 U.S.C. § 101(36). Generally, then, any lien created or effected by judicial process is a judicial lien, even if the lien was not specifically created in a court order or decree. The method of creation of the lien, rather than the method of its enforcement, is the deciding factor in determining whether or not a lien is a judicial lien. See In re Carpenter, 252 B.R. 905 (ED VA, 2000), and In re Smith, 401 B.R. 674 (ED PA, 2009).

judicial lien, what constitutes

Liens created in divorce decrees, support orders, and property settlement agreements approved by the court are judicial liens, regardless of how the lien is designated in the decree, order, or agreement. See In re Haynes, 157 B.R. 646 (SD IN, 1992); In re Ray, 104 B.R. 217 (WD MO, 1989); In re West, 54 B.R. 855 (MD FL, 1985); In re Pederson, 875 F.2d 781 (9th Cir., 1989). In Keller v. Johnson, 375 F.3d 668 (8th Cir., 2004), the court stated that bankruptcy courts should look to state law to determine if a lien arising from a marital dissolution decree is a judicial lien. Similarly, judgment liens are also universally considered to be judicial liens for purposes of Section 522(f)(1)(A) even though the judgment may have to be recorded to be effective. See In re Tolson, 338 B.R. 359 (CD IL, 2005); In re Shurtleff, 170 B.R. 54 (ND NY, 1994); In re Stone, 119 B.R. 222 (ED WA, 1990). See In re Rettemnier, 113 B.R. 757 (SD FL, 1990), where a lien that arose from the issuance of a writ by a court clerk was found to be a judicial lien. See also, In re Schick, 308 B.R. 189 (NJ, 2004) (lien against a debtor's property based upon unpaid motor vehicle surcharges was held to be a statutory lien, and not a judicial lien).

judicial liens, types of

Attachment, execution, and garnishment liens are also universally held to be judicial liens for purposes of Section 522(f)(1)(A). See In re Rodriguez, 278 B.R. 749 (ND TX, 2002); In re Lafoon, 278 B.R. 767 (ED TN, 2002); In re Weatherspoon, 101 B.R. 533 (ND IL, 1989); In re Yetter, 112 B.R. 301 (SD IA, 1990); In re Austin, 73 B.R. 75 (VT, 1987); In re Coston, 65 B.R. 224 (NM, 1986); In re Challinor, 79 B.R. 19 (MT, 1987). Liens of this type cease to exist, and therefore may not be avoided under Section 522(f)(1)(A), when the garnishment, attachment or execution process has been terminated, either by a court order awarding the funds or property to the creditor or by the turning over of the funds or property to the creditor. See In re Weatherspoon, 101 B.R. 533 (ND IL, 1989). However, turning over of garnished wages by the employer to the sheriff may not, of itself, extinguish a garnishment lien for purposes of Section 522(f). See In re Yetter, 112 B.R. 301 (SD IA, 1990).

garnishment liens, avoidability of under §522(f)

wage assignment liens, avoidability of

Liens resulting from voluntary wage assignments should be distinguished from garnishment or attachment liens. Wage assignment liens are consensual liens and not judicial liens because the assignment is created by an agreement and not by judicial process, and therefore may not be avoided under Section 522(f)(1)(A). See In re Rosol, 114 B.R. 560 (ND IL, 1989); Simon v. Mercury Fin. Co., 153 B.R. 217 (ND IL, 1993).

other liens, avoidability of under §522(f)

Liens of attorneys against debtors' awards for damages for personal injuries and liens for unpaid services performed by an attorney are not avoidable under Section 522(f)(1)(A) because they are created by statute and not by judicial process. See In re Sacco, 99 B.R. 647 (WD PA, 1989); In re Thorogood, 22 B.R. 725 (ED NY, 1982); In re Felizardo, 255 B.R. 85 (SD FL, 2000). Similarly, liens of hospitals against personal injury awards of a debtor are also statutory in nature and therefore not avoidable under Section 522(f)(1)(A). See In re Pohrman, 146 B.R. 570 (OR, 1992); In re Nelson, 92 B.R. 837 (MN, 1988). The lien of a homeowners' association for unpaid assessments was held to be statutory and therefore not avoidable under Section 522(f)(1)(A) in Phillippy v. Corkscrew Woodlands Assoc., 178 B.R. 67 (MD PA, 1994).

workers' comp. lien, avoidability of under §522(f)

mechanics lien, avoidability of under §522(f)

A lien against a debtor's workers' compensation benefits created by agreement between the debtor and the state public welfare division whereby the debtor assigned his rights to future workers' compensation benefits to the state in exchange for public assistance payments was found to be statutory and therefore not avoidable under Section 522(f)(1)(A) in In re Herrick, 27 B.R. 824 (MA, 1983), even though the assignment had been submitted to and approved by the state industrial accident board, which, the debtor argued, was quasi-judicial in nature. A mechanics' lien was held to be an avoidable judicial lien under Vermont law in In re Bernstein, 62 B.R. 545 (VT, 1986). However, in In re Wisner, 77 B.R. 395 (ND NY, 1987), a mechanics' lien was found to be a statutory lien under New York law and therefore not avoidable by the debtor under Section 522(f)(1)(A). See also In re Chambers, 264 B.R. 818 (ND WV, 2001); In re Thames, 349 B.R. 659 (ID, 2005).

judicially enforced consensual lien, avoidability of under §522(f)

What about the situation where, prior to bankruptcy, a creditor employs judicial process to enforce a consensual or other nonjudicial lien? Does the lien then become judicial? In In re Lodek, 61 B.R. 66 (WD TX, 1986), an equitable lien imposed against the debtor's home because the debtor had illegally taken funds from the creditor and used the funds to improve the debtor's home was not a judicial lien because the lien arose by operation of law and the judicial acts in enforcing the lien merely protected the preexisting lien of the creditor. Similarly, in In re Sanders, 61 B.R. 381 (KS, 1986), the enforcement of a consensual lien through judicial process did not convert the lien to a judicial lien for purposes of Section 522(f)(1)(A). The court stated that the origin of the creditor's interest, and not the means of enforcement, determines the nature of the lien. In Midlantic Nat. Bank v. Deseno, 17 F.3d 642 (3d Cir., 1994), the court held that a foreclosure judgment is not a judicial lien because it is the product of a mortgage agreement. See In re Krueger, 127 B.R. 252 (ID, 1991) for a similar ruling. In Banknorth, N.A. v. Hart, 328 F.3d 45 (1st Cir., 2003) a debtor's deficiency judgment arising from a mortgage foreclosure was determined to be a non-consensual judicial lien. See also In re Criscuolo, 386 B.R. 389 (CT, 2008).

In most states and under federal law, tax liens arise automatically by statute upon the happening of the act giving rise to the lien. Obviously, then, most tax liens are statutory in nature and are therefore not avoidable under Section 522(f)(1)(A). See In re Cox, 349 B.R. 4 (ED CA, 2006); In re Shurtleff, 170 B.R. 54 (ND NY, 1994); In re Ridgley, 81 B.R. 65 (OR, 1987); In re Rench, 129 B.R. 649 (KS, 1991). However, in In re Frost, 111 B.R. 306 (CD CA, 1990), a California personal property tax lien was avoidable under Section 522(f)(1)(A) as a judicial lien because the statute imposing the tax stated that a lien for taxes thereunder shall have the force, effect, and priority of a judgment lien.

tax liens, avoidability of under §522(f)

The "interest of the debtor in property" requirement for lien avoidance. Section 522(f)(1) provides in part that "the debtor may avoid the fixing of a lien on an interest of the debtor in property...." Therefore, in order to have standing to avoid a judicial lien under Section 522(f)(1)(A), the debtor must have an interest in the secured property (i.e., the property to which the lien is attached) when avoidance of the lien is sought. See In re Vizard, 327 B.R. 515 (MA, 2005); In re Carilli, 65 B.R. 280 (ED NY, 1986); In re Trammel, 63 B.R. 878 (ED VA, 1986) (holding under Section 522(f)(1)(A) a debtor may avoid only those liens fixed on the debtor's own property and that once a debtor transfers title to the encumbered property to someone else he or she loses the right to avoid liens under Section 522(f)). The debtor's interest in the secured property must exist both when the bankruptcy case is filed and at the time when lien avoidance is sought. See In re Rosol, 114 B.R. 560 (ND IL, 1989); In re Kudrna, 173 B.R. 934 (ID, 1994).

§522(f)(1)(A), interest in property requirement, general aspects

Of course, an ownership interest in the secured property by the debtor constitutes a sufficient interest to support lien avoidance under Section 522(f)(1)(A). An interest in property that is less than a full ownership can also support a Section 522(f)(1)(A) lien avoidance proceeding. The debtor's interest in the subject property must be sufficient to enable the debtor to sustain a claim of exemption for the property. In In re Laird, 6 B.R. 273 (ED PA, 1980), the court held that a common law arbitration award in the debtor's favor constituted a sufficient interest in the awarded funds to enable the debtor to claim an exemption under 11 U.S.C. § 522(d)(5), even though the award had not been validated and did not yet have the force of law.

interest in property, what constitutes

The debtor need not have any "equity" in the secured property in order to seek lien avoidance under Section 522(f)(1)(A). In In re Shurtleff, 170 B.R. 54 (ND NY, 1994), the court held that the debtor could avoid judgment liens against his bank account even though the liens exceeded the amount in the account. It was not necessary for a debtor to have equity in the secured property in order to have an interest in the property because the purpose of Section 522(f) was to enable the debtor to create equity in the property by extinguishing the liens. See also In re May, 340 B.R. 633 (WD AR, 2006); In re Taras, 304 B.R. 912 (ND GA, 2004); In re Cheek, 111 B.R. 828 (ED MO, 1990); In re Hermansen, 84 B.R. 729 (CO, 1988); In re Citrone, 159 B.R. 144 (SD NY, 1993).

lien avoidance, necessity of equity in property

transfer of interest in property, effect of on lien avoidance

If the debtor's entire interest in the secured property has been transferred, either voluntarily or involuntarily, prior to the time that avoidance of the lien is sought, then the debtor will not have an interest in the property and may not avoid judicial liens against it under Section 522(f)(1)(A). See In re Pfiester, 449 B.R. 422 (Bankr. D. N.M. 2011) (holding debtor could not claim exemption on prepetition transfer of property which was subject of trustee's preference avoidance action). Issues of this type typically arise in cases where the debtor has property that was subject to a prebankruptcy garnishment or foreclosure proceeding wherein the debtor's interest in the property had been reduced or eliminated. In In re Roberson, 7 B.R. 34 (ID, 1980), the court held that a prebankruptcy sheriff's execution sale of the debtor's truck had transferred the debtor's entire interest in the truck to the creditor and that the debtor, therefore, did not have an interest in the truck for purposes of Section 522(f)(1)(A).

time of transfer, effect of on lien avoidance

It is important in cases of this type to determine when under local law the debtor's entire or last remaining interest in the property is transferred to the creditor. If under local law the debtor was deemed to have retained a legal or equitable interest in the secured property when the bankruptcy case was filed, then the debtor will normally be deemed to have a sufficient interest in the property to avoid a lien against the property under Section 522(f)(1)(A).

garnishment lien, effect of local law on avoidability under §522(f)

In cases where the debtor seeks to avoid a garnishment lien on wages in the hands of the employer or other personal property, whether or not the debtor retains an interest in the wages or property often depends on when under local law title to the wages or property is transferred to the creditor. If, under local law, title to the funds or property passes to the creditor at the commencement of garnishment proceedings and the debtor has no significant rights in the garnishment proceeding, then the debtor will most likely be deemed to have an insufficient interest in the funds or property to avoid a lien against the funds or property under Section 522(f)(1)(A). See In re Antley, 18 B.R. 207 (MD GA, 1982); In re Woodman, 8 B.R. 686 (WD WI, 1981).

garnishment lien, avoidability under §522(f)

In most states, however, title to garnished funds or property does not pass to the creditor until the final order of transfer in the garnishment proceeding. Therefore, if the debtor's bankruptcy case is filed prior to the entry of the final order of transfer in the garnishment proceeding, the debtor will be deemed to have retained an interest in the garnished funds or property sufficient to sustain a motion to avoid the garnishment lien under Section 522(f)(1)(A). See In re Mason, 153 B.R. 8 (RI, 1993); In re Buzzell, 56 B.R. 197 (MD, 1986); In re Harville, 63 B.R. 371 (WD KY, 1986); General Motors Acceptance Corp. v. Bates, 161 B.R. 965 (ND IL, 1993); In re Ford, 29 B.R. 364 (WD MO, 1983); In re Moore, 56 B.R. 7 (MD AL, 1985).

garnishment, transfer order voidability of

If the final order of transfer in the garnishment proceeding is entered after the filing of the bankruptcy case, the transfer order will be voidable as being in violation of the automatic stay in the bankruptcy case. Because the transfer order is voidable, the debtor will be deemed to have retained an interest in the transferred property for purposes of Section 522(f)(1)(A). See In re Yetter, 112 B.R. 301 (SD IA, 1990).

The final requirement in establishing a valid interest of the debtor in the secured property for purposes of Section 522(f)(1)(A) is that of showing that the debtor's interest in the property predated the attachment of the creditor's lien to the property. The reason for this requirement is that only liens that attached to the subject property after the debtor acquired his or her interest in the property may be avoided under Section 522(f)(1)(A).

preacquisition liens, nonavoidability of

The preexisting interest requirement described above was imposed by the Supreme Court in Farrey v. Sanderfoot, 500 U.S. 291, 111 S. Ct. 1825 (1991). In that case a house that had been jointly owned by a married couple was awarded to the debtor in a divorce decree which also granted a lien to the debtor's ex-wife to secure her share of the value of the house. Subsequently, the debtor filed bankruptcy and attempted to avoid his ex-wife's lien against the house under Section 522(f)(1)(A). The Supreme Court held that since the debtor's interest in the house in its present form arose out of the same decree that created the ex-wife's lien, the debtor's interest in the property did not predate the attachment of the ex-wife's lien to the property and therefore the lien could not be avoided under Section 522(f)(1)(A). Specifically, the court held that Section 522(f)(1)(A) requires the debtor to have possessed the interest in the property to which the lien attached before the lien attached.

Farrey v. Sanderfoot, preexisting interest requirement

The Sanderfoot rule is used primarily in cases where the debtor is attempting to avoid a divorce-created lien. The 1994 and 2005 amendments to Section 522(f)(1)(A) excluding judicial liens securing debts for DSOs from avoidability under that section has greatly reduced the applicability of the Sanderfoot rule.

preexisting interest requirement, when applicable

But the rationale of the Sanderfoot rule applies to liens of any type, not just divorce-related liens. For example, in General Motors Acceptance Corp. v. Garcia, 155 B.R. 173 (ND IL, 1993), the court was faced with the issue of whether the Sanderfoot rule rendered unavoidable a lien created by a wage deduction proceeding as applied to wages earned after the filing of the lien. Applying the Sanderfoot rationale, the court ruled the wage-deduction lien was avoidable under Section 522(f)(1)(A) because the debtor's interest in his wages arose by virtue of his employment contract and therefore predated the attachment of the wage-deduction lien as a matter of public policy. See also General Motors Acceptance Corp. v. Bates, 161 B.R. 965 (ND IL, 1993).

preexisting interest requirement in lien avoidance, when applicable

lien avoidance under §522(f)(1)(A), valid exemption requirement

The valid exemption requirement for lien avoidance. Only judicial liens on exempt property may be avoided by the debtor under Section 522(f)(1)(A). Therefore, the debtor must be entitled to, and must properly claim, a valid exemption with respect to the secured property in order to avoid a lien on the property under Section 522(f)(1)(A). The debtor may claim an exemption for purposes of Section 522(f)(1)(A) under either a state or federal exemption statute, whichever is applicable in the case. See Owen v. Owen, 500 U.S. 305, 111 S. Ct. 1833 (1991). However, a debtor who fails to claim or establish an exemption with respect to the secured property under either state or federal law may not avoid a lien against the property under Section 522(f)(1)(A). See In re Wall, 127 B.R. 353 (ED VA, 1991).

lien avoidance, importance of stacking exemptions

Because the amount of a judicial lien that may be avoided under Section 522(f)(1)(A) is limited by the amount of the exemption claimed by the debtor with respect to the secured property, it will usually behoove the debtor to claim the largest possible exemption with respect to the property. To this end, it may be in the debtor's interest to "stack" his or her exemptions with respect to the secured property. "Stacking" exemptions is accomplished by applying more than one exemption to the same property. This is usually accomplished by applying all or a portion of a so-called wildcard exemption to the property in addition to the listed exemption.

stacking exemptions in lien avoidance, examples

For example, if the federal bankruptcy exemptions (11 U.S.C. § 522(d)) were applicable to a debtor who wished to avoid a $5,000 judgment lien against his or her automobile, the debtor could apply the $3,450 automobile exemption under 11 U.S.C. § 522(d)(2) plus $1,150 (or the amount needed) of the wildcard exemption under 11 U.S.C. § 522(d)(5) to the automobile. See In re Bagley, 1 B.R. 116 (ED PA, 1979); In re Hawley, 24 B.R. 42 (MD PA, 1982); In re Marino, 39 B.R. 830 (MD PA, 1984). "Stacking" is also permissible with respect to state exemption laws. See, e.g., In re Keinath, 102 B.R. 699 (CD IL, 1986); In re Harris, 139 B.R. 386 (ED NC, 1992); In re Smith, 119 B.R. 757 (ED CA, 1990).

objections to exemptions, filing requirements

11 U.S.C. § 522(l) provides that property claimed by the debtor as exempt is deemed exempt unless a timely objection is filed. Bankruptcy Rule 4003(b) provides that the trustee or any creditor may file objections to the debtor's list of exempt property within 30 days after the meeting of creditors or the filing of any amendments to the list of exempt property by the debtor. A judgment lien creditor who does not properly object to the debtor's list of exempt property is likely estopped from litigating the issue in an ensuing motion to avoid liens under Section 522(f)(1)(A) filed by the debtor. See Campbell v. Stewart, 313 B.R. 313 (B.A.P. 10th Cir., 2004); In re Hahn, 60 B.R. 69 (MN, 1986).

Other courts have ruled to the contrary on this issue and have permitted creditors to contest the debtor's exemptions for purposes of Section 522(f)(1)(A) even if they have not previously objected to the exemptions. See In re Fonke, 321 B.R. 199 (SD TX, 2005), In re Maylin, 155 B.R. 605 (ME, 1993), In re Streeper, 158 B.R. 783 (ND IA, 1993), and In re Thompson, 263 B.R. 134 (WD OK, 2001). However, the Supreme Court has ruled that the 30 day period for filing objections to the debtor's list of exempt property is mandatory and that the exemptions claimed by the debtor must be granted if an objection or request for extension of time is not filed during that period, even if the claimed objections are clearly improper. See Taylor v. Freeland & Kronz, 503 U.S 638, 112 S. Ct. 1644 (1992).

objecting to exemptions, applicable rules

A judicial lien may be avoided under Section 522(f)(1)(A) even if state law defines an exemption in such a way as to exclude the interest in the property that is encumbered by the lien from the exemption. In Owen v. Owen, 500 U.S. 305, 111 S. Ct. 1833 (1991), the Supreme Court held that a lien is avoidable under Section 522(f)(1)(A) even if the interest secured by the lien is excluded under state law from the debtor's exemption. In that case a judgment lien was recorded against the debtor before the debtor purchased his home. Under state law a debtor's homestead exemption was not effective against preexist¬ing liens, which meant that under state law the debtor's homestead exemption was not effective against the preexisting judgment lien. The court ruled that the debtor could avoid the preexisting judgment lien under Section 522(f)(1)(A) regardless of its status under state law because under federal law the lien was deemed to have impaired the debtor's home¬stead exemption. The court also ruled that for purposes of lien avoidance under Section 522(f)(1)(A), state and federal exemptions must be treated in the same manner and that once an exemption was created certain types of liens could not be excluded or waived from the application of the exemption.

lien avoidance, effect of state exemption laws

Because Section 522(f)(1) is prefaced by the words "Notwithstanding any waiver of exemptions," the debtor may avoid a judicial lien against exempt property even if the debtor has waived the exemption with respect to the property subject to the lien. See In re Smith, 119 B.R. 757 (ED CA, 1990), and Owen v. Owen, 500 U.S. 305, 111 S. Ct. 1833 (1991).

waiver of exemptions, effect in lien avoidance

lien avoidance under §522(f)(1)(A), impairment of exemption requiremnt

The impairment of exemption requirement for lien avoidance. Section 522(f)(1) provides that a debtor may avoid the fixing of a lien "to the extent that such lien impairs an exemption to which the debtor would have been entitled...." The extent to which a lien impairs an exemption has been the subject of much litigation since the adoption of Section 522(f) in 1978. The cases construing this term, some of which are set forth below, have been far from uniform in their construction. The 1994 amendments to Section 522(f) attempted to clarify this issue by adopting a simple arithmetic method of determining the extent to which a lien impairs an exemption. This method is set forth in Section 522(f)(2)(A), which provides in essence that a lien shall be considered to impair an exemption to the extent that the sum of (1) the dollar amount of that lien, plus (2) the dollar amount of all other valid liens against the property, plus (3) the amount in dollars of the exemption that the debtor could claim if there were no liens on the property, exceeds the value of the debtor's interest in the property in the absence of liens.

impairment of exemption, illustration of calculations

avoidance of lien, amount of, limitation

Section 522(f)(2)(A) can best be explained by an illustration. Suppose, for example, that the debtors' home, which they own in fee simple, is valued at $70,000 in the absence of liens, is subject to a $50,000 first mortgage lien, a $15,000 second mortgage lien, a $35,000 judgment lien, and the debtors' $20,000 homestead exemption. Under Section 522(f)(2)(A) the $35,000 judgment lien is deemed to impair the debtors' exemption in the amount of $50,000 ($50,000 first mortgage lien + $15,000 second mortgage lien + $35,000 judgment lien + $20,000 homestead exemption - $70,000 value of debtor's interest in property = $50,000). This means that the entire amount of the judgment lien may be avoided by the debtors under Section 522(f)(1)(A) even though their equity in the home prior to the attachment of the judgment lien was only $5,000. However, if the market value of the property exceeds the sum of all consensual (i.e., non-judicial) liens against property plus the amount of the debtor's exemption with respect to the property, then the judicial lien may be avoided only to the extent of the debtor's exemption. See In re Haney, 453 B.R. 42 (Bankr. E. D. N.Y. 2011 (each lien's avoidance is assessed in reverse order under state law); In re Silveira, 141 F.3d 34 (1st Cir., 1998); In re Hanger, 217 B.R. 592 (B.A.P. 9th Cir., 1997). In other words, a judgment creditor may retain its lien to the extent that the debtor's equity in the property exceeds the amount of his or her exemption. If the property in question is owned jointly by the debtor and a nondebtor, it has been held that the debtor's surplus equity in the property must be calculated after deducting all joint encumbrances from the total value of the property and not from the debtor's fractional interest in the property. See Wiget v. Nielsen, 197 B.R. 665 (B.A.P. 9th Cir., 1996); In re Young, 471 B.R. 715 (Bankr. E. D. Tenn. 2012) (holding joint debtors entitled to aggregate homestead exemptions).

impairment of exemption, two liens, applicable rule

Section 522(f)(2)(B) provides that if the secured property is subject to more than one lien, a lien that has been avoided shall not be considered in making the arithmetic calculation described above with respect to the other liens. Therefore, if a debtor wishes to avoid two judicial liens against the same property, the calculation with respect to the first lien to be avoided would be made in the manner described above and the amount of both liens would be counted in calculating the extent to which the lien impairs the debtor's exemption. However, when the second judicial lien is avoided, the amount of the first judicial lien (i.e., the one already avoided) would not be counted in calculating the extent to which the second lien impairs the debtor's exemption.

Section 522(f)(2)(C) provides that the arithmetic method of calculating the extent to which a lien impairs an exemption (i.e., the method described above) shall not be applied with respect to a judgment arising out of a mortgage foreclosure. This means that if a foreclosure lien is avoided under Section 522(f)(1)(A) the arithmetic method described above may not be used to determine the extent to which the lien impairs the debtor's exemption. It is not clear what method should be used.

§522(f)(1)(A), when not applicalbe

All previous case-law interpretations of the term "impair an exemption" that are not in accord with the definition set forth in Section 522(f)(2)(A) were effectively overruled by the adoption of that section in 1994. See In re Holland, 151 F.3d 547 (6th Cir., 1998). Specifically overruled, according to the legislative history of the 1994 amendment, were the cases, including In re Chabot, 992 F.2d 891 (9th Cir., 1993), that limited the impairment amount to the amount of the debtor's exemption. Also overruled were Menell v. First Nat. Bank, 37 F.3d 113 (3d Cir., 1994); In re Gonzalez, 149 B.R. 9 (MA, 1993) and other cases limiting the impairment amount to the amount of the debtor's equity in the exempt property. It would appear that Section 522(f)(2) also overruled In re Dixon, 885 F.2d 327 (6th Cir., 1989), David Dorsey Distrib. v. Sanders, 39 F.3d 258 (10th Cir., 1994), and other cases holding that because the state homestead exemption applies only to execution sale situations, it could never impair an exemption of the debtor in a bankruptcy case. See In re Jakubowski, 198 B.R. 262 (ND OH, 1996). Section 522(f)(2) overrules In re Arango, 992 F.2d 611 (6th Cir., 1993) and other cases holding that jointly-owned property is not impaired in bankruptcy cases for purposes of Section 522(f)(1)(A). Finally, Section 522(f)(2) was intended to overrule In re Simonson, 758 F.2d 103 (3d Cir., 1985) and other cases holding that a judicial lien could not be avoided if it was senior to a nonavoidable mortgage lien and the amount of the mort¬gages against the property exceeded its value. In In re Cisneros, 257 B.R. 332 (NM, 2000), the court stated that whether a lien "impairs" an exemption may be determined in every case by applying the Section 522(f)(2) formula, regardless of any state law limitations on the application of exemptions. It was held that a judgment lien impaired the debtor's homestead even if state law did not allow the lien to attach to the homestead.

§522(f)(1)(A), effect of on prior case law

lien avoidance, exclusion of DSO liens

The domestic support obligation exclusion to lien avoidance. To be avoidable under Section 522(f)(1)(A), a judicial lien must be a lien other than a judicial lien that secures a debt to a spouse, former spouse, or child of the debtor, for a domestic support obligation. As defined in 11 U.S.C. § 101(14A), a DSO now encompasses the prior term used in 522(f)(1)(A), which was alimony, maintenance or support. Therefore, all cases prior to the 2005 amendments to the Bankruptcy Code pertaining to applicable issues of alimony, maintenance, and support are relevant to the new section 522(f)(1)(A). A judicial lien securing alimony or child support may not be avoided under Section 522(f)(1)(A). See, e.g., In re Brasslett, 233 B.R. 177 (ME, 1999); In re Allen, 217 B.R. 247 (SD IL, 1998). To be excludable (i.e., for the lien securing the debt to be nonavoidable under Section 522(f)(1)(A)), the debt must have been incurred in connection with a valid and enforceable separation agreement, divorce decree or other order of a court of record, must not have been assigned to another entity either voluntarily or by operation of law, and the liabilities designated as alimony, maintenance or support must actually be in the nature of alimony, maintenance or support.

property settlement liens, avoidability of under §522(f)

Property settlement debts are generally not in the nature of alimony, maintenance, or support and are therefore dischargeable under Section 523(a). See, e.g., In re Brody, 3 F.3d 35 (2d Cir., 1993); In re Morel, 983 F.2d 104 (8th Cir., 1992). Because the wording in Section 522(f)(1)(A) is identical to the wording in Section 523(a)(5), judicial liens securing property settlement obligations of the debtor are avoidable under Section 522(f)(1)(A) unless they are nonavoidable for other reasons. However, see Section 523(a)(15), making property settlement debts nondischargeable, and thus potentially ineligible for lien avoidance under the doctrines discussed immediately below.

lien avoidance, dischargeable debt requirement

The dischargeable debt requirement for lien avoidance. While nothing in Section 522(f) specifically requires a debt to be dischargeable in order for the lien securing the debt to be avoidable under Section 522(f)(1)(A), several courts have imposed this requirement. A debtor may not avoid a lien under Section 522(f)(1)(A) if the debt secured by the lien is nondischargeable. See, e.g., In re Citrone, 159 B.R. 144 (SD NY, 1993); In re De Cosmo, 163 B.R. 227 (WD NY, 1994); In re Rouse, 145 B.R. 546 (WD MI, 1992); In re Ray, 104 B.R. 217 (WD MO, 1989); Brockman v. Brockman, 143 B.R. 703 (SD IA, 1992). The rationale of these cases is that a debtor's "fresh start" would not be enhanced by the avoidance of a lien securing a nondischargeable debt and that the avoidance of such liens is contrary to the overall intent and purpose of the Bankruptcy Code.

At least one court, however, has refused to recognize the dischargeable debt requirement for lien avoidance under Section 522(f)(1)(A). See In re Hulvey, 102 B.R. 703 (CD IL, 1988) (holding the nondischargeable nature of a debt for civil damages was not a bar to the avoidance of a judicial lien securing the debt). Also, in In re Allen, 217 B.R. 945 (MD FL, 1998) the court permitted a Chapter 7 debtor to avoid a lien under Section 522(f)(1) even though the debtor was denied a discharge in the case. The court stated that the underlying nature of the debt which is secured by a judicial lien has no bearing on the debtor's right to avoid the lien.

lien avoidance permitted, non-dischargeable debt

What if a debtor fraudulently transfers or conceals assets and then attempts to avoid a judicial lien against the assets when they are recovered by the trustee? One court has held that fraud of the debtor is not a proper issue in a lien avoidance proceeding under Section 522(f)(1)(A). See In re Marino, 39 B.R. 830 (MD PA, 1984); In re Belmore, 68 B.R. 889 (MD PA, 1987); but see In re Forbes, 58 B.R. 706 (SD FL, 1986) (later proceeding in 65 B.R. 58) (refusing to permit the debtor to exempt (and avoid liens against) any portion of a judgment for unpaid wages because the debtor had failed to disclose the existence of the judgment in his bankruptcy schedules). See also In re Jones, 305 B.R. 276 (SD OH, 2003) (holding fraudulent mortgages cannot be considered when conducting the 11 U.S.C. § 522(f)(2)(A) impairment calculation).

lien avoidance, effect of fraudulent transfer or concealment of assets

Avoiding security interests under Section 522(f)(1)(B). Section 522(f)(1)(B) provides that a debtor may avoid a lien against exempt property of the debtor, to the extent that the lien impairs an exemption of the debtor, if the lien is a nonposessory, nonpurchase money security interest in any of the following types of property:

avoiding security interests under §522(f)(1)(B), types of property

(1) household furnishings, household goods, wearing apparel, appliances, books, animals, crops, musical instruments, or jewelry held primarily for the personal, family, or household use of the debtor or a dependent thereof,

(2) implements, professional books, or tools, of the trade of the debtor or of a dependent thereof, or

(3) professionally prescribed health aids of the debtor or a dependent thereof.

As indicated earlier in this section, the purposes of Section 522(f)(1)(B) are: (1) to permit debtors to avoid nonpurchase related liens of creditors against personal property that is exempt to the debtor and is of a type that is likely to be of considerable "fresh start" value to the debtor and of little monetary value to the creditor; and (2) prevent creditors with liens of this type from coercing debtors into reaffirming debts secured by this type of property. See In re Wetzel, 46 B.R. 254 (WD VA, 1984).

§522(f)(1)(B), purposes of

The terms "security interest" and "lien" will be used interchangeably throughout the discussion of Section 522(f)(1)(B). Because a security interest is a form of lien, the terms are synonymous for purposes of this discussion. To avoid a security interest under Section 522(f)(1)(B), a debtor must satisfy the following requirements with respect to the lien and the property subject to the lien (i.e., the secured property):

security interest as lien

avoiding security interests under §522(f)(1)(B), requirements

(1) The lien sought to be avoided must be a nonpossessory, nonpurchase money security interest.

(2) The secured property must qualify under one of the three types or categories of property listed in Section 522(f)(1)(B).

(3) The debtor must have an interest in the secured property.

(4) The debtor must claim a valid exemption with respect to the secured property.

(5) The lien must impair an exemption of the debtor in the secured property.

(6) If it is applicable to the debtor, the $5,850 property limitation in Section 522(f)(3) must be complied with.

lien avoidance requirements, applicability

All debtors seeking to avoid liens under Section 522(f)(1)(B) must satisfy requirements (1) through (5) above. Most debtors do not have to comply with requirement (6) above. The only debtors who need to comply with requirement (6) above are those who claim exemptions under a state law that either provides for an unlimited exemption of a debtor's equity in certain types of property or prohibits the avoidance of a lien on exempt property. Each of the above requirements is discussed separately below.

§522(f)(1)(B), designation of prior to 1994 amendments

Prior to the 1994 amendments to Section 522(f), the provisions of what is now Section 522(f)(1)(B) were set forth in Section 522(f)(2). Therefore, all cases prior to 1995 refer to Section 522(f)(2) when discussing the avoidance of nonpossessory, nonpurchase money security interests under what is now Section 522(f)(1)(B).

lien avoidance under §522(f)(1)(B), security interest requirements

The nonpossessory, nonpurchase money security interest requirement. To be avoidable under Section 522(f)(1)(B) a lien must be a nonpossessary, nonpurchase money security interest. The three specific requirements for avoidability under this general requirement are (1) the interest being avoided must be a "security interest" under the Bankruptcy Code, (2) the security interest being avoided must not be a purchase-money security interest, and (3) the security interest being avoided must not be a possessory security interest.

The first specific requirement for avoidability under Section 522(f)(1)(B) is that the interest sought to be avoided must be a security interest under the Bankruptcy Code. If the interest of the creditor in the collateral is not a security interest it may not be avoided under Section 522(f)(1)(B). A "security interest" is defined in the Bankruptcy Code as a lien created by an agreement. See 11 U.S.C. § 101(51). A security interest, then, is a consensual lien created by a security agreement. A "security agreement" is defined in the Bankruptcy Code as an agreement that creates or provides for a security interest. See 11 U.S.C. § 101(50). Generally, any writing signed by the debtor that describes the collateral and establishes the intent of the parties to create a security interest is a security agreement. See In re Data Entry Service Corp., 81 B.R. 467 (ND IL, 1988).

security interest, what constitutes

The second specific requirement for avoidability under Section 522(f)(1)(B) is that the security interest sought to be avoided must not be a purchase-money security interest, which is determined under state law. See In re Billings, 838 F.2d 405 (10th Cir., 1988); Klanish v. Penn Furniture Co., 56 B.R. 184 (WD PA, 1986).

purchase money security interest, governing law

A "purchase-money security interest" is defined in article 9-107 of the Uniform Commercial Code, as adopted in most states, as a security interest that is (1) taken or retained by the seller of the collateral to secure all or part of its price, or (2) taken by a person who by making advances or incurring an obligation gives value to enable the debtor to acquire rights in or the use of collateral if such value is in fact so used. This definition is applicable to lien avoidance proceedings under Section 522(f)(1)(B). See, e.g., In re Coomer, 8 B.R. 351 (ED TN, 1980).

purchase money security interest, definition of

A purchase-money security interest may be obtained either by the seller of the goods constituting the collateral or by a bank or other third party who furnishes the funds or value used to purchase the goods. For a valid purchase-money security interest to exist, there must be a valid security agreement that creates a security interest in favor of either the seller of the goods or the entity that supplies the funds or value used to purchase the goods.

purchase money security interest, who may obtain

A valid purchase-money security interest exists for purposes of Section 522(f)(1)(B) even if the debtor receives the goods before receiving the proceeds of the loan as long as the purpose of the loan was to enable the debtor to acquire the goods. See In re Sherwood, 79 B.R. 399 (WD WI, 1986). That the transfer of a valid purchase-money security interest from the seller of the goods to another entity does invalidate the purchase-money security interest, see In re Brooks, 74 B.R. 418 (ND GA, 1987).

purchase money security interest, validity of

purchase money security interest, effect of refinancing, transformation rule

In bankruptcy cases disputes as to the existence of purchase-money security interests most often arise in situations where the original purchase-money security interest has been refinanced, consolidated, or otherwise altered by the parties. The general rule is that the refinancing of a purchase-money security interest wherein the original debt is repaid by the proceeds of the new loan transforms the purchase-money security into a nonpurchasemoney security interest for purposes of Section 522(f)(1)(B) under the so-called "transformation rule." See In re Psick, 61 B.R. 308 (MN, 1985); In re Faughn, 69 B.R. 18 (ED MO, 1986); Rosen v. Associates Fin. Svs. Co., 17 B.R. 436 (SC, 1982); In re Richardson, 47 B.R. 113 (WD WI, 1985); In re Janz, 67 B.R. 553 (ND, 1986). The "transformation rule" is most likely to be invoked by the court if the new financing arrangement is significantly different from the original one. See In Barley, 74 B.R. 450 (ND IN, 1987); In re Hillard, 198 B.R. 620 (ND AL, 1996).

transformation rule, when not applicable

However, if it is clear from the documents and from the circumstances of the refinancing that the parties did not intend to extinguish the original purchase-money security interest, a transformation may be deemed not to have occurred. Such a finding is most likely to be made if the refinancing is done by the original lender and not by a new lender. See In re Clark, 156 B.R. 693 (SD FL, 1993); In re Hatfield, 117 B.R. 387 (CD IL, 1990); In re Hemingson, 84 B.R. 604 (MN, 1988).

purchase money security interest, refinancing of, effect of state law

In In re Billings, 838 F.2d 405 (10th Cir., 1988), state law determined whether the refinancing of a purchase-money security interest extinguished the creditor's purchase-money security interest for purposes of Section 522(f)(1)(B). The court held that under state law the refinancing of a purchase-money loan wherein the old note and security agreement are cancelled and replaced by a new note and security agreement does not automatically extinguish the creditor's purchase-money security interest where the parties did not intend to extinguish the original security interest and where the original collateral remained and almost no new funds were advanced. See also In re Short, 170 B.R. 128 (SD IL, 1994); In re Hansen, 85 B.R. 821 (ND IA, 1988); In re Krueger, 172 B.R. 572 (ND OH, 1994).

purchase money security interest, effect of loan consolidation

Loan consolidations are also a fruitful source of litigation on the issue of whether a purchase-money security interest has been extinguished. The general rule is that the consolidation of an earlier loan in a transaction wherein new funds are advanced by the creditor or new properties are added on as collateral extinguishes the creditor's purchase-money security interest in the property securing the earlier loan. See In re Freeman, 956 F.2d 252 (11th Cir., 1992); In re Challinor, 79 B.R. 19 (MT, 1987); In re Snipes, 86 B.R. 1006 (WD MO, 1988); In re Wandler, 77 B.R. 735 (ND, 1987). In some states, however, a creditor's purchase-money security interest is preserved in a loan consolidation. See In re Crispin, 139 B.R. 187 (ED TX, 1992).

The third specific requirement for avoidability under Section 522(f)(1)(B) is that the security interest sought to be avoided must not be a possessory security interest. Whether a creditor possesses a valid possessory security interest in collateral is determined under state law. Generally, a possessory security interest arises when a creditor has actual physical possession of the collateral in accordance with the provisions of the security agreement. See In re Vann, 177 B.R. 704 (KS, 1995); Wood v. Provident Fin. Co., 13 B.R. 245 (ED NC, 1981).

possessory security interest, what constitutes

The issue of whether or not a creditor has a possessory security interest in its collateral usually arises in cases where the debtor is seeking to avoid the creditor's security interest in property that has been repossessed by the creditor. In In re Meadows, 75 B.R. 357 (WD VA, 1987), the court held that the fact that the secured creditor took possession of exempt collateral prior to the filing of the bankruptcy case, as permitted in the security agreement, did not give the creditor a possessory security interest in the collateral because the security was not a possessory security interest when it attached. See also In re Schultz, 101 B.R. 68 (ND IA, 1989).

possessory security interest, effect of repossession

Similarly, in In re McFarland, 38 B.R. 370 (ND IA, 1983), the creditor did not have a possessory security interest in repossessed property because the property was in the debtor's possession when the creditor's security interest attached. In In re Vann, 177 B.R. 704 (KS, 1995), the court held that in order to create a possessory security interest that is not avoidable under Section 522(f)(2)(B), there must be an agreement providing that the secured party will posses the collateral and the secured party must in fact possess the collateral as provided in the agreement.

possessory security interests, what constitutes

However, in In re Sanders, 61 B.R. 381 (KS, 1986), the court held that upon the repossession of its collateral, a secured creditor's nonpossessory security interest became a possessory security interest that could not be avoided under Section 522(f)(1)(B). In In re Wenrich, 38 B.R. 665 (NM, 1984), the court held that a secured creditor did not have a possessory security interest in property that was owned by the debtor but was being kept in storage by a third party.

possessory security interest, existence of

The types of property against which security interests may be avoided. Only security interests in the following types or categories of property may be avoided under Section 522(f)(1)(B):

lien avoidance under §522(f)(1)(B), types of property

(1) household furnishings, household goods, wearing apparel, appliances, books, animals, crops, musical instruments, or jewelry that are held primarily for the personal, family, or household use of the debtor or a dependent thereof;

(2) implements, professional books, or tools, of the trade of the debtor or a dependent thereof; or

(3) professionally prescribed health aids for the debtor or a dependent thereof.

property subject to security interest, claiming exemptions on, effect of state law

Even though the descriptions of the above-listed proper¬ties are identical to those appearing in the federal bankruptcy exemptions (see 11 U.S.C. § 522(d)(3),(4),(6),(9)), security interests may be avoided under Section 522(f)(1)(B) against property of this type regardless of whether the debtor is claiming exemptions under the federal bankruptcy exemptions or under a state exemption statute. Further, security interests may be avoided under Section 522(f)(1)(B) against qualifying property that is exempt under state law even if state law either prohibits lien avoidance by a debtor or defines an exemption so as to exclude the secured interest from the exemption. See In re Pelter, 64 B.R. 492 (WD OK, 1986), and In re Jackson, 55 B.R. 343 (MD NC, 1985). Even if a state "opts out" of the federal bankruptcy exemptions, the avoidance of liens and security interests under Section 522(f) remains a federally-created right that cannot be taken away by the state in the guise of either opting out or limiting the interest in property to which a state exemption applies. See Owen v. Owen, 500 U.S. 305, 111 S. Ct. 1833 (1991).

property subject to security interest, claiming exemptions on

When a debtor chooses or is forced by the opting out of the local state to use exemptions provided under state law, it is often difficult to determine whether a security interest against a particular item of property can be avoided under Section 522(f)(1)(B). This is because property exempt under state law is not usually identified in the same manner as the property listed in Section 522(f)(1)(B). Section 522(f)(1)(B) initially determines whether the property qualifies for lien avoidance. That is, the property must be of a type listed in Section 522(f)(1)(B) to qualify for lien avoidance. If the property is of a type listed in Section 522(f)(1)(B), it qualifies for lien avoidance as long as it is exempt to the debtor under any applicable state or federal exemption law. For example, in In re Stallsworth, 133 B.R. 470 (SD IN, 1991), the court permitted the debtor to avoid a lien against a tool of trade even though the state exemption laws contained no exemption for tools of trade. In that case the court permitted the debtor to exempt the tool of trade under the state wildcard (i.e., "any property") exemption.

lien avoidance under §522(f)(1)(B), property requirements

To avoid a security interest in property listed in Section 522(f)(1)(B)(i), the property must be (1) of a type listed therein, (2) exempt to the debtor under an applicable state or federal exemption law, and (3) held primarily for the personal, family, or household use of the debtor or a dependent of the debtor. Even if a particular item of property is exempt and qualifies by description, if the property either is not or cannot be consumed or used by the debtor or his or her dependents, the property does not qualify for lien avoidance under Section 522(f)(1)(B). For example, in In re Duss, 79 B.R. 821 (WD WI, 1987), the court held that the debtor could not avoid a security interest on 30 acres of hay, even though the hay was obviously a crop and was exempt under state law, because the hay was not consumable and was therefore not held primarily for the personal, family or household use of the debtor or his dependents. See also In re Dana, 136 B.R. 813 (NE, 1990) (520 bushels of wheat).

The descriptions of several of the types of property listed in Section 522(f)(1)(B)(i) are general in nature and subject to differing interpretations. Foremost among these are household furnishings, and appliances. While these terms are often used interchangeably, the term "household goods" is the most nebulous and difficult to construe of these terms. Not surprisingly, it has been the subject of much bankruptcy litigation.

§522(f)(1)(B)(i) property, definitions of

The term "implements, professional books, or tools, of the trade of the debtor" appearing in Section 522(f)(1)(B)(ii) has also been the subject of much bankruptcy litigation. A state exemption statute providing that the exemption for tools of trade does not apply to defeat a security interest or pledge of otherwise exempt property does not preclude the avoidance of such liens against the property under Section 522(f)(1)(B). See, e.g., In re Day, 75 B.R. 22 (AZ, 1987); Owen v. Owen, 500 U.S. 305, 111 S. Ct. 1833 (1991).

§522 (f)(1)(B)(ii) property, effect of state law

To qualify for lien avoidance under Section 522(f)(1)(B)(ii), an item of personal property must qualify as an implement, professional book, or tool of trade and must qualify for an exemption under an applicable state or federal exemption law. See In re Neal, 140 B.R. 634 (WD TX, 1992). If a debtor uses the federal bankruptcy exemptions (11 U.S.C. § 522(d)(1) et seq.), the item of personal property upon which the lien is to be avoided need only qualify as a tool of trade, etc. under Section 522(f)(1)(B)(ii), because the applicable exemption statute (11 U.S.C. § 522(d)(6)) and Section 522(f)(1)(B)(ii) are worded identically. However, if a debtor claims exemptions under a state exemption statute, it will be necessary to qualify the item of personal property separately under Section 522(f)(1)(B)(ii) and the state statute unless the state exemption statute is worded identically to Section 522(f)(1)(B)(ii).

§522 (f)(1)(B)(ii) property, claiming exemptions on

A debtor who exempts tools of trade under a state exemption statute is not bound by the $2,025 limitation set forth in 11 U.S.C. § 522(d)(6). See In re Thompson, 867 F.2d 416 (7th Cir., 1989). Such a debtor may be bound by the $5,850 lien avoidance limitation set forth in Section 522(f)(3), however. This limitation is discussed below in this section.

tools of trade exemption, limitations on

Because the Bankruptcy Code does not contain a definition of "tools of trade," many courts look to state law for guidance. See In re Thompson, 867 F.2d 416 (7th Cir., 1989). For example, in In re Newbury, 70 B.R. 1 (KS, 1985), the court held that breeding cattle did not constitute a tool of trade of a farmer because the Kansas exemption statute listed cattle separately from tools. See also In re Gray, 303 B.R. 632 (WD MO, 2003). However, in In re Heape, 886 F.2d 280 (10th Cir., 1989), the Court of Appeals ruled that breeding cattle were tools of the trade of a livestock farmer under the Kansas exemption statute. Dairy cattle are specialized tools of the trade of a dairy farmer. See, e.g., In re Cook, 66 B.R. 3 (WD WI, 1985); but see In re Sticha, 60 B.R. 717 (MN, 1986); In re Patterson, 64 B.R. 120 (WD WI, 1986). See also In re Nuckolls, 71 B.R. 593 (WD VA, 1987) (restaurant equipment not tool of trade under Virginia statute); In re Nash, 142 B.R. 148 (ND TX, 1992) (stating "tools of trade" takes on the character of the statute providing the exemption, be it state or federal).

tools of trade, what constitutes

tools of trade, what constitutes

Generally, "tools of trade" are not restricted to small hand tools, but may include large items of equipment used in the debtor's trade. See In re Jones, 87 B.R. 738 (MD GA, 1988); In re Stallsworth, 133 B.R. 470 (SD IN, 1991); In re La Fond, 791 F.2d 623 (8th Cir., 1986) (holding that in determining whether the debtor may avoid liens on farm equipment under Section 522(f)(1)(B) as tools of trade, it is not enough that the equipment be commonly understood to be implements or tools of the debtor's trade, but instead the test is the reasonable necessity of the item to the debtor's particular trade or business. In that case the court ruled that a tractor, a plow, a wagon and silage box, a haybine, and a cylinder and hoses were tools of the trade of a farmer). In In re Neal, 140 B.R. 634 (WD TX, 1992), a computer system was held to be a tool of trade for purposes of Section 522(f)(1)(B). However, in In re Thompson, 867 F.2d 416 (7th Cir., 1989), the court ruled that the debtor could not avoid a security interest on tractors and other large items of farm equipment worth many thousands of dollars for public policy reasons. But the $5,850 limitation on lien avoidance now set forth in Section 522(f)(3) has rendered this ruling moot.

motor vehicles as tool of trade

A motor vehicle was found not to be a tool of trade for purposes of Section 522(f)(1)(B) in the following cases: In re Garcia, 451 B.R. 909 (C. D. Cal. 2011); In re Belsome, 434 F.3d 774 (5th Cir., 2005); In re Villa, 74 B.R. 497 (MT, 1987); In re Graham, 62 B.R. 64 (ED MO, 1985); In re Johnson, 160 B.R. 613 (MN, 1993). However, a motor vehicle was found to be a tool of trade for purposes of Section 522(f)(1)(B) in the following cases: In re Vasina, 337 B.R. 684 (NE, 2006), In re Stallsworth, 133 B.R. 470 (SD IN, 1991), In re Baker, 139 B.R. 468 (WD MO, 1992), and In re Vann, 177 B.R. 704 (KS, 1995). It depends on the particular trade or occupation of the debtor and the necessity of the vehicle in the debtor's trade or business. See In re King, 451 B.R. 884 (Bankr. D. Iowa, 2011) (debtor entitled to prove motor vehicle was "tool of the trade" notwithstanding that debtor claimed exemptions under state law, which did not permit vehicles to be "tools of the trade").

tools of trade, avoiding liens against, effect of abandonment of trade

Generally, held that the temporary abandonment of a trade or occupation by a debtor does not preclude the debtor from avoiding liens on the tools of that trade as long as it is shown that the debtor intends to resume the trade or occupation in the foreseeable future. See In re La Fond, 791 F.2d 623 (8th Cir., 1986); In re Jones, 87 B.R. 738 (MD GA, 1988); In re Janz, 67 B.R. 553 (ND, 1986); In re Banke, 275 B.R. 317 (ND IA, 2002). However, liens against tools or implements of the trade of the debtor may not be avoided under Section 522(f)(1)(B) if the debtor has abandoned the trade or occupation and has no present intention of returning to that trade or occupation. See In re Psick, 61 B.R. 308 (MN, 1985); Johnson v. Border State Bank, 230 B.R. 608 (B.A.P. 8th Cir., 1999).

§522(f)(1)(B), interest of debtor in property requirements

The "interest of the debtor in property" and exemption require-ments. To have standing to avoid a security interest in household goods, tools of trade, or any other property under Section 522(f)(1)(B), the debtor must have an interest in the property when avoidance of the security interest is sought. This does not mean that the debtor must have an "equity" in the property. A debtor may avoid a security interest in personal property in which the debtor has no "equity" in the economic sense. See In re Shearer, 132 B.R. 313 (WD VA, 1991); In re Gray, 87 B.R. 591 (ED MO, 1988); In re Leonard, 866 F.2d 335 (10th Cir., 1989); Owen v. Owen, 500 U.S. 305, 111 S. Ct. 1833 (1991).

However, the debtor must have a present legal or equitable interest in the property in order to have standing under Section 522(f)(1)(B). If the debtor's entire interest in the property was transferred prior to the filing of the bankruptcy case, the debtor has no standing to avoid a security interest in the property under Section 522(f)(1)(B). For further reading on this subject see the discussion of this issue above in this article with respect to the avoidance of judicial liens under Section 522(f)(1)(A).

interest of debtor in property, what constitutes

As indicated above, in order to avoid a security interest in personal property under Section 522(f)(1)(B), the debtor must claim a valid exemption with respect to the property. The exemption, which must be properly listed and claimed by the debtor in the schedules filed in the case, may be claimed under either state or federal law, whichever is applicable to the debtor in the case. See Owen v. Owen, 500 U.S. 305, 111 S. Ct. 1833 (1991); In re Neal, 140 B.R. 634 (WD TX, 1992).

§522(f)(1)(B), valid exemption requirement

If a debtor is claiming exemptions under a state exemption statute, the state does not have to specifically exempt "household goods," "tools of trade," or any other item of personal property listed in Section 522(f)(1)(B). It is only necessary that the item of personal property in question be exempt under an exemption of some type. See In re Jones, 87 B.R. 738 (MD GA, 1988), where the debtor was permitted to exempt tools of trade under the state wildcard (i.e. "any property") exemption statute.

state exemption laws, requirements of for lien avoidance

Because the amount of a security interest that may be avoided against personal property is dependent upon the amount of the exemption claimed by the debtor against the property, it may behoove the debtor to claim the largest possible exemption against the property. To this end, it is permissible for a debtor to "stack" exemptions with respect to property against which a security interest is sought to be avoided under Section 522(f)(1)(B). Exemption "stacking" is accomplished by applying more than one exemption to the same property. A debtor claiming exemptions under state law may stack exemptions by applying the state tools of trade exemption and the state wildcard exemption to the same property. See, e.g., In re Jones, 87 B.R. 738 (MD GA, 1988); In re Allman, 58 B.R. 790 (CD IL, 1986). "Stacking" is permitted with respect to the federal bankruptcy exemptions under 11 U.S.C. § 522(d)(1) et seq. See, e.g.,, see In re Marino, 39 B.R. 830 (MD PA, 1984). For further reading on the valid exemption requirement, see the discussion on that subject above in this article with respect to the avoidance of judicial liens under Section 522(f)(1)(A).

lien avoidance, validity of exemption stacking

In order to avoid a security interest under Section 522(f)(1)(B), the security interest must impair an exemption of the debtor. This means that a debtor may avoid a security interest under Section 522(f)(1)(B) only to the extent that the security interest impairs the debtor's exemption in the property that is subject to the security interest. See 11 U.S.C. § 522(f)(1).

§522(f)(1)(B), impairment of exemption requirement

impairment of exemption, what constitutes

The extent to which a lien or security interest impairs an exemption of the debtor is set forth in Section 522(f)(2)(A). Section 522(f)(2)(A) provides that for purposes of Section 522(f), a lien shall be considered to impair an exemption to the extent that the sum of the lien being avoided, plus all other liens on the property, plus the amount of the exemption that the debtor could claim if there were no liens on the property exceeds the value that the debtor's interest in the property would be if there were no liens on the property.

impairment of exemption, illustration

Suppose, for example, that a debtor wishes to avoid a $3,000 nonpossessory, nonpurchase money security interest in household goods valued at $2,000, upon which the debtor is entitled to a $2,000 exemption. The debtor's exemption is deemed to be impaired for purposes of Section 522(f)(1)(B) in the amount of $3,000 (the $3,000 lien being avoided plus the debtor's $2,000 exemption, less the $2,000 value of the property), which means that in this case the entire $3,000 security interest may be avoided by the debtor.

impairment of exemption, rule when 2 or more liens

Section 522(f)(2)(B) provides that if secured property is subject to more than one lien, a lien that has been avoided shall not be considered in making the impairment calculation with respect to the other liens. Suppose that a debtor has tools of trade valued at $4,000 which are subject to two nonpossessory, nonpurchase money security interests consisting of lien A in the amount of $5,000 and lien B in the amount of $1,000. Suppose further that the debtor is entitled to a $1,500 exemption with respect to the property. If the debtor avoids lien A first, that lien is deemed to impair the debtor's exemption in the amount of $3,500 ($5,000 + $1,000 + $1,500 - $4,000 = $3,500), which means that lien A could be avoided in the amount of $3,500. If lien B is then avoided, it would not be deemed to impair the debtor's exemption in any amount ($1,000 + $1,500 - $4,000 = -$1,500), which means that lien B could not be avoided. However, if lien B was avoided first, it could be avoided in its entirety because it would be deemed to impair the debtor's exemption in the amount of $3,500 ($5,000 + $1,000 + $1,500 - $4,000 = $3,500). Lien A could then be avoided in the amount of $2,500 ($5,000 + $1,500 - $4,000 = $2,500).

exemption stacking, importance of in lien avoidance

In the above example if the debtor had "stacked" his or her exemptions and applied $2,500 of a wildcard or other applicable exemption to the property in addition to the $1,500 tool of trade exemption, both liens could have been avoided in their entirety, regardless of the order of avoidance. Lien B, if avoided first, would impair the debtor's combined exemptions in the amount of $6,000 ($5,000 + $1,000 + $4,000 (combined exemption amount) - $4,000 = $6,000) and lien A would then impair the exemption in the amount of $5,000 ($5,000 + $4,000 - $4,000 = $5,000). If lien A was avoided first, it would again be completely avoided ($5,000 + $1,000 + $4,000 - $4,000 = $6,000), as would lien B ($1,000 + $4,000 - $4,000 = $1,000). This example illustrates the importance of "stacking" exemptions for purposes of lien avoidance under Section 522(f). For further reading on the impairment of exemption requirement, see the discussion above in this section on the impairment of exemption requirement with respect to the avoidance of judicial liens under Section 522(f)(1)(A).

The $5,850 limitation on security interest avoidance. Section 522(f)(3) provides that if a debtor claims his or her exemptions under state law, either voluntarily or because the state has opted out of the federal bankruptcy exemptions, and if the state law either allows an exemption of an unlimited amount with respect to the debtor's equity in the property or prohibits the avoidance of a consensual lien on exempt property, the debtor may not avoid a security interest in the following types of property of the debtor or a dependent thereof to the extent that the value of the property exceeds $5,850: (1) implements, professional books, or tools of the trade, or (2) farm animals or crops.

lien avoidance, $5,850 limitation, applicable property

Section 522(f)(3) was enacted in 1994, apparently in response to In re Patterson, 825 F.2d 1140 (7th Cir., 1987), and In re Thompson, 867 F.2d 416 (7th Cir., 1989), which held that a debtor could avoid liens in an unlimited amount against the debtor's tools of trade when the state exemption laws placed no limit on the amount of its tools of trade exemption. See also In re La Fond, 791 F.2d 623 (8th Cir., 1986), (allowing the debtor to avoid liens against items of farm equipment worth many thousands of dollars).

$5, 850 lien avoidance limitation, reason for

Suppose that a debtor owns tools of trade valued at $10,000, claims his exemptions under a state law that provides an unlimited exemption for a debtor's equity in tools of trade, and wishes to avoid a $7,000 nonpossessary, nonpurchase money security interest in the tools of trade. While it is not clear how Section 522(f)(3) functions with respect to Section 522(f)(2)(A), the debtor could avoid the security interest only in the amount of $5,850 because under Section 522(f)(3) the security interest could not be avoided against the property to the extent that the property exceeds $5,850 in value.

$5, 850 lien avoidance limitation, illustration

The most important thing to remember about Section 522(f)(3) is that it only applies when each of the following two conditions are present: (1) the debtor is claiming his or her exemptions under state law, and (2) state law either permits an exemption in an unlimited amount with respect to the debtor's equity in the secured property or prohibits the avoidance of a consensual lien on the secured property. See In re Ehlen, 207 B.R. 179 (WD WI, 1996). Section 522(f)(3) is never applicable to a debtor who uses the federal bankruptcy exemptions. Like other exemption provisions, Section 522(f)(3) applies separately to each debtor in a joint case. See 11 U.S.C. § 522(m).

$5, 850 lien avoidance limitation, applicability of

Bibliography. For further reading on the issues discussed in this article, see the annotations and articles listed below:

Annotations:

Avoidance under §522(f) of Bankruptcy Code of 1978 of Judicial Liens on Debtor's Exempt Property. 124 ALR Fed 465

Avoidance Under § 522(f)(1) of Bankruptcy Code (11 U.S.C.A. § 522(f)(1)) of Judicial Lien on Debtor's Exempt Real Property. 14 ALR Fed 2d 593

Avoidance under 11 U.S.C. § 522(f)(2) of the Bankruptcy Code of 1978 of Nonpossessory, Nonpurchase-money Security Interests in Debtor's Exempt Personal Property. 55 ALR Fed 353

Articles:

A tale of two codes: Examining Section 522(f) of the Bankruptcy Code, Section 9-103 of the Uniform Commercial Code, and the Proper Role of State Law in Bankruptcy. 79 Wash. U. L Q 863, Fall 2001.

Divorce, Bankruptcy and Metaphysics: Avoidance of Marital Liens Under Section 522(f) of the Bankruptcy Code. 31 Family Law Quarterly 513, Fall, 1997.

Security interests in exempt property after the 1994 Amendments to the Bankruptcy Code. 4 Am. Bkcy. Inst. L.R. 57, Spring, 1996.

Judicial lien avoidance and the homestead exemption. 3 J. Bankruptcy Law & Practice 319, May - June, 1994.

Security interests on exempt personal property; their fate in bankruptcy. 2 J. Bankruptcy Law & Practice, 247, July - Aug., 1993.

Divorce liens under Section 522(f) of the federal Bankruptcy Code: resolving tensions between family and bankruptcy law. 67 NYU L Rev 879, October, 1992.

Bankruptcy Law - avoidance of divorce liens under Section 522(f)(1) of the Bankruptcy Code: all's fair in love and divorce. 14 W. New England L. Rev. 221, 1992.

Farrey v. Sanderfoot: judicial liens created pursuant to a divorce decree - are they still avoidable in bankruptcy? 31 Univ. of Louisville J. Family Law 143, 1992-93.

Lien Avoidance Under Section 522(f); can it be Utilized by the Debtor after the Closing of his Bankruptcy Case. 38 Pers. Finance L. Q. Rep 7, Winter, 1984.

1.06. To what extent are debts for educational loans and benefits nondischargeable in bankruptcy?

Text of statute. Section 523(a)(8) of the Bankruptcy Code (11 U.S.C. § 523(a)(8)) provides:

523. Exceptions to discharge

(a) A discharge under section 727, 1141, 1228(a), 1228(b), or 1328(b) of this title does not discharge an individual debtor from any debt –

* * * * * *

(8) unless excepting such debt from discharge under this paragraph would impose an undue hardship on the debtor and the debtor's dependents, for – §523(a)(8), text of

(A)(i) an educational benefit overpayment or loan made, insured, or guaranteed by a governmental unit, or made under any program funded in whole or in part by a governmental unit or nonprofit institution; or

(ii) an obligation to repay funds received as an educational benefit, scholarship, or stipend; or

(B) any other educational loan that is a qualified education loan, as defined in section 221(d)(1) of the Internal Revenue Code of 1986, incurred by a debtor who is an individual;

Introduction. Section 523(a)(8) was enacted in the Bankruptcy Reform Act of 1978. As originally enacted, only educational loans made by government units and nonprofit institutions of higher education were excepted from discharge, and there was a required payment period for dischargeability of 5 years. The scope of Section 523(a)(8) was broadened by Congress in 1979, 1984, and 1990 in attempts to prevent abuse in the student loan program. In 1990 the length of the payment period required for dischargeability was increased from 5 to 7 years. In 1998 the provision providing for dischargeability after a payment period of 7 years was removed from the statute, leaving it in its present form. §523(a)(8), history of

Section 523(a)(8)(B) was added in 2005. This section provides that any educational loan that is a qualified education loan under section 221(d)(1) of the Internal Revenue Code is nondischargeable unless the debt is dischargeable under the "undue hardship" exception to nondischargeability. A qualified education loan is defined in 26 U.S.C. § 221(d)(1) as follows: §523(a)(8)(B), addition of

(1) Qualified education loan

qualified education loan, definition of

The term "qualified education loan" means any indebtedness incurred by the taxpayer solely to pay qualified higher education expenses –

(A) which are incurred on behalf of the taxpayer, the taxpayer's spouse, or any dependent of the taxpayer as of the time the indebtedness was incurred,

(B) which are paid or incurred within a reasonable period of time before or after the indebtedness is incurred, and

(C) which are attributable to education furnished during a period during which the recipient was an eligible student.

Such term includes indebtedness used to refinance indebtedness which qualifies as a qualified education loan. The term "qualified education loan" shall not include any indebtedness owed to a person who is related (within the meaning of section 267(b) or 707(b)(1)) to the taxpayer or to any person by reason of a loan under any qualified employer plan (as defined in section 72(p)(4)) or under any contract referred to in section 72(p)(5).

§523(a)(8)(B), effect of

There is no requirement in section 523(a)(8)(B), or in the above definition of a qualified educational loan, that the loan or other obligation be made by a nonprofit or governmental entity. Therefore, Section 523(a)(8)(B) has the effect of extending student loan nondischargeability to loans and obligations owed to profit-making and other non-governmental entities such as private credit unions. The only educational loans that appear to be dischargeable are loans and obligations owed to a family member or to an entity owned or controlled by the debtor (see 26 U.S.C. § 267(b) for a list of such entities), loans made by an employer from a tax-qualified employee benefit plan, and, as described above, loans the nondischarge of which would impose an undue hardship on the debtor and his or her dependents.

student loans, nondischargeability under section 1328(a)

Under the 2005 BAPCPA amendments student loans and other educational obligations remain nondischargeable in chapter 13 cases even if the discharge is granted under Section 1328(a). The fact that section 1328(a) is not included in the first line of section 523(a)(8) does not render student loans dischargeable under section 1328(a). See 11 U.S.C. § 1328(a)(2).

§523(a)(8), applicability of in Chapter 7 cases, Chapter 13 cases

The nondischargeability provisions of Section 523(a)(8) are applicable to Chapter 7 cases and to all Chapter 13 cases, regardless of the type of discharge that is granted in the case. In cases filed prior to November 5, 1990, student loans were dischargeable in Chapter 13 cases wherein the debtor received a completed-plan discharge under 11 U.S.C. § 1328(a). As of that date 11 U.S.C. § 1328(a) was amended so as to except debts of a kind specified in Section 523(a)(8) from a Chapter 13 completed-plan discharge. Therefore, in Chapter 13 cases filed after November 5, 1990, student loans are nondischargeable to the extent provided in Section 523(a)(8), regardless of the type of Chapter 13 discharge received by the debtor.

The nondischargeability provisions of Section 523(a)(8) are self-executing. This means that it is not necessary for a creditor to file an objection or complaint, or even to appear, in the debtor's bankruptcy case in order for the debt to be nondischargeable. To obtain discharge of a student loan, the debtor must institute an adversary proceeding and give adequate notice of such proceeding to the creditor. See In re Ruele, 296 B.R. 146 (ND OH, 2003). A student loan creditor may seek the post-bankruptcy collection of a student loan or benefit without having to file a complaint or otherwise appear in the debtor's bankruptcy case. See Buford v. Higher Education Assistance Foundation, 85 B.R. 579 (KS, 1988); In re Barth, 86 B.R. 146 (WD WI, 1988). Also, the dischargeability of a student loan may be determined in a state court because the issue is not within the exclusive jurisdiction of the bankruptcy court. See In re Craig, 56 B.R. 479 (WD MO, 1985).

§523(a)(8), self executing nature of

Section 523(a)(8) of the Bankruptcy Code provides in essence that a loan or benefit that meets the educational qualifications set forth therein is not dischargeable in a bankruptcy case unless nondischarge of the debt will impose an undue hardship on the debtor and his or her dependents. To be nondischargeable, then, a loan or benefit must meet both of the following conditions:

§523(a)(8), general requirements for non-dischargeabiliy

> (1) The loan or benefit must be either (a) made, insured or guaranteed by a governmental unit, (b) made under a program funded wholly or in part by a governmental unit or non-profit institution, or (c) for an obligation to repay funds received as an educational benefit, scholarship or stipend regardless of the source of the funds.
>
> (2) Nondischarge of the debt will not impose an "undue hardship" on the debtor and his or her dependents.

If a loan or benefit fails to meet either of the conditions listed above, the loan or benefit does not qualify for nondischargeability under Section 523(a)(8) and is therefore dischargeable in a bankruptcy case. The above conditions are discussed separately below.

student loan or benefit, when dischargeable

The source of loan requirements for nondischargeability. To be nondischargeable under 11 U.S.C. § 523(a)(8) a debt must be (1) for an educational benefit, overpayment or loan that was either (a) made, insured, or guaranteed by a governmental unit or (b) made under a program that is funded in whole or in part by a governmental unit or a nonprofit institution, or (2) for an obligation to repay funds that were received as an educational benefit, scholarship or stipend regardless of the source of the funds or benefits. A loan or benefit that does not qualify under one of these categories is not nondischargeable under Section 523(a)(8) and is therefore dischargeable (unless it is nondischargeable under another provision of Section 523(a)).

student loan or benefit, educational requirements for non-dischargeability

The primary consideration in determining whether a debt qualifies for nondischargeability under Section 523(a)(8) on this ground is whether the funds or benefits given to the debtor were given for educational purposes, not whether the funds or benefits were technically considered a grant or a loan at the time of the transfer. See U.S. Dept. of Health & Human Services v. Smith, 807 F.2d 122 (8th Cir., 1986) (holding a physician's grant under the Physician Shortage Area Scholarship Program constituted a nondischargeable loan because the debtor failed to reside in a physician shortage area and, under the terms of the grant, became obligated to repay all funds advanced to him under the program with interest). In Smith, the fact that the loan was contingent did not prevent it from being nondischargeable under Section 523(a)(8). See also In re Burks, 244 F.3d 1245 (11th Cir., 2001). A consolidation loan made to consolidate pre-existing student loans is also generally nondischargeable under Section 523(a)(8). See, e.g., Levernier v. Educ. Credit Mgmt. Corp., 307 B.R. 684 (CD CA, 2004); In re Flint, 238 B.R. 676 (ED MI, 1999); In re Shaffer, 237 B.R. 617 (ND TX, 1999).

§523(a)(8), educational requirement of

Unpaid tuition can qualify as a loan in two situations: where actual funds have changed hands between the institution and the student, or where there is an agreement whereby the institution extends credit to the student. In re Chambers, 348 F.3d 650 (7th Cir., 2003); In Mackay v. Vanderbilt Univ., 366 B.R. 144 (OR, 2007), a system whereby a student could charge tuition and related educational expenses to an account which was to be paid monthly was a student loan under 11 U.S.C. § 523(a)(8).

unpaid tuition as an "educational loan"

In HEMAR Service Corp., Inc. v. Pilcher, 149 B.R. 595 (B.A.P. 9th Cir., 1993) the court stated that to be nondischargeable under Section 523(a)(8) the actual loan itself need not be funded by a nonprofit institution as long as the loan was obtained through a loan program that was funded in part by nonprofit institutions. In In re Joyner, 171 B.R. 762 (ED PA, 1994), the court held that the portion of a student loan obligation attributable to room and board was nondischargeable because it conferred an educational benefit on the debtor. In In re Merchant, 958 F.2d 738 (6th Cir., 1992), educational loans made by commercial lenders and guaranteed by private educational institutions were nondischargeable under Section 523(a)(8). Private student loans made by a family member do not qualify for nondischargeability under Section 523(a)(8). See, e.g., In re Reis, 274 B.R. 46 (MA, 2002). Likewise, a salary advance by a hospital to enable a debtor-doctor to pay off a student loan was not an educational loan under Section 523(a)(8). See, e.g., In re Lakemaker, 241 B.R. 577 (ND IL, 1999).

source of funds, requirements for non-dischargeability

However, in In re Roberts, 149 B.R. 547 (CD IL, 1993), the court found the credit union in question to be a nonprofit institution and held that the debtor's student loan obtained therefrom was nondischargeable under Section 523(a)(8). The court also stated that since the focus of Section 523(a)(8) is on the nature and character of the loan and not on how the recipient actually spends the proceeds of the loan, it was irrelevant whether the debtor actually spent the loan proceeds for educational purposes. In In re Murphy, 282 F.3d 868 (5th Cir., 2002), the court stated that it is the purpose, not the use of a loan that determines its dischargeability under Section 523(a)(8) and that students may not discharge the portion of their student loans that were not spent on tuition or books. A student loan remains nondischargeable even if a portion of the loan proceeds were received by the debtor after he had left school. See, e.g., In re Mehta, 262 B.R. 35 (NJ, 2001) (holding that a student's nonpayment of tuition does not constitute an extension of credit or a loan for purposes of Section 523(a)(8)). See also In re Feyes, 228 B.R. 887 (ND OH, 1998).

credit union as nonprofit institution

proceeds of loan, how spent, effect on dischargeability

Generally, consolidation loans are "educational loans" under Section 523(a)(8), and are therefore non-dischargeable just like the preexisting student loans they pay off. See In re Levernier, 244 B.R. 458 (CD CA, 1999); In re Lapusan, 244 B.R. 423 (SD IL, 2000); In re Gallagher, 333 B.R. 169 (NH, 2005). However, in In re McBurney, 357 B.R. 536 (B.A.P. 9th Cir., 2006), a consolidation loan made post-petition was deemed to extinguish the pre-petition student loans, and was not subject to an undue hardship attack under Section 523(a)(8).

consolidation loans

The "undue hardship" exception to nondischargeability. Section 523(a)(8) provides that a qualifying student loan is nondischargeable unless nondischarge of the debt will impose an undue hardship on the debtor and the debtor's dependents. See In re Vermaas, 302 B.R. 650 (NE, 2003). Otherwise stated, a qualifying student loan is dischargeable if not discharging the debt will impose an undue hardship on the debtor and his or her dependents. The Bankruptcy Code does not contain a definition of the term "undue hardship" which means that its meaning has been judicially determined.

undue hardship, requirement for dischargeability

Not surprisingly, the term "undue hardship" has been the subject of much bankruptcy litigation. There are two general lines of cases on the issue of what constitutes an undue hardship. One line of cases emanates from In re Johnson, 5 BCD 532 (ED PA, 1979) and adopts a 3 part test for determining undue hardship that is discussed in the next two paragraphs. The other, more recent, line of cases follow the criteria set forth in Brunner v. New York State Higher Education Services Corp., 831 F.2d 395 (2d Cir., 1987), which is discussed below. Some courts, however, follow neither line of cases in determining undue hardship.

undue hardship, definition of, lines of cases

The so-called Johnson test for determining the existence of an undue hardship under Section 523(a)(8) utilizes a 3 part test. The first part is a mechanical test where the court considers the debtor's vocational profile, including current employment and income, future employment and income prospects, educational level, work skills, health, family support obligations and practical marketability of work skills. In applying this part of the test the debtor has the burden of showing that his or her income and other financial resources will be insufficient to maintain a minimal or poverty-line standard of living for the debtor and his or her dependents for the foreseeable future if the student loan obligation is not discharged.

undue hardship, what constitutes, Johnson test

The second part of the Johnson test is a good-faith test whereby the debtor must show that he or she is minimizing current living expenses and maximizing personal and professional resources. The third part of the Johnson test is a policy determination whereby the court must determine whether the discharge of the student loan would constitute an abuse of the bankruptcy discharge. In applying this part of the test the court must consider the relative size of the debtor's student loan debt as compared to the total amount of the debtor's debts (i.e., whether the debtor is filing bankruptcy primarily to discharge the student loan) and any personal, professional and financial benefit received by the debtor from the education financed by the student loan. See, e.g., In re Kopf, 245 B.R. 731 (Bankr. D. Maine 2000); In re Frech, 62 B.R. 235 (MN, 1986); In re Connor, 83 B.R. 440 (ED MI, 1988); In re Correll, 105 B.R. 302 (WD PA, 1989); In re Fox, 189 B.R. 115 (ND OH, 1995).

Johnson test for undue hardship, requirements of

undue hardship, what constitutes, Brunner test

In Brunner v. New York State Higher Education Services Corp., 831 F.2d 395 (2d Cir., 1987), the court set forth the following test (the Brunner test) for establishing undue hardship in student loan cases: The debtor must prove (1) that if the loan is not discharged he or she cannot maintain, based on current income and expenses, a minimal standard of living for the debtor and his or her dependents; (2) that this state of affairs is likely to persist for a significant portion of the loan repayment period; and (3) that he or she has made a good faith effort to repay the loan. See also In re Cox, 338 F.3d 1228 (11th Cir. 2003).

Brunner test for undue hardship, general aspects

The Brunner test abandons the policy portion of the Johnson test on the grounds that it is irrelevant for purposes of dischargeability whether or not the debtor has benefitted from the education financed by the student loan. See In re Robertson, 999 F.2d 1132 (7th Cir., 1993) (rejecting the Johnson test and adopting the Brunner test for the 7th Circuit). Under the Brunner test the "fresh start" policy of the Bankruptcy Code must be balanced against the Congressional goal of preventing abuse in the student loan program. See, e.g., Cheesman v. Tennessee Student Assistance Corp., 25 F.3d 356 (6th Cir., 1994); Mathews v. Higher Ed. Assistance Found., 166 B.R. 940 (KS, 1994); Raymond v. Northwest Ed. Loan Ass'n., 169 B.R. 67 (WD WA, 1994); Sands v. United Student Aid Funds, 166 B.R. 299 (WD MI, 1994); In re Pena, 155 F.3d 1108 (9th Cir., 1998); In re Brown, 247 B.R. 228 (ND OH, 2000); Ulm v. Educ. Credit Mgmt. Corp., 304 B.R. 915 (SD GA, 2004).

undue hardship, burden of proof

Under either test, the burden of proof on the issue of undue hardship rests with the debtor. See In re Nixon, 453 B.R. 311 (Bankr. S. D. Ohio 2011); In re Durrani, 311 B.R. 496 (ND IL, 2004). The legal standard is a preponderance of the evidence under F.R.B.P. 4007(a)-(b). See Educ. Credit Mgmt. Corp. v. Mersmann, 318 B.R. 537 (B.A.P. 10th Cir., 2004). Further, the hardship proven by the debtor must truly be undue if the loan is to be dischargeable. In In re Frech, 62 B.R. 235 (MN, 1986), the court stated that a debtor does not establish undue hardship by proof that continuing responsibility for student loans would bring about unpleasantness or garden-variety hardship. The court stated that the hardship necessary to discharge a student loan must be long term and there must be no hope of repayment, not simply a present inability to repay the loan.

undue hardship, what constitutes, general requirements

In In re Ballard, 60 B.R. 673 (WD VA, 1986), the court stated that undue hardship means more than unpleasantness associated with the payment of a just debt, and that a finding of undue hardship is reserved for exceptional cases and requires the presence of unique or extraordinary circumstances which would render it unlikely that the debtor would be able to repay the debt. Demonstrating undue hardship sufficient to warrant nondischargeability under Section 523(a)(8) requires the debtor to show that, even with the advantage of a Chapter 7 discharge, her present circumstances and future prospects do not give the debtor the resources to repay the student loan and provide a minimal standard of living for the debtor and her dependents. See In re Kopf, 245 B.R. 731 (ME, 2000); In re Kennedy, 2011 WL 87242 (Bankr. E. D. Tenn. 2011) (expenditures on internet, cell phone, gym, and cigarettes generally unnecessary to maintain standard of living); but see In re Nixon, 453 B.R. 311 Bankr. S. D. Ohio 2011); In re Miller 409 B.R. 299 (Bankr. E. D. Penn. 2009) ("minimal standard of living" lies somewhere between poverty and mere difficulty). However, the hardship standard does not require an absolute certainty of hopelessness. See In re Anelli, 262 B.R. 1 (MA, 2000).

As a practical matter, the great majority of the reported cases on the issue of undue hardship have held that an undue hardship had not been established and that the debtor's student loan was therefore nondischargeable. See, e.g., In re Sorber, 358 B.R. 68 (ND NY, 2006); O'Hearn v. Educ. Credit Mgmt. Corp., 339 F.3d 559 (7th Cir., 2003); In re Holmes, 319 B.R. 620 (ND MO, 2004); In re Buchanan, 276 B.R. 744 (ND WV, 2002); Reyes v. Okla. State Regents for Higher Ed., 154 B.R. 320 (ED OK, 1993);In re Bey, 95 B.R. 376 (WD PA, 1989). In In re Garcia, 135 B.R. 437 (SD FL, 1992) a student loan was found to be nondischargeable even though the creditor agreed to the dischargeability of the debt on undue hardship grounds.

undue hardship, existence of, majority of cases

Undue hardship is likely to be found only where the debtor's plight is clearly dismal. For example, in In re Reilly, 118 B.R. 38 (MD, 1990), the debtor's student loan was discharged on the grounds of undue hardship even though the debtor had never made any payments on the loan, which was small ($2,762), where it was established that the debtor's monthly income was $1,076 and that the debtor was a divorced mother of 3 young children, received little or no support from her ex-husband who was incurably ill, lived with her parents, and her earnings were unlikely to increase. In In re Turner, 69 B.R. 62 (MN, 1986), a similar ruling was entered where it was shown that the debtors had a monthly income of $1,060, monthly expenses of $1,102, and that there was no realistic chance of earning significantly more, a good probability that their expenses would increase and no realistic possibility of paying off the student loans. See also Oyler v. Educ. Credit Mgmt. Corp., 300 B.R. 255 (B.A.P. 6th Cir., 2003).

undue hardship, existence of, cases finding

On the other hand, where debtor establishes that he or she suffers from a disability, the debtor realistically expect a bankruptcy court to rule in the debtor's favor on the issue of undue hardship. In most reported cases where the debtor has established that he or she suffers from a permanent disability or an incurable illness, the court has found the debtor's student loan to be dischargeable on the grounds of undue hardship. See In re Marcotte, 455 B.R. 460 (Bankr. S.C. 2011) (chronic pain from pre-loan accident); In re Nanton-Marie, 303 B.R. 228 (SD FL, 2003) (57 year old with advanced glaucoma); In re Ford, 269 B.R. 673 (B.A.P. 8th Cir., 2001) (62 year-old debtor with arthritis); O'Brien v. Household Bank FSB, 165 B.R. 456 (WD MO, 1994) (chronic fatigue syndrome); In re Correll, 105 B.R. 302 (WD PA, 1989) (undisclosed injury); In re Alliger, 78 B.R. 96 (ED PA, 1987) (back injury); In re Wilson, 76 B.R. 19 (RI, 1987) (physical disability); In re Wilcox, 57 B.R. 479 (MD GA, 1985) (crippling arthritis); In re Dresser, 33 B.R. 63 (ME, 1983) (post traumatic stress disorder); In re Dockery, 36 B.R. 41 (ED TN, 1984) (heart attack); In re Dyer, 40 B.R. 872 (ED TN, 1984) (agoraphobia); In re Connolly, 29 B.R. 978 (MD FL, 1983) (physical and emotional disorders); In re Brown, 247 B.R. 228 (ND OH, 2000).

undue hardship, disability of debtor, effect of

undue hardship, disabled debtor, requirements

A finding of undue hardship may be denied, however, if the court is not convinced that the debtor in fact suffers from a disability. See In re Gearhart, 94 B.R. 392 (WD PA, 1989). A finding of undue hardship may also be denied if there is evidence that the debtor's disability is not permanent and will be cured in the foreseeable future. See In re Bowen, 37 B.R. 171 (MD FL, 1984). See also Ford v. Tennessee Student Assistance Corp., 151 B.R. 135 (MD TN, 1993) (holding that an undue hardship had not been established where it was shown that the debtor was unemployed, received disability benefits and food stamps, and was unable to pay her bankruptcy filing fee, but where it was also shown that the debtor's disability was at most 50 percent, the debtor had made little attempt to find employment and maximize her income, and the debtor's student loan represented most of her total unsecured debt). In In re McClain, 272 B.R. 42 (NH, 2002) a debtor who was suffering from emotional and psychiatric problems had the burden of showing how these problems impair his ability to work. In In re Kelly, 351 B.R. 45 (ED NY, 2006), the court stated that the debtor failed to prove that her depressive disorder and social phobia were likely to continue into the indefinite future. The court also made note of the lack of effort the debtor had made toward repaying the loans.

§523(a)(8), power of court in rulings under

While in most cases the bankruptcy court will find that an undue hardship either exists or does not exist for purposes of Section 523(a)(8), the court has the authority under 11 U.S.C. § 105 to discharge a portion of the student loan debt, to defer payments on the debt for a specified period, or to discharge the entire debt and stay the order of discharge pending an improvement in the debtor's condition. In Cheesman v. Tennessee Student Assistance Corp., 25 F.3d 356 (6th Cir., 1994), where the court held that the bankruptcy court had the power under 11 U.S.C. § 105, after ruling that the debtor's student loan was dischargeable on the grounds of undue hardship, to stay its order for 18 months on the ground that the debtor's financial situation might improve thereby making the discharge unwarranted. The court stated that by proceeding in this fashion the bankruptcy court was correctly attempting to balance the Bankruptcy Code's goal of providing fresh starts for Chapter 7 debtors with Congress's goal of preventing abuse in the student loan program. In In re Hornsby, 144 F.3d 433 (6th Cir., 1998), the court held that where total discharge of a student loan is not warranted, a bankruptcy court has the power to take action short of total discharge under its authority to issue orders necessary to carry out provisions of the Bankruptcy Code.

In Woyame v. Career Ed. & Management, 161 B.R. 198 (ND OH, 1993), the court ruled that of the debtor's $11,157 total student loan debt, $8,872 was nondischargeable and $2,285 was dischargeable as imposing an undue hardship on the debtor. The court ruled that a bankruptcy court may, in its discretion, determine that equity requires a reduction in the amount of nondischargeable debt to a level that will not impose an undue hardship on the debtor and thereby enable the debtor to repay the nondischarged portion of the debt. See also In re Nixon, 453 B.R. 311 (Bankr. S. D. Ohio 2011); In re Mort, 272 B.R. 181 (WD VA, 2002); In re Nary, 253 B.R. 752 (ND TX, 2000); In re Brown, 239 B.R. 204 (SD CA, 1999); In re Grine, 254 B.R. 191 (ND OH, 2000); In re England, 264 B.R. 38 (ID, 2001). However, in In re Skaggs, 196 B.R. 865 (WD OK, 1996), the court held that it did not have the power to discharge only a portion of a student loan or to modify the terms of the loan, it only had the authority to determine the dischargeability of the entire debt. See also In re Griggs, 252 B.R. 866 (NH, 2000); In re Richardson, 334 B.R. 311 (MA, 2005).

partial dischargeability of student loan debt, power of court to order

In In re Conner, 89 B.R. 744 (ND IL, 1988), the court found the debtor's student loan obligation to be nondischargeable under Section 523(a)(8), but ordered that payments on the loan be deferred without interest for four years because the debtor's obligation for his daughters' educations should end in four years whereupon the debtor should be able to repay his student loan without an undue hardship.

order of dis-chargeability, deferment of

Dischargeability of co-obligors and nonstudent obligors. Comakers, guarantors, accommodation parties, cosigners and other co-obligors are typically non-students who receive no personal educational benefit from the student loan they have become obligated for. Are their obligations also nondischargeable under Section 523(a)(8) or is that section applicable only to debtors who actually receive the benefit from the student loan? Most courts have held that the nondischargeability provisions of Section 523(a)(8) are equally applicable to debtors and codebtors and that a qualifying student loan obligation is nondischargeable to a non-student cosigner or guarantor unless the cosigner or guarantor can establish an undue hardship. See In re O'Neal, 390 B.R. 821 (SC, 2008).

§523(a)(8), applicability to co-obligors

Because there is no legislative history indicating an intent to exempt non-student codebtors from the nondischargeability provisions of Section 523(a)(8) and because it is the type of loan and not by whom or how the proceeds are spent that dictates the dischargeability of a loan, most courts have held that Section 523(a)(8) is fully applicable to non-student cosigners, guarantors and other codebtors. See In re Pelkowski, 990 F.2d 737 (3d Cir., 1993); In re Wilcon, 143 B.R. 4 (MA, 1992); In re Varma, 149 B.R. 817 (ND TX, 1992); In re Barth, 86 B.R. 146 (WD WI, 1988); In re Selmonosky, 93 B.R. 785 (ND GA, 1988); In re Hawkins, 139 B.R. 651 (ND OH, 1991); Owens v. Nebraska Higher Ed. Loan Program, 161 B.R. 829 (NE, 1993); Education Resources Inst. v. Garelli, 162 B.R. 552 (OR, 1994); Webb v. Student Loan Funding Corp., 151 B.R. 804 (ND OH, 1992).

§523(a)(8), applicability to co-obligors, majority rule

Several courts have extended this rule to situations where the nonstudent debtor is the only obligor of the student loan. In In re Salter, 207 B.R. 272 (MD FL, 1997), a loan taken by the debtor to pay for his daughter's preparatory school tuition was held to be an "educational" loan even though the debtor did not obtain or use the proceeds personally and even though he was the only obligor on the note. See also In re Norris, 239 B.R. 247 (MD AL, 1999); James v. United Student Aid Funds, 226 B.R. 885 (SD CA, 1998).

§523(a)(8), applicability to co-obligors, minority rule

A few courts have ruled that the nondischargeability provisions of Section 523(a)(8) are applicable only to student borrowers and are not applicable to non-student obligors usually because the loans are not deemed to be "educational" with respect to non-student obligors who received no benefit from the loan. See In re Pryor, 234 B.R. 716 (WD TN, 1999); In re Zobel, 80 B.R. 950 (ND IA, 1986); In re Meier, 85 B.R. 805 (WD WI, 1986); In re Kirkish, 144 B.R. 367 (WD MI, 1992); In re Bawden, 55 B.R. 459 (MD AL, 1985); In re Washington, 41 B.R. 211 (ED VA, 1984).

Bibliography. For further reading on the issues discussed in this article, see the annotations and articles listed below.

Annotations:

Applicability to obligations of nonstudent co-obligors of exception to discharge in bankruptcy for educational loans under 11 USC 523(a)(8). 120 ALR Fed 609.

Validity, construction, and application of statutes, regulations, or policies allowing denial of student loans, student loan guarantees, or educational services to debtors who have had student loans scheduled in bankruptcy. 107 ALR Fed. 192.

Rights and obligations of Federal Government under 20 USC 1080 when student borrower defaults on federally insured loan. 73 ALR Fed 303.

Bankruptcy discharge of student loan on ground of undue hardship under Section 523(a)(8)(B) of Bankruptcy Code of 1978. 144 ALR Fed 1.

Articles:

Burden of Proof, Undue Hardship, and Other Arguments for Student Debtor Under 11 U.S.C. § 523(a)(8)(B). 243 JC & UL, Winter, 1998.

Nondischargeability of educational debts under Section 523(a)(8) of the Bankruptcy Code: equitable treatment of cosigners and guarantors? 11 Bankruptcy Dev. J. 481, 1994-95.

Non-student cosigners and Section 523(a)(8) of the Bankruptcy Code. 1991 Univ. of Chicago Legal F. 357, 1991.

Student Loan Bankruptcy: Establishing "Undue Hardship" in South Dakota. 27 SD L. Rev. 282 (Spring, 1982).

Educational Loans in Bankruptcy. 2 N Illinois U. L. Rev. 325, 1982.

Kosel, Running the Gauntlet of "Undue Hardship" - the Discharge of Student Loans in Bankruptcy. 11 Golden Gate U. L. Rev. 457 (Spring, 1981).

Skipping Out on Alma Mater: Some Problems Involving the Collection of Federal Student Loans. 15 Columbia Journal of Law & Social Problems 317 (1980).

1.07 To what extent are divorce-related debts nondischargeable in bankruptcy?

Text of statutes. Sections 523(a)(5) and 523(a)(15) of the Bankruptcy Code (11 U.S.C. § 523(a)(5), (15)) are applicable to the subject discussed in this article. They provide as follows:

523. Exceptions to discharge

(a) A discharge under section 727, 1141, 1228(a), 1228(b), or 1328(b) of this title does not discharge an individual debtor from any debt -

* * * * * *

Section 523(a)(5), text of

(5) for a domestic support obligation;

* * * * * *

Section 523(a)(15), text of

(15) to a spouse, former spouse, or child of the debtor and not of the kind described in paragraph (5) that is incurred by the debtor in the course of a divorce or separation or in connection with a separation agreement, divorce decree or other order of a court of record, or a determination made in accordance with State or territorial law by a governmental unit;

divorce-related debt, what constitutes

Introduction. This article covers the dischargeability of divorce-related debts in Chapter 7 and Chapter 13 bankruptcy cases. Divorce-related debts include debts for accrued and unpaid alimony, maintenance or support (a domestic support obligation or "DSO"), property-settlement debts, debts for attorneys' fees, court costs and other fees related to divorce or separation proceedings, marriage-related debts that were assigned to or assumed by a debtor in a divorce or separation proceeding, and debts resulting from a debtor's divorce or separation-related requirement to hold a spouse or former spouse harmless from certain obligations. The dischargeability of each type of divorce or separation-related debt is discussed separately below in this article.

history of Sections 523(a)(5) & (15)

Section 523(a)(5) was enacted in the Bankruptcy Reform Act of 1978. Minor amendments to this section were made in 1981, 1984, 1986, and 1996, when "section 408(a)(3)" in subparagraph (A) was substituted for "section 402(a)(26)." Section 523(a)(15) was enacted in the Bankruptcy Reform Act of 1994 and is applicable to cases filed after October 21, 1994. Section 523(a)(18) was enacted in the Welfare Reform Act of 1996. The BAPCPA amendments of 2005 altered sections 523(a)(5) and (a)(15). The BAPCPA amendments of 2005 eliminated section 523(a)(18). The matters that were dealt with under the old section 523(a)(18) prior to the BAPCPA are now dealt with under section 523(a)(5).

Section 523(a)(5) now provides simply that domestic support obligations are nondischargeable. A domestic support obligation is defined as follows in 11 U.S.C. § 101(14A):

domestic support obligation, definition of

> (14A) The term "domestic support obligation" means a debt that accrues before, on, or after the date of the order for relief in a case under this title, including interest that accrues on that debt as provided under applicable nonbankruptcy law notwithstanding any other provision of this title, that is –
>
> (A) owed to or recoverable by –
>
> (i) a spouse, former spouse, or child of the debtor or such child's parent, legal guardian, or responsible relative; or
>
> (ii) a governmental unit;
>
> (B) in the nature of alimony, maintenance, or support (including assistance provided by a governmental unit) of such spouse, former spouse, or child of the debtor or such child's parent, without regard to whether such debt is expressly so designated;
>
> (C) established or subject to establishment before, on, or after the date of the order for relief in a case under this title, by reason of applicable provisions of –
>
> (i) a separation agreement, divorce decree, or property settlement agreement;
>
> (ii) an order of a court of record; or
>
> (iii) a determination made in accordance with applicable nonbankruptcy law by a governmental unit; and
>
> (D) not assigned to a nongovernmental entity, unless that obligation is assigned voluntarily by the spouse, former spouse, child of the debtor, or such child's parent, legal guardian, or responsible relative for the purpose of collecting the debt.

To be nondischargeable under the amended section 523(a)(5), the debt must be (1) owed to (or recoverable by) either a spouse, former spouse, or child of the debtor or a governmental unit, (2) in the nature of alimony, maintenance or support, (3) made in connection with lawful divorce or governmental support determination proceeding, and (4) not assigned to a nongovernment entity unless the assignment is voluntary and for purposes of collection.

domestic support obligation, elements of non-dischargeability

property settlement debts, dischargeability of

The BAPCPA greatly broadened the scope of nondischargeability of property settlement debts under section 523(a)(15) by removing the ability to pay and the relative harm provisions (subparagraphs (A) and (B)) that formerly limited nondischargeability under this section. Consequently, under the amended Section 523(a)(15) virtually all property settlement and other divorce-related debts that are not in the nature of alimony, maintenance or support appear to be nondischargeable in chapter 7 cases. The BAPCPA amendments to Section 523(a)(15) have rendered moot the previous body of case law interpreting the relative harm and ability to pay provisions. Under post BAPCPA law, all debts incurred by a debtor to a spouse, former spouse or child of the debtor that are incurred in the course of a divorce or separation are nondischargeable. Further, such debts are now automatically nondischargeable because Section 523(c)(1) of the Bankruptcy Code was amended by the BAPCPA so as to remove the requirement of filing a request to determine dischargeability for debts that are nondischargeable under Section 523(a)(15). Therefore, the nondischargeability provisions of Section 523(a)(15) are now automatically applicable in chapter 7 cases without the necessity of filing a request to determine dischargeability under Section 523(c)(1). However, property settlement debts remain dischargeable in chapter 13 cases wherein the debtor receives a Section 1328(a) completed plan discharge. See 11 U.S.C. § 1328(a)(2). It should also be noted that the BAPCPA amended Section 522(c) of the Bankruptcy Code to provide that property exempted by the debtor in a bankruptcy case shall be liable for domestic support obligations of the debtor during and after the case. See 11 U.S.C 522(c)(1).

Sections 523(a)(5) & (15) applicability in Chapter 7 cases

Sections 523(a)(5) and 523(a)(15) are both applicable in Chapter 7 cases, which means that in Chapter 7 cases divorce-related debts may be nondischargeable under either of these sections. For Chapter 7 debtors, then, divorce-related debts must be screened for nondischargeability under each of these sections. For example, a divorce-related debt may be dischargeable under Section 523(a)(5) because it is not a DSO but may be nondischargeable under the criteria of Section 523(a)(15).

Sections 523(a)(5) & (15), applicability in Chapter 13 cases

Section 523(a)(5) is also applicable to all Chapter 13 cases, regardless of the type of discharge received by the debtor. See 11 U.S.C. § 1328(a). Section 523(a)(15) is not applicable to Chapter 13 cases in which the debtor receives a completed plan discharge under 11 U.S.C. § 1328(a). However, Section 523(a)(15) is applicable to Chapter 13 cases in which the debtor receives a "best-efforts" discharge under 11 U.S.C. § 1328(b).

determining dischargeability of debts under Section 523(a)(5) & (15)

The nondischargeability provisions of Sections 523(a)(5) and (a)(15) are self-executing in both Chapter 7 and Chapter 13 cases, which means that it is not necessary for a creditor to file an objection or a request to determine dischargeability, or even to appear in the debtor's bankruptcy case in order for a covered debt to be nondischargeable. See In re Ball, 181 B.R. 384 (WD AR, 1995). This also means that the dischargeability of a debt covered by Section 523(a)(5) and (a)(15) may be determined at a later time by another court and not necessarily by a bankruptcy court. See Kaylo v. Kaylo, 183 B.R. 557 (WD AR, 1995). A debtor's discharge will automatically exclude both Section 523(a)(5) and (a)(15) debts from the discharge unless a complaint for determination is filed and results in a determination of discharge.

Determining the nature of a divorce-related debt or obligation. The definition of a DSO revolves around the obligation being in the nature of either alimony, maintenance or support. Therefore, although removed from Section 523(a)(5) by the BAPCPA, a discussion of whether a debt is in the nature of alimony, maintenance or support is still relevant. See In re Phegley, 443 B.R. 154, 157 (B.A.P. 8th Cir. 2011); In re Boller, 393 B.R. 569 (ED TN, 2008). Only debts in the nature of alimony, maintenance or support are nondischargeable under Section 523(a)(5). Debts that are not in the nature of alimony, maintenance or support (such as property settlement debts) are dischargeable under this section. Therefore, the key issue in determining the dischargeability of a particular divorce-related debt is determining whether the debt is a property settlement debt or is in the nature of alimony, maintenance or support. See In re Baron, 283 B.R. 328 (MD FL, 2002). Note, however, that even if a debt is not in the nature of alimony, maintenance or support (i.e., is a property settlement debt), all or a portion of the debt may be nondischargeable under Section 523(a)(15). The nondischargeability of property settlement debts under Section 523(a)(15) is discussed under another heading below in this article.

property settlement debts, dischargeability of

It is clear that although state law may be looked to for guidance, federal bankruptcy law controls the determination of whether a particular debt is in the nature of alimony, maintenance or support for purposes of Section 523(a)(5). See In re Pylant, 467 B.R. 246 (Bankr. M. D. Ga. 2012); In re Mills, 313 B.R. 395 (WD PA, 2004); Carlin-Blume v. Carlin, 314 B.R. 286 (SD NY, 2004); In re Reines, 142 F.3d 970 (7th Cir., 1998); In re Yeates, 807 F.2d 874 (10th Cir., 1986); In re Biggs, 907 F.2d 503 (5th Cir., 1990); In re Seibert, 914 F.2d 102 (7th Cir., 1990); In re Sillins, 264 B.R. 894 (ND IL, 2001); In re Brody, 3 F.3d 35 (2d Cir., 1993) (holding a state court's determination that the provisions of a separation agreement effected a nonmodifiable property distribution between the parties is not binding on a bankruptcy court in determining whether an obligation is in the nature of alimony, maintenance or support for purposes of Section 523(a)(5)). On the other hand, in In re Boller, 393 B.R. 569 (ED TN, 2008) the bankruptcy court held that an award designated as "support" by the state court and that has the indicia of a support award should be conclusively presumed to be a support obligation.

determining whether debt is property settlement or support, factors, burden of proof

Dischargeability is favored under the Bankruptcy Code and the objecting creditor normally has the burden of proof in establishing the nondischargeability of a divorce-related debt under Section 523(a)(5). See In re Johnson, 397 B.R. 289 (MD NC, 2008); In re Norbut, 387 B.R. 199 (SD OH, 2008); In re Reines, 142 F.3d 970 (7th Cir., 1998); Tilley v. Jessee, 789 F.2d 1074 (4th Cir., 1986); Roberts v. Poole, 80 B.R. 81 (ND TX, 1987); In re Midnet, 84 B.R. 776 (MD FL, 1988). However, in Stahl v. Stahl, 261 B.R. 164 (WD PA, 2001), the court stated that although exceptions to discharge are generally strictly construed in favor of the debtor and against the objector, this policy is tempered in Section 523(a)(5) cases by the intent of Congress to protect former spouses and dependent children in matters involving alimony, maintenance and support. In In re Bailey, 254 B.R. 901 (B.A.P. 6th Cir., 2000), the court stated that the terms "alimony" and "support" are to be given a broad construction to promote the congressional policy that favors enforcement of obligations for spousal and child support. See also, In re Kemp, 232 F.3d 652 (8th Cir., 2000). The degree of proof required to establish nondischargeability under Section 523(a)(5) is that of preponderance of the evidence. See Grogan v. Garner, 498 U.S. 279, 111 S.Ct. 654 (1991).

non-dischargeability of divorce debt, burden of proof

degree of proof

property settlement or support debt, intention of parties or court

There are three overriding factors that bankruptcy courts look at when determining if a divorce-related obligation is a non-dischargeable support obligation: (1) the actual language and substance of the agreement; (2) the parties' financial circumstances at the time of the agreement; and (3) the function that the obligation served at the time of the divorce or settlement agreement. See In re Tyndall, 360 B.R. 68 (DE, 2007). Generally, the key issue in determining whether a particular obligation is a property settlement debt or is a debt in the nature of alimony, maintenance or support is the intention of the parties or the divorce court at the time of the making of agreement or order creating the obligation. See In re Farelli, 347 B.R. 501 (WD PA, 2006), In re Hoberg, 300 B.R. 752 (CD CA, 2003), In re Brody, 3 F.3d 35 (2d Cir., 1993), In re Biggs, 907 F.2d 503 (5th Cir., 1990), and In re Sampson, 997 F.2d 717 (10th Cir., 1993) (stating the critical question in determining whether an obligation is in the nature of alimony, maintenance or support is the function served by the obligation at the time of the divorce). If the obligation effectively functioned as the former spouse's source of income at the time of the divorce, it is in substance a support obligation regardless of the terminology of the agreement or order. See Cummings v. Cummings, 244 F.3d 1263 (11th Cir., 2001). A bankruptcy court is free to consider all relevant evidence which goes to the state court's intent and need not limit its inquiry to any certain category or type of evidence when determining the intent of a state divorce court in making an ambiguously worded award. Foiles v. Taylor, 174 B.R. 692 (ED VA, 1994); Young v. Young, 35 F.3d 499 (10th Cir., 1994).

present needs of the parties, irrelevance of in bankruptcy case

Also, the present needs of the parties (i.e., their needs at the time of the filing of the bankruptcy case) generally are not relevant to the issue of whether a particular debt is in the nature of alimony, maintenance or support and should not be considered. See In re Wendt, 381 B.R. 217 (SD TX, 2007); In re Cotten, 318 B.R. 583 (WD OK, 2004); In re Mills, 313 B.R. 395 (WD PA, 2004); Draper v. Draper, 790 F.2d 52 (8th Cir., 1986); Sylvester v. Sylvester, 865 F.2d 1164 (10th Cir., 1989); Fitzgerald v. Fitzgerald, 9 F.3d 517 (6th Cir., 1993). In In re Chedrick, 98 B.R. 731 (WD PA, 1989) the court stated that for purposes of determining whether a divorce-related obligation was in the nature of alimony, maintenance or support the court may consider the financial circumstances and economic positions of the parties at the time of the agreement and should not inquire into the current relative financial conditions of the parties or any other circumstances existing at the time the bankruptcy petition was filed. The court stated that if the financial condition of the debtor's spouse changes so that it is equal to or superior to that of the debtor, the debtor's remedy is not to discharge the debt in bankruptcy but rather to petition the divorce court for a modification of the agreement in light of the changed circumstances. See also In re Fryman, 67 B.R. 112 (ED WI, 1986) (holding the debtor's support obligations to the state and his former spouse were nondischargeable under Section 523(a)(5) even though the debtor's spouse and children were no longer in need of support). In Lane v. Lane, 267 B.R. 679 (DE, 2001), the fact that under state law the debtor's former spouse was not entitled to alimony did not mean that an award of property to the former spouse in the divorce decree did not actually function as support for purposes of Section 523(a)(5). See also Richardson v. Edwards, 127 F.3d 97 (D.C. Cir., 1997); but see In re Westerfield, 403 B.R. 545 (ED TN, 2009) (using the "present needs" test of the ex-spouse).

A bankruptcy court should look beyond the labels state courts or the parties gave to the obligations at the time of the divorce when determining the nondischargeability of divorce-related debts under Section 523(a)(5). Dennis v. Dennis, 25 F.3d 274 (5th Cir., 1994). The court stated that the factors which should be considered by a bankruptcy court in determining whether a divorce obligation constitutes alimony, maintenance, or support under Section 523(a)(5) include the disparity of the parties' earning capacities, their relative business opportunities, their physical condition, their educational background, their probable future financial needs, and the benefits that each party would likely have received had the marriage continued. See also In re Benich, 811 F.2d 943 (5th Cir., 1987).

divorce debts, dischargeability of under Section 523(a)(5), factors considered

Courts use the following factors were to determine whether an obligation was in the nature of alimony, maintenance or support: (1) whether the obligation terminates upon the death or remarriage of the former spouse, (2) whether the obligation is payable in a lump sum or in periodic payments, (3) the disparity, if any, in the earning powers of the parties, (4) the structure and terms of the agreement or order, (5) whether enforceability of the obligation is by attachment or contempt, (6) whether the parties have children whose support is in question, (7) whether the former spouse is directly or indirectly benefitted by payment of the obligation, (8) the ages and physical and emotional conditions of the parties, (9) the existence of a legal or moral obligation by the debtor to pay alimony or support, (10) the circumstances that contributed to the separation of the parties, and (11) the tax treatment of the obligation by the parties. See, e.g., In re Phegley, 443 B.R. 154 (B.A.P. 8th Cir. 2011); In re Mac Donald, 194 B.R. 283 (ND GA, 1996); In re Swartz, 339 B.R. 497 (WD MO, 2006).

divorce debt, property settlement vs. support, relevant factors

In In re Brody, 3 F.3d 35 (2d Cir., 1993), the intent of the parties at the time the separation agreement was executed determines whether an obligation created by the agreement is in the nature of alimony, maintenance or support for purposes of Section 523(a)(5). The court further stated that all evidence, direct or circumstantial, which tends to illuminate the subjective intention of the parties at the time of execution is relevant to the issue of intent and that labels given an obligation by the parties or by a state court are not dispositive of the issue. The court held that the bankruptcy court did not err in finding the debtor's $1,000,000 installment obligation to his former spouse to be in the nature of nondischargeable alimony, maintenance or support even though the obligation was characterized as a "distributive award" in the separation agreement. See also Foiles v. Taylor, 174 B.R. 692 (ED VA, 1994).

divorce debt, property settlement vs. support, intention of parties

The parties' intent at the time of the divorce should be the initial inquiry in determining whether an obligation is in the nature of alimony, maintenance or support for purposes of Section 523(a)(5). In re Sampson, 997 F.2d 717 (10th Cir., 1993). In Sampson, the court further stated that such an inquiry should not turn on one party's post hoc explanation as to his or her state of mind at the time of the divorce, even if uncontradicted, but rather the critical issue is the shared intent of the parties at the time of the divorce.

divorce debt, property settlement vs. support, intention of parties

divorce debt, property settlement vs. support, importance of tax treatment by parties

The manner in which the parties have treated the payment of a divorce-related obligation for income tax purposes is relevant to the issue of whether the obligation is in the nature of property settlement or alimony, maintenance or support because it manifests the intentions of the parties. See Cox v. Cox, 292 B.R. 141 (ED TX, 2003); In re Corke, 161 B.R. 64 (KS, 1993). In Holloway v. Kelley, 151 B.R. 790 (SD TX, 1992), the debtor was held to be estopped from claiming that his obligation to his former spouse was in the nature of property settlement because the debtor had taken four years of alimony income tax deductions for his payment obligations. In Robb-Fulton v. Robb, 23 F.3d 895 (4th Cir., 1994), the court held that quasi-estoppel precluded the debtor from asserting that his $3,000 monthly payment obligation under a settlement agreement was dischargeable support for his ex-wife's disabled daughter rather than nondischargeable alimony where the debtor had claimed the payments as deductible alimony on his income tax returns. See also, In re Davidson, 947 F.2d 1294 (5th Cir., 1991) and In re McGunn, 284 B.R. 855 (ND IL, 2002). In both In re Zeitchik, 369 B.R. 900 (ED NC, 2007) and In re Hysock, 75 B.R. 113 (DE, 1987), a divorce-related obligation was found to be in the nature of a property settlement in part because the debtor's spouse did not report the payments as alimony income on her federal income tax returns. However, in In re Bailey, 285 B.R. 15 (ND OK, 2002), the court refused to apply quasi-estoppel with respect to the parties' tax treatment of divorce payments and found them to be dischargeable property settlement payments because they were intended to compensate the ex-wife for awarding the marital business to the debtor. See also In re Kelley, 216 B.R. 806 (ED TN, 1998).

existence of support debt, issues in determining

In In re Perlin, 30 F.3d 39 (6th Cir., 1994), the court held that the following issues must be considered in determining whether a particular obligation was in the nature of alimony, maintenance or support for purposes of Section 523(a)(5): (1) whether there was an intent to create a support obligation; (2) whether the obligation has the effect of providing the support necessary to satisfy the daily needs of the former spouse and children; and (3) whether the amount of support represented by the obligation is not so excessive that it is manifestly unreasonable under traditional concepts of support. These same factors have been applied in In re Shain, 344 B.R. 821 (WY KY, 2006), In re Wilson, 342 B.R. 268 (WD KY, 2006), and In re Ker, 365 B.R. 807 (SD OH, 2007).

existence of support debt, factors in determining

In In re Singer, 787 F.2d 1033 (6th Cir., 1986) it was held that a debt may be deemed to be in the nature of support for purposes of Section 523(a)(5) even if it is characterized as property settlement in the settlement agreement if no other provisions have been made for spousal support and the circumstances indicate that the spouse needs and is entitled to support. The court stated that the factors to be considered in determining whether the obligation is in the nature of support include the presence of minor children, an imbalance in the relative income of the parties, and the nature and duration of the obligation. The termination of an obligation upon the majority of a child or the remarriage of a spouse is an indication of alimony or support while an indefinite length is an indication of property settlement.

A factor that is often considered in determining whether a divorce-related obligation is in the nature of property settlement or alimony, maintenance or support is whether the obligation is payable for a limited period or for an indefinite period. An obligation to pay a periodic amount for an extended period is usually an indication that the obligation is in the nature of alimony, maintenance or support, especially if the obligation terminates upon the majority of a child or the death or remarriage of the recipient spouse. See Alticor, Inc., v. Grissum, 198 S.W. 2d 629 (MO. App., 2006); In re Sorah, 163 F.3d 397 (6th Cir., 1998); Forsdick v. Turgeon, 812 F.2d 801 (2d Cir., 1987); In re Goin, 808 F.2d 1391 (10th Cir., 1987); Nowak v. Nowak, 183 B.R. 568 (NE, 1995); Sadowsky v. Larson, 169 B.R. 945 (ND, 1994); In re Jackson, 102 B.R. 524 (MD LA, 1989); In re Levy, 63 B.R. 449 (WD LA, 1986); In re Foss, 87 B.R. 167 (KS, 1988); In re Bell, 61 B.R. 171 (SD TX, 1986); In re Myers, 61 B.R. 891 (ND GA, 1986).

existence of support debt, importance of duration of payments

On the other hand, the requirement of a lump sum payment or the payment of a sum certain in installments over a limited period is often construed as an indication that the obligation was intended to be in the nature of property settlement. See Duffy v. Taback, 331 B.R. 137 (SD NY, 2005); In re Sanabria, 275 B.R. 204 (NJ, 2002); In re Mac Donald, 194 B.R. 283 (ND GA, 1996); In re Foege, 195 B.R. 815 (MD FL, 1996); In re Schmiel, 94 B.R. 373 (ED PA, 1988) (where a lump sum award of $50,494 to the debtor's spouse in a state court divorce proceeding was found to be a dischargeable property settlement award). See In re Petty, 333 B.R. 472 (MD FL, 2005) where a payment of one-half of the proceeds from the sale of the family business was determined to be a property settlement. In In re Duffy, 331 B.R. 137 (SD NY, 2005), the sum of $240,000, payable in $2,000 monthly installments over ten years was deemed to be a property settlement despite the state court's use of "spousal maintenance" and the debtor's treatment of the payments as alimony for tax purposes. See also Wright v. Wright, 184 B.R. 318 (ND IL, 1995), where $94,200 of a $135,000 lump sum award was found to be a dischargeable property settlement debt. See also, In re Kerzner, 259 B.R. 253 (SD NY, 2001). However, a lump sum award or payment has been held to be in the nature of nondischargeable alimony, maintenance or support where other factors indicate that the award or payment was intended to provide maintenance or support for the recipient spouse. See In re Zaino, 316 B.R. 1 (RI, 2004); In re Cox, 68 B.R. 307 (MD FL, 1986); In re Goin, 808 F.2d 1391 (10th Cir., 1987); In re Mendez, 275 B.R. 482 (WD PA, 2001); and In re Smith, 218 B.R. 254 (SD GA, 1997).

lump sum payment, inference of property settlement

The relative income or earning capacity of the parties at the time of the divorce or separation is often an important factor in determining whether a divorce-related obligation is in the nature of alimony, maintenance or support. See In re Phegley, 443 B.R. 154 (B.A.P. 8th 2011); In re Swartz, 339 B.R. 497 (WD MO, 2006); In re MacGibbon, 383 B.R. 749 (WD WA, 2008); In re Goin, 808 F.2d 1391 (10th Cir., 1987); Dennis v. Dennis, 25 F.3d 274 (5th Cir., 1994). If the income or earning capacity of the debtor is significantly greater than that of the spouse, the obligation is likely to be construed as alimony, maintenance or support unless a provision for adequate alimony, maintenance or support is contained elsewhere in the agreement or order. See In re Sampson, 997 F.2d 717 (10th Cir., 1993); In re Patalano, 68 B.R. 30 (RI, 1986); In re Combs, 101 B.R. 609 (B.A.P. 9th Cir., 1989). However, if the parties had approximately equal income at the time of the agreement or order, an ambiguously-worded obligation is likely to be found to be in the nature of property settlement. See Young v. Young, 181 B.R. 555 (ED OK, 1995).

support vs. property settlement debt, earning capacities of parties, importance of

support debt, excessive amount, dischargeability of

If the amount of support or alimony provided for in a divorce-related obligation is so excessive that it is manifestly unreasonable under traditional concepts, the excessive amount of the obligation may be found not to be in the nature of alimony, maintenance or support for purposes of Section 523(a)(5). See In re Perlin, 30 F.3d 39 (6th Cir., 1994), In re Sullivan, 62 B.R. 465 (ND MS, 1986), In re Skaggs, 91 B.R. 1018 (SD OH, 1988), and In re Portaro, 108 B.R. 142 (ND OH, 1989). The excessive amount of the support or alimony must be determined by the bankruptcy court and the amount so determined is dischargeable, while the balance is nondischargeable under Section 523(a)(5). See In re Harrison, 82 B.R. 900 (SD OH, 1988).

support debt, excessive amount, what constitutes

postpetition interest, dischargeability of

In In re Sullivan, 62 B.R. 465 (ND MS, 1986), the debtor's child support obligation as contained in a consent decree was manifestly unreasonable where it exceeded the debtor's total income. In In re Erler, 60 B.R. 220 (WD KY, 1986), the debtor's support obligation of paying his former spouse's car payments in the total amount of $4,824 was found to be excessive under the facts of the case and was reduced by the court to $2,000 for purposes of nondischargeability under Section 523(a)(5). The remainder of the obligation was dischargeable. However, in Henry v. Henry, 239 B.R. 812 (ND, 1999), the court stated that while whether a state court award constitutes support for purposes of Section 523(a)(5) is a question of federal law, whether the amount of the award is excessive or unreasonable is a question wholly and exclusively within the purview of the state court's jurisdiction. That postpetition interest on a nondischargeable child support obligation is also nondischargeable, see In re Foross, 242 B.R. 692 (B.A.P. 9th Cir., 1999). Note that the definition of a DSO includes the phrase "including interest that accrues on that debt".

debts owed to spouse's attorney, non-dischargeability of

The dischargeability under Section 523(a)(5) of debts for divorce-related attorney's fees and litigation expenses. Section 523(a)(5) provides nondischargeability only for DSOs. DSOs include debts in the nature of alimony, support, or maintenance that are owed to a spouse, former spouse or child of the debtor and that have not been assigned to another nongovernmental entity, unless it is voluntarily assigned for collection purposes. It is evident that a literal reading of Section 523(a)(5) and the definition of a DSO does not provide nondischargeability for attorney fee obligations of a spouse, former spouse or child of the debtor that are by court order or agreement payable by the debtor directly to the other party's attorney. However, the great majority of cases have held that debts owed by the debtor to the attorney for the debtor's spouse, former spouse, or child for services related to the attainment of alimony, maintenance or support for the spouse or child are nondischargeable under Section 523(a)(5) even if they are payable directly to the attorney and not to the spouse, former spouse or child. See In re Rogawski, 462 B.R. 435 (Bankr. E. D. N.Y. 2011) (payale to wife's attorney); In re Golio, 393 B.R. 56 (ED NY, 2008); In re Rehkow, 239 Fed. Appx. 341 (9th Cir., 2007); In re Bearden, 330 B.R. 214 (ND IL, 2005); In re Maddigan, 312 F.3d 589 (2d Cir., 2002); In re McNamara, 275 B.R. 832 (ED MI, 2002); In re Kline, 65 F.3d 749 (8th Cir., 1995). That an attorney creditor has standing to file a complaint to determine the dischargeability of such a debt under Section 523(a)(5), see Martin v. Morello, 185 B.R. 753 (ED TN, 1995). The assignment clause in Section 523(a)(5)(A) precluding nondischargeability for assigned debts does not pertain to assignments by a spouse to the spouse's attorney. See, e.g., In re Adams, 246 F.3d 662 (4th Cir., 2001); In re Thomas, 222 B.R. 174 (ED MO, 1998).

The interpretation of Section 523(a)(5) followed by most courts is that where state law permits an award of attorney fees to be based on the financial circumstances of the parties and where the facts show that the recipient had need of such award, a Bankruptcy Court may find that the award had a support function and is therefore nondischargeable under Section 523(a)(5). See In re Prater, 231 B.R. 819 (MD FL, 1999); In re Anderson, 62 B.R. 448 (MN, 1986); In re Snider, 62 B.R. 382 (SD TX, 1986); In re Schmiel, 94 B.R. 373 (ED PA, 1988) (stating that if the spouse or dependent children can show any nexus, however scant, between their maintenance and support and the debtor's payment of an attorney's fee award, the award is nondischargeable under Section 523(a)(5)).

non-dischargeability of debts owed to spouse's attorney, reasons for

Finding an award of attorneys' fees to be in the nature of nondischargeable alimony, maintenance or support serves two functions: (1) it prevents the spouse or former spouse from having to divert money needed to support herself and her children in order to pay legal fees, and (2) it permits the former spouse to have the benefit of adequate legal representation in the divorce proceeding. In re Michaels, 157 B.R. 190 (MA, 1993).

non-dischargeability of debts owed to spouse's attorney, reasons for

A few courts, however, have construed Section 523(a)(5) literally and have held that debts for alimony or support-related attorneys' fees that are payable directly to the former spouse's attorney, either by agreement, court order or assignment, are dischargeable because of the Bankruptcy Code's presumption of dischargeability and because such debts are not specifically protected from discharge by Section 523(a)(5). See In re Brooks, 371 B.R. 761 (ND TX, 2007); Ricci v. Simmons, 179 B.R. 645 (ED MO, 1995); In re Skinner, 68 B.R. 45 (WD OK, 1986). In In re Gentilini, 365 B.R. 251 (SD FL, 2007), a state court judgment requiring the debtor to pay his former wife's attorney's fees was held dischargeable despite being in the nature of a support obligation because the law firm's right to enforce the retainer agreement had expired due to the running of the statute of limitations.

debts owed to spouse's attorney, held dischargeable

As indicated above, most courts have held that a debtor's obligations for attorney fees, court costs, and related expenses incurred by a spouse, former spouse, or child of the debtor in connection with an award of alimony, maintenance or support are nondischargeable under Section 523(a)(5) if the debts are deemed to be in the nature of alimony, maintenance or support. See In re Peters, 964 F.2d 166 (2d Cir., 1992); Joseph v. J. Huey O'Toole, PC, 16 F.3d 86 (5th Cir., 1994); Rosenblatt v. Wittlin, 176 B.R. 76 (SD FL, 1994); Kahoe v. Williams, 151 B.R. 605 (MD FL, 1993). However, attorney's fee obligations and related expenses incurred by a spouse or former spouse of the debtor in connection with a property settlement are dischargeable under Section 523(a)(5) because such fees and expenses are not in the nature of alimony, maintenance or support. See In re Klem, 362 B.R. 585 (WD NY, 2007); In re Kijewski, 91 B.R. 48 (ND IL, 1988); Wester v. Wester, 187 B.R. 358 (MD FL, 1995); In re Rice, 94 B.R. 617 (WD MO, 1988).

fees owed to spouse's attorney for property settlement services, dischargeability of

Several courts have held that if the attorney fees assessed against the debtor in the divorce case were incurred partly for the attainment of alimony, maintenance or support and partly for property settlement purposes, only the portion related to alimony, maintenance or support are nondischargeable under Section 523(a)(5). See In re Schmiel, 94 B.R. 373 (ED PA, 1988); In re Boggess, 105 B.R. 470 (SD IL, 1989). Note, however, that all or a portion of attorney fee obligations related to property settlement may be nondischargeable under Section 523(a)(15).

non-dischargeability of spouse's attorney's fees, importance of intention of court in making award

Additionally, several courts have held that an award of attorney's fees may be treated as being in the nature of alimony, maintenance or support for purposes of Section 523(a)(5) even if a portion of the fees were incurred for property settlement purposes if the attorney's fee award itself was intended to be in the nature of alimony, maintenance or support. See In re Joseph v. J. Huey O'Toole, 16 F.3d 86 (5th Cir., 1994), where the court stated that an attorney's fee award granted pursuant to a divorce decree is not nondischargeable under Section 523(a)(5) because the fees tangentially relate to alimony, maintenance or support. Rather, the court stated, the obligation is nondischargeable if the fee award reflects a balancing by the divorce court of the parties' financial needs after considering such matters as disparity in earning capacity, relative business opportunities, physical condition, the probable future need for support, educational background, and the benefits they would have received had the marriage continued. The court stated that an attorney's fee award is but one factor to be considered in making an equitable division of an estate. The court then held that the entire attorney's fee award assessed to the debtor by the divorce court was nondischargeable under Section 523(a)(5) even though a portion of the fees may have been related to property settlement matters.

non-dischargeability of spouse's attorney's fees, importance of intention of court in making award

A similar rationale is found in Ewing v. Ewing, 180 B.R. 443 (ED VA, 1994), where an award of attorney's fees, commissioner's fees, and court costs was held to be nondischargeable under Section 523(a)(5) despite the fact that the state court had refused to award spousal support to the former spouse, because the divorce decree, the commissioner's report, and the underlying nature of the obligation indicated that the state court and commissioner had intended for the award of fees and costs to be in the nature of support and maintenance. See also Robertson v. Robertson, 187 B.R. 159 (ED VA, 1995); CaterCorp., Inc. v. Henicheck, 186 B.R. 211 (ED VA, 1995).

non-dischargeability of spouse's attorney's fees, importance of intention of court in making award

In Burns v. Burns, 149 B.R. 578 (ED MO, 1993), the court found the debtor's obligation to pay for his former spouse's attorney fees to be nondischargeable under Section 523(a)(5) even though the fees were payable directly to the former spouse's attorney and there was no language in the dissolution decree indicating that the fees were incidental to maintenance or support, because from the record it was evident that the state court intended for the award of attorney's fees to serve a maintenance function. In Wright v. Wright, 184 B.R. 318 (ND IL, 1995), the court held that the entire attorney's fee award assigned to the debtor by the divorce court constituted nondischargeable support for purposes of Section 523(a)(5) even though $94,200 of a $135,000 divorce court award to the debtor's spouse was found to be a dischargeable property settlement debt.

Note that the nondischargeability provisions of Section 523(a)(5) do not cover fees owed to the debtor's own attorney that were incurred in connection with a divorce or separation. Therefore, the debtor's obligation to his or her own attorney in a divorce or separation proceeding are not protected from discharge by Section 523(a)(5). Accordingly, such fees are dischargeable unless they are nondischargeable under another subsection of Section 523. In In re Rios, 901 F.2d 71 (7th Cir., 1990), the court held that a debtor's debt to her former attorney for representation in a paternity and child support action was dischargeable under Section 523(a)(5) because the debtor's liability for her own attorney's fees is not a debt owed "to a spouse, former spouse, or child of the debtor" and because there was no court order imposing the liability as required by Section 523(a)(5).

fees owed to debtor's own attorney, dischargeability of

Divorce-related expenses other than attorney fee obligations may also constitute nondischargeable alimony, maintenance or support under Section 523(a)(5). In Baillargeon v. Stacey, 164 B.R. 210 (NH, 1994), and Walker v. Laing, 187 B.R. 531 (WD VA, 1995), guardian ad litem fees were held to be in the nature of support and therefore nondischargeable under Section 523(a)(5) even though the fees were payable to a third party and not to the debtor's child. In In re Laney, 53 B.R. 231 (ND TX, 1985), attorney's fees owed to a guardian ad litem who represented the debtor's child in a custody dispute were held to be a debt incurred for the support of the child and therefore nondischargeable under Section 523(a)(5). See also In re Burnes, 405 B.R. 654 (WD MO, 2009); Spear v. Constantine, 183 B.R. 335 (MA, 1995) (attorney fees owed to a guardian ad litem in a custody dispute were nondischargeable); Taylor v. Foiles, 176 B.R. 420 (ED VA, 1994) (commissioners' fees in a divorce case were nondischargeable). In In re Seibert, 914 F.2d 102 (7th Cir., 1990), the costs of a paternity action imposed upon the debtor father were held nondischargeable under Section 523(a)(5) as being part of the debtor's underlying support obligation. In In re Slater, 188 B.R. 852 (ED WA, 1995), an award of attorney's fees to a legal assistance office in connection with an attempt to collect child support from the debtor was found nondischargeable under Section 523(a)(5). In Sinton v. Blaemire, 229 B.R. 665 (MA, 1999), an award of attorney fees to an attorney appointed by a state court to represent the debtor's minor children in a custody and support dispute were found to be in the nature of support and therefore nondischargeable under Section 523(a)(5).

divorce or support-related fees and costs, non-dischargeability of

attorney fees in custody actions, non-dischargeability of

Is a debtor's obligation to pay a former spouse's attorney's fees in a child custody dispute nondischargeable under Section 523(a)(5)? Yes, said the court in Jones v. Jones, 9 F.3d 878 (10th Cir., 1993), ruling that the term "support" as used in Section 523(a)(5) encompasses the issue of custody in the absence of unusual circumstances and holding that court-ordered attorney's fees arising from a post-divorce custody action are deemed to be in the nature of nondischargeable support. Ruling that a custody debt could be in the nature of support under Section 523(a)(5) even though it would not legally qualify as alimony or support under state law, the court held a custody-related attorney-fee obligation to be nondischargeable under Section 523(a)(5). See also In re Moers, 206 Fed. Appx. 327 (5th Cir., 2006); In re Peterson, 18 FLW Fed. B. 207 (SD FL, 2005); In re Peters, 124 B.R. 433 (SD NY, 1991); In re Dahlin, 94 B.R. 79 (ED VA, 1988); In re Vazquez, 84 B.R. 848 (SD FL, 1988); In re Snider, 62 B.R. 382 (SD TX, 1986); Filbeck v. Clegg, 189 B.R. 818 (ED TN, 1995); In re Strickland, 90 F.3d 444 (11th Cir., 1996) (attorney's fee award against the debtor in a post-divorce custody action was nondischargeable under Section 523(a)(5) because it was based on relative need and ability to pay). In Berman v. Mobley, 238 B.R. 486 (MD FL, 1998), the debtor's obligation to pay his ex-wife's attorney's fees was held nondischargeable under Section 523(a)(5) as being in the nature of support even though the debtor was not ordered by the divorce court to pay his ex-wife spousal or child support and, as the custodial parent of the minor children, received child support payments from his ex-wife.

attorney fees in custody or visitation cases, when dischargeable

However, in Adams v. Zentz, 963 F.2d 197 (8th Cir., 1992), the court held that under the facts of the case the debtor's obligation to pay her former spouse's attorney's fees arising from a custody dispute was not in the nature of support under Section 523(a)(5) and was therefore dischargeable. Similarly, in In re Shaw, 67 B.R. 911 (MD FL, 1986), the court held that attorney fees assessed against the debtor in connection with a visitation rights issue were not related to support for purposes of Section 523(a)(5) and were therefore dischargeable.

this heading, scope of discussion under

The dischargeability under Section 523(a)(5) of marital obligations owed to third parties. In a divorce or separation proceeding it is common for debts and obligations incurred during the marriage to be assigned to or assumed by one of the spouses. The issue addressed under this heading is the extent to which third-party debts and obligations assigned to or assumed by the debtor are nondischargeable under Section 523(a)(5) of the Bankruptcy Code.

3rd-party marital debts, whether viewed as support or property settlement, importance of

Like other divorce-related debts, marital debts and obligations that were assigned to or assumed by the debtor in a divorce or separation proceeding are nondischargeable under Section 523(a)(5) only if the obligation, or the payment thereof, is deemed to be a DSO, and therefore in the nature of alimony, maintenance or support. If the obligation is deemed to be in the nature of property settlement, it is dischargeable under Section 523(a)(5), but may be nondischargeable under Section 523(a)(15).

One of the tests for determining whether a third-party obligation is in the nature of alimony, maintenance, or support is whether the parties, in the case of an agreement, or the court, in the case of an order, intended the obligation to be in the nature of alimony, maintenance or support. See In re Anderson, 62 B.R. 448 (MN, 1986); In re Young, 72 B.R. 450 (RI, 1987); Ozey v. Ozey, 166 B.R. 169 (ND OK, 1994). The "present needs" test is not applicable in cases involving the nondischargeability of divorce-related third-party obligations owed by the debtor. See In re Rowles, 66 B.R. 628 (ND OH, 1986). The fact that a debt or obligation that is in the nature of alimony, maintenance or support is owed or payable to a third party and not to the spouse, former spouse, or child of the debtor, as required by a literal reading of Section 523(a)(5) does not prevent the obligation from being nondischargeable under Section 523(a)(5). See Livengood v. Idaho, 157 B.R. 678 (ID, 1993).

3rd-party marital debts, importance of intent in determining dischargeability

In determining whether a third-party obligation is in the nature of alimony, maintenance or support, much depends upon the nature of the particular debt or obligation. For example, a third-party debt incurred for food, clothing or housing is more likely to be deemed alimony, maintenance or support than a third-party debt incurred for the purchase of investment property. In Manzi v. Geenty, 283 B.R. 103 (CT, 2002), a debt owed to a court-appointed guardian ad litem for the debtor's minor children from a previous marriage for services rendered to the children in connection with the debtor's divorce was held to be a nondischargeable debt for child support.

3rd-party marital debt, nature of debt, importance of

Debts owed to third parties for medical and dental care are universally held to be in the nature of alimony, maintenance or support and therefore nondischargeable under Section 523(a)(5). See In re Woods, 309 B.R. 22 (WD MO, 2004); In re Seibert, 914 F.2d 102 (7th Cir., 1990); Livengood v. Idaho, 157 B.R. 678 (ID, 1993); In re Young, 72 B.R. 450 (RI, 1987); In re Spurgeon, 80 B.R. 477 (WD MO, 1986). Debts owed to third parties for medical and dental insurance are also normally held to be in the nature of alimony, maintenance or support and therefore nondischargeable under Section 523(a)(5). See In re Bowers, 357 B.R. 663 (MD FL, 2006); In re Kemp, 242 B.R. 178 (B.A.P. 8th Cir., 1999); In re Stone, 79 B.R. 633 (MD, 1987); Hubbard v. Woodall, 185 B.R. 743 (ED KY, 1995). In In re Merrill, 252 B.R. 497 (B.A.P. 10th Cir., 2000) the debtor's obligations to pay his former spouse's automobile insurance and life insurance expenses were nondischargeable support expenses under Section 523(a)(5).

3rd-party debts for medical care or insurance, non-dischargeability of

Obligations owed by the debtor to a governmental agency for pregnancy, child birth, and related expenses incurred on behalf of the debtor's child or spouse and imposed on the debtor by a valid agreement or order are normally deemed to be in the nature of support and are nondischargeable under Section 523(a)(5) even though the debts are not owed to the debtor's spouse or child. See In re Seibert, 914 F.2d 102 (7th Cir., 1990) (holding costs of a paternity action were also nondischargeable under Section 523(a)(5)); Mullally v. Carter, 67 B.R. 535 (ND IL, 1986); In re Burton, 132 B.R. 575 (ND IN, 1988); and In re Oberley, 153 B.R. 179 (ND OH, 1993); In re Chang, 163 F.3d 1138 (9th Cir., 1998).

3rd-party debts to governmental entities for medical expenses, non-dischargeability of

mortgage on spouse's home, dischargeability of debt for

A debtor's obligation to pay a mortgage indebtedness on the post-marriage home of a former spouse or child of the debtor is usually held to be in the nature of nondischargeable support or alimony. See In re Busch, 369 B.R. 614 (B.A.P. 1st Cir.0, 2007); In re Walden, 312 B.R. 187 (CD IL, 2004); In re Gianakas, 917 F.2d 759 (3d Cir., 1990); In re Robinson, 921 F.2d 252 (10th Cir., 1990); In re Ploski, 44 B.R. 911 (NH, 1984); In re Mizen, 72 B.R. 251 (ND OH, 1987); In re Delaine, 56 B.R. 460 (ND AL, 1985); Slider v. Slider, 176 B.R. 7 (WD PA, 1994); In re Coverdale, 65 B.R. 126 (MD FL, 1986). However, in In re Tosti, 62 B.R. 131 (NJ, 1986), a mortgage obligation on a former spouse's property was held to be in the nature of a dischargeable property settlement obligation because the divorce court intended the payment to equalize the distribution of property between the spouses. See also In re Mader, 228 B.R. 787 (MD FL, 1998); In re McKenzie, 55 B.R. 220 (ED TN, 1985). A debtor's obligations to make automobile and furniture payments for the former spouse may also be nondischargeable under Section 523(a)(5). See, e.g., In re Carlisle, 205 B.R. 812 (WD LA, 1997); In re Marriage of Weis, 232 P.3d 789 (Colo. 2010) (agreement to use home sale proceeds to pay off joint creditor was DSO).

obligations for educational expenses, when non-dischargeable

Obligations for educational expenses incurred during the marriage by the debtor's children or former spouse are usually held to be in the nature of support or alimony and therefore nondischargeable under Section 523(a)(5). See In re Shaw, 299 B.R. 107 (WD PA, 2003); Ozey v. Ozey, 166 B.R. 169 (ND OK, 1994); In re Portaro, 108 B.R. 142 (ND OH, 1989); Bush v. Bush, 154 B.R. 69 (SD OH, 1993); In re Rowles, 66 B.R. 628 (ND OH, 1986). In In re Pierce, 95 B.R. 154 (ND CA, 1988), the debtor's obligation to provide financial support for his children's college education was held to be a nondischargeable support obligation under Section 523(a)(5) even though the obligation might not have been enforceable under state law because it was for post-majority support without a contractual undertaking. See also Warren v. Warren, 160 B.R. 395 (ME, 1993); In re Casler, 94 B.R. 741 (MD FL, 1988).

obligations for educational expenses, dischargeability of

In In re Brown, 74 B.R. 968 (CT, 1987), the debtor's obligation to pay for his child's post-high school education was nondischargeable even though under state law the debtor's support obligation ended when the child attained the age of majority. However, in In re Motley, 69 B.R. 406 (ND OH, 1987), the debtor's obligation to pay his daughter's private school tuition was a dischargeable property settlement debt under the terms of the debtor's divorce decree. See also Cowell v. Hale, 279 B.R. 618 (MA, 2002).

Whether credit card and charge account obligations imposed on the debtor by a divorce agreement or decree constitute nondischargeable alimony, maintenance, or support depends on the nature of the items or services purchased or obtained and on the intent of the parties in acquiring the items or services. See In re Fussell, 303 B.R. 539 (SD GA, 2003); In re Calhoun, 715 F.2d 1103 (6th Cir., 1983); In re Williams, 703 F.2d 1055 (8th Cir., 1983). In In re Coverdale, 65 B.R. 126 (MD FL, 1986), a charge account obligation for the purchase of goods which may or may not be awarded to the spouse and which may or may not be retained by her was classified as a dischargeable property settlement debt. In In re Hiller, 44 B.R. 764 (ND OH, 1984), a credit card obligation imposed on the debtor in a divorce decree was held to be a dischargeable property settlement debt under the terms of the decree. See also In re Hodge, 265 B.R. 908 (ND OH, 2001); In re Midnet, 84 B.R. 776 (MD FL, 1988). However, in In re Luman, 238 B.R. 697 (ND OH, 1999), a former spouse's credit card debt that was assigned to the debtor in the divorce decree was found to be a nondischargeable debt under Section 523(a) because it was clearly intended by the divorce court to be in the nature of support. See also, Hayes v. Hayes, 235 B.R. 885 (WD TN, 1999).

spouse's credit card & charge account obligations, dischargeability of

However, if the spouse or former spouse will be rendered unable to support herself and her dependents if the debtor's obligation is discharged, the obligation is likely to be found to be in the nature of nondischargeable support. See In re Petoske, 16 B.R. 412 (ED NY, 1982); In re Harke, 24 B.R. 645 (ED MO, 1982); In re Sermersheim, 97 B.R. 885 (ND OH, 1989), where the court held a credit card obligation to be in the nature of nondischargeable alimony but found that it would be manifestly unreasonable to hold the debtor liable for the accrued interest on the obligation and therefore found the accrued interest on the obligation to be in the nature of a dischargeable property settlement obligation.

spouse's credit card & charge account obligations, dischargeability of

The dischargeability under Section 523(a)(5) of divorce-related hold-harmless debts. In divorce or separation proceedings it is not uncommon for one spouse to agree or be ordered to hold the other spouse harmless from one or more debts or obligations. The issue addressed under this heading is the extent to which debts and obligations incurred by a debtor under a hold-harmless provision in a divorce-related agreement or order are nondischargeable under Section 523(a)(5) of the Bankruptcy Code as a DSO.

this heading, scope of discussion under

Like other divorce-related debts, to be a nondischargeable DSO obligation under Section 523(a)(5), a debt or obligation incurred by a debtor under a hold-harmless provision in a divorce-related agreement or order must be in the nature of alimony, maintenance or support. If such a debt or obligation is found to be in the nature of property settlement, it is dischargeable under Section 523(a)(5) but may be nondischargeable under Section 523(a)(15).

hold-harmless debts, whether viewed as support or property settlement, importance of

Whether a debt or obligation incurred by a debtor under a hold-harmless provision is deemed to be in the nature of alimony, maintenance or support depends on the type of debt incurred, the role or purpose of the hold-harmless provision in the agreement or order, and the intention of the parties or the court with respect to the provision. In In re Shimp, 59 B.R. 553 (ND OH, 1986), the court stated that hold-harmless clauses do not, in and of themselves, constrain a Bankruptcy Court to find that obligations incurred thereunder are in the nature of alimony, maintenance or support for purposes of Section 523(a)(5). The court stated that hold-harmless obligations are in the nature of alimony, maintenance or support only if the hold-harmless clause, taken as a whole, operates as

hold-harmless debts, dischargeability of, factors

hold-harmless debts, dischargeability of, factors

alimony, maintenance, or support. In In re Dean, 277 B.R. 381 (CD IL, 2002) a divorce decree that provided for the debtor to hold his ex-wife harmless from a tax liability and specifically linked the debtor's assumption of this obligation to a corresponding reduction in child support created a debt that was nondischargeable under Section 523(a)(5). In In re Harden, 351 B.R. 643 (CD IL, 2006), the court enumerated four factors to consider when determining if a hold-harmless provision imposes an obligation in the nature of nondischargeable support. The factors to be considered are: (1) whether the agreement includes provisions for payments to the ex-spouse; (2) whether the hold-harmless provision was intended to balance the parties' incomes; (3) whether the provision is located within property allocation provisions of the agreement; and, (4) whether the hold-harmless provision describes the character and method of payment.

hold-harmless debts, dischargeability of, cases

In Ianke v. Ianke, 185 B.R. 297 (ED MO, 1995), the debtor's obligation to indemnify and hold harmless his former spouse as to certain credit card debts and attorney's fees was found to be in the nature of maintenance and support and therefore nondischargeable under Section 523(a)(5) where the debtor's income and income potential greatly exceeded that of his former spouse. On the other hand, in In re Portaro, 108 B.R. 142 (ND OH, 1989), the debtor's obligation to hold his former spouse harmless from mortgage liabilities on rental properties conveyed to the debtor in the divorce decree was found to be in the nature of property settlement and therefore dischargeable under Section 523(a)(5).

dischargeability of hold-harmless debts, importance of context of provision in order

As indicated above, whether an obligation incurred by a debtor under a divorce-related hold-harmless provision is deemed to be in the nature of alimony, maintenance or support often depends on the context of the provision in the applicable agreement or order. For example, in In re Boggess, 105 B.R. 470 (SD IL, 1989), the debtor's obligation to hold his former spouse harmless from liability for all marital debts was found not to be in the nature of alimony, maintenance or support where the divorce court found that each spouse had sufficient income to support themselves and clearly expressed its intent not to award maintenance or support. Similarly, in Moore v. Moore, 78 B.R. 304 (ND FL, 1987), the debtor's agreement to hold his spouse harmless from all marital debts was found not to be in the nature of alimony, maintenance or support where there were no minor children and the spouse was employed, earned as much as the debtor, and had expressly waived alimony in the agreement. In In re Brock, 58 B.R. 797 (SD OH, 1986), the debtor's obligation to hold his former spouse harmless from a second mortgage was found not to be in the nature of alimony, maintenance or support, and therefore dischargeable under Section 523(a)(5), because, considering the income and assets of both parties, it was impossible to conclude that the debtor's hold-harmless obligation was in the nature of support.

If the debtor's spouse or former spouse did not request or was not in need of support or alimony, a hold-harmless obligation is likely to be found to be in the nature of a property settlement obligation. In In re Arosemena, 63 B.R. 55 (MD FL, 1986), the debtor's obligation to hold his former spouse harmless from a debt owed to the former spouse's mother was found to be a dischargeable property settlement obligation where the former spouse had not requested alimony, maintenance or support and the marriage had lasted only 9 months. In In re Hudgens, 57 B.R. 184 (MD LA, 1986), the debtor's obligation to hold his spouse harmless from a community debt was held to be a dischargeable property settlement obligation in part because the spouse had agreed not to seek alimony. See also In re Boggess, 105 B.R. 470 (SD IL, 1989); Moore v. Moore, 78 B.R. 304 (ND FL, 1987), supra. See In re Findley, 245 B.R. 526 (ND OH, 2000) and In re Davis, 261 B.R. 659 (SD OH, 2001) (finding hold harmless obligations to be in the nature of property settlement debts).

hold-harmless debts, dischargeable, cases holding

However, in In re Lord, 93 B.R. 678 (ED MO, 1988), the debtor's obligation to hold his former spouse harmless from all marital debts was found to be in the nature of nondischargeable alimony, maintenance or support where the former spouse was in poor health, legally blind, and unable to sustain meaningful employment, while the debtor was in good health and earned $30,000 per year. In that case the underlying debt (i.e., the debtor's obligation to the third party creditor) was found to be dischargeable because it was payable to a third party and not to the former spouse, but the debtor's obligation to hold his former spouse harmless from the debt was found to be nondischargeable under Section 523(a)(5).

hold-harmless debts, non-dischargeable, case holding

In In re Horton, 69 B.R. 42 (ED MO, 1986), the debtor's obligation to hold his former spouse harmless from specified creditors was found to be in the nature of nondischargeable maintenance where the separation agreement provided that the debtor was made responsible for the debts in lieu of providing maintenance to the former spouse and where disparate incomes of the parties indicated that the obligation was intended to provide support for the former spouse. Similarly, in In re MacDonald, 69 B.R. 259 (NJ, 1986), the debtor's obligation to hold his former spouse harmless from certain business loans that she had cosigned was found to be in the nature of alimony, maintenance or support and therefore nondischargeable under Section 523(a)(5) where the circumstances were such that the former spouse's support would have been inadequate if she had to pay the obligations.

hold-harmless debts, non-dischargeable, cases holding

The dischargeability under Section 523(a)(5) of debts owed or assigned to governmental entities. As indicated above in this article, debts for DSOs that have been validly assigned to the Federal Government or to a state or political subdivision thereof remain nondischargeable under Section 523(a)(5). Also, nondischargeability for support debts owed to states and municipalities is provided for in 42 U.S.C. § 656(b). Read together, these statutes clearly reflect the intent of Congress to prevent the discharge of debts for alimony, maintenance and support that are assigned, either in fact or by operation of law, to a governmental entity.

debts assigned to governmental entity, non-dischargeability of, statutory authority non-dischargeability of debts assigned to governmental entity under Section 523(a)(5)

A debt for child or spousal support owed by the debtor under an enforceable agreement or order that has been validly assigned to the state or county or an agency thereof by the debtor's spouse or child are nondischargeable under Section 523(a)(5). See In re Schauer, 391 B.R. 430 (ED WI, 2008); In re Roy, 315 B.R. 108 (ND, 2004); In re Seibert, 914 F.2d 102 (7th Cir., 1990); In re Petty, 60 B.R. 86 (MD AL, 1986); In re Jones, 94 B.R. 99 (ND OH, 1988); Kidd v. Clermont County Child Support Enforcement Agency, 177 B.R. 876 (SD OH, 1995) (holding the amount owed by the debtor to the county agency for medical expenses incurred in connection with a child born out of wedlock was nondischargeable under Section 523(a)(5) because the child's mother upon receipt of her public assistance automatically assigned to the agency her right to medical support from the debtor).

non-dischargeability of debts assigned to governmental entity, effect of conditions subsequent

In In re Lhamon, 139 B.R. 849 (ND OH, 1991), the fact that the debtor and his former spouse had remarried did not affect the nondischargeable nature of the debtor's liability to the state for child support obligations previously assigned to the state by the debtor's spouse as a condition of receiving AFDC benefits. In Donelson v. Missouri Dept. of Social Services, 153 B.R. 995 (WD MO, 1993), the subsequent emancipation of the debtor's son did not affect the nondischargeable nature of the debtor's obligation to the state, to whom the child support claim had been assigned by the son's mother in order to receive AFDC benefits.

debt assigned to governmental entity, requirement of valid order

For an assignment of a DSO to a governmental unit to be valid, an agreement or order setting forth the debtor's obligation must exist and the assignment to the governmental unit must be clear and effective. In In re Ramirez, 795 F.2d 1494 (9th Cir., 1986), the court held that an assignment of support rights to a county welfare agency in order to obtain AFDC benefits did not render the assigned claim nondischargeable under Section 523(a)(5) where there was no support order or separation agreement requiring the debtor to support his children.

debts assigned to governmental entity, necessity of valid assignment

In Godden v. Kansas Dept. of Social & Rehab Servs., 156 B.R. 36 (WD MO, 1993), the court held that the debtor's support obligation to the State of Kansas as assignee was dischargeable under Section 523(a)(5) because the assignment was ineffective in that it failed to differentiate between child and spousal support, rendering it impossible to determine the amount of support assigned to the state. In Matter of Saafir, 192 B.R. 964 (NE, 1996), a judgment debt owed by the debtor to the Kansas Department of Social and Rehabilitation Services for reimbursement of assistance extended by the state to the debtor's child while a ward of the state was ruled dischargeable, even though it was in the nature of child support, because it was not a debt owed to a spouse, former spouse or child of the debtor and did not arise from an assignment to the state of a support obligation.

In Browning v. County of Stanislaus, 161 B.R. 841 (ED CA, 1993), the county's claim for support against the debtor was based partly on an AFDC assignment made by the mother of the debtor's child and partly on a California statute that provides counties with a limited right of reimbursement from absent parents when aid is provided. The court held that the county's claim against the debtor was nondischargeable to the extent that it was based on the AFDC assignment but was dischargeable to the extent that it was based on the California statute because the portion of the debt based on the California statute was owed directly to the county. The court further held that the portion of the county's claim that was based on the AFDC assignment was nondischargeable even though no court order, agreement or determination establishing support was in existence when the bankruptcy case was filed or when the AFDC assignment was made. An AFDC assignment is valid for purposes of Section 523(a)(5)(A) if it is made before the debtor's liability arises under local law. See, e.g., In re Pierson, 47 B.R. 258 (NE, 1985).

debts assigned to governmental entity, dischargeability of, general aspects

Bibliography. For further reading on the issues discussed in this article, see the annotations and articles listed below.

Annotations:

Debts for alimony, maintenance and support as exceptions to bankruptcy discharge under §523(a)(5) of Bankruptcy Code of 1978. 69 ALR Fed 403.

Articles:

The Dischargeability of Property Settlement and Hold Harmless Agreements in Bankruptcy: An Overview of Section 523(a)(15). 31 Family Law Quarterly 409, Fall, 1997.

Using Bankruptcy Court to Modify Domestic Relations Decrees: Problems Created by Sections 523(a)(2)(A), (a)(4), and (a)(6) of the Bankruptcy Code. 31 Family Law Quarterly 433, Fall, 1997.

Does the new exception to discharge in bankruptcy give the marital creditor a benefit or a trompe l'oeil? 6 J. Bankruptcy L. & Pract. 51, Nov - Dec., 1996.

Protection for family support and maintenance in consumer bankruptcies. 69 Wis. Lawyer 14, Fall, 1996.

Bankruptcy meets family law: a presumptive approach to the dischargeability of equitable distribution awards. 5 J. Bankruptcy L. & Pract. 83, Nov. - Dec., 1995.

Protecting the former spouse's property settlement under the Bankruptcy Reform Act of 1994. 69 Fla. B.J. 52, Dec. 1995.

1.08 What constitutes a debt for willful and malicious injury and to what extent are such debts nondischargeable in bankruptcy?

Text of statute. Section 523(a)(6) of the Bankruptcy Code (11 U.S.C. § 523(a)(6)) is applicable to the subject discussed in this article. It provides as follows:

Section 523(a)(6), text of

523. Exceptions to discharge

(a) A discharge under section 727, 1141, 1228(a), 1228(b), or 1328(b) of this title does not discharge an individual debtor from any debt -

. . . .

(6) for willful and malicious injury by the debtor to another entity or to the property of another entity;

Section 523(a)(6), applicability to Chapter 7 and Chapter 13 cases

Introduction. Section 523(a)(6) was enacted in the Bankruptcy Reform Act of 1978 and has remained unchanged. Section 523(a)(6) is applicable to Chapter 7 cases and to Chapter 13 cases where the debtor receives a "best-efforts" discharge under 11 U.S.C. § 1328(b). Section 523(a)(6) is not applicable to Chapter 13 cases where the debtor receives a completed plan discharge under 11 U.S.C. § 1328(a). Therefore, debts for willful and malicious injury are nondischargeable only in Chapter 7 cases and in Chapter 13 cases wherein the debtor receives a "best-efforts" discharge under 11 U.S.C. § 1328(b). Such debts are dischargeable in Chapter 13 cases wherein the debtor receives a completed plan discharge under 11 U.S.C. § 1328(a). See In re Caldwell, 895 F.2d 1123 (6th Cir., 1990), and Mason v. Young, 237 F.3d 1168 (10th Cir., 2001).

Section 523(a)(6), necessity of filing request to determine dischargeability of debt

Nondischargeability under Section 523(a)(6) is not self-executing. This means that a debt meeting the criteria of Section 523(a)(6) (i.e., a debt for willful and malicious injury) will be discharged unless the creditor successfully challenges the dischargeability of the debt in the bankruptcy proceeding. For a debt to be nondischargeable under Section 523(a)(6), the creditor to whom the debt is owed must file a request to determine the dischargeability of the debt within the required period and the bankruptcy court, after notice and a hearing, must find the debt to be nondischargeable under this Section. See 11 U.S.C. § 523(c)(1). The burden of proof on the issue of nondischargeability is on the creditor, who must establish nondischargeability by a preponderance of the evidence. See Grogan v. Garner, 498 U.S. 279, 111 S.Ct. 654 (1991); In re Mayerson, 254 B.R. 407 (ND OH, 2000).

The procedure for determining the dischargeability of debts under Section 523(a)(6) is governed by 11 U.S.C. § 523(c)(1) and by Bankruptcy Rule 4007(c) in Chapter 7 cases and Bankruptcy Rule 4007(d) in Chapter 13 cases wherein the debtor requests a discharge under 11 U.S.C. § 1328(b). In a Chapter 7 case the creditor to whom the debt is owed must file a complaint to determine the dischargeability of the debt within 60 days after the first date set for the meeting of creditors, unless, on the motion of a party in interest made within the 60-day period, the court for cause extends the time for such filing. See Bankruptcy Rule 4007(c). In a Chapter 13 case in which the debtor has requested a discharge under 11 U.S.C. § 1328(b), the time for filing complaints to determine the dischargeability of debts under Section 523(a)(6) must be fixed by the court. At least 30 days notice of the time so fixed must be given to all creditors. See Bankruptcy Rule 4007(d).

procedure for filing request to determine dischargeability under Section 523(a)(6)

Section 523(a)(6) provides that neither a Chapter 7 discharge nor a Chapter 13 discharge granted under Section 1328(b) discharges the debtor from a liability or claim for personal injury or property damage caused by a willful and malicious act of the debtor. Nondischargeability under Section 523(a)(6) depends on the nature of the act giving rise to the liability and not on the relationship between the parties. Therefore, nondischargeability under Section 523(a)(6) is generally limited to intentional torts and is not imposed for simple breach of contract, negligence, or even recklessness. See In re Catalanotto, 366 B.R. 566 (ED LA, 2007); In re Elwood, 319 B.R. 371 (ED PA, 2005); In re Lazzara, 287 B.R. 714 (ND IL, 2002); In re Allen, 75 B.R. 742 (CD CA, 1987); In re Braen, 94 B.R. 35 (NJ, 1988); In re Keller, 106 B.R. 639 (B.A.P. 9th Cir., 1989).

Section 523(a)(6), general applicability

It is important to note that for a claim or liability to be nondischargeable under Section 523(a)(6), the act or acts of the debtor must be both willful and malicious. See In re D'Amato, 330 B.R. 749 (ED MO, 2005); In re Littleton, 942 F.2d 551 (9th Cir., 1991); In re Schultz, 89 B.R. 28 (ED WI, 1988); In re McCune, 85 B.R. 834 (WD MO, 1988). However, most courts have held that specific intent by the debtor to cause harm to the person or property of the injured party is not required for nondischargeability under Section 523(a)(6). See In re Thirtyacre, 36 F.3d 697 (7th Cir., 1994); In re Braen, 94 B.R. 35 (NJ, 1988); In re Erickson, 89 B.R. 850 (ID, 1988) (holding under Section 523(a)(6) the focus is not on the debtor's intent to cause injury but rather on the debtor's intent to perform the act that gives rise to the injury). Thus, to establish nondischargeability it is usually only necessary to show that the debtor intended to perform the malicious act and not that the debtor specifically intended to harm the person or property of the injured creditor. A few courts have held that to establish nondischargeability under Section 523(a)(6), a creditor must show a specific intent by the debtor to injure the creditor. See In re Zaidan, 86 B.R. 296 (SD FL, 1988); In re Pasek, 983 F.2d 1524 (10th Cir., 1993); In re Elwood, 319 B.R. 371 (ED PA, 2005).

non-dischargeability under Section 523(a)(6), necessity of intent to injure non-dischargeable willful and malicious injuries, types of

Generally, any willful and malicious act committed by the debtor that proximately causes foreseeable injury to the person or property of another entity may create a debt for willful and malicious injury that is nondischargeable under Section 523(a)(6). The types of acts or conduct that may give rise to a nondischargeable debt under Section 523(a)(6) may be categorized as follows: intentional personal torts, intentional vehicular torts, intentional conversion, aggravated breach of contract, failure to carry workers' compensation insurance, and intentional waste. Each category of willful and malicious misconduct is discussed separately below following the discussions of the definition and proof of willful and malicious injury.

willful misconduct, what constitutes

The definition and proof of willful and malicious injuries. As indicated above, to be nondischargeable under Section 523(a)(6), the act or acts of the debtor that gave rise to the debt must have been both willful and malicious. For purposes of Section 523(a)(6), "willful" means deliberate or intentional. See Chrysler Credit Corp. v. Perry Chrysler Plymouth, Inc., 783 F.2d 480 (5th Cir., 1986); Wheeler v. Laudani, 783 F.2d 610 (6th Cir., 1986). The test for willfulness under Section 523(a)(6) is whether the debtor intentionally performed the acts that caused the debtor's injury. In In re Elwood, 319 B.R. 371 (ED PA, 2005). Accordingly, "willful" conduct is conduct that is volitional and deliberate and over which the debtor exercises meaningful control, as opposed to unintentional, accidental, or even reckless conduct. See In re Posta, 866 F.2d 364 (10th Cir., 1989). Recklessness or reckless disregard does not generally constitute "willfulness" for purposes of Section 523(a)(6). See, e.g., Hope v. Walker, 48 F.3d 1161 (11th Cir., 1995); In re Ikner, 883 F.2d 986 (11th Cir., 1989); Kawaauhau v. Geiger, 523 U.S. 57, 118 S. Ct. 974 (1998) (holding "willfulness" under Section 523(a)(6) requires deliberate or intentional injury, not merely deliberate or intentional acts that lead to injury). The willfulness requirement of Section 523(a)(6) is met only when the debtor has a subjective motive to inflict injury or when the debtor believes that injury is substantially certain to result from his own conduct. See Carrillo v. Su, 290 F.3d 1140 (9th Cir., 2002).

malicious misconduct, what constitutes

The term "malicious," for purposes of Section 523(a)(6), means without just cause or excuse or in conscious disregard of one's duties. See Chrysler Creditor Corp. v. Perry Chrysler Plymouth, Inc., 783 F.2d 480 (5th Cir., 1986); Wheeler v. Laudani, 783 F.2d 610 (6th Cir., 1986); Leslie v. Leslie, 181 B.R. 317 (ND OH, 1995). Implied or constructive malice is sufficient for purposes of Section 523(a)(6). See Chrysler Credit Corp. v. Rebhan, 842 F.2d 1257 (11th Cir., 1988); Barnett Bank v. Ussery, 179 B.R. 737 (SD GA, 1995). The test for malicious conduct under Section 523(a)(6) focuses on the debtor's actual knowledge or reasonable foreseeability that his or her conduct will result in injury to the creditor and not on the wrongfulness of the debtor's act. See In re Posta, 866 F.2d 364 (10th Cir., 1989). Malice may generally be inferred from the nature of a wrongful act. See, e.g., In re Littleton, 942 F.2d 551 (9th Cir., 1991). Recklessness or reckless disregard by the debtor can be used to establish malice but not willfulness. See, e.g., Sims v. Morris, 185 B.R. 939 (ND GA, 1994). To prove malice, it need not be shown that the debtor specifically intended to injure the creditor, but it must be shown that the debtor knew or should reasonably have foreseen that his or her conduct would result in injury to the creditor. See In re Britton, 950 F.2d 602 (9th Cir., 1991); Smith v. Assevero, 185 B.R. 951 (ND GA, 1995).

To be both "willful" and "malicious," then, the act giving rise to the injury or claim must have been intentionally and deliberately committed by the debtor without just cause or excuse. See In re Littleton, 942 F.2d 551 (9th Cir., 1991); Hope v. Walker, 48 F.3d 1161 (11th Cir., 1995). Under the Supreme Court's ruling in Kawaauhau v. Geiger, supra, to establish nondischargeability under Section 523(a)(6) it is also necessary to show that the debtor intended the consequences of his or her acts and not merely that the debtor intended to commit the act itself. This means that to establish nondischargeability under Section 523(a)(6) it must be shown that the debtor specifically intended to cause harm or injury. See In re Bundick, 303 B.R. 90 (ED VA, 2003).

willful and malicious conduct, what constitutes

The burden of proof in establishing the nondischargeability of a debt under Section 523(a)(6) is on the creditor. As explained above in this article, the holder of a claim that is allegedly nondischargeable under Section 523(a)(6) must file a complaint to determine the dischargeability of the debt (or claim) within a prescribed period in order to prevent the debt from being discharged. After filing the complaint, the creditor must prove by a preponderance of the evidence that the claim (or debt) in question was proximately caused by the willful and malicious acts of the debtor. See In re Littleton, 942 F.2d 551 (9th Cir., 1991); Chrysler Credit Corp. v. Rebhan, 842 F.2d 1257 (11th Cir., 1987); Century 21 Balfour Real Estate v. Menna, 16 F.3d 7 (1st Cir., 1994).

willful and malicious injury, burden of proof

In Grogan v. Garner, 498 U.S. 279, 111 S.Ct. 654 (1991), the Supreme Court held that the standard of proof imposed on creditors in establishing the nondischargeability of a debt under Section 523(a)(6) is the ordinary preponderance of the evidence standard. Clear and convincing evidence is not required. A creditor seeking to have a debt held nondischargeable under Section 523(a)(6) must also prove that the debt in question was proximately caused by debtor's willful and malicious conduct and not by the creditor's own intervening conduct. See Century 21 Balfour Real Estate v. Menna, 16 F.3d 7 (1st Cir., 1994).

willful and malicious injury, standard of proof

To establish nondischargeability under Section 523(a)(6), willful and malicious injury must be proven by competent evidence. Willful and malicious misconduct by the debtor can not generally be proven by imputing the acts of another to the debtor. See, e.g., In re Maltais, 202 B.R. 807 (MA, 1996). In In re Schulcz, 79 B.R. 726 (SD OH, 1987), willful and malicious injury under Section 523(a)(6) was not established by the affidavit of an attorney who was involved in a state court proceeding against the debtor. In In re Pavelka, 79 B.R. 228 (ED PA, 1987), the court held that willful and malicious injury under Section 523(a)(6) was not established by the admission into evidence of a promissory note given by the debtor in settlement of a civil suit for conversion where the settlement contained no admission by the debtor of intentional or willful wrongdoing. Duress or compulsion may constitute justification or excuse that will prevent an intentional injury from being a malicious one. See In re Russell, 262 B.R. 449 (ND IN, 2001).

willful and malicious injury, ineffective evidence

Often, the conduct complained of in a Section 523(a)(6) nondischargeability proceeding has been the subject of a prior case in a state court. What effect or weight does a prior judgment or finding of a state court have in a Section 523(a)(6) bankruptcy proceeding? The general rule is that if the issues raised in the bankruptcy proceeding were raised and resolved in a prior judicial proceeding involving the same parties, the doctrines of collateral estoppel and res judicata preclude the issues from being tried again in the bankruptcy court. See In re Jacobs, 381 B.R. 128 (ED PA, 2008); Stahl v. Gross, 288 B.R. 655 (ED NY, 2003); Bukowski v. Patel, 266 B.R. 838 (ED WI, 2001); In re Evans, 252 B.R. 366 (ND MS, 2000). A bankruptcy court must apply the rules of collateral estoppel used in the local state. See

collateral estoppel, applicability in Section 523(a)(6) proceeding

collateral estoppel, applicability in Section 523(a)(6) proceeding

In re McNallen, 62 F.3d 619 (4th Cir., 1995); In re Abbo, 192 B.R. 891 (ND OH, 1996); In re Martino, 220 B.R. 129 (MD FL, 1998). However, federal law controls the issue of whether the debt arose from a willful and malicious injury inflicted by the debtor. See In re Price, 264 B.R. 8 (ED AR, 2001).

In In re Caldwell, 60 B.R. 214 (ED TN, 1986), the court held that the debtor was collaterally estopped from relitigating the factual issues determined in a state court action for false arrest, false imprisonment, and malicious prosecution against the debtor because state law required the same showing of maliciousness and willfulness as is required under Section 523(a)(6). In Pulley v. Longfitt, 182 B.R. 35 (WD AR, 1995), while the imposition of punitive damages in a state court proceeding will support a finding of willful and malicious misconduct for purposes of Section 523(a)(6), a failure of the state court to impose punitive damages does not preclude the creditor from establishing willful and malicious misconduct in the bankruptcy proceeding. See also In re Peterson, 332 B.R. 678 (DE, 2005). In In re McNallen, 62 F.3d 619 (4th Cir., 1995), a state court judgment against the debtor based on the debtor's intentionally tortious treatment of his mother was found to have collaterally estopped the debtor from litigating the issues of willfulness and maliciousness in the bankruptcy court. In Ball v. A.O. Smith Corp., 451 F.3d 66 (2d Cir., 2006), an attorney debtor was collaterally estopped from re-litigating the original sanctioning court's finding that the attorney's conduct in filing a lawsuit that was clearly time-barred was done with malice enough to be non-dischargeable.

collateral estoppel, use of to prove willful and malicious injury under Section 523(a)(6)

On the other hand, if the issues litigated in the state court proceeding were not identical to the issues raised in the Section 523(a)(6) bankruptcy proceeding, the doctrines of res judicata and collateral estoppel are not applicable and the judgment or finding of the state court on the issues are not binding on the bankruptcy court. See Gable v. Olson, 355 B.R. 660 (ED TN, 2006) and In re Ikner, 883 F.2d 986 (11th Cir., 1989). Specifically, if the issues of the willfulness and maliciousness of the debtor's conduct were not raised in the state court, the state court finding or judgment is not binding on the bankruptcy court. See In re Robinson, 76 B.R. 145 (WD MO, 1987). In Confer v. Confer, 277 B.R. 374 (SD OH, 2002), a state court default judgment against the debtor was held to be an insufficient basis for applying the doctrine of collateral estoppel. See also In re Andress, 345 B.R. 358 (ND OK, 2006); but see In re Edie, 314 B.R. 6 (UT, 2004).

collateral estoppel, when not applicable in Section 523(a)(6) proceeding

In In re Pickens, 3 BAMSL 1747 (ED MO, 1985), the court stated the doctrine of collateral estoppel was not applicable to a state court award of punitive damages unless the state court in adjudicating the issue of wrongful detention determined that issue by using standards identical to those set forth in Section 523(a)(6). The court held that the definition of willful and wanton misconduct in the Missouri jury instruction was not sufficiently similar to the willful and malicious requirement of Section 523(a)(6) to warrant collateral estoppel. See also Haenline v. Neal, 179 B.R. 234 (ID, 1995), where the court held that a state court verdict against the debtor for sexual battery did not establish the Section 523(a)(6) requirement of malicious injury because the elements of sexual battery under state law did not require the debtor's conduct to have necessarily caused injury as is required under Section 523(a)(6). See In re Fulgham, 70 B.R. 168 (NM, 1986), for a similar ruling.

collateral estoppel, when not applicable in Section 523(a)(6) proceeding

Regardless of whether the doctrines of res judicata and collateral estoppel are found to be applicable for purposes of determining the nondischargeability of a debt under Section 523(a)(6), once the existence of willful and malicious injury has been established by the creditor, the doctrine of res judicata is almost always imposed for the purposes of determining the amount of the debt (i.e., the extent of the injury or the amount of the creditor's damages resulting from the injury). That the amount of a state court judgment will be recognized by the bankruptcy court as the amount of the nondischargeable debt in a Section 523(a)(6) proceeding, see Stokes v. Ferris, 150 B.R. 388 (WD TX, 1992), In re Mc Donald, 73 B.R. 877 (ND TX, 1987), In re Morton, 100 B.R. 607 (ND GA, 1989), In re Green, 138 B.R. 622 (NM, 1992), Katahn Assocs., Inc. v. Wien, 155 B.R. 479 (ND IL, 1993), and Metromedia Co. v. Fugazy, 157 B.R. 761 (SD NY, 1993). The amount of an arbitration award may also be recognized as the amount of a Section 523(a)(6) debt. See, e.g., Pollock v. Marx, 171 B.R. 218 (ND TX, 1994). Even the amount of a default judgment entered against the debtor in a state court has been recognized by a bankruptcy court as constituting the amount of a nondischargeable debt under Section 523(a)(6). See Daghighfekr v. Mekhail, 161 B.R. 685 (B.A.P. 9th Cir., 1993) and State Farm Fire & Cas. Co. v. Edie, 314 B.R. 6 (UT, 2004). However, in Colwell v. Lucas, 186 B.R. 67 (ED VA, 1995), the court held that a state court default judgment was insufficient to establish the amount of the debt in a Section 523(a)(6) proceeding.

res judicata, use of to establish amount of non-dischargeable debt under Section 523(a)(6)

It is common in state court actions based on willful and malicious conduct for a court or jury to assess punitive damages against the debtor. Therefore, many state court judgments against Section 523(a)(6) debtors contain awards for both compensatory and punitive damages. In most districts the entire amount of a state court judgment against a debtor, including an award for punitive damages, are nondischargeable under Section 523(a)(6). See In re Miera, 926 F.2d 741 (8th Cir., 1991), where the court held that both the compensatory and the punitive damages portion of a state court judgment against the debtor were nondischargeable under Section 523(a)(6) because both types of damages stemmed from the same willful and malicious injury and Section 523(a)(6) does not distinguish between debts that are compensatory and those that are punitive in nature. In In re Harper, 378 B.R. 836 (ED AR, 2007) a state court jury verdict imposing treble damages on a conversion claim was held to be non-dischargeable under Section 523(a)(6). See also In re Britton, 950 F.2d 602 (9th Cir., 1991); Stokes v. Ferris, 150 B.R. 388 (WD TX, 1992); Reynolds-Marshall v. Hallum, 162 B.R. 51 (ME, 1993); Brown v. Benson, 180 B.R. 796 (WD PA, 1995). Awards for treble damages are also generally nondischargeable under Section 523(a)(6). See, e.g., Metromedia Co. v. Fugazy, 157 B.R. 761 (SD NY, 1993); Katahn Assocs., Inc. v. Wien, 155 B.R. 479 (ND IL, 1993).

punitive damages as non-dischargeable debt under Section 523(a)(6)

punitive damages, held dischargeable under Section 523(a)(6)

A few courts have held that punitive damages are not nondischargeable under Section 523(a)(6) because they do not constitute compensation for injury but rather are imposed to punish the wrongdoer and to deter others from committing like offenses. See In re Alwan Bros. Co., 105 B.R. 886 (CD IL, 1989); In re Van Loan, 114 B.R. 760 (MD FL, 1990); Nguyen v. Van Quach, 187 B.R. 615 (ND IL, 1995).

attorneys' fees as non-dischargeable debt under Section 523(a)(6)

The general rule followed in most districts is that all damages that were found to have originated from the claim against the debtor for malicious and willful misconduct are nondischargeable under Section 523(a)(6). This includes compensatory damages, punitive damages, and attorney's fees, if awarded by the state court. See Nolan v. Smith, 321 B.R. 542 (CO, 2005); In re McGuffey, 145 B.R. 582 (ND IL, 1992). An award of attorney fees entered in connection with a debt for willful and malicious injury is also generally nondischargeable under Section 523(a)(6). See,e.g., Mills v. Ellerbee, 177 B.R. 731 (ND GA, 1995); A.U. Pharmaceuticals v. Whitner, 179 B.R. 699 (ED OK, 1995). See also, Florida v. Ticor Title Ins. Co., 164 B.R. 636 (B.A.P. 9th Cir., 1994) (where, in addition to attorneys fees, discovery sanctions imposed against the debtor by the state court were also found to be nondischargeable under Section 523(a)(6)).

attorneys' fees held dischargeable under Section 523(a)(6)

On the other hand, in Avery v. Sotelo, 179 B.R. 214 (SD CA, 1995), an award of attorneys fees in a sexual harassment action against the debtor was found to be dischargeable under Section 523(a)(6) even though the creditor's claims for loss of income, pain and suffering, and punitive damages were nondischargeable. In Adams v. Zentz, 157 B.R. 145 (WD MO, 1993), an award of attorney fees entered in a state court action against the debtor for wrongfully denying visitation and custodial rights to the debtor's former spouse was found to be dischargeable because the debtor did not intend to cause economic harm to the former spouse.

intentional personal torts, non-dischargeability of under Section 523(a)(6)

The dischargeability of debts for intentional personal torts. Intentional personal torts include physical and sexual assault, assault by firearm, harassment, libel and slander, and professional malpractice. Because assaults are by definition willful and malicious, debts for injuries caused by physical or sexual assault are almost always nondischargeable under Section 523(a)(6). In In re Cunningham, 59 B.R. 743 (ND IL, 1986), the court, in finding a default judgment for assault and battery against the debtor to be nondischargeable under Section 523(a)(6), stated that debts based on traditional intentional torts such as assault and battery, as well as the more recent torts such as infliction of emotional distress, are nondischargeable under Section 523(a)(6), provided that the debtor's acts in committing the tort were both willful and malicious. In In re Miller, 156 F.3d 598 (5th Cir., 1998) the court stated that either any tort substantially certain to result in injury or any tort motivated by a desire to inflict injury meets the requirement of "willful and malicious injury" under Section 523(a)(6). In In re Mitchell, 256 B.R. 256 (ND OH, 2000) a debt for injuries received due to an assault were held to be non-dischargeable where the debtor plead guilty to aggravated assault in the criminal action and had a default judgment entered against her in the civil matter.

A debt for physical assault was found to be nondischargeable under Section 523(a)(6) in In re Thirtyacre, 36 F.3d 697 (7th Cir., 1994), where the court held that intoxication by the debtor is not a defense to nondischargeability under Section 523(a)(6) because a finding of specific intent to injure the victim is not required. See In re Mitchell, 256 B.R. 256 (B.A.P. 10th Cir., 1997); In re Domingue, 59 B.R. 5 (MD LA, 1986); In re Siefke, 61 B.R. 220 (MT, 1986); In re Hartley, 75 B.R. 165 (WD MO, 1987) (holding the throwing of a firecracker into a basement where an employee was cleaning tires with gasoline constituted willful and malicious conduct despite the debtor's assertion that he merely intended to scare the employee, because the debtor acted willfully and knew or should reasonably have known that injury was likely to result).

debts for physical assault, non-dischargeability

A debt for injuries caused by the intentional shooting of a victim is nondischargeable under Section 523(a)(6), even if no punitive damages were awarded in the underlying action. See, e.g., In re Levin, 434 B.R. 910 (S. D. Fla. 2010); In re Ratcliff, 199 B.R. 185 (WD MO, 1996); In re Gaebler, 88 B.R. 62 (ED PA, 1988); In re Morton, 100 B.R. 607 (ND GA, 1989) (finding a $75,000 state court judgment against the debtor for intentional shooting and assault and battery to be nondischargeable under Section 523(a)(6)). In Morton, the court stated that while all injuries from gunshot wounds are not the result of willful and malicious conduct within the meaning of Section 523(a)(6), shootings which are not accidental and not in self defense are generally deliberate and malicious. In Delaney v. Corley, 185 B.R. 521 (WD LA, 1995), the court held that the discharge of a gun that resulted from tapping the gun on the windshield of a vehicle could not be construed as a deliberate and intentional act for purposes of Section 523(a)(6). See also In re Ayala, 335 B.R. 763 (Bankr. D. Wyo. 2005) (discharge of shotgun into girlfriend's leg no intentional and damages dischargeable).

gun-shot injuries, non-dischargeability under Section 523(a)(6)

Damages for sexual assault are also nondischargeable under Section 523(a)(6). See Dorer v. Moberg, 156 B.R. 810 (MN, 1993) (finding a former employee's claim against the debtor arising from a non-consensual sexual encounter to be nondischargeable under Section 523(a)(6)). The debtor acted willfully because he knew from the employee's actions and verbal protestations that she did not wish to have sex and that he acted maliciously because nonreciprocal or forced sex is substantially certain to cause harm to the victim. The court stated that the fact that the debtor did not physically threaten the employee and the fact that the employee did not attempt to leave and ultimately acquiesced to the sexual act did not render the claim dischargeable because physical brutality by the debtor is not required and the victim is not required to use every possible means to avoid the injury. In In re Love, 347 B.R. 362 (WD MO, 2006) a minor child's damage award was held to be non-dischargeable by the debtor because the debtor was found guilty of sexually molesting 4 children while working as a Santa Claus. In Fischer v. Hanson, 171 B.R. 869 (MN, 1994), a debt owed to the debtor's former girlfriend for the transmission to her of venereal disease was found to have resulted from a willful and malicious injury because the debtor knew he had the disease, knew the disease was sexually communicable, and intentionally had sex with the girl without telling her of the disease. See also Gray v. Gray, 322 B.R. 682 (ND AL, 2005); Ridley v. Holt, 310 B.R. 675 (ND TX, 2004); In re Halverson, 226 B.R. 22 (MN, 1998); Johnson v. Fors, 259 B.R. 131 (B.A.P. 8th Cir., 2001); In re Maxwell, 456 B.R. 408 (Bankr. E. D. Mo. 2011) (holding former boyfriend must prove former girlfriend desired for him to contract HPV or was substantially certain he would contract it).

damages for sexual assault, non-dischargeability under Section 523(a)(6)

debts for intentional personal tort, when dischargeable

Not every intentional personal tort creates a nondischargeable debt, however. In Holmes v. Robinson, 140 B.R. 245 (CD IL, 1992), the debtor injured a friend's knee while attempting to give the friend a "bear hug." The court found the debt to be dischargeable because even though the debtor had acted willfully, he had not acted maliciously because there was no showing that the debtor had any knowledge that the bear hug would result in harm to the friend. In Kresmery v. Service Am. Corp., 227 B.R. 10 (CT, 1998), an employment discrimination claim was held not to qualify for nondischargeability under Section 523(a)(6). See also In re Bullard, 449 B.R. 379 (B.A.P. 8th 2011) (damages caused by throwing a glass during a barroom brawl dischargeable given lack of evidence that, inter alia, actions were targeted at creditor).

intentional personal torts of employee, not imputed to debtor under Section 523(a)(6)

In order for a debt resulting from an intentional personal tort to be nondischargeable under Section 523(a)(6) it must have been committed by or at the direction of the debtor. The willful and malicious acts of another may not be imputed to the debtor for purposes of Section 523(a)(6). See In re Eggers 51 B.R. 452 (ED TN, 1985); In re Whitacre, 93 B.R. 584 (ND OH, 1988); In re Albano, 143 B.R. 323 (CT, 1992) (holding the willfulness and maliciousness of the debtor's "bouncer" in assaulting a patron in a restaurant owned by the debtor could not be imputed to the debtor under the doctrine of respondent superior). The patron's claim against the debtor was found not to be protected from discharge by Section 523(a)(6) and was therefore dischargeable. In In re Taneff, 190 B.R. 501 (WD NY, 1996), a tavern owner who served drinks to a person who later injured the creditor in a car accident was found not to have acted willfully and maliciously for purposes of Section 523(a)(6).

damages for sexual harassment, non-dischargeability of under Section 523(a)(6)

Damages for sexual harassment are also nondischargeable under Section 523(a)(6) even in the absence of proof of specific intent to injure. See, e.g., In re Jones, 300 B.R. 133 (B.A.P. 1st Cir., 2003); In re Turner, 204 B.R. 988 (B.A.P. 9th Cir., 1997); In re Gee, 173 B.R. 189 (WD WA, 1994). A claim for physical and mental injuries resulting from the sexual harassment of a co-employee by the debtor was found to be nondischargeable under Section 523(a)(6) in Avery v. Sotelo, 179 B.R. 214 (SD CA, 1995), where the court found the debtor's acts of harassment to be willful and malicious because they were intentionally committed and in violation of state and federal employment laws. See also In re Porter, 363 B.R. 78 (ED AR, 2007). In In re Cunningham, 59 B.R. 743 (ND IL, 1986), the debtor's conduct in harassing the plaintiff was found to have created a nondischargeable debt because the debtor's acts of harassment were willful and malicious in that the debtor must have known that his conduct would cause harm to the plaintiff and yet he proceeded to engage in the conduct. See also, In re Wilson, 216 B.R. 258 (ED WI, 1997); In re Spagnolo, 473 B.R. 518 (S. D. N.Y. 2012) (unwanted touching not willful).

debts for libel and slander, non-dischargeability of under Section 523(a)(6)

A debt for libel meets the nondischargeability requirements of Section 523(a)(6) if the debtor knew the published statements were false but not if the debtor acted with a reckless disregard for the truth or falsity of the statements. See, e.g., Jett v. Sicroff, 401 F.3d 1101 (9th Cir., 2005); Wheeler v. Laudani, 783 F.2d 610 (6th Cir., 1986); In re Durrance, 84 B.R. 238 (MD FL, 1988). A debt for slander is nondischargeable under Section 523(a)(6) if the debtor had no cause or excuse for publicizing the defamatory information. See, e.g., Merritt v. Thompson, 162 B.R. 748 (ED MI, 1993); In re Litwok, 246 B.R. 1 (ED NY, 2000). Malicious prosecution claims are likewise nondischargeable under Section 523(a)(6). See, e.g., Abbo v. Rossi, McCreery & Assoc., 168 F.3d 930 (6th Cir., 1999) and K & K Ins. Group, Inc. v. Houston, 305 B.R. 111 (MD FL, 2003).

Debts for professional malpractice are nondischargeable under Section 523(a)(6) if the creditor establishes that the debt resulted from malpractice that was intentionally carried out without just cause and that necessarily produced harm to the victim. See Perkins v. Scharffe, 817 F.2d 392 (6th Cir., 1987) (holding acts of a podiatrist in unnecessarily using a contaminated needle to inject the patient's foot, in failing to perform tests when the infection became apparent and then ignoring test results, and in failing to hospitalize the patient when it was urgently needed, were willful and malicious for purposes of Section 523(a)(6)). See also Kawaauhau v. Geiger, 172 B.R. 916 (ED MO, 1994); Smith v. Assevero, 185 B.R. 951 (ND GA, 1995); Fernandez v. McMahon, 183 B.R. 948 (MD FL, 1995); In re Aviles, 59 B.R. 138 (SD FL, 1986); In re Britton, 950 F.2d 602 (9th Cir., 1991).

debts for medical malpractice, non-dischargeability of under Section 523(a)(6)

Malpractice claims against attorneys may also be nondischargeable under Section 523(a)(6) if the acts of the attorney were shown to be willful and malicious. See In re Cole, 378 B.R. 215 (ND IL, 2007) and Mingus v. Lombardo, 310 B.R. 819 (SD OH, 2003) (holding the lack of direct evidence pertaining to the willful and malicious nature of an attorney's malpractice in a will and estate matter precluded a determination of nondischargeability under Section 523(a)(6)). In Kosac v. Clark, 179 B.R. 898 (AZ, 1995), a claim for professional malpractice against an attorney was found to be nondischargeable under Section 523(a)(6) where the attorney had directed the client to walk out in the middle of a state court trial resulting in the entry of a large judgment against the client. The court held that the attorney's acts were willful because they were intentional and were malicious because it was reasonably foreseeable that the client would incur a large judgment. See also In re Kane, 470 B.R. 902 (Bankr. S. D. Fla. 2012) (holding attorneys acted with specific intent to injury co-counsel in structuring settlement agreement); In re Keller, 106 B.R. 639 (B.A.P. 9th Cir., 1989) (involving a professional malpractice claim against an attorney); Ball v. A.O. Smith Corp., 321 B.R. 100 (ND NY, 2005) (sanctions awarded against an attorney debtor under Fed. R. Civ. P. 11 and 28 U.S.C. § 1927 were held to be nondischargeable).

damages for attorney's malpractice, non-dischargeability of under Section 523(a)(6)

The dischargeability of debts for vehicular torts. Most nondischargeability proceedings involving vehicular torts involve the issue of the debtor's intoxication. Section 523(a)(9), which as enacted on July 10, 1984, deals with the nondischargeability of debts for death or personal injury caused by the debtor's operation of a motor vehicle, vessel, or aircraft while intoxicated. Prior to the enactment of Section 523(a)(9), the issue of nondischargeability of such debts was resolved under Section 523(a)(6). Since the enactment of Section 523(a)(9), however, the nondischargeability of debts for death or personal injuries for driving while intoxicated is normally resolved under that section exclusively. Some courts, however, have permitted creditors to proceed alternatively under Section 523(a)(6) or Section 523(a)(9). See In re Moore, 53 B.R. 259 (SD OH, 1985); In re Hudson, 73 B.R. 649 (B.A.P. 9th Cir., 1987). Nondischargeability for drunk driving injuries may also be established under Section 523(a)(6). See, e.g., In re Dale, 199 B.R. 1014 (SD FL, 1995).

debts for driving while intoxicated, non-dischargeability under Section 523(a)(9) property damage debts caused by DWI, nondischargeability of

Section 523(a)(9) deals only with the nondischargeability of debts for death or personal injury. Therefore, the nondischargeability of debts for property damage caused by the debtor's driving while intoxicated must be resolved under Section 523(a)(6). See Hartford Ins. Group, Inc. v. Chapin, 155 B.R. 323 (WD NY, 1993); In re Williams, 175 B.R. 17 (MD TN, 1994). The issue of nondischargeability of debts for death or personal injury caused by the debtor's operation of a motor vehicle, vessel or aircraft while intoxicated is discussed in article 1.09 of this handbook.

debts for vehicular torts, cases finding debts dischargeable

In In re Noller, 56 B.R. 36 (ED WI, 1985), the conduct of the debtor in driving at a speed of 90 to 95 miles per hour and passing in a "no passing" zone, while constituting reckless conduct, did not in and of itself constitute willful misconduct for purposes of Section 523(a)(6). In In re Ikner, 883 F.2d 986 (11th Cir., 1989), a debt based upon a state court judgment against the debtor for wantonness arising from an automobile accident was not excepted from discharge under Section 523(a)(6) because the judgment creditor did not prove by inference or innuendo that the debtor intended the accident or resulting injury to occur and did not prove that the debtor acted maliciously, either with special malice or with implied or constructive malice. In In re Granda, 98 B.R. 598 (SD FL, 1989), a debt arising from the striking of a pedestrian by the debtor while driving his parents' uninsured car was found to be dischargeable under Section 523(a)(6), even though the state court found recklessness and awarded punitive damages, because it was not shown that the debtor intentionally hit the pedestrian.

debts for vehicular torts, cases finding debts dischargeable

In In re Frazee, 60 B.R. 109 (WD MO), the claim of a person injured in an automobile accident that resulted from the debtor's driving at excessive speed was not protected from discharge under Section 523(a)(6) because excessive speed alone does not constitute willful and malicious conduct for purposes of Section 523(a)(6). In Boyce v. Greenway, 180 B.R. 179 (WD TX, 1995), a state court judgment against the debtor for wrongful death and personal injuries was dischargeable because the jury in the state court case found that the debtor was not guilty of gross negligence. Leaving the scene of an accident, while willful in and of itself, does not, without more, establish willful and malicious conduct for purposes of Section 523(a)(6). See, e.g., In re Frazee, 60 B.R. 109 (WD MO, 1986); In re Wells, 44 B.R. 1006 (SD FL, 1984); DeBlasio v. Groff, 301 B.R. 644 (NJ, 2003) (holding a debtor's guilty plea in state court to operating a motor vehicle during a period of license suspension causing death did not constitute willful and malicious conduct, and the underlying debt was therefore dischargeable).

In Konefal v. Kaperonis, 156 B.R. 736 (SD NY, 1993), a debt owed to a person who was injured as a result of the debtor's drag racing on a public street was found to be nondischargeable under Section 523(a)(6). Willfulness was established by showing that the debtor intentionally engaged in the unlawful act of drag racing, was traveling at an excessive rate of speed alongside another vehicle, ran through a red light, and did not slow down prior to the collision. Reckless driving, without more, does not establish nondischargeability under Section 523(a)(6). See, e.g., In re Kokenge, 279 B.R. 541 (ED TN, 2002). In In re Adams, 147 B.R. 407 (WD MI, 1992), the court held that willful conduct and implied malice existed for purposes of Section 523(a)(6) where it was established that the debtor operated his vehicle without insurance and on a suspended license and accelerated through a red light at a congested intersection.

debts for vehicular torts, cases finding debts non-dischargeable under Section 523(a)(6)

Creditors of debtors who drive without liability insurance often attempt to protect their uninsured claims from dischargeability under Section 523(a)(6). These attempts have usually been unsuccessful, however, because it is generally held that failing to obtain insurance prior to driving, without more, does not constitute willful and malicious conduct for purposes of Section 523(a)(6). See In re Caffey, 248 B.R. 920 (ND GA, 2000); In re Fate, 100 B.R. 141 (MA, 1989); Pechan v. Moore, 98 B.R. 488 (NE, 1988); In re Eberhardt, 92 B.R. 773 (ED TN, 1988). Likewise, the failure of a parent to provide liability insurance on a vehicle driven by a minor son or daughter does not constitute willful and malicious conduct for purposes of Section 523(a)(6). See Myrick v. Ballard, 186 B.R. 297 (ND GA, 1994); Beyerdoerfer v. Bex, 143 B.R. 835 (ED KY, 1992); In re Granda, 98 B.R. 598 (SD FL, 1989). However, in Barnett Bank, N.A. v. Ussery, 179 B.R. 737 (SD GA, 1995), the court held that the debtor's intentional failure to carry insurance that was required by state law inflicts willful and malicious injury when a third party suffers an injury that would have been compensable if the mandated insurance had been obtained.

driving without insurance as willful and malicious conduct, cases

The dischargeability of debts for intentional conversion. Judging from the number of reported cases, the intentional conversion of money or property by the debtor is the most common type of willful and malicious act covered by Section 523(a)(6). The conversion of money or property by the debtor, done intentionally and without justification or excuse to the injury of another person, constitutes willful and malicious injury within the meaning of Section 523(a)(6). See, e.g., In re Cecchini, 780 F.2d 1440 (9th Cir., 1986); In re Riso, 978 F.2d 1151 (9th Cir., 1992); In re Pasek, 983 F.2d 1524 (10th Cir., 1993); In re Guillory, 285 B.R. 307 (CD CA, 2002); In re Shaffer, 305 B.R. 771 (SC, 2004); In re Fowers, 360 B.R. 888 (ND IN, 2007).

intentional conversion as willful and malicious injury under Section 523(a)(6)

intentional conversion, definition of under Section 523(a)(6)

For purposes of Section 523(a)(6), conversion may consist of either (1) an unauthorized act which deprives the owner of his or her property, either permanently or for an indefinite period, or (2) the wrongful exercise of dominion and control over another's property to the exclusion of the owner's rights or that is inconsistent with rights of the owner. See In re Barnes, 369 B.R. 298 (WD TX, 2007); Printy v. Dean Witter Reynolds, Inc., 110 F.3d 853 (1st Cir., 1997); In re Burdick, 65 B.R. 105 (ND IN, 1986); In re Van Loan, 114 B.R. 760 (MD FL, 1990); In re Mace, 82 B.R. 864 (SD OH, 1987). In First Nat. Bank v. Stanley, 66 F.3d 664 (4th Cir., 1995), the court held that the debtor's use of an extra $72,000 that the bank mistakenly added to his line of credit amounted to a wrongful conversion of the line of credit which rendered the resulting debt nondischargeable under Section 523(a)(6). In In re Banks, 225 B.R. 738 (CD CA, 1998), the failure of the debtor, who was an attorney, to pay his client a portion of the proceeds of a settlement was a willful and malicious injury under Section 523(a)(6). See also Superior Metal Prods v. Martin, 321 B.R. 437 (ND OH, 2004).

conversion, requirements for non-dischargeability under Section 523(a)(6)

Not every conversion constitutes willful and malicious conduct for purposes of Section 523(a)(6). Davis. v. Aetna, 293 U.S. 328 (1934). A creditor seeking to prove the nondischargeability of a debt for conversion under Section 523(a)(6) must establish by a preponderance of the evidence not only that a conversion has occurred, but that the conversion was willful and malicious. See In re Grim, 293 B.R. 156 (ND OH, 2003); In re Littleton, 942 F.2d 551 (9th Cir., 1991); In re Bren, 284 B.R. 681 (MN, 2002); Bukowski v. Patel, 266 B.R. 838 (ED WI, 2001); In re Evans, 252 B.R. 366 (ND MS, 2000); In re Luce, 960 F.2d 1277 (5th Cir., 1992). A debt resulting from an innocent or technical conversion is not protected from discharge by Section 523(a)(6). See, e.g., In re Pavelka, 79 B.R. 228 (ED PA, 1987); In re Brinsfield, 78 B.R. 364 (MD GA, 1987); In re Hurst, 94 B.R. 442 (ND OH, 1988); In re Cilek, 115 B.R. 974 (WD WI, 1990) (stating injury under Section 523(a)(6) may include common law conversion, but willful and malicious injury does not follow as a matter of course from every act of conversion). A debtor's issuance of a bad check does not, without more, satisfy the willfulness requirement of Section 523(a)(6). See, e.g., In re Paul, 266 B.R. 686 (ND IL, 2001). However, the issuance of a counterfeit check will almost always result in a nondischargeability ruling. See In re Corner, 299 B.R. 462 (SD OH, 2003).

debts for innocent or technical conversion, dischargeability

In In re Brubaker, 57 B.R. 736 (WD VA, 1986), the court stated that while Section 523(a)(6) includes willful and malicious conversion, willful and malicious injury does not follow from every act of conversion. A conversion may be innocent or technical, such as an unauthorized assumption of dominion without willfulness or malice. See In re Strojny, 337 B.R. 150 (WD MI, 2006) (overpayment received due to incorrectly calculated invoice). A debt founded upon a technical conversion without a conscious intent to violate the rights of another or under a mistake or misapprehension may be discharged. Whether a conversion is willful and malicious depends on the facts and circumstances of each case. In In re Trantham, 286 B.R. 650 (WD TN, 2002), a patent infringement claim against the debtor was held dischargeable in a Section 523(a)(6) proceeding because the intentional nature of patent infringement standing alone, was insufficient to satisfy the "willful and malicious" requirement of Section 523(a)(6). However, copyright or trademark infringement can constitute willful and malicious misconduct if there are aggravating circumstances. See In re Blankfort, 217 B.R. 138 (SD NY, 1998).

For an act of conversion to be willful under Section 523(a)(6) it must be deliberate or intentional and not negligent or accidental. See In re Burdick, 65 B.R. 105 (ND IN, 1986); In re Kapnison, 65 B.R. 221 (NM, 1986). For a conversion to be malicious under Section 523(a)(6) it must be targeted at the creditor in the sense that the conversion is certain or almost certain to cause financial harm to the creditor. See In re Martin, 70 B.R. 146 (MD AL, 1987). A conversion is malicious if the debtor knew or should reasonably have known that the act of conversion would result in financial harm to the creditor. See In re Harris, 107 B.R. 210 (NE, 1989).

debts for conversion, requirements for non-dischargeability under Section 523(a)(6)

Perhaps the most common form of intentional conversion is the sale of secured property by the debtor wherein the debtor retains the proceeds of the sale without the consent of the secured creditor. The sale by the debtor of property subject to a security interest constitutes willful and malicious conduct rendering the claim of the secured creditor nondischargeable under Section 523(a)(6). See In re Dickerson, 372 B.R. 827 (ND MS, 2007); In re Shaffer, 305 B.R. 771 (SC, 2004); In re Van Loan, 114 B.R. 760 (MD FL, 1990); Moog Employees Fed. Credit Union v. Kibler, 172 B.R. 740 (WD NY, 1994) (the debtor's acts in dismantling and selling the parts of an automobile that was subject to a security interest were a willful and malicious conversion of secured property for purposes of Section 523(a)(6)). See also In re Cox, 243 B.R. 713 (ND IL, 2000).

sale of secured property as intentional conversion

Even if the debtor is not the actual owner of property sold in violation of the security agreement, the debt created thereby may nevertheless be nondischargeable under Section 523(a)(6) if the debtor instigated the conversion and pocketed the proceeds therefrom. In Ford Motor Credit Co. v. Owens, 807 F.2d 1556 (11th Cir., 1987), the sale by a corporate car dealership of a creditor's collateral and the retention of the proceeds by the debtor, who was the president and majority shareholder of the dealership, rendered the debtor liable for a willful and malicious conversion. See also In re Tarrant, 84 B.R. 831 (MD FL, 1988); In re Smith, 56 B.R. 699 (ED PA, 1986); In re Wheeler, 73 B.R. 220 (WD MO, 1987); In re Ridsdale, 286 B.R. 238 (WD NY, 2002).

sale of secured property as intentional conversion

To render a debt for the conversion of secured property nondischargeable under Section 523(a)(6), the secured creditor must prove that the debtor acted both willfully and maliciously in converting the secured property to his own use. See In re Vandrovec, 61 B.R. 191 (ND, 1986); Security Bank v. Wehri, 212 B.R. 963 (ND, 1997). In order to prevail under Section 523(a)(6), a secured creditor must show that the debtor had a subjective, conscious intent to injure the secured creditor. See Farmers and Merchants Bank v. Alexander, 70 B.R. 419 (MD GA, 1987). The mere failure by the debtor to pay over to the secured creditor the proceeds received from the sale of secured property does not establish willfulness and maliciousness for purposes of Section 523(a)(6). See In re Cilek, 115 B.R. 974 (WD WI, 1990) and In re Bennett, 293 B.R. 760 (CD IL, 2003). Willfulness and malice may not be inferred from a deliberate sale of collateral in violation of a security agreement without proof of specific intent to injure the creditor. See Deere & Co. v. Contella, 166 B.R. 26 (WD NY, 1994).

conversion of secured property, proof requirements for non-dischargeability willful and malicious conversion of secured property, acts not constituting

In In re Eberle, 61 B.R. 638 (MN, 1985), a willful and malicious conversion under Section 523(a)(6) had not occurred where a bank official had personally observed the debtor's practice of selling property that was subject to the bank's security interest for at least 6 months and did nothing to stop the practice. In In re McCune, 85 B.R. 834 (WD MO, 1988), the debtor's liability for transferring collateral in violation of a security agreement was held to be dischargeable because the debtor understood that her actions were in contravention of the agreement. In In re Littleton, 942 F.2d 551 (9th Cir., 1991), the debtor's conduct in selling the creditor's collateral and using the proceeds for other business purposes was not malicious because the actions would not have necessarily produced harm in light of the debtor's good faith and sincere intention to keep the business going.

conversion of secured property, measure of damages

To establish a nondischargeable claim for the willful and malicious conversion of secured property under Section 523(a)(6), the injured creditor must prove that damages were incurred as a result of the conversion. The general rule is that only the value of the collateral at the time of the unlawful conversion, and not the entire debt owed to the creditor, is nondischargeable under Section 523(a)(6). See In re Modicue, 926 F.2d 452 (5th Cir., 1991); In re Burdick, 65 B.R. 105 (ND IN, 1986). In Bonfiglio v. Harkema, 171 B.R. 245 (ED MI, 1994), the court stated that where a debtor is found liable for conversion under Section 523(a)(6), the appropriate measure of damages is the amount of the injury caused by the conversion rather than any other sum owed by the debtor). Therefore, only the value of the collateral at the time it was unlawfully sold by the debtor is nondischargeable. The court held that the amount of damages for an unlawful conversion depend upon the value of the converted property and not by the face value of the security interest that was impaired by the conversion. In In re Gerken, 69 B.R. 251 (WD MO, 1986), a bank had not established damages from the debtor's conversion of collateral under Section 523(a)(6) where it presented only evidence of loans made to the debtor, with no evidence of the balance due.

mis-appropriation of funds or property as intentional conversion under Section 523(a)(6)

Of course there are many forms of conversion that do not involve the sale of collateral. The retention or misappropriation by the debtor of funds or property known to belong to another is a common form of willful and malicious conversion. An act of theft creates a debt that is nondischargeable under Section 523(a)(6). See Erickson v. Roehrich, 169 B.R. 941 (ND, 1994); Sunco Sales, Inc. v. Latch, 820 F.2d 1163 (11th Cir., 1987). In In re Salamone, 62 B.R. 690 (ED PA, 1986), a debt arising from the debtor's intentional misappropriation of her employer's customer list and the use of the list in her own business was found to be nondischargeable under Section 523(a)(6). In In re Cecchini, 780 F.2d 1440 (9th Cir., 1986), a debt that arose from the debtor's conversion of payments collected by the debtor as agent for the property owner was found to be nondischargeable under Section 523(a)(6) because the debtor willfully withheld the funds from the owner with direct knowledge of the resulting injury to the property owner. The diversion by the debtor of insurance premiums held in trust for the insurance company was willful and malicious conversion in In re Coover, 70 B.R. 554 (SD FL, 1987).

The retention by the debtor of medical insurance proceeds which he had previously assigned to his physician was a willful and malicious conversion under Section 523(a)(6) in In re Hopkins, 65 B.R. 967 (ND IL, 1986). The sale by the debtor of property assigned to his ex-wife in a divorce order was held to be a willful and malicious conversion for purposes of Section 523(a)(6) in Sateren v. Sateren, 183 B.R. 576 (ND, 1995). In Chrysler Credit Corp. v. Perry Chrysler Plymouth, Inc., 783 F.2d 480 (5th Cir., 1986), a nondischargeable debt was found to have been created when the debtor took money belonging to the creditor and used it to gamble with the intent of winning enough to save the debtor's business.

mis-appropriation of funds or property as intentional conversion under Section 523(a)(6)

The diversion or misappropriation of money or property, even though willful, does not create a nondischargeable debt under Section 523(a)(6) unless the conversion is also shown to be malicious. In In re Martin, 70 B.R. 146 (MD AL, 1986), the conversion by the debtor, a contractor, of funds assigned to a supplier was found not to be malicious (and therefore dischargeable) because substantially all of the funds were used by the debtor to pay materialmen and labor in an effort to keep the business going so that the debtor could repay the supplier. In Bethesda Hospital v. Kessnick, 174 B.R. 481 (SD OH, 1994), the cashing by the debtor of medical benefit checks that were intended for the hospital was held not to be malicious because the checks did not prominently state that they were for benefits that had been assigned to the hospital and because the debtor was not fully aware of the purpose of the checks. In American Honda Fin. Corp. v. Loder, 77 B.R. 213 (ND IA, 1987), a debt created by the passing of a bad check was found to be dischargeable because the debtor believed he had sufficient funds to cover the check when it was written.

conversion of funds, requirement of maliciousness for non-dischargeability

The dischargeability of debts for aggravated breach of contract. While a debt created by the unintentional or unavoidable breach of a contract (i.e., simple breach of contract) is clearly not protected from discharge by Section 523(a)(6), the intentional breach of an enforceable contract by the debtor, if willful and malicious, may give rise to a debt that is nondischargeable under Section 523(a)(6). See In re Riso, 978 F.2d 1151 (9th Cir., 1992), where the court stated that simple breach of contract is not covered by Section 523(a)(6) and that intentional breach of contract is excepted from discharge only when accompanied by willful and malicious conduct. See also In re Phillips, 882 F.2d 302 (8th Cir., 1989) (holding the breach of a security agreement, if both willful and malicious, may be sufficient to render the debt secured thereby nondischargeable under Section 523(a)(6)). See also In re Penton, 299 B.R. 701 (SD GA, 2003).

aggravated breach of contract, what constitutes

breach of covenant not to compete as willful and malicious injury

Several courts have held that the intentional breach by the debtor of a covenant not to compete gives rise to a debt that is nondischargeable under Section 523(a)(6). See In re Andress, 345 B.R. 358 (ND OK, 2006); In re Hallahan, 936 F.2d 1496 (7th Cir., 1991) (holding the debtor's willful breach of an enforceable covenant not to compete rendered the resulting debt nondischargeable under Section 523(a)(6)). See also Carter v. Trammell, 172 B.R. 41 (WD AR, 1994). A debt for the breach of a covenant not to compete may be nondischargeable under Section 523(a)(6) even if the debtor relies on the advice of counsel in breaching the covenant. See, e.g., Traditional Industries, Inc. v. Ketaner, 149 B.R. 395 (ED VA, 1992). However, in In re Pasek, 983 F.2d 1524 (10th Cir., 1993), the debtor's violation of a covenant not to compete was not willful and malicious for purposes of Section 523(a)(6) where the former employer acted in violation of its agreement with the debtor and the debtor relied on the advice of counsel in disregarding the covenant.

justifiable breach of contract as not willful and malicious under Section 523(a)(6)

If the debtor's conduct in breaching a contract can be justified under any reasonable circumstance, the debt created by the breach is not protected from discharge by Section 523(a)(6). See In re Gehl, 325 B.R. 269 (ND IA, 2005). In In re Clementi, 58 B.R. 167 (ED WI, 1985), the debtor's failure to maintain possession of a vehicle which was collateral for a loan, while a violation of her loan agreement, was not willful and malicious for purposes of Section 523(a)(6) because the debtor was unaware of the possession requirement in the agreement and because the other person wrongfully refused to return the vehicle to the debtor. The court stated that while willful injury does not require hatred or ill will toward the creditor, it does require a showing that the debtor knows that injury will be caused to the creditor and nevertheless proceeds in the face of this knowledge to intentionally breach the contract. See also, In re Cloyd, 238 B.R. 328 (ED MI, 1999), and In re Jercich, 243 B.R. 747 (B.A.P. 9th Cir., 2000).

breach of contract, held not willful and malicious

In Vaugn v. Quinn, 170 B.R. 1013 (ED MO, 1994), a homeowner's claim for breach of a construction contract was found to be dischargeable because the debtor's conduct in breaching the contract, while negligent and reckless to the point where punitive damages were awarded by a state court, did not rise to the level of maliciousness required under Section 523(a)(6). However, see Sinha v. Clark, 330 B.R. 702 (CD IL, 2005) for a contrary ruling wherein a $14,597 debt was held to be nondischargeable by a debtor contractor because the evidence suggested that the debtor knew that his faulty workmanship would cause damage to plaintiffs' home, yet he continued to work and collect payments under the contract. See In re Martinez, 49 BCD 173 (CD CA, 2008) for a similar ruling. In In re Buckley, 65 B.R. 283 (SD, 1986), the court held that the debtor's conduct in leasing his property and collecting the rents therefrom without notifying the mortgagee in violation of the mortgage agreement did not constitute willful and malicious conduct for purposes of Section 523(a)(6). In In re Bafford, 61 B.R. 631 (WD TN, 1985), the debtor's failure to maintain insurance coverage on his secured property and failure to notify the secured creditor of the lapse in insurance coverage in violation of the security agreement was not willful and malicious because the debtor was unable to pay the insurance premiums as a result of being laid off at work and failed to notify the secured creditor because he believed that he would soon be reemployed and have the funds with which to pay the insurance premiums.

The dischargeability of debts for failure to carry workers' compensation insurance. The courts are divided on the issue of whether a failure by the debtor to carry statutorily required workers' compensation insurance renders an employee's claim for benefits nondischargeable under Section 523(a)(6). In In re Strauss, 99 B.R. 396 (ND IL, 1989), a debt to an employee for a workers' compensation claim was held nondischargeable under Section 523(a)(6) solely because of the debtor's failure to carry statutorily-required workers' compensation insurance. In Hester v. Saturday, 138 B.R. 132 (SD GA, 1991), the workers' compensation claim of a former employee of the debtor was ruled nondischargeable under Section 523(a)(6) because the debtor intentionally and deliberately failed to carry the required insurance. The court stated that the fact that the debtor could not afford the insurance did not negate the willful and malicious act of deliberately not providing the required insurance coverage.

failure to carry workers' comp. insurance as willful and malicious conduct

In Carter v. Verhelst, 170 B.R. 657 (WD AR, 1993), a workers' compensation claim against an uninsured debtor was found to be nondischargeable under Section 523(a)(6) because the debtor's decision not to carry the required insurance was willful, the debtor knew the insurance was required by law, and the debtor represented to the employee that he was carrying workers' compensation insurance and the employee relied upon this representation in working for the debtor. In In re Peel, 166 B.R. 735 (WD OK, 1994), a worker's compensation claim against the debtor was held nondischargeable because the debtor withheld money from the employee's wages to purchase the insurance and then willfully and maliciously failed to do so.

failure to carry workers' comp. insurance as willful and malicious conduct

However, in Collora v. Leahy, 170 B.R. 10 (ME, 1994), a debt for a workers' compensation claim against the debtor was dischargeable because the employee failed to show that the debtor intentionally failed to carry the required insurance and that the debtor acted in a manner that was certain or almost certain to cause the employee harm. In Bailey v. Chatham, 171 B.R. 703 (ND GA, 1994), the court held that the debtor's failure to carry workers' compensation insurance did not give rise to a willful and malicious injury under Section 523(a)(6) because the debtor's failure to obtain workers' compensation insurance did not directly and necessarily create a willful injury. The court stated that such an injury cannot be characterized as malicious because there was no substantial certainty that an employee would suffer harm if the insurance was not provided. Other cases holding that the debtor's failure to carry workers' compensation insurance does not render an employee's claim for workers' compensation nondischargeable under Section 523(a)(6) include Vizzini v. Vizzini, 348 B.R. 339 (ED LA, 2005), Tiberi v. Annan, 161 B.R. 872 (RI, 1993), Morton v. Kemmerer, 156 B.R. 806 (SD IN, 1993), Silva v. Frias, 153 B.R. 6 (RI, 1993), In re Mazander, 130 B.R. 534 (ED MO, 1991), and Szewczyk v. Wojtaszek, 164 B.R. 604 (ND IL, 1994).

failure to carry workers' comp. insurance as not causing willful and malicious injury

failure to carry workers' comp. insurance as not causing willful and malicious injury

In In re Popa, 140 F.3d 317 (1st Cir., 1998), the court held that under the definition of "willful injury" set forth by the Supreme Court in Kawaauhau v. Geiger, supra, the debtor's intentional failure to carry worker's compensation insurance did not constitute an actual intent to cause injury and therefore did not make the employee's worker's compensation claim nondischargeable under Section 523(a)(6). In finding the employee's claim to be dischargeable, the court in Nicholson v. Adkins, 183 B.R. 702 (MD NC, 1995), held that willfulness and malice were not established by the employee in the absence of evidence that the lapse in coverage was intentional or deliberate rather than a negligent oversight or evidence that the debtor actually represented coverage that was not provided. The court also held that the fact that the employee's job involved some heavy construction and a certain degree of danger did not establish maliciousness under Section 523(a)(6) where the employee's duties were not so inherently dangerous that injuries were substantially certain to occur.

intentional waste as willful and malicious conduct

The dischargeability of debts for intentional waste. A few courts have held that the commission by the debtor of intentional waste with respect to rented or mortgaged property to the extent that the landlord or creditor's interest in the property is impaired constitutes willful and malicious injury under Section 523(a)(6). In In re Mills, 73 B.R. 638 (B.A.P. 9th Cir., 1987), the court held that a debtor who willfully permitted mortgaged hotel property to deteriorate to the point where many of the units were in violation of building and sanitary codes and the restrooms and showers were unusable, intentionally committed waste against the property rendering the secured creditor's deficiency nondischargeable under Section 523(a)(6). In In re Berry, 84 B.R. 717 (WD WA, 1987), the debtor's abandonment of open vats of highly dangerous chemicals on rented property and his failure to properly contain the chemicals constituted willful and malicious conduct under Section 523(a)(6) rendering the landlord's claim for the expenses of cleaning up the chemicals nondischargeable under Section 523(a)(6).

Bibliography. For further reading on the issues discussed in this article, see the annotations and articles listed below.

Annotations:

When does medical practitioner's treatment of patient constitute "willful and malicious injury," so as to make practitioner's debt arising from such treatment nondischargeable under §523(a)(6) of Bankruptcy Act (11 USCS §523(a)(6)). 77 ALR Fed 918.

Debtor's traffic-related liability as "willful and malicious injury" excepted by 11 USCS §523(a)(6) from bankruptcy discharge. 85 ALR Fed 643.

Claim or Judgment Based on Aggravated or Felonious Assault and Battery or Assault or Battery Using Deadly Weapon as Liability for Willful and Malicious Injury Within § 523(a)(6) of Bankruptcy Code (11 U.S.C.A. § 523(a)(6)) and Predecessor Statute, Barring Discharge of Such Liability. 27 ALR Fed 2d 1

Claim or Judgment Based on Sexual Offense or Misconduct as Liability for Willful and Malicious Injury Within § 523(a)(6) of Bankruptcy Code and Predecessor Statute, Barring Discharge of Such Liability. 18 ALR Fed 2d 465

Conversion as wilful and malicious injury to property within provision of Bankruptcy Act preventing discharge from liability for such injury. 98 ALR 1454

Articles:

Alice's Restaurant: An Analysis of the Dischargeability of Punitive Damages Under Section 523(a)(2)(A), (a)(4) and (a)(6) of the Bankruptcy Code. 28 U. Memphis L. Rev. 951 (Spring, 1998).

Tort claims and judgments as debts for "willful and malicious injury" nondischargeable under Section 523(a)(6) of the Bankruptcy Code. 100 Comm. L.J. 498, Winter, 1995.

Collateral estoppel in Section 523(a) dischargeability proceedings: when is a default judgment actually litigated? 12 Bankruptcy Dev. J. 321, 1996.

Attorney malpractice judgments, bankruptcy discharge, and professional responsibility. 4 J. Bankruptcy L. & Pract. 219, Mar. - Apr., 1995.

When a sting is overkill: an argument for the discharge of punitive damages in bankruptcy. 94 Columbia L. Rev. 2724, Dec., 1994.

Section 523(a)(6): Willful and malicious exception from discharge: the "implied malice" standard. 16 U Dayton L Rev 155, Fall 1990.

1.09 To what extent are debts caused by drunk driving dischargeable in bankruptcy?

Text of statute. Section 523(a)(9) of the Bankruptcy Code (11 U.S.C. § 523(a)(9)) is applicable to the subject discussed in this article. It provides as follows:

523. Exceptions to discharge

> (a) A discharge under section 727, 1141, 1228(a), 1228(b), or 1328(b) of this title does not discharge an individual debtor from any debt -
>
> * * * * * *
>
> (9) for death or personal injury caused by the debtor's operation of a motor vehicle, vessel, or aircraft if such operation was unlawful because the debtor was intoxicated from using alcohol, a drug, or another substance;

Section 523(a)(9), text of

Section 523(a)(9), history of statute, intention of Congress

Introduction. Section 523(a)(9) was originally enacted on July 10, 1984. Prior to that time the nondischargeability of debts for driving while intoxicated was decided under Section 523(a)(6) of the Bankruptcy Code, which deals with the nondischargeability of debts for willful and malicious injury. In its original form Section 523(a)(9) required the entry of a judgment for damages against the debtor in order for the debt to be nondischargeable and was not limited to debts for death or personal injury. In its current form Section 523(a)(9) does not require the existence of a judgment against the debtor for nondischargeability and is limited to debts for death or personal injury. Section 523(a)(9) in its present form was enacted on November 15, 1990. The intent of Congress in enacting Section 523(a)(9) in its present form was to protect victims of drunk driving and to deter drunk driving by ensuring that those who cause personal injury or death by drunk driving do not escape liability under the bankruptcy laws. See In re Dale, 199 B.R. 1014 (SD FL, 1995); In re Mellott, 187 B.R. 578 (ND OH, 1995); In re Felski, 277 B.R. 732 (ED MI, 2002).

BAPCPA amendments, effect of

Section 523(a)(9) was amended in 2005 by the addition of the words "vessel, or aircraft" after "motor vehicle." The 2005 BAPCPA also added a new paragraph 10 to Section 507(a), thus providing priority status to personal injury and death claims "resulting from the operation of a motor vehicle or vessel if such operation was unlawful because the debtor was intoxicated from using alcohol, a drug, or another substance." (See 11 U.S.C. § 507(a)(10)).

As indicated above, prior to the enactment of Section 523(a)(9) in 1984 the nondischargeability of debts incurred while driving while intoxicated was decided under Section 523(a)(6), which provides nondischargeability for debts for willful and malicious injury. Since the enactment of Section 523(a)(9), the dischargeability of debts for death or personal injury caused by intoxicated driving has been handled almost exclusively under that section. Some courts, however, have permitted creditors to proceed alternately under Section 523(a)(9) or Section 523(a)(6). See In re Moore, 53 B.R. 259 (SD OH, 1985); In re Hudson, 73 B.R. 649 (B.A.P. 9th Cir., 1987). Nondischargeability for a debt for personal injuries caused by drunk driving may be established under Section 523(a)(6). See, e.g., In re Dale, 199 B.R. 1014 (SD FL, 1995). As a practical matter, however, there is little to be gained by proceeding under Section 523(a)(6) because of the difficulty of proving the willfulness and maliciousness. See In re Hostetler, 44 B.R. 886 (MD FL, 1984). The nondischargeability of debts for willful and malicious injury under Section 523(a)(6) is discussed in article 1.08 of this handbook.

DWI debts for death or personal injury, non-dischargeability under Section 523(a)(6)

In its original form, Section 523(a)(9) provided nondischargeability for property damage debts resulting from intoxicated driving and for debts for fines and surcharges assessed against debtors for driving while intoxicated, as well as nondischargeability for debts for death or personal injury. In its present form, however, only debts for death or personal injury are nondischargeable under Section 523(a)(9). Debts for property damage are not nondischargeable under Section 523(a)(9) in its present form. See, e.g., In re Williams, 175 B.R. 17 (MD TN, 1994); In re Spencer, 168 B.R. 142 (ND TX, 1994); In re Brisson, 186 B.R. 205 (ED VA, 1995). Debts for motor vehicle department fines and surcharges assessed against debtors for drinking-driving offenses are not protected from discharge by Section 523(a)(9) in its present form. See, e.g., Matter of Kent, 190 B.R. 196 (NJ, 1995).

Section 523(a)(9), debts covered by

Property damage debts resulting from a debtor's intoxicated driving may be nondischargeable under Section 523(a)(6) if the required showing of willfulness and maliciousness can be made. See In re Dale, 199 B.R. 1014 (SD FL, 1995), and In re Chapin, 155 B.R. 323 (WD NY, 1993). Nondischargeability for such debts may be difficult to prove under Section 523(a)(6), however, because it is generally held that property damage debts caused by a debtor's drunk driving are not per se nondischargeable under Section 523(a)(6). See In re Fall, 192 B.R. 16 (NH, 1995), In re Brisson, 186 B.R. 205 (ED VA, 1995), and In re Chapin, 155 B.R. 323 (WD NY, 1993).

debts for property damage caused by DWI, non-dischargeability under Section 523(a)(6)

Section 523(a)(9) is fully applicable in all Chapter 7 cases and in all Chapter 13 cases regardless of the type of discharge obtained by a Chapter 13 debtor. See 11 U.S.C. § 1328(a)(2), (c)(2). This means that debts for death or personal injury incurred by the debtor as a result of driving while intoxicated are not dischargeable by individual or joint debtors in either a Chapter 7 case or a Chapter 13 case or in a case filed under any other chapter of the Bankruptcy Code by an individual debtor.

Section 523(a)(9), applicability to Chapter 7 and Chapter 13 cases

non-dischargeability under Section 523(a)(9), creditor action unnecessary

The nondischargeability provisions of Section 523(a)(9) are self-executing. This means that it is not necessary for a creditor to file an objection or complaint, or even to appear in the debtor's bankruptcy case in order for the debt to be nondischargeable. Therefore, a creditor may seek the post-bankruptcy collection or prosecution of a claim for death or personal injuries caused by the debtor's driving while intoxicated without having to file a complaint in or otherwise obtain relief from the bankruptcy court. Because nondischargeability under Section 523(a)(9) is self-executing, the bankruptcy court does not have exclusive jurisdiction to decide the issue of nondischargeability under Section 523(a)(9). That other courts, including state courts, may determine the issue of the nondischargeability of a debt under Section 523(a)(9) if the issue has not been previously determined by the bankruptcy court, see In re Anderson, 74 B.R. 463 (ED WI, 1987).

Section 523(a)(9), requirements for non-dischargeability

Establishing the elements of nondischargeability. Section 523(a)(9) in its present form provides simply that debts for personal injury or death that result from the operation of a motor vehicle, vessel or aircraft by the debtor while intoxicated are nondischargeable. The creditor is not required to obtain a judgment against the debtor or even to have filed a case against the debtor in another court. There is also no requirement to show that the debtor has been convicted of a drunk-driving offense in a state or local court. See In re Hart, 347 B.R. 635 (WD MI, 2006). To establish nondischargeability under Section 523(a)(9) a creditor need only show that the debtor was in fact intoxicated under state law, that the debtor operated a motor vehicle while so intoxicated, and that the creditor's claim for death or personal injury resulted therefrom.

establishing non-dischargeability under Section 523(a)(9), burden of proof

In any event, Section 523(a)(9) is generally liberally construed in favor of the debtor and strictly construed against the creditor. See In re Mellott, 187 B.R. 578 (ND OH, 1995). To prevail in a Section 523(a)(9) dispute, a creditor must establish nondischargeability by a preponderance of the evidence. See In re Mellott, supra; In re Race, 198 B.R. 740 (WD MO, 1996) (stating that in order to establish nondischargeability under Section 523(a)(9) the burden is on the creditor to prove each element of nondischargeability by a preponderance of the evidence).

establishing non-dischargeability under Section 523(a)(6), matters to prove

As indicated above, to establish nondischargeability under Section 523(a)(9) a creditor need only prove by a preponderance of the evidence that the debtor was legally intoxicated under state law while operating a motor vehicle and that the debt in question arose from the operation of the vehicle. It need not be shown that the debtor has been convicted of a drunk-driving offense under state or local law, it is not necessary to show that there has been a factual finding of legal intoxication in a state proceeding, and it is not always necessary to show the results of a blood alcohol test on the debtor in order to prove nondischargeability under Section 523(a)(9). See In re Dale, 199 B.R. 1014 (SD FL, 1995); In re Phalen, 145 B.R. 551 (ND OH, 1992); Whitson v. Middleton, 898 F.2d 950 (4th Cir., 1990) (stating that in determining whether a debt is nondischargeable under Section 523(a)(9), it is sufficient for courts to determine first that liability was incurred as a result of the debtor's operation of an automobile and second that the debtor was legally intoxicated while driving, and nondischargeability does not require a legal determination by a state court that liability resulted from driving while intoxicated). See also In re Wiggins, 180 B.R. 676 (MD AL, 1995); Hildebrand v. Kugler, 170 B.R. 291 (ED VA, 1994) (holding the term "unlawful" in Section 523(a)(9) refers to the debtor's conduct and whether it is prohibited under state law and not to whether the debtor could be lawfully prosecuted for that conduct in the state courts).

A creditor is also not required to prove that the debtor's intoxication "caused" the accident that gave rise to the creditor's injuries. See In re Hodak, 119 B.R. 516 (WD PA, 1990); In re Dale, 199 B.R. 1014 (SD FL, 1995) (stating nondischargeability under Section 523(a)(9) may be established upon a mere showing that the debtor was driving while intoxicated without showing that the debtor's intoxication was the principal or sole cause of the accident).

establishing non-dischargeability under Section 523(a)(6), matters to prove

Proving intoxication in the bankruptcy court. A bankruptcy court must apply state law for purposes of determining whether the debtor's operation of the vehicle was "unlawful" for purposes of Section 523(a)(9). See In re Tulloch, 373 B.R. 370 (NJ, 2007); In re Barnes, 266 B.R. 397 (B.A.P. 8th Cir., 2001); In re Jackson, 77 B.R. 120 (ND OH, 1987). This means that a bankruptcy court must apply state law, including the state blood-alcohol presumption levels for establishing intoxication, in determining whether the debtor was intoxicated while driving. See In re Spencer, 168 B.R. 142 (ND TX, 1994), Whitson v. Middleton, 898 F.2d 950 (4th Cir., 1990); In re Mellott, 187 B.R. 578 (ND OH, 1995). See also In re Wiggins, 180 B.R. 676 (MD AL, 1995) (stating that to establish nondischargeability under Section 523(a)(9) it must be shown that the debtor was legally intoxicated under state law and that liability for the debt for death or personal injuries resulted from the debtor's operation of the vehicle).

Section 523(a)(9), applicability of state law

In In re Mellott, 187 B.R. 578 (ND OH, 1995), the court held that evidence showing that the debtor drove with a blood-alcohol content of more than .10%, the amount required for conviction under state law, established the debtor's intoxication for purposes of Section 523(a)(9). In In re Brisson, 186 B.R. 205 (ED VA, 1995), the court found that the debtor was driving while intoxicated for purposes of Section 523(a)(9) where the debtor pled guilty to reckless driving in the state court, the accident victim presented evidence of the debtor's intoxication, and the debtor admitted having at least two drinks within two hours of the accident.

DWI, proof of, requirements

In In re Phelan, 145 B.R. 551 (ND OH, 1992), the court held that the preponderance of the evidence established that the debtor was legally intoxicated at the time of the accident in question even though the debtor was never convicted of driving under the influence, where the debtor pleaded guilty to aggravated vehicular homicide and was given a 10 year license revocation and ordered to attend alcohol counseling, and witnesses stated that the debtor had consumed four cans of beer prior to the accident. In In re Dale, 199 B.R. 1014 (SD FL, 1995), the court held that the evidence supported a finding that the debtor was driving while intoxicated for purposes of Section 523(a)(9) where, even though the debtor drank beer after the accident, the medical examiner testified that the debtor's blood alcohol level was still more than .10% at the time of the accident, the debtor offered no scientific evidence to contradict the medical examiner's retrograde extrapolation testimony, and other witnesses testified as to the debtor's conduct after the accident and as to his abnormal driving prior to the accident. However, in In re Barnes, 266 B.R. 397 (B.A.P. 8th Cir., 2001), the court ruled that a nondischargeability complaintant needed to produce expert testimony regarding the rate at which alcohol dissipates from the blood stream when the debtor-motorist had .05% BAC three hours after the accident.

DWI by debtor, proof of, when established

In In re Race, 198 B.R. 740 (WD MO, 1996), the creditor failed to prove that the debtor was intoxicated at the time of a motorboat accident where the debtor and other witnesses testified that the debtor was not impaired at the time of the accident, there was no evidence that the debtor had anything

DWI by debtor, proof of, when established

to drink within two hours of the accident, the debtor's swollen face and red eyes were explained by the debtor's broken nose and the presence of gasoline in the water into which the debtor fell after the accident, and the officer who smelled alcohol on the debtor's breath was biased against the debtor. Similarly, in In re Spencer, 168 B.R. 142 (ND TX, 1994), the court held that the creditor failed to prove by a preponderance of the evidence that the debtor was intoxicated as defined in the state DWI statute in a case where the debtor was not charged with DWI in the state court. In In re Crump, 321 B.R. 879 (ND OH, 2004) the court ruled that where a test of the debtor's blood alcohol level was not administered within the required time period under Ohio state law and was therefore inadmissible under state law, the debtor's admission to consuming alcohol the night before the collision coupled with the debtor's poor judgment in failing to stop for a stop sign were insufficient to establish the debtor's intoxication at the time of the accident

DWI, proof of, when not established

If the issues of the debtor's intoxication and liability for the debt in question have been previously determined in a state judicial proceeding, the doctrines of res judicata and collateral estoppel may preclude a retrial of these issues in the bankruptcy court. See In re Tyler, 98 B.R. 396 (ND IL, 1989) (holding a bankruptcy court is authorized to determine the Section 523(a)(9) issues either from the evidence submitted to it or by the application of the doctrines of res judicata or collateral estoppel).

collateral estoppel, applicability to Section 523(a)(9) proceeding

In In re Race, 198 B.R. 740 (WD MO, 1996), the court held that the party seeking to assert collateral estoppel against another has the burden of establishing all of the elements of collateral estoppel, that a bankruptcy court must apply the doctrine of collateral estoppel adopted in the local state, and that under local law collateral estoppel applies only when the issues in the present action are identical to the issues in the prior adjudication, where the prior adjudication resulted in a judgment on the merits, where the party against whom estoppel is asserted is the same party or is in privity with the party in the prior adjudication, and where the party against whom estoppel is asserted had a full and fair opportunity to litigate the issue in the prior adjudication.

collateral estoppel, elements of

If the creditor has obtained a prior judgment against the debtor and if the judgment included an award of punitive damages, the question arises as to whether the punitive damage award is nondischargeable under Section 523(a)(9). In In re Dale, 199 B.R. 1014 (SD FL, 1995), the court held that Section 523(a)(9) applies to all sorts of debts and that both compensatory and punitive damages are nondischargeable thereunder. However, in Sellers v. Friend, 147 B.R. 584 (ND OK, 1992), the court ruled that punitive damages do not represent compensation for personal injury and are therefore not protected from discharge by Section 523(a)(9). In Longhenry v. Wyatt, 246 B.R. 234 (MD, 2000), a claim for consortium loss was found to fall within the definition of "personal injury" under Section 523(a)(9) and was therefore nondischargeable. Note that if a judgment against the debtor contains an award for property damage, that portion of the judgment is dischargeable because Section 523(a)(9) does not apply to property damage. See In re Spencer, 168 B.R. 142 (ND TX, 1994).

punitive damages, non-dischargeability of under Section 523(a)(9)

Also, debts based upon imputed or vicarious liability for driving while intoxicated are not protected from discharge by Section 523(a)(9). See In re Lewis, 77 B.R. 972 (SD FL, 1987) (where a debt incurred as a result of the operation of a motor vehicle while intoxicated by the debtor's daughter was found to be dischargeable under Section 523(a)(9)); In re Taneff, 172 B.R. 744 (WD NY, 1994) (reversed on other grounds in 190 B.R. 501) (holding that Section 523(a)(9) is not broad enough to apply to a debt owed by a bar owner under a dram shop statute for the sale of intoxicating liquor to a patron who later drove while intoxicated); In re Austin, 36 B.R. 306 (MD TN, 1984).

debts for imputed liability, dischargeability of under Section 523(a)(9)

Obviously, an automobile is the most common motor vehicle involved in Section 529(a)(9) matters. However, a motor boat has been deemed to be a vessel. See In re Race, 198 B.R. 740 (WD MO, 1996). A snowmobile has also been deemed to be a motor vehicle in In re Dunn, 203 B.R. 414 (ED MI, 1996). However, the court in In re Schumucker, 409 B.R. 477 (ND IN, 2007) determined that the term "vessel" was not broad enough to encompass a horse and buggy that an intoxicated debtor was operating.

vessel, what constitutes

Annotations:

Exception of Debt from Discharge as One for Death or Personal Injury Resulting from Debtor's Unlawful Operation of Motor Vehicle, Vessel, or Aircraft While Intoxicated, 11 U.S.C.A. § 523(a)(9). 53 ALR Fed 2d 347.

Articles:

Interpreting the nondischargeability of drunk driving debts under Section 523(a)(9) of the Bankruptcy Code: a case of judicial legislation. 49 Maryland L. Rev. 156, 1990.

Cheers? The drunk-driving exception to discharge. 63 Am. Bankruptcy L.J. 213, April 1989.

Drunk and dischargeable. 59 Wis. Bar Bulletin 11, Fall 1986.

1.10 To what extent are tax debts and debts for tax penalties and interest nondischargeable in bankruptcy?

Text of statutes. Sections 523(a)(1) and 523(a)(7) of the Bankruptcy Code (11 U.S.C. § 523(a)(1), (7)) are applicable to the subject discussed in this article. They provide as follows:

523. Exceptions to discharge

(a) A discharge under section 727, 1141, 1228(a), 1228(b), or 1328(b) of this title does not discharge an individual debtor from any debt -

Section 523(a)(1), text of

(1) for a tax or a customs duty -

(A) of the kind and for the periods specified in section 507(a)(3) or 507(a)(8) of this title, whether or not a claim for such tax was filed or allowed;

(B) with respect to which a return, or equivalent report or notice, if required -

(i) was not filed or given; or

(ii) was filed or given after the date on which such return, report, or notice was last due, under applicable law or under any extension, and after two years before the date of the filing of the petition; or

(C) with respect to which the debtor made a fraudulent return or willfully attempted in any manner to evade or defeat such tax;

. . . .

Section 523(a)(7), text of

(7) to the extent such debt is for a fine, penalty, or forfeiture payable to and for the benefit of a governmental unit, and is not compensation for actual pecuniary loss, other than a tax penalty -

(A) relating to a tax of a kind not specified in paragraph (1) of this subsection; or

(B) imposed with respect to a transaction or event that occurred before three years before the date of the filing of the petition;

history of statutes

Introduction. Section 523(a)(1) was enacted in the Bankruptcy Reform Act of 1978. Section 507(a)(6) in subparagraph (1)(A) was changed to "section 507(a)(7)" in 1986 and to "section 507(a)(8)" in 1994 to correspond to subparagraph number changes in Section 507. In 2005, the BAPCPA amended section 523(a)(1)(B) by broadening the scope of tax debts which are nondischargeable under this section primarily because of the expansion of the type of document the nonfiling (or nongiving) of which will result in nondischargeability under this subsection. Section 523(a)(7) was also enacted in the Bankruptcy Reform Act of 1978 and has remained unchanged since its enactment.

Note that under the BAPCPA amendments debts that are incurred to pay a tax to a governmental unit, other than the United States, that would be nondischargeable under 11 U.S.C. § 523(a)(1) are nondischargeable. See 11 U.S.C. § 523(a)(14A). Debts incurred to pay a nondischargeable tax owed to the United States were nondischargeable prior to the BAPCPA and remain so. See 11 U.S.C. § 523(a)(14).

non-dischargeability of debts incurred to pay taxes(9)

Tax debts that are nondischargeable under sections 523(a)(1)(B) and (C) are now nondischargeable in a Chapter 13 case wherein the debtor receives a completed plan discharge under section 1328(a) of the Bankruptcy Code. See 11 U.S.C. § 1328(a)(2). However, tax debts that are nondischargeable under subsections 523(a)(1)(A) and 523(a)(7) are dischargeable under a section 1328(a) completed plan discharge, even after the BAPCPA amendments. Nonpriority tax claims and tax penalties are not accorded priority under 11 U.S.C. § 1322(a)(2) and are therefore dischargeable under 11 U.S.C. § 1328(a).

Sections 523(a)(1) & (7), applicability to Chapter 7 and Chapter 13 cases(9)

Section 523(a)(1) provides, in essence, that debts for the following types of taxes are nondischargeable:

types of non-dischargeable tax debts(9)

(1) taxes that are accorded priority under 11 U.S.C. § 507(a)(8);

(2) taxes with respect to which a return or equivalent report or notice was not filed or given;

(3) taxes with respect to which a return was filed late but within 2 years of the bankruptcy filing date;

(4) taxes with respect to which the debtor filed a fraudulent return; and

(5) taxes which the debtor willfully attempted to evade or defeat.

Note that the categories of tax debts listed above are not mutually exclusive and that a tax debt may qualify for nondischargeability under more than one of the categories. To be nondischargeable a tax debt need only qualify under one of the above categories. If a debt is dischargeable under one category but nondischargeable under another category, the debt is nondischargeable. The nondischargeability of each type of tax debt listed above is discussed separately below.

tax debts, when non-dischargeable under more than one category(9)

Section 523(a)(7) provides, in essence, that all tax penalties are nondischargeable except (1) penalties imposed on dischargeable tax debts and (2) penalties imposed with respect to transactions or events that occurred more than 3 years prior to the bankruptcy filing date. Otherwise stated, debts for tax penalties are dischargeable only if the tax upon which the penalty was imposed is dischargeable or if the transaction or event upon which the penalty was imposed occurred more than 3 years prior to the bankruptcy filing date. The nondischargeability of tax penalties and interest is discussed separately below in this article.

tax penalties, when non-dischargeable under Section 523(a)(7)

The nondischargeability provisions of Section 523(a)(1) and 523(a)(7) are self-executing. This means that it is not necessary for the holder of the claim to file an objection or a request to determine dischargeability of the debt, or even to appear in the debtor's bankruptcy case, in order for the debt to be

Sections 523(a)(1) & (7), necessity of creditor action(9)

Sections 523(a)(1) & (7), necessity of creditor action

nondischargeable. See In re Newman, 402 B.R. 908 (MD FL, 2009) (holding that nondischargeability was not affected by the fact that the IRS classified part of a tax liability owed by the debtor as a general unsecured claim rather than a priority claim). In Newman, the court ruled that the classification designated in the proof of claim could not be used by the debtor to compromise the nondischargeable nature of the debt. The dischargeability or nondischargeability of a tax debt may also be determined at a later time by another court.

priority tax debts, when non-dischargeable

The dischargeability of priority tax debts. Tax debts that qualify for priority under 11 U.S.C. § 507(a)(8) are nondischargeable under Section 523(a)(1)(A), whether or not a claim for the tax was filed or allowed in the bankruptcy case. Tax debts that qualify for priority under 11 U.S.C. § 507(a)(3) are also nondischargeable under Section 523(a)(1)(A). However, because 11 U.S.C. § 507(a)(3) deals only with business-related claims in involuntary bankruptcy cases it is not applicable to Chapter 7 consumer cases and Chapter 13 cases and will not be further discussed in this article.

Section 507(a)(8) accords priority to 9 categories of tax claims:

Section 507(a)(8), text of

> (8) Eighth, allowed unsecured claims of governmental units, only to the extent that such claims are for -
>
> (A) a tax on or measured by income or gross receipts for a taxable year ending on or before the date of the filing of the petition-
>
> (i) for which a return, if required, is last due, including extensions, after three years before the date of the filing of the petition;
>
> (ii) assessed within 240 days before the date of the filing of the petition, exclusive of –
>
> (I) any time during which an offer in compromise with respect to that tax was pending or in effect during that 240 day period, plus 30 days; and
>
> (II) any time during which a stay of proceedings against collections was in effect in a prior case under this title during that 240 day period, plus 90 days; or
>
> (iii) other than a tax of a kind specified in section 523(a)(1)(B) or 523(a)(1)(C) of this title, not assessed before, but assessable, under applicable law or by agreement, after, the commencement of the case;
>
> (B) a property tax incurred before the commencement of the case and last payable without penalty after one year before the date of the filing of the petition;
>
> (C) a tax required to be collected or withheld and for which the debtor is liable in whatever capacity;
>
> (D) an employment tax on a wage, salary, or commission of a kind specified in paragraph (4) of this subsection earned from the debtor before the date of the filing of the petition, whether or not actually paid before such date, for which a return is last due, under applicable law or under any extension, after three years before the date of the filing of the petition;
>
> (E) an excise tax on -
>
> (i) a transaction occurring before the date of the filing of the petition for which a return, if required, is last due, under applicable law or under any extension, after three years before the date of the filing of the petition; or
>
> (ii) if a return is not required, a transaction occurring during the three years immediately preceding the date of the filing of the petition;
>
> (F) a customs duty arising out of the importation of merchandise-
>
> (i) entered for consumption within one year before the date of the filing of the petition;
>
> (ii) covered by an entry liquidated or reliquidated within one year before the date of the filing of the petition; or
>
> (iii) entered for consumption within four years before the date of the filing of the petition but unliquidated on such date, if the Secretary of the Treasury certifies than failure to liquidate such entry was due to an investigation pending on such date into assessment of antidumping or countervailing duties or fraud, or if information needed for the proper appraisement or classification of such merchandise was not available to the appropriate customs officer before such date;
>
> or

(G) a penalty related to a claim of a kind specified in this paragraph and in compensation for actual pecuniary loss.

An otherwise applicable time period specified in this paragraph shall be suspended for any period during which a governmental unit is prohibited under applicable nonbankruptcy law from collecting a tax as a result of a request by the debtor for a hearing and an appeal of any collection action taken or proposed against the debtor, plus 90 days; plus any time during which the stay of proceedings was in effect in a prior case under this title or during which collection was precluded by the existence of 1 or more confirmed plans under this title, plus 90 days. §507(a)(8), text of

11 U.S.C. § 507(a)(8), as set forth above, accords priority to the 9 categories of tax debts listed and described below. Because they are accorded priority under 11 U.S.C. § 507(a)(8), debts for these types of taxes are nondischargeable under Section 523(a)(1)(A). Each category of these debts is discussed separately below.

(1) Debts for income or gross receipts taxes for which a tax return, if required, was last due, including extensions, within 3 years prior to the bankruptcy filing date. See 11 U.S.C. § 507(a)(8)(A)(i). An income tax debt is dischargeable under this provision if the tax return was last due, including extensions, more than 3 years prior to the bankruptcy filing date. See In re Paradis, 477 B.R. 295 (Bankr. D. Maine 2012); In re Borck, 81 B.R. 142 (SD FL, 1987). It is important to note that the 3 year period for nondischargeability is tied to the due date of the tax return and not to the due date of the tax or date when the tax return was actually filed. See In re Wood, 78 B.R. 316 (MD FL, 1987). In In re Resnick, 52 B.R. 90 (MA, 1985), the debtor's debt for his 1976 federal income taxes was nondischargeable because his bankruptcy case was filed on January 2, 1980 which was within 3 years of the April 15, 1997 due date of his 1976 federal income tax return. See also Muhle v. IRS, 175 B.R. 34 (NE, 1994). In Elkins v. IRS, 369 B.R. 741 (SD GA, 2007), the debtor filed his 2001 tax return, after requesting an extension, on October 15, 2002, which indicated that he owed taxes for 2001. He subsequently filed for chapter 7 bankruptcy on October 14, 2005. The debtor's tax liability was nondischargeable because the bankruptcy code contemplates a calendar year instead of a specific number of days. The court ruled that the lookback period for determining dischargeability is 3 calendar years, not 1,095 days.

income tax debts whose return was due within 3 years of bankruptcy, non-dischargeability of

time period, how to calculate

Even if the debtor's tax return was originally due more than 3 years prior to the bankruptcy filing date, the tax debt is nondischargeable if the debtor obtained an extension whereby the due date for filing the return was extended to a date that was within 3 years of the bankruptcy filing date. See In re Hofmann, 76 B.R. 853 (SD FL, 1987). The 3 year period of limitation for nondischargeability may be suspended or tolled by agreement, by an applicable statute, or by the filing of a bankruptcy case. This issue is discussed under a separate heading below in this article. Note that the term "return" in 11 U.S.C. § 507(a)(8)(A)(i) has been construed to include effective substitutes for formal tax returns if such are permitted under state law. See In re Lamborn, 181 B.R. 98 (ND OK, 1995); U.S. v. Black, 725 F. Supp. 2d 1279 (E. D. Wash. 2010).

3 year period for tax return, what constitutes

debts for income taxes assessed within 240 days of bankruptcy, non-dischargeability of

(2) Debts for income or gross receipts taxes that were assessed within 240 days prior to the bankruptcy filing date. See 11 U.S.C. § 507(a)(8)(A)(ii). It should be noted that the 240 day period is automatically expanded by any period plus 30 days during which an offer in compromise with respect to the tax was made during the 240 day period. An income tax debt is dischargeable under this provision if the tax was "assessed" more than 240 days prior to the bankruptcy filing date. The 240 day period of limitation for nondischargeability may be suspended or tolled by agreement, by an applicable statute, or by the filing of a bankruptcy case. This issue is discussed under a separate heading below in this article.

assessment of taxes, what constitutes

The critical term under this provision is "assessed." The term "assessed" or "assessment" is not defined in the Bankruptcy Code. When dealing with federal taxes, most courts use the definition of "assessment" found in the federal tax regulations. See 26 CFR 301.6203-1 (2013), where an assessment is defined as "the date the summary record is signed by an assessment officer." The "summary record" is a form signed by the IRS and sent to the taxpayer notifying the taxpayer of the taxes due. In Harris v. U.S., 228 B.R. 740 (AZ, 1998), a tax assessment became final under state law upon the expiration of time for appealing the assessment and not when the state revenue department began collection proceedings.

assessment of income taxes, what constitutes

In Hartman v. U.S., 110 B.R. 951 (KS, 1990), the debtor received a "notice of deficiency" form from the IRS more than 240 days prior to the bankruptcy filing date but the "summary record" was actually signed by the assessment officer within 240 days of the bankruptcy filing date. The court adopted the definition of assessment in the IRS regulations (see above) and found the tax debt to be nondischargeable because it was assessed within 240 days of the bankruptcy filing date. See also In re King, 961 F.2d 1423 (9th Cir., 1992) (holding an "assessment" occurred under state law when the tax became final under state law and not when notice of the tax liability was sent to the debtor). However, in Wernimont v. Dept. of Revenue & Finance, 183 B.R. 181 (ND IA, 1994), the date of assessment under state law was held to be the date of notice of assessment, which was more than 240 days prior to the bankruptcy filing date and rendered the debt dischargeable. In In re Harris, 228 B.R. 740 (AZ, 1998), the court ruled that a tax assessment became final under Arizona law upon the expiration of the time to appeal the assessment, instead of the time the department of revenue issued its collection letter and commenced collection proceedings. But see In re O'Connell, 246 B.R. 332 (B.A.P. 8th Cir. 2000) (holding state law definition of "assessment" not controlling).

Note that an income tax debt may be nondischargeable either because the tax return was due within 3 years of the bankruptcy filing date or because the tax was assessed within 240 days of the bankruptcy filing date. See Linder v. U.S., 139 B.R. 950 (CO, 1992). Therefore, even if the tax return was due more than 3 years prior to the bankruptcy filing date, the tax debt will be nondischargeable if the tax was "assessed" within 240 days of the bankruptcy filing date. See Frary v. U.S., 117 B.R. 541 (AK, 1990).

income tax debt, when non-dischargeable

(3) Debts for income or gross receipts taxes that were not assessed prior to the commencement of the bankruptcy case but which are assessable after the commencement of the case either by applicable law or by agreement. See 11 U.S.C. § 507(a)(8)(A)(iii). A tax that was assessable, yet not assessed, before a debtor filed a bankruptcy petition is nondischargeable under section 507(a)(8)(A)(iii). See Martinez v. U.S., 323 B.R. 650 (ED LA, 2005). This nondischargeability provision does not apply to taxes that were not assessed because the tax return was either not filed, filed late, or fraudulent. This provision is applicable to debts for taxes that were not assessed because income was not reported on the debtor's tax return. With respect to this provision, it should be noted that while the IRS is normally required to assess taxes within 3 years after the return is filed, it has 6 years to assess in cases where the taxpayer omits from gross income an amount in excess of 25 percent of the amount of gross income shown on the return. See 26 U.S.C. § 6501(e)(1)(A). This means that a federal income tax debt that was due 6 years prior to the bankruptcy filing date may be nondischargeable under this provision if the debtor understated his or her income by more than 25 percent. See Edwards v. U.S., 74 B.R. 661 (ND OH, 1987), and Blake v. I.R.S., 154 B.R. 590 (MD AL, 1992).

unreported income, tax debts for, non-dischargeability of

(4) Debts for property taxes incurred prior to the commencement of the bankruptcy case and last payable without penalty within one year prior to the bankruptcy filing date. See 11 U.S.C. § 507(a)(8)(B). Property taxes incurred prior to the commencement of the case that were last payable without a penalty more than a year prior to the bankruptcy filing date are dischargeable under this provision. See, e.g., In re Howe, 455 B.R. 148 (Bankr. W. D. Wis. 2011) (Town's untimely proof of claim not entitled to priority).

incurred property taxes payable within 1 year of bankruptcy, non-dischargeability of

(5) Debts for any tax required to be collected or withheld for which the debtor is liable in any capacity. See 11 U.S.C. § 507(a)(8)(C). This provision is primarily applicable to "trust fund" taxes withheld by an employer for the benefit of its employees. In re Musbruckers, 227 B.R. 434 (B.A.P. 8th Cir. 1998). Debts for corporate withholding taxes owed by a debtor as a principal or responsible person of the corporation under 26 U.S.C. § 6672 are nondischargeable under this provision. See, e.g., In re Paris, 355 B.R. 867 (MD FL, 2006); Tashjian v. IRS, 325 B.R. 56 (MA, 2005); In re Campbell, 242 B.R. 327 (WD VA, 1999); In re Gust, 229 B.R. 44 (SD GA, 1998); In re Mosbrucker, 227 B.R. 434 (B.A.P. 8th Cir., 1998); In re Stanmock, Inc., 103 B.R. 228 (B.A.P. 9th Cir., 1989). Debts for unpaid sales and use taxes required by state law to be collected for the state by the debtor as a licensed retailer are also generally held to be nondischargeable under this provision. See McDonough v. Iowa Dep't of Revenue, 346 B.R. 492 (SD IA, 2006); Rosenow v. Illinois, 715 F.2d 277 (7th Cir., 1983) Shank v. Washington State Dept. of Revenue, 792 F.2d 829 (9th Cir., 1986); De Chiaro v. New York State Tax Comm., 760 F.2d 432 (2d Cir., 1985); In re Peiffer, 126 B.R. 364 (ND AL, 1991); but see In re Hansen, 470 B.R. 535 (B.A.P. 9th Cir. 2012) (holding unpaid unemployment insurance taxes that company of Chapter 7 debtor was responsible for were not a tax contemplated by Section 523(a)(1)(A)).

withholding taxes, debts for, non-dischargeability of

sales tax debts, dischargeability of

unemployment taxes, debts for, non-dischargeability of

(6) Debts for unemployment taxes due with respect to wages, salaries or commissions earned by employees from the debtor prior to the bankruptcy filing date for which a return was due within 3 years of the bankruptcy filing date. See 11 U.S.C. § 507(a)(8)(D). Note that the limitations on claims for wages, salaries and commissions set forth in 11 U.S.C. § 507(a)(4) have been held not to be applicable to this provision. See State v. Pierce, 935 F.2d 709 (5th Cir., 1991). Also because this provision applies only to wages "earned from the debtor," a debtor's liability for corporate unemployment taxes is dischargeable under this provision. See Ndosi v. Minnesota, 116 B.R. 687 (MN, 1990). However, in Tashjran v. IRS, 325 B.R. 56 (MA, 2005), a debtor was not allowed to discharge debts incurred prior to filing a petition which pertained to responsible officer liabilities for unpaid withholding taxes.

excise taxes, debts for, non-dischargeability of

(7) Debts for excise taxes on pre-bankruptcy transactions for which a return was due within 3 years prior to the bankruptcy filing date or, if a tax return was not required, on transactions that occurred within 3 years prior to the bankruptcy filing date. See 11 U.S.C. § 507(a)(8)(E). For this provision to be applicable, the tax in question must be an excise tax. See In re Quiroz, 450 B.R. 699 (Bankr. E. D. Mich. 2011). The question of whether a tax is an excise tax for purposes of the Bankruptcy Code is a federal question for the federal courts to decide. A state cannot force a fee or tax to be treated as an excise tax for bankruptcy purposes merely by labeling it as an excise tax. See U.S. v. Mansfield Tire & Rubber, 942 F.2d 1055 (6th Cir., 1991).

excise tax, what constitutes

An "excise tax" has been defined as an indirect tax imposed on the performance of an act or the carrying on of an occupation, employment or privilege. See New Neighborhoods Inc. v. West Virginia Workers' Compensation Fund, 886 F.2d 714 (4th Cir., 1989) (holding a debt for premiums owed by an employer to the state workers' compensation fund was found to be an excise tax for bankruptcy purposes). A motor carrier tax was found to be a nondischargeable excise tax in In re Dawson, 98 B.R. 519 (OR, 1989); In re Fagan, 465 B.R. 472 (Bankr. E. D. Mich. 2012). A corporate tax for which the debtor is personally liable under state law as a corporate officer is generally a nondischargeable excise tax under this section. See, e.g., In re McAdam, 402 B.R. 473 (NH, 2009); In re George, 95 B.R. 718 (B.A.P. 9th Cir., 1989). Unpaid workers' compensation premiums is a nondischargeable excise tax. See, e.g., In re Voightman, 239 B.R. 380 (B.A.P. 8th Cir., 1999).

debts for customs duties, non-dischargeability of

(8) Debts for customs duties arising out of the importation of certain merchandise. See 11 U.S.C. § 507(a)(8)(F). Because debts of this type are seldom, if ever, incurred by consumer Chapter 7 or Chapter 13 debtors, they will not be discussed here.

(9) Debts for tax penalties that are in compensation for actual pecuniary loss by the taxing authority. See 11 U.S.C. § 507(a)(8)(G). Penalties that are punitive in nature are dischargeable under this provision but may be nondischargeable under Section 523(a)(7), which is discussed below in this article. Most federal tax penalties are punitive in nature and are therefore dischargeable under this provision. See, e.g., In re Jackson, 80 B.R. 213 (CO, 1987); In re Henderberg, 108 B.R. 407 (ND NY, 1989). However, the 100% penalty imposed against responsible corporate officers for failing to turn over withholding taxes was found to be in compensation for actual pecuniary loss and therefore nondischargeable under this provision in In re Matlock, 104 B.R. 389 (ND OK, 1989), and In re Coleman, 19 B.R. 529 (KS, 1982).

nonpunitive tax penalties, debts for, non-dischargeability of

A bankruptcy court may look beyond the label of a tax penalty to determine whether it is actually punitive in nature. See U.S. v. Dumler, 983 F.2d 161 (10th Cir., 1992) (holding a 10 percent surcharge imposed on the debtor by the IRS for an early withdrawal from a tax-qualified pension plan was punitive in nature and not compensation for actual pecuniary loss, and therefore dischargeable under Section 523(a)(1)(A)); see also Mounier v. U.S., 232 B.R. 186 (SD CA, 1998). Some courts have held that prepetition interest on tax claims constitutes a nonpunitive, and therefore nondischargeable, penalty under this provision. See In re Reich, 66 B.R. 554 (CO, 1986); In re Avant, 110 B.R. 264 (WD TX, 1989). The dischargeability of interest on tax debts is discussed under a separate heading below in this article.

nonpunitive tax penalty, what constitutes

The dischargeability of tax debts for which a return or equivalent report or notice was not filed or given. Section 523(a)(1)(B)(i) provides that tax debts with respect to which a tax return or equivalent report or notice was not filed or given are nondischargeable regardless of when the taxes or the return was due. There is no period of limitation with respect to the nondischargeability of taxes for which a return or equivalent report or notice, if required, was not filed or given. The age or staleness of a tax liability is irrelevant under this provision. See In re Woodley, 92 AFTR 2d 5288 (MD FL, 2003) and In re Haywood, 62 B.R. 482 (ND IL, 1986).

taxes for which return was not filed or given, non-dischargeability of

Not surprisingly, disputes often arise as to what constitutes the filing of a tax return for purposes of Section 523(a)(1)(B)(i). To qualify as a return, generally: (1) it must purport to be a return; (2) it must be executed under penalty of perjury; (3) it must contain sufficient data to allow calculation of a tax; and (4) if must represent an honest and reasonable attempt to satisfy the requirements of the tax law. In re Wagoman, 475 B.R. 239 (B.A.P. 10th Cir. 2012) (applying the "Beard" test). In Smith v. U.S., 186 B.R. 411 (ND OH, 1995), the court held that for purposes of Section 523(a)(1)(B), a bankruptcy court could apply the "physical delivery rule" whereby documents are deemed "filed" only when they are delivered to and received by the IRS. See also Crump v. U.S., 282 B.R. 859 (ND OH, 2002); Campbell v. U.S., 186 B.R. 731 (ND FL, 1995). See In re Pizzuto, 384 B.R. 105 (NJ, 2008) (holding that delivering a delinquent tax return to an IRS Special Agent did not qualify as filing a return).

filing of tax return, what constitutes

tax return filed by IRS, effect of

It is clear that to be deemed "filed" a tax return must be filed by the taxpayer and not by the taxing authority. See U.S. v. Hatton, 220 F.3d 1057 (9th Cir., 2000), and In re Thompson, 272 B.R. 612 (MD, 2002). Several courts have held that the filing of an unsigned tax return for the debtor by the IRS or other taxing authority does not constitute the filing of a return for purposes of Section 523(a)(1)(B)(i). See In re Bergstrom, 949 F.2d 341 (10th Cir., 1991), In re Eastwood, 164 B.R. 989 (ED AR, 1994), In re Chapin, 148 B.R. 304 (CD IL, 1992), and In re Gushue, 126 B.R. 202 (ED PA, 1991). In Brown v. U.S., 280 B.R. 760 (MD GA, 2002), neither a substitute return filed by the IRS nor an installment agreement signed by the debtor was found to constitute the filing of tax return for purposes of Section 523(a)(1)(B)(i).

filing of tax return, what constitutes

In In re Arenson, 134 B.R. 934 (NE, 1991), the filing by the debtor of an amended return to challenge an IRS tax assessment was held not to constitute the filing of a tax return for purposes of Section 523(a)(1)(B)(i) where the original return was never filed. In Blutter v. U.S., 177 B.R. 209 (SD NY, 1995), the court held that an IRS notice of assessment received by the state taxing authority following an IRS audit which revealed improper deductions was not a valid substitute for a state tax return and that the debtor's failure to inform the state of the changes in his federal tax liability rendered his state tax debt nondischargeable under Section 523(a)(1)(B)(i). The addition of a jurat clause to an income tax form by the debtor was held to have rendered the form invalid as a tax return and made the resulting tax nondischargeable under Section 523(a)(1)(B)(i). See Carroll v. U.S., 310 B.R. 621 (MN, 2004); In re Schmitt, 140 B.R. 571 (WD OK, 1992). However, in In re Jackson, 184 F.3d 1046 (9th Cir., 1999) the court held that the debtor's failure to report an IRS reassessment of it's federal income tax liability to the state tax board as required by state law did not constitute a failure to file a tax return for purposes of Section 523(a)(1)(B)(i).

tax return filed by IRS, when valid

In In re Gless, 181 B.R. 414 (NE, 1993) a tax return filed pursuant to 26 U.S.C. § 6020(a) prepared by the IRS with the cooperation of the debtor and signed by the debtor constituted the filing of a tax return for purposes of Section 523(a)(1)(B)(i). See also Lowrie v. U.S., 162 B.R. 864 (NV, 1994) (where the signing and filing by the debtor of dummy tax returns (Form 1902-B) prepared by an IRS agent was held to constitute the filing of a return for purposes of Section 523(a)(1)(B)(i) because the agent represented that the dummy forms would be a valid substitute for the 1040 return and because the dummy returns contained sufficient information to permit the IRS to assess an accurate income tax for the period in question). In Mathis v. U.S., 249 B.R. 324 (SD FL, 2000), an IRS form 4549 filed by the debtor was found to qualify as a "return" for purposes of Section 523(a)(1)(B)(i). However, in Hamer v. U.S., 328 B.R. 825 (ND AL, 2005), the court held that substitute returns prepared by the I.R.S. pursuant to IRC § 6020(b) did not qualify as filed returns.

filing of tax return held valid, cases

In Elmore v. U.S., 165 B.R. 35 (SD IN, 1994), the filing of a tax return by the debtor as part of a U.S. Tax Court petition was found to constitute the filing of a return for purposes of Section 523(a)(1)(B)(i). In Berard v. United States, 181 B.R. 653 (MD FL, 1995), the court held, for purposes of Section 523(a)(1)(B)(i), a form could be considered a filed return if it supplies the IRS with all of the information necessary to compute the debtor›s tax liability and the debtor effectively assented to the assessment of the tax. If the taxing authority did not require the debtor to file a tax return for the period in question, then nondischargeability for the tax debt may not be obtained under Section 523(a)(1)(B)(i). See In re Olson, 174 B.R. 543 (ND, 1994); Woods v. IRS, 285 B.R. 284 (SD IN, 2002), (holding the debtor's tax returns, although filed late and after the IRS made its involuntary assessment, were found to be facially complete and accurate and therefore "returns" for purposes of Sections 507(a)(8)(A)(i) and 523(a)(1)(B)(i)); In re Hetzler, 262 B.R. 47 (NJ, 2001).

return not required, effect of

If the debtor alleges that a tax return was filed and the IRS or other taxing authority has no record of the return, the burden of proof is essentially on the debtor to show that the tax return was filed as alleged. See In re Shorton, 375 B.R. 26 (MA, 2007); In re Clark, 138 B.R. 579 (ED AR, 1991); D'Avanza v. U.S., 101 B.R. 787 (MD FL, 1989). Note that 26 U.S.C. § 7502(c)(1) provides that if the taxpayer sends a tax return by registered mail, the registration is prima facie evidence that the return was filed. As a practical matter, in the absence of registered mail it is very difficult for the debtor to prove that a tax return was filed when the taxing authority states that it has no record of the return. See Brown v. U.S., 167 B.R. 249 (SD AL, 1994). Tax returns filed after the tax has been assessed is not the filing of a tax return for purposes of Section 523(a)(1)(B)(i). See, e.g., In re Walsh, 260 B.R. 142 (MN, 2001); U.S. v. Ralph, 266 B.R. 217 (MD FL, 2001). However, other courts have held that post-assessment 1040s that are signed by the debtor constitute returns. See Colsen v. U.S., 446 F.3d 836 (8th Cir., 2008); U.S. v. Klein, 312 B.R. 443 (SD FL, 2004).

disputed filing of tax return, burden of proof

The dischargeability of tax debts for which a late or fraudulent return, report or notice was filed. Section 523(a)(1)(B)(ii) provides nondischargeability for tax debts with respect to which the tax return, report or notice if required, was filed after the date on which the return was due, either by operation of law or under any extension, if the last due date for the return was within 2 years of the bankruptcy filing date. See In re Casano, 473 B.R. 504 (Bankr. E. D. N.Y. 2012). If a late tax return, report or notice was filed more than 2 years before the bankruptcy filing date, the tax debt from that return, report or notice is dischargeable under this section. It should be noted that most tax debts that are nondischargeable under this section are also nondischargeable under Section 523(a)(1)(A), which incorporates 11 U.S.C. § 507(a)(8)(A)(i) and its 3 year period of limitation for nondischargeability. A tax debt may be nondischargeable under Section 523(a)(1)(A) even if it is dischargeable under Section 523(a)(1)(B)(ii). See, e.g., Etheridge v. Illinois, 127 B.R. 421 (CD IL, 1989); Luke v. IRS, 142 B.R. 160 (WD MI, 1992). As a practical matter, Section 523(a)(1)(B)(ii) is applicable only in a limited number of situations, such as where an amended tax return was filed within 2 years of the bankruptcy filing date. See In re Greenstein, 95 B.R. 583 (ND IL, 1989); In re Izzo, 287 B.R. 158 (ED MI, 2002). The 2 year period of limitation set forth in this section may be suspended by agreement, by an applicable statute, or by the filing of a bankruptcy case. See Jones v. U.S., 177 B.R. 541 (ND OH, 1994). The issue of suspending periods of limitation for tax debts is discussed under a separate heading below in this article.

debts for taxes due under late tax return, report or notice non-dischargeability of fraudulent tax return, debts for taxes due under, no period of limitation

Section 523(a)(1)(C) provides nondischargeability for tax debts with respect to which the debtor filed a fraudulent tax return. There is no period of limitation for establishing nondischargeability under this section, which means that a tax debt for which a fraudulent return was filed is nondischargeable regardless of when or how long ago the fraudulent return was filed.

filing fraudulent return, elements of proof

To establish fraud for purposes of Section 523(a)(1)(C), the taxing authority must establish the following elements by a preponderance of the evidence: (1) the existence of a false return filed by the debtor (2) knowledge by the debtor of the falsity of the return, (3) an intent to evade the tax in question, and (4) underpayment of the tax in question. See Hopkins v. U.S., 133 B.R. 102 (ND OH, 1991). It must be shown that the debtor acted deliberately and willfully in filing the false return. Actual fraud must be shown because constructive fraud does not satisfy Section 523(a)(1)(C). See In re Gathwright, 102 B.R. 211 (OR, 1989); Kirk v. U.S., 98 B.R. 51 (MD FL, 1989). If the debtor was not aware of the falsity of the return, the return is not fraudulent and the tax is dischargeable under this section. However, if it is established that the debtor signed a return which he or she knew was false and if the falsity resulted in an underpayment of tax, fraud is committed and the tax is nondischargeable under this section. See In re Carey, 326 B.R. 816 (ED CA, 2005); In re Meyers Way Dev. Ltd. Partnership, 116 B.R. 239 (WD WA, 1990).

tax debt for fraudulent return, extent of non-dischargeability

Note that if the filing of a fraudulent return is established, the entire tax debt resulting from the return is nondischargeable. Nondischargeability is not limited to the tax that resulted from the false or omitted information. See In re Harris, 59 B.R. 545 (WD VA, 1986) (holding that even though only a portion of the tax liability resulting from the debtor's tax return was attributable to the false information contained in the return, the entire unpaid tax liability resulting from the return was nondischargeable under Section 523(a)(1)(C)).

non-dischargeability of debt for fraudulent tax return, collateral estoppel not applicable

Note that the Internal Revenue Code contains a provision which permits the IRS to assess a penalty if any part of a tax underpayment is due to fraud. See 26 U.S.C. § 6653(b). Many courts construe this provision and the fraudulent return provision of Section 523(a)(1)(C) similarly. See Carapella v. U.S., 115 B.R. 365 (MD FL, 1990), Gathwright v. U.S., 102 B.R. 211 (OR, 1989), and Kirk v. U.S., 98 B.R. 51 (MD FL, 1989). However, because the two statutes are not identical, it has been held that a finding of liability or nonliability under 26 U.S.C. § 6653(b) in another proceeding is not binding on the bankruptcy court under the doctrines of collateral estoppel and res judicata when ruling on the nondischargeability of a tax debt under Section 523(a)(1)(C). See Graham v. IRS, 973 F.2d 1089 (3d Cir., 1992); Levinson v. U.S., 969 F.2d 260 (7th Cir., 1992).

tax evasion debts, non-dischargeability of

The dischargeability of willfully evaded tax debts. Section 523(a)(1)(C) provides nondischargeability for debts with respect to taxes which the debtor willfully attempted in any manner to evade or defeat. The broad provisions of this section have been the subject of much bankruptcy litigation. Nondischargeability under this section has been imposed against tax protesters and others who have attempted to defeat the federal income tax by concealing their income or assets or through the use of fraudulent tax evasion schemes or improper deductions.

Note that the Internal Revenue Code contains a provision that is similar to the willful evasion provision in Section 523(a)(1)(C). The Internal Revenue Code provision provides that it is a felony to willfully attempt in any manner to evade or defeat any tax imposed by the Internal Revenue Code or the payment thereof. See 26 U.S.C. § 7201(a). This provision differs from the willful evasion provision in Section 523(a)(1)(C) in that it contains the words "or the payment thereof" at the end of the provision. Because of the failure of Congress to include the words "or the payment thereof" in Section 523(a)(1)(C), some courts have concluded that an intentional failure to pay taxes does not constitute an attempt to evade or defeat the tax for purposes of Section 523(a)(1)(C). See Haas v. IRS, 48 F.3d 1153 (11th Cir., 1995); In re Gathwright, 102 B.R. 211 (OR, 1989). Other courts have refused to interpret Section 523(a)(1)(C) in this manner and have held that an intentional failure to pay a tax is an attempt to evade or defeat the tax for purposes of Section 523(a)(1)(C). See Jones v. U.S., 116 B.R. 810 (KS, 1990); Fridrich v. IRS, 156 B.R. 41 (NE, 1993); U.S. v. Sumpter, 170 B.R. 908 (ED MI, 1994); U.S. v. Freidus, 165 B.R. 537 (ED NY, 1994); Pierce v. U.S., 184 B.R. 338 (ND IA, 1995); Wright v. IRS, 191 B.R. 291 (SD NY, 1995).

taxes intentionally not paid, non-dischargeability of

To be nondischargeable under the willful evasion provision of Section 523(a)(1)(C), the debtor's attempt to evade or defeat the tax need not be fraudulent; it need only be willful. See Goff v. IRS, 180 B.R. 193 (WD TN, 1995); U.S. v. Jacobs, 490 F.3d 913 (11th Cir., 2007). To establish willfulness under Section 523(a)(1)(C) it must be shown that the law imposed a duty on the debtor, that the debtor was aware of this duty, and that the debtor voluntarily and intentionally violated that duty. See Cheek v. U.S., 498 U.S. 192, 111 S.Ct. 604 (1991), which was a case under 26 U.S.C. § 7201 that several courts have applied to Section 523(a)(1)(C) cases. See U.S. v. Sumpter, 170 B.R. 908 (ED MI, 1994); Howard v. U.S., 167 B.R. 684 (MD FL, 1994).

evaded taxes, necessity of willfulness

In U.S. v. Freidus, 165 B.R. 537 (ED NY, 1994), the court stated that a willful attempt to evade a tax debt under Section 523(a)(1)(C) will be found where the debtor has a duty to pay the tax, the debtor knew that the duty to pay existed, and the debtor voluntarily and intentionally violated that duty. However, in U.S. v. Hedgecock, 160 B.R. 380 (OR, 1993), the court held that nondischargeability under the willful evasion provision of Section 523(a)(1)(C) does not depend on evidence that the debtor intentionally violated a known duty, but rather it need only be shown that the debtor's conduct amounted to an intentional and knowing effort to evade or defeat a tax. See also U.S. v. Toti, 149 B.R. 829 (ED MI, 1993). In Pierce v. U.S., 184 B.R. 338 (ND IA, 1995), the standard of willfulness in Section 523(a)(1)(C) was held to be where the debtor acted voluntarily, consciously or intentionally, or with a reckless disregard of the existence of a duty to pay taxes. In U.S. v. Fretz, 244 F.3d 1323 (11th Cir., 2001), the court stated that while the willfulness requirement of Section 523(a)(1)(C) is not satisfied when it is shown that the debtor filed accurate tax returns and simply failed to pay the taxes, if it is shown that the debtor intentionally failed to file tax returns and did not pay the tax, willfulness is established without further evidence of affirmative conduct by the debtor. See also Griffith v. U.S., 206 F.3d 1389 (11th Cir., 2000).

willful attempt to evade tax, what constitutes

willful attempt to evade tax, what constitutes

In U.S. v. Sumpter, 170 B.R. 908 (ED MI, 1994), the court held that the debtor's transfer of real estate to his children's trust, if for the purpose of thwarting the government's attempt to collect taxes owed by the debtor, would constitute a willful attempt to evade or defeat a tax debt under Section 523(a)(1)(C). In Pierce v. U.S., 184 B.R. 338 (ND IA, 1995), the existence of a 5 year pattern by the debtor of filing late tax returns, not paying taxes, filing frivolous law suits and bankruptcy petitions, and transferring property to trusts constituted a willful attempt to evade or defeat a tax debt under Section 523(a)(1)(C). See also Jones v. Ga. Dept. of Revenue, 158 B.R. 535 (ND GA, 1993); Laurin v. U.S.,x 161 B.R. 73 (WY, 1993); Dube v. U.S., 169 B.R. 886 (ND IL, 1994).

nonpayment of tax, when not willful

If the debtor has a valid or believable reason for not paying a tax or not filing a tax return, nondischargeability under Section 523(a)(1)(C) is likely to be denied. See In re Lindros, 459 B.R. 842 (Bankr. M. D. Fla. 2011); Billingsley v. U.S., 146 B.R. 775 (SD IL, 1992). In In re Gathwright, 102 B.R. 211 (OR, 1989), nondischargeability for a tax debt was denied where the court found that the debtor's failure to file tax returns was because of the debtor's financial stress, an incorrect belief that no taxes were owed, and a desire to await the outcome of an audit. In Miller v. U.S., 176 B.R. 266 (MD FL, 1994), the court held that the mere failure to file tax returns for 6 years, without more, did not establish nondischargeability under Section 523(a)(1)(C) in a case where the debtors cooperated with the IRS, did not attempt to mislead the IRS, and made a partial tax payment prior to filing bankruptcy. See Williams v. U.S., 164 B.R. 352 (MD FL, 1994), for a similar ruling.

willful tax evasion, evidence required to prove

While the filing of false W-4 withholding statements for the purpose of preventing the withholding of taxes constitutes evidence of a willful attempt to evade or defeat a tax, additional evidence of willful evasion is usually required in order to establish a willful attempt to evade or defeat the tax under Section 523(a)(1)(C). See In re Peterson v. U.S., 152 B.R. 329 (WY, 1993); Smith v. U.S., 169 B.R. 55 (SD IN, 1994); Ketchum v. U.S., 177 B.R. 628 (ED MO, 1995). In Gillis v. IRS, 251 B.R. 920 (SD GA, 2000), the debtor's single act of refusing to allow an IRS officer to enter the debtor's residence to make a levy pursuant to a court order was held sufficient to establish willfulness for purposes of Section 523(a)(1)(C).

willful tax evasion, badges of fraud, what constitutes

In cases where the debtor has attempted to defeat a tax through the fraudulent conveyance or concealment of assets or income, some courts employ the "badges of fraud" approach used in fraudulent conveyance litigation. See Pierce v. U.S., 184 B.R. 338 (ND IA, 1995). For purposes of Section 523(a)(1)(C), "badges of fraud" include repeated significant understatements of income, failure to file tax returns, implausible or inconsistent behavior by the taxpayer with respect to the transfer or handling of assets, and failure to cooperate with the taxing authority. See Berzon v. U.S., 145 B.R. 247 (ND IL, 1992); U.S. v. Sumpter, 170 B.R. 908 (ED MI, 1994); Sly v. U.S., 318 B.R. 194 (ND FL, 2004). See also, U.S. v. Ryan, 286 B.R. 141 (WD MO, 2002) (holding the debtor's tax liability was found to be nondischargeable under Section 523(a)(1)(C) because the debtor had engaged in a pattern of evasive conduct that clearly constituted a willful attempt to avoid the payment of a tax liability).

The dischargeability of debts for tax penalties. Section 523(a)(7) provides in essence that debts for fines, penalties or forfeitures that are payable to a governmental unit and that are not in compensation for actual pecuniary loss are nondischargeable except that penalties on dischargeable tax debts are dischargeable and tax penalties imposed with respect to transactions or events that occurred more than 3 years prior to the bankruptcy filing date are dischargeable. In addition, 11 U.S.C. § 507(a)(8)(G), which is incorporated by Section 523(a)(1)(A), provides nondischargeability for penalties imposed with respect to priority tax debts if the penalty is in compensation for actual pecuniary loss. The nondischargeability of tax penalties under Section 523(a)(1)(A) (i.e., penalties for actual pecuniary loss) is discussed above in this article in item (9) under the heading of "The dischargeability of priority tax debts." The dischargeability of such penalties will not be further discussed here.

Section 523(a) (7), essential provisions of

nonpunitive tax penalties, non-dischargeability of

The general rule under Section 523(a)(7) is that tax penalties, because they are payable to a government unit and are punitive in nature (and therefore not in compensation for actual pecuniary loss), are nondischargeable. See In re Lopez, 475 B.R. 418 (Bankr. E. D. Pa. 2012); In re Nam, 254 B.R. 834 (ED PA, 2000). Only if a tax penalty qualifies under subpart (A) or (B) of Section 523(a)(7) is it dischargeable. Under subpart (A) of Section 523(a)(7), a tax penalty is dischargeable if it relates to (i.e., was imposed with respect to) a dischargeable tax debt. Therefore, if the underlying tax debt is found to be dischargeable under any provision of Section 523(a)(1), then the penalty imposed with respect to that tax is dischargeable under Section 523(a)(7)(A). See In re Meyers Dev. Ltd. Partnership, 116 B.R. 239 (WD WA, 1990).

tax penalties, non-dischargeability of, general rule

penalties on dischargeable tax debts, dischargeability of

Section 523(a)(7)(B) provides that a tax penalty imposed with respect to a transaction or event that occurred less than 3 years prior to the bankruptcy filing date is nondischargeable. See In re Allen, 272 B.R. 913 (ED VA, 2002). This means that tax penalties assessed with respect to a tax return that was filed more than 3 years prior to the bankruptcy filing date are dischargeable. See In re Bergstom, 949 F.2d 341 (10th Cir., 1991) and Polston v. U.S., 239 B.R. 277 (MD PA, 1999). It should be noted, however, that the 3 year period of limitation specified in Section 523(a)(7)(B) may be tolled or suspended by agreement, by the filing of a bankruptcy case or by an applicable statute. See In re Linder, 139 B.R. 950 (CO, 1992). This issue is discussed below in this article under a separate heading.

penalties on taxes more than 3 years overdue, dischargeability of

tolling of 3 year period

The general rule is that because subparts A and B of Section 523(a)(7) are connected by the conjunction "or," a tax penalty is dischargeable if it is covered under either subpart. This means that a penalty assessed with respect to a nondischargeable tax, while nondischargeable under subpart A, may nevertheless be dischargeable under subpart B of 523(a)(7) if it qualifies thereunder. This rule is followed by most courts. See In re Roberts, 906 F.2d 1440 (10th Cir., 1990), In re Burns, 887 F.2d 1541 (11th Cir., 1989), In re Hopkins, 131 B.R. 308 (ND TX, 1991), and In Pierce v. U.S., 184 B.R. 338 (ND IA, 1995).

tax penalties, when dischargeable, general rule

tax penalty on return more than 3 years old held dischargeable

In In re Frary, 117 B.R. 541 (AK, 1990), penalties were assessed by the IRS with respect to taxes for which the return was due more than 3 years prior to the bankruptcy filing date. However, the taxes were assessed by the IRS within 240 days of the bankruptcy filing date and were therefore nondischargeable. The court held that the "transaction or event" that gave rise to the penalty was the debtor's failure to file his return and pay the taxes when due and not the assessment of the taxes and that the penalties were dischargeable (even though the tax was nondischargeable) because the transaction or event that gave rise to the penalty occurred more than 3 years prior to the bankruptcy filing date.

tax penalty on return more than 3 years old, when non-dischargeable

Some courts, however, have ruled that penalties assessed with respect to nondischargeable tax debts are nondischargeable even if they were imposed with respect to a transaction or event that occurred more than 3 years prior to the bankruptcy filing date. See Cassidy v. Comm., 814 F.2d 477 (7th Cir., 1987); but see 892 F.2d 637 (for a later proceeding in the same case that implicitly disapproves this ruling). The reason for such rulings is that subpart A indirectly incorporates an extendable 3 year period of limitation for nondischargeability by rendering penalties imposed on nonpriority tax debts dischargeable and that to avoid contradiction the intent of Congress was that subpart B should apply only to penalties that do not relate directly to a tax, such as late-filing penalties, negligence penalties, and civil fraud penalties. See In re Carlton, 19 B.R. 73 (NM, 1982); In re Oldfield, 121 B.R. 249 (ED AR, 1990); In re Harris, 59 B.R. 545 (WD VA, 1986) (In re Feingold, 474 B.R. 293 (Bankr. S. D. Fla. 2012) (holding penalties assessed in attorney discipline action nondischargeable).

tax debt interest, types of in bankruptcy cases

The dischargeability of interest on tax debts. In bankruptcy cases two types of interest may be claimed with respect to a tax debt by the IRS or other taxing authority: prepetition interest and postpetition interest. The dischargeability of postpetition interest is usually an issue only in Chapter 11 reorganization cases, but may be an issue in a Chapter 13 case, especially if a Section 1328(b) discharge is granted. The dischargeability of postpetition interest on tax debts is seldom an issue in Chapter 7 consumer cases unless there are sufficient assets in the debtor's estate from which to pay the tax debt.

prepetition interest on tax debt, dischargeability of, general rule

The general rule is that prepetition interest on nondischargeable tax debts is nondischargeable to the same extent as the tax upon which the interest has accrued. See In re Hardee, 137 F.3d 337 (5th Cir., 1998), In re Miller, 284 B.R. 121 (ND CA, 2002), Leahey v. U.S., 169 B.R. 96 (NJ, 1994), and Pierce v. U.S., 184 B.R. 338 (ND IA, 1995). It is generally held that matured prepetition interest on a tax debt constitutes part of the taxing authority's claim and is therefore nondischargeable to the same extent as the underlying tax debt. See In re Larson, 862 F.2d 112 (7th Cir., 1988), and Ward v. Bd. of Equalization, 204 F.3d 888 (9th Cir., 2000). A few courts have held that prepetition interest on a tax debt constitutes a nonpunitive penalty under 11 U.S.C. § 507(a)(8)(G) and is therefore nondischargeable under Section 523(a)(1)(A). See In re Reich, 66 B.R. 554 (CO, 1986), and In re Avant, 110 B.R. 264 (WD TX, 1989). Of course, if the underlying tax debt is found to be dischargeable, then the interest that has accrued on the tax debt is also dischargeable.

Postpetition interest (i.e., interest that accrues on a tax debt during the pendency of a bankruptcy case) on a nondischargeable tax debt is also generally held to be nondischargeable. See Bruning v. U.S., 376 U.S. 358, 84 S.Ct. 906 (1964); Matter of Johnson, 146 F.3d 252 (5th Cir., 1998); Burns v. U.S., 887 F.2d 1541 (11th Cir., 1989); In re Hanna, 872 F.2d 829 (8th Cir., 1989); In re Reich, 66 B.R. 554 (CO, 1986); Pierce v. U.S., 184 B.R. 338 (ND IA, 1995). Even if a nondischargeable tax debt is paid by the trustee, a debtor may remain personally liable for any unpaid postpetition interest that accrues on the debt during the pendency of the case. See In re Stine, 81 B.R. 641 (ND FL, 1988) (holding that a Chapter 7 debtor may be liable for postpetition interest on a nondischargeable tax debt up to the date of payment of the debt by the trustee).

postpetition interest on tax debt, dischargeability of

Suspending periods of limitation for tax debts. Sections 523(a)(1) and 523(a)(7) both specify periods of limitation (or lookback periods), the expiration of which will render a tax debt or penalty dischargeable. For example, an income tax debt is dischargeable if 3 or more years have expired between the last due date of the tax return and the bankruptcy filing date, provided that the tax was assessed more than 240 days prior to the bankruptcy filing date. Both of these lookback periods, however, may be suspended or tolled by agreement, by the application of another statute, or by the filing of a bankruptcy case.

periods of limitation for tax debt non-dischargeability, examples of

A long line of cases developed the general rule that the filing of a bankruptcy case tolls the periods of limitation specified in Sections 523(a)(1) and 523(a)(7) for the period during which the holder of the claim is precluded by the automatic stay from collecting the claim. See Young v. U.S., 535 U.S. 43,122 S. Ct. 1036 (2002); In re Klingshirn, 147 F.3d 526 (6th Cir., 1998); In re Taylor, 81 F.3d 20 (3d Cir., 1996); Molina v. U.S., 99 B.R. 792 (SD OH, 1988); Florence v. IRS, 115 B.R. 109 (SD OH, 1990); Bowling v. U.S., 147 B.R. 383 (ED VA, 1992); Jones v. U.S., 177 B.R. 541 (ND OH, 1994); In re Harris, 167 B.R. 680 (MD FL, 1994); Clark v. IRS, 184 B.R. 728 (ND TX, 1995).

filing of bankruptcy case, effect of on periods of limitation, general rule

The BAPCPA codified this line of cases with an unnumbered paragraph at the end of section 507(a)(8). The new paragraph reads as follows:

section 507(a)(8), new paragraph

> An otherwise applicable time period specified in this paragraph shall be suspended for any period during which a governmental unit is prohibited under applicable nonbankruptcy law from collecting a tax as a result of a request by the debtor for a hearing and an appeal of any collection action taken or proposed against the debtor, plus 90 days; plus any time during which the stay of proceedings was in effect in a prior case under this title or during which collection was precluded by the existence of 1 or more confirmed plans under this title, plus 90 days.

section 507(a)(8), text of new paragraph

Priority now extends to tax debts for taxes assessed during the 240 day period prior to filing a case, plus any time that a stay was in effect, plus 90 days. If a hearing or an appeal is requested for a tax debt, the time is also extended during any such action.

Section 507(a)(8) effect of new paragraph

payment of non-dischargeable tax claim by codebtor or guarantor, non-dischargeability of payors claim

Subrogated nondischargeability for tax debts. 11 U.S.C. § 509(a) provides that "an entity that is liable with the debtor on, or that has secured, a claim of a creditor against the debtor, and that pays such claim, is subrogated to the rights of such creditor to the extent of such payment." If a codebtor or surety of a debtor pays a nondischargeable tax debt of the debtor, this provision is generally construed to render nondischargeable the resulting debt owed to the subrogee by the debtor or the debtor's estate. See In re Stephenson, 100 AFTR 2d 6787 (ED VA, 2007), In re Fields, 926 F.2d 501 (5th Cir., 1991), Travelers Indem. Co. v. Rose, 139 B.R. 878 (WD TN, 1992), and In re Woerner, 19 B.R. 708 (KS, 1982). The provision in 11 U.S.C. § 507(d) that provides that a subrogee of a claim under 11 U.S.C. § 507(a)(8) is not subrogated to the priority rights of the claim does not prevent the subrogated claim from being nondischargeable under Section 523(a)(1). See In re Cooper, 83 B.R. 544 (CD IL, 1988), and In re Norris, 107 B.R. 592 (ED TN, 1989). Note that the claim of a subrogee who paid a nondischargeable federal tax may also be nondischargeable under 11 U.S.C. § 523(a)(14) which provides nondischargeability for debts incurred to pay a nondischargeable federal tax.

payment of tax claim by debtor's spouse, non-dischargeability of spouse's claim against debtor

If a separated or divorced spouse pays a nondischargeable tax debt that is owed by both spouses jointly but the payment of which was assigned to the other spouse in the divorce or separation proceeding, the claim of the paying spouse against the other spouse is generally held to be nondischargeable under Section 523(a)(1). See In re Cooper, 83 B.R. 544 (CD IL, 1988), In re Lane, 82 B.R. 544 (HI, 1988); In re Caffrey, 77 B.R. 219 (WD MO, 1987). However, in In re Campbell, 74 B.R. 805 (MD FL, 1987), the court held that as a matter of law there can be no subrogation of a federal tax claim and that the ex-wife of the debtor, who paid the tax for the debtor upon the debtor's promise to indemnify her, may not assert that her claim against the debtor for indemnification is nondischargeable under Section 523(a)(1).

payment of tax debt by surety, non-dischargeability of surety's claim

A surety or guarantor of the debtor who pays a nondischargeable tax debt owed by the debtor is subrogated to the taxing authority's right of nondischargeability for the debt under Section 523(a)(1). See, e.g., In re Fields, 926 F.2d 501 (5th Cir., 1991); In re Waite, 698 F.2d 1177 (11th Cir., 1983); Travelers Indem. Co. v. Rose, 139 B.R. 878 (WD TN, 1992); In re Norris, 107 B.R. 592 (ED TN, 1989); In re Trasks' Charolais, 84 B.R. 646 (SD, 1988); In re Hancock, 36 B.R. 709 (SD IL, 1984).

non-dischargeability of subrogee's claim, requirements

In order for a subrogated claim to be nondischargeable under Section 523(a)(1), the subrogee must have a valid right of subrogation to the claim. In In re Smothers, 60 B.R. 733 (WD KY, 1986), the court held that the claim against the debtor of a partner of the debtor who paid state partnership taxes on the debtor's behalf was dischargeable under Section 523(a)(1) even though the agreement between the parties provided that the debtor would pay the taxes and indemnify the partner for any taxes paid by the partner, because the partner paid the taxes as part of his legal obligation as a partner and was not entitled to subrogation for paying his own obligation.

Bibliography. For further reading on the issues discussed in this article, see the annotations and articles listed below.

Annotations:

Debts Arising From Tax Penalties as Exceptions to Bankruptcy Discharge Under Sections 523(a)(7)(A) and (B) of the Bankruptcy Code of 1978. 157 ALR Fed 313.

Treatment under 11 U.S.C. § 507(a)(7) of sales and use tax claims arising prior to filing of bankruptcy petition. 107 ALR Fed 526.

Codebtor's subrogation rights under 11 U.S.C. § §509. 86 ALR Fed 886.

Extensions of time under §108(c) of the Bankruptcy Code. 83 ALR Fed 528.

Right of taxing authority to collect post-petition interest on tax claim in bankruptcy or related proceedings. 13 ALR Fed 877.

Debts Arising from Penalties as Exceptions to Bankruptcy Discharge Under §§ 523(a)(7), (13) and 1328(a) of Bankruptcy Code of 1978 (11 U.S.C.A. §§ 523(a)(7), (13), and 1328(a)). 150 ALR Fed 159.

Articles:

Borrowing from the taxpayer: state and local tax claims in bankruptcy. 4 Am. Bankruptcy Instit. L. Rev. 201, Spring, 1996.

Discharging tax liability in bankruptcy. 42 Pract. Lawyer 41, Mar. 1996.

"Willfulness" and attempts to evade or defeat taxes under the Bankruptcy Code's Section 523(a)(1)(C) exception to discharge. 3 Am. Bankruptcy Instit. L. Rev. 469, Winter, 1995.

Property taxes in bankruptcy: Section 546(b), Section 506(c), and lien survival. 2 J. Bankruptcy L. & Pract. 277, July - Aug., 1993.

When tax evaders go bankrupt: the bankruptcy exception to debt discharge and "willfulness" in tax crimes. 27 Suffolk Univ. L. Rev. 5, Spring, 1993.

Prepetition tax levies on intangible property: the aftermath of Whiting Pools. 9 Bankruptcy Dev. J. 587, 1993.

Tax claims in bankruptcy. 67 Am. Bankruptcy L.J. 343, Summer, 1993.

1.11 To what extent are debts obtained by fraud, false pretenses, or false financial statements nondischargeable in bankruptcy?

Text of statute. Section 523(a)(2) of the Bankruptcy Code (11 U.S.C. § 523(a)(2)) is applicable to the subject discussed in this article. It provides as follows:

523. Exceptions to discharge

(a) A discharge under section 727, 1141, 1228(a), 1228(b), or 1328(b) of this title does not discharge an individual debtor from any debt -

* * * * * *

(2) for money, property, services, or an extension, renewal, or refinancing of credit, to the extent obtained by -

(A) false pretenses, a false representation, or actual fraud, other than a statement respecting the debtor's or an insider's financial condition;

Section 523(a)(2), text of

(B) use of a statement in writing -

(i) that is materially false;

(ii) respecting the debtor's or an insider's financial condition;

(iii) on which the creditor to whom the debtor is liable for such money, property, services, or credit reasonably relied; and

(iv) that the debtor caused to be made or published with intent to deceive; or

(C)(i) for purposes of subparagraph (A) –

(I) consumer debts owed to a single creditor and aggregating more than $600 for luxury goods or services incurred by an individual debtor on or within 90 days before the order for relief under this title are presumed to be nondischargeable; and

(II) cash advances aggregating more than $875 that are extensions of consumer credit under an open end credit plan obtained by an individual debtor on or within 70 days before the order for relief under this title, are presumed to be nondischargeable; and

(ii) for purposes of this subparagraph –

(I) the terms "consumer", "credit", and "open end credit plan" have the same meanings as in section 103 of the Truth in Lending Act; and

(II) the term "luxury goods or services" does not include goods or services reasonably necessary for the support or maintenance of the debtor or a dependent of the debtor.

Section 523(a)(2), history of statute

Introduction. Section 523(a)(2) was enacted in the Bankruptcy Reform Act of 1978. Originally this section contained only subparts A and B. Subpart C was added in 1984, when minor revisions throughout the section were made. In 1994 the presumptive amount for luxury goods and services in subpart C was increased from $500 to $1,000, the presumptive prebankruptcy period for luxury goods and services was increased from 40 days to 60 days, and the presumptive prebankruptcy period for cash advances was increased from 20 days to 60 days. In 1998 the presumptive amounts were raised to $1,150.

In 2005, the BAPCPA amended section 523(a)(2)(C) so as to broaden the scope of presumptively nondischargeable consumer debts for luxury goods or services by lowering the amount of a covered debt from $1150 to $500 and by extending the period in which a covered debt may be incurred from 60 days to 90 days prior to bankruptcy. For example, under prior law a consumer debt for luxury goods of $1000 would have been dischargeable. Under the BAPCPA amendment this debt would be presumptively nondischargeable. Under prior law a $5,000 debt for luxury goods incurred 65 days prior to bankruptcy would be dischargeable. Under the BAPCPA amendment this debt would be presumptively nondischargeable

§523(a)(2), BAPCPA amendments to

The BAPCPA amendment also broadened the scope of nondischargeable cash advances by lowering the amount of a covered debt from $1150 to $750 and by extending the period in which a covered debt may be incurred from 60 days to 70 days prior to bankruptcy. However, the BAPCPA amendment did not change the definition of "luxury goods or services" and the definition of "open end credit plan" in section 103 of the Truth in Lending Act is identical to that provided under prior law. See 15 U.S.C. § 1602(i). The definitions of "consumer" and "credit" in section 103 of the Truth in Lending Act also do not change prior law. See 15 U.S.C. § 1602(e), (h). In 2010, the dollar amounts contained in section 523(a)(2)(C)(i) were adjusted to $600 and $875, pursuant to 11 U.S.C. § 104(b). The dollar amounts are scheduled for adjustment again in April, 2013.

§523(a)(2), BAPCPA amendments to

dollar amount changes pursuant to § 104(b)

It should be noted that debts for fraud or defalcation while acting in a fiduciary capacity are nondischargeable under Section 523(a)(4) of the Bankruptcy Code. The nondischargeability of debts under that section is not discussed in this article.

fiduciary fraud, non-dischargeability of debts for

Section 523(a)(2) is applicable to Chapter 7 cases and to Chapter 13 cases wherein the debtor is granted a "best efforts" discharge under 11 U.S.C. § 1328(b), as well as to Chapter 13 cases wherein the debtor receives a completed plan discharge under 11 U.S.C. § 1328(a).

Section 523(a)(2), applicability to Chapter 7 and Chapter 13 cases

Nondischargeability under Section 523(a)(2) is not self-executing. This means that a debt meeting the criteria of Section 523(a)(2) (i.e., a debt obtained by fraud, falsity, or a false written financial statement) will be discharged unless the creditor successfully challenges the dischargeability of the debt in the debtor's bankruptcy proceeding. For a debt to be nondischargeable under Section 523(a)(2), then, the creditor to whom the debt is owed must file a request to determine the dischargeability of the debt within the required period and the bankruptcy court, after notice and a hearing, must find the debt to be nondischargeable. See 11 U.S.C. § 523(c)(1). Unless the debt is presumed to be nondischargeable under Section 523(a)(2)(C), the burden of proof on the issue of nondischargeability is on the creditor, who must establish nondischargeability by a preponderance of the evidence. See Grogan v. Garner, 498 U.S. 279, 111 S.Ct. 654 (1991).

non-dischargeability under Section 523(a)(2), necessity of creditor action

Section 523(a)(2), determining dischargeability of debt under, procedure in Chapter 7 case

The procedure for determining the dischargeability of debts under Section 523(a)(2) is governed by 11 U.S.C. § 523(c)(1) and by Bankruptcy Rule 4007(c) in Chapter 7 cases and Bankruptcy Rule 4007(d) in Chapter 13 cases wherein the debtor requests a discharge under 11 U.S.C. § 1328(b). Nondischargeability hearings are core proceedings under 28 U.S.C. § § 157(b). See In re Smith, 84 B.R. 175 (AZ, 1988). There is no right to a jury trial in nondischargeability hearings. See Goodale v. Duffy, 317 B.R. 49 (RI, 2004). In a Chapter 7 case the creditor to whom the debt is owed must file a complaint to determine the dischargeability of the debt within 60 days after the first date set for the meeting of creditors, unless, on the motion of a party in interest made within the 60-day period, the court for cause extends the time for such filing. See Bankruptcy Rule 4007(c). A creditor who fails to meet these time requirements may not challenge the dischargeability of a debt under Section 523(a)(2). See In re Thomason, 288 B.R. 809 (SD IL, 2002); In re Hill, 811 F.2d 484 (9th Cir., 1987). This deadline may not be extended for excusable neglect. See, e.g., In re Gordon, 988 F.2d 1000 (9th Cir., 1993); In re Nordin, 299 B.R. 915 (B.A.P. 8th Cir., 2003).

determination of dischargeability procedure in Chapter 13 cases

In a Chapter 13 case where the debtor has requested a discharge under 11 U.S.C. § 1328(b) the time for filing complaints to determine the dischargeability of debts under Section 523(a)(2) must be fixed by the court. At least 30 days' notice of the time so fixed must be given to all creditors. See Bankruptcy Rule 4007(d).

attorney's fees, when recoverable by debtor in Section 523(a)(2) proceeding

If a creditor files a complaint to determine the dischargeability of a consumer debt under Section 523(a)(2) and is unsuccessful, the debtor is entitled to recover the costs and attorney fees that he or she incurred in the contested proceeding if the court finds that the creditor's position was not substantially justified and does not find that such an award would be unjust. See 11 U.S.C. § 523(d). The subject of recovering attorney fees in nondischargeability proceedings is discussed in article 1.16 of this handbook. It should also be noted that if a debt that is nondischargeable under Section 523(a)(2) is based on a contract that provides for a recovery of the creditor's attorneys fees, then the attorney fee portion of the debt may also be nondischargeable under Section 523(a)(2). See Chase Manhattan Bank v. Birkland, 98 B.R. 35 (WD WA, 1988); In re Martin, 761 F.2d 1163 (6th Cir., 1985).

creditor's attorney's fees, when non-dischargeable under Section 523(a)(2)

Section 523(a)(2) contains three subparts, each of which provides nondischargeability for a particular type of debt. Generally speaking, a debt is nondischargeable under Section 523(a)(2)(A) if it was obtained by fraud or falsity, while a debt is nondischargeable under Section 523(a)(2)(B) if it was obtained by the use of a false written financial statement. Under Section 523(a)(2)(C), debts of more than $550 incurred within 90 days of filing for luxury goods or services or cash advances are presumed to have been obtained by fraud or falsity.

It is important to note the presence of the phrase "to the extent obtained by" in Section 523(a)(2). This phrase has been interpreted to mean that if only a portion of a debt owed to a creditor was obtained by fraud, falsity, or a false written financial statement, only that portion of the debt is nondischargeable under Section 523(a)(2), even if the entire indebtedness arose out of the same general transaction. See South Div. Credit Union v. McFarland, 179 B.R. 87 (ND IL, 1995) (where the unpaid balance of an existing loan that was consolidated with a new loan was held dischargeable despite the fact that the new loan was nondischargeable under Section 523(a)(2)(B) because it was obtained by the use of a false financial statement). See also Medley v. Owen, 181 B.R. 288 (WD VA, 1995). However, if the due date of the original loan was extended by the creditor because of the debtor's fraud or false representations, it too will be nondischargeable under Section 523(a)(2). See Cho Hung Bank v. Kim, 62 F.3d 1511 (9th Cir., 1995) (holding it is not necessary for the creditor to show that "new money" was lent to the debtor in order to obtain nondischargeability under Section 523(a)(2)). See also In re Duncan, 123 B.R. 383 (CD CA, 1991).

Section 523(a)(2), extent of non-dischargeability under

consolidated loans, extent of non-dischargeability under Section 523(a)(2)

In In re Britton, 950 F.2d 602 (9th Cir., 1991), the creditor had obtained a state court judgment based on a jury verdict against the debtor for $53,000 in compensatory damages and $250,000 for punitive damages. Of the $53,000 compensatory damage award, $45,000 was for fraud. The court held that only the $45,000 fraud portion of the $303,000 judgment was nondischargeable under Section 523(a)(2). The balance of the judgment was held to be dischargeable under Section 523(a)(2), although the court noted that the punitive damage portion of the judgment may have been nondischargeable under Section 523(a)(6). See also Medley v. Owen, 181 B.R. 288 (WD VA, 1995); Hilliard v. Peel, 166 B.R. 735 (WD OK, 1994). See article 1.08 of this handbook for a discussion of the nondischargeability of punitive damages under Section 523(a)(6) of the Bankruptcy Code.

multipart judgments, extent of non-dischargeability under Section 523(a)(2)

In order to be nondischargeable under Section 523(a)(2) a debt must be for money, property, services, or an extension, renewal or refinancing of credit. If none of these items were furnished by the creditor, the debt owed to the creditor is dischargeable under this section. See In re Ables, 302 B.R. 917 (MD FL, 2003) and In re Burgess, 955 F.2d 134 (1st Cir., 1992). In order to establish nondischargeability under Section 523(a)(2), the money, property, services, or credit must have been received by the debtor from the creditor and not from someone else. See Richard v. Dougherty, 179 B.R. 316 (MD FL, 1995); but see In re Clark, 330 B.R. 702 (CD IL, 2005) (where a $14,597 judgment was not technically "obtained" by the debtor, but the debt arose directly from the debtor's fraudulent conduct, and was therefore nondischargeable). In Jacobs v. Mones, 169 B.R. 246 (DC, 1994), the court held that to be nondischargeable under Section 523(a)(2), a debt must be for money, property or services obtained from the creditor either by the debtor or for the benefit of the debtor. The extension of a due date on a loan has been held to constitute an extension of credit under Section 523(a)(2). See In re Brandon, 297 B.R. 308 (SD GA, 2002); Cho Hung Bank v. Kim, 63 F.3d 1511 (9th Cir., 1995). See also Norris v. First Nat. Bank, 70 F.3d 27 (5th Cir., 1995). However, in In re Booher, 284 B.R. 191 (WD PA, 2002) a forbearance by the creditor from exercising an acceleration right in an equipment lease because of the debtor's false financial statement was held not to constitute an "extension of credit" for purposes of Section 523(a)(2).

non-dischargeability under Section 523(a)(2), foundational requirements

extension of credit, what constitutes

Section 523(a)(2), categories of non-dischargeability

For purposes of discussion, nondischargeability under Section 523(a)(2) may be divided into four general categories: (1) nondischargeability for false pretenses or false representations under Section 523(a)(2)(A), (2) nondischargeability for fraud under Section 523(a)(2)(A), (3) nondischargeability based on a false written financial statement under Section 523(a)(2)(B), and (4) the presumption of nondischargeability for certain consumer debts under Section 523(a)(2)(C). Each category is discussed separately below.

non-dischargeability under Section 523(a)(2), types of conduct required

The applicable provision of Section 523(a)(2) depends on whether the conduct complained of was an oral statement, an act, or a written statement. Nondischargeability for false pretenses or false representations under Section 523(a)(2)(A) is usually based on oral representations made by the debtor or written representations of matters other than the debtor's financial condition. Nondischargeability for fraud under Section 523(a)(2)(A) is broad based and may include a wide range of acts, representations or nondisclosures perpetrated or committed by the debtor. Nondischargeability under Section 523(a)(2)(B) is based on false written financial statements made by the debtor.

Section 523(a)(2), general aspects

Sections 523(a)(2)(A) and (B) are mutually exclusive because Section 523(a)(2)(A) contemplates representations of a nonwritten nature, while Section 523(a)(2)(B) expressly contemplates written representations. See, e.g, In re Reder, 60 B.R. 529 (MN, 1986). In interpreting Section 523(a)(2)(A) fraud is distinguishable from false pretenses and representations. See, e.g., Recoveredge, L.P. v. Pentecost, 44 F.3d 1284 (5th Cir., 1995). It should be noted, however, that many courts lump false pretenses, false representations and fraud together when dealing with Section 523(a)(2)(A).

Section 523(a)(2)(A), provisions of

The nondischargeability of debts obtained by false pretenses or false representations. Section 523(a)(2)(A) provides in part that debts for money, property, services, or an extension, renewal, or refinancing of credit are nondischargeable to the extent that they were obtained by false pretenses or false representations. Statements with respect to the debtor's financial conditions are expressly excluded from the operation of Section 523(a)(2)(A), presumably because they are covered under Section 523(a)(2)(B). Because it is often difficult to distinguish false pretenses and representations from fraud, many courts do not distinguish between the two and lump them together in their rulings.

false pretenses or representations, elements to be proven

Generally, in order to to establish nondischargeability for false pretenses or false representations under Section 523(a)(2)(A) a creditor must establish each of the following elements by a preponderance of the evidence:

(1) that the debtor made a representation or pretense to the creditor that was materially false;

(2) that the debtor knew the representation or pretense was false when it was made;

(3) that the debtor made the representation or pretense with an intent to deceive or defraud the creditor; and

(4) that the creditor justifiably relied on the misrepresentation or pretense to its detriment.

See Grogan v. Garner, 498 U.S. 279, 111 S.Ct. 654 (1991); In re Treadwell, 637 F.3d 855 (8th Cir. 2011); In re Schnuella, 441 B.R. 616 (B.A.P. 8th 2011); Blackstone Enterprises, Inc. v. Abejuela, 349 B.R. 536 (ND IL, 2006), In re Foxworth, 17 FLW Fed. B. 239 (ND FL, 2004), In re Biondo, 180 F.3d 126 (4th Cir., 1999), In re Ophaug, 827 F.2d 340 (8th Cir., 1987), In re Kirsh, 973 F.2d 1454 (9th Cir., 1992), In re Coston, 977 F.2d 175 (5th Cir., 1992).

A materially false representation may not be established solely by showing that the debtor failed to perform a promised act. To establish nondischargeability under Section 523(a)(2)(A) it must be shown that when the promise was made the debtor did not intend to perform the act. See In re Baker, 298 B.R. 815 (SD FL, 2003); In re Scarlata, 979 F.2d 521 (7th Cir., 1992); In re Widner, 285 B.R. 913 (WD VA, 2002). Several courts have ruled that the breach by the debtor of a promise to perform a future act, without more, does not constitute a misrepresentation for purposes of Section 523(a)(2)(A). See Namvar v. Baker, 298 B.R. 815 (SD FL, 2003); Carlan v. Dover, 185 B.R. 85 (ND GA, 1995) (where the debtor's failure to keep a promise to provide a mortgage as security for his loan from the creditor was held to be a promise to perform a future act and not a materially false representation for purposes of Section 523(a)(2)(A)).

failure to perform future act as false representation

In In re Roeder, 61 B.R. 179 (WD KY, 1986), the failure by the debtor to fulfill a promise to turn over his income tax refund to the creditor was held not to be a materially false representation under Section 523(a)(2)(A). In In re Allison, 960 F.2d 481 (5th Cir., 1992) the court stated that while the breach of a promise to perform a future act does not constitute a false representation under Section 523(a)(2)(A), a misrepresentation by the debtor of his intention to perform a future act may constitute a false representation under Section 523(a)(2)(A) if it is proven that when the representation was made the debtor had no intention of performing the act. In In re Young, 181 B.R. 555 (ED OK, 1995), the court stated that to find misrepresentation in connection with a broken promise for purposes of Section 523(a)(2)(A), it is not enough to show that the promise was not performed, it must be shown that there was no reasonable basis to believe that the debtor would perform when the promise was made. See also Orsine v. Orsine, 254 B.R. 184 (ND OH, 2000).

failure to perform promised act as false representation

Similarly, statements of opinion made by the debtor do not, without more, constitute false representations for purposes of Section 523(a)(2)(A). Representations as to the value of property made by the debtor are generally statements of opinion and, as such, are not false representations under Section 523(a)(2)(A). See, e.g., Loomas v. Evans, 181 B.R. 508 (SD CA, 1995).

statements of opinion as false representations

While a few courts have held that a mere nondisclosure cannot constitute a false representation or pretense under Section 523(a)(2)(A) (see In re Reder, 60 B.R. 529 (MN, 1986), and In re Weinberg, 81 B.R. 145 (SD FL, 1987)), it is generally held that under the appropriate circumstances a deliberate failure by the debtor to disclosure relevant information can constitute a false representation or pretense under Section 523(a)(2)(A). See In re Martin, 299 B.R. 234 (CD IL, 2003); Mendez v. Cram, 178 B.R. 537 (MD FL, 1995); Resolution Trust Corp. v. Roberti, 183 B.R. 991 (CT, 1995); In re Wyatt, 87 B.R. 874 (ED VA, 1988).

nondisclosure of information as false pretense or representation

importance of debtor's belief in truth of representation

To establish nondischargeability for false representation under Section 523(a)(2)(A), the creditor must show that the debtor knew or should reasonably have known when the representation was made that it was false. See Recoveredge, L.P. v. Pentecost, 44 F.3d 1284 (5th Cir., 1995); In re Siriani, 967 F.2d 302 (9th Cir., 1992). If the debtor in good faith believed the representation was true when made, then the debt is dischargeable under this section even if the representation later turns out to be false. See In re Villalobos, 462 B.R. 712 (Bankr. S. D. Iowa 2011). In Bank One Lafayette, N.A. v. Larisey, 185 B.R. 877 (MD FL, 1995), a debt for the purchase of new carpeting just prior to bankruptcy was found to be dischargeable under Section 523(a)(2) because of the debtor's belief that funds to pay the debt would be generated either by the sale of the house in which the carpeting was installed or by a new job that the debtor had hoped to obtain.

false representation, importance of showing intent to deceive

It is clear that for a debt to be nondischargeable under Section 523(a)(2)(A) on the basis of false representation or false pretenses, the misrepresentation must be made by the debtor with the present intent of deceiving or defrauding the creditor. See In re Bowden, 326 B.R. 62 (ED VA, 2005); Bonnett v. National Bank of Petersburg, 73 B.R. 715 (CD IL, 1987); In re Hunter, 83 B.R. 803 (MD FL, 1988). An intent to deceive may also be inferred from the debtor's acts or established by the surrounding circumstances. See In re Hultquist, 101 B.R. 180 (B.A.P. 9th Cir., 1989); Kuper v. Spar, 176 B.R. 321 (SD NY, 1994); In re Black, 787 F.2d 503 (10th Cir., 1986). However, an intent to deceive cannot be inferred from the use of a credit card by an insolvent debtor. See In re Way, 260 B.R. 291 (MD FL, 2000) (holding that a credit card holder did not make an implied representation of intention or ability to pay by using a credit card while insolvent). See also Chase Bank v. Brumbaugh, 383 B.R. 907 (ND OH, 2007); Citibank v. Olwan, 312 B.R. 476 (ED NY, 2004). However, in MBNA Am. Bank, N.A. v. Hostetter, 328 B.R. 674 (ND IN, 2005), the court ruled that a card issuer can make a prima facie case of nondischargeability under section 523(a)(2)(A) by presenting evidence that a debtor, based upon her income, debt structure, and fixed expenses could not even make the minimum payments on the card while keeping current on other obligations. At the time the debtor incurred a $5,574.40 credit card debt, she owed $169,478.00 in other credit card debt.

reliance by creditor on debtors mis-representation, level of reliance required

justifiable reliance, what constitutes

To establish nondischargeability under Section 523(a)(2)(A) on the basis of false representations or pretenses the creditor justifiably relied on the debtor's misrepresentations. In Field v. Mans, 516 U.S. 59, 116 S.Ct. 437 (1995), the Supreme Court rejected the standards of "reasonable reliance" and "reliance in fact" in favor of the standard of "justifiable reliance." "Justifiable reliance" is reliance that is both actual and justifiable under the circumstances. Quoting from Restatement (2nd) of Torts, the court stated "[a]lthough the plaintiff's reliance on the misrepresentation must be justifiable... this does not mean that his conduct must conform to the standard of the reasonable man. Justification is a matter of the qualities and characteristics of the particular plaintiff, and the circumstances of the particular case, rather than of the application of a community standard of conduct to all cases." Justifiable reliance, therefore, is less demanding of the creditor (and therefore easier to prove) than reasonable reliance, but more demanding (and therefore harder to prove) than reliance in fact or actual reliance. See Universal Bank v. Stephens, 302 B.R. 218 (ND OH, 2003) (holding a credit card issuer's lack of conducting a credit check on the debtor was evidence that there was no justifiable reliance on the debtor's fraudulent representations).

In Field v. Mans, the issue before the court was the level of reliance required to establish "actual fraud" under Section 523(a)(2)(A). The case, while dealing with Section 523(a)(2)(A), did not involve allegations of false pretenses or false representations. Footnote 8 of the court's opinion stated: "Although we do not mean to suggest that the requisite level of reliance would differ if there should be a case of false pretense or representation but not of fraud, there is no need to settle that here." Technically, then, Field v. Mans does not specify the level of reliance necessary to establish false pretenses or false representations. However, until the court rules otherwise it is probably safe to assume that "justifiable reliance" is sufficient in false pretense or false representation cases because it is difficult to imagine that different standards of reliance would be required for conduct as closely related as fraud and false pretenses or representations.

justifiable reliance, importance of in false representation

The nondischargeability of debts obtained by actual fraud. Section 523(a)(2)(A) provides in part that debts for money, property, services, or an extension, renewal or refinancing of credit are nondischargeable to the extent that they were obtained by actual fraud. Statements with respect to the debtor's financial condition are excluded from the operation of Section 523(a)(2)(A), presumably because they are covered under Section 523(a)(2)(B). See In re Sacco, 270 B.R. 382 (WD PA, 2001).

Section 523(a)(2)(A), provisions of with respect to actual fraud

In Field v. Mans, 516 U.S. 59, 116 S.Ct. 437 (1995), the Supreme Court held that the term "actual fraud" in Section 523(a)(2)(A) incorporates the general common law definition of fraud rather than its definition under the law of any particular state. Actual fraud under Section 523(a)(2)(A), is any deceit, artifice, trick or design involving direct and active operation of mind, used to circumvent and cheat another person. Recoveredge, L.P. v. Pentecost, 44 F.3d 1284 (5th Cir., 1995). Something said, done or omitted with the design of perpetrating what is known to be cheat or deception. Fraud may consist of silence, concealment, or intentional nondisclosure of material fact, as well as affirmative misrepresentation of material fact. See, e.g., In re Schmidt, 70 B.R. 634 (ND IN, 1986); In re Van Horne, 823 F.2d 1285 (8th Cir., 1987).

actual fraud, what constitutes

In order to prove actual fraud under Section 523(a)(2)(A) a creditor must prove the following factors by a preponderance of the evidence:

actual fraud, matters to be proven

(1) that the debtor made a representation or concealment;
(2) that the debtor knew the representation or concealment was false or fraudulent when it was made or made the representation or concealment with a reckless disregard for the truth;
(3) that the representation or concealment was intended to deceive the creditor;
(4) that the creditor justifiably relied on the representation or concealment; and
(5) that the creditor sustained a loss as a result of the representation or concealment.

See Recoveredge, L.P. v. Pentecost, 44 F.3d 1284 (5th Cir., 1995), In re Alport, 144 F.3d 1163 (8th Cir., 1998), In re Rembert, 141 F.3d 277 (6th Cir., 1998), Rodriquez v. Volpentesta, 187 B.R. 261 (ND IL, 1995), In re Mayerson, 254 B.R. 407 (ND OH, 2000), and In re Nappy, 269 B.R. 277 (ED NY, 1999).

Section 523(a)(2)(A), type of fraud required

Generally, in order to render a debt nondischargeable under Section 523(a)(2)(A) the fraud must involve moral turpitude or intentional wrongdoing by the debtor. It must affirmatively appear that the false representation or fraudulent concealment was knowingly and fraudulently made. Fraud implied in law, which may exist without bad faith, is insufficient to establish nondischargeability under Section 523(a)(2)(A). See In re Foreman, 906 F.2d 123 (5th Cir., 1990); In re Maranzino, 67 B.R. 394 (KS, 1986); In re Van de Water, 180 B.R. 283 (NM, 1995). In Cohen v. De La Cruz, 523 U.S. 213, 118 S. Ct. 1212 (1998), a debt for a treble damages award based on an order by a local rent control administrator to refund excessive rents was held to be nondischargeable as a debt obtained by actual fraud by the debtor/landlord under Section 523(a)(2)(A). In re Vanarthos, 445 B.R. 257 (Bankr. S. D. N.Y. 2011 (holding credit card charges in month prior to bankruptcy created inference of fraud); but see In re May, 448 B.R. 197 (W. D. Mich. 2011) (holding cash advances just prior to bankruptcy not fraudulent under circumstances).

fraudulently incurred credit card debt.

Credit card debt is often incurred fraudulently prior to bankruptcy. Courts consider may factors when determining whether debtor fraudulently incurred credit card debt that he did not intend to repay, including: (1) length of time between charges and filing of bankruptcy petition; (2) whether bankruptcy attorney was consulted before charges were incurred; (3) number of charges; (4) financial condition of debtor when charges were made; (5) whether charges exceeded credit limit of account; (6) whether there were multiple charges on same day (7) whether debtor was employed; (8) financial sophistication of debtor; (9) whether debtor's spending habits suddenly changed; (10) whether purchases were made for luxuries or necessities.; and (11) debtor's lack of ability to repay debt, including whether he was hopelessly insolvent at time charges were incurred. In re Vanarthos, 445 B.R. 257 (Bankr. S.D.N.Y. 2011).

justifiable reliance by creditor, definition of

In Field v. Mans, 516 U.S. 59, 116 S.Ct. 437 (1995), the Supreme Court held that the level or standard of reliance by a creditor on the debtor's misrepresentation or concealment necessary to establish actual fraud under Section 523(a)(2)(A) was that of justifiable reliance. Justifiable reliance is reliance that is justified under the circumstances of the case. See the discussion of justifiable reliance under the previous heading in this article.

Field v. Mans, facts of case

In Field v. Mans, supra, the creditors sold a parcel of real estate to a corporation controlled by the debtor. The debtor supplied part of the purchase price and personally guaranteed a promissory note for the balance. The note was secured by a second mortgage on the property and contained a due-on-sale clause. A few months after the sale title to the property was conveyed by the debtor to a partnership without the creditors' consent and in violation of the due-on-sale clause in the note. The debtor then sent the creditors a letter requesting a waiver of the due-on-sale provision in the note but did not disclose the fact that title to the property had been transferred. The waiver was not granted by the creditors. Three years later the debtor filed Chapter 11 bankruptcy, whereupon the creditors discovered that the property had been transferred in violation of the due-on-sale clause in the note. The creditors then filed a complaint in the bankruptcy proceeding alleging that the $150,000 balance of the note was due when the property was transferred and that the resulting debt was nondischargeable under the actual fraud provisions of Section 523(a)(2)(A). The bankruptcy court ruled that although the creditors had relied to their detriment on the debtor's misrepresentation and concealment in extending credit to the debtor (i.e., in not demanding payment under the due-on-sale clause), the debt was dischargeable because the reliance was not reasonable under circumstances because a reasonably prudent person would have checked the real estate records for a conveyance after receiving the debtor's request for a waiver of the due-on-sale clause. The Supreme Court ruled that the bankruptcy court had erred in applying the "reasonable man" standard for reliance and remanded the case with instructions to determine whether justifiable reliance had been established by the creditors; that is, whether the creditors reliance on the debtor's misrepresentation was justified under the circumstances of the case.

In In re Kirsh, 973 F.2d 1454 (9th Cir., 1992), an attorney who relied on the debtor's misrepresentation about property without researching the real estate records did not justifiably rely on the false representations for purposes of establishing actual fraud under Section 523(a)(2)(A). In In re Oh, 278 B.R. 844 (CD CA, 2002), the debtor was found to have induced a bank to open a checking account by falsely representing that he was the owner of a business. The court held that overdrafts on the account paid by the bank were nondischargeable under Section 523(a)(2)(A) because the bank relied on the false representations in opening the account and but for opening the account the bank would not have sustained the loss. See also In re Vann, 67 F.3d 277, (11th Cir., 1995); Sedlacek, 327 B.R. 872 (ED TN, 2005).

justifiable reliance, what constitutes, cases

A wide range of acts have been held to constitute actual fraud under Section 523(a)(2)(A). The undertaking of a financial obligation without intending to repay it constitutes actual fraud under Section 523(a)(2)(A). See, e.g., In re Tipple, 80 B.R. 93 (ND OH, 1987); In re Rusu, 188 B.R. 325 (ND GA, 1995). Causing another female to falsely pose as the debtor's wife for the purpose of signing loan documents was held to constitute actual fraud under Section 523(a)(2)(A) in Automotive Fin. Servs. v. Youndblood, 167 B.R. 870 (WD TN, 1994). Obtaining the renewal of a note from his mother-in-law 4 days before leaving his wife and 12 days before filing for divorce was held to constitute actual fraud under Section 523(a)(2)(A) in In re Van Horne, 823 F.2d 1285 (8th Cir., 1987), because the debtor failed to disclose his intent to leave and the family relationship was the only reason the note was renewed. However, the issuance of a worthless check to purchase goods, in itself, was held not to constitute actual fraud under Section 523(a)(2)(A) in In re Hunter, 83 B.R. 803 (MD FL, 1988). See also, Gadtke v. Bren, 284 B.R. 681 (MN, 2002), where the signing of a lien waiver by the creditor in exchange for the debtor's check, which was subsequently dishonored, was held not to constitute fraud under Section 523(a)(2)(A) absent a showing that the debtor knew or intended at the time of issuance that the check would be dishonored. Finally, in Archer v. Warner, 538 U.S. 314, 123 S.Ct. 1462 (2003), the Supreme Court held that Section 523(a)(2)(A) is broad enough to cover a fraud debt that was embodied in a subsequent agreement that settled the fraud debt, thus making the settlement agreement nondischargeable even though it released the debtor from every state-law claim.

actual fraud, what constitutes, cases

The nondischargeability of debts obtained by false written financial statements. Section 523(a)(2)(B) provides that debts for money, property, services, or an extension, renewal or refinancing of credit are nondischargeable to the extent that they were obtained by the use of a statement in writing that is materially false with respect to the debtor's financial condition, upon which the creditor reasonably relied, and that the debtor caused to be made or published with an intent to deceive.

Section 523(a)(2)(B), provisions of

non-dischargeability under Section 523(a)(2)(B), matters to be proven

Generally, to establish the nondischargeability of a debt under Section 523(a)(2)(B), a creditor must prove the following by a preponderance of the evidence:

(1) that the debt in question was for money, property, services or an extension, renewal or refinancing of credit;

(2) that a written statement with respect to the debtor's financial condition was used to obtain the debt;

(3) that the written statement was materially false as to the debtor's financial condition;

(4) that the creditor reasonably relied upon the written statement in providing the debtor with money, property, services, or an extension of credit; and

(5) that the debtor published or caused the written statement to be made with an intent to deceive the creditor.

See In re Oster, 474 Fed. Appx. 422 (6th Cir. 2012); In re Schnuelle, 441 B.R. 616 (B.A.P. 8th 2011); In re Kroh, 87 B.R. 1004 (WD MO, 1988); In re Herke, 92 B.R. 962 (SD FL, 1988) (stating nondischargeability under Section 523(a)(2)(B) requires active and intentional wrongdoing by misrepresentation and deceit).

The foundational requirement in (1) above that the debt be for money, property, services, or an extension of credit is discussed above in the Introduction segment of this article.

written financial statement, what constitutes

As for requirement (2) above that a written statement with respect to the debtor's financial condition be used to obtain the debt, for purposes of Section 523(a)(2)(B) a statement respecting the debtor's financial condition requires a balance sheet, profit and loss statement, or accounting document and not a mere statement as to a single asset or liability. See In re Sansoucy, 136 B.R. 20 (NH, 1992). In In re Cassel, 322 B.R. 363 (CD IL, 2005), oral statements were not included in Section 523(a)(2)(B). The signing of a lease did not constitute the use of a statement in writing for purposes of Section 523(a)(2)(B) in Lewis v. Chew, 182 B.R. 341 (ND AL, 1995). A short check issued by the debtor was held not to be a "statement in writing" for purposes of Section 523(a)(2)(B) in In re Lahiri, 225 B.R. 582 (ED PA, 1998) and In re Brzakala, 305 B.R. 705 (ND IL, 2004). A credit card application was held not to be a written statement with respect to debtor's financial condition for purposes of Section 523(a)(2)(B) in Signet Bank/Virginia v. Hale, 139 B.R. 41 (MD FL, 1992), because it did not require any information regarding the debtor's liabilities or assets except home ownership. However, in First Int'l Bank v. Kerbaugh, 162 B.R. 255 (ND, 1993), a credit card application was not a valid written statement with respect to the debtor's financial condition for purposes of Section 523(a)(2)(B). Obviously, much depends on the type and extent of the financial information required in the application. Generally, a statement that does not set forth the debtor's net worth or overall financial condition is insufficient to establish nondischargeability under Section 523(a)(2)(B). See In re Kirsh, 973 F.2d 1454 (9th Cir., 1992); Gehlhausen v. Olinger, 160 B.R. 1004 (SD IN, 1993); Jokay Co. v. Mercado, 144 B.R. 879 (CD CA, 1992); In re Chivers, 275 B.R. 606 (UT, 2002).

To form the basis of nondischargeability under Section 523(a)(2)(B), a written financial statement must have been either signed by the debtor, prepared by the debtor, or adopted and used by the debtor. See In re Martin, 299 B.R. 234 (CD IL, 2003); In re Kaspar, 200 B.R. 399 (CO, 1996); First Fed. S. & L. Assn. v. Kelley, 163 B.R. 27 (ED NY, 1993); Riggs Nat. Bank v. Ross, 180 B.R. 130 (ED VA, 1994). See also, Southern Commerce Bank v. Katzman, 178 B.R. 883 (MD FL, 1995) (holding a financial statement made by the debtor's spouse that was not signed by the debtor and did not contain information supplied by the debtor was found to be insufficient to establish nondischargeability under Section 523(a)(2)(B)). See also Shelley v. Shelley, 18 FLW Fed B 275 (ND FL, 2005) (ruling that a forbearance agreement, standing alone, is not a financial agreement or financial statement).

written financial statement, preparation and signing requirements

In order for a financial statement be "materially false," for purposes of Section 523(a)(2)(B) it generally requires an important or substantial untruth in or omission from the statement. A statement is materially false if it substantially overstates assets, substantially understates liabilities, or omits significant liabilities. See Norris v. First Nat. Bank, 70 F.3d 27 (5th Cir., 1995). Statements that are essentially correct with respect to the debtor's assets and liabilities, or that the debtor reasonable believes are true, are usually not materially false for purposes of Section 523(a)(2)(B). See In re Cacciatori, 465 B.R. 545 (Bankr. C. D. Cal. 2012); In re Frugh, 133 B.R. 870 (ND OH, 1991); First Am. Bank v. Bodenstein, 168 B.R. 23 (ED NY, 1994) (holding that to be materially false under Section 523(a)(2)(B), a financial statement must paint a substantially untruthful picture of the debtor's financial condition by misrepresenting information of the type that normally affects the decision to extend credit); see also In re Adams, 312 B.R. 576 (MD NC, 2004); In re Schnuelle, 441 B.R. 616 (B.A.P. 8th 2011) (Chapter 12 debtor acted with reckless disregard where he failed to verify the information submitted); In re White, 472 B.R. 883 (E. D. Mo. 2011) (holding public assistance nondischargeable where debtor under-reported income in order to qualify).

materially false financial statement, what constitutes

Some courts use the "but for" test to determine if a financial statement is materially false. See Union Planters Bank Nat'l Ass'n v. Martin, 306 B.R. 591 (CD IL, 2004). A financial statement is more likely to be materially false if the creditor would not have permitted the debtor to incur the debt if the statement had accurately represented the debtor's financial condition. See Shawmut Bank, N.A. v. Goodrich, 999 F.2d 22 (1st Cir., 1993), and Ferraro v. Phillips, 185 B.R. 121 (ED NY, 1995). On the other hand, if it is shown that credit would have been extended even if the financial statement had been accurate, the financial statement is not likely to be found to be materially false even if the misstatements or omissions are fairly substantial. See In re Spilotros, 105 B.R. 708 (MD FL, 1989), and In re Di Marco, 105 B.R. 128 (SD FL, 1989).

materially false financial statement, importance of reliance by creditor

A loan application that stated the debtor's income as $9,578.22 per month when the income was actually only $2,917.00 per month was deemed to be materially false in In re De Julio, 322 B.R. 456 (MD FL, 2005). A financial statement was found to be materially false in In re Galizia, 108 B.R. 63 (WD PA, 1989) where the debtor incorrectly listed a computer that he did not own as an asset, failed to show a security interest in a tractor that was listed as an asset, and over-valued his office furniture. In In re Bartlett, 128 B.R. 775 (WD MO, 1991), a financial statement was found to be materially false because the debtor listed her income as $500 per month when she had no income. In In re Calvo, 111 B.R. 1003 (MD FL, 1990), a financial statement was found to be materially false because the debtor over-valued his boat by $80,000. In In re Graham, 122 B.R. 447 (MD FL, 1990), a financial statement that grossly misstated the debtors' income, falsely stated that the debtors owned their home, and falsely stated the debtor's period of employment was found to be materially false. Omitting large, yet unmatured loan

materially false financial statement, cases

guaranties was found to be materially false in In re Martin, 306 B.R. 591 (CD IL, 2004).

materially false financial statement, requirements

Financial statements that do not contain all of the debtor's outstanding obligations are usually found to be materially false. See In re Capelli, 261 B.R. 81 (CT, 2001); In re Torres, 139 B.R. 659 (ND OH, 1991); In re Barron, 126 B.R. 255 (ED TX, 1991). A failure to list a $128,000 mortgage on her financial statement was material falsity in In re Harasymiw, 895 F.2d 1170 (7th Cir., 1990). Financial statements that list as assets properties that are not owned by the debtor are also likely to be found to be materially false. See In re Hodges, 116 B.R. 558 (ND OH, 1990); In re Pretner, 110 B.R. 942 (CO, 1990); Ag Credit, ACA v. Walton, 165 B.R. 610 (ND OH, 1994); In re Gemme, 459 B.R. 493 (Bankr. D. Mass. 2011).

financial statement held not materially false, cases

On the other hand, in Benjelloun v. Robbins, 178 B.R. 299 (MA, 1995), a financial statement was not materially false even though it substantially over-valued the debtor's real estate where the debtor's estimates of value were based on an appraisal of the property that was made before a dramatic decline in real estate values. The inclusion by the debtor of deferred income as "income" on a loan application form was held not to have rendered the statement materially false for purposes of Section 523(a)(2)(B) in Berr v. FDIC, 172 B.R. 299 (B.A.P. 9th Cir., 1994). In AVCO Fin. Servs. v. Abdul' Faruq, 175 B.R. 618 (ED VA, 1994), the debtor's failure to disclose a debt on a credit application was held not to be a material omission because under the creditor's lending standards the loan would have been approved even if the debt had been disclosed. In Ramsey Nat. Bank & Trust Co. v. Dammen, 167 B.R. 545 (ND, 1994), the court held that the debtor's financial statement was not materially false where the bank loan office assisted in the preparation of the statement and any inaccuracies in the statement were either known to the bank or readily apparent on the face of the document and where most of the information on the statement was estimated. See also In re Grider, 453 B.R. 716 (Bankr. W. D. Ky. 2011) (omission of debt which debtor believed bank was not taking security interest was insufficient to establish fraud).

false financial statement, burden of proof

The creditor bears the burden of proof on the issue of whether a financial statement is materially false. See In re Weaver, 316 B.R. 705 (WD WI, 2004). In In re West, 108 B.R. 157 (SD OH, 1989), the court held that a financial statement signed by the debtor for a loan extension was not materially false because the creditor failed to submit evidence proving that the information on the statement was materially false on the day that the application was completed. That a creditor seeking nondischargeability under Section 523(a)(2)(B) must submit evidence of the falsity of the financial statement in question and may not rely on the asset values set forth in the debtor's bankruptcy schedules to establish falsity, see ITT Commercial Fin. Corp. v. Walz, 115 B.R. 353 (ND FL, 1990).

reliance by creditor on false financial statement, requirement of

Requirement (4) above requires the creditor to have reasonably relied on the debtor's financial statement in extending credit to the debtor or in providing the debtor with money, property or services. The level of creditor reliance required under Section 523(a)(2)(B) is "reasonable reliance," while the level of creditor reliance required under Section 523(a)(2)(A) is "justifiable reliance." "Reasonable reliance" means that the creditor is held to the standard of conduct of a reasonable person under the circumstances. See Field v. Mans, 516 U.S. 59, 362, 116 S.Ct. 437 (1995). Reasonable reliance, it should be noted, includes actual reliance, so if it is shown that the creditor did not actually rely on the false statement in extending credit to the debtor (i.e., if the statement was not used or if the credit would have been extended even if the statement had not been false), then reasonable reliance is not established. See AVCO Fin. Servs. v. Abdul' Faruq, 175 B.R. 618 (ED VA, 1994); Commonwealth Land Title Ins. Co. v. Homer, 168 B.R. 790 (ND GA, 1994); In re West, 108 B.R. 157 (SD OH, 1989).

reasonable reliance, definition

reasonable reliance, what constitutes, factors

The reasonableness of a creditor's reliance on the debtor's representations must be determined on a case-by-case basis in light of the totality of circumstances. In re Vann, 67 F.3d 277, 280 (11th Cir. 1995); In re Brooks, 457 B.R. 840 (N.D. Ala. 2011); In re Bonnett, 895 F.2d 1155 (7th Cir., 1989). A creditor's failure to follow its own established lending procedures can preclude a finding of reasonable reliance. See In re Harasymiw, 895 F.2d 1170 (7th Cir., 1990). Whether a creditor's reliance was reasonable in a particular case is a factual determination to be made in light of the totality of the circumstances, including (1) whether the creditor had a close personal relationship or friendship with the debtor that justified trust in the debtor's representations; (2) whether there had been any previous business dealings with the debtor that gave rise to a relationship of trust; (3) whether the debt was incurred for personal or commercial reasons; (4) whether there were any "red flags" in the transaction or representations that would have alerted a prudent lender to the possibility that the representations were not accurate, and (5) whether even minimal investigation would have revealed the inaccuracy of the debtor's representations. See In re Adams, 312 B.R. 576 (MD NC, 2004), In re De Julio, 322 B.R. 456 (MD FL, 2005), In re Ledford, 970 F.2d 1556 (6th Cir., 1992), In re Coston, 991 F.2d 257 (5th Cir., 1993), and In re McCormick, 283 B.R. 680 (WD PA, 2002). See also, In re Gertsch, 237 B.R. 160 (B.A.P. 9th Cir., 1999), where the court stated that in the absence of other factors, a creditor demonstrates reasonable reliance by showing that it followed its normal business practice.

reliance on false financial statement, importance of creditor's standards

In Pittsburgh Police Fed. Credit Union v. Lundy, 165 B.R. 157 (WD PA, 1994), two credit unions whose loan committees approved or rejected loans using objective standards and set formulas were held to have reasonably relied on the debtor's inaccurate loan applications even though the debtor's father was the president of one of the credit unions and his uncle was president of the other, but neither was on the loan committee. In First Int'l Bank v. Kerbaugh, 162 B.R. 255 (ND, 1993), the creditor actually and reasonably relied on the debtor's false credit card application where the creditor conducted a commercially reasonable investigation of the information supplied and there was nothing on the face of the application that should reasonably have put the creditor on notice that the application was grossly inaccurate. See also In re Larrieu, 230 B.R. 256 (ED PA, 1999).

reasonable reliance, when not established, cases

In Citizens Bank v. Broyles, 55 F.3d 980 (4th Cir., 1995), there was no reasonable reliance where the creditor was uncertain about the debtor's factual statements and failed to inquire further. In Household Fin. Corp. v. Kahler, 187 B.R. 508 (ED VA, 1995), the creditor's reliance on the debtor's representations was not reasonable because even a minimal investigation would have revealed the falsity of the representations. In In re Ruwart, 114 B.R. 725 (CO, 1990), the creditor's reliance on the debtor's financial statement was found not reasonable partly because the statement was found not to have been a material factor in the extending of credit and partly because no effort was made to verify the accuracy of the statement. In Sinclair Oil Corp. v. Jones, 31 F.3d 659 (8th Cir., 1994), the creditor's reliance on the debtor's financial statement was not reasonable because the debtor's unpaid accounts with the creditor should have alerted the creditor to investigate further. See also In re Keim, 236 B.R. 400 (B.A.P. 8th Cir., 1999); In re Osborne, 257 B.R. 14 (CD CA, 2000).

false financial statement, requirement of

Requirement (5) above requires the financial statement to have been made or published by the debtor with an intent to deceive. Generally, intent to deceive may be inferred where the debtor knew that his or her financial statement was materially false. See In re Sheridan, 57 F.3d 627 (7th Cir., 1995). An intent to deceive may also be inferred from the totality of the circumstances. See, e.g., In re Rental Journal, Inc., 111 B.R. 1012 (SD FL, 1989); In re Wyatt, 87 B.R. 874 (ED VA, 1988). Likewise, an intent to deceive may also be inferred where it is shown that the debtor displayed a reckless disregard for the truth or accuracy of the information on the financial statement. See In re Rigg, 310 B.R. 725 (WD AR, 2004); In re Black, 787 F.2d 503 (10th Cir., 1986); First Am. Bank v. Bodenstein, 168 B.R. 23 (ED NY, 1994).

intent to deceive, when not established, case

On the other hand, where the debtor made an honest or understandable mistake or acted in good faith, an intent to deceive may not be inferred from his or her conduct. See Gen. Elec. Capital Corp. v. Acosta, 406 F.3d 367 (5th Cir., 2005); Equitable Bank v. Miller, 39 F.3d 301 (11th Cir., 1994); In re Rodgers, 115 B.R. 678 (CD CA, 1990); In re Frugh, 133 B.R. 870 (ND OH, 1991). See also First of Am. Bank v. Bourdon, 160 B.R. 117 (ND IN, 1993) (holding the foolishness or imprudence of the debtor's purchase was not sufficient to prove intent to deceive under Section 523(a)(2)(B)).

intent to deceive, importance of business acumen

In determining whether a debtor who had submitted a false financial statement acted in good faith or was attempting to deceive the creditor, the courts often consider the experience and business acumen of the debtor. A debtor with business experience and acumen is more likely to have an intent to deceive than a person who is inexperienced or unsophisticated in business matters. See Frankfort Bank v. Chryst, 177 B.R. 486 (ED PA, 1994); In re Jordan, 927 F.2d 221 (5th Cir., 1991); Equitable Bank v. Miller, 39 F.3d 301 (11th Cir., 1994); In re Moore, 118 B.R. 64 (ND TX, 1990); In re Bixel, 215 B.R. 772 (SD CA, 1997).

Other factors that may determine whether the court will infer an intent to deceive include the extent of the inaccuracy or falsity of the financial statement and whether the debtor independently informed the creditor of the truth as to the information requested in the statement. See In re Barron, 126 B.R. 255 (ED TX, 1991); In re Vermont, 98 B.R. 581 (MD FL, 1989); Sinclair Oil Corp. v. Jones, 31 F.3d 659 (8th Cir., 1994); In re Jacobe, 121 B.R. 299 (ED VA, 1990) (holding that an intent to deceive the creditor could not be inferred from the falsity of the debtor's financial statement because it had been prepared for a third party and not for the creditor).

intent to deceive, existence of, factors

The presumptive nondischargeability of consumer debts and cash advances incurred within 90 days of bankruptcy. Section 523(a)(2)(C) provides that consumer debts for luxury goods or services of more than $600 incurred within 90 days of the bankruptcy filing date and certain cash advances of more than $875 obtained within 70 days of the bankruptcy filing date are presumed to be nondischargeable under Section 523(a)(2)(A). This means that debts of this type are presumed to have been obtained by false pretenses, false representations, or actual fraud for purposes of Section 523(a)(2)(A).

Section 523(a)(2)(C), provisions of

If a creditor produces prima facie evidence that the debtor either purchased luxury goods or services of more than $600 from the creditor within 90 days of bankruptcy or obtained cash advances of more than $875 from the creditor within 70 days of bankruptcy, the debtor's intent not to repay the debt is presumed under Section 523(a)(2)(A) and actual fraud under Section 523(a)(2)(A) is presumptively established. However, the debtor may rebut the presumption by producing evidence of either an intent to repay the debt or that the debt is not covered by Section 523(a)(2)(C) (i.e., was not for luxury goods or services or was not a covered cash advance). See In re Cline, 282 B.R. 493 (WD WA, 2002); In re Powell, 213 B.R. 306 (WD VA, 1997); In re Orecchio, 109 B.R. 285 (SD OH, 1989); In Koch, 83 B.R. 898 (ED PA, 1988). The debtor may also rebut the Section 523(a)(2)(C) presumption by showing that his credit card was used within the applicable period without his knowledge or permission. See In re Weiler, 244 B.R. 305 (ED PA, 2000).

presumptive non-dischargeability under Section 523(a)(2)(C), procedure

Section 523(a)(2)(C) also provides that luxury goods or services do not include goods or services reasonably acquired for the support or maintenance of the debtor or a dependent of the debtor. Generally, what constitutes luxury goods or services depends on the facts and circumstances of a particular case and must be determined in light of the debtor's circumstances. See In re Faulk, 69 B.R. 743 (ND IN, 1986); In re Herran, 66 B.R. 323 (SD FL, 1986). Items that constitute luxury goods or services include expensive jewelry, Christmas gifts, expensive floral arrangements, high-end clothing and expensive cosmetics. See In re Lebovitz, 344 B.R. 556 (WD TN, 2006); In re Meseck, 284 B.R. 901 (ND IA, 2002); In re Barthol, 75 B.R. 305 (SD OH, 1987); In re Herran, 66 B.R. 323 (SD FL, 1986).

luxury goods, what constitutes

luxury goods, what constitutes

Items that are not to constitute luxury goods or services include moderately priced clothing, "Barbie" dolls and accessories, and a new Chevrolet Lumina automobile. See In re Barger, 85 B.R. 756 (SD OH, 1988), Sears Roebuck & Co. v. Johannsen, 160 B.R. 328 (WD WI, 1993), and In re McDonald, 129 B.R. 279 (MD FL, 1991). The debtor's use of a credit card to purchase a van to be used by himself, his wife and his three children did not constitute a luxury item in In re Park, 375 B.R. 153 (WD PA, 2007). That gambling debts are "luxury goods", see In re Simpson, 319 B.R. 256 (MD FL, 2003).

cash advance under Section 523(a)(2)(C), what constitutes

To be covered by Section 523(a)(2)(C) (i.e., to be presumed nondischargeable), a cash advance must be an extension of consumer credit under an open end credit plan as defined in the Consumer Credit Protection Act. This means cash advances under a plan wherein the creditor reasonably contemplates repeated transactions, which prescribes the terms of such transactions, and which provides for a finance charge on the unpaid balance. See 15 U.S.C. § 1602(i). Cash advances on credit cards is the most common type of cash advance covered by Section 523(a)(2)(C). However, in In re Manning, 280 B.R. 171 (SD OH, 2002), the debtor's use of a bank's credit card balance transfer offer to pay off the balance owing on another credit card was held not to constitute a cash advance under Section 523(a)(2)(C). See also, In re Green, 296 B.R. 173 (CD IL, 2003); see also In re May, 448 B.R. 197 (W. D. Mich. 2011). A cash loan to the debtor within 60 days of bankruptcy is not covered under Section 523(a)(2)(C) even if the loan proceeds were used to purchase luxury goods. See, e.g., In re Neal, 113 B.R. 607 (B.A.P. 9th Cir., 1990); In re Woods, 66 B.R. 984 (ED PA, 1986).

collateral estoppel, use of for state court fraud judgments

Collateral estoppel in Section 523(a)(2) proceedings. It is not uncommon for a creditor to have obtained a judgment grounded in fraud or false pretenses against the debtor in a state court. The question that often arises in Section 523(a)(2) proceedings is whether the state court judgment has a collateral estoppel effect on the issue of the nondischargeability of the judgment in the bankruptcy case. In Grogan v. Garner, 498 U.S. 279, 111 S.Ct. 654 (1991), the Supreme Court held that collateral estoppel could be used by a creditor with a state court fraud judgment against the debtor in the Bankruptcy case to establish the nondischargeability of its judgment under Section 523(a)(2)(A).

collateral estoppel, use of in Section 523(a)(2) proceedings

Additionally, the Supreme Court in Grogan v. Garner, supra, held that because the standard of proof required to establish nondischargeability under Section 523(a)(2) is preponderance of the evidence (and not the higher standard of clear and convincing evidence), all creditors who have obtained fraud judgments, the elements of which are the same as those required to establish fraud under Section 523(a)(2)(A), may obtain nondischargeability of the judgment in the bankruptcy court under the doctrine of collateral estoppel. See 498 U.S. at 285. Therefore, even if clear and convincing evidence is required to establish fraud under state law, the doctrine of collateral estoppel may be used to establish the nondischargeability of the debt under Section 523(a)(2)(A) in the bankruptcy proceeding, provided that the elements of fraud under state law are the same as those under Section 523(a)(2)(A). The elements of fraud under Section 523(a)(2)(A) are described above in this article under the heading of "The dischargeability of debts obtained by actual fraud."

If the issue of fraud was actually litigated in the prior proceeding, the doctrine of collateral estoppel is clearly applicable in the bankruptcy proceeding, provided that the elements of fraud are the same in both cases. See In re Livingston, 389 B.R. 1 (ED MI, 2008); In re Wellinger, 371 B.R. 249 (ED MI, 2007). But what if the issue of fraud was not actually litigated in the prior case? In Bush v. Balfour Beatty Bahamas, 62 F.3d 1319 (11th Cir., 1995), a default judgment in a prior action conclusively established the elements necessary for the bankruptcy court to hold the debt nondischargeable for fraud under Section 523(a)(2)(A) where the debtor actively participated in the prior case over an extended period of time and a default judgment based upon fraud was ultimately entered against the debtor as a sanction. In In re Herwig, 77 B.R. 662 (SD IL, 1987), the doctrine of collateral estoppel was applied by the bankruptcy court to a default judgment for fraud against the debtor by a state court in a case where the debtor filed an answer and counterclaim but failed to appear at trial and the judgment was entered after the presentation of evidence by the creditor. See also In re Uhrig, 306 B.R. 687 (MD FL, 2004).

collateral estoppel, when applicable to default judgments

On the other hand, in Brandenberger v. Chinnery, 181 B.R. 954 (WD MO, 1995), the debtor was held not to be collaterally estopped from litigating the issue of fraud in the bankruptcy court because the fraud judgment in the prior case had been entered against the debtor pursuant to a settlement agreement and the issue of fraud had not been actually litigated in the prior case wherein the debtor was not represented by counsel, and because the issue of nondischargeability under Section 523(a)(2) is the exclusive province of the bankruptcy court. In In re Manuel, 76 B.R. 105 (ED MI, 1987), the court refused to apply the doctrines of collateral estoppel or res judicata to a state court consent judgment dismissing the creditor's fraud claims against the debtor with prejudice because the parties did not stipulate to findings of fact in the state court case and the issue of fraud had therefore not been litigated and decided.

collateral estoppel, when not applicable to default judgments

Bibliography. For further reading on the issues discussed in this article, see the annotations and articles listed below.

Annotations:

Credit Card Debt as Nondischargeable Under Bankruptcy Code Provision Concerning Nondischargeability of Individual Debt Obtained Through False Pretenses, False Representations, or Actual Fraud Other Than Statement Respecting Debtor's or Insider's Financial Condition. 158 ALR Fed. 189.

What constitutes a materially false statement in loan or credit application under Bankruptcy Code provision concerning nondischargeability of certain debts obtained through use of false written statement respecting financial condition (11 USCS §523(a)(2)(B)). 93 ALR Fed 821.

What constitutes intent to deceive in loan or credit application under bankruptcy code provision concerning nondischargeability of certain debts obtained through use of false written statement respecting financial condition (11 USCS §523(a)(2)(B)). 94 ALR Fed 437.

What constitutes reliance on loan or credit application under bankruptcy code provision concerning nondischargeability of certain debts obtained through use of false written statement respecting financial condition (11 USCS §523(a)(2)(B)). 94 ALR Fed 516.

What constitutes reliance on loan or credit application under Bankruptcy Code provision concerning nondischargeability of individual debt obtained through false pretenses, false representation, or actual fraud, other than statement respecting debtor's or insider's financial condition. 97 ALR Fed 402.

Articles:

Proving Fraud in Credit Card Dischargeability Actions: a Permanent State of Flux. 102 Com. L.J. 233, Fall, 1997.

Discharging Credit Card Debt in Bankruptcy. 9 Prac. Litig. 49, May 1998.

A Game of Chance: The Dischargeability of Credit Card Gambling Debt Under 11 U.S.C. § §523(a)(2)(A). 28 Univ. of Memphis L. Rev., 985, Spring, 1998.

The Fallacy of Conflicting Theories for Analyzing Credit Card Fraud Under 11 USC Section 523(a)(2)(A). 4 J Bankr L & Prac 641, September/October 1995.

Punitive damages - the dischargeability debate continues. Are punitive damages dischargeale under 11 U.S.C. § 523(a)(2)(A)? 10 Bankruptcy Dev. J. 423, 1994; 11 Bankruptcy Dev. J. 707, 1994-95.

1.12 To what extent are debts owed to unlisted or improperly listed creditors dischargeable in bankruptcy?

Text of Statute. Section 523(a)(3) of the Bankruptcy Code (11 U.S.C. § 523(a)(3)) is applicable to the subject discussed in this article. It provides as follows:

523. Exceptions to discharge

(a) A discharge under section 727, 1141, 1228(a), 1228(b), or 1328(b) of this title does not discharge an individual debtor from any debt -

. . . .

(3) neither listed nor scheduled under section 521(1) of this title, with the name, if known to the debtor, of the creditor to whom such debt is owed, in time to permit -

(A) if such debt is not of a kind specified in paragraph (2), (4), or (6) of this subsection, timely filing of a proof of claim, unless such creditor had notice or actual knowledge of the case in time for such timely filing; or

(B) if such debt is of a kind specified in paragraph (2), (4), or (6) of this subsection, timely filing of a proof of claim and timely request for a determination of dischargeability of such debt under one of such paragraphs, unless such creditor had notice or actual knowledge of the case in time for such timely filing and request;

Section 523(a)(3), text of Section 523(a)(3), text of

Introduction. It is not uncommon for a debtor to fail to list a creditor on the debtor's bankruptcy schedules or to list an incorrect address for a scheduled creditor. The dischargeability of debts owed to such creditors is governed by Section 523(a)(3) of the Bankruptcy Code. Section 523(a)(3) was enacted in the Bankruptcy Reform Act of 1978 and has not been amended since its enactment. Section 523(a)(3) provides, in essence, that debts that are not properly listed on the debtor's bankruptcy schedules are nondischargeable unless the creditor had notice or actual knowledge of the case in time to file a proof of claim and, if applicable, a complaint to determine the dischargeability of the debt.

Section 523(a)(3), essential provision

The nondischargeability provisions of Section 523(a)(3) are applicable to Chapter 7 cases of individual debtors and to Chapter 13 cases wherein the debtor receives a "best efforts" discharge under 11 U.S.C. § 1328(b). Section 523(a)(3) is not applicable to Chapter 7 cases of corporate debtors or to Chapter 13 cases wherein the debtor receives a "completed plan" discharge under 11 U.S.C. § 1328(a). It should be understood, however, that the inapplicability of Section 523(a)(3) to Chapter 13 cases of this type does not mean that unlisted debts are discharged by a Section 1328(a) discharge. By definition, a Section 1328(a) discharge discharges only debts that are either provided for in the plan or disallowed under 11 U.S.C. § 502. See 11 U.S.C. § 1328(a). Because unlisted debts are not dealt with in the plan and are not disallowed under 11 U.S.C. § 502, they are not discharged by a Section 1328(a) discharge. See In re Schroff, 94 B.R. 279 (ED NY, 1988); In re Hamilton, 179 B.R. 749 (SD GA, 1995); In re Chirillo, 84 B.R. 120 (ND IL, 1988).

Section 523(a)(3), applicability to Chapter 7 and Chapter 13 cases

BAPCPA, amendment to §1328(a)

To this end, in 2005 the BAPCPA amended Section 1328(a) of the Bankruptcy Code so as to specifically make debts that are nondischargeable under Section 523(a)(3) nondischargeable in a Chapter 13 case wherein the debtor receives a completed plan discharge under section 1328(a). This BAPCPA amendment does not change existing law, however, because, as explained above, unlisted debts are not dealt with in a Chapter 13 plan and are therefore not dischargeable under a section 1328(a) discharge in any event.

non-dischargeability under Section 523 (a)(3), necessity of creditor action

The nondischargeability provisions of Section 523(a)(3) are self-executing. This means it is not necessary for an unlisted or improperly listed creditor to file an objection or request a determination of dischargeability in the bankruptcy case in order for its claim to be nondischargeable. Further, determining the nondischargeability of a debt under Section 523(a)(3) is not within the exclusive province of the bankruptcy court, which means that such a determination may be made by any state or federal court of record. See In re Dabbs, 72 B.R. 73 (ND AL, 1987); In re Cheely, 280 B.R. 763 (MD GA, 2002) (holding the issue could be litigated in one of three ways: (1) in the creditor's civil lawsuit on the claim, where the debtor could assert a bankruptcy discharge as an affirmative defense and the civil court could decide the issue; (2) either the creditor or the debtor could move to reopen the bankruptcy case under Bankruptcy Rule 4007(b) for the purpose of filing a complaint to determine the dischargeability of the debt; or (3) the debtor could bring an action to the bankruptcy court to enforce the discharge injunction).

dischargeability of unlisted, factors governing

Whether a debt owed to an unlisted or improperly listed creditor is nondischargeable in a particular case depends on the following factors: (1) whether the case is a Chapter 7 "no asset" case, (2) whether the omission of the creditor from the debtor's schedules was inadvertent or was intentional or fraudulent, (3) whether the creditor had sufficient and timely notice of or actual knowledge of the case, and (4) whether the debt is of a type covered by Section 523(a)(3)(A) or of a type covered by Section 523(a)(3)(B).

The dischargeability of unlisted debts in Chapter 7 "no-asset" cases. For the reasons given below, a substantially different rule with respect to the nondischargeability of unlisted debts under Section 523(a)(3) is generally applied in Chapter 7 "no-asset" cases. The general rule now followed by most bankruptcy courts is that in Chapter 7 "no-asset" cases (i.e., in cases wherein a notice of no dividend is given under Bankruptcy Rule 2002(e)), debts owed to unlisted or improperly listed creditors are dischargeable under Section 523(a)(3) even if the creditor did not receive notice or have knowledge of the bankruptcy case until after the discharge was granted and the case was closed, provided that (1) the omission of the creditor from the debtor's schedules was inadvertent and not intentional or fraudulent and (2) the debt is not of a kind specified in Section 523(a)(3)(B) (i.e., is not a debt obtained by fraud, falsity or a false financial statement and is not a debt for fiduciary fraud or willful or malicious injury). See In re Nielsen, 383 F.3d 922 (9th Cir., 2004); In re Houston, 310 B.R. 224 (MD AL, 2004); In re Madaj, 149 F.3d 467 (6th Cir., 1998); In re Stone, 10 F.3d 285 (5th Cir., 1994); In re Beezley, 994 F.2d 1433 (9th Cir., 1993); In re Baitcher, 781 F.2d 1529 (11th Cir., 1986); Peacock v. State Farm Auto. Ins. Co., 139 B.R. 421 (ED MI, 1992); In re Raanan, 181 B.R. 480 (CD CA, 1995); In re Bulbin, 122 B.R. 161 (DC, 1990); In re Presley, 288 B.R. 732 (WD VA, 2003); In re Herzigi, 238 B.R. 5 (ED NY, 1998); American Credit Services v. Tucker, 143 B.R. 330 (WD NY, 1992). See also Miller v. Schuchardt, 159 B.R. 849 (ED AR, 1993) (holding that the omitted creditor's alleged deprivation of being unable to elect a trustee, examine the debtor at the meeting of creditors, object to the debtor's list of exempt property, and object to the debtor's discharge was insufficient to warrant nondischargeability of the omitted creditor's debt under Section 523(a)(3)).

dischargeability of unlisted debts in "no-asset" cases, general rule

The rationale behind the above-stated general rule is that in Chapter 7 "no-asset" cases the creditors are normally notified not to file claims unless they are later instructed to do so, which means that in such cases there is no bar date for filing proofs of claim unless creditors are later instructed to file claims. Because there is no bar date for filing proofs of claim, the nondischargeability requirement in Section 523(a)(3)(A) can not be complied with in that the creditor will, when it is later notified of the case, receive notice of the case in time to permit the timely filing of a proof of claim. Therefore, the debt is not nondischargeable under Section 523(a)(3)(A) and is therefore dischargeable unless it either qualifies for nondischargeability under Section 523(a)(3)(B) (i.e., is of a kind specified in 11 U.S.C. § 523(a)(2), (4), or (6)), or the omission of the creditor from the debtor's schedules was intentional or fraudulent. See In re Stone, 10 F.3d 285 (5th Cir., 1994).

dischargeability of unlisted debts in "no-asset" cases, rationale of rule

It has been held, however, that if, for whatever reason, a bar date for filing claims is established in a "no-asset" Chapter 7 case, the general rule described above is not applicable and an omitted debt is nondischargeable under Section 523(a)(3)(A) unless it can be shown that the creditor had notice or actual knowledge of the case in time to file a claim prior to the bar date. See In re Corgiat, 123 B.R. 388 (ED CA, 1991); In re Bosse, 122 B.R. 410 (CD CA, 1990).

"no-asset" case, rule if bar date established in

non-dischargeability of unlisted debt in "no-asset" case, intentional or fraudulent omission of debt

If in a Chapter 7 "no-asset" case that the debtor intentionally or fraudulently failed to list a creditor on his or her bankruptcy schedules, then the general rule described above is not applicable and the debt owed to the unlisted creditor is nondischargeable under Section 523(a)(3)(A) unless the creditor had notice or actual knowledge of the case in time to timely file a proof of claim. See In re Stone, 10 F.3d 285 (5th Cir., 1994); Raines v. Brooker, 183 B.R. 299 (MD FL, 1995); In re Raanan, 181 B.R. 480 (CD CA, 1995) (stating that in the case of intentionally omitted creditors the equitable doctrines of laches and estoppel justify an exception to the rule that unlisted debts in a "no-asset" Chapter 7 case are automatically discharged if they fall under Section 523(a)(3)(A)). If the failure to list a creditor was attributable solely to negligence or inadvertence, however, the unlisted debt is dischargeable. See In re Stone, supra. However, in Karras v. Hansen, 165 B.R. 636 (ND IL, 1994), the court held that a Chapter 7 debtor's failure to schedule a debt in a "no-asset" case does not preclude discharge of the debt even if the debt was intentionally omitted because the right to file claims continues indefinitely and there is nothing to distribute to creditors in any event. See also White v. Nielsen, 383 F.3d 922 (9th Cir., 2004); In re Cruz, 254 B.R. 801 (SD NY, 2000) (holding that inquiring into the debtor's state of mind surrounding the omission of a creditor in a Chapter 7 "no asset" case for the purpose of determining whether Section 523(a)(3) is applicable is irrelevant).

omitted Section 523(a)(2), (4) or (6) debts, non-dischargeability of, general rule

Because deadlines for filing complaints to determine the dischargeability of debts under 11 U.S.C. § 523(a)(2), (4) or (6) are normally imposed in Chapter 7 "no-asset" cases, the reasoning applied to debts covered by Section 523(a)(3)(A) does not apply with respect to debts covered by Section 523(a)(3)(B). Generally, therefore, debts covered by Section 523(a)(3)(B) (i.e., debts obtained by fraud, falsity or false financial statements, debts for fiduciary fraud, and debts for willful and malicious injury) are nondischargeable under Section 523(a)(3) unless the creditor had notice or actual knowledge of the claim in time to permit the timely filing of a request to determine the dischargeability of the debt. See In re Rey, 324 B.R. 449 (ED NY, 2005); In re Padilla, 84 B.R. 194 (CO, 1987); In re Stone, 10 F.3d 285 (5th Cir., 1994); In re James, 184 B.R. 147 (ND AL, 1995) (stating that the purpose of Section 523(a)(3)(A) is to protect a creditor's right to file a proof of claim and participate in distribution and nothing else, whereas the purpose of Section 523(a)(3)(B) is to protect a creditor's right to file a complaint to determine the dischargeability of its claim, a right which, under Bankruptcy Rule 4007(c), may not be extended once it has expired). See In re Fauchier, 71 B.R. 212 (B.A.P. 9th Cir., 1987); In re Purcell, 362 B.R. 465 (ED CA, 2007) (where a debtor failed to include certain tax assessment debts in his schedules; the court ruled that, although the taxing authority would have received nothing from the estate, its lien survived the bankruptcy, and the debt was not discharged).

To obtain nondischargeability under Section 523(a)(3)(B) in a "no-asset" Chapter 7 case, an omitted creditor must do more than merely allege that its claim is of a kind covered by Section 523(a)(3)(B). A creditor must prove it actually has such a claim. See In re Candelaria, 121 B.R. 140 (ED NY, 1990) (stating the mere passage of time beyond which a determination of dischargeability may be sought does not alone trigger nondischargeability under Section 523(a)(3)(B), and that unless the creditor can show that its claim actually comes within the dischargeability exceptions of 11 U.S.C. § 523(a)(2), (4) or (6), there is no reason to deny the debtor the benefit of a full discharge in a no-asset case simply because he inadvertently omitted a debt); see also In re Haga, 131 B.R. 320 (WD TX, 1991); In re Bosse, 122 B.R. 410 (CD CA, 1990) (holding that mere allegations of nondischargeability are insufficient and that to establish nondischargeability under Section 523(a)(3)(B) an omitted creditor must independently have a claim that would be nondischargeable under 11 U.S.C. § 523(a)(2), (4) or (6) and must prove that claim in the present case).

omitted Section 523(a)(2), (4) or (6) debt, duties of creditor

Debtors in Chapter 7 "no-asset" cases occasionally attempt to reopen a closed case in order to amend the schedules by adding the name and address of an omitted creditor. Most courts now refuse to permit the reopening of such cases for this purpose because there is nothing to be gained thereby. If the omitted debt is of a kind covered by Section 523(a)(3)(A), it is dischargeable upon notice to the creditor and if the debt is of a kind covered by Section 523(a)(3)(B) it is nondischargeable and will remain nondischargeable even if the creditor is added to the schedules because the time for filing determination of dischargeability requests for such debts has expired and cannot under Bankruptcy Rule 4007(c) be extended. See In re Madaj, 149 F.3d 467 (6th Cir., 1998), In re Beezley, 994 F.2d 1433 (9th Cir., 1993), In re Walendy, 118 B.R. 774 (CD CA, 1990), In re Renfro, 164 B.R. 337 (WD WA, 1994), and In re Karamitsos, 88 B.R. 122 (SD TX, 1988); American Standard Ins. Co. v. Bakehorn, 147 B.R. 480 (ND IN, 1992) (holding that omitted creditors are not denied due process if they are added to the schedules after the case has been closed because such an act has no effect on the dischargeability of the debt).

omitted debt, "no-asset" case, necessity of reopening case

Because the debtor is not permitted to reopen a "no-asset" case for the purpose of adding an omitted creditor does not mean that the case may not be reopened for the purpose of determining the dischargeability of an omitted debt, especially if the creditor alleges that the omitted debt is of a kind specified in Section 523(a)(3)(B). See In re Ford, 87 B.R. 641 (NV, 1988); In re Padilla, 84 B.R. 194 (CO, 1987); In re Dabbs, 72 B.R. 73 (ND AL, 1987) (refusing to reopen a case for the purpose of determining the dischargeability of a debt owed to an omitted creditor because the bankruptcy court does not have sole jurisdiction to determine the nondischargeability of a debt under Section 523(a)(3)).

reopening "no-asset" case to determine dischargeability of debt

non-dischargeability of unlisted debt in asset cases, general rule

The dischargeability of unlisted debts in cases other than Chapter 7 "no-asset" cases. The general rule in cases that are not Chapter 7 "no-asset" cases (i.e., in cases where a notice of no dividend under Bankruptcy Rule 2002(e) is not given) is that debts owed to unlisted or improperly listed creditors are nondischargeable unless the creditor had notice or actual knowledge of the case in time to permit the timely filing of a proof of claim and, if the debt is of the kind specified in 11 U.S.C. § 523(a)(2), (4) or (6), in time to permit the timely filing of a request to determine the dischargeability of the debt. See In re Fauchier, 71 B.R. 212 (B.A.P. 9th Cir., 1987), Beverly Lumber Co. v. Nicholson, 170 B.R. 153 (WD MO, 1994), In re Geris, 240 B.R. 228 (WD VA, 1999), In re Bosse, 122 B.R. 410 (CD CA, 1990), and Omni Mfg. v. Smith, 21 F.3d 660 (5th Cir., 1994).

non-dischargeability of unlisted debt in asset cases, reason for rule

The reason that cases of this type (i.e., Chapter 7 asset cases and cases under Chapters 11, 12 and 13) are treated differently than Chapter 7 "no-asset" cases is that in cases of this type a bar date for filing proofs of claim is established and the "timely filing of a proof of claim" requirements of Section 523(a)(3)(A) are applicable to omitted creditors, whereas in Chapter 7 "no-asset" cases a bar date is not established. Also, in cases of this type there are likely to be assets available for distribution to creditors and an unlisted creditor would not receive its portion of the distribution. In other words, omitted creditors are more severely prejudiced in cases of this type than in Chapter 7 "no-asset" cases. See Omni Mfg. v. Smith, 21 F.3d 660 (5th Cir., 1994).

determining dischargeability of unlisted debt in asset cases, issues

The important issues in cases of this type are (1) whether the creditor was given sufficient and timely notice of the case, and (2) whether the creditor had actual knowledge of the case within the required time. It is generally held that if a creditor's name and address is correctly listed on the debtor's schedules, the creditor is presumed to have received timely notice of the case and may not claim nondischargeability under Section 523(a)(3). See L.F. Rothschild & Co. v. Angier, 84 B.R. 274 (MA, 1988), and In re Strong, 64 B.R. 54 (ED TN, 1986). Further, if a creditor is properly scheduled and notified of the case, the notice is effective as to all claims against the debtor, even if some of the claims are not listed in the debtor's schedules (at least in a Chapter 7 case). See In re Mandukich, 87 B.R. 296 (SD NY, 1988).

adequacy of creditor's address in schedules, burden of proof

In In re Walker, 125 B.R. 177 (ED MI, 1990), the court stated that a creditor is duly scheduled and listed for purposes of Section 523(a)(3) if the address provided by the debtor is sufficiently accurate to permit delivery by the U.S. Postal Service to the appropriate party. A creditor who challenges the accuracy of the listed address has the burden of establishing that the address provided by the debtor is so incorrect as to fall short of this threshold. If the creditor establishes the inadequacy of the address, the burden shifts to the debtor to show that, notwithstanding the incorrect address, the creditor had timely notice or actual knowledge of the case. In In re Fauchier, 71 B.R. 212 (B.A.P. 9th Cir., 1987), the court held that there is no requirement in cases of this type to show that the debtor acted in bad faith in improperly listing a debt. The court stated that the burden is on the debtor to use reasonable diligence in completing the schedules and if a creditor proves that an address in incorrect, the debtor must justify the inaccuracy in the schedules, with carelessness, inadvertence, and relying on the debtor's own knowledge being insufficient justification.

It is not necessary for a creditor to have received formal notice from the court of the debtor's bankruptcy case in order for its claim to be discharged, as long as the notice is received in sufficient time prior to the bar date to permit the creditor to inquire and file a proof of claim. In In re Sam, 894 F.2d 778 (5th Cir., 1990), the court held that even though the creditor did not receive the 30 day notice required under Bankruptcy Rule 4007(c), he received timely notice for purposes of Section 523(a)(3) when he received notice of the automatic stay 18 days prior to the bar date. See also In re Bateman, 254 B.R. 866 (MD, 2000). However, in In re Dewalt, 961 F.2d 848 (9th Cir., 1992), the court held the creditor's receipt of notice of the case 7 days prior to the bar date was insufficient for purposes of Section 523(a)(3). In Mitchell Constr. Co. v. Smith, 180 B.R. 311 (ND GA, 1995), notice of the bankruptcy case received on the day that time expired for filing nondischargeability complaints was found to be inadequate notice of the case for purposes of Section 523(a)(3)(B); see also In re Harris, 447 B.R. 254 (W. D. Ark. 2011). adequate notice of case, what constitutes

Generally, in the case of large corporate or governmental creditors notice must be given to the proper department or office of the creditor in order to be effective for purposes of Section 523(a)(3). In In re Senall, 64 B.R. 325 (MD FL, 1986), it was held that for purposes of nondischargeability under Section 523(a)(3) notice of the debtor's bankruptcy sent to the Pasadena branch of the creditor bank did not constitute adequate notice to the Los Angeles branch of the bank. In U.S., SBA v. Bridges, 894 F.2d 108 (5th Cir., 1990), notice of the debtor's bankruptcy sent to the Biloxi office of the SBA was held not to constitute adequate notice to the Jackson office of the SBA for purposes of Section 523(a)(3). However, in In re Van Cloostere, 94 B.R. 131 (SD IL, 1988), a letter sent by the debtor's attorney to the Illinois Department of Agriculture informing them of the debtor's bankruptcy was found to constitute adequate notice of the case for purposes of Section 523(a)(3). In In re Anderson, 196 B.R. 839 (WD MO, 1996) notice of the debtor's bankruptcy given to the only two directors and shareholders of the creditor corporation was held to constitute notice to the corporation. adequate notice to large creditors, what constitutes

Notice to a corporation did not constitute adequate notice under Section 523(a)(3) to a creditor who was an officer, director and shareholder of the corporation in In re Strong, 64 B.R. 54 (ED TN, 1996). However, several courts have held that timely notice given to a creditor's attorney constitutes adequate notice of the case for purposes of Section 523(a)(3). See In re Price, 871 F.2d 97 (9th Cir., 1989), In re Slaiby, 57 B.R. 770 (NH, 1985), In re Walker, 103 B.R. 281 (UT, 1989), Hatch v. Hatch, 175 B.R. 429 (MA, 1994), and In re Van Cloostere, 94 B.R. 131 (SD IL, 1988). However, in Carpet Services v. Hutchinson, 187 B.R. 533 (SD TX, 1995), the court held that scheduling the address of a creditor in care of the office of its state-court attorney did not constitute adequate notice under Section 523(a)(3). In In re Ellett, 317 B.R. 134 (ED CA, 2004), the court ruled that pre-petition taxes owed to the state franchise tax board were not discharged in the debtor's chapter 13 case because an erroneous social security number for the debtor on the bankruptcy notice sent to the tax board vitiated the effectiveness of the notice. adequate notice of case, what constitutes

actual knowledge of case, what constitutes

Even if notice of the debtor's bankruptcy case is not given to a creditor, the debt owed to the creditor may be dischargeable if it is shown that the creditor had actual knowledge of the case in time to permit the filing of a proof of claim and, if applicable, a request to determine the dischargeability of the debt under 11 U.S.C. § 523(a)(2), (4) or (6). See In re Rey, 324 B.R. 449 (ED NY, 2005) (where the creditor, without formally receiving notice, still attended the meeting of creditors simply "to see what it was all about."). Again, in most cases actual knowledge of the case by the creditor's attorney constitutes actual knowledge by the creditor. See In re Walker, 103 B.R. 281 (UT, 1989); In re Compton, 891 F.2d 1180 (5th Cir., 1990). Oral notice, if proven, is generally sufficient to constitute actual notice. See, e.g., Rowe v. Steinberg, 253 B.R. 524 (ED MI, 2000). However, knowledge by a creditor that the debtor was contemplating bankruptcy does not constitute actual knowledge of the case for purposes of Section 523(a)(3). See In re Gray, 57 B.R. 927 (RI, 1986); In re Brown, 267 B.R. 877 (WD OK, 2001).

Bibliography. For further reading on the issues discussed in this article, see the annotations and articles listed below.

Annotations:

Reopening Bankruptcy Case, Pursuant to § 350(b) of the Bankruptcy Code (11 U.S.C.A. § 350(b)), to Add or Properly Schedule Omitted Creditor or Debt Where Deadline Was Set for Filing Proof of Claim. 12 A.L.R. Fed. 2d 359.

Reopening Bankruptcy Case, Pursuant to § 350(b) of the Bankruptcy Code (11 U.S.C.A. § 350(b)), to Add or Properly Schedule Omitted Creditor or Debt in "No Asset" Case in Which Deadline Was Not Set for Filing Proof of Claim. 25 A.L.R. Fed. 2d 1.

Articles:

Discharging unscheduled debts: creating equal justice for creditors by restoring integrity to Section 523(a)(3). 10 Bankruptcy Dev. J. 571, 1994.

The emerging harmless innocent omission defense to nondischargeability under Bankruptcy Code §523(a)(3)(A): making sense of the confusion over reopening cases and amending schedules to add omitted debts. 69 Am. Bankruptcy L.J. 33, Winter, 1995.

We left them off the list - now what? Unscheduled creditors in Chapter 7 bankruptcies. 54 La. L. Rev. 389, 1993.

The unscheduled creditor in a Chapter 7 no-asset case. 64 Am. Bankruptcy L.J. 281, July 1990.

1.13 To what extent can a debtor's retirement funds and IRAs survive a bankruptcy case?

Text of Statutes. Sections 522(b)(1), (b)(3)(C), (b)(4), (d)(10)(E), (d)(12), (n) and 541(b)(5), (b)(6), and (c)(2) of the Bankruptcy Code (11 U.S.C. § 522(b)(1), 11 U.S.C. § 522(b)(3)(C), 11 U.S.C. § 522(b)(4), 11 U.S.C. § 522(d)(10)(E), 11 U.S.C. § (d)(12), 11 U.S.C. § 522(n), 11 U.S.C. § 541(b)(5), 11 U.S.C. § 541(b)(6), and 11 U.S.C. § 541(c)(2)) are applicable to the subject discussed in this article. These statutes provide as follows:

522. Exemptions

* * * * * *

(b)(1) Notwithstanding section 541 of this title, an individual debtor may exempt from property of the estate the property listed in either paragraph (2) or, in the alternative, paragraph (3) of this subsection. Section 522(b)(1), text of

* * * * * *

(b)(3) Property listed in this paragraph is –

* * * * * *

(C) retirement funds to the extent that those funds are in a fund or account that is exempt from taxation under section 401, 403, 408, 408A, 414, 457, or 501(a) of the Internal Revenue Code of 1986. Sections 522(b)(3)(C) and (4), text of

* * * * * *

(4) For purposes of paragraph (3)(C) and subsection (d)(12), the following shall apply:

(A) If the retirement funds are in a retirement fund that has received a favorable determination under section 7805 of the Internal Revenue Code of 1986, and that determination is in effect as of the date of the filing of the petition in a case under this title, those funds shall be presumed to be exempt from the estate.

(B) If the retirement funds are in a retirement fund that has not received a favorable determination under such section 7805, those funds are exempt from the estate if the debtor demonstrates that –

(i) no prior determination to the contrary has been made by a court or the Internal Revenue Service; and

(ii)(I) the retirement fund is in substantial compliance with the applicable requirements of the Internal Revenue Code of 1986; or

(II) the retirement fund fails to be in substantial compliance with the applicable requirements of the Internal Revenue Code of 1986 and the debtor is not materially responsible for that failure.

(C) A direct transfer of retirement funds from 1 fund or account that is exempt from taxation under section 401, 403, 408, 408A, 414, 457, or 501(a) of the Internal Revenue Code of 1986, under section 401(a)(31) of the Internal Revenue Code of 1986, or otherwise, shall not cease to qualify for exemption under paragraph (3)(C) or subsection (d)(12) by reason of such direct transfer.

(D)(i) Any distribution that qualifies as an eligible rollover distribution within the meaning of section 402(c) of the Internal Revenue Code of 1986 or that is described in clause (ii) shall not cease to qualify for exemption under paragraph (3)(C) or subsection (d)(12) by reason of such distribution.

(ii) A distribution described in this clause is an amount that –

(I) has been distributed from a fund or account that is exempt from taxation under section 401, 403, 408, 408A, 414, 457, or 501(a) of the Internal Revenue Code of 1986; and

(II) to the extent allowed by law, is deposited in such a fund or account not later than 60 days after the distribution of such amount.

. . . .

(d) The following property may be exempted under subsection (b)(1) of this section:

Section 522(d)(10) (E), text of

. . . .

(10) The debtor's right to receive -

. . . .

(E) a payment under a stock bonus, pension, profitsharing, annuity, or similar plan or contract on account of illness, disability, death, age, or length of service, to the extent reasonably necessary for the support of the debtor and any dependent of the debtor, unless -

(i) such plan or contract was established by or under the auspices of an insider that employed the debtor at the time the debtor's rights under such plan or contract arose;

(ii) such payment is on account of age or length of service; and

(iii) such plan or contract does not qualify under section 401(a), 403(a), 403(b), or 408 of the Internal Revenue Code of 1986.

* * * * * *

(d) The following property may be exempted under subsection (b)(2) of this section:

* * * * * *

Section 522(d)(12), text of

(12) Retirement funds to the extent that those funds are in a fund or account that is exempt from taxation under section 401, 403, 408, 408A, 414, 457, or 501(a) of the Internal Revenue Code of 1986.

* * * * * *

Section 522(n), text of

(n) For assets in individual retirement accounts described in section 408 or 408A of the Internal Revenue Code of 1986, other than a simplified employee pension under section 408(k) of such Code or a simple retirement account under section 408(p) of such Code, the aggregate value of such assets exempted under this section, without regard to amounts attributable to rollover contributions under section 402(c), 402(e)(6), 403(a)(4), 403(a)(5), and 403(b)(8) of the Internal Revenue Code of 1986, and earnings thereon, shall not exceed $1,171,650 in a case filed by a debtor who is an individual, except that such amount may be increased if the interests of justice so require.

541. Property of the estate

* * * * * *

(b) Property of the estate does not include -

* * * * * *

Section 541(b)(5) and (b)(6), text of

(5) funds placed in an education individual retirement account (as defined in section 530(b)(1) of the Internal Revenue Code of 1986) not later than 365 days before the date of the filing of the petition in a case under this title, but –

(A) only if the designated beneficiary of such account was a child, stepchild, grandchild, or stepgrandchild of the debtor for the taxable year for which funds were placed in such account;

(B) only to the extent that such funds –

(i) are not pledged or promised to any entity in connection with any extension of credit; and

(ii) are not excess contributions (as described in section 4973(e) of the Internal Revenue Code of 1986); and

(C) in the case of funds placed in all such accounts having the same designated beneficiary not earlier than 720 days nor later than 365 days before such date, only so much of such funds as does not exceed $5,850;

(6) funds used to purchase a tuition credit or certificate or contributed to an account in accordance with section 529(b)(1)(A) of the Internal Revenue Code of 1986 under a qualified State tuition program (as defined in section 529(b)(1) of such Code) not later than 365 days before the date of the filing of the petition in a case under this title, but –

(A) only if the designated beneficiary of the amounts paid or contributed to such tuition program was a child, stepchild, grandchild, or stepgrandchild of the debtor for the taxable year for which funds were paid or contributed;

(B) with respect to the aggregate amount paid or contributed to such program having the same designated beneficiary, only so much of such amount as does not exceed the total contributions permitted under section 529(b)(6) of such Code with respect to such beneficiary, as adjusted beginning on the date of the filing of the petition in a case under this title by the annual increase or decrease (rounded to the nearest tenth of 1 percent) in the education expenditure category of the Consumer Price Index prepared by the Department of Labor; and

(C) in the case of funds paid or contributed to such program having the same designated beneficiary not earlier than 720 days nor later than 365 days before such date, only so much of such funds as does not exceed $5,850;

. . . .

(c)(2) A restriction on the transfer of a beneficial interest of the debtor in a trust that is enforceable under applicable nonbankruptcy law is enforceable in a case under this title. Section 541(c)(2), text of

Introduction. This article deals with the exclusion or exemption in a bankruptcy case of the debtor's interest in the assets and funds of retirement plans and IRAs. It does not deal with the exemption of periodic benefit payments which the debtor was either receiving or had the right to receive at the time of bankruptcy. It should be noted, however, that a debtor's periodic retirement benefits are usually exempt, either under Section 522(d)(10)(E) of the Bankruptcy Code or under a state exemption law. This article deals with the protection of retirement funds that have been accumulated by or on behalf of a debtor either in a retirement or pension plan of some type or in an individual retirement account (IRA). scope of article

The statutes set forth above were enacted in the Bankruptcy Reform Act of 1978. Sections 522(b)(3), 522(b)(4), 522(d)(12), 522(n), 541(b)(5) and 541(b)(6) were amended by the BAPCPA. The BAPCPA did not amend sections 522(d)(10)(E) or 541(c)(2). history of statutes

In 2005, the BAPCPA amendments to section 522(b) provided that debtors who claim their exemptions under state law and not under the federal bankruptcy exemptions, either by choice or because state law requires them to do so, may exempt retirement funds and IRAs that are qualified (i.e., tax-deferred) under the Internal Revenue Code, regardless of whether these funds are exempt under state law. If, as is often the case, the Internal Revenue Service has not specifically ruled on the qualification of a particular fund or IRA, the fund or IRA may be exempted by showing that the fund or IRA is in substantial compliance with the requirements of the Internal Revenue Code or, if not in substantial compliance, that the failure to comply is not the fault of the debtor. Also, the direct transfer of retirement funds from a qualified fund or IRA to another account (i.e., a withdrawal of funds from a retirement account) does not cause the debtor to lose the exemption. The same rule applies to rollover distributions if the funds are deposited in the new account within 60 days after the distribution. It is important to note that retirement funds and IRAs may be exempted under section 522(b)(3) whether or not the funds or IRAs are ERISA-qualified. They need only be qualified under the Internal Revenue Code to be exempt under this section. Under the BAPCPA amendments tax-qualified IRAs may be exempted by the debtor regardless of whether they are exempt under state law. Section 522(b), BAPCPA amendments to and explanation of

Section 522(d), BAPCPA amendments

The BAPCPA amendments to Section 522(d) set forth above essentially provide that a debtor's retirement funds and IRAs may be exempted by a debtor who claims his or her exemptions under the federal bankruptcy exemptions, to the extent that the funds or IRAs are qualified (i.e., tax-deferred) under the Internal Revenue Code. While Section 522(d)(12), as set forth above, does not refer to IRAs by name, Sections 408 and 408A of the Internal Revenue Code deal with IRAs and these sections are listed in Section 522(d)(12) of the Bankruptcy Code, which clearly means that IRAs may be exempted under this section.

Section 522(d), BAPCPA amendments to

Under the BAPCPA amendment to Section 522(d) a debtor's tax-qualified retirement funds and IRAs are exempt under Section 522(d)(12) regardless of the construction given to section 522(d)(10)(E) by the courts. In this regard, it should be noted that the Supreme Court in Rousey v. Jacoway, 544 U.S. 320, 125 S. Ct. 1561 (2005) held that IRAs may be exempted by a debtor under Section 522(d)(10)(E) of the Bankruptcy Code. It appears, then, that a debtor claiming his or her exemptions under the federal bankruptcy exemptions may exempt his or her IRAs either under Section 522(d)(10)(E) or under the new Section 522(d)(12).

Section 522(n), explanation of

Section 522(n) establishes a $1,171,650 exemption limit under Section 522 for IRAs that are not established under a simplified employee pension plan or a simple retirement account. This exemption limit may be increased if the interests of justice so require.

Section 541(b), BAPCPA amendments to

The 2005 BAPCPA amendments to Section 541(b) provide that funds placed by the debtor in a qualified educational IRA or used to purchase tuition credits or certificates under a qualified state tuition program are not includable in the debtor's bankruptcy estate, provided that the beneficiary of the account or tuition credit is a child, stepchild, grandchild or stepgrandchild of the debtor and that the funds were contributed by the debtor 365 days or more prior to bankruptcy. Also, the funds in an educational IRA must not be pledged or encumbered. The excludable amount of tuition credits may not exceed the amount that is qualified under the Internal Revenue Code. There is a $5,475 per beneficiary excludable limit for educational IRAs or tuition credits that were placed or contributed by the debtor within 720 days of bankruptcy.

retirement funds, exclusion or exemption from estate

The status of a debtor's retirement funds in bankruptcy depends primarily on the type of plan or account wherein the funds have accrued or accumulated. Depending on the status of the funds, they may either be excludable from (i.e., do not become the property of) the bankruptcy estate under Section 541(c)(2) or exempted from (i.e., removed from) the bankruptcy estate under Section 522(d)(10)(E) or a state exemption law.

As indicated above, the protection accorded retirement funds in bankruptcy depends primarily on the type of plan or account in which the funds have accrued or accumulated. For purposes of bankruptcy, retirement plans and accounts may be categorized as follows: (1) employer-sponsored retirement plans that are qualified under ERISA (the Employees Retirement Income Security Act of 1974); (2) employer-sponsored retirement plans that are not qualified under ERISA; and (3) individual retirement accounts (IRAs), which may or may not be part of a simplified employee pension plan (SEP). The protection accorded each type of retirement plan or IRA in bankruptcy is discussed separately below in this article.

retirement funds, categories of

The subject discussed in this article and the statutes set forth above are applicable to both Chapter 7 and Chapter 13 cases. While the importance of protecting a debtor's retirement benefits is usually more critical in Chapter 7 cases, the same protections are available to Chapter 13 debtors. The Section 541(c)(2) exclusion may be employed by a Chapter 13 debtor. See, e.g., In re Harshbarger, 66 F.3d 775 (6th Cir., 1995).

protection of retirement funds, Chapter 7 & 13 cases

The survivability in bankruptcy of funds in retirement plans that are covered by ERISA. To retain deductibility for its contributions to an employee benefit or retirement plan, an employer must qualify the plan under the Internal Revenue Code. In addition, certain types of employee benefit and retirement plans are covered by ERISA and must therefore comply with the requirements of ERISA. One of the eligibility requirements under both ERISA and the Internal Revenue Code is that the plan must contain a nonalienation provision prohibiting creditors of plan participants from attaching or garnisheeing the funds and benefits of the plan. See respectively, 29 U.S.C. § 1056(d)(1) and 26 U.S.C. § 401(a)(13)(A). While all qualified pension plans and most other qualified plans that provide retirement benefits must comply with both ERISA and the Internal Revenue Code, some types of defined contribution employee benefit plans are not covered by ERISA and are required only to qualify under the Internal Revenue Code. Simplified employee benefit plan (SEPs) and Keogh plans are examples of plans of this type. A significant difference between ERISA and the Internal Revenue Code is that under ERISA substantive rights are vested in plan participants (i.e., in employees) to enforce required plan provisions, while under the Internal Revenue Code the only penalty imposed on an employer for not complying with statutory plan requirements is loss of tax qualification.

retirement plans covered by ERISA, requirements

Patterson v. Shumate, holding of case

In Patterson v. Shumate, 504 U.S. 753, 112 S.Ct. 2242 (1992), the Supreme Court held that a debtor's interest in an ERISA-qualified pension plan is excluded from the debtor's bankruptcy estate under Section 541(c)(2) of the Bankruptcy Code because of the ERISA-required nonalienation provision in the plan. The court ruled that the words "applicable nonbankruptcy law" appearing in Section 541(c)(2) included not only state law but federal nonbankruptcy law as well. Because the ERISA-qualified pension plan was required by federal law to contain a nonalienation clause prohibiting creditors of plan participants from attaching or garnisheeing the funds and benefits of the plan, under Section 541(c)(2) these restrictions were enforceable against the bankruptcy trustee. Therefore the debtor's interest in the funds and benefits of the plan did not become part of the debtor's bankruptcy estate and remained the separate property of the debtor in much the same manner as exempt property.

plans covered by ERISA, exclusion of funds from bankruptcy estate

Under Patterson v. Shumate, a debtor's interest in any type of pension plan that is covered by ERISA is clearly excludable from the debtor's bankruptcy estate under Section 541(c)(2). See In re Chilton, 674 F.3d 486 (5th Cir. 2012) (pre-petition inherited IRA funds were "retirement funds"); In re Radcliffe, 563 F.3d 627 (7th Cir., 2009); In re Chambers, 384 B.R. 460 (ED TX, 2008); In re Rueter, 11 F.3d 850 (9th Cir., 1993); Matter of Dunn, 988 F.2d 45 (7th Cir., 1993); In re Carbaugh, 278 B.R. 512 (B.A.P. 10th Cir., 2002). In Traina v. Sewell, 180 F.3d 707 (5th Cir., 1999), and In re Baker, 114 F.3d 636 (7th Cir., 1997), an ERISA-qualified plan was held excludable from the debtor's estate even if the plan was not tax-qualified under Section 401 of the Internal Revenue Code. In In re Conner, 73 F.3d 258 (9th Cir., 1996), a debtor's ERISA-qualified pension and profit-sharing plan, including the debtor's after-tax contributions over which the debtor had control and could withdraw at any time, was excludable from the debtor's bankruptcy estate. It has also been held that a debtor's right to receive a lump sum distribution under a plan does not prevent the plan funds from being excludable under Section 541(c)(2). See Whetzal v. Alderson, 32 F.3d 1302 (8th Cir., 1994). The termination of the debtor's employment by the plan-sponsoring employer does not prevent the debtor's interest in an ERISA-qualified profit-sharing plan from being excludable under Section 541(c)(2) even though the debtor is entitled to a lump sum payment upon termination. See, e.g., Winkler v. Gorham, 164 B.R. 728 (WD NC, 1994); see also In re Pellegrini, 467 B.R. 117 (W. D. Mich. 2012) (judgment funds against investment company who defrauded debtor which were not yet in tax exempt account did not qualify for exclusion).

exclusion of retirement funds from estate under Section 541(c)(2), requirements

To exclude retirement funds from a bankruptcy estate under Section 541(c)(2), a debtor must show that the plan in question is in fact ERISA-qualified. That is, the debtor must show that the plan contains a nonalienation provision that is required by and enforceable under ERISA. See In re Reed, 985 F.2d 1026 (9th Cir., 1993). ERISA qualification is most likely to be lacking in retirement plans of small employers, especially if the debtor is an owner of the employer who sponsored the plan. For example, if a plan does not qualify under ERISA because its sole participants are the owners of the employer and no other employees are covered by the plan, then the owners' interest in the plan is not excludable under Section 541(c)(2). See Watson v. Proctor, 161 F.3d 593 (9th Cir., 1998), In re Kaplan, 189 B.R. 882 (ED PA, 1995), Fugarino v. Hartford Life & Acc. Ins. Co., 969 F.2d 178 (6th Cir., 1992), and In re Orkin, 170 B.R. 751 (MA, 1994). See also In re Acosta, 182 B.R. 561 (ND CA, 1994), where the court held that a sole shareholder of a corporation did not qualify as an employee under ERISA because a sole shareholder is deemed to be an employer under ERISA and is therefore prohibited from receiving benefits under an ERISA plan. The right to a Section 541(c)(2) exclusion may also be lost if the plan is not administered in the manner prescribed by ERISA. See In re Harris, 188 B.R. 444 (MD FL, 1995). Fraudulent or preferential payments made to a pension plan do not qualify for the Section 541(c)(2) exclusion. See, e.g., Bell v. Beckwith, 5 F.3d 150 (6th Cir., 1993).

Section 541(c)(2) exclusion, when lost

As indicated above, to qualify for a Section 541(c)(2) exclusion, the plan in question must not only contain a nonalienation clause, it must be required by ERISA to contain the clause. Therefore, a Section 541(c)(2) exclusion will be denied if it is shown that the plan in question is not required by ERISA to contain a nonalienation clause even if the plan in fact contains such a clause. See In re Kellogg, 179 B.R. 379 (MA, 1995) (where a nonalienation clause in a simplified employee pension plan (a SEP) could not support a Section 541(c)(2) exclusion because ERISA does not require SEPs to contain nonalienation clauses).

Section 541(c)(2) exclusion, when denied

How does a court determine whether a plan is ERISA-qualified for purposes of the Section 541(c)(2) exclusion? Some courts employ a two-part test whereby it is first determined whether the plan is subject to or covered by ERISA and then whether the plan in question includes a nonalienation clause that is enforceable under ERISA. See In re Baker, 195 B.R. 386 (ND IL, 1996), In re Bennett, 185 B.R. 4 (ED NY, 1995), and In re Hanes, 162 B.R. 733 (ED VA, 1994). It should be noted, however, that a plan that is qualified under the Internal Revenue Code but is not covered by ERISA may not qualify for the Section 541(c)(2) exclusion (unless it qualifies as a spendthrift trust under state law) because the Internal Revenue Code, unlike ERISA, does not give plan beneficiaries enforcement rights. See In re Acosta, 182 B.R. 561 (ND CA, 1994), In re Kellogg, 179 B.R. 379 (MA, 1995), and In re Witwer, 148 B.R. 930 (CD CA, 1992).

Section 541(c)(2) exclusion, qualification for, tests used

In addition to the Section 541(c)(2) exclusion, some courts have held that a debtor's interest in an ERISA-qualified plan is exempt under 29 U.S.C. § 1056(d)(1) which is made applicable to the debtor by 11 U.S.C. § 522(b)(2)(A). 29 U.S.C. § 1056(d)(1) is the ERISA provision requiring plans to include a nonalienation clause. 11 U.S.C. § 522(b)(2)(A) permits debtors who do not elect, or are prohibited by state law from electing, to claim exemptions under the federal bankruptcy exemptions (11 U.S.C. § 522(d)) to claim as exempt property that is exempt under federal nonbankruptcy law. Cases wherein such an exemption has been allowed include In re Komet, 104 B.R. 799 (WD TX, 1989), In re Messing, 114 B.R. 541 (ED TN, 1990), In re White, 131 B.R. 526 (MA, 1991), and In re Hennessey, 135 B.R. 711 (MA, 1992). Cases wherein such an exemption was denied have held that ERISA does not constitute "other federal law" for exemption purposes. See In re Dyke, 943 F.2d 1435 (5th Cir., 1991), In re Rosenquist, 122 B.R. 775 (MD FL, 1990), and In re Conroy, 110 B.R. 492 (MT, 1990). It should be noted, however, that the rationale of these cases was expressly rejected by the Supreme Court in Patterson v. Shumate, supra, in connection with the Section 541(c)(2) exclusion.

plans covered by ERISA, exemption of funds under §522(b)(2)(A)

ERISA qualification, types of plans requiring

What types of retirement plans are subject to ERISA for purposes of the Section 541(c)(2) exclusion? Under 29 U.S.C. § 1002(1) and 1003, ERISA applies to any employee benefit plan established or maintained by an employer or a union except governmental plans, church plans, workers' compensation or unemployment plans, and excess benefit plans. An "employee benefit plan" is defined in ERISA as an employee benefit pension plan, an employee welfare benefit plan, or a plan that is both an employee benefit pension plan and an employee welfare benefit plan. However, under ERISA only employee welfare pension plans (or "pension plans") are required to contain nonalienation clauses. Therefore, plans that are not employee welfare pension plans do not qualify for the Section 541(c)(2) exclusion in bankruptcy cases.

ERISA, types of plans covered by

Clearly all traditional (i.e., defined-benefit) pension plans are subject to ERISA for purposes of the Section 541(c)(2) exclusion. See In re Conner, 73 F.3d 258 (9th Cir., 1996). 401(k) plans and profit-sharing plans are subject to ERISA for purposes of the Section 541(c)(2) election. See, e.g., IRS v. Wingfield, 284 B.R. 787 (ED VA, 2002); In re Nudo, 147 B.R. 68 (ND NY, 1992); In re Harline, 950 F.2d 669 (10th Cir., 1991); In re Moore, 907 F.2d 1476 (4th Cir., 1990). In In re Hthiy, 283 B.R. 447 (ED MI, 2002) a debtor's 50% interest in her ex-husband's 401(k) plan that was received by the debtor in a qualified domestic relations order (QDRO) was excludable from the debtor's bankruptcy estate under Section 541(c)(2). See aksi U.S. v. Rogers, 558 F. Supp. 2d 774 (ND OH, 2008) and In re Lalchandani, 279 B.R. 880 (B.A.P. 1st Cir., 2002) (similar rulings dealing with the debtor's interest in a QDRO). On the other hand, Keogh plans, simplified employee pension plans (SEPs), and individual retirement accounts (IRAs) are not subject to ERISA for purposes of the Section 541(c)(2) exclusion. See In re Walker, 959 F.2d 894 (10th Cir., 1992), In re Meehan, 173 B.R. 818 (SD GA, 1994), and In re Taft, 171 B.R. 497 (ED NY, 1994). In In re Segovia, the court ruled that a long term incentive compensation plan (LTICP) established by Wells Fargo was not an ERISA qualified plan because it did not, either expressly, or based on surrounding circumstances, possess a retirement purpose, nor did it defer any income as required by ERISA. See In re Segovia, 404 B.R. 896 (ND CA, 2009.) Note, however, that a debtor's interest in plans or accounts that are not subject to ERISA may be exempt or excludable under either state law or other federal law. The protection of funds in non-ERISA plans and accounts is discussed below in this article.

The exemption of retirement funds and IRAs under Section 522(d) (10)(E) and similar state exemption statutes. The exemption provided in Section 522(d)(10)(E) of the Bankruptcy Code may be used by debtors only in those states that have not "opted out" of the federal bankruptcy exemptions under 11 U.S.C. § 522(b). A few states have enacted exemption statutes similar to Section 522(d)(10)(E) and this discussion may be relevant to debtors in those states as well as to debtors in states where the Section 522(d)(10)(E) exemption may be used. The exemptability of funds in retirement plans under Section 522(d)(10)(E) will be discussed first, followed by a discussion of the exemptability of IRAs under Section 522(d)(10)(E). The Section 522(d)(10)(E) requirement that the funds be reasonably necessary for the support of the debtor is discussed at the end of this article.

Section 522(d) (10)(E), when applicable

For its funds to qualify for exemption under Section 522(d)(10)(E), a retirement plan must be a stock bonus, pension, profitsharing, annuity or similar plan or contract. In addition, payments under the plan must be on account of illness, disability, death, age, or length of service. For a holding that a debtor's Roth IRA meets the exemption requirements of Section 522(d)(10)(E), see In re Bramlette, 333 B.R. 911 (ND GA, 2005). Finally, the plan must not have been established by or under the auspices of an insider that employed the debtor when the debtor's rights under the plan arose if payments under the plan are on account of age or length of service and the plan does not qualify under 26 U.S.C. § 401(a), 403(a), 403(b), or 408. See In re Krebs, 527 F.3d 82 (3d Cir., 2008).

Section 522(d) (10)(E), general requirements

A plan need not be tax-qualified for its funds to be exempt under Section 522(d)(10)(E). See In re Goff, 706 F.2d 574, 587 (5th Cir., 1983). Tax-qualification is required only if the plan was established by or under the auspices of an insider that employed the debtor and payments under the plan are on account of age or length of service. Generally then, if the debtor is not an insider with respect to the plan, the plan may be exempt under Section 522(d)(10)(E) without tax-qualification, but if the debtor is an insider with respect to the plan then tax-qualification is required for exemption. Insiders include directors and officers of corporations, general partners of partnerships, and persons in control of plan sponsors. See 11 U.S.C. § 101(31) for the full Bankruptcy Code definition of "insider."

tax qualification, when required under Section 522(d)(10)(E)

Unlike most state exemption statutes, Section 522(d)(10)(E) does not specifically exempt the funds in a retirement plan; it exempts only "the debtor's right to receive a payment" under the plan. Not surprisingly, there is a split of authority over whether Section 522(d)(10)(E) applies only to distributions from a plan to which the debtor has an immediate and present right to receive or to the debtor's interest in the accumulated and undistributed funds of the plan. One line of cases holds that a debtor must be presently entitled to receive benefits under the plan when the bankruptcy case is filed in order for the plan funds to be exempt under Section 522(d)(10)(E). See In re Clark, 711 F.2d 21 (3d Cir., 1983); In re Chick, 135 B.R. 201 (CT, 1991); Dale v. Puerner, 264 B.R. 875 (WD MI, 2001).

Section 522(d)(10) (E), exemption requirements

Section 522(d)(10)(E), necessity of present right to benefits, general rule

The other line of cases holds that it is not necessary for the debtor to have begun receiving benefits under the plan prior to bankruptcy in order to qualify the plan funds for exemption under Section 522(d)(10)(E). See In re Bowder, 262 B.R. 919 (MN, 2001); In re Marsella, 188 B.R. 731 (RI, 1995); In re Cilek, 115 B.R. 974 (WD WI, 1990); In re Carmichael, 100 F.3d 375 (5th Cir., 1996).

Sections 522(d)(10)(E) and 522(12), interplay between

It should be noted that the 2005 BAPCPA amendments to the Bankruptcy Code have made exempting retirement funds and IRAs possible under either Section 522(d)(10)(E) or Section 522(d)(12). Section 522(d)(12) exempts retirement funds from the bankruptcy estate to the extent that such funds are exempt from taxation by the I.R.C. Also note that Section 522(n) limits the IRA exemption to $1,171,650, except where justice requires that such amount be increased.

Bibliography. For further reading on the issues discussed in this article, see the annotations and articles listed below.

Annotations:

Retirement Fund Benefits or Refunds of Retirement Fund Contributions as "Property" of Bankruptcy Estate Under Section 541 of Bankruptcy Code of 1978. 174 ALR Fed. 587.

Individual retirement accounts as exempt property in bankruptcy. 133 ALR Fed 1.

Articles:

Revisiting the scope and implications of Patterson v. Shumate in light of In re Lyons. 3 Am. Bankruptcy Instit. L. Rev. 379, Winter 1995.

ERISA qualified pension plan benefits as property of the bankruptcy estate: the unanswered questions after Patterson v. Shumate. 16 Campbell L. Rev. 303, Summer 1994.

Protecting pension assets in personal bankruptcy. 68 St. Johns L. Rev. 409, Spring 1994.

After Shumate, some retirement plan benefits are more equal than others in bankruptcy. 21 J. Corp. Taxation 23, Spring 1994.

Patterson v. Shumate: the impact of bankruptcy on divorced women. 15 Women's Rights L. Rep. 73, Fall 1993.

Prebankruptcy planning with ERISA-qualified pension plans and individual retirement accounts after Patterson v. Shumate. 29 Williamette L. Rev. 893, Fall 1993.

ERISA-related claims in bankruptcy, 3 J Bankr L & Prac 76 (1993).

1.14 What types of prefiling transfers are avoidable in bankruptcy?

Text of Statutes. Sections 544, 547(b), 547(c), 547(h), 547(i), 548(a)(1) and 548(e) of the Bankruptcy Code (11 U.S.C. § 544, 574(b), 547(c), 547(h), 547(i), 548(a)(1), 548(e)) are applicable to the subject discussed in this article. These statutes provide as follows:

544. Trustee as lien creditor and as successor to certain creditors and purchasers

(a) The trustee shall have, as of the commencement of the case, and without regard to any knowledge of the trustee or of any creditor, the rights and powers of, or may avoid any transfer of property of the debtor or any obligation incurred by the debtor that is voidable by - Section 544, text of

(1) a creditor that extends credit to the debtor at the time of the commencement of the case, and that obtains, at such time and with respect to such credit, a judicial lien on all property on which a creditor on a simple contract could have obtained such a judicial lien, whether or not such a creditor exists;

(2) a creditor that extends credit to the debtor at the time of the commencement of the case, and obtains, at such time and with respect to such credit, an execution against the debtor that is returned unsatisfied at such time, whether or not such a creditor exists; or

(3) a bona fide purchaser of real property, other than fixtures, from the debtor, against whom applicable law permits such transfer to be perfected, that obtains the status of a bona fide purchaser and has perfected such transfer at the time of the commencement of the case, whether or not such a purchaser exists.

(b)(1) Except as provided in paragraph (2), the trustee may avoid any transfer of an interest of the debtor in property or any obligation incurred by the debtor that is voidable under applicable law by a creditor holding an unsecured claim that is allowable under section 502 of this title or that is not allowable only under section 502(e) of this title.

(2) Paragraph (1) shall not apply to a transfer of a charitable contribution (as that term is defined in section 548(d)(3)) that is not covered under section 548(a)(1)(B), by reason of section 548(a)(2). Any claim by any person to recover a transferred contribution described in the preceding sentence under Federal or State law in a Federal or State court shall be preempted by the commencement of the case.

547. Preferences

. . . .

(b) Except as provided in subsections (c) and (i) of this section, the trustee may avoid any transfer of an interest of the debtor in property - Section 547(b), text of

(1) to or for the benefit of a creditor;

(2) for or on account of an antecedent debt owed by the debtor before such transfer was made;

(3) made while the debtor was insolvent;

(4) made -

(A) on or within 90 days before the date of the filing of the petition; or

(B) between ninety days and one year before the date of the filing of the petition, if such creditor at the time of such transfer was an insider; and

(5) that enables such creditor to receive more than such creditor would receive if -

(A) the case were a case under chapter 7 of this title;

(B) the transfer had not been made; and

(C) such creditor received payment of such debt to the extent provided by the provisions of this title.

*   *   *   *   *   *

(c) The trustee may not avoid under this section a transfer -

(1) to the extent that such transfer was -

Section 547(c), text of

(A) intended by the debtor and the creditor to or for whose benefit such transfer was made to be a contemporaneous exchange for new value given to the debtor; and

(B) in fact a substantially contemporaneous exchange;

(2) to the extent that such transfer was in payment of a debt incurred by the debtor in the ordinary course of business or financial affairs of the debtor and the transferee, and such transfer was –

(A) made in the ordinary course of business or financial affairs of the debtor and the transferee; or

(B) made according to ordinary business terms;

(3) that creates a security interest in property acquired by the debtor-

(A) to the extent such security interest secures new value that was -

(i) given at or after the signing of a security agreement that contains a description of such property as collateral;

(ii) given by or on behalf of the secured party under such agreement;

(iii) given to enable the debtor to acquire such property; and

(iv) in fact used by the debtor to acquire such property; and

(B) that is perfected on or before 30 days after the debtor receives possession of such property;

(4) to or for the benefit of a creditor, to the extent that, after such transfer, such creditor gave new value to or for the benefit of the debtor -

(A) not secured by an otherwise unavoidable security interest; and

(B) on account of which new value the debtor did not make an otherwise unavoidable transfer to or for the benefit of such creditor;

(5) that creates a perfected security interest in inventory or a receivable or the proceeds of either, except to the extent that the aggregate of all such transfers to the transferee caused a reduction, as of the date of the filing of the petition and to the prejudice of other creditors holding unsecured claims, of any amount by which the debt secured by such security interest exceeded the value of all security interests for such debt on the later of -

(A)(i) with respect to a transfer to which subsection (b)(4)(A) of this section applies, 90 days before the date of the filing of the petition; or

(ii) with respect to a transfer to which subsection (b)(4)(B) of this section applies, one year before the date of the filing of the petition; or

(B) the date on which new value was first given under the security agreement creating such security interest;

(6) that is the fixing of a statutory lien that is not avoidable under section 545 of this title;

(7) to the extent such transfer was a bona fide payment of a debt for a domestic support obligation;

(8) if, in a case filed by an individual debtor whose debts are primarily consumer debts, the aggregate value of all property that constitutes or is affected by such transfer is less than $600; or

(9) if, in a case filed by a debtor whose debts are not primarily consumer debts, the aggregate value of all property that constitutes or is affected by such transfer is less than $5,850.

*   *   *   *   *   *

(h) The trustee may not avoid a transfer if such transfer was made as a part of an alternative repayment schedule between the debtor and any creditor of the debtor created by an approved nonprofit budget and credit counseling agency.

Section 547(h), text of

(i) If the trustee avoids under subsection (b) a transfer made between 90 days and 1 year before the date of the filing of the petition, by the debtor to an entity that is not an insider for the benefit of a creditor that is an insider, such transfer shall be considered to be avoided under this section only with respect to the creditor that is an insider.

Section 547(i), text of

548. Fraudulent transfers and obligations

(a)(1) The trustee may avoid any transfer (including any transfer to or for the benefit of an insider under an employment contract) of an interest of the debtor in property, or any obligation (including any obligation to or for the benefit of an insider under an employment contract) incurred by the debtor, that was made or incurred on or within 2 years before the date of the filing of the petition, if the debtor voluntarily or involuntarily - Section 548(a)(1), text of

(A) made such transfer or incurred such obligation with actual intent to hinder, delay, or defraud any entity to which the debtor was or became, on or after the date that such transfer was made or such obligation was incurred, indebted; or

(B)(i) received less than a reasonably equivalent value in exchange for such transfer or obligation; and

(ii)(I) was insolvent on the date that such transfer was made or such obligation was incurred, or became insolvent as a result of such transfer or obligation;

(II) was engaged in business or a transaction, or was about to engage in business or a transaction, for which any property remaining with the debtor was an unreasonably small capital;

(III) intended to incur, or believed that the debtor would incur, debts that would be beyond the debtor's ability to pay as such debts matured; or

(IV) made such transfer to or for the benefit of an insider, or incurred such obligation to or for the benefit of an insider, under an employment contract and not in the ordinary course of business.

(2) A transfer of a charitable contribution to a qualified religious or charitable entity or organization shall not be considered to be a transfer covered under paragraph (1)(B) in any case in which -

(A) the amount of that contribution does not exceed 15 percent of the gross annual income of the debtor for the year in which the transfer of the contribution is made; or

(B) the contribution made by a debtor exceeded the percentage amount of gross annual income specified in subparagraph (A), if the transfer was consistent with the practices of the debtor in making charitable contributions.

* * * * * *

(e)(1) In addition to any transfer that the trustee may otherwise avoid, the trustee may avoid any transfer of an interest of the debtor in property that was made on or within 10 years before the date of the filing of the petition, if – Section 548(e), text of

(A) such transfer was made to a self-settled trust or similar device;

(B) such transfer was by the debtor;

(C) the debtor is a beneficiary of such trust or similar device; and

(D) the debtor made such transfer with actual intent to hinder, delay, or defraud any entity to which the debtor was or became, on or after the date that such transfer was made, indebted.

(2) For the purposes of this subsection, a transfer includes a transfer made in anticipation of any money judgment, settlement, civil penalty, equitable order, or criminal fine incurred by, or which the debtor believed would be incurred by –

(A) any violation of the securities laws (as defined in section 3(a)(47) of the Securities Exchange Act of 1934 (15 U.S.C. § 78c(a)(47))), any State securities laws, or any regulation or order issued under Federal securities laws or State securities laws; or

(B) fraud, deceit, or manipulation in a fiduciary capacity or in connection with the purchase or sale of any security registered under section 12 or 15(d) of the Securities Exchange Act of 1934 (15 U.S.C. § 78I and 78o(d)) or under section 6 of the Securities Act of 1933 (15 U.S.C. § 77f).

purpose of article

Introduction. The ability of a bankruptcy trustee to avoid prebankruptcy transfers is one of the most complex and heavily litigated areas of bankruptcy law. Volumes have been written on the subject. The intent of this article is to give the reader an overview of the law on the subject, especially with respect to the types of transfers that are most likely to be encountered in Chapter 7 consumer cases and Chapter 13 cases. The purpose of this article is to inform the reader of the types of transfers that may be avoidable in bankruptcy and not necessarily to assist the reader in determining the avoidability of a particular transfer.

avoidable transfers, a summary

Prebankruptcy transfers either by the debtor or of property of the debtor, may be avoidable under three separate provisions of the Bankruptcy Code: Sections 544, 547(b) and 548(a). Section 544 is the so-called "strong arm clause" of the Bankruptcy Code whereunder transfers and liens that are avoidable under state law may be avoided by the bankruptcy trustee. Section 547(b) deals with preferential transfers and permits the trustee to avoid as preferential any transfer made by the debtor within 90 days of bankruptcy to a creditor for the payment of an antecedent debt if the transfer enabled the creditor to receive more than other creditors of the same class. If the transfer was made to an insider, the preference period is one year instead of 90 days. Section 548(a)(1) deals with fraudulent transfers and permits the trustee to avoid as fraudulent any transfer of real or personal property made by the debtor within one year of bankruptcy if the transfer was made by the debtor with actual intent to hinder, delay or defraud creditors or if the debtor received less than a reasonably equivalent value in exchange for the transfer. In summary, then, there are three types of prebankruptcy transfers that may be set aside by a bankruptcy trustee: (1) transfers that are avoidable under state law, (2) preferential transfers, and (3) fraudulent transfers.

avoidance powers, when debtor may exercise

The avoidance powers of the bankruptcy trustee under Sections 544, 547(b), 547(c), 547(h), 547(i), 548(a)(1), and 548(e) are applicable in both Chapter 7 and Chapter 13 cases. While avoidance powers under these Sections are conferred upon debtors in possession in Chapter 11 cases by 11 U.S.C. § 1107, they are not available to Chapter 7 or Chapter 13 debtors except as provided in 11 U.S.C. § 522(h). See In re Merrick, 151 B.R. 260 (ID, 1993). Under 11 U.S.C. § 522(h) a Chapter 7 or Chapter 13 debtor may avoid prebankruptcy transfers of property if (1) the property will be exempt to the debtor if recovered, (2) the transfer is avoidable by the trustee, (3) the trustee has not attempted to recover the property, (4) the property was not voluntarily transferred by the debtor, and (5) the debtor either did not conceal the property or could have avoided the transfer under 11 U.S.C. § 522(f)(2). See 11 U.S.C. § 522(h).

transferred property, recovery of by trustee

If a transfer is avoided by the trustee under Section 544, 547(b), 547(c), 547(h), 547(i), 548(a)(1), or 548(e) the trustee may recover the transferred property, or the value of thereof, from the transferee or from a subsequent transferee. See 11 U.S.C. § 550(a). Even the subsequent bankruptcy of a transferee does not bar recovery of the property by the debtor's trustee. See In re Croft Plumbing Service, 53 B.R. 654 (MD FL, 1985). If the transferred property has depreciated or disappeared, the trustee may recover a money judgment against the transferee. See In re Computer Universe, Inc., 58 B.R. 28 (MD FL, 1986). However, the trustee is not generally entitled to an award of attorney's fees against the transferee. See In re Candor Diamond Corp., 76 B.R. 342 (SD NY, 1987).

It should be noted that since the passage of the Religious Liberty and Charitable Donation Protection Act of 1998, charitable or religious donations made by the debtor of up to 15 percent of the debtor's gross income are not avoidable by the trustee. See 11 U.S.C. § 544(b)(2), 548(a)(2), (d)(3), (4).

charitable contributions, avoidability of

Transfers avoidable by state law under Section 544. Transfers that are avoidable under state law are also avoidable in bankruptcy under Section 544, which is often referred to as the "strong arm clause." Generally, under Section 544 the bankruptcy trustee may avoid transfers of and liens on the debtor's property that could be avoided by creditors under state law. More specifically, Section 544(a) permits the trustee to avoid prebankruptcy transfers of money or property by the debtor that were avoidable under local law on the bankruptcy filing date by a general creditor with an unsatisfied judicial lien, by a creditor with an unsatisfied writ of execution, or by a bonafide purchaser of real property from the debtor, whether or not such a creditor or purchaser actually exists. Section 544(b)(1) permits the trustee to avoid prebankruptcy transfers of the debtor that were avoidable under local law on the bankruptcy filing date by an existing unsecured creditor. Because the substantive rights of the trustee under Section 544 are derived from state law, the extent of the trustee's rights, remedies and powers under Section 544 are governed by state law. See In re Stanton, 254 B.R. 357 (ED TX, 2000), and Phillips v. Chandler, 215 B.R. 684 (ED VA, 1997).

Section 544(a), provisions of

Section 544(b)(1), provisions of

The purpose of the "strong arm clause" is to prevent undisclosed transfers, unperfected security interests, and secret liens from depleting the debtor's estate. See In re LMJ, Inc., 159 B.R. 926 (NV, 1993). To this end, certain defenses that may be available to transferees and lienholders against the debtor under local law are not available against the bankruptcy trustee. One court has described the bankruptcy trustee as "the perfect litigant without flaw". See Rinn v. First Union Nat. Bank of Maryland, 176 B.R. 401 (MD, 1995). Specifically, the trustee is not charged with actual knowledge with respect to the transfer or lien in question, even if the debtor or a creditor has actual knowledge of the transaction. In addition defenses based on estoppel and equity are not available against the trustee under Section 544. Therefore, a transfer or lien may be avoidable by the trustee under Section 544 even though it may be valid and therefore not avoidable as between the parties under local law. However, the trustee is charged with constructive knowledge of recorded liens, transfers, and security interests and with notice of open possession by the transferee. See Citizen's Sav. Bank v. Covey, 284 B.R. 650 (CD IL, 2002), and In re Henderson, 284 B.R. 515 (ND GA, 2002).

Section 544, purpose of

defenses not available against trustee

The types of prebankruptcy transfers that are most likely to be avoidable under Section 544(a) include unperfected security interests in the debtor's property, unrecorded or unperfected liens against the debtor's property, and unrecorded transfers of interests in real property of the debtor. In this regard, it should be understood that it is the status of the security interest, lien or transfer on the bankruptcy filing date that controls. Unless local law so permits, a creditor or the debtor may not perfect or record a transfer after the bankruptcy filing date so as to defeat the trustee's Section 544 avoidance powers. See In re Spring Creek Invest., N.V., Inc., 71 B.R. 157 (ND TX, 1987). In In re Levine, 134 F.3d 1046 (11th Cir., 1998), the transfer by the debtor of nonexempt assets to various insurance companies for the purpose of purchasing annuities that were exempt under state law was held to have been a fraudulent transfer under state (Florida) law and was therefore avoidable by the trustee under Section 544(a). However, in In re Howe, 232 B.R. 534 (B.A.P. 1st Cir., 1999), it was held that the exempting of property by the debtor under Section 522(b) of the Bankruptcy Code does not constitute a "transfer" for purposes of Section 544(a).

Section 544(a), types of transfers avoidable under

The type of transfers most likely to be avoidable under Section 544(b) are transfers made in violation of a state fraudulent conveyance statute. If a transfer is avoidable under a state fraudulent conveyance law, it is usually avoidable by the trustee under Section 544(b). For example, transfers of real or personal property by the debtor for inadequate consideration are usually avoidable under Section 544(b). Transfers that were made in violation of the state bulk sales law may also be avoided under Section 544(b). See In re Interstate Cigar Co., 278 B.R. 8 (ED NY, 2002).

Section 544(b), types of transfers avoidable under

It should be noted that no time limits or look-back periods are imposed by the Bankruptcy Code with respect to the avoidability of transfers under Section 544. Therefore, unless a time limitation is imposed by local law, a transfer may be avoided by the trustee under Section 544 regardless of when the transfer occurred.

Section 544, time limits

Any security interest in property of the debtor that requires the recording of a financing statement or other document in order to be perfected under state law may be avoided by the trustee under Section 544(a) if the recording requirements of the local Uniform Commercial Code (UCC) have not been complied with. See In re Pickle Logging, Inc., 286 B.R. 181 (MD GA, 2002), where a security interest in equipment was avoided because the equipment was incorrectly described on the security agreement. A creditor who used a debtor's nickname instead of his legal name was held to have an unperfected security interest subject to the trustee's avoidance powers. See In re Kinderknecht, 308 B.R. 71 (BAP10, 2004). In In re Newman, 993 F.2d 90 (5th Cir., 1993), the court held that an annuity contract in which a creditor held a security interest was a general intangible under the UCC and that the creditor's failure to file a financing statement with respect to its security interest rendered the security interest avoidable under Section 544(a). For the position that the trustee prevails over a consignor without proper perfection, see In re International Home Design, Inc., 28 B.R. 584 (WD MD, 1983). That a purchase money security interest in property is avoidable under Section 544(a) if the security interest is not perfected under the UCC, see Grabscheid v. Calvert Sales, 39 F.3d 669 (6th Cir., 1994). That a security interest in certificates of deposit, as general intangibles under the UCC, is avoidable by the trustee under Section 544(a) if a financing statement has not been filed, see In re Cambridge Biotech Corp., 178 B.R. 34 (MA, 1995). That a security interest in the debtor's automobile can be avoided under Section 544(a) if the security interest does not appear on the certificate of title, see In re Milcher, 86 B.R. 103 (WD MI, 1988). See also In re Hicks, 491 F.3d 858 (7th Cir., 2007).

unperfected security interests, avoidability under Section 544(a)

Prebankruptcy assignments by debtors of interests in real or personal property may be avoided by the trustee under Section 544(a) if the assignment was not recorded or otherwise perfected as required under state law prior to the bankruptcy filing date. See In re Pryor, 215 B.R. 362 (ND OH, 1997) (improperly recorded mortgage held avoidable), In re Bygaph, Inc., 56 B.R. 596 (SD NY, 1986) (unrecorded assignment of lease held avoidable); In re Haynes, 41 B.R. 423 (MD TN, 1984) (unrecorded quit claim deed), In re Currie, 57 B.R. 224 (MD LA, 1986) (unrecorded assignment of rents held avoidable), In re Yates, 58 B.R. 257 (ED TN, 1986) (unrecorded assignment of judgment held avoidable); In re Bourgeois, 58 B.R. 657 (WD LA, 1986) (assignment of accounts receivable to bank held avoidable because it was not recorded until 4 days after the bankruptcy filing date); WFC Realty Co. v. Monzack, 170 B.R. 31 (RI, 1994) (unperfected assignment of interest in general partnership held avoidable); and In re Kroskie, 315 F.3d 644 (6th Cir., 2003) (unperfected lien on mobile home held avoidable).

prebankruptcy assignments, avoidability under Section 544(a)

Unperfected liens against the debtor's property may also be avoided by the trustee under Section 544(a). An unperfected mechanics' or materialman's lien may be avoided under this section. See In re Ernest & Assoc., 59 B.R. 495 (WD TX, 1985). In In re Nicholson, 57 B.R. 672 (NV, 1986) an unperfected lien for attorney's fees in a personal injury case of the debtor was held avoidable. An unrecorded equitable lien against the debtor's property was held avoidable in In re Sullivan, 82 B.R. 133 (CO, 1988). An IRS tax lien was held avoidable in LMS Holding Co. v. U.S., 149 B.R. 681 (ND OK, 1992), because it had not been properly filed.

unperfected liens, avoidability under Section 544(a)

It should be noted that while the recording of a lien after the bankruptcy filing date is usually ineffective against the trustee under Section 544(a), if local law permits a later recording to relate back to a prebankruptcy event, such as the time of performance of the service for which the lien exists, then the postbankruptcy recording of the lien may perfect the lien and prevent the trustee from avoiding it under Section 544(a). See In re Maas, 69 B.R. 245 (MD FL, 1986).

relation back of lien recording, when applicable

Transfers that are avoidable under local law because of a defect in the instrument of conveyance may also be avoided by the trustee under Section 544(a). A recorded but legally defective mortgage was held avoidable by the trustee under Section 544(a) in In re Ryan, 851 F.2d 502 (1st Cir., 1988). An improperly executed mortgage was held avoidable by the trustee under Section 544(a) in In re Taylor, 58 B.R. 793 (WD LA, 1986). In In re Haynes, 41 B.R. 423 (MD TN, 1984), the interest of a creditor who had released its lien against the debtor's property in return for a quit-claim deed that was never recorded was avoided by the trustee under Section 544(a)(3). In In re Cascade Oil Co., 65 B.R. 35 (KS, 1986), an unrecorded assignment of an oil and gas lease was avoided under Section 544(a)(3) because under local law an oil and gas lease constituted an interest in real property. In In re Kline, 242 B.R. 306 (WD NC, 1999), a properly executed deed of trust was avoided because it was recorded in the wrong county.

defective transfers, avoidability under Section 544(a)

unrecorded deeds, avoidability under Section 544(a)

In In re Allen, 75 B.R. 572 (ED MO, 1987), the trustee was allowed to avoid the interest of a prebankruptcy purchaser of the debtor's real property who had only an unrecorded quit-claim deed to the property. However, in In re Flether Oil Co., 124 B.R. 501 (ED MI, 1990), the trustee was not allowed to avoid an unrecorded quit-claim deed to the debtor's property because the transferee was living in open possession of the property, which under local law gave a bonafide purchaser of the property notice of the transferee's claim to the property. In Michael v. Martinson, 49 F.3d 499 (9th Cir., 1995), the court held that the trustee could not use Section 544(a)(3) to avoid the debtor's unrecorded homestead interest in his own property.

avoidability of fraudulent transfers under Section 544(b)(1), charitable contribution exception

fraudulent transfers, avoidability under Section 544(b)(1)

As indicated earlier in this article, under Section 544(b)(1) the trustee may avoid transfers made by the debtor in violation of state fraudulent conveyance or fraudulent transfer laws. It should be noted, however, that transfers by the debtor for charitable contributions of up to 15 percent of the debtor's gross income are protected from avoidability under Section 544(b)(1) by the provisions of Section 544(b)(2). A prebankruptcy transfer of funds from the debtor to his or her spouse made in violation of the state fraudulent conveyance statute was held avoidable under Section 544(b)(1) in Butler v. Nations Bank, N.A., 58 F.3d 1022 (4th Cir., 1995). See also In re Carpenter, 56 B.R. 704 (RI, 1986), where the prebankruptcy transfer by the debtor of his residence to his wife was avoided by trustee under Section 544(b) and where the court also held that the debtor was barred by 11 U.S.C. § 522(g)(1) from claiming a homestead exemption in the property after it was recovered by the trustee. See also In re Carbaat, 357 B.R. 553 (ND CA, 2006).

fraudulent transfers, avoidability under Section 544(b)(1)

Transfers by the debtor of nonexempt property for exempt property can be avoided by the trustee under Section 544(b)(1). For example, in Gigandet v. Covington, 171 B.R. 294 (MD TN, 1994), the transfer by the debtor of nonexempt fire insurance proceeds into an exempt single premium life insurance policy together with the transfer of a remainder interest in real estate to her children were held avoidable under Section 544(b)(1) because the transfers violated the state fraudulent conveyance law. The creation by the debtor of a spendthrift trust in his own favor was held avoidable under Section 544(b)(1) in Barash v. Morris, 144 B.R. 401 (CD IL, 1992) because it was created in violation of the state fraudulent conveyance act. See In re Guillot, 250 B.R. 570 (MD LA, 2000), for a similar ruling.

transfers for no consideration, avoidability under Section 544(b)(1)

An acceptance by the debtor of title to property in joint tenancy with his or her spouse may constitute an avoidable transfer under Section 544(b)(1) if the debtor provides all of the consideration for the property. See In re Herbst, 76 B.R. 882 (MA, 1987). The transfer of the debtor's farm to a religious society for no monetary consideration was avoided under Section 544(b) in In re Zarling, 70 B.R. 402 (ED WI, 1987) because the transfer was fraudulent as to creditors under the state fraudulent conveyance statute. A transfer of property to the debtor's grandparents for no consideration was avoided under Section 544(b)(1) in In re Steele, 79 B.R. 503 (MD FL, 1987) for the same reason.

Preferential transfers avoidable under Section 547(b). A transfer of an interest in real or personal property made by an insolvent debtor to a creditor for the payment of an antecedent debt within 90 days prior to the bankruptcy filing date is avoidable by the trustee as a preference under Section 547(b) if the transfer enabled the creditor to receive more than it would have received in a Chapter 7 liquidation case had the transfer not been made. If the creditor is an insider, the preference (or look-back) period is one year instead of 90 days. An antecedent debt is a debt that existed prior to the transfer.

Section 547(b), general provisions of

The primary purpose of Section 547(b) is to effectuate the Bankruptcy Code policy of equal distribution of estate assets to creditors of the same class. Section 547(b) implements this policy by preventing a debtor from favoring one creditor over another of the same class on the eve of bankruptcy. See In re Microage Corp., 288 B.R. 855 (AZ, 2003). Accordingly, a creditor that receives a greater payment than others in its class may be required under Section 547(b) to return the money or property received on the eve of bankruptcy. The motives of the debtor and creditor are irrelevant with respect to a Section 547(b) action. See In re Fordu, 209 B.R. 854 (B.A.P. 6th Cir., 1997).

Section 547(b), purpose of

Because "insiders" are more likely to be favored by insolvent debtors, the period of avoidability is increased from 90 days to one year with respect to transfers to them. For individual debtors, insiders include relatives and general partners of the debtor and corporations and partnerships controlled by the debtor. See 11 U.S.C. § 101(31). Relatives include persons related by affinity or consanguinity within the 3rd degree. See 11 U.S.C. § 101(45).

insider, what constitutes

For a transfer to be avoidable under Section 547(b) all of the following conditions must exist:

avoidability under Section 547(b), required conditions

(1) The transfer must be of an interest of the debtor in property.

(2) The transfer must be to or for the benefit of a creditor for or on account of an antecedent debt owed by the debtor prior to the transfer.

(3) The transfer must be made while the debtor was insolvent and within 90 days prior to the bankruptcy filing date (or within one year prior to the bankruptcy filing date if the preferred creditor was an insider).

(4) The transfer must enable the creditor to receive more than it would have received in a Chapter 7 liquidation case had the transfer not occurred.

transfer of interest in property, what constitutes

insolvent debtor, presumption

The word "transfer" was amended by the BAPCPA and is broadly defined in the Bankruptcy Code to include every mode of voluntarily or involuntarily parting with an interest in property, including the creation of a lien, the retention of title as a security interest, and the foreclosure of a debtor's equity of redemption. See 11 U.S.C. § 101(54). However, for purposes of Section 547, a transfer is not made until the debtor has acquired rights in the property transferred. See 11 U.S.C. § 547(e)(3). The term "interest in property" has been broadly construed to include any interest that would constitute property of the estate under 11 U.S.C. § 541 had it not been transferred. See In re Lewis W. Shurtleff, Inc., 778 F.2d 1416 (9th Cir., 1985). That a debtor does not have an equitable interest in property that he holds in trust for another, see Poss v. Morris, 260 F.3d 654 (6th Cir., 2001). For a ruling holding that a debtor general contractor holds funds in trust for the benefit of unpaid subcontractors, see In re IT Group, Inc., 326 B.R. 270 (DE, 2005). For purposes of Section 547, a debtor is presumed to have been insolvent during the 90 day period immediately preceding the bankruptcy filing date. See 11 U.S.C. § 547(f).

1 year preference period, when applicable to creditor

While a 90 day preference period is normally applied to all creditors except insiders, it has been held that if an insider is benefitted by a transfer, the one-year preference period (rather than the 90 day preference period) is applicable in determining whether the transfer is voidable under Section 547(b) even though the transfer was made to the creditor and not to the insider. See In re Sufolla, 2 F.3d 977 (9th Cir., 1993), where the court held that if an insider has guaranteed an obligation of the debtor, the Section 547(b) preference period with respect to payments made by the debtor to the creditor on such an obligation should be one year instead of 90 days. See also, Hirsch v. Va. Tarricone, 286 B.R. 256 (SD NY, 2002); In re Global Aviation Holdings Inc., 478 B.R. 142 (Bankr. E.D.N.Y. 2012).

Section 547(i), effect on debtors

The BAPCPA added a new subsection (i) to section 547 pertaining to transfers to insiders. Under the new section 547(i), if the debtor transfers money or property to a non-insider creditor of an insider between 90 days and one year prior to bankruptcy, the trustee cannot avoid the transfer as between the non-insider creditor and debtor, but can avoid any transfer of liability as between the debtor and the insider

The Bankruptcy Code excludes certain types of transfers from avoidability under Section 547(b). See 11 U.S.C. § 547(c), which provides that the following types of transfers are not avoidable as preferences under Section 547(b):

transfers not avoidable under Section 547(b)

(1) contemporaneous exchanges for new value,
(2) payments of debts incurred in the ordinary course of the debtor's business,
(3) transfers creating purchase money security interests securing new value that are perfected within 30 days,
(4) transfers to creditors who then give new value to the debtor,
(5) certain transfers creating perfected security interests in inventory or receivables,
(6) transfers that fix valid statutory liens, such as mechanics liens,
(7) payments for domestic support obligations, and
(8) transfers of less than $600 made by consumer debtors.
(9) for a debtor with primarily non-consumer debts, transfers of less than $5,475. See 11 U.S.C. § 547(c).

It should be noted that under (4) above, the "new value" defense to a preferential transfer is available only to the extent of the new value received by the debtor in the transaction. See Gray v. Oppenheimer, 262 B.R. 172 (MA, 2001). Under (8) above, it has been held that two or more transfers to the same creditor within 90 days of bankruptcy may be added together for purpose of reaching the $600 minimum. See In re Clark, 217 B.R. 89 (WD KY, 1995). Finally, it should be understood that setoffs are not avoidable under section 547(b). Prebankruptcy setoffs are not considered "transfers" for purposes of Section 547(b) and must be dealt with under 11 U.S.C. § 553. See Jarboe v. U.S. Small Bus. Admin., 137 B.R. 835 (ND OK, 1992).

new value defense, extent of

setoffs, not avoidable under Section 547(b)

In addition to the limitations placed on a trustee's ability to avoid any of the nine types of transfers enumerated in section 547(c), the BAPCPA added a new subsection (h). Under section 547(h), a trustee is not allowed to avoid any transfers made by the debtor to a creditor that were made in connection with a debt repayment plan or schedule that is created by an approved credit counseling service. This section is meant to bolster the credit counseling requirement and general debtor education thrust of the BAPCPA.

Section 547(h), effect of

Section 547(b) is generally applicable only to transfers to unsecured creditors. Creditors who become fully secured more than 90 days prior to the bankruptcy filing date are not subject to attack under Section 547(b). See In re Missionary Baptist Foundation, Inc., 796 F.2d 752 (5th Cir., 1986). However, a creditor who becomes fully secured within the applicable preference period of Section 547(b) may be subject to attack under Section 547(b) if it's security interest was perfected by virtue of an avoidable preference. In this regard it should be noted that payments made by a debtor to a partially-secured creditor during the preference period are presumed to have been first applied to the unsecured portion of the debt and may therefore by avoidable under Section 547(b). See Drabkin v. A. I. Credit Corp., 800 F.2d 1153 (CA DC, 1986).

Section 547(b), applicability to secured creditors

While the Bankruptcy Code contains no such requirement, several courts have held that to constitute an avoidable preference under Section 547(b) the transfer in question must have diminished the debtor's estate. See In re Standard Food Service, Inc., 723 F.2d 820 (11th Cir., 1984). Therefore a transfer within the Section 547(b) preference period from the debtor to a solvent creditor in exchange for the creditor's promissory note has been held not to be an avoidable preference under Section 527(b) because the exchange was for present value and the debtor's estate was not diminished by the transfer. See In re Southern Industrial Banking Corp., 48 B.R. 306 (ED TN, 1985).

avoidable preference, necessity of diminishing debtor's estate

earmarking doctrine, requirements

Another court-imposed rule applicable to avoidable preferences under Section 547(b) is the so-called "earmarking doctrine." Under this doctrine the payment of an existing debt within the preference period with earmarked funds does not constitute a preference, provided that the earmarked funds were never in the debtor's control, because one creditor is simply substituted for another and the estate is not diminished. See In re Fox, 382 B.R. 800 (KS, 2008) and In re Hartley, 825 F.2d 1067 (6th Cir., 1987). This doctrine is premised on the Section 547(b) requirement that to be an avoidable preference the transfer must be of an interest of the debtor in property. Because the funds come from a third party, an interest of the debtor is not being transferred and the debtor's estate is therefore not diminished by the earmarked transfer. See In re Heitkamp, 137 F.3d 1087 (8th Cir., 1998).

earmarking doctrine, when applicable

For a transaction to qualify as nonpreferential under the earmarking doctrine there must be an agreement between the new lender and the debtor that the new funds will be used only to pay a specified antecedent debt, the agreement must be carried out according to its terms, and there must be no diminution of the debtor's estate because of the transaction. See In re Bohlen Enterprises, Ltd., 859 F.2d 561 (8th Cir., 1988), and Adams v. Anderson, 223 F.3d 1004 (9th Cir., 2000). Of course, if the debtor controls the disposition of funds and independently designates the creditor to whom the funds will be paid, the earmarking doctrine does not apply and the transfer is avoidable as a preference under Section 547(b). The earmarking doctrine has also been held not to be applicable in situations where an unsecured debt owed by the debtor is paid off with the proceeds of a secured loan of the debtor because the lien resulting from the transaction diminishes the debtor's estate. See In re Van Huffel Tube Corp., 74 B.R. 579 (ND OH, 1987); In re Crystal Medical Products, Inc., 240 B.R. 290 (ND IL, 1999); In re Visionary Imaging, LLC, 450 B.R. 876 (Bankr. E. D. Mo. 2011).

earmarking doctrine, when applicable

The earmarking doctrine has been held applicable to situations where the guarantor or cosigner of a note supplies funds for the specific purpose of paying off the note. See Brown v. First Nat. Bank, 748 F.2d 490 (8th Cir., 1984). It has also been held applicable to situations where a family member or other third party provides funds to cover a short check or to pay off a specified debt within the preference period. See In re Hartley, 825 F.2d 1067 (6th Cir., 1987), and In re Borgman, 48 B.R. 666 (WD MO, 1985).

tearmarking doctrine, credit card transfers

The earmarking doctrine appears not to apply to the now common practice of using an offer from a credit card issuer to pay another card. The general theory asserted by the courts is that the debtor has control of the funds, and they are not earmarked for specific payment of the previously incurred debt (even when the funds never passed through the debtor's account). See In re Egidi, 571 F.3d 1156 (11th Cir., 2009), In re Perry, 343 B.R. 685 (10th Cir., 2008), In re Wells, 561 F.3d 633 (6th Cir., 2009), and In re Dilworth, 383 B.R. 415 (ND OH, 2007).

The transfer of funds or property by a debtor to an attorney during the preference period for the payment of an antecedent fee obligation (i.e., for services previously rendered) is clearly an avoidable preference under Section 547(b). See In re Day Telecommunications, Inc., 70 B.R. 904 (ED NC, 1987) and In re American Metro Comm. Corp., 274 B.R. 641 (DE, 2002). The retention by an attorney, pursuant to a contingent fee agreement, of a fee from funds collected for the debtor by the attorney during the preference period may or may not be an avoidable preference depending on whether the attorney had a valid lien on the proceeds under local law that was perfected prior to the preference period. If the contingent fee agreement does not contain the requisite elements of a valid equitable or attorney's lien under local law, the funds retained by the attorney during the preference period may be recovered by the trustee as an avoidable preference under Section 547(b). See Kallen v. Litas, 47 B.R. 977 (ND IL, 1985). However, if under local law the contingent fee agreement creates a valid equitable or attorney's lien on the proceeds of the recovery prior to the preference period, then the collection and retention of an attorney's fee during the preference period does not constitute a voidable preference under Section 547(b). See In re Brass Kettle Restaurant, Inc., 790 F.2d 574 (7th Cir., 1986), and In re Sin-ko, Inc., 72 B.R. 651 (ND OH, 1987). Payments made by a debtor to an attorney for future services are not transfers on account of an antecedent debt and are therefore not avoidable under Section 547(b) if made during the preference period. See Meeks v. Perroni, 234 B.R. 899 (ED AR, 1999). Note, however, that a debtor's attorney is not automatically an "insider." In re Premiere Network Services, Inc., 333 B.R. 126 (N. D. Tex. 2005).

transfers to attorneys during preference period, avoidability of

Most tax payments made by or on behalf of the debtor during the preference period are not avoidable under Section 547(b) because tax claims are usually priority claims and would be collectible by the creditor in a Chapter 7 case if the transfer had not been made. See In re Kohout, 236 B.R. 365 (ND OH, 1999). Also, payments of trust fund taxes to the Internal Revenue Service (i.e., employee income and FICA taxes, excise taxes, etc.) are not avoidable under Section 547(b) because such payments are held in a statutory trust. See Begier v. U.S. IRS, 878 F.2d 762 (3d Cir., 1989). However, the payment of nondesignated funds to the Internal Revenue Service during the preference period may constitute an avoidable preference if the funds were not applied to trust fund debts by the IRS. See In re L & S Concrete Services, Inc., 129 B.R. 208 (ED WA, 1991).

tax payments during preference period, avoidability of transfer

The time that a transfer is deemed to have occurred is important under Section 547(b) because only transfers that are deemed to have occurred during the preference period are avoidable. For purposes of Section 547(b), a transfer is deemed to have occurred at the time the transfer takes effect pursuant to the agreement between the parties if the transfer is perfected within 10 days thereafter. If the transfer is not perfected within 10 days thereafter, the transfer is deemed to have occurred when the transfer was perfected if the perfection occurs prior to the bankruptcy filing. The transfer is deemed to have occurred immediately prior to the bankruptcy filing date if the transfer is not perfected until after the later of the bankruptcy filing date or the expiration of the 10 day post-transfer perfection period described above in this paragraph. See 11 U.S.C. § 547(e)(2).

time of transfer under Section 547(b), rules

real property, time of transfer under Section 547(b)

A transfer of an interest in real property, other than fixtures, is deemed to be perfected when a legitimate bonafide purchaser of the property from the debtor cannot under local law acquire an interest in the property superior to that of the transferee. See 11 U.S.C. § 547(e)(1)(A). Interests under contracts for the sale of real estate are included under the above rule. Transfers of interests in fixtures and personal property are deemed to be perfected when the transferee's interest cannot under local law be avoided under a judicial lien. See 11 U.S.C. § 547(e)(1)(B).

garnishments, time of transfer under Section 547(b)

Funds garnisheed by a creditor from the debtor's employer during the preference period are recoverable under Section 547(b) if under local law the transfer is deemed to have occurred during the preference period. The time of transfer of garnisheed funds depends on the wording and interpretation of the local garnishment statute. In some cases the time of transfer is deemed to have been the time that the writ of garnishment was served on the employer. See Miller v. Kibler, 182 B.R. 26 (ED KY, 1995), and Harpley v. Hines, 153 B.R. 925 (MD FL, 1993). Courts sitting in other states have held that a transfer does not occur until the final order of garnishment is issued. See Freedom Group v. Lapham-Hickey Steel Corp., 50 F.3d 408 (7th Cir., 1995). Other courts have held that the transfer occurs when the wages are actually earned by the debtor. See In re Johnson, 239 B.R. 416 (MD AL, 1999), In re Baker, 246 B.R. 379 (ED MO, 2000), and Taylor v. Mississippi Learning Inst., 151 B.R. 772 (ND MS, 1993). In In re Price, 272 B.R. 828 (WD NY, 2002) the court held that since the transfer of property under Section 547 must be determined under federal rather than state law, a levy on the debtor's wages was a transfer that occurred at the time of payment of the wages.

checks, time of transfer under Section 547(b)

divorce-related transfers, validity of under Section 547(b)

For purposes of determining whether a transfer occurs within the Section 547(b) preference period, the time of transfer with respect to checks can be important. In Barnhill v. Johnson, 503 U.S. 393, 118 L.Ed. 2d 39, 112 S.Ct. 1396 (1992), the Supreme Court clarified the law on the subject by ruling that for purposes of Section 547(b) a transfer occurs when the check is honored by the bank, regardless of when the check was issued by the debtor or received by creditor. Property transferred by the debtor within 90 days of bankruptcy pursuant to a valid, noncollusive divorce decree is not normally held to be a preferential transfer under Section 547(b). See In re Hope, 231 B.R. 403 (DC, 1999), and In re Parker, 241 B.R. 722 (OR, 1999).

fraudulent transfers, avoidability of under Section 544(a)(1)

Fraudulent transfers avoidable under Section 548(a)(1). Section 548(a)(1) is the fraudulent transfer section of the Bankruptcy Code. This section permits the bankruptcy trustee to avoid transfers made by the debtor within two years prior to the bankruptcy filing date that unlawfully deplete the debtor's estate to the detriment of creditors. Transfers within two years of bankruptcy that are tainted by either actual fraud or constructive fraud may be avoided by the trustee under this section. It should be noted that some transfers that are avoidable under this section may also be avoidable under Section 544(b)(1) as being in violation of a state fraudulent conveyance law.

Section 548(a)(1)(A) deals with actual fraud. It provides, in essence, that the trustee may avoid any transfer of an interest of the debtor in property made within two years before the bankruptcy filing date if the transfer was made with actual intent by the debtor to hinder, delay or defraud existing or future creditors. See 11 U.S.C. § 548(a)(1)(A).

Section 548(a)(1)(A), provisions of

Section 548(a)(1)(B) deals with constructive fraud. It provides, in essence, that the trustee may avoid any transfer of an interest of the debtor in property made within two years before the bankruptcy filing date if the debtor received less than a reasonably equivalent value in exchange for the transfer and was insolvent, undercapitalized, or unable to pay his or her debts, either when the transfer occurred or as a result of the transfer. See 11 U.S.C. § 548(a)(1)(B).

Section 548(a)(1)(B), provisions of

It should be noted that Section 548(a)(1) also permits the trustee to avoid fraudulent obligations incurred by the debtor within two years of bankruptcy. However, because this article deals only with avoidable transfers made by the debtor, the avoidance of obligations under Section 548(a) will not be discussed.

fraudulent obligations, avoidability of under section 548(a)(1)

It should also be noted that transfers by the debtor of charitable contributions to qualified religious or charitable entities are not avoidable under Section 548(a)(1) if the amount of the contributions in any year do not exceed 15 percent of the debtor's annual gross income or, if in excess of 15 percent, is consistent with the debtor's practices in this regard. See 11 U.S.C. § 548(a)(2). See 11 U.S.C. § 548(d)(3) and (4) for the definitions of "charitable contributions" and "qualified religious or charitable entity or organization."

charitable contributions by debtor, avoidability of under Section 548(a)(1), exception

For a transfer to be avoidable under Section 548(a)(1), whether for actual fraud under subpart (A) or for constructive fraud under subpart (B), there must be a (1) "transfer" of (2) "an interest of the debtor in property" that was (3) "made within two years before the date of the filing of the petition." These three elements must be present in order for a transfer to be avoidable under Section 548(a)(1), regardless of the type of fraud involved. These elements will be discussed first below, followed by discussions of the requirements of actual fraud under subpart (A) and constructive fraud under subpart (B).

Section 548(a)(1), general requirements for avoidability under

A "transfer" is defined in the Bankruptcy Code to mean "every mode, direct or indirect, absolute or conditional, voluntary or involuntary, of disposing of or parting with property or with an interest in property, including the creation of a lien, the retention of title as a security interest and the foreclosure of the debtor's equity of redemption." See 11 U.S.C. § 101(54). It is clear both from the definition of transfer and from the appearance of the words "voluntarily or involuntarily" in Section 548(a)(1) that both voluntary and involuntary transfers are covered by (and therefore avoidable under) Section 548(a)(1). The debtor's granting of a security interest constitutes a "transfer". See In re Jordan, 392 B.R. 428 (ID, 2008).

transfer, what constitutes, types of

Voluntary conveyances are clearly "transfers" for purposes of Section 548(a). Therefore, just about any type of voluntary transfer made by the debtor within one year of bankruptcy is subject to avoidability under Section 548(a)(1), regardless of to whom the transfer is made.

voluntary transfers, avoidability of under Section 548(a)(1) involuntary transfer, time of, how determined

Involuntary transfers (i.e., foreclosures, repossessions, etc.) are usually triggered by the debtor's failure to fulfill an obligation owed to a creditor. A repossession or foreclosure sale is clearly a "transfer" under Section 548(a). See In re Littleton, 888 F.2d 90 (11th Cir., 1989). The only question is when the transfer occurs. If there is no redemption period with respect to the repossession or foreclosure, then the transfer occurs at the time of the repossession or sale. However, if under local law the debtor has a specified period during which to redeem the property, some courts have held that for purposes of Section 548(a)(1) the "transfer" does not occur until the expiration of the redemption period. See In re Cole, 81 B.R. 326 (ED PA, 1988). Other courts have held that the "transfer" occurs for purposes of Section 548(a)(1) at the time of the foreclosure sale. See In re Butler, 862 F.2d 1015 (3d Cir., 1988). Much depends on the phraseology of the local statute and the rights created thereunder. The time of the transfer can be important in determining whether the transfer occurred during the two year look-back period of Section 548(a)(1).

avoidable involuntary transfers, types of

Other types of involuntary transfers that may be subject to avoidability under Section 548(a)(1) include (1) the perfection of a security interest in the debtor's property, (2) the attachment of a lien on the debtor's property, (3) the garnishment of the debtor's wages or bank account, (4) the filing of a lis pendens on the debtor's property, and (5) the termination of a lease of property to the debtor. Some courts have held that the termination of the debtor's rights under an executory contract may also constitute an avoidable transfer under Section 548(a)(1). See In re Sheppard's Dental Centers, Inc., 65 B.R. 274 (SD FL, 1986).

time of transfer, garnishments, foreclosures

As indicated above, the time at which a transfer is deemed to have occurred can be important under Section 548(a)(1), especially in determining whether the transfer occurred within two years of bankruptcy. The time of transfer with respect to garnishments is discussed above in this article with respect to preferential transfers. The time of transfer with respect to foreclosures and repossessions is discussed two paragraphs above.

time of transfer, determination of, rules

The time of transfer can be difficult to determine with respect to transfers of security interests in the debtor's property. In this regard, Section 548(d)(1) of the Bankruptcy Code states that for purposes of Section 548 a transfer is deemed to be made when the transfer is so perfected that under local law a good-faith purchaser of the property from the debtor cannot acquire an interest in the property superior to that of the transferee. If such a transfer is not perfected prior to the commencement of the case, the transfer is deemed to have been made immediately prior to the bankruptcy filing date. See 11 U.S.C. § 548(d)(1). Under this provision fraudulent security interests which are created prior to the two-year look-back period of Section 548(a)(1) but which are not perfected under local law until a time within the two-year period or which are not perfected prior to the bankruptcy filing date are avoidable by the trustee under Section 548(a). See In re Emerald Oil Co., 807 F.2d 1234 (5th Cir., 1987), and In re Ozark Restaurant Equip. Co., 850 F.2d 342 (8th Cir., 1988) (interpreting Section 548(a) prior to the BAPCPA amendment increasing the look-back period from one year to two years).

As indicated above, only the transfer of "an interest of the debtor in property" may be avoided under Section 548(a)(1). While the term "interest of the debtor in property" is not defined in the Bankruptcy Code, it is generally held to mean any interest in property which if recovered would be includable in the debtor's bankruptcy estate. See In re Wallace, 66 B.R. 834 (ED MO, 1986). Under this definition, transfers of property by the debtor which if recovered would not be property of the estate may not be avoided by the trustee.

interest of debtor in property, what constitutes

Under the above definition, the transfer by the debtor of property held by the debtor in trust, either to another trustee or to the beneficial owner, may not be avoided by the trustee under Section 548(a)(1), if the trust is valid and was not fraudulently created. See In re Torrez, 63 B.R. 751 (B.A.P. 9th Cir., 1986), and In re Welborn, 75 B.R. 243 (MT, 1987). Payments made under a letter of credit issued by the debtor's bank have been held not to constitute the transfer of an interest of the debtor in property because it is the bank's funds and not the debtor's that are transferred. See Kupetz v. Continental Illinois Nat. Bank & Trust Co., 77 B.R. 754 (B.A.P. 9th Cir., 1986) (affirmed in 845 F.2d 842 (9th Cir., 1987)). It has also been held that the transfer by the debtor of property in which the debtor has no equity does not constitute the transfer of an interest of the debtor in property for purposes of Section 548(a). See In re Central States Press, 57 B.R. 418 (WD MO, 1985). For a holding that a debtor's use of a credit card to pay a preexisting debt when the debtor was insolvent did not involve an "interest of the debtor in property", see In re Perry, 343 B.R. 685 (UT, 2005).

interest of debtor in property, transfers not constituting

It has been held that an involuntary transfer of property that is exempt to the debtor does not constitute the transfer of an interest of the debtor in property for purposes of Section 548(a)(1) because if recovered the property could be exempted by the debtor and would therefore not be property of the estate. See In re Turner, 45 B.R. 649 (SD OH, 1985). Voluntary transfers of exempt property by the debtor are avoidable under Section 548(a)(1), however, because the debtor is precluded from claiming an exemption in such property. See 11 U.S.C. § 522(g). Under this theory it would appear that transfers by the debtor of property that would be excludable from debtor's estate under 11 U.S.C. § 541(c)(2), such as the debtor's interest in an ERISA-qualified retirement plan, would also not be avoidable under Section 548(a)(1). However, transfers by the debtor of nonexempt property into exempt property on the eve of bankruptcy are often avoidable under this section. See In re Loomer, 222 B.R. 618 (NE, 1998), and In re Pulliam, 279 B.R. 916 (MD GA, 2002).

transfers of exempt property, avoidability of under Section 548(a)(1)

Under Section 548(a)(1)(A), which is the actual fraud provision of Section 548(a)(1), the trustee may avoid the transfer of an interest of the debtor in property made within two years of bankruptcy if the transfer was made with actual intent to hinder, delay or defraud existing or future creditors of the debtor. The important issue under this provision, in addition to the general Section 548(a)(1) issues discussed in the preceding paragraphs, is whether the transfer was made with an actual intent to defraud. To be avoidable under Section 548(a)(1)(A) the transfer must also be prejudicial to creditors, but that condition almost always exists.

Section 548(a)(1)(A), requirements for avoidability under

actual fraud, what constitutes

Actual fraud for purposes of Section 548(a)(1)(A) has been defined as any deceit, artifice, trick, or design involving the direct and active operation of the mind used to circumvent and cheat another. See In re Sentinel Management Group, Inc., 689 F.3d 855 (7th Cir. 2012) (requiring a creditor to show that the main purpose of the transfer was to prevent a lawful creditor from collecting the debt); In re Landbank Equity Corp., 83 B.R. 362 (ED VA, 1987). The intent to hinder, delay or defraud (i.e., the actual fraudulent intent) must be that of the debtor-transferor, as the intent of the transferee is irrelevant. See In re Rubin Bros. Footwear, Inc., 119 B.R. 416 (SD NY, 1990), and In re Metro Shippers, Inc., 78 B.R. 747 (ED PA, 1987). In this regard it should be noted that transfers involving actual fraud must by definition be voluntary transfers.

actual fraud, when inferred

Because direct proof of actual fraudulent intent is rarely available, the courts have held that actual fraud may be inferred or implied when the existence of certain indicia or badges of fraud are established. See Kelly v. Armstrong, 141 F.3d 799 (8th Cir., 1998) and Kaler v. McLaren, 236 B.R. 882 (ND, 1999). The existence of a significant number of the following circumstances has been held to constitute "badges of fraud" sufficient to support an inference of actual fraudulent intent by the debtor for purposes of Section 548(a)(1)(A):

badges of fraud, list of

(1) where a close personal or business relationship exists between the debtor and the transferee;
(2) where the debtor received inadequate consideration for the transfer;
(3) where the debtor was insolvent or heavily in debt at the time of the transfer;
(4) where the debtor's entire estate was transferred;
(5) where the debtor retained control or possession of the transferred property or retained certain important benefits from the property;
(6) where the transfer was concealed or secretly made;
(7) where litigation against the debtor was pending or threatened at the time of the transfer;
(8) where the transfer was made outside of the debtor's usual course of business;
(9) where numerous transfers occurred without a rational business purpose or explanation;
(10) where the filing of the bankruptcy case was obviously delayed in an attempt to avoid the two-year look-back period of Section 548(a); or
(11) where the debtor was unable to satisfactorily explain transactions that were obviously suspicious or indicative of fraud.

actual fraud, proof of, requirements

The existence of a single badge of fraud is usually insufficient to support an inference of actual fraud, but the existence of several badges will normally support such an inference. See In re FBN Food Services, Inc., 185 B.R. 265 (ND IL, 1995), and In re Warner, 87 B.R. 199 (MD FL, 1988). Other factors, however, may mitigate against an inference of actual fraud even if several badges of fraud are shown to exist. Included here are such factors as the occurrence of the transfer during a relatively profitable period for the debtor and a lack of business sophistication on the part of the debtor. See In re Zeman, 60 B.R. 764 (ND IA, 1986).

Under Section 548(a)(1)(B), which is the constructive fraud provision of Section 548(a)(1), the trustee may avoid the transfer of an interest of the debtor in property made within two years of bankruptcy if the debtor received less than a reasonably equivalent value in exchange for the transfer and was insolvent, undercapitalized, or unable to pay his or her debts at the time of the transfer or became such by reason of the transfer. See 11 U.S.C. § 548(a)(1)(B). Generally, under Section 548(a)(1)(B) a transfer is avoidable as fraudulent if certain objective criteria with respect to the transfer can be established, regardless of whether the debtor actually intended to hinder, delay or defraud creditors.

Section 548(a)(1)(B), requirements of for constructive fraud

The principal requirement for avoidability for constructive fraud under Section 548(a)(1)(B) is that the debtor received less than a reasonably equivalent value in exchange for the transfer. If the debtor received a reasonably equivalent value in exchange for the transfer, the estate was not diminished by the transfer and the transfer is not avoidable. See In re Jeffrey Bigelow Design Group, Inc., 956 F.2d 479 (4th Cir., 1992).

avoidability under Section 548(a)(1)(B), main requirement

The first step in determining whether the debtor received a reasonably equivalent value in exchange for the transfer is that of determining whether "value" of a kind recognized by the Bankruptcy Code was received by the debtor in exchange for the transfer. "Value" is defined in Section 548(d)(2)(A) of the Bankruptcy Code to mean property or the satisfaction or securing of a present or antecedent debt of the debtor. However, value does not include an unperformed promise to furnish support to the debtor or to a relative of the debtor. See 11 U.S.C. § 548(d)(2)(A). Therefore, if the debtor received in exchange for the transfer either property or the payment or securing of a present or antecedent debt, then value was received for the transfer and the question is whether the value was sufficient to constitute a reasonably equivalent value. If the debtor received neither property nor the payment or securing of a present or antecedent debt, then value was not received for the transfer.

value, what constitutes under Section 548(a)(1)(B)

As indicated above, to have received value in exchange for a transfer, the debtor must have received either property or the payment or securing of a present or antecedent debt. "Property" is not defined in the Bankruptcy Code but is generally defined to include anything that is the subject of ownership, real or personal, corporeal or incorporeal, tangible or intangible, visible or invisible. See In re Falk, 88 B.R. 957 (MN, 1988). Consideration such as good will and forbearance from suit has been held to constitute property and therefore value under Section 548(a)(1)(B). The payment by the transferee of a debt guaranteed by the debtor has also been held to constitute value for purposes of Section 548(a)(2). However, such consideration as love and affection, disclaimers of the right to inherit the debtor's property, and promises of future consideration have been held not to constitute value for purposes of Section 548(a)(1). See Lim v. Greenfield, 273 B.R. 128 (ED MI, 2002), where a transfer of property by the debtor from himself to himself and his wife in tenancy by the entireties in exchange for the wife's inchoate dower rights was held not to have been made for reasonably equivalent value.

property, what constitutes

value, what constitutes

satisfaction of debt as value, requirements

Under Section 548(a)(1)(B), value, by definition, includes the satisfaction or securing of a present or antecedent debt of the debtor. A partial satisfaction of an indebtedness of the debtor is sufficient to constitute value. That is, a present or antecedent debt need not be satisfied in its entirety in order to constitute value under this section. See In re Crane, 6 B.R. 7 (ND AL, 1980). However, the satisfaction of a debt that is void or unenforceable does not constitute value. See In re Abramoff, 92 B.R. 698 (WD TX, 1988). While the securing by the transferee of a present or antecedent debt of the debtor constitutes value even if the security interest is not perfected until a later date, the security interest securing the debt must be granted contemporaneously with the transfer and not a later date. See In re Kelley, 7 B.R. 384 (SD, 1980). Also, to constitute value the debt secured must be a debt of the debtor and not the debt of a principal or spouse of the debtor. See In re Fair Oaks, Ltd., 168 B.R. 397 (B.A.P. 9th Cir., 1994).

reasonably equivalent value, what constitutes

The Bankruptcy Code does not define the term "reasonably equivalent value." What constitutes reasonably equivalent value under Section 548(a)(1)(B) depends greatly on the type of transfer involved and the context of the transfer. For example, if marketable property is transferred, reasonably equivalent value is generally equated to fair market value. See In re Ozark Restaurant Equip. Co., 850 F.2d 342 (8th Cir., 1988). Reasonably equivalent value has a different meaning when used with respect to involuntary transfers, such as foreclosures or repossessions, and sales of partial interests. In BFP v. Resolution Trust Corp., 511 U.S. 531, 114 S.Ct. 1757 (1994), the Supreme Court held that for purposes of Section 548(a)(1)(B) the price brought at a regularly conducted, noncollusive foreclosure sale of real estate is conclusively presumed to constitute reasonably equivalent value. In In re Washington, 232 B.R. 340 (ED VA, 1999), the sale of property assessed at $20,000 for $8,000 at a forced sale was held to constitute reasonably equivalent value where the state's tax sale foreclosure procedures gave the delinquent taxpayer adequate protection. See also In re Neal, 478 B.R. 261 (B.A.P. 6th Cir. 2012).

reasonably equivalent value, how to determine

Regardless of the type of transfer, however, the important factor in determining whether a reasonably equivalent value was received is what the debtor received and not what the transferee gave. The issue is whether the debtor received a value that was reasonably equivalent under the circumstances to that surrendered in the transfer and not on whether the value surrendered by the transferee was reasonably equivalent to that received by the transferee. See In re United Energy Corp., 944 F.2d 589 (9th Cir., 1991). It should also be understood that reasonably equivalent value may come from a person other than the transferee under the so-called indirect benefit rule. See In re Jeffrey Bigelow Design Group, Inc., 956 F.2d 479 (4th Cir., 1992).

For a transfer to be avoidable for constructive fraud under Section 548(a)(1)(B) it must also be shown that the debtor was insolvent, under capitalized, or unable to pay its debts, either at the time of the transfer or as a result of the transfer. See 11 U.S.C. § 548(a)(1)(B)(ii). For individual and corporate debtors "insolvent" is defined in the Bankruptcy Code to mean a financial condition such that the sum of the debtor's debts is greater than the fair value of all of the debtor's property except exempt property and property that has been fraudulently transferred, concealed or removed. See 11 U.S.C. § 101(32). Thus, a debtor is insolvent for purposes of Section 548(a)(1)(B) if liabilities exceed nonexempt assets. The insolvency must occur either on the date of the transfer or within a reasonable time either before or after the transfer. See In re Kaylor Equip & Rental, Inc., 56 B.R. 58 (ED TN, 1985). Contingent liabilities and assets must be realistically and appropriately discounted in determining insolvency. See In re Xonics Photochemical, Inc., 841 F.2d 198 (7th Cir., 1988). The burden of proof on the issue of the debtor's insolvency is on the trustee. See Burdick v. Lee, 256 B.R. 837 (MA, 2001).

insolvency of debtor under Section 548(a)(2), what constitutes

Section 548(e) permits the trustee to avoid transfers of money or property made by the debtor within 10 years prior to bankruptcy to a self-settled trust or similar device of which the debtor is a beneficiary upon a showing that the debtor made the transfer with actual intent to hinder, delay or defraud any entity to which the debtor was indebted to at the time of the transfer or became indebted to after the transfer. This new provision gives the trustee new powers to attack self-settled trusts of debtors. To do so, however, it appears that the trustee will have to show that the debtor actually intended to hinder, delay or defraud actual creditors. It may not be enough if the trustee merely shows that the debtor created and transferred assets to such a trust while he or she was indebted, because the statute does not provide for a presumption of fraud in such a situation.

Section 548(e), effect of

Bibliography. **For further reading on the issues discussed in this article, see the annotations and articles listed below.**

Annotations:

Calculation of 90-day period between transfer of interest in debtor's property and filing of debtor's petition in bankruptcy, for purpose of determining whether transfer is avoidable under 11 USCS §547(b), as made by counting backward from date petition was filed or by counting forward from date of transfer. 117 ALR Fed. 333.

When is transfer from debtor for «new value» within meaning of §§547(a)(2) and 547(c) of Bankruptcy Code of 1978. 111 ALR Fed 409.

Power of trustee in bankruptcy to defeat rights of beneficiary of constructive trust under §544(a) of Bankruptcy Code. 96 ALR Fed 100.

What falls within «contemporaneous exchange» exception to bankruptcy trustee›s power to avoid transfer of property by debtor, under §547(c)(1) of Bankruptcy Code. 77 ALR Fed 14.

Insider within meaning of Bankruptcy Code of 1978. 71 ALR Fed 197.

Right of creditor to set aside fraudulent transfer as affected by bankruptcy of debtor. 158 A.L.R. 1274.

Articles:

The correct application of Section 547(e)(2): deciding whether Wage garnishment transfers are preferential. 12 Bankruptcy Dev. J. 219, 1995.

Debtors who convert their assets on the eve of bankruptcy: villains or victims of the fresh start? 70 N.Y.U. L. Rev. 235, May 1995.

Robbing Peter to pay Paul: charitable donations as fraudulent transfers. 100 Dick. L.R. 103, Fall 1995.

The small preference exception of Bankruptcy Code Section 547(c)(7). 55 Ohio St. L.J. 675, 1994.

Lawsuits, contingent-fee contracts and bankruptcy. 47 Okla. L. Rev. 515, Fall 1994.

The subsequent new value exception under Section 547(c)(4) of the Bankruptcy Code - judicial gloss is creditors' loss. 24 Mem. St. U. L. Rev 667, Summer 1994.

Preference conundrums. 98 Com LJ 1, Spring, 1993.

Preferences in bankruptcy. 112 Banking L.J. 422, May 1995.

In re CHG International Incorporated [897 F2d 1479]: the ordinary course of business exception; what you see is what you get. 22 Golden Gate U L Rev 31, Spring 1992.

The effective date of a transfer by check under section 547(b) of the Bankruptcy Code: transfer upon delivery or honor? 70 Wash ULQ 209, Spring 1992.

Is there a one-year preference period for non-insiders? 64 Am. Bankruptcy L.J. 383, Fall 1990.

1.15 Under what circumstances and to what extent may a debtor recover damages for a violation of the automatic stay?

Text of statutes. Sections 105(a) and 362(k) of the Bankruptcy Code (11 U.S.C. § 105(a), 362(k)) provide as follows:

105. Power of court

Section 105(a), text of

(a) The court may issue any order, process, or judgment that is necessary or appropriate to carry out the provisions of this title. No provision of this title providing for the raising of an issue by a party in interest shall be construed to preclude the court from, sua sponte, taking any action or making any determination necessary or appropriate to enforce or implement court orders or rules, or to prevent an abuse of process.

362. Automatic stay

* * * * * *

Section 362(k), text of

(k)(1) Except as provided in paragraph (2), an individual injured by any willful violation of a stay provided by this section shall recover actual damages, including costs and attorneys' fees, and, in appropriate circumstances, may recover punitive damages.

(2) If such violation is based on an action taken by an entity in the good faith belief that subsection (h) applies to the debtor, the recovery under paragraph (1) of this subsection against such entity shall be limited to actual damages.

damages for relief from stay, history of

Introduction. The automatic stay is one of the fundamental protections accorded debtors by the Bankruptcy Code. Accordingly, violations of the automatic stay are treated as serious matters by bankruptcy courts, especially if the person injured by the violation is the debtor. Because in consumer cases the person most often injured by a violation of the automatic stay is the debtor, this article is devoted primarily to the rights of individual debtors to recover damages for violations of the automatic stay. It should be understood, however, that the bankruptcy trustee and, on occasion, other parties may also be damaged by violations of the automatic stay and may be entitled to recover damages therefor.

damages for violation of stay, history of

Prior to 1984 damage awards for violations of the automatic stay were made by bankruptcy courts under their Section 105(a) contempt powers. Then, in the Bankruptcy Amendments and Federal Judgeship Act of 1984, Congress created a separate right of damages for individuals injured by willful violations of the automatic stay in Section 362(h).

§362(k), BAPCPA amendments to

In 2005, the BAPCPA redesignated Section 362(h) as Section 362(k) and amended its provisions. Except for the proviso referring to paragraph (2), Section 362(k)(1) is identical to Section 362(h) as it existed prior to the BAPCPA. Because of the change of sections, actions to recover damages for violations of the automatic stay must now be brought under Section 362(k)(1) instead of Section 362(h).

Section 105(a) of the Bankruptcy Code permits a bankruptcy court to enforce and implement its orders and rulings through contempt proceedings. See In re Taylor, 379 B.R. 388 (MD FL, 2007). Because the automatic stay is deemed to be a court order for purposes of implementation and enforcement, a bankruptcy court can hold willful violators of the stay in contempt and award damages to parties injured by the violation. Section 362(k) of the Bankruptcy Code creates a separate right of damages for individuals injured by willful violations of the automatic stay. Therefore, a debtor or other aggrieved individual who is damaged by a willful violation of the automatic stay may be awarded damages either in a civil contempt proceeding under Section 105(a) or in a proceeding filed under Section 362(k). Sections 105(a) and 362(k), it should be noted, are applicable to cases filed under any chapter of the Bankruptcy Code, including Chapter 7 and Chapter 13 cases.

Section 105(a), general provisions

Sections 105(a) & 362(k), applicability of

It is clear that Section 362(k) was intended to supplement, and not replace, the civil contempt remedies available under Section 105(a). See 130 Cong. Record H 1942 (March 26, 1984); In re Colon, 114 B.R. 890 (ED PA, 1990). Therefore, an individual debtor or other injured individual may seek damages under either Section 105(a) or Section 362(k), although only one recovery is permitted. However, it has been held that an individual debtor's sole remedy is under Section 362(k). See Eskanos & Adler, P.C. v. Roman, 283 B.R. 1 (B.A.P. 9th Cir., 2002). Because only one recovery is permitted and because the procedures for obtaining recovery under the Sections 105(a) and 362(k) are substantially different, it is usually advisable to seek relief under one section or the other and not under both. In deciding whether to proceed under Section 362(k) or Section 105(a), the following factors should be considered:

Sections 105(a) & 362(k), relief under, choice of

relief under Section 105(a) vs. Section 362(k), factors

(1) The assessment of compensatory damages in a civil contempt proceeding under Section 105(a) is subject to a stricter standard than is the assessment of actual damages in a proceeding under Section 362(k).

(2) Punitive damages may be awarded under Section 362(k) but are seldom awarded in civil contempt proceedings under Section 105(a). See In re Aponte, 82 B.R. 738 (ED PA, 1988).

(3) Civil contempt proceedings under Section 105(a) must comply with the notice and procedural requirements of Bankruptcy Rule 9020 and require the filing of a complaint and the initiation of an adversary proceeding under Part VII of the Bankruptcy Rules. A proceeding under Section 362(k), on the other hand, is treated as a contested matter and may be initiated by the filing of a motion under Bankruptcy Rule 9014. See Patton v. Shade, 263 B.R. 861 (CD IL, 2001) and In re Timbs, 178 B.R. 989 (ED TN, 1994).

(4) A proceeding under Section 362(k) is a core proceeding and may be heard and decided by the bankruptcy court. See In re Johnson, 390 B.R. 414 (B.A.P. 10th Cir., 2008); In re Bethea, 275 B.R. 284 (ND IL, 2002); Budget Serv. Co. v. Better Homes of Virginia, 804 F.2d 289 (4th Cir., 1986). Civil contempt proceedings under Section 105(a) are treated as non-core proceedings and are subject to de novo review by the district court. See Bankruptcy Rule 9020(c); Brown v. Ramsay, 3 F.3d 1174 (8th Cir., 1993).

Section 362(k), when preferable to Section 105(a)

Because it is less expensive and easier to file and implement and because of the availability of punitive damages thereunder, Section 362(k) is usually preferable to Section 105(a) for individual debtors who have been damaged by a willful violation of the automatic stay. Section 105(a) may be preferable for corporate and other nonindividual debtors and for bankruptcy trustees seeking damages on behalf of the estate. Because Section 362(k) is clearly preferable to Section 105(a) for most Chapter 7 and Chapter 13 debtors, it will be discussed first below. A discussion of the civil contempt remedies available under Section 105(a) follows the discussion of Section 362(k).

Section 362(k) provides that an individual injured by a willful violation of the automatic stay shall recover actual damages, including costs and attorneys' fees and may recover punitive damages. To recover either actual or punitive damages under Section 362(k), then, the following conditions or requirements must be satisfied:

recovering damages under Section 362(k), requirements

(1) The debtor or other person seeking relief must be an individual.

(2) The entity from whom damages is sought must have violated at least one provision of the automatic stay as set forth in 11 U.S.C. § 362.

(3) The stay violation complained of must have been willfully committed.

(4) The person seeking relief must have been injured and incurred actual damages as a proximate result of the stay violation. See In re Adams, 212 B.R. 703 (MA, 1997).

These requirements are discussed separately under the appropriate headings in the paragraphs below.

individual under Section 362(k), what constitutes

The "individual" requirement of Section 362(k). The first requirement for recovering damages of any type under Section 362(k) is that the person seeking damages must be an "individual." While the term "individual" is not separately defined in the Bankruptcy Code, it is clear that a natural person is an "individual" for purposes of Section 362(k). A more difficult question is whether the term "individual" in Section 362(k) also includes debtors who are corporations, partnerships, or limited liability companies. Most courts have held that the context in which the term "individual" is used in Section 362(k) implies a natural person and it therefore was not intended to provide relief for corporations, partnerships, and other creatures of statute. See In re Spookyworld, Inc., 318 B.R. 1 (MA, 2003), In re Chateaugay Corp., 920 F.2d 183 (2d Cir., 1993), In re Just Brakes Corporate Systems, Inc., 108 F.3d 881 (8th Cir., 1997), and Johnston Environmental Corp. v. Knight, 991 F.2d 613 (9th Cir., 1993). Generally, in those circuits corporate, partnership, and limited liability company debtors may not recover damages of any type under Section 362(k).

Some courts, however, have held that limiting recovery to natural persons would be unfair and would defeat the purpose of Section 362(k). These courts have held that Congress must therefore have intended to include corporate debtors as individuals for purposes of Section 362(k). See In re Diamond Indus. Corp., 265 B.R. 707 (VI, 2001), Budget Service Co. v. Better Homes of Virginia, Inc., 804 F.2d 289 (4th Cir., 1986), and In re Atlantic Business and Community Corp., 901 F.2d 325 (3d Cir., 1990). In those circuits corporate debtors generally may recover damages under Section 362(k). In several circuits the issue of corporate eligibility under Section 362(k) has not been decided.

corporation as individual, cases

Another question is whether a bankruptcy trustee is an "individual" for purposes of Section 362(k). In In re Pace, 67 F.3d 187 (9th Cir., 1995), the court held that even though the trustee was a natural person, he represented the bankruptcy estate, which was not a natural person, and therefore the trustee was not an "individual" for purposes of the old Section 362(h) and could not recover damages under that section. See also In re C. W. Min. Co., 477 B.R. 176 (B.A.P. 10th Cir., 2012). However, in Martino v. First National Bank, 186 B.R. 414 (ND IL, 1995), the court rejected this narrow construction and held that in the absence of clear language to the contrary in the Bankruptcy Code, a Chapter 7 trustee may be considered an "individual" for purposes of the old Section 362(h) and could recover actual damages sustained by the bankruptcy estate as a result of a willful violation of the automatic stay. See also In re Fas Mart Convenience Stores, Inc., 318 B.R. 370 (ED VA, 2004) (where a Chapter 11 trustee was deemed to have standing to pursue sanctions for violating the automatic stay).

bankruptcy trustee as individual, cases

The stay violation requirement of Section 362(k). The second requirement for recovering damages of any type under Section 362(k) is that the entity against whom damages are sought must have violated a stay that is specified in Section 362 of the Bankruptcy Code. If the action complained of did not constitute a violation of at least one of the stays provided for in Section 362, then damages may not be recovered under Section 362(k). Violations of the Section 1301 stay of acts against codebtors and violations of the permanent injunction issued under 11 U.S.C. § 524(a) in conjunction with the issuance of a discharge are not compensable under Section 362(k). Such violations may be punishable (and compensable) under Section 105(a), however. See In re Wagner, 87 B.R. 612 (CD CA, 1988).

Section 362(k) recovery, necessity of automatic stay violation

Section 362(a) describes the scope of the automatic stay and provides that the filing of a bankruptcy petition operates as a stay, applicable to all entities, of the eight categories of acts listed therein. Section 362(b) limits the scope of the stay and provides that the filing of a bankruptcy petition does not operate as a stay as to the types of acts specified therein. Section 362(c) deals with the duration of the stay and provides that, unless relief from the stay is earlier granted, the automatic stay of acts against property of the estate continues until the property is no longer property of the estate and the stay of all other covered acts continues until the earlier of the granting of a discharge or the dismissal or closing of the case. To be entitled to relief under Section 362(k), then, the debtor must show that the acts complained of incurred after the filing of the bankruptcy petition and prior to the termination of the stay, were of a type prohibited by Section 362(a), and were not of a type permitted under Section 362(b).

violation of automatic stay, what constitutes

collection of non-dischargeable debt as stay violation

Section 362(a), it should be noted, does not distinguish between dischargeable and nondischargeable debts, which means that the automatic stay precludes the postpetition collection of nondischargeable debts during the period of the stay. See In re Copley, 383 B.R. 621 (SD WV, 2008). A creditor who wishes to collect or enforce a nondischargeable debt while the bankruptcy case is pending must first obtain relief from the stay. Otherwise, the creditor is in violation of the stay and may be liable for damages under Section 362(k). See In re Price, 179 B.R. 209 (ED CA, 1995), and In re Tweed, 76 B.R. 636 (ED TN, 1987).

violation of §362(a)(6), what constitutes

Any act by a creditor during the duration of the stay that is in violation of Section 362(a) and is not expressly permitted by Section 362(b) constitutes a violation of the automatic stay and may entitle the debtor to actual damages under Section 362(k). See Patton v. Shade, 263 B.R. 861 (CD IL, 2001); In re Price, 42 F.3d 1068 (7th Cir., 1994). In consumer cases the stay provision that is most likely to be violated is the Section 362(a)(6) stay which prohibits any act to collect, assess or recover a claim against the debtor that arose before the commencement of the bankruptcy case. The Section 362(a)(6) stay is strictly construed by most courts and even minor violations of this are likely to result in an award of damages to the debtor under Section 362(k). For example, in In re Colon, 102 B.R. 421 (ED PA, 1989) the state Department of Transportation and Traffic Court were found to have willfully violated the automatic stay for purposes of the old Section 362(h) by sending letters to the debtor attempting to collect a fine that was listed in the debtor's bankruptcy schedules after receiving notice of the debtor's bankruptcy filing and by threatening to have the debtor arrested if the fine was not paid.

contact with debtor as stay violation

In In re Baker, 183 B.R. 30 (RI, 1995) a creditor's direct postpetition contact with the Chapter 7 debtors while the debtors were represented by counsel was held to be a willful violation of Section 362(a)(6) entitling the debtors to an award of damages under the old Section 362(h). Even the making of postpetition phone calls to the debtor by a creditor for the purpose of attempting to collect a prepetition debt is a violation of Section 362(a)(6) and may entitle the debtor to actual damages under Section 362(k). See In re Wingard, 382 B.R. 892 (WD PA, 2008), In re Goodfellow, 298 B.R. 358 (ND IA, 2003) and Mc Henry v. Key Bank, 179 B.R. 165 (B.A.P. 9th Cir., 1995). The "bona fide error" defense contained in the Fair Debt Collection Practices Act is no defense to a willful violation of the automatic stay. See In re Wingard, 382 B.R. 892 (WD PA, 2008). However, the postpetition contact by the creditor must be for the purpose of collecting a prepetition debt. Additionally, disparaging words spoken by the creditor to the debtor about the debtor's bankruptcy filing do not constitute a willful stay violation for purposes of Section 362(k) if the creditor does not also demand payment of the debt. See Gordan v. Dennis Burlin Sales, Inc., 174 B.R. 257 (ND OH, 1994).

Several courts have held that the sending of computer-generated collection notices to a debtor by an institutional lender after being notified of the debtor's bankruptcy is a violation of the Section 362(a)(6) stay and entitles the debtor to an award of actual damages under Section 362(k). See In re Brock Utils. & Grading, 185 B.R. 719 (ED NC, 1995) (stating creditors who send computer-generated collection notices have a responsibility and obligation to ensure that such notices are not sent to bankruptcy debtors and that actual damages, attorney's fees and punitive damages may be appropriate when creditors ignore this responsibility); see also In re Campion, 294 B.R. 313 (B.A.P. 9th Cir., 2003); In re Georgetown Steel Co., LLC, 318 B.R. 313 (SC, 2004). This rule also applies to the Internal Revenue Service and other institutional governmental units. See In re Price, 103 B.R. 989 (ND IL, 1989); Matthews v. U.S., 184 B.R. 594 (SD AL, 1995).

collection notice as stay violation

Other willful violations of the automatic stay that may entitle a debtor to damages under Section 362(k) include the following:

(1) The commencement or continuation of an action against the debtor in a nonbankruptcy forum to recover a prepetition claim in violation of 11 U.S.C. § 362(a)(1). A landlord willfully violated the automatic stay by filing an unlawful detainer action against the debtor after receiving notice of the debtor's bankruptcy filing in Johnston Environmental Corp. v. Knight, 991 F.2d 613 (9th Cir., 1993). In Eskanos & Adler, P.C. v. Leetien, 309 F.3d 1210 (9th Cir., 2002), a law firm willfully violated the automatic stay by delaying the dismissal of its state court action against the debtor for over a month without a contemporaneous explanation. In Stamper v. Stamper, 17 B.R. 216 (SD OH, 1982), the debtor's wife willfully violated the automatic stay by seeking a contempt of court order against the debtor in a state court proceeding after receiving notice of the debtor's bankruptcy filing. Proceeding against a debtor in a family court matter was sanctionable in In re Sutton, 250 B.R. 771 (SD FL, 2000). A postpetition action commenced by the debtor's wife to collect child support arrearages was a willful violation of the automatic stay entitling the debtor to actual damages in In re Tweed, 76 B.R. 636 (ED TN, 1987). However, in In re Nelson, 994 F.2d 42 (1st Cir., 1993), the debtor's former spouse did not willfully violated the automatic stay by pursuing a postpetition equity action in the state court to preserve her rights in marital property that she reasonably believed was not part of the bankruptcy estate. With respect to actions against the debtor that are related to a domestic support obligation, paternity, child custody or visitation, dissolution of marriage (except property division) or domestic violence it should be noted that 11 U.S.C. § 362(b)(2) provides that the filing of a bankruptcy petition does not operate as a stay of such actions. However, see In re Caffey, 384 B.R. 297 (SD AL, 2008).

prosecution of legal action as stay violation

judgment enforcement as stay violation

(2) An attempt to enforce a prepetition judgment against the debtor in violation of 11 U.S.C. § 362(a)(2). In In re Braught, 307 B.R. 399 (SD NY, 2004), a creditor was liable to a debtor couple for actual damages and attorney's fees where the creditor failed to take affirmative action to vacate a judgment for a month after the debtors filed their petition. See also In re Johnston, 321 B.R. 262 (AZ, 2005). In In re Grosse, 96 B.R. 29 (ED PA, 1989), a creditor's attorney was found to have willfully violated the automatic stay by permitting an attachment to continue against the debtor's property and by failing to dissolve a writ of garnishment on the debtor's bank account after receiving notice of the debtor's bankruptcy filing. An attempt by a judgment creditor to enforce a nondischargeable judgment with knowledge of the debtor's bankruptcy and without obtaining relief from the automatic stay was found to be a willful violation of the automatic stay entitling the debtor to damages under Section 362(h) in In re Watson, 78 B.R. 267 (CD CA, 1987). Filing a judgment to create a lien on real property postpetition is a stay violation. See In re Jackson, 403 B.R. 95 (ID, 2009).

lien enforcement as stay violation

(3) An attempt to obtain, create, perfect or enforce either a lien against property of the bankruptcy estate or, if the lien secures a prepetition claim, a lien against property of the debtor in violation of 11 U.S.C. § 362(a)(4) or (5). Most postpetition repossessions and foreclosures by secured creditors are prohibited by these provisions of Section 362(a). In In re Franklin Mortgage & Invest. Co., 143 B.R. 295 (DC, 1992), a willful violation of the automatic stay occurred when a creditor's attorney, with knowledge of the debtor's bankruptcy filing, sent a notice of sale to the state court clerk directing the clerk to give notice of a judicial sale of the debtor's property. In In re Pierre, 77 B.R. 951 (SD FL, 1987), the debtor's mortgagee was willfully violated the automatic stay by refusing to dismiss a foreclosure action upon being notified of the debtor's bankruptcy filing. In In re Knaus, 889 F.2d 773 (8th Cir., 1989), a creditor who, prior to the bankruptcy filing, had seized equipment belonging to the debtor pursuant to a state court writ of execution was willfully violated the automatic stay when it refused to turn the property over to the debtor under 11 U.S.C. § 542(a) after being notified of the debtor's bankruptcy. See also In re Bolen, 295 B.R. 803 (SC, 2002).

setoff as stay violation

(4) The setoff of a prepetition debt owed by a creditor to the debtor against a claim of the creditor against the debtor in violation of 11 U.S.C. § 362(a)(7). This is a favorite tactic of banks and other financial institutions. An attempt by a creditor to exercise a right of setoff after receiving notice of the filing of a bankruptcy case by the debtor constitutes a willful violation of the automatic stay entitling the debtor to damages under the old Section 362(h). See, e.g., Citizens Bank v. Strumpf, 37 F.3d 155 (4th Cir., 1994); In re Jim Nolker Chevrolet-Buick-Oldsmobile, Inc., 121 B.R. 20 (WD MO, 1990).

willful violation of stay, what constitutes

The "willful violation" requirement of Section 362(k). The third requirement for recovery under Section 362(k) is that the stay violation must have been willfully committed. Only willful violations of the automatic stay are compensable under Section 362(k). The general rule is that a willful violation of the automatic stay is established when it is shown that a creditor or other violator was aware of the stay and intentionally committed an act that was in violation of the stay, regardless of whether the violator knew that the act violated the stay. See In re Tyson, 450 B.R. 754 (Bankr. Tenn. 2001); In re Kline, 472 B.R. 98 (B.A.P. 10th Cir. 2012); In re Radcliffe, 563 F.3d 627 (7th Cir., 2009); Randolph v. IMBS, Inc., 368 F.3d 726 (7th Cir., 2004); In re Crysen/Montenay Energy Co., 902 F.2d 1098 (2d Cir., 1990); In re Schwartz, 954 F.2d 569 (9th Cir., 1992).

To establish liability under Section 362(k) it is not necessary to show a specific intent by the creditor to violate the automatic stay. See Ellison v. C.I.R., 385 B.R. 158 (SD WV, 2008); In re Banks, 253 B.R. 25 (ED MI, 2000); In re Midway Indus. Contractors, 167 B.R. 139 (ND IL, 1994). In addition, it is not necessary to show a demand by the debtor to cease the offending action and a refusal by the offending party to do so. See In re Braught, 307 B.R. 399 (SD NY, 2004); In re Chateaugay Corp., 112 B.R. 526 (SD NY, 1990), reversed on other grounds in 920 F.2d 183 (2d Cir., 1993). It is also not necessary to show bad faith on the part of the creditor or other violator in order to recover actual damages under Section 362(k). See In re Huron Electric Co., 180 B.R. 496 (ND OH, 1995). It is sufficient to show that the creditor was aware of the stay (or of the filing of the bankruptcy case that gave rise to the stay) and intentionally committed an act that is found to be in violation of the stay. See In re Cain, 272 B.R. 304 (WY, 2001); In re Midway Ind. Contractors, 167 B.R. 139 (ND IL, 1994); In re James, 112 B.R. 687 (ED PA, 1990).

willful violation of stay, general aspects

It is not a defense to an action for actual damages under Section 362(k) to show that a creditor or other violator acted on the advice of counsel in committing the act that was in violation of the stay. See In re Taylor, 884 F.2d 478 (9th Cir., 1989) (holding a creditor's good-faith reliance on the advice of its attorney that the stay had been validly terminated was not a defense to the debtor's claim for actual damages under the old Section 362(h)); see also In re General Homes Corp., 181 B.R. 870 (SD TX, 1994). Similarly, a good-faith belief by a creditor that its actions were not in violation of the automatic stay is not defense to an action for actual damages under Section 362(k). See In re Radcliffe, 563 F.3d 627 (7th Cir., 2009), In re University Medical Center, 973 F.2d 1065 (3d Cir., 1992), Taborski v. U.S., 141 B.R. 959 (ND IL, 1992), and In re Ramirez, 183 B.R. 583 (B.A.P. 9th Cir., 1995) (where the acts of a judgment creditor, his attorney, and the marshall's keeper in confiscating the debtor's files and equipment after receiving notice of the filing of the bankruptcy case were found to be willful violations of the automatic stay entitling the debtor to actual damages under the old Section 362(h) even though the violators believed they had a right to take the property after the state court denied the debtor's motion to release the levy). Creditors may not violate the stay simply because they have doubts as to the validity of the discharge. See Espinosa v. United Student Aid Funds, Inc., 553 F.3d 1193 (9th Cir. 2008), aff'd 130 S. Ct. 1367 (2010). See also In re Campbell, 361 B.R. 831 (SD TX, 2007) (stating where it is irrelevant to the issue of willfulness that the creditor believes in good faith that it has a right to the property).

willful stay violation, effect of reliance on advice of counsel

technical violations of stay, compensability under §362(k)

On the other hand, generally technical, trivial, or inadvertent violations of the automatic stay, even if they are willfully committed, will not support an award of actual damages under Section 362(k). See In re Hamrick, 175 B.R. 890 (WD NC, 1994); In re Red Ash Coal & Coke Corp., 83 B.R. 399 (WD VA, 1988); In re Advanced Professional Home Health Care, Inc., 94 B.R. 95 (ED MI, 1988); In re Uiterwyk Corp., 81 B.R. 658 (MD FL, 1987), where the court held that although the credit union had technically violated the automatic stay by placing a hold on the debtor's bank account, sanctions would not be imposed under the old Section 362(h) because the credit union's conduct constituted only a technical violation of the stay and had not resulted in any actual damage to the debtor. A technical violation of the automatic stay is generally held to be a minor or inadvertent violation that resulted in little or no injury or damage to the debtor or other aggrieved individual. See In re Costello, 176 B.R. 592 (MD FL, 1994); In re Freunscht, 53 B.R. 110 (VT, 1985) (holding that while a creditor's attorney's action in writing the debtor's attorney seeking reaffirmation by the debtor of a prepetition debt may have been a technical violation of the automatic stay, because the letter was sent to the attorney and not to the debtor no actual injury occurred and therefore the violation was technical only and no damages would be awarded). In In re Skeen, 248 B.R. 312 (ED TN, 2000) a debtor technically violated the automatic stay by making two telephone calls to the debtor, even though the creditor did not have actual knowledge of the bankruptcy was held to be a technical violation of the automatic stay not entitling the debtor to damages under the old Section 362(h)).

technical stay violation, failure to cure, effect of under §362(k)

It is clear, however, that a non-compensable technical violation can escalate into a compensable violation under Section 362(k) if the creditor fails to correct or reverse the technical violation and its effect on the debtor. See In re Matthews, 184 B.R. 594 (SD AL, 1995); In re Herron, 177 B.R. 866 (ND OH, 1995) (holding that while the action of a student loan creditor in requesting the IRS to intercept the debtor's tax refund in order to satisfy its prepetition debt was initially only a technical violation, the creditor's refusal to reverse the intercept procedure after the filing of the debtor's Chapter 13 plan wherein the creditor was to be paid in full constituted a compensable willful violation entitling the debtor to damages under the old Section 362(h)).

refusal to undo nonwillful violation as willful violation

Even a nonwillful (i.e., unknowing) violation of the automatic stay can become a willful violation if the violator refuses to undo the act that violated the stay. In In re James, 112 B.R. 687 (ED PA, 1990), state officials unknowingly obtained a default judgment against the debtor in violation of the automatic stay. The court held that even though obtaining the judgment was not a willful violation, the failure of the state officials to undo the default judgment after being advised of the stay constituted a willful act entitling the debtor to damages under the old Section 362(h). In In re Tarrant, 190 B.R. 704 (SD GA, 1995), a utility provider, without knowledge of the debtor's bankruptcy, terminated the debtor's electrical service and then, after receiving notice of the bankruptcy, refused to restore service to the debtor in an effort to collect from the debtor a utility bill owed by the debtor's wife. The court stated that since the utility provider did not terminate service with knowledge of the debtor's bankruptcy, its actions in terminating the service constituted a noncompensable (i.e., nonwillful) violation of the stay that could have been remedied without adverse consequences if service to the debtor had been immediately restored upon receiving notice of the bankruptcy filing. The court held that when the utility provider failed to take the steps necessary to remedy its error, the noncompensable violation was transformed into a willful violation that was compensable under the old Section 362(h). In In re Meadows, 379 B.R. 737 (SD OH, 2008), a creditor who obtained estate funds by presenting a check of debtor postpetition, was guilty of "willfully" violating the automatic stay by not immediately returning the funds to the estate.

The "injury" requirement for recovery under Section 362(k). The fourth requirement for relief under Section 362(k) is that the debtor or other injured individual must show that he or she suffered an injury or incurred actual damages as a reasonable and proximate result of the stay violation. The burden is placed on the debtor to show damages and causation by a preponderance of the evidence. See In re Sharon, 200 B.R. 181 (SD OH, 1996). However, see In re Grisard-Von Roey, 373 B.R. 441 (SC, 2007) where the court adopted a "clear and convincing" standard. Even if a willful violation of the automatic stay is shown, if the debtor fails to show that he or she suffered damages as a reasonable and proximate result of the violation, an award under Section 362(k) will not be made. See Martino v. First Nat. Bank, 164 B.R. 955 (ND IL, 1994); Mc Henry v. Key Bank, 179 B.R. 165 (B.A.P. 9th Cir., 1995) (although a creditor's actions in making phone calls to the debtor for the purpose of collecting a secured debt and one week later repossessing the debtor's vehicle constituted willful violations of the automatic stay, the conduct was held not to warrant an award of actual damages under the old Section 362(h) because the debtor had intended to turn the secured property over to the creditor anyway and therefore suffered no actual damages other than annoyance, inconvenience and an invasion of the debtor's right of privacy, which were held insufficient to justify an award under the old Section 362(h)); see also In re Skeen, 248 B.R. 312 (ED TN, 2000).

actual damages, necessity of under §362(k)

In In re Price, 179 B.R. 209 (ED CA, 1995), a Chapter 13 debtor suffered no injury from a stay violation by the District Attorney's office where the District Attorney had violated the automatic stay by continuing to accept the debtor's child support arrearage payments under its state court wage assignment order after receiving notice of the debtor's bankruptcy. No injury to the debtor was found to have occurred, however, because the child support obligation was nondischargeable in the case and because collection of the child support was in keeping with the debtor's plan, which provided for payment in full of the debtor's child support obligation. In Aiello v. Providian Fin. Corp., 239 F.3d 876 (8th Cir., 2002), the court held that emotional injury is not compensable under the old Section 362(h) when there is no financial loss to hitch it to. See also Patton v. Shade, 263 B.R. 861 (CD IL, 2001). However, some courts hold that economic injury is not required for a finding of emotional distress damages. See In re Stinson, 128 Fed. Appx. 30 (9th Cir., 2005); In re Feldmeier, 335 B.R. 807 (OR, 2005) (awarding $10,000 in emotional distress damages against a law firm that violated the stay while attempting to collect a debt); see also In re Herbts, 2012 WL 1212248 (Bank. W. D. Wis. 2012) (holding no injury from bank's refusal to return pre-petition repossessed collateral).

actual damages, when not established

non-economic damages

actual damages, necessity of proof

In a Section 362(k) proceeding it is important that the debtor or other injured individual present competent evidence of the actual damages that were incurred as a proximate result of the stay violation. See In re Mayer, 254 B.R. 396 (ND OH, 2000). Mental anguish can be "injury" under Section 362(k) and can support an award of damages. See, e.g., Fleet Mtg. Group v. Kaneb, 196 F.3d 265 (1st Cir., 1999); In re Johnson, 253 B.R. 857 (SD OH, 2000). If the debtor presents no evidence of actual damages, an award of actual damages under Section 362(k) cannot be made even if proof of a willful violation of the automatic stay is made because such an award would be based on speculation and conjecture, which is not permissible. See In re Falls Bldg., Ltd., 94 B.R. 471 (ED TN, 1988); In re Allen, 83 B.R. 678 (ED MO, 1988); In re Kuck, 111 B.R. 995 (SD AL, 1990).

actual damages necessity of award of under §362(k)

The amount of actual damages recoverable under Section 362(k). Section 362(k) provides that an individual injured by a willful violation of the automatic stay "shall recover actual damages, including costs and attorneys' fees..." In In re Brock Utilities & Grading, 185 B.R. 719 (ED NC, 1995), the court stated that the automatic stay serves a crucial function in bankruptcy cases and willful violations under Section 362(k) are serious matters warranting mandatory imposition of the sanctions that Congress has prescribed. Several courts have held that because of the words "shall recover" an award of actual damages is mandatory upon the finding of a willful violation of the automatic stay and injury to the debtor. See Patton v. Shade, 263 B.R. 861 (CD IL, 2001); Ramirez v. Fuselier, 183 B.R. 583 (B.A.P. 9th Cir., 1995); In re Timbs, 178 B.R. 989 (ED TN, 1994); In re Inslaw, Inc., 83 B.R. 89 (DC, 1988) reversed on other grounds in 932 F.2d 1467 (CA DC, 1991). In In re Hendry, 214 B.R. 473 (ED VA, 1997), a creditor's willful violation of the automatic stay mandated an award of compensatory damages unless the creditor could show cause for the violation.

actual damages, necessity of awarding to injured person

In addition, any damages must be awarded to the injured party and not to a creditor of the injured party or the injured party's estate. In Stainton v. Lee, 139 B.R. 232 (B.A.P. 9th Cir., 1992), the District Court held that the Bankruptcy Court, having found that a willful violation of the automatic stay occurred and that the debtor's damages amounted to $6,900, was required to award the entire amount to the debtor as the injured party and did not have the discretion to allocate the award between the debtor's creditors and the debtor's bankruptcy estate. This rule is apparently not applicable to the debtor's attorney, however, because in In re Johnson, 138 B.R. 352 (RI, 1992), damages were awarded under the old Section 362(h) directly to the debtor's attorney for services rendered on behalf of the debtor in obtaining relief from a stay violation. Note that a debtor's claim for damages under Section 362(k) by definition cannot exist until after the bankruptcy case is filed. This means that in a Chapter 7 case the claim does not become property of the bankruptcy estate and may be retained by the debtor. See 11 U.S.C. § 541. However, in a Chapter 13 case nonexempt property acquired by debtor during the case becomes property of the estate. See 11 U.S.C. § 1306(a). This means that in a Chapter 13 case damages recovered by the debtor under Section 362(k) may become property of the estate and be distributable to creditors under the plan.

The debtor or other injured party may seek damages either against the creditor at whose direction or for whose benefit the stay was violated or against the attorney or other agent who actually committed the act that was in violation of the automatic stay. See In re Mullarkey, 81 B.R. 280 (NJ, 1987) (damages assessed against creditor's attorney and not against creditor), and In re Grosse, 84 B.R. 377 (ED PA, 1988). In In re Carpio, 213 B.R. 744 (WD MO, 1997), damages were assessed against a creditor who at the time of the violation had no actual knowledge of the debtor's bankruptcy filing because the creditor's attorney knew of the filing and the attorney's knowledge was imputed to the creditor.

actual damages, from whom recoverable

Section 362(k) provides for the recovery of "actual damages, including costs and attorneys' fees." Generally, two factors determine the amount of actual damages awarded in a Section 362(k) proceeding: (1) the amount of provable damages incurred by the debtor or other injured individual as a result of the stay violation, exclusive of attorneys' fees; and (2) the amount of attorneys' fees reasonably incurred in obtaining relief from the stay violation.

actual damages, what constitutes

The normal rules of damages are applied in assessing non-attorney fee damages under Section 362(k). For example, if the violator uses or damages the debtor's property during or in the process of violating the stay, the debtor may recover damages for the use of the property or the costs of repairing the damaged property. See Matter of Sielaff, 164 B.R. 560 (WD MI, 1994) (allowing a debtor to recover $76.25 for 305 miles put on a wrongfully repossessed automobile by the repossessing creditor). In In re Diviney, 211 B.R. 951 (ND OK, 1997), the debtor was awarded the value of his vehicle which was repossessed and sold by the creditor in violation of the automatic stay. Personal injuries suffered by the debtor as a result of the stay violation are also compensable under Section 362(k). In In re Flynn, 185 B.R. 89 (SD GA, 1995), a $5,000 award for emotional distress suffered by the debtor as a result of a freeze put on her bank account in violation of the automatic stay was entered against the violator in a pre-BAPCPA Section 362(h) proceeding. See also In re Johnson, 478 B.R. 235 (Bankr. S. D. Miss. 2012) (holding debtor is entitled to emotional distress for willful violation of stay only if debtor can show a specific, discernable injury to emotional state).

property damage and personal injury as actual damages

A debtor who is forced to miss work or who otherwise loses income as a proximate result of a stay violation may recover the lost income from the violator under Section 362(k). See In re Hiers, 76 B.R. 640 (ED TN, 1987); In re Grace, 85 B.R. 464 (SD OH, 1988); In re Brown, 213 B.R. 317 (WD KY, 1997); In re Cox, 214 B.R. 635 (ND AL, 1997). The burden of proof in establishing lost income, however, is on the injured party. See In re Sharon, 200 B.R. 181 (SD OH, 1996).

lost income as actual damages

attorneys' fees as actual damages, when recoverable

In recovering attorneys' fees under Section 362(k), the general rule is that attorneys' fees incurred by the debtor in nullifying, correcting, or seeking relief from a stay violation, including the prosecution of a Section 362(k) proceeding, may be recovered from the violator. In In re NWFX, Inc., 81 B.R. 500 (WD AR, 1987), the court awarded the sum of $2,490 to the debtor for attorneys' fees incurred in defending a state court action against the debtor that was commenced by a creditor in violation of the automatic stay, in seeking removal of the action, and in prosecuting the motion for sanctions under the old Section 362(h) in the Bankruptcy Court. See also In re Summers, 213 B.R. 825 (ND OH, 1996) ($500.00 in attorney's fees awarded against creditor who filed garnishment proceeding against debtor in violation of the automatic stay); In re Davis, 74 B.R. 406 (ND OH, 1987) ($1,254 in attorneys' fees awarded to Chapter 13 debtor against state liquor control agency); In re Classe, 75 B.R. 543 (ED MO, 1987) ($977.50 in attorneys' fees awarded to Chapter 13 debtor against former wife). A showing of bad faith by the creditor is not necessary to recover attorneys' fee under Section 362(k). See In re Huron Elect. Co., 180 B.R. 496 (ND OH, 1995). In Patton v. Shade, 263 B.R. 861 (CD IL, 2001), the court held that even though the debtor is not entitled to compensatory damages, he may nevertheless be entitled to attorney fees and punitive damages under the old Section 362(h). Appellate attorney's fees may be recovered by the debtor under Section 362(k). See, e.g, In re Shade, 261 B.R. 213 (CD IL, 2001); Beard v. Walsh, 219 B.R. 873 (B.A.P. 9th Cir., 1998).

attorneys' fees as actual damages, requirement of necessity

To be recoverable under Section 362(k), the attorneys' fees incurred by the debtor must have been reasonably necessary to remedy the wrong to the debtor created by the stay violation. For example, if the stay violation could have been remedied by a simple phone call or letter to the creditor, the attorneys' fees incurred in filing a legal proceeding against the creditor are not likely to be recoverable under Section 362(k). See In re Price, 179 B.R. 70 (SD OH, 1995) (stating an attorney's fee award for a creditor's violation of the automatic stay should be circumscribed to what it would have cost to resolve the matter in a non-litigious manner where the creditor's actions were not in bad faith and mechanisms were in place to cease the stay violation). See also In re Houchens, 85 B.R. 152 (ND FL, 1988) (awarding only $50 for attorneys' fees because the misunderstanding with the violating creditor could have been resolved with a simple phone call instead of the legal proceedings initiated by the debtor's attorney); In re Johnson, 478 B.R. 235 (Bankr. S. D. Miss. 2012) (awarding $13,215).

attorneys' fees as actual damages, when not allowed

Attorney fees may not be recovered under Section 362(k) if the stay violation was caused or contributed to by acts of the debtor or the debtor's attorney. See In re Belcher, 189 B.R. 16 (SD FL, 1995) (where $20 in attorneys' fees was awarded to the debtor for a stay violation instead of the $1400 requested by the debtor because much of the delay in obtaining relief from the stay violation was caused by the debtor and her attorney). In Houseworth v. Three Rivers Fed. Credit Union, 177 B.R. 557 (ND OH, 1994), the court held that the Chapter 7 debtor was entitled to no attorneys' fees for a stay violation that consisted of not terminating automatic withdrawals from the debtor's account upon the filing of the bankruptcy case because the debtor contributed to the violation when her attorney sent a misleading letter to the creditor after the filing of the case.

Awards of attorneys' fees against governmental units to be consistent with 28 U.S.C. § 2412(d)(2)(A), which caps hourly rates at $125 unless the court determines that an increase in the cost of living or other special factors justify a higher fee. See Price v. U.S., 42 F.3d 1068 (7th Cir., 1994), and U.S. v. Flynn, 185 B.R. 89 (SD GA, 1995).

attorneys fees against governmental units, limitation of

Recovering punitive damages under Section 362(k). With respect to punitive damages, Section 362(k) provides that an individual injured by a willful violation of the automatic stay may, in appropriate circumstances, recover punitive damages. The key words here are "appropriate circumstances." The requirements of a willful violation of the automatic stay and the suffering of an injury by the debtor or other damaged individual are the same for punitive damages as for actual damages. These requirements are discussed above in this article.

recovering punitive damages under §362(k), requirements

It is important to note that section 362(k)(2) limits the debtor's right to recover punitive damages in situations where section 362(h), as that section was amended by the BAPCPA, is applicable. Section 362(h), as it now exists after the BAPCPA amendments, provides that the automatic stay is terminated with respect to personal property that either secures a claim or is subject to an unexpired lease if the debtor fails to timely file a statement of intention dealing with the property or fails to perform the action specified in the statement in a timely manner. In essence, then, section 362(k)(2) provides that a creditor is not liable for punitive damages for willfully violating the automatic stay if the creditor can show that he or she in good faith believed that the debtor had either failed to timely file a statement of intention dealing with the personal property in question or failed to perform the action specified in the statement of intention with respect to the property in question in a timely manner.

§362(k) limitations on punitive damages

The general rule is that punitive damages for a willful violation of the automatic stay are recoverable under Section 362(k) only if the offending party's conduct was malicious, oppressive, egregious, or in bad faith. See In re Hutchings, 348 B.R. 847 (ND AL, 2006), Ramirez v. Fuselier, 183 B.R. 583 (B.A.P. 9th Cir., 1995), and In re Lewis, 211 B.R. 970 (ND AL, 1997). In In re Knaus, 889 F.2d 773 (8th Cir., 1989), the court stated that an award of punitive damages under the old Section 362(h) requires not only a willful violation of the automatic stay, but also a finding of appropriate circumstances, such as egregious, intentional misconduct by the violator. See also, In re Cox, 214 B.R. 635 (ND AL, 1997), and In re Hodge, 367 B.R. 843 (MD AL, 2007).

punitive damages, requirement of egregious conduct

Note that punitive damages may be awarded under Section 362(k) against a corporate entity as well as against a natural person. See In re Baker, 140 B.R. 88 (VT, 1992). However, punitive damages may not be awarded against a governmental unit. See 11 U.S.C. § 106(a)(3); U.S. v. Flynn, 185 B.R. 89 (SD GA, 1995).

punitive damages, against whom recoverable

punitive damages, relevant factors

Relevant factors courts consider when determining whether punitive damages should be awarded for a willful violation of the automatic stay include the following: (1) the nature of the creditor's conduct, (2) the creditor's ability to pay damages, (3) the motive of the creditor, and (4) any provocation by the debtor. In re Seaton, 462 B.R. 582 (Bankr. E. D. Va. 2011). In In re Aponte, 82 B.R. 738 (ED PA, 1988), the court stated that in assessing punitive damages under the old Section 362(h), the court must consider the act itself together with the motive of the wrongdoer and relations between the parties. The court stated that the award should be gauged by the gravity of the offense and set at a level sufficient to ensure that it will punish and deter. The court concluded that the violator's financial position must be considered because the award must be sufficient to sting the violator's pocketbook. Therefore, in Section 362(k) proceedings wherein punitive damages are sought, the financial resources of the violator are relevant. Also relevant are the attitude and motives of the violator, the previous or general practices of the violator in bankruptcy cases, and the state of the relations between the violator and the debtor or other injured individual. See also, In re Shade, 261 B.R. 213 (CD IL, 2001), and In re Baggs, 283 B.R. 726 (CD IL, 2002), where the court awarded the debtor $300 in punitive damages and $450 in attorney's fees against a car dealer who sent a threatening collection letter, even though the debt in question was for only $100 and the debtor suffered emotional stress but no other damages. See also In re Hromidko, 302 B.R. 629 (ND IA, 2003) where the court ruled that a creditor's status as a sophisticated player in the credit industry is relevant when determining punitive damages.

punitive damages, amount of

In In re Kortz, 283 B.R. 706 (ND OH, 2002), punitive damages in the amount of $51,500 were awarded to the debtors where it was shown that the creditor contacted the debtors on 15 occasions after the filing of the bankruptcy case demanding payments and making threats despite knowledge of the bankruptcy filing. In In re Brown, 213 B.R. 317 (WD KY, 1997), punitive damages in the amount of $6,300 (triple the amount of the creditor's claim) were assessed against a creditor who intentionally violated the automatic stay by filing a criminal proceeding against the debtor to coerce the payment of a prepetition debt. In In re Diviney, 225 B.R. 762 (B.A.P. 1st Cir.0, 1998), punitive damages in the amount of $40,000 were awarded against a large bank who repossessed and sold the debtor's vehicle in "reckless disregard" of the automatic stay. The award was 10-times the amount of the debtor's actual damages and was awarded to deter future actions of this nature by the bank. $9,000 in punitive and actual damages plus attorney's fees were awarded against a creditor who threatened to collect a listed debt through violence in Varela v. Ocasio, 272 B.R. 815 (B.A.P. 1st Cir., 2002).

punitive damages, award of for wrongful repossession

Punitive damages are often assessed against secured creditors who repossess property in willful violation of the automatic stay. See In re Velichko, 473 B.R. 64 (Bankr. S. D. N. Y. 2012) (awarding actual and punitive damages, and attorney fees, for creditor's refusal to return vehicle after repossession). In In re Depew, 51 B.R. 1010 (ED TN, 1985), punitive damages in the amount of $1,000 were assessed against a bank which, with notice of the debtor's bankruptcy, repossessed the debtor's vehicle in willful violation of the automatic stay and made no attempt to obtain relief from the stay. In In re Mullarkey, 81 B.R. 280 (NJ, 1987), punitive damages in the amount $1,000 were assessed against a secured creditor's attorney who, in willful violation of the automatic stay, directed the sheriff to sell property of the bankruptcy estate. In In re Grace, 85 B.R. 464 (SD OH, 1988), a $250 punitive damage award was entered against a secured creditor who attempted to repossess the debtors' vehicle and then threatened the debtors if they did not reaffirm the entire amount of the creditor's claim. In Davis v. Gatorwheel, Inc., 265 B.R. 453 (ND FL, 2001), $4500 in punitive damages were awarded against a car dealer for repossessing and refusing to return the debtor's car.

On the other hand, in McHenry v. Key Bank, 179 B.R. 165 (B.A.P. 9th Cir., 1995), the actions of a secured creditor in making a phone call to the debtor for the purpose of collecting a debt and then a week later repossessing the debtors vehicle, both in willful violation of the automatic stay, were not sufficiently egregious or continuing to warrant an award of punitive damages because the debtor intended to turn the vehicle over to the creditor in any event. In In re Joslyn, 75 B.R. 590 (NH, 1987), a creditor who willfully violated the automatic stay by repossessing the debtor's vehicle was not liable for punitive damages under the old Section 362(h) because there was no evidence that the creditor had previously engaged in conduct of this type.

punitive damages, when not awarded under §362(k)

Punitive damages may also be awarded in cases where the creditor or other violator fails or refuses to take affirmative action necessary to terminate a pending proceeding against the debtor or the debtor's property upon receiving notice of the debtor's bankruptcy. In In re Timbs, 178 B.R. 989 (ED TN, 1994), the court held that punitive damages under Section 362(h) were appropriate where, despite knowledge of the debtor's bankruptcy, the creditor's attorney consciously chose to take no action to stop garnishment of the debtor's wages and publicly criticized the bankruptcy court's ruling on the matter rather than complying with or appealing the ruling.

punitive damages, award of for failing to stop proceedings

In In re Brock Utilities & Grading, 185 B.R. 719 (ED NC, 1995), the court stated that creditors who send computer-generated collection notices to bankruptcy debtors may be liable for punitive damages under Section 362(k) if they ignore their responsibility of ensuring that such notices are not sent. In Citizens Bank v. Strumpf, 37 F.3d 155 (4th Cir., 1994), an award of punitive damages based on the continuation by the bank of an administrative hold on the debtor's bank account in willful violation of the automatic stay in an attempt to buy time while seeking relief from the automatic stay was upheld on appeal.

punitive damages, award of for failing to stop procedures

Recovering damages against governmental units under Section 362(k). Because it is "applicable to all entities," the automatic stay is clearly applicable to governmental units, whether federal, state, or local. See 11 U.S.C. § 101(2), 362(a). To recover damages against a governmental unit, however, there must be a waiver of sovereign immunity. Section 106 of the Bankruptcy Code, entitled "Waiver of sovereign immunity," provides for a waiver of sovereign immunity to a certain extent with respect to specified sections of the Bankruptcy Code, including Section 362. Prior to the enactment of the Bankruptcy Reform Act of 1994, there was much litigation and confusion over the extent to which Section 106, as it was then worded, constituted a valid waiver of federal sovereign immunity. In 1992 the Supreme Court, in U.S. v. Nordic Village, Inc., 503 U.S. 30, 112 S. Ct. 1011 (1992) concluded that Section 106, as it was then worded, did not provide for a waiver of federal sovereign immunity for the purpose of recovering a tax payment from the United States in a bankruptcy case.

§362(k), effect of against governmental units, sovereign immunity waiver of federal sovereign immunity by §106, extent of

The Bankruptcy Reform Act of 1994 substantially rewrote Section 106 and rendered most of the pre-1994 cases dealing with that section moot. Section 106(a) now clearly provides for a waiver of federal sovereign immunity with respect to claims for actual damages recovered against the United States under Section 362(k). See In re Talbot, 124 F.3d 1201 (10th Cir., 1997); In re Brown, 211 B.R. 1020 (SD GA, 1997); In re Milto, 210 B.R. 687 (MD, 1997). In addition, if a governmental unit files a claim in the case against which the debtor's claim under Section 362(k) is a compulsory counterclaim, sovereign immunity with respect to the counterclaim is waived by the provisions of Section 106(b). See In re Pinkstaff, 974 F.2d 113 (9th Cir., 1992); In re Burke, 146 F.3d 1313 (11th Cir., 1998).

§106, legislative history

punitive damages, governmental unit

The legislative history of the Bankruptcy Reform Act of 1994 indicates that one of the purposes of the Section 106 revisions was to overrule U.S. v. Nordic Village, Inc., supra, and similar cases. See Congressional Record of Oct. 4, 1994, p. H10766. It should be noted, however, that Section 106(a)(3) specifically excludes awards of punitive damages from the power of bankruptcy courts to enter judgments and orders against governmental units, so it would appear that punitive damages may not be awarded against a governmental unit under in a Section 362(k) proceeding. See U.S. v. Flynn, 185 B.R. 89 (SD GA, 1995).

waiver of sovereign immunity by §106, effect of against states

While Section 106(a) now quite clearly provides for a waiver of federal sovereign immunity with respect to claims for actual damages under Section 362(k), a more difficult question is whether this statute also provides for a waiver of sovereign immunity with respect to state or local governmental units. In Seminole Tribe of Florida v. Florida, 517 U.S. 44, 116 S. Ct. 1114 (1996), the Supreme Court held that under the 11th Amendment to the Constitution Congress could constitutionally waive a state's sovereign immunity only through an express waiver pursuant to a valid exercise of power. While this case did not specifically deal with Section 106 of the Bankruptcy Code, other courts have generally held that the waiver of sovereign immunity in Section 106 insofar as it applies to Section 362(k) proceedings against states is an unconstitutional exercise of congressional power and is therefore an invalid waiver of sovereign immunity with respect to state governmental units. See In re Lush Lawns, Inc., 203 B.R. 418 (ND OH, 1996); In re Rose, 214 B.R. 372 (WD MO, 1997), In re Louis;Harris, 213 B.R. 796 (CT, 1997); In re NVR, 206 B.R. 831 (ED VA, 1997); In re Sacred Heart Hospital, 133 F.3d 237 (3d Cir., 1998); In re Fernandez, 123 F.3d 241 (5th Cir., 1997) (modified in 130 F.3d 1138); In re Creative Goldsmiths, 119 F.3d 1140 (4th Cir., 1997). However, other courts hold that Section 106(a) contains an unmistakably clear waiver of sovereign immunity and held that the state, as the holder of a student loan, was not immune from suit in a bankruptcy court. In re Hood, 319 F.3d 755 (6th Cir., 2003) aff'd 541 U.S. 440 (2004); In In re Omine, 329 B.R. 343 (MD FL, 2005) (Florida Dept. of Revenue was found liable for actual damages, sanctions, and attorney fees for violating the stay); In re Berkebile, 444 B.R. 326 (W. D. Penn. 2001) (finding 106(a) is a clear waiver of sovereign immunity); In re DBSI, Inc., 463 B.R. 709 (Bankr. Del. 2012) (holding sovereign immunity was abrogated with respect to fraudulent transfers).

Section 106(b) of the Bankruptcy Code (11 U.S.C. § 106(b)) provides that a governmental unit that files a proof of claim in the case is deemed to have waived sovereign immunity with respect to a claim of the debtor against the governmental unit that is property of the estate and that arose out of the same transaction or occurrence as the governmental unit's claim. Therefore, a state may waive sovereign immunity by filing a proof of claim in the case. See In re Straight, 143 F.3d 1387 (10th Cir., 1998), and In re Fennelly, 212 B.R. 61 (NJ, 1997). In In re Koehler, 204 B.R. 210 (MN, 1997), the court held that while the waiver of sovereign immunity in Section 106(a) was unconstitutional with respect to state governmental units under the 11th Amendment, sovereign immunity was validly waived with respect to the state governmental unit under Section 106(b) to the extent that the debtor's damages did not exceed the amount demanded in the counterclaim filed by the governmental unit.

waiver of sovereign immunity in §106(b), validity of with respect to states

Civil contempt remedies under Section 105(a). Civil contempt remedies for willful violations of the automatic stay are sought primarily by bankruptcy trustees, corporate debtors and other nonindividual entities who are not eligible for relief under Section 362(k). That civil contempt remedies under Section 105(a) are available to trustees and debtors who are not eligible for relief under Section 362(k), see In re Soll, 181 B.R. 433 (AZ, 1995), In re Prairie T. Ry., 125 B.R. 217 (ND IL, 1991), In re Pace, 67 F.3d 187 (9th Cir., 1995), and In re Ormond Beach Assocs. Ltd. Partnership, 185 B.R. 408 (CT, 1995).

civil contempt remedies, availability of

The automatic stay is deemed to be an order of the bankruptcy court for purposes of enforcement. See In re Stonegate Sec. Services, Ltd., 56 B.R. 1014 (ND IL, 1986). Because the automatic stay constitutes an injunction with the force of a court order, a knowing violation of the automatic stay gives rise to the remedy of civil contempt. See In re Stephen W. Grosse, P.C., 84 B.R. 377 (ED PA, 1989) (affirmed in 96 B.R. 29 and 879 F.2d 856), and In re Shropshire, 25 B.R. 128 (WD WA, 1982). In a civil contempt proceeding the court may award the injured party compensatory damages, costs, and attorney's fees. See In re O'Connor, 42 B.R. 390 (ED AR, 1984). However, an award of damages as a civil contempt remedy is not mandatory and must be based on a showing of actual damage. See In re Colon, 114 B.R. 890 (ED PA, 1990). Punitive damages may not be awarded in a civil contempt proceeding under Section 105(a). See In re Wagner, 87 B.R. 612 (CD CA, 1988). However, in In re Dynamic Tours & Transp., Inc., 359 B.R. 336 (MD FL, 2006), $50,000 in punitive damages were awarded under Section 105(a) against a large corporate creditor.

civil contempt remedy for stay violation, general aspects

Sanctions under 105(a) must meet one or both of the following purposes: (1) to compel or ensure compliance with a court order, or (2) to compensate parties for losses caused by refusal to follow court's order. See In re C. W. Min. Co., 477 B.R. 176 (B.A.P. 10th Cir. 2012). To establish liability for civil contempt under Section 105(a), it must be shown that a specific and definite court order (such as the automatic stay) was violated by a party with knowledge of the order. See In re Tel-A-Communications Consultants, Inc., 50 B.R. 250 (CT, 1985). Even if the violator acted in good faith and relied on the advice of counsel in committing the act in question, civil contempt liability may be imposed if the act in fact constituted a violation of the stay. See In re General Homes Corp., 181 B.R. 870 (SD TX, 1994). Some courts have held that prior to the initiation of civil contempt proceedings it is incumbent upon the debtor or other injured party to make an effort to remedy the stay violation without resorting to litigation. See In re Houchens, 85 B.R. 152 (ND FL, 1988). Other courts have refused to impose this obligation on the debtor because such an obligation would defeat the policy of the stay by unfairly shifting the burden of creditor compliance to the debtor. See Price v. Pediatric Academic Ass'n, 175 B.R. 219 (SD OH, 1994).

civil contempt remedy for stay violation, general rules

civil contempt proceeding, procedure

The procedure for contempt proceedings is governed by Bankruptcy Rule 9020. This rule provides that contempt, other than contempt committed in the presence of the bankruptcy judge, may be determined by the bankruptcy judge after a hearing on notice. The notice must be in writing, must state the essential facts constituting the alleged contempt, and must state the time and place of the hearing, allowing a reasonable time for the preparation of a defense. The notice may be given on the court's own initiative or on the application of the United States attorney or an attorney appointed by the court for that purpose. See Bankruptcy Rule 9020(b).

order of contempt by bankruptcy court, effect of

An order of contempt entered by a bankruptcy court has the same force and effect as an order of contempt entered by a district court unless the entity held in contempt within 10 days after service of the order on the entity serves and files objections prepared in the manner prescribed for filing objections to proposed findings of facts and conclusions of law in a non-core proceeding. If objections are timely filed, the order of contempt must be reviewed de novo by the district court in the manner prescribed for reviews in non-core proceedings. See Bankruptcy Rules 9020(b), (c) and 9033. In essence, then, a civil contempt proceeding is a non-core proceeding in the bankruptcy court.

contempt powers of bankruptcy court

Finally, note that while bankruptcy courts clearly have the power to remedy contempt, it is not clear whether they have the power to punish contempt. See Brown v. Ramsay, 3 F.3d 1174 (8th Cir., 1993); In re Just Brakes Corporate Systems, Inc., 108 F.3d 881 (8th Cir., 1997). Awarding compensatory damages for stay violations would appear to be remedial in nature and therefore within the power of the bankruptcy court. See In re Lovato, 203 B.R. 747 (WY, 1996) (awarding the debtor reasonable attorneys' fees and costs against the IRS for willfully violating a discharge injunction).

Bibliography. For further reading on the issues discussed in this article, see the annotations and articles listed below.

Annotations:

Validity of Section 106(a) of Bankruptcy Code Providing Waiver of Governmental Immunity in Title 11 Proceedings. 190 ALR Fed. 453.

Remedies and Damages for Violations of the Automatic Stay Provisions of the Bankruptcy Code by Parties Other Than the Federal Government. 153 ALR Fed. 463.

Federal Government's Liability for Damages Under 11 USC 362(h) for Willful Violation of Automatic Stay in Bankruptcy. 117 ALR Fed 1.

Violation of Automatic Stay Provisions of 1978 Bankruptcy Code as Contempt of Court. 57 ALR 927.

Articles:

Defining the Limits of Federal Court Jurisdiction Over States in Bankruptcy Courts. 28 St. Mary's Law Journal 575 (Spring, 1997).

Who Can Waive State Immunity? 15 Am. Bkcy. Inst. Journal 10 (Dec. 1996-Jan. 1997).

Sovereign Immunity in Bankruptcy: The Next Chapter. 70 Am. Bkcy. Law Journal 195 (Spring, 1996).

Congressional Response to Hoffman and Nordic Village: Amended Section 106 and Sovereign Immunity. 69 Am. Bkcy. Law Journal 311 (Summer, 1995).

Staying True to Repose: Including Corporate Debtors under § 362(h) of the Federal Bankruptcy Code, 76 Ind. L.J. 243 (Winter, 2001).

1.16 Under what circumstances may a debtor recover costs and attorney's fees from a creditor who challenges the dischargeability of a debt?

Text of statute. Section 523(d) of the Bankruptcy Code (11 U.S.C. § 523(d)) provides as follows:

523. Exceptions to discharge

§523(d), text of

> (d) If a creditor requests a determination of dischargeability of a consumer debt under subsection (a)(2) of this section, and such debt is discharged, the court shall grant judgment in favor of the debtor for the costs of, and a reasonable attorney's fee for, the proceeding if the court finds that the position of the creditor was not substantially justified, except that the court shall not award such costs and fees if special circumstances would make the award unjust.

Introduction: Section 523(d) is written in mandatory language. It requires the court to assess against the creditor the costs and attorneys' fees incurred by the debtor in a proceeding to determine the dischargeability of a debt if all of the following conditions exist:

§523(d), requirements for recovery under

(1) nondischargeability of the debt was sought by the creditor under Section 523(a)(2) of the Bankruptcy Code, which provides nondischargeability for debts obtained by fraud, false pretences or false financial statements,

(2) the debt for which nondischargeability was sought is a consumer debt,

(3) the debt for which nondischargeability was sought is found to be dischargeable,

(4) the creditor's position in seeking nondischargeability of the debt was not substantially justified, and

(5) special circumstances making an award of costs and attorneys fee against the creditor unjust do not exist.

§523(d), legislative history of

Section 523(d) was originally enacted in the Bankruptcy Reform Act of 1978. In 1984 Section 523(d) was revised to its present form. Prior to the 1984 revision, costs and attorney's fees were awardable to the debtor if the challenged debt was found to be dischargeable unless such an award would be clearly inequitable. The 1984 revision removed the "clearly inequitable" exception to recovery and substituted the present language denying recovery if the creditor's position is substantially justified or if special circumstances exist which would make such an award unjust.

The legislative purpose of Section 523(d) was to deter creditors from challenging the dischargeability of debts on the basis of questionable false financial statements or weak fraud or false pretense allegations in hopes of extracting settlements from honest debtors who were reluctant to incur (or unable to afford) the expenses of defending such actions. See Senate Report 989, page 80 (95th Congress, 2nd Session 1978). In other words, the threat of assessing the debtor's costs and attorney's fees against creditors with weak fraud, false pretense or false financial statement cases is intended to deter such creditors from challenging the dischargeability of debts on these grounds. See In re Rocco, 239 B.R. 297 (ED PA, 1999).

§523(d), purpose of

Note that Section 523(d) works only in favor of the debtor. Prevailing creditors have no statutory right to attorney's fees under Section 523(d). See In re Claybrook, 385 B.R. 842 (ED TX, 2008); In re LeBlanc, 346 B.R. 706 (MD LA, 2006). It does not permit the court to assess a creditor's costs and attorney's fee against the debtor if the creditor prevails on the nondischargeability issue. See In re Bonnifield, 154 B.R. 743 (ND CA, 1993), where the court stated that assessing a successful creditor's costs and attorney's fee against the debtor would defeat the legislative purpose of Section 523(d) by restoring the balance of power in Section 523(a)(2) nondischargeability situations to the creditor.

§523(d), applicability of

Note, however, that if the creditor prevails on the nondischargeability issue, and an agreement between the parties permits the creditor to recover its costs and attorney's fee from the debtor, and it is valid under local state law, generally the costs and attorney's fees incurred by the creditor in a nondischargeability proceeding may be added to the debt and that the entire debt, including the costs and attorney's fees, and are nondischargeable. See In re Ashland, 307 B.R. 317 (MA, 2004); In re Rowland, 316 B.R. 759 (SD GA, 2004); TranSouth Financial Corp. of Florida v. Johnson, 931 F.2d 1505 (11th Cir., 1991); Matter of Sheridan, 105 F.3d 1164 (7th Cir., 1997); Matter of Luce, 960 F.2d 1277 (5th Cir., 1992); In re Martin, 761 F.2d 1163 (6th Cir., 1985); In re Ellingsworth, 212 B.R. 326 (WD MO, 1997). A prevailing creditor in a nondischargeability proceeding may also be entitled to recover its costs (but not its attorneys' fees) under Bankruptcy Rule 7054(b). See In re Dunston, 146 B.R. 269 (CO, 1992).

recovery of costs and attorney›s fees by creditor, when permitted

Each of the conditions or requirements for recovery under Section 523(d) are discussed separately below under the appropriate headings. Also discussed below is the extent to which costs and attorneys' fees may be recovered by the debtor under Section 523(d) and the procedure for obtaining such a recovery.

scope of article

recovery under §523(d), requirement of proceeding under §523(a)(2)

The requirement that nondischargeability be sought under Section 523(a)(2). By its express wording Section 523(d) is applicable only to determinations of dischargeability sought by creditors under Section 523(a)(2) of the Bankruptcy Code. As indicated above, Section 523(a)(2) provides nondischargeability for debts obtained by fraud, false pretenses, or false financial statements. Therefore, in order for a debtor to obtain an award of costs and attorney's fees under Section 523(d), nondischargeability must be sought by the creditor on the grounds of fraud, false pretenses or the use of a false financial statement. See Manufacturers Hanover Trust Co. v. Hudgins, 72 B.R. 214 (ND IL, 1987) (holding that Section 523(d) was applicable to nondischargeability challenges under Section 523(a)(2)(A) (i.e., on the grounds of false pretenses, false representations, or actual fraud), notwithstanding the legislative history of Section 523(d) which indicates that it was intended to apply only to nondischargeability challenges under Section 523(a)(2)(B) (i.e., on the grounds of false financial statements)). See article 1.11 of this handbook for an in-depth discussion of the nondischargeability of debts obtained by fraud, false pretenses or false financial statements under Section 523(a)(2) of the Bankruptcy Code.

§523(d), inapplicability to proceedings not under §523(a)(2)

As indicated above, it is clear that costs and attorney's fees are recoverable under Section 523(d) only in cases where nondischargeability is sought by a creditor under Section 523(a)(2). For example, Section 523(d) is not applicable to proceedings where nondischargeability of a divorce-related debt was unsuccessfully sought under Section 523(a)(5) of the Bankruptcy Code. See In re Shearer, 124 B.R. 862 (ND FL, 1990). Nor is Section 523(d) applicable to unsuccessful attempts to obtain nondischargeability of debts for willful and malicious injury under Section 523(a)(6) of the Bankruptcy Code. See In re Chiok, 53 B.R. 697 (OR, 1985). In addition, it is clear that Section 523(d) is not applicable to unsuccessful attempts to bar a debtor's discharge under Section 727 of the Bankruptcy Code. See In re Floyd, 322 B.R. 205 (MD FL, 2005); In re Outlaw, 66 B.R. 413 (ED NC, 1986); In re Wolmer, 57 B.R. 128 (ND IL, 1986).

consumer debt requirement of §523(d), burden of proof

The "consumer debt" requirement for recovery. In providing for the recovery of costs and attorneys' fees, Section 523(d) explicitly refers to a "consumer debt." It is clear, therefore, that in order for a debtor to recover costs and attorney's fees from a creditor under Section 523(d) the debt for which nondischargeability is unsuccessfully sought must be a consumer debt. See In re Burns, 894 F.2d 361 (10th Cir., 1990). The burden of proof on the issue of whether the debt in question is a consumer debt is on the debtor. See In re Austin, 73 B.R. 937 (WD LA, 1987).

consumer debt, definition of

As defined in 11 U.S.C. § 101(8), a "consumer debt" is a debt incurred by an individual primarily for a personal, family, or household purpose. The first requirement of a consumer debt is that it be incurred by an individual and not by a corporation or other nonindividual. Therefore, if a debt was incurred by a corporation, it is not a consumer debt even if an individual debtor is also liable for the debt as a guarantor or otherwise. See In re Ethridge, 80 B.R. 581 (MD GA, 1987).

In determining whether a debt incurred by an individual is a consumer debt for purposes of Section 523(d), the determining factor is the purpose for which the debt was primarily incurred. If the debt was incurred primarily for a personal, family, or household purpose, it is a consumer debt, even if the debt is secured by real property. See Guaranty S & L Assoc. v. Lowe, 109 B.R. 698 (WD VA, 1990). In Ciancioso v. Ciancioso, 187 B.R. 438 (ED NY, 1995), a debt incurred primarily to pay off the debtor's brother in exchange for the relinquishment by the brother of the debtor's inheritance was found to be a consumer debt for purposes of Section 523(d) because it was incurred primarily for a personal or family purpose. In In re Burgess, 22 B.R. 771 (MD TN, 1982), an unsecured debt incurred by the debtors to purchase real estate which they intended to use as their home was found to be a consumer debt. In In re Vianese, 195 B.R. 572 (ND NY, 1995), a gambling debt incurred by the debtors was found to be a consumer debt for purposes of Section 523(d) where neither debtor earned a living by gambling and the debt, while incurred in hopes of generating a profit, was incurred primarily for personal purposes.

consumer debt, what constitutes, cases

On the other hand, debts that were incurred primarily for business-related or profit-motive purposes are not consumer debts for purposes of Section 523(d). In In re Baker, 206 B.R. 507 (ND IL, 1997), a debtor who admitted that his credit card debt was incurred in connection with his business was not permitted to recover attorneys' fees under Section 523(d). In In re Burns, 894 F.2d 361 (10th Cir., 1990), a debt in the form of a loan that was incurred by the debtor primarily for the purpose of investing the loan proceeds in the stock market was found not to be a consumer debt for purposes of Section 523(d). In In re Bernstein, 71 B.R. 259 (SD FL, 1987), a $39,000 debt incurred to pay attorney's fees incurred by the debtor's adult son in defending an indictment for business-related fraud was found not to be a consumer debt for purposes of Section 523(d), even though it was obviously incurred for a family purpose. Debts incurred primarily for business-related purposes are not consumer debts for purposes of Section 523(d). See, e.g., In re Panaia, 65 B.R. 865 (MA, 1985); In re Walter, 50 B.R. 521 (DE, 1985). In In re Melcher, 322 B.R. 1 (CO, 2005), a debt that was incurred by the debtor due to damages caused to a neighbor's property was not a consumer debt. In In re Dains, 384 B.R. 241 (WD MO, 2008) a parent's loan to a debtor for use in the debtor's business was deemed not to be a consumer debt.

consumer debt, what does not constitute, cases

The "dischargeable debt" requirement for recovery. Section 523(d) clearly states that the debt for which nondischargeability is sought by the creditor must be found by the court to be dischargeable in order for the debtor to recover costs and attorney's fees. In other words, in order to be awarded costs and attorney's fees under Section 523(d), the debtor must prevail on the Section 523(a)(2) nondischargeability issue.

§523(d), dischargeable debt requirement

Not all nondischargeability complaints go to trial. Is recovery under Section 523(d) permitted if the complaint is settled or dismissed prior to trial? In In re Randolph, 28 B.R. 811 (ED VA, 1983), the court held that the involuntary dismissal of the creditor's nondischargeability complaint prior to trial did not preclude the debtor from pursuing his claim for costs and attorney's fees under Section 523(d). However, if the Section 523(a)(2) nondischargeability issue is compromised and settled by the debtor prior to trial, or if the creditor's complaint is voluntarily dismissed prior to trial, recovery under Section 523(d) may be denied. See In re Sawicki, 12 B.R. 515 (WD WI, 1981); In re Begley, 12 B.R. 839 (CT, 1981); In re Kirsch, 65 B.R. 297 (ND IL, 1986). However, in In re D'Alessandria, 20 FLW Fed B 258 (SD FL, 2006) a partial award was granted when the creditor dismissed during litigation.

recovery under §523(d) when case dismissed or settled

The "substantial justification" exception to recovery. If the other requirements of Section 523(d) are complied with, the court is required to grant judgment in favor of the debtor for the costs and attorney's fees incurred in the dischargeability proceeding if the court also finds that the position of the creditor in requesting the determination of dischargeability was not substantially justified. Therefore, if the court finds that the position of the creditor in filing the complaint to determine dischargeability was substantially justified, then the debtor is not entitled to an award of costs and attorney's fees under Section 523(d). Note that the "substantially justified" standard was derived from the Equal Access to Justice Act (28 U.S.C. § 2412(d)), under which the losing party must make a strong showing in order to avoid being assessed with the other party's costs and attorney's fees. See In re Gilliam, 2012 WL 1191854 (B.A.P. 9th Cir. 2012) (holding substantial justification requires a "reasonable basis on both law and fact") (not selected for publication); Carthage Bank v. Kirkland, 121 B.R. 496 (SD MS, 1990).

recovery under §523(d), substantial justification exception

The burden of proof on the issue of substantial justification is clearly on the creditor. See FCC Nat. Bank v. Dobbins, 151 B.R. 509 (WD MO, 1992); In re Carolan, 204 B.R. 980 (B.A.P. 9th Cir., 1996); In re Kurtz, 213 B.R. 253 (ND NY, 1997) (stating that on a motion for an award of costs and attorney's fees under Section 523(d), the debtor must initially establish that the creditor sought a determination of nondischargeability under Section 523(a)(2), that the debt was found to be dischargeable, and that the debt was a consumer debt, whereupon the burden shifts to the creditor to prove that its action in initiating the proceeding was substantially justified). Generally, to establish substantial justification under Section 523(d) a creditor must show that it's unsuccessful dischargeability action had a reasonable basis in fact and law. See In re Harvey, 172 B.R. 314 (B.A.P. 9th Cir., 1994); In re Poirier, 214 B.R. 53 (CT, 1997); In re Williamson, 181 B.R. 403 (WD MO, 1995).

substantial justification, burden of proof

In determining whether substantial justification exists for purposes of Section 523(d), the court must first examine the creditor's evidence and determine whether the creditor was justified in seeking a determination of nondischargeability. If the court finds that the creditor's evidence was not sufficient to sustain each necessary element on which the creditor had the burden of proof under Section 523(a)(2), then the creditor was not substantially justified in seeking a determination of nondischargeability for the debt in question. In In re Woods, 69 B.R. 999 (ED PA, 1987), the court stated that because a creditor can determine whether evidence to meet the necessary standard exists by examining the debtor at the meeting of creditors, it should be able to ascertain prior to filing the complaint to determine dischargeability whether the facts are sufficient to meet the burden required for substantial justification under Section 523(d). The court held that the existence of only a short period of time between the obtaining of the loan by the debtor and the filing of the bankruptcy petition, without more, is not sufficient to establish substantial justification for seeking nondischargeability of the debt for fraud under Section 523(a)(2)(A). In In re Miller, 250 B.R. 294 (ED KY, 2000), the creditor's complaint was held not substantially justified because the creditor did not attend the meeting of creditors and did not schedule a Rule 2004 examination or otherwise concern itself with the facts of the transaction until after the filing of the adversary proceeding. See also In re Flowers, 391 B.R. 178 (MD AL, 2008) (where a creditor's lack of any pre-filing investigation merited an award of attorney fees to the debtor).

substantial justification, proof of, requirements, cases

If the creditor produces no evidence of nondischargeability at the trial or fails to appear at the trial, then the debtor is clearly entitled to recover reasonable costs and attorney's fees under Section 523(d). See In re Powell, 213 B.R. 306 (WD VA, 1997), and In re Bernard, 85 B.R. 864 (CO, 1988). If summary judgment on the nondischargeability complaint is entered against the creditor, substantial justification is likely to be found not to exist. See In re Snyder, 75 B.R. 130 (SD OH, 1987). If a creditor produces no evidence or witnesses at trial other than the debtors and loses the case, substantial justification is likely to be found not to exist. See Manufacturers Hanover Trust Co. v. Hudgins, 72 B.R. 214 (ND IL, 1987). If neither the legal arguments nor the factual situation advanced by the creditor provides a reasonable basis for initiating the dischargeability proceeding, then substantial justification is not established under Section 523(d). See In re Rhodes, 93 B.R. 622 (SD IL, 1988).

substantial justification, when not established, cases

A showing of good faith on the part of the creditor in filing the dischargeability complaint does not necessarily establish substantial justification. See In re Harvey, 172 B.R. 314 (B.A.P. 9th Cir., 1994) (stating court was not limited to an examination of the creditor's initial decision to seek nondischargeability for the debt, but rather that costs and attorney's fee could be awarded to the debtor under Section 523(d) if the court finds that the creditor proceeded with its case past the point where it knew or should have known that it could not carry its burden of proof). In In re Williamson, 181 B.R. 403 (WD MO, 1995), the court stated that even if the creditor had a reasonable basis for initiating the dischargeability proceeding, that basis becomes unreasonable if the creditor continues to pursue the proceeding after it knew or should have known that it could not prevail. See also In re Talarico, 234 B.R. 182 (MD FL, 1999); In re Poirier, 214 B.R. 53 (CT, 1997).

substantial justification after filing of case, requirements, cases

In order to establish substantial justification, an unsuccessful creditor must have exercised reasonable diligence in determining and assessing its case for nondischargeability under Section 523(a)(2). See In re Williams, 224 B.R. 523 (B.A.P. 2d Cir., 1998); In re Park, 375 B.R. 153 (WD PA, 2007). The mere showing of a dishonored check, with nothing more, is not a substantially justified position. See In re Bullock, 322 B.R. 176 (MD AL, 2005). In First Card v. Leonard, 158 B.R. 839 (CO, 1993), the court found that substantial justification for seeking nondischargeability did not exist because the creditor undertook no discovery to ascertain the facts prior to trial and was negligent in extending $7,500 in preapproved credit to the debtor without inquiring into the debtors' credit worthiness or financial circumstances. In FCC Nat'l Bank/First Card v. Friend, 156 B.R. 257 (WD MO, 1993), substantial justification for seeking nondischargeability for credit card fraud under Section 523(a)(2)(A) was found lacking because the tests used by the creditor in determining whether to litigate nondischargeability of credit card debts were inaccurate in that they were not in keeping with the requirements set forth in the Bankruptcy Code and applicable case law. Credit card issuers who challenge the dischargeability of their credit card claims often have a difficult time establishing substantial justification when they do not prevail. See In re Cameron, 219 B.R. 531 (WD MO, 1998); In re Nguyen, 235 B.R. 76 (ND CA, 1999); In re Akins, 235 B.R. 34 (WD TX, 1999).

substantial justification, general requirements, cases

substantial justification, when established, cases

Generally, however, a creditor is substantially justified if it establishes a prima facie case of nondischargeability at the nondischargeability hearing, even if the debtor produces sufficient additional or rebuttal evidence at the hearing to prevail on the nondischargeability issue. See In re Schoenlein, 157 B.R. 824 (ND OH, 1993); In re Kurtz, 213 B.R. 253 (ND NY, 1997). See also In re Melcher, 322 B.R. 1 (CO, 2005) (stating that each of the creditor's elements had some plausibility, which required a finding of substantial justification). In In re Carolan, 204 B.R. 980 (B.A.P. 9th Cir., 1996), the court held that the substantial justification standard should not be read so as to create a presumption that the position of the creditor was not substantially justified simply because it lost on the nondischargeability issue. The court stated that if it is shown, either at the dischargeability trial or otherwise, that the creditor, even though not prevailing on the nondischargeability issue, had sufficient facts on each element on which it had the burden of proof to constitute a reasonable basis for filing and maintaining the nondischargeability proceeding, then substantial justification is established and the creditor is not liable for the debtor's costs and attorney's fees under Section 523(d).

recovery under §523(d), special circumstances exception

The "special circumstances" exception to recovery. In addition to the substantial justification exception to recovery, Section 523(d) also provides that the court shall not award costs and attorney's fees to the debtor if special circumstances would make the award unjust. The term "special circumstances" is not defined in the Bankruptcy Code and the legislative history of 1984 Bankruptcy Code amendments (when this clause was added to Section 523(d)) provides little guidance as to its meaning. However, in In re Hingson, 954 F.2d 428 (7th Cir., 1992), the court stated that the "special circumstances" clause in Section 523(d) does not provide bankruptcy judges with a license to base their decisions on idiosyncratic notions of equity, fair dealing or family justice, but rather it should be interpreted with reference to traditional equity principles.

special circumstances, what does not constitute

In Carthage Bank v. Kirkland, 121 B.R. 496 (SD MS, 1990), the court stated that the application of equity principles to the "special circumstances" clause in Section 523(d) must be tempered by the statute's stated goal of deterring creditors from filing unwarranted exceptions to discharge. The court also stated that in determining whether "special circumstances" exist under Section 523(d), the focus of the analysis should be on the creditor and not on the debtor. In that case the court held that neither the abbreviated nature of the first meeting of creditors, the debtor's resistance to the taking of his deposition by the creditor, the vagueness and evasiveness of the debtor's answers at the deposition, the materially false information in the debtor's financial statements, nor the creditors altruistic motives in making loans to the debtor constituted special circumstances making an award of costs and attorney's fees unjust.

In FirstBanks v. Goss, 149 B.R. 460 (ED MI, 1992), the court found that special circumstances making an award unjust did not exist where the creditor claimed it did not receive notice of the trial date but did not attend the meeting of creditors nor conduct any discovery in the nondischargeability proceeding. However, in Middlefield Bank v. Kassoff, 146 B.R. 194 (ND OH, 1992), the court found that special circumstances existed to make an award of costs and attorney's fees under Section 523(d) unjust where the creditor filed 7 counts of nondischargeability only one of which was under Section 523(a)(2) and where only one of the contested debts was a consumer debt.

special circumstances, what constitutes

Amounts recoverable by the debtor under Section 523(d). Once liability is established under Section 523(d), the court is required to enter judgment against the creditor and in favor of the debtor for the costs of, and a reasonable attorney's fee for, the nondischargeability proceeding. Therefore, a successful debtor is entitled to an award equal to its costs incurred in the nondischargeability proceeding plus a reasonable attorney's fee incurred in the proceeding. It is clear from the wording of Section 523(d) that the debtor is entitled to recover only the costs incurred in the nondischargeability proceeding and not the costs of the entire bankruptcy proceeding. Therefore, the key issues in most instances are what constitutes a reasonable rate for the attorney's services and to what extent are the services rendered by the attorney are includible in the award. Note that while pro se debtors are not entitled to recover attorney's fees under Section 523(d) because none have been incurred, they may recover their costs. See In re Welch, 208 B.R. 107 (SD NY, 1997); In re Williamson, 181 B.R. 403 (WD MO, 1995).

recovery under §523(d), extent of

pro se debtors, rights of under §523(d)

It is not unusual for a creditor to either object to the dischargeability of several debts, some of which are not consumer debts, or to object to the dischargeability of a consumer debt on several grounds in addition to Section 523(a)(2). As indicated above, creditor liability under Section 523(d) is limited to consumer debts whose dischargeability is challenged under Section 523(a)(2). Therefore, legal services rendered by the debtor's attorney with respect to debts or dischargeability challenges that are not covered by Section 523(d) are not recoverable under Section 523(d). However, common issues of law and fact are often presented by debts or dischargeability challenges that are covered by Section 523(d) and those that are not and it can be very difficult or impossible to allocate or apportion the legal services between covered and non-covered debts or challenges. In such cases many courts allow the entire amount of dual or overlapping fees under Section 523(d), as long as the total amount is reasonable, rather than attempting to parcel out the services spent defending only the covered debt or challenge. See FCC Nat'l Bank v. Dobbins, 151 B.R. 509 (WD MO, 1992) (where $937.50 was approved as a reasonable amount for attorney's fees despite the fact that much of the chargeable time was spent defending a non-covered Section 523(a)(1) dischargeability challenge). See also In re Stahl, 222 B.R. 507 (WD NC, 1998) (where debtor's attorney fees of $17,575 for defending an adversary action brought by an extremely aggressive attorney were found to be reasonable).

overlapping cases, recovery of attorney's fees for

attorney's fees in overlapping cases, flat fee situations

In In re Dayton, 306 B.R. 322 (ND CA, 2004), a chapter 7 debtor was entitled to recover her attorney's fees which resulted from a creditor's adversary proceeding that was not substantially justified. Despite the fact that the debtor and her attorney had entered into a flat fee agreement prior to filing, she was entitled to an award based on the market rate for services performed by the attorney for both the adversary proceeding and the motion for attorney's fees.

attorney's fees in overlapping cases, amount awardable

In In re Watson, 44 B.R. 183 (MD TN, 1984), the court approved an attorney's fee award of $3,107 under Section 523(d) (computed at $65 per hour) for successfully defending the dischargeability of two debts, one a consumer debt and the other a business debt. Even though fraud and conversion were alleged only with respect to the consumer debt, where there were common issues of fact with respect to the dischargeability of both debts, the dischargeability of the two debts were tried together, and it was impossible to apportion the attorney's time between the two debts.

attorney's fees, amount awardable under §523(d), cases

The determination of the amount of attorneys' fees to award under Section 523(d) is clearly within the authority of the bankruptcy judge. See In re Poskanzer, 55 B.R. 329 (NJ, 1985) (where an attorney's fee of $1,725 was approved as reasonable even though the creditor's complaint was ultimately dismissed as not being timely filed). In Carthage Bank v. Kirkland, 121 B.R. 496 (SD MS, 1990), legal expenses incurred in the filing on behalf of the debtor of an unsuccessful motion for summary judgment on the Section 523(a)(2) nondischargeability issues were awardable under Section 523(d) because the motion was not frivolous or unreasonable.

attorney's fees for §523(d) services, recovery of

In FirstBanks v. Goss, 149 B.R. 460 (ED MI, 1992), an attorney's fee award of $1,380 was approved as being well within the ballpark for the defense of consumer dischargeability litigation. However, the court refused to award additional attorney's fees for the preparation of a brief on the Section 523(d) issues. In essence, the court awarded attorney's fees for the time spent by the attorney on the Section 523(a)(2) dischargeability issues but not for time spent on the Section 523(d) creditor liability issues. However, in In re Woods, 69 B.R. 999 (ED PA, 1987), the court explicitly held that time spent by the debtor's attorney on the Section 523(d) creditor liability issues was chargeable against the creditor in addition to the time spent on the Section 523(a)(2) dischargeability issues. See In re Goldstein, 345 B.R. 412 (MA, 2006), for an award of $1000 under Section 523(d) for an inadvertent violation of the automatic stay.

appellate attorney's fees, recovery of under §523(d)

It is not clear whether appellate attorney's fees are awardable under Section 523(d). In In re Wiencek, 58 B.R. 485 (ED VA, 1986), the court held that Section 523(d) mandates an award of attorney's fees for appellate representation in a Section 523(a)(2) nondischargeability proceeding and that the bankruptcy court is the appropriate forum for hearing such fee applications. However, in In re Vasseli, 5 F.3d 351 (9th Cir., 1993) Section 523(d) did not grant the bankruptcy court the authority to award attorney's fees for legal representation on appeal. The court held that under Rule 38 of the Federal Rules of Appellate Procedure the appellate court and not the bankruptcy court has the authority to make such awards. In In re Williams, 224 B.R. 523 (B.A.P. 2d Cir., 1998), the court stated that in the absence of a motion for fees, Section 523(d) alone does not authorize the bankruptcy court to award attorney's fees for appellate representation.

The procedure for obtaining an award under Section 523(d). The proper method of obtaining an award of costs and attorney's fees against a creditor under Section 523(d) is for the debtor to file an application or motion for an award of costs and attorney's fees under Section 523(d) with the bankruptcy court within a reasonable time after the conclusion of the dischargeability proceeding. See In re Kurtz, 213 B.R. 253 (ND NY, 1997). The matter is a contested matter governed by Bankruptcy Rule 9014, which requires reasonable notice to the party against whom relief is sought and an opportunity to be heard. See In re Smith, 54 B.R. 299 (SD IA, 1985). It is now clear that because of the mandatory language in Section 523(d) the debtor does not have to file a counterclaim seeking an award under Section 523(d) in order to recover under that Section. See In re Williamson, 181 B.R. 403 (WD MO, 1995). See also In re Melcher, 322 B.R. 1 (CO, 2005) where the debtors' failure to plead a request for attorney's fees in their answer was not fatal to their ability to request fees at a later time. See also In re Bullock, 322 B.R. 176 (MD AL, 2005).

§523(d) proceeding, procedure

While the motion or application for an award of costs and attorney's fees under Section 523(d) must normally be filed within a reasonable time after the conclusion of the nondischargeability proceeding, if the unsuccessful creditor is the federal government, the motion or application should be filed within 30 days after the date of the nondischargeability judgment. See 28 U.S.C. § 2412(d)(1)(B) (requiring that motions for attorney's fees against the federal government under the Equal Access to Judgment Act be filed within 30 days of the judgment. This provision may be applicable to bankruptcy proceedings involving the federal government). See also 11 U.S.C. § 106(a)(3).

§523(d) proceeding, procedure when creditor is U.S.

Bibliography. For further reading on the issues discussed in this article, see the annotations and articles listed below.

Annotations: None available.

Articles:

Fee Shifting in Bankruptcy: Deterring Frivolous, Fraud-Based Objections to Discharge. 76 N.C. Law Review 97 (Nov., 1997).

1.17 To what extent may a debtor avoid liens securing unallowed claims under Section 506(d) of the Bankruptcy Code?

Text of statute. Section 506(d) of the Bankruptcy Code (11 U.S.C. § 506(d)) is applicable to the subject discussed in this article. It provides as follows:

506. Determination of secured status

§506(d), text of

(d) To the extent that a lien secures a claim against the debtor that is not an allowed secured claim, such lien is void, unless –

(1) such claim was disallowed only under section 502(b)(5) or 502(e) of this title; or

(2) such claim is not an allowed secured claim due only to the failure of any entity to file a proof of such claim under section 501 of this title.

lien avoidance, importance of in bankruptcy

Introduction. Lien avoidance is an important aspect of many consumer bankruptcy cases. Liens that are not avoided survive the bankruptcy case and are enforceable against the debtor's post-bankruptcy property to the full extent permitted under local law. See In re Hermansen, 84 B.R. 729 (CO, 1988). Even if the debt that gave rise to the lien is discharged, the lien, if not avoided, survives the bankruptcy case and may seriously impede the debtor's post-bankruptcy fresh start. It is important, therefore, that liens be avoided to the full extent permitted under the Bankruptcy Code.

lien avoidance by debtor, methods of

Generally, liens may be avoided by the debtor under Sections 522(f), 522(h), and 506(d). The avoidance of liens on exempt property under Section 522(f) is discussed in article 1.05 of this handbook. The avoidance of nonconsensual liens on exempt property under Section 522(h) is discussed in article 1.18 of this handbook. The avoidance of liens securing unallowed claims under Section 506(d) is discussed in this article.

avoidance of liens under §506(d), exceptions and limitations

§506(d), applicability of in bankruptcy cases

Section 506(d) provides that liens securing disallowed claims are void. This proviso, however, is subject to three statutory exceptions and one court-imposed exception. The first statutory exception to the Section 506(d) rule voiding liens that secure disallowed claims is that liens securing unmatured claims for domestic support obligations may not be avoided, even though such claims are not allowable. The second statutory exception is that liens securing claims of codebtors or guarantors of the debtor for reimbursement or contribution may not be avoided if the claim is disallowable only because the codebtor or guarantor has not paid the creditor on the claim. The third statutory exception is that liens securing claims that were not allowed in the bankruptcy case only because the claim was not filed may not be avoided. In addition, the Supreme Court has ruled that a lien may not be avoided or reduced under Section 506(d) solely because the claim to which the lien relates is not fully secured. In other words, a lien securing an undersecured claim may not be reduced or "stripped down" under Section 506(d) to the value of the secured property. Except for the lien stripping limitations, which are generally limited to Chapter 7 cases, Section 506(d) is applicable to cases filed under any chapter of the Bankruptcy Code, including Chapter 13.

Section 506(d) was originally enacted in the Bankruptcy Reform Act of 1978. In 1984 paragraphs (1) and (2) of Section 506(d) were revised to their present form. The purpose of the 1984 amendment was to ensure that liens securing claims for unmatured alimony, maintenance or support could not be avoided under this section and to make it clear that a lien could not be avoided under this section solely because proof of the underlying claim was not filed in the bankruptcy case. See Senate Report No. 98-65, 98th Congress 1st Sess. 79 (1983).

§506(d), legislative history

The status of "lien stripping." In Dewsnup v. Timm, 502 U.S. 410, 112 S. Ct. 773, (1992), the Court held that "lien stripping" was not permitted under Section 506(d) of the Bankruptcy Code. Prior to that decision several courts had held that a lien on the debtor's property could be avoided under Section 506(d) to the extent that the lien secured a claim that was not an "allowed secured claim." This so-called "lien stripping" was accomplished by bifurcating a lien securing an undersecured claim into secured and unsecured portions in the manner provided in 11 U.S.C. § 506(a) for the bifurcation of an undersecured claim into secured and unsecured portions. Lien stripping was based in part on the language of Section 506(d), which provides that a lien is void to the extent that it secures a claim that is not an "allowed secured claim." The courts supporting lien stripping held that the portion of the lien securing the unsecured portion of an undersecured claim did not secure an "allowed secured claim" and was therefore void under Section 506(d). The Supreme Court, in Dewsnup v. Timm, ruled that this interpretation of Section 506(d) was incorrect.

lien stripping under §506(d), prior to Dewsnup v. Timm

In Dewsnup v. Timm the debtors owned farmland valued by the bankruptcy court at $39,000 that was subject to a consensual lien (a deed of trust) securing a $120,000 note. The debtors defaulted on the note and prior to foreclosure filed for bankruptcy relief under Chapter 7. The debtors then sought to avoid the creditor's lien under Section 506(d) to the extent that the lien exceeded the $39,000 value of the property. In other words, the debtors sought to use Section 506(d) to reduce the creditor's lien from $120,000 to $39,000 by stripping from the lien the portion securing the unsecured portion of the claim.

Dewsnup v. Timm, facts of case

The Supreme Court refused to allow the debtors to strip the creditor's lien in this manner. The court decided that Section 506(d) should be interpreted independently of Section 506(a). In other words, the court held that the claim bifurcation provisions of Section 506(a) were not applicable to the lien avoidance provisions of Section 506(d). Specifically, the court held that the phrase "allowed secured claim" in Section 506(d) should be construed independently of Section 506(a) and means a secured claim that has been allowed in the case. The court held that the phrase "allowed secured claim" did not mean the secured portion of an allowed undersecured claim. Therefore, the court held, only a lien securing a secured claim that was not allowed in the case may be avoided under Section 506(d), provided that the lien otherwise qualifies for avoidance under Section 506(d).

Dewsnup v. Timm, holding of case

Dewsnup v. Timm, applicability to cases under other chapters

Dewsnup v. Timm was a Chapter 7 case and the Supreme Court expressly limited its holding to the facts and circumstances of that case. Consequently, most lower courts have limited the lien stripping prohibitions in Dewsnup v. Timm to Chapter 7 cases. See In re Janssen, 311 B.R. 518 (ED MO, 2004). Lien stripping is generally not prohibited by the rule of Dewsnup v. Timm in cases under Chapters 11, 12 and 13. Liens, other than those secured only by the debtor's principal residence and those incurred within 910 days of the petition filing for personal use automobiles, may be reduced or stripped down to the judicially determined value of the secured property in a Chapter 13 case. See, e.g., In re Aubain, 296 B.R. 624 (ED NY, 2003); In re Robert, 313 B.R. 545 (ND NY, 2004); In re Pond, 252 F.3d 122 (2d Cir., 2001); In re Bellamy, 962 F.2d 176 (2d Cir., 1992); Sapos v. Provident Inst. of Savings, 967 F.2d 918 (3d Cir., 1992); Lomas Mortgage USA v. Wiese, 980 F.2d 1279 (9th Cir., 1992); In re Mc Donough, 166 B.R. 9 (MA, 1994); In re Butler, 139 B.R. 258 (ED OK, 1992); In re Gibbons, 164 B.R. 207 (NH, 1993). But see 11 U.S.C. 1325(a) (hanging paragraph). These cases have generally held that the provisions in Chapter 13 permitting the debtor to modify the rights of secured creditors (other than those secured only by a security interest in the debtor's principal residence and "910" creditors) distinguish a Chapter 13 case from the Chapter 7 case dealt with in Dewsnup v. Timm. These provisions are found in 11 U.S.C. § 1322(b)(2), 1325(a)(5), and 1327(c). See In re Orkwis, 457 B.R. 243 (Bankr. E.D. N.Y. 2011) (holding Dewsnup prohibition applies to lien on Chapter 13 debtor's residence if there is any equity above senior lien). Similar rulings permitting lien stripping have been made in Chapter 11 and Chapter 12 cases. See Wade v. Bradford, 39 F.3d 1126 (10th Cir., 1994), and In re Crook, 966 F.2d 539 (10th Cir., 1992). Note, however, that lien stripping is not permitted in a Chapter 13 case if the case is converted to Chapter 7. See In re Jordan, 164 B.R. 89 (ED MO, 1994).

lien stripping in converted Chapter 13 case

Some courts have further limited the effect of Dewsnup v. Timm by limiting it to cases where the secured creditor has some security in the secured property. The courts in these cases have held that Dewsnup v. Timm is not applicable to Chapter 7 cases where the creditor, by virtue of the existence of senior secured interests in the secured property, is completely unsecured. See Chong Woo Yi v. Citibank, N.A., 219 B.R. 394 (ED VA, 1998); In re Zempel, 244 B.R. 625 (WD KY, 1999); In re Howard, 184 B.R. 644 (ED NY, 1995); In re Geyer, 203 B.R. 726 (SD CA, 1996); In re Vaillancourt, 197 B.R. 464 (MD PA, 1996). In In re Duncan, 60 B.R. 345 (MD AL, 1986), the court held that a judgment lien that attaches to nothing because there is no property in the estate is not an allowed secured claim and is therefore void under Section 506(d). See also In re Fisette, 455 B.R. 177 (B.A.P. 8th Cir. 2011) (chapter 13 debtor may strip off wholly unsecured lien on principal residence). Other courts have ruled to the contrary, holding that Dewsnup v. Timm prevents lien stripping even in cases where the creditor is completely undersecured. See In re Webster, 287 B.R. 703 (ND OH, 2002), In re Virello, 236 B.R. 199 (SC, 1999), In re Talbert, 268 B.R. 811 (WD MI, 2001), In re Fitzmaurice, 248 B.R. 356 (WD MO, 2000), In re Cater, 240 B.R. 420 (MD AL, 1999), In re Madjerac, 157 B.R. 499 (ME, 1993), and In re Wolkup, 183 B.R. 884 (ED CA, 1995). The question, obviously, is whether a completely undersecured claim is an "allowed secured claim" under Section 506(d) as that phrase was interpreted by the Supreme Court in Dewsnup v. Timm. The lower courts are divided on the issue.

lien stripping where creditor is completely undersecured

Dewsnup v. Timm dealt with a consensual lien. However, generally the lien stripping prohibitions of Dewsnup v. Timm are equally applicable to nonconsensual liens. See In re Esler, 165 B.R. 583 (MD, 1994). Therefore, nonconsensual liens such as tax liens and judgment liens may not be stripped down in Chapter 7 cases. See In re Place, 173 B.R. 911 (ED AR, 1994); In re Doviak, 161 B.R. 379 (ED TX, 1993); Crossroads of Hillsville v. Payne, 179 B.R. 486 (WD VA, 1995); In re Rombach, 159 B.R. 311 (CD CA, 1993). On the other hand, in In re Howard, 184 B.R. 644 (ED NY, 1995), a chapter 7 case, a nonconsensual judgment lien held by a creditor may be avoided under Section 506(a) and (d) where, because of a large first mortgage, the judgment lien is wholly unsecured.

lien stripping, nonconsensual lien

The avoidability of liens securing claims for unmatured domestic support obligations. Section 506(d)(1) provides, in part, that liens securing disallowed claims are void unless the claim is disallowed only under Section 502(b)(5) of the Bankruptcy Code. Section 502(b)(5) provides that claims for unmatured domestic support obligations are not allowable in bankruptcy cases. Therefore, liens securing claims for future domestic support obligations may not be avoided under Section 506(d) even though the underlying claim is not allowable.

liens securing future support obligation, nonavoidability of

The avoidability of liens securing claims of codebtors or guarantors for reimbursement or contribution. Section 506(d)(1) provides, in part, that liens securing disallowed claims are void unless the claim is disallowed only under Section 502(e) of the Bankruptcy Code. Section 502(e) provides that a claim for reimbursement or contribution by a codebtor or guarantor of the debtor is not allowable to the extent that the claim is contingent or to the extent that codebtor or guarantor elects a subrogation remedy under Section 509 of the Bankruptcy Code. A claim for reimbursement or contribution is contingent to the extent that the codebtor or guarantor has not paid the underlying obligation owed by the debtor. The reason for the requirement of prepayment by codebtor or guarantor is to prevent both the codebtor or guarantor and the underlying creditor from collecting from the estate on the same underlying claim. However, the codebtor or guarantor may perfect its claim for reimbursement or contribution after the filing of the bankruptcy case by paying the underlying obligation to the creditor. See 11 U.S.C. § 502(e)(2). In order to preserve the enforcement rights of a codebtor or guarantor who later perfects itsv claim by paying the underlying obligation, the lien securing the claim of the codebtor or guarantor is protected from avoidance under Section 506(d). See 11 U.S.C. § 506(d)(1). Therefore, a lien securing the claim of a codebtor or guarantor for reimbursement or contribution may not be avoided under Section 506(d) even though the claim is not allowable because it is still contingent.

liens securing claims of codebtors, nonavoidability of

liens securing unfiled claims, nonavoidability and survival of

The avoidability of liens securing unfiled claims. Section 506(d)(2) provides that a lien securing a claim that was not an allowed secured claim in the bankruptcy case only because a proof of claim was not filed is not void. This is the most widely used and frequently litigated exception to the avoidability of liens securing unallowed claims under Section 506(d). Under this provision, a lien securing an unfiled claim survives the bankruptcy case even if the debtor's personal liability for the unfiled claim is discharged. See Estate of Lellock v. Prudential Ins. Co., 811 F.2d 186 (3d Cir., 1987).

enforcement of liens securing unfiled claims, effect of discharge injunction

Note that a creditor with a lien securing an unfiled but discharged claim is not enjoined by the discharge injunction from enforcing its lien against the debtor's property after the bankruptcy case. The discharge injunction, as set forth in 11 U.S.C. § 524(a)(2), enjoins only acts against the debtor to recover debts as a personal liability of the debtor. Because surviving liens are enforceable "in rem" against property of the debtor, their postbankruptcy enforcement is not a violation of the discharge injunction. See In re Hermansen, 84 B.R. 729 (CO, 1988).

lien securing unfiled claim, necessity of avoiding in bankruptcy court

To avoid a lien securing an unfiled claim under Section 506(d), the debtor must either file a proof of claim on behalf of the creditor and then object to its allowance or file a proceeding in the bankruptcy court to avoid the lien. If the debtor does nothing, a lien securing an unfiled claim will survive the bankruptcy case even if the claim was listed in the debtor's schedules as being unsecured. See Pierce v. Woodard, 29 B.R. 612 (ED NC, 1983). Even if the lien securing an unfiled claim was unperfected (and therefore avoidable) at the time of the bankruptcy filing, if it is not affirmatively avoided in the bankruptcy case the lien will pass through the bankruptcy case unaffected by Section 506(d) and may later be perfected and enforced by the creditor. See In re Eakin, 153 B.R. 59 (ID, 1993) (holding that a discharged creditor with an unperfected security interest in the debtor's mobile home who had not filed a claim in the bankruptcy case could foreclose on its lien after the bankruptcy case because the lien had not been avoided in the bankruptcy case even though it could have been).

lien securing unfiled claim, necessity of filing claim in order to avoid lien

Under Section 506(d)(2), a lien securing a claim that is not an allowed secured claim is void unless the claim was not allowed solely because proof of the claim was not filed. If the creditor chooses not to file a proof of claim, the debtor may do so but only after the expiration of the time for filing proofs of claim. See Bankruptcy Rule 501(c). If the debtor wishes to avoid a lien securing an unfiled claim, must the debtor wait until after the expiration of the time for filing proofs of claim before doing so? In other words, is it necessary for a proof of claim to be filed in order to contest the validity of the lien securing the claim? Most courts have answered this question in the negative, holding that it is not necessary that proof of a claim be filed in order to contest the validity of the lien securing the claim. See In re Brown, 73 B.R. 740 (WD WI, 1987); In re Duncan, 60 B.R. 345 (MD AL, 1986); In re Shumate, 42 B.R. 462 (ED TN, 1984).

The procedure for avoiding liens under Section 506(d). In most cases the proper procedure for avoiding a lien under Section 506(d) is to file an adversary proceeding under Bankruptcy Rule 7001. However, if a debtor wishes to value collateral and thereafter avoid an unsecured lien, he or she may do so by motion. In re Sadala, 294 B.R. 180 (MD FL, 2003). In In re Williams, 277 B.R. 78 (MD, 2002) the court ruled that, as a co-owner of property, a debtor's spouse (a non-debtor) was a necessary party to the debtor's motion to avoid a secured creditor's lien because the motion sought to amend interests in the real property. See Bankruptcy Rule 7001(2); Cen-Pen Corp. v. Hanson, 58 F.3d 89 (4th Cir., 1995); Wright v. Commercial Credit Corp, 178 B.R. 703 (ED VA, 1995). If the claim upon which the lien is based has not been filed, the proper procedure may be to file a claim on the creditor's behalf under Bankruptcy Rule 501(c) and then file an objection to the claim. If the claim is disallowed on any grounds other than the two grounds listed in Section 506(d)(1), then the lien is automatically avoided under Section 506(d) without further action. See In re Folendore, 862 F.2d 1537 (11th Cir., 1989). In a Chapter 13 case a lien may be avoided under Section 506(d) in the plan confirmation process if proper notice of the intent to avoid the lien is given. See In re Pence, 905 F.2d 1107 (7th Cir., 1990); In re Wolf, 162 B.R. 98 (NJ, 1993).

procedure for avoiding liens under §506(d)

Bibliography. For further reading on the issues discussed in this article, see the annotations and articles listed below.

Annotations:

Special Commentary: Bifurcation and Avoidance, or "stripping" of Liens, Security Interests, and Encumbrances Held by Undersecured Creditors by Rehabilitating and Liquidating Debtors in Bankruptcy. 158 ALR Fed. 1.

Articles:

Dewsnup v. Timm: The Supreme Court on "Lien Stripping." 63 Okla. B.J. 1265 (May, 1992).

Determination of Secured Status & Section 506 Lien-Stripping: Is There Life for Lien-Stripping After Dewsnup? 11 ABI Newsletter 6 (1992).

Undersecured Creditors in Bankruptcy: Dewsnup, Nobleman, and the Decline of Priority. 25 Ariz. St. L.J. 547 (1993).

Modifying Wholly Unsecured Unsecured Home Mortgage Loans in Chapter 13: If They're Under Water, Let 'em Drown. 7 J. Bkcy L & Prac. 625 Sept./Oct., 1998.

1.18 To what extent may a debtor avoid nonconsensual liens on exempt property under Section 522(h) of the Bankruptcy Code?

Text of statute. Section 522(h) of the Bankruptcy Code (11 U.S.C. § 522(h)) provides as follows:

522. Exemptions

§522(h), text of

(h) The debtor may avoid a transfer of property of the debtor or recover a setoff to the extent that the debtor could have exempted such property under subsection (g)(1) of this section if the trustee had avoided such transfer, if -

(1) such transfer is avoidable by the trustee under section 544, 545, 547, 548, 549, or 724(a) of this title or recoverable by the trustee under section 553 of this title; and

(2) the trustee does not attempt to avoid such transfer.

§522(h), legislative history, use of in addition to §522(f)

Introduction. Section 522(h) was enacted in the Bankruptcy Reform Act of 1978 and, except for the correction of a spelling error in 1986, has remained unchanged since its enactment. The debtor's right to avoid nonconsensual liens and other involuntary transfers of interests in exempt property under Section 522(h) is in addition to the debtor's right to avoid liens on exempt property under Section 522(f) of the Bankruptcy Code. See article 1.05 of this handbook for a discussion of the debtor's right to avoid liens on exempt property under Section 522(f).

§522(h), scope and function of

Section 522(g) of the Bankruptcy Code permits a debtor to claim exemptions on property recovered by the trustee if the debtor did not voluntarily transfer the property and did not conceal the existence of the property. See In re Buelow, 287 B.R. 446 (ND IA, 2002). However, the primary obligation of a bankruptcy trustee is to the estate and not to the debtor. Therefore, a bankruptcy trustee is not likely to attempt to recover exempt property because the property will go to the debtor and not to the estate. To overcome this obstacle to a debtor's right to fully exercise his or her exemptions and obtain a fresh start, Section 522(h) of the Bankruptcy Code permits a debtor to avoid transfers of property or recover setoffs to the extent that the debtor could have exempted the transferred property under Section 522(g) if the trustee could have avoided the transfer or recovered the setoff but did not do so. In essence, then, Section 522(h) permits a debtor to exercise his or her Section 522(g) exemption rights in cases where the trustee does not attempt to avoid an involuntary transfer of property that may be claimed as exempt by the debtor.

involuntary transfers, types of that are avoidable under §522(h)

Only involuntary or nonconsensual transfers may be avoided by the debtor under Section 522(h). Involuntary or nonconsensual transfers include transfers resulting from judgment liens, statutory liens, tax liens, garnishments, attachments, executions, and foreclosures. It is transfers of this type that are most often avoidable by the debtor under Section 522(h). Wage garnishments, homestead foreclosures, attachments or repossessions of exempt property, and the filing of judgment or statutory liens on exempt property are examples of the types of transfers that may be avoidable by the debtor under Section 522(h). See In re Smoot, 237 B.R. 875 (MD, 1999) permitting a Chapter 13 debtor to recover the proceeds of a wage garnishment under Section 522(h)).

Note that if a debtor avoids a transfer or recovers a setoff under Section 522(h), the debtor may recover the exempt portion of the property in question under Section 550 of the Bankruptcy Code. Under Section 550 the exempt property may be recovered by the debtor either from the initial transferee or from a subsequent transferee. However, because the debtor is subject to the same recovery limitations as the trustee, the debtor may not recover exempt property from a good faith transferee who took the property for value without knowledge of the avoidability of the transfer in question. See 11 U.S.C. § 522(i)(1), 550(b). A bankruptcy case may be reopened for the purpose of lien avoidance under Section 522(h). See, e.g., In re Levy, 256 B.R. 563 (NJ, 2000).

§550, use of by debtor to recover transferred property

While it is most often used by Chapter 7 debtors, Section 522(h) may be used by individual debtors under any chapter of the Bankruptcy Code, including Chapter 13. A Chapter 13 debtor has standing to avoid a transfer under Section 522(h). See In re Herring, 224 B.R. 858 (ND GA, 1997); In re Talbot, 254 B.R. 63 (CT, 2000) (stating the exempt property recovered in the Section 522(h) proceeding would be preserved for the benefit of the debtors rather than the estate). Because they have no exempt property, corporate and other nonindividual debtors have no standing to avoid transfers under Section 522(h).

§522(h), applicability of in Chapter 7 and 13 cases

The requirements for avoiding liens under Section 522(h). Section 522(h) of the Bankruptcy Code provides that the debtor may avoid the transfer of property that the debtor could have exempted under Section 522(g)(1) of the Bankruptcy Code had the trustee avoided the transfer, provided that (1) the transfer is avoidable by the trustee and (2) the trustee does not attempt to avoid the transfer. Section 522(g)(1), permits the debtor to claim exemptions on property recovered by the trustee if the avoided transfer of the property by the debtor was not voluntary and if the debtor did not conceal the property. Applying the provisions of Sections 522(h) and 522(g)(1), the debtor generally must meet the following five requirements in order to have standing to avoid a lien or other transfer under Section 522(h):

§522(h), provisions of

§522(g)(1), provisions of

(1) the transfer that is sought to be avoided must not have been voluntarily or consensually made by the debtor;

§522(h), requirements for use of by debtor

(2) the debtor must not have concealed the existence of transferred property in the bankruptcy case;

(3) the trustee must not have attempted to avoid the transfer in question;

(4) the transfer in question must be avoidable by the trustee under Sections 544, 545, 547, 548, 549 or 724(a) of the Bankruptcy Code or be recoverable by the trustee as a setoff under Section 553 of the Bankruptcy Code; and

(5) the debtor must be able to exercise all or part of an applicable exemption on the transferred property if it is recovered.

See, e.g., In re De Marah, 62 F.3d 1248 (9th Cir., 1995); In re James, 257 B.R. 673 (B.A.P. 8th Cir., 2001); In re Dalip, 194 B.R. 597 (ND IL, 1996); In re Perkins, 169 B.R. 455 (MD GA, 1994); In re Humphrey, 165 B.R. 578 (MD, 1993).

§522(h) requirements, cases establishing

§522(h), requirement of involuntary transfer

The first requirement for transfer avoidance by the debtor under Section 522(h) is that the transfer in question must not have been voluntarily or consensually made by the debtor. Under Section 522(g)(1)(A), which is incorporated by Section 522(h), the debtor may not exercise an exemption on recovered property if the transfer by the debtor of the property in question was voluntary or consensual. This means that the debtor may avoid a lien or other transfer under Section 522(h) only if the interest in property in question was involuntarily or nonconsensually transferred from the debtor. Voluntary or consensual transfers of interests in property of the debtor may not be avoided by the debtor under Section 522(h). See In re Gingery, 48 B.R. 1000 (CO, 1985); In re Driver, 133 B.R. 476 (SD IN, 1991); In re Kildow, 232 B.R. 686 (SD OH, 1999).

voluntary transfer, what constitutes, cases

It is sometimes difficult to determine whether a particular transfer was voluntary or involuntary for purposes of Section 522(h). The granting of a mortgage or security interest by the debtor is usually a voluntary transfer regardless of the circumstances of the transfer. See In re Patton, 314 B.R. 826 (KS, 2004); In re Ulrich, 203 B.R. 691 (CD IL, 1997); In re Terry, 56 B.R. 538 (VT, 1986) (holding the granting of a mortgage in the settlement of a lawsuit against the debtor was a voluntary transfer). In In re Dalip, 194 B.R. 597 (ND IL, 1996), an agreement by the debtor to give the IRS a portion of the proceeds from the sale of his house for a tax lien payment was a voluntary transfer for purposes of Section 522(h). In In re Trevino, 96 B.R. 608 (ED NC, 1989), a transfer of cash and a trailer to his father by the debtor in repayment of past financial assistance was found to be a voluntary transfer for purposes of Section 522(h). The execution by the debtor of a wage assignment was found to be a voluntary transfer for purposes of Section 522(h) in In re Whisenton, 40 B.R. 468 (DC, 1984). However, in Berman v. Forti, 232 B.R. 653 (MD, 1999), transfers resulting from judicial liens that arose automatically by operation of state law when a judgment creditor filed a consent judgment after the debtors had voluntarily settled a lawsuit by giving promissory notes were held to be involuntary for purposes of Section 522(h).

voluntary vs. involuntary transfer, effect of pressure or coercion by transferee

Several courts have held that if the debtor can show that he or she was pressured, harassed, insulted, or shamed into making the transfer, then the transfer may be deemed involuntary for purposes of Section 522(h). See In re Corwin, 135 B.R. 922 (SD FL, 1992), and In re Reaves, 8 B.R. 177 (SD, 1981). A payment to a creditor by the debtor to obtain the release of a wage garnishment was held to be an involuntary transfer for purposes of Section 522(h) in In re Via, 107 B.R. 91 (WD VA, 1989). In In re Washkowiak, 62 B.R. 884 (ND IL, 1986), the payment by the debtors of a perfected judgment lien on the day after they sold their home because the title company withheld funds from the sale proceeds to satisfy the lien was held not to be a voluntary transfer for purposes of Section 522(h) because the judgment supporting the lien was not entered with the debtor's consent. However, the burden of proof is on the debtor to establish that he or she was unduly coerced, harassed or threatened into making the transfer in question. See In re Corwin, 135 B.R. 922 (SD FL, 1992), where the threat by the creditor of "very serious legal ramifications" was held insufficient to make the granting of a homestead lien by the debtor involuntary for purposes of Section 522(h).

The second requirement for transfer avoidance by the debtor under Section 522(h) is that the existence of the transferred property must not have been concealed by the debtor. This generally means that in order to avoid the transfer of an interest in property under Section 522(h), the existence of the property must have been voluntarily disclosed by the debtor, either in the bankruptcy schedules or otherwise. See In re Fox, 80 B.R. 753 (WD PA, 1987); In re Fabian, 122 B.R. 678 (WD PA, 1990). In Glass v. Hitt, 60 F.3d 565 (9th Cir., 1995), the debtor had forfeited his right to claim a homestead exemption under Section 522(g) by voluntarily transferring the homestead to his son 37 days prior to the bankruptcy filing and concealing the existence of the property at the time of the filing. See also In re Yasipour, 238 B.R. 289 (MD PA, 1999).

§522(h), requirement of nonconcealment

The third requirement for transfer avoidance by the debtor under Section 522(h) is that the trustee must not have previously attempted to avoid the transfer. See In re Hill, 152 B.R. 204 (SD OH, 1993). Section 522(h)(2) explicitly provides that the debtor may avoid a transfer under Section 522(h) only if the trustee does not attempt to avoid the transfer. It is clear, therefore, that the availability to the debtor of Section 522(h) is limited to cases where the trustee has chosen not to exercise its avoiding powers. See In re Wilkinson, 196 B.R. 311 (ED VA, 1996); In re Prejean, 64 B.R. 71 (WD LA, 1986). If the trustee has attempted to avoid the transfer in question, Section 522(h) is not available to the debtor and he or she must act under Section 522(g) to claim an exemption on the recovered property. See In re Gingery, 48 B.R. 1000 (CO, 1985).

§522(h), requirement of no action by trustee

The fourth requirement for transfer avoidance by the debtor under Section 522(h) is that the lien or other transfer in question must be avoidable by the trustee under Sections 544, 545, 547, 548, 549 or 724(a) of the Bankruptcy Code or recoverable as a setoff by the trustee under Section 553 of the Bankruptcy Code. If the transfer is not avoidable by the trustee under one of these sections it is not avoidable by the debtor under Section 522(h). The types of transfers that are avoidable by the trustee under these sections of the Bankruptcy Code are discussed under the next heading below in this article.

§522(h), requirement of avoidability by trustee

§522(h), requirement of applicable exemption

The fifth and final requirement for lien avoidance by the debtor under Section 522(h) is that the debtor must be able to claim an exemption on all or a portion of the recovered property. In other words, the debtor may avoid liens and recover property under Section 522(h) only to the extent that the recovered property is or will be exempt to the debtor in the bankruptcy case. See Owen v. Treadway, 169 B.R. 261 (ME, 1994). If the debtor has already claimed and received his or her maximum exemption on the type of property that is sought to be recovered by the avoidance of the lien in question, then the debtor may not avoid the lien under Section 522(h). For example, if the debtor has already claimed the maximum allowable homestead exemption on his or her residence, the debtor will not be permitted to avoid a nonconsensual lien on the residence under Section 522(h). See 11 U.S.C. § 522(j); In re Jones, 21 B.R. 469 (SC, 1982). Also, if the property in question is fully encumbered without reference to the lien that is sought to be avoided so that the debtor will have no equity in the property to exempt if the lien is avoided then the debtor may not avoid the lien in question under Section 522(h). See In re Bickleman, 71 B.R. 135 (ED PA, 1987). However, if the debtor can exempt even a portion of the property sought to be recovered by avoiding the lien in question, then the debtor may avoid the lien, whereupon the excess value of the recovered property will remain subject to the lien unless the balance of the lien is subsequently avoided by the trustee. See In re Pruitt, 72 B.R. 436 (ED NY, 1987) (permitting the debtor to avoid a mortgage foreclosure sale under Section 522(h) as a fraudulent transfer even though the debtor was entitled to exempt only a $10,000 portion of the $110,000 property whose transfer was avoided).

§522(h), requirement of timeliness

If the debtor chooses to avoid a lien or other transfer under Section 522(h), it is important that the debtor act in a timely manner. If the debtor fails to act timely to reclaim the exempt property and the trustee acts in reliance on the debtor's apparent disinterest in the property, the debtor may be denied permission to reclaim the property under Section 522(h). See In re Sandoval, 470 B.R. 195 (Bankr. N.M. 2012). This procedural requirement is in addition to the five substantive requirements described above.

§522(h), types of transfers avoidable under

The types of liens that are avoidable under Section 522(h). As indicated above, to be avoidable by the debtor under Section 522(h) a lien or other transfer must be avoidable by the trustee under Sections 544, 545, 547, 548, 549 or 724(a) of the Bankruptcy Code or recoverable as a setoff by the trustee under Section 553 of the Bankruptcy Code. The various types of liens or other transfers that are avoidable by the trustee under these Code sections (and therefore avoidable against exempt property by the debtor under Section 522(h)) are listed and discussed below.

transfers avoidable by state law under §544

(1) Transfers that are avoidable by the trustee under state law as provided in Section 544 of the Bankruptcy Code. Section 544 is the so-called "strong arm" clause of the Bankruptcy Code whereunder transfers that are avoidable by creditors under state law are avoidable by the trustee in a bankruptcy case. See article 1.14 of this handbook for a discussion of these avoidance powers.

(2) Transfers resulting from statutory liens that are avoidable by the trustee under Section 545 of the Bankruptcy Code. Under Section 545 statutory liens that arise from bankruptcy or insolvency filings, statutory liens that are not perfected or enforceable against bona fide purchasers of the property on the bankruptcy filing date, and statutory liens for rent or distress of rent are avoidable by the trustee.

transfers by statutory liens avoidable under §545

(3) Transfers that are avoidable by the trustee as preferences under Section 547 of the Bankruptcy Code. A transfer made by an insolvent debtor to a creditor for the payment of an antecedent debt within 90 days prior to the bankruptcy filing date is avoidable by the trustee as a preference under Section 547 if the transfer enabled the creditor to receive more than it would have received in a Chapter 7 liquidation case had the transfer not occurred. If the creditor is an insider, the preference or look-back period is one year instead of 90 days. See article 1.14 of this handbook for a discussion of the trustee's Section 547 avoidance powers.

transfers avoidable as preferences under §547

Of interest to consumer debtors is the provision in Section 547(c)(8) providing that in cases filed by individuals whose debts are primarily consumer debts a transfer of less than $600 is not an avoidable transfer. This means that involuntary transfers of exempt property by consumer debtors of less than $600 may not be avoided by the debtor as a preference under Section 522(h). See In re Lewis, 116 B.R. 54 (MD, 1990). However, if the amount of the transfer exceeds $600, the entire exempt amount of the transfer is avoidable as a preference under Section 522(h). See In re Vickery, 63 B.R. 222 (ED TN, 1986). See also In re Hailes, 77 F.3d 873 (5th Cir., 1996) (holding that the debtor, who was seeking to recover exempt wages that were garnished over a period of several weeks prior to the filing of the bankruptcy case, could total the amounts of the weekly garnishments within the 90 day preference period to exceed the $600 "safe harbor" of Section 547(c)(8) for purposes of transfer avoidance under Section 522(h)).

avoidable preferences under §522(h), effect of $600 transfer limitation

(4) Transfers that are avoidable by the trustee as a fraudulent transfer under Section 548 of the Bankruptcy Code. Under Section 548 the trustee may avoid transfers made by the debtor within one year prior to the bankruptcy filing date that unlawfully deplete the debtor's estate to the detriment of creditors. Transfers within one year of bankruptcy that are tainted by either actual or constructive fraud may be avoided by the trustee under Section 548. See article 1.14 of this handbook for a discussion of the trustee's Section 548 avoidance powers.

fraudulent transfers avoidable under §548

(5) Postpetition transfers that are avoidable by the trustee under Section 549 of the Bankruptcy Code. Under Section 549 the trustee can avoid most unauthorized postpetition transfers of estate property.

postpetition transfers avoidable under §549

tax penalty liens avoidable under §724(a)

(6) Tax liens that are avoidable by the trustee under Section 724(a) of the Bankruptcy Code. Under Section 724(a) the trustee can avoid tax liens that secure tax penalties that are not compensation for actual pecuniary loss suffered by the taxing authority. While Section 522(h) confers the power to avoid tax liens of this type to the debtor if the trustee fails to act, it should be noted that Section 522(c)(2)(B) of the Bankruptcy Code provides that exempt property of the debtor is, and after the case remains, liable for debts secured by properly filed tax liens. At least one court has held that Section 522(c)(2)(B) prevents the debtor from avoiding liens for tax penalties against exempt property under Section 522(h). See In re De Marah, 62 F.3d 1248 (9th Cir., 1995).

setoffs recoverable under §553

(7) Transfers in the form of setoffs that are recoverable by the trustee under Section 553 of the Bankruptcy Code. Under Section 553(b) the trustee can recover all or a portion of most setoffs that occur within 90 days prior to the bankruptcy filing date. In consumer bankruptcy and Chapter 13 cases setoffs are usually made by banks who set off their claim against the debtor's bank account. See In re Riggsby, 34 B.R. 440 (ED TN, 1983) (holding that the debtor was entitled to avoid the entire amount of a setoff pursuant to Section 522(h) and 553(b) because the bank setoff the entire amount of the debtor's pay check against two loans within 90 days of the bankruptcy filing date); In re Moses, 91 B.R. 994 (MD FL, 1988).

§522(h), proceedings under, procedure

The procedure for avoiding liens under Section 522(h). The proper procedure for avoiding a lien or other transfer under Section 522(h) and for recovering the transferred property under Section 550 is to file an adversary proceeding under Bankruptcy Rule 7001. See Bankruptcy Rule 7001(1), (2). If necessary in the case, the debtor should also request the court to preserve the avoided transfer because such transfers are not automatically preserved for the debtor. See 11 U.S.C. § 522(i)(2), which provides that an avoided transfer "may be preserved." (Under 11 U.S.C. § 551, it should be noted, avoided transfers are automatically preserved for the trustee.)

Bibliography. For further reading on the issues discussed in this article, see the annotations and articles listed below.

Annotations: None available.

Articles:

Avoidance of preferential transfers of exempt property. 215 N.Y.L.J. 3 (Jan. 18, 1996).

CHAPTER TWO

CHAPTER 7 BANKRUPTCY ISSUES

The articles in this chapter deal with issues that arise under the provisions of Chapter 7 of the Bankruptcy Code. Therefore, the articles in this chapter pertain only to Chapter 7 cases and are not applicable to Chapter 13 cases or to cases arising under any other chapter of the Bankruptcy Code.

2.01 Under what circumstances and by whom may a Chapter 7 case be dismissed for cause under Section 707(a) of the Bankruptcy Code?

Text of statute. **Section 707(a) of the Bankruptcy Code (11 U.S.C. § 707(a)) provides:**

707. Dismissal

(a) The court may dismiss a case under this chapter only after notice and a hearing and only for cause, including -

(1) unreasonable delay by the debtor that is prejudicial to creditors;

(2) nonpayment of any fees or charges required under chapter 123 of title 28; and

(3) failure of the debtor in a voluntary case to file, within fifteen days or such additional time as the court may allow after the filing of the petition commencing such case, the information required by paragraph (1) of section 521, but only on a motion by the United States trustee. §707(a), text of

Introduction. A Chapter 7 case may be dismissed on either of two grounds: (1) for "cause" under Section 707(a) of the Bankruptcy Code, or (2) for "abuse" under Section 707(b) of the Bankruptcy Code. See, e.g., In re McFadden, 477 B.R. 686 (Bankr. N. D. Ohio 2012); In re Jabarin 395 B.R. 330 (Bankr. E. D. Penn. 2008) (discussing common law under 707(a)). Dismissals for "cause" under Section 707(a) are discussed in this article and dismissals for "abuse" under Section 707(b) are discussed in article 2.02, infra. The only other grounds for the dismissal of a voluntary Chapter 7 case are debtor ineligibility under 11 U.S.C. § 109(g) and abstention under 11 U.S.C. § 305. Debtor ineligibility under Section 109(g) is discussed in article 1.01, supra. The doctrine of abstention is seldom applicable in Chapter 7 consumer cases and such cases are rarely dismissed on this ground. grounds for dismissal of Chapter 7 cases

A Chapter 7 case may, of course, be dismissed for any of the three causes listed in Section 707(a). Dismissals for nonpayment of the filing fee are seldom contested as it is clear that nonpayment of the filing fee constitutes grounds for dismissal. See In re Taylor, 252 B.R. 709 (WD TN, 2000). Dismissals for the debtor's failure to obtain required prepetition credit counseling have been deemed dismissals for cause. See In re Dyer, 381 B.R. 200 (WD NC, 2007) (also invoking 11 U.S.C. § § 109(h).) The nondisclosure of assets is grounds for dismissal under Section 707(a)(3). See In re Moses, 792 F. Supp. 529 (ED MI, 1992). Failure to attend the meeting of creditors has been deemed to be cause for dismissal under Section 707(a). See In re Sochia, 231 B.R. 158 (WD NY, 1999). Dismissal for failing to file required information may only be sought by the United States trustee. In re Young, 92 B.R. 782 (ND IL, 1988). §707(a), listed causes for dismissal

§707(a), nonlisted causes for dismissal

Note that the three causes of dismissal listed in Section 707(a) are illustrative and not exclusive, and that causes of dismissal other than those listed in the statute may be raised under Section 707(a). See United States v. Pedigo, 329 B.R. 47 (SD IN, 2005); In re Éclair Bakery, Ltd., 255 B.R. 645 (SD NY, 2000); In re Creazzo, 172 B.R. 657 (MD FL, 1994). Several other causes of dismissal, including dismissals for bad faith by the debtor, are discussed below in this article.

dismissals under §707(a), general aspects

A Chapter 7 case may be dismissed for cause under Section 707(a) at the request of either the debtor or another party in interest. In other words, a dismissal under Section 707(a) may be voluntary or involuntary. A creditor, the trustee, or the United States trustee may seek the involuntary dismissal of a Chapter 7 case under Section 707(a). As noted above, however, only the United States trustee may seek dismissal on the grounds of the failure of the debtor to timely file the required schedules and statements. Voluntary and involuntary dismissals are discussed separately below. The ultimate decision whether to grant dismissal lies within the discretion of the bankruptcy court. See In re Hopper, 404 B.R. 302 (ND IL, 2009).

dismissals under §707(a), procedure

A request for dismissal under Section 707(a), whether voluntary or involuntary, is a contested matter governed by Bankruptcy Rules 1017(d) and 9014. Section 707(a) dismissals are contested matters under Bankruptcy Rule 9014 and may be initiated by the filing of a motion. The motion must satisfy the requirements of Bankruptcy Rule 9013. At least 21 days notice of the hearing on the motion must be served on the trustee and all creditors. See Bankruptcy Rules 1017(a) and 2002(a).

§522(h), proceedings under, procedure

Voluntary dismissal. A voluntary dismissal is a dismissal at the request of the debtor. While it is clear that a debtor has the right to seek the dismissal of his or her Chapter 7 case under Section 707(a), it is equally clear that such a dismissal may be ordered by the court only upon a showing of cause by the debtor. A debtor has no absolute right to dismiss his Chapter 7 case. See In re Acosta-Rivera, 557 F.3d 8 (PR, 2009). Unlike a Chapter 13 debtor, a Chapter 7 debtor is not entitled to a dismissal of the bankruptcy case as a matter of right. See In re Watkins, 229 B.R. 907 (ND IL, 1999) and In re Schwartz, 178 B.R. 340 (ED NY, 1995). A Chapter 7 case may be dismissed by the court at the request of the debtor only upon a showing of cause. See In re Maixner, 288 B.R. 815 (B.A.P. 8th Cir., 2003); In re Hopkins, 261 B.R. 822 (ED PA, 2001).

cause for voluntary dismissal, general rule

Generally, a Chapter 7 case may be dismissed by the court at the request of the debtor only if it is shown that the benefit to be gained by the debtor from the dismissal (or the detriment that will be incurred by the debtor if the case is not dismissed) outweighs the prejudicial effect of the dismissal, if any, on the creditors and other parties in interest. See In re Cohara, 324 B.R. 24 (B.A.P. 6th Cir., 2005); In re Bartee, 317 B.R. 362 (B.A.P. 9th Cir., 2004); In re Eichelberger, 225 B.R. 437 (ED MO, 1998); Turpen v. Eide, 244 B.R. 431 (B.A.P. 8th Cir., 2000); In re Anderson, 79 B.R. 482 (SD CA, 1987). The debtor, as the moving party, has the burden of proof on these issues in a voluntary dismissal proceeding under Section 707(a).

When determining if cause for voluntary dismissal is warranted, courts consider several factors. Among the factors considered are: (1) whether dismissal is in the best interest of the debtor; (2) whether dismissal is in the best interest of the creditors; (3) whether dismissal would result in a manipulation of the bankruptcy system; (4) whether all, or a significant portion of creditors have consented; (5) whether dismissal will result in a prejudicial delay in payment to creditors; (6) whether payment of claims can be handled through other proceedings; (7) whether an objection to discharge, an objection to exemptions, or a preference claim is pending; and (8) whether dismissal is justified by any case-by-case compelling equitable principles. See, e.g., In Re Hopper, 404 B.R. 302 (ND IL, 2009); In re Jaborin, 395 B.R. 330 (Bankr. E.D. Penn. 2008) (adopting balancing test).

considerations for "cause" to voluntarily dismiss

In order to establish cause for the voluntary dismissal of a Chapter 7 case, the debtor must give a reason for the dismissal. The debtor's reason for seeking dismissal may have a significant effect on the extent and type of cause that must be established by the debtor to obtain the dismissal. For example, cause for a dismissal sought because the debtor has had a genuine change of heart or fortune and has decided to attempt to repay his or her creditors is much easier to establish than cause for a dismissal sought because of the discovery of undisclosed assets or because the debtor wishes to refile the case in order to discharge postpetition debts.

reason for voluntary dismissal, effect of on cause

Whatever the reason for seeking voluntary dismissal, to obtain dismissal a Chapter 7 debtor must show that the benefit to be obtained by the debtor from the dismissal outweighs the detriments, if any, that will be suffered by creditors and other parties in interest by reason of the dismissal. In In re Schwartz, 58 B.R. 923 (SD NY, 1986), the court held that in determining whether cause exists for the voluntary dismissal of a Chapter 7 case, the test is whether dismissal is in the best interests of the debtor and the creditors. The court stated that as to the best interest of creditors, the issue is one of prejudice and if they claim to be prejudiced by delay the issue is whether the delay will be unreasonable. In In re Stairs, 307 B.R. 698 (CO, 2004), the debtor's motion to dismiss was denied under Section 707(a) because the debtor's creditors had been stayed from collection efforts for 15 months, which caused prejudice to the creditors. In In re MacDonald, 73 B.R. 254 (ND OH, 1987), the court refused to grant the debtor a voluntary dismissal of his Chapter 7 case because dismissal would be prejudicial to creditors who must then pursue their claims in state court after the delay resulting from the automatic stay. However, in In re McDaniel, 350 B.R. 616 (MD FL, 2006), the debtor was allowed to dismiss against the objection of a tax creditor because she was given incorrect legal advice concerning the "look-back" period pertaining to non-dischargeable tax debts.

cause for voluntary dismissal, test for establishing

A common reason for seeking the voluntary dismissal of a Chapter 7 case is that for whatever reason the debtor has more nonexempt assets than were contemplated when the case was filed. Unanticipated assets may exist either because a claimed exemption was not allowed or because the debtor had assets that were either unknown to the debtor when the case was filed or were not disclosed by the debtor in the bankruptcy schedules. In cases of this type the burden on the debtor in obtaining dismissal is substantial. See In re Fulton, 339 B.R. 698 (ND IA, 2006.)

voluntary dismissal, reasons for requesting

voluntary dismissal, unexpected assets, cases

In In re Cohara, 324 B.R. 24 (B.A.P. 6th Cir., 2005), a debtor received payments from an annuity for injuries incurred in an auto accident and attempted to dismiss her case under Section 707(a). The court refused to dismiss, stating that the debtor presented no evidence that creditors would not be prejudiced and failed to support her claim of needing the annuity payments to pay medical expenses with appropriate medical evidence. In In re Mauk, 56 B.R. 445 (ND OH, 1985), the debtors filed a motion to dismiss their Chapter 7 case because of the existence of an unexpected equity in their property. In refusing to dismiss the case, the court ruled that creditors should not be forced to resort to nonbankruptcy collection proceeding to collect their claims and that the debtors could more easily dispose of the property without paying creditors if the bankruptcy case was dismissed. For similar rulings, see In re Maixner, 288 B.R. 815 (B.A.P. 8th Cir., 2003). In In re Higbee, 58 B.R. 71 (CD IL, 1986), the debtor sought the dismissal of her Chapter 7 case on the grounds that her pending personal injury claim may be worth $200,000 rather than the $2,000 she anticipated when the bankruptcy case was filed. In refusing to dismiss the case, the court ruled that a dismissal could easily cause the creditors to lose the only asset available to them. The court stated that even though the entire proceeds of her claim might ultimately be paid to creditors in the bankruptcy case, the debtor must accept the unfortunate consequences of her voluntary election to file under Chapter 7. See also In re Klein, 39 B.R. 530 (ED NY, 1984).

voluntary dismissal, general rules

In In re Rodriguez, 57 B.R. 465 (SD FL, 1985), the debtors moved for the dismissal of their Chapter 7 case because a claimed exemption was not allowed by the court. The court held that the case should not be dismissed because the debtors provided no tangible assurance that creditors would be paid if the case was dismissed. Of course, if it is clearly established that creditors will be paid in full outside of bankruptcy, a voluntary dismissal will usually be granted. See In re Cleland, 150 B.R. 63 (KS, 1992). If the advantages of dismissal outweigh the disadvantages, the case may be dismissed upon the request of the debtor, even if the debtor failed to disclose an important asset. See In re Schwartz, 58 B.R. 923 (SD NY, 1986).

voluntary dismissal, postpetition debts, cases

Another common reason for seeking the voluntary dismissal of a Chapter 7 case is the incurrence by the debtor of substantial postpetition debts which the debtor wishes to discharge by dismissing the existing case and refiling under Chapter 7 so as to include the postpetition debts. Here, too, the burden on the debtor in establishing cause for the dismissal is substantial. In In re Branisel, 130 B.R. 502 (ND OH, 1991), the debtor sought the dismissal of her Chapter 7 case so that she could file another Chapter 7 case and include debts for medical expenses incurred after the filing of the present case. The court refused to dismiss the case because allowing dismissal of the case would circumvent 11 U.S.C. § 727(a)(8), which precludes the granting of a discharge if the debtor has been granted a discharge within the previous 8 years. In In re McCullough, 229 B.R. 374 (ED VA, 1999), the court held that the desire of the debtor, whose minor son was involved in a postpetition automobile accident, to dismiss the case in order to refile another Chapter 7 case listing potential tort claimants from the accident as creditors did not rise to the level of cause for dismissal.

In In re Compston, 161 B.R. 636 (ND OH, 1993), the debtors moved for the dismissal of their Chapter 7 case so that they could file another Chapter 7 case and include debts that had resulted from a postpetition automobile accident. The court refused to dismiss the case because (1) dismissal for the sole purpose of filing a new petition would circumvent 11 U.S.C. § 727(a)(8), (2) postpetition creditors had not been notified of the motion to dismiss as required by Bankruptcy Rule 1017(a), (3) it had not been established that a dismissal would not prejudice the rights of postpetition creditors; and (4) the debtors are not without recourse if dismissal is denied because they are not precluded from discharging the postpetition debts in a Chapter 13 case.

voluntary dismissal, postpetition debts, reasons for denial

In In re Sheets, 174 B.R. 254 (ND OH, 1994), the court denied the debtors' motion to dismiss their no-asset Chapter 7 case for the purpose of refiling the case so as to discharge postpetition debts because (1) there had been no showing of "cause" in that the debtors will always be incurring new debts, (2) such a dismissal would circumvent the 6 (now 8) year requirement in 11 U.S.C. § 727(a)(8), and (3) the debtors have the alternate recourse of filing under Chapter 13. See also In re Haney, 241 B.R. 430 (ED AR, 1999). In In re Astin, 77 B.R. 537 (WD VA, 1987), the debtor sought the dismissal of his Chapter 7 case for the purpose of enabling the debtor to perfect his homestead exemption and refile the case. The court ruled that in the absence of the consent of all creditors the debtor was not entitled to the dismissal of his case because the rights of creditors would clearly be prejudiced by such a dismissal. See also In re Hague, 256 B.R. 352 (MA, 2000) (refusing to find cause for voluntary dismissal when the debtors' attorney stated that debtors would undoubtedly refile to take advantage of a recently-increased homestead exemption).

voluntary dismissal, postpetition debts, cases

Involuntary dismissal. An involuntary dismissal is a dismissal at the request of a party other than the debtor. Cause for involuntary dismissal under Section 707(a) includes (1) unreasonable delay that is prejudicial to creditors, (2) nonpayment of the filing fee, and (3) upon the motion of the United States trustee only, the failure of the debtor in a voluntary case to file the required statements and schedules within 14 days after the filing of the petition or within such other period as may be allowed by the court. See 11 U.S.C. § 707(a).

involuntary dismissals, causes for

It is clear, however, that cause for involuntary dismissal under Section 707(a) is not limited to these three causes. See, e.g., In re Dinova, 212 B.R. 437 (B.A.P. 2d Cir. 1997) (notice and hearing required prior to dismissal); In re Éclair Bakery, 255 B.R. 121 (SD NY, 2000); In re Brown, 88 B.R. 280 (HI, 1988); In re Creazzo, 172 B.R. 657 (MD FL, 1994). Causes for dismissal under Section 707(a) include lack of good faith by the debtor in the filing or conduct of the case, a failure by the debtor to obey an order of the court, the filing of a second Chapter 7 case during the pendency of an existing Chapter 7 case (the second case was dismissed). See respectively, In re Bingham, 68 B.R. 933 (MD PA, 1987); In re Ladd, 82 B.R. 476 (ND IN, 1988); In re Weeks, 134 B.R. 972 (MD FL, 1991).

involuntary dismissal, causes not listed in §707(a)

Perhaps the most common cause for dismissal under Section 707(a) (other than nonpayment of the filing fee) is lack of good faith (or the presence of bad faith) by the debtor. It is clear that lack of good faith by the debtor constitutes cause for dismissal under Section 707(a). See In re Blumenberg, 263 B.R. 704 (ED NY, 2001); In re Zick, 931 F.2d 1124 (6th Cir., 1991); In re Khan, 172 B.R. 613 (MN, 1994) (defining good faith as whether the debtor is in bankruptcy with the intent to receive the type of relief that Congress made available under Chapter 7 and is willing to responsibly carry out the duties that Congress imposed on debtors as the cost of receiving such relief). In Zick, the court stated that bad faith is shown by a pervasive and orchestrated effort by the debtor to obtain the benefits of bankruptcy while intentionally and fraudulently taking action to avoid the duties and detriments of bankruptcy. In In re Bingham, 68 B.R. 933 (MD PA, 1987), the court held that good faith is an implicit jurisdictional requirement of a Chapter 7 case and that once the debtor's good faith has been put into question, the debtor has the burden of proving that the petition was filed in good faith. The bankruptcy court must look at the totality of circumstances surrounding both the objective and subjective considerations in each case to determine whether "cause" exists to dismiss a case. See In re Am. Telecom Corp., 304 B.R. 867 (ND IL, 2004).

involuntary dismissal, bad faith, what constitutes

In a Chapter 7 trustee's motion to dismiss, the court found that errors in the debtor's schedules and an increased amount of certain claimed expenses were sufficient to undermine the debtors' good faith and shift the burden to her to produce affirmative proof of her good faith intention in filing her petition. See In re Mottilla, 306 B.R. 782 (MD PA, 2004). In Tamecki v. Frank, 229 F.3d 205 (3d Cir., 2000), the court held, in affirming the dismissal of the debtor's case, that the debtor failed to meet his burden of proving good faith, which had shifted to him once the trustee called his good faith into question by challenging his accumulation of large credit card debts just prior to filing. Likewise, in Huckfeldt v. Huckfeldt, 39 F.3d 829 (8th Cir., 1994), the court held that the debtor's Chapter 7 case was properly dismissed on the grounds of bad faith where it was established that the debtor had filed the case for the obvious purpose of forcing his ex-wife into bankruptcy. Using the bankruptcy system as a litigation tactic constitutes bad faith and will merit dismissal. See In re Am. Telecom Corp., 304 B.R. 867 (ND IL, 2004).

involuntary dismissal, bad faith, cases

In In re Zick, 931 F.2d 1124 (6th Cir., 1991), the debtor's Chapter 7 case was properly dismissed for cause under Section 707(a) where it was established that the debtor's petition was filed in bad faith as evidenced by the debtor's manipulations which reduced the number of creditors to one, namely his former employer who had obtained a mediation award against the debtor for breach of a covenant not to compete, and the debtor's failure to make any efforts to pay this debt while paying all other debts and continuing his extravagant lifestyle. The court held that the debtor's petition was clearly filed in response to the mediation award and not for the intended purposes of Chapter 7.

involuntary dismissal, bad faith, case

In In re Brown, 88 B.R. 280 (HI, 1988), a debtor's Chapter 7 petition had not been filed in good faith and was therefore dismissed for cause under Section 707(a) where it was shown that the sole creditor of the ophthalmologist debtor was a former patient with a $400,000 medical malpractice judgment against the debtor, that the debtor had made no effort to pay any portion of the judgment and had not changed his luxurious lifestyle, and that the debtor had transferred the profits of his lucrative medical practice to himself and his wife as tenants by the entirety under the guise of rent.

involuntary dismissal, bad faith, case

However, in In re Josey, 169 B.R. 138 (SD OH, 1994), the court refused to dismiss a Chapter 7 case for cause under Section 707(a) holding that the fact that the debtors were nonneedy, without more, does not constitute sufficient bad faith to require dismissal. The court held that bad conduct by the debtors must be shown to establish bad faith. See also In re Etcheverry, 221 B.R. 524 (CO, 1998).

involuntary dismissal, bad faith, case

In Buck v. Buck, 166 B.R. 106 (MD TN, 1993), the court also refused to dismiss a Chapter 7 case for cause under Section 707(a) where just prior to filing the debtor learned that his wages were about to be garnished in the amount of $42,000 as the result of a state court judgment. In that case there was no evidence of a lavish lifestyle by the debtor and the debtor was experiencing cash flow problems and was unable to pay the $42,000 judgment. The court held that there was no evidence of fraud or misconduct by the debtor and that the debtor was legitimately in need of bankruptcy protection. See Deglin v. Keobapha, 279 B.R. 49 (CT, 2002).

involuntary dismissal, bad faith, case

Several courts have held that a Chapter 7 debtor's ability to repay all or a substantial portion of his or her debts out of current or projected income does not of itself constitute bad faith or cause for dismissal under Section 707(a). See In re Hopkins, 261 B.R. 822 (ED PA, 2001); In re Marks, 174 B.R. 37 (ED PA, 1994); In re Khan, 172 B.R. 613 (MN, 1994); In re Young, 92 B.R. 782 (ND IL, 1988); Perniciaro v. Natale, 136 B.R. 344 (ED NY, 1992); In re Frisch, 76 B.R. 801 (CO, 1987); In re Bridges, 135 B.R. 36 (ED KY, 1991). To rule otherwise would render Section 707(b) unnecessary and meaningless. See In re Cecil, 71 B.R. 730 (WD VA, 1987). Several courts, however, have dismissed the Chapter 7 cases of debtors who maintain lavish life styles on the grounds of bad faith. See In re Griffieth, 209 B.R. 823 (ND NY, 1996); In re Lacrosse, 244 B.R. 583 (MD PA, 1999); In re Emge, 226 B.R. 396 (WD KY, 1998); Walton v. Smith, 229 B.R. 895 (SD GA, 1997); In re Stallman, 198 B.R. 491 (WD MI, 1996).

involuntary dismissal under §707(a), debtor's ability to pay debts as cause

involuntary dismissal, grounds not constituting cause

In In re Latimer, 82 B.R. 354 (ED PA, 1988), the court held that postpetition payments by the debtor to creditors, whether selectively or otherwise, does not constitute cause for dismissal under Section 707(a) because such payments are authorized by 11 U.S.C. § 524(f). The court also held that the debtors' alleged manipulation of their property for the purpose of maximizing their exemptions (i.e., exemption planning) does not constitute cause for dismissal under Section 707(a). The court in that case also held that the fact that the debtors planned to file a Chapter 13 case subsequent to their Chapter 7 also did not constitute cause for dismissal of the Chapter 7 case. The fact that the debtors timed the filing of their Chapter 7 case so as to take advantage of 11 U.S.C. § 541(a)(5)(A) (property properly in estate if acquired by bequest, devise or inheritance within 180 days after the date of filing) and 11 U.S.C. § 541(c)(2) (restricted beneficial interests in trust not includible in estate) was held not to constitute cause for dismissal under Section 707(a) in In re Kragness, 63 B.R. 459 (OR, 1986).

involuntary dismissal, grounds not constituting cause

In In re Fekos, 148 B.R. 10 (WD PA, 1992), a Chapter 7 debtor's refusal to answer questions at a Bankruptcy Rule 2004 examination wherein the debtor claimed his Fifth Amendment privilege against self incrimination did not constitute cause for dismissal under Section 707(a). In In re Causey, 211 B.R. 336 (WD AR, 1997) and In re Rodriguez, 255 B.R. 118 (SD NY, 2000), the debtor's failure to attend the meeting of creditors was not cause for dismissal of the case under Section 707(a). In In re Churchill, 178 B.R. 478 (NE, 1995) the concealment of assets by the debtor did not constitute cause for dismissal under Section 707(a) even though such misconduct may result in the denial of the debtor's discharge. In In re Abrahams, 163 B.R. 606 (SD FL, 1993), the death of the Chapter 7 debtor did not constitute cause for dismissal of the case under Section 707(a).

involuntary dismissal, grounds constituting cause

On the other hand, in In re Harris, 226 B.R. 924 (SD FL, 1998), the failure of the debtor to perform matters listed in her statement of intention, or to perform alternatives thereto, was cause for dismissal under Section 707(a) for unreasonable delay that was prejudicial to creditors. In In re Moses, 227 B.R. 98 (ED MI, 1998), the debtor's case was dismissed for cause under Section 707(a) because of the debtor's failure to provide the trustee with sufficient information with which to administer the estate.

§707(a), sanctions

If a debtor's case is dismissed under Section 707(a) for conduct the court deems to cause a showing of bad faith, the debtor may also be sanctioned. In In re Am. Telecom Corp., 304 B.R. 867 (ND IL, 2004), the court awarded attorneys fees against the debtor under Fed. R. Bakr. P. 9011 as a sanction for its bad faith petitio.

Bibliography. For further reading on the issues discussed in this article, see the annotations and articles listed below.

Annotations: None available.

Articles:

The implied requirement of "good faith" filing: where are the limits of bad faith? 1993 Det. C.L. Rev. 1591, Winter 1993.

Bad faith dismissals in bankruptcy cases. 39 Pract. Lawyer 75, April 1993.

Debtor trap: The ironies of Section 707(a). Comment. 7 Bankruptcy Dev. J. 175, 1990.

2.02 Under what circumstances may a Chapter 7 case be dismissed for "abuse" under Section 707(b) of the Bankruptcy Code?

Text of statute. Section 707(b) of the Bankruptcy Code (11 U.S.C. § 707(b)) provides as follows:

707. Dismissal of a case or conversion to a case under chapter 11 or 13

* * * * * *

§707(b), text of

(b)(1) After notice and a hearing, the court, on its own motion or on a motion by the United States trustee, trustee (or bankruptcy administrator, if any), or any party in interest, may dismiss a case filed by an individual debtor under this chapter whose debts are primarily consumer debts, or, with the debtor's consent, convert such a case to a case under chapter 11 or 13 of this title, if it finds that the granting of relief would be an abuse of the provisions of this chapter. In making a determination whether to dismiss a case under this section, the court may not take into consideration whether a debtor has made, or continues to make, charitable contributions (that meet the definition of "charitable contribution" under section 548(d)(3)) to any qualified religious or charitable entity or organization (as that term is defined in section 548(d)(4)).

(2)(A)(i) In considering under paragraph (1) whether the granting of relief would be an abuse of the provisions of this chapter, the court shall presume abuse exists if the debtor's current monthly income reduced by the amounts determined under clauses (ii), (iii), and (iv), and multiplied by 60 is not less than the lesser of –

(I) 25 percent of the debtor's nonpriority unsecured claims in the case, or $7,025, whichever is greater; or

(II) $11,725.

(ii)(I) The debtor's monthly expenses shall be the debtor's applicable monthly expense amounts specified under the National Standards and Local Standards, and the debtor's actual monthly expenses for the categories specified as Other Necessary Expenses issued by the Internal Revenue Service for the area in which the debtor resides, as in effect on the date of the order for relief, for the debtor, the dependents of the debtor, and the spouse of the debtor in a joint case, if the spouse is not otherwise a dependent. Such expenses shall include reasonably necessary health insurance, disability insurance, and health savings account expenses for the debtor, the spouse of the debtor, or the dependents of the debtor. Notwithstanding any other provision of this clause, the monthly expenses of the debtor shall not include any payments for debts. In addition, the debtor's monthly expenses shall include the debtor's reasonably necessary expenses incurred to maintain the safety of the debtor and the family of the debtor from family violence as identified under section 302 of the Family Violence Prevention and Services Act, or other applicable Federal law. The expenses included in the debtor's monthly expenses described in the preceding sentence shall be kept confidential by the court. In addition, if it is demonstrated that it is reasonable and necessary, the debtor's monthly expenses may also include an additional allowance for food and clothing of up to 5 percent of the food and clothing categories as specified by the National Standards issued by the Internal Revenue Service.

(II) In addition, the debtor's monthly expenses may include, if applicable, the continuation of actual expenses paid by the debtor that are reasonable and necessary for care and support of an elderly, chronically ill, or disabled household member or member of the debtor's immediate family (including parents, grandparents, siblings, children, and grandchildren of the debtor, the dependents of the debtor, and the spouse of the debtor in a joint case who is not a dependent) and who is unable to pay for such reasonable and necessary expenses.

(III) In addition, for a debtor eligible for chapter 13, the debtor's monthly expenses may include the actual administrative expenses of administering a chapter 13 plan for the district in which the debtor resides, up to an amount of 10 percent of the projected plan payments, as determined under schedules issued by the Executive Office for United States Trustees.

(IV) In addition, the debtor's monthly expenses may include the actual expenses for each dependent child less than 18 years of age, not to exceed $1,775 per year per child, to attend a private or public elementary or secondary school if the debtor provides documentation of such expenses and a detailed explanation of why such expenses are reasonable and necessary, and why such expenses are not already accounted for in the National Standards, Local Standards, or Other Necessary Expenses referred to in subclause (I). §707(b), text of

(V) In addition, the debtor's monthly expenses may include an allowance for housing and utilities, in excess of the allowance specified by the Local Standards for housing and utilities issued by the Internal Revenue Service, based on the actual expenses for home energy costs if the debtor provides documentation of such actual expenses and demonstrates that such actual expenses are reasonable and necessary.

(iii) The debtor's average monthly payments on account of secured debts shall be calculated as the sum of –

(I) the total of all amounts scheduled as contractually due to secured creditors in each month of the 60 months following the date of the filing of the petition; and

(II) any additional payments to secured creditors necessary for the debtor, in filing a plan under chapter 13 of this title, to maintain possession of the debtor's primary residence, motor vehicle, or other property necessary for the support of the debtor and the debtor's dependents, that serves as collateral for secured debts;

divided by 60.

(iv) The debtor's expenses for payment of all priority claims (including priority child support and alimony claims) shall be calculated as the total amount of debts entitled to priority, divided by 60.

(B)(i) In any proceeding brought under this subsection, the presumption of abuse may only be rebutted by demonstrating special circumstances, such as a serious medical condition or a call or order to active duty in the Armed Forces, to the extent such special circumstances that justify additional expenses or adjustments of current monthly income for which there is no reasonable alternative.

(ii) In order to establish special circumstances, the debtor shall be required to itemize each additional expense or adjustment of income and to provide –

(I) documentation for such expense or adjustment to income; and

(II) a detailed explanation of the special circumstances that make such expenses or adjustment to income necessary and reasonable.

(iii) The debtor shall attest under oath to the accuracy of any information provided to demonstrate that additional expenses or adjustments to income are required.

(iv) The presumption of abuse may only be rebutted if the additional expenses or adjustments to income referred to in clause (i) cause the product of the debtor's current monthly income reduced by the amounts determined under clauses (ii), (iii), and (iv) of subparagraph (A) when multiplied by 60 to be less than the lesser of –

(I) 25 percent of the debtor's nonpriority unsecured claims, or $7,025, whichever is greater; or

(II) $11,725.

(C) As part of the schedule of current income and expenditures required under section 521, the debtor shall include a statement of the debtor's current monthly income, and the calculations that determine whether a presumption arises under subparagraph (A)(i), that show how each such amount is calculated.

(D) Subparagraphs (A) through (C) shall not apply, and the court may not dismiss or convert a case based on any form of means testing –

(i) if the debtor is a disabled veteran (as defined in section 3741(1) of title 38), and the indebtedness occurred primarily during a period during which he or she was -

(I) on active duty (as defined in section 101(d)(1) of title 10); or

(II) performing a homeland defense activity (as defined in section 901(1) of title 32); or

(ii) with respect to the debtor, while the debtor is –

(I) on, and during the 540-day period beginning immediately after the debtor is released from, a period of active duty (as defined in section 101(d)(1) of title 10) of not less than 90 days; or

(II) performing, and during the 540-day period beginning immediately after the debtor is no longer performing, a homeland defense activity (as defined in section 901(1) of title 32) performed for a period of not less than 90 days:

if after September 11, 2001, the debtor while a member of a reserve component of the Armed Forces or a member of the National Guard, was called to such active duty or performed such homeland defense activity.

(3) In considering under paragraph (1) whether the granting of relief would be an abuse of the provisions of this chapter in a case in which the presumption in paragraph (2)(A)(i) does not arise or is rebutted, the court shall consider –

(A) whether the debtor filed the petition in bad faith; or

(B) the totality of the circumstances (including whether the debtor seeks to reject a personal services contract and the financial need for such rejection as sought by the debtor) of the debtor's financial situation demonstrates abuse.

(4)(A) The court, on its own initiative or on the motion of a party in interest, in accordance with the procedures described in rule 9011 of the Federal Rules of Bankruptcy Procedure, may order the attorney for the debtor to reimburse the trustee for all reasonable costs in prosecuting a motion filed under section 707(b),
§707(b), text of including reasonable attorneys' fees, if –

(i) a trustee files a motion for dismissal or conversion under this subsection; and

(ii) the court –

(I) grants such motion; and

(II) finds that the action of the attorney for the debtor in filing a case under this chapter violated rule 9011 of the Federal Rules of Bankruptcy Procedure.

(B) If the court finds that the attorney for the debtor violated rule 9011 of the Federal Rules of Bankruptcy Procedure, the court, on its own initiative or on the motion of a party in interest, in accordance with such procedures, may order –

(i) the assessment of an appropriate civil penalty against the attorney for the debtor; and

(ii) the payment of such civil penalty to the trustee, the United States trustee (or the bankruptcy administrator, if any).

(C) the signature of an attorney on a petition, pleading, or written motion shall constitute a certification that the attorney has –

(i) performed a reasonable investigation into the circumstances that gave rise to the petition, pleading, or written motion; and

(ii) determined that the petition, pleading, or written motion –

(I) is well grounded in fact; and

(II) is warranted by existing law or a good faith argument for the extension, modification, or reversal of existing law and does not constitute an abuse under paragraph (1).

(D) The signature of an attorney on the petition shall constitute a certification that the attorney has no knowledge after an inquiry that the information in the schedules filed with such petition is incorrect.

(5)(A) Except as provided in subparagraph (B) and subject to paragraph (6), the court, on its own initiative or on the motion of a party in interest, in accordance with the procedures described in rule 9011 of the Federal Rules of Bankruptcy Procedure, may award a debtor all reasonable costs (including reasonable attorneys' fees) in contesting a motion filed by a party in interest (other than a trustee or a United States trustee (or bankruptcy administrator, if any)) under this subsection if –

(i) the court does not grant the motion; and

(ii) the court finds that –

(I) the position of the party that filed the motion violated rule 9011 of the Federal Rules of Bankruptcy Procedure; or

(II) the attorney (if any) who filed the motion did not comply with the requirements of clauses (i) and (ii) of paragraph (4)(C), and the motion was made solely for the purpose of coercing a debtor into waiving a right guaranteed to the debtor under this title.

(B) A small business that has a claim of an aggregate amount less than $1,175 shall not be subject to subparagraph (A)(ii)(I).

(C) For purposes of this paragraph –

(i) the term "small business" means an unincorporated business, partnership, corporation, association, or organization that –

(I) has fewer than 25 full-time employees as determined on the date on which the motion is filed; and

(II) is engaged in commercial or business activity; and

(ii) the number of employees of a wholly owned subsidiary of a corporation includes the employees of –

(I) a parent corporation; and

(II) any other subsidiary corporation of the parent corporation.

(6) Only the judge or United States trustee (or bankruptcy administrator, if any) may file a motion under section 707(b), if the current monthly income of the debtor, or in a joint case, the debtor and the debtor's spouse, as of the date of the order for relief, when multiplied by 12, is equal to or less than –

(A) in the case of a debtor in a household of 1 person, the median family income of the applicable State for 1 earner;

§707(b), text of

(B) in the case of a debtor in a household of 2, 3, or 4 individuals, the highest median family income of the applicable State for a family of the same number or fewer individuals; or

(C) in the case of a debtor in a household exceeding 4 individuals, the highest median family income of the applicable State for a family of 4 or fewer individuals, plus $625 per month for each individual in excess of 4.

(7)(A) No judge, United States trustee (or bankruptcy administrator, if any), trustee, or other party in interest may file a motion under paragraph (2) if the current monthly income of the debtor, including a veteran (as that term is defined in section 101 of title 38), and the debtor's spouse combined, as of the date of the order for relief when multiplied by 12, is equal to or less than –

(i) in the case of a debtor in a household of 1 person, the median family income of the applicable State for 1 earner;

(ii) in the case of a debtor in a household of 2, 3, or 4 individuals, the highest median family income of the applicable State for a family of the same number or fewer individuals; or

(iii) in the case of a debtor in a household exceeding 4 individuals, the highest median family income of the applicable State for a family of 4 or fewer individuals, plus $625 per month for each individual in excess of 4.

(B) In a case that is not a joint case, current monthly income of the debtor's spouse shall not be considered for purposes of subparagraph (A) if –

(i)(I) the debtor and the debtor's spouse are separated under applicable nonbankruptcy law; or

(II) the debtor and debtor's spouse are living separate and apart, other than for the purpose of evading subparagraph (A); and

(ii) the debtor files a statement under penalty of perjury –

(I) specifying that the debtor meets the requirement of subclause (I) or (II) of clause (i); and

(II) disclosing the aggregate, or best estimate of the aggregate, amount of any cash or money payments received from the debtor's spouse attributed to the debtor's current monthly income.

Introduction. Section 707(b) was added to the Bankruptcy Code in 1984 at the request of the consumer credit lobby which claimed that many debtors were abusing Chapter 7 by discharging debts that they could legitimately repay if forced to do so. Originally a dismissal under Section 707(b) could only be initiated upon the motion of the court. In 1986 Section 707(b) was amended to provide that a motion to dismiss on the grounds of substantial abuse of Chapter 7 may be initiated by either the United States trustee or the court. In 1998 the last sentence in Section 707(b) was added precluding the court from considering charitable or religious contributions made by the debtor as disposable income for purposes of dismissals under Section 707(b). In 2005, section 707(b) was amended to a degree not seen since it was enacted in 1984. Section 707(b) was amended by the BAPCPA to permit the case trustee, the U.S. trustee, the bankruptcy administrator, and any party in interest (subject to some standing issues discussed below) to move for dismissal of an individual's Chapter 7 case if abuse is found under the means test established by the BAPCPA. The BAPCPA changed the former standard of "substantial abuse" to "an abuse," thus lowering the bar for finding reason to dismiss or convert to a Chapter 13 case. In any event, this amendment is best understood as a codification of pre-BAPCA caselaw. In re Ng, 477 B.R. 118 (B.A.P. 9th Cir. 2012).

§707(b), legislative history

charitable contributions by debtor, consideration of by court

In most districts all Chapter 7 cases are examined by the case trustee or the United States trustee shortly after filing for the possibility of abuse. Of particular interest to the United States trustee (and the court) are the figures appearing in Official Form B22A (Statement of Current Monthly Income and Means Test Calculation), Schedule I (Current Income of Individual Debtor) and Schedule J (Current Expenditures of Individual Debtor) filed by individual debtors. In addition, facts or circumstances discovered by the Chapter 7 trustee at the meeting of creditors indicating abuse may also be considered by the United States trustee in deciding whether to file a motion to dismiss for abuse under Section 707(b).

§707(b) motions to dismiss, information for, how obtained

The requirements for abuse dismissals after the BAPCPA. The procedural requirements for abuse dismissals under Section 707(b) are set forth in Bankruptcy Rule 1017(e), which provides as follows:

Rule 1017(e), text of

> (e) DISMISSAL OF INDIVIDUAL DEBTOR'S CHAPTER 7 CASE OR CONVERSION TO A CASE UNDER CHAPTER 11 OR 13 FOR ABUSE. The court may dismiss or, with the debtor's consent, convert an individual debtor's case for abuse under §707(b) only on motion and after a hearing on notice to the debtor, the trustee, the United States trustee, and any other entity as the court directs.
>
> (1) Except as otherwise provided in § 704(b)(2), a motion to dismiss a case for abuse under §707(b) or (c) may be filed only within 60 days after the first date set for the meeting of creditors under §341(a), unless, on request filed before the time has expired, the court for cause extends the time for filing the motion to dismiss. The party filing the motion shall set forth in the motion all matters to be considered at the hearing. In addition, a motion to dismiss under § 707(b)(1) and (3) shall state with particularity the circumstances alleged to constitute abuse.
>
> (2) If the hearing is set on the court's own motion, notice of the hearing shall be served on the debtor no later than 60 days after the first date set for the meeting of creditors under §341(a). The notice shall set forth all matters to be considered by the court at the hearing.

The debtor's attorney should be aware of the time restriction imposed on abuse dismissal proceedings by Bankruptcy Rule 1017(e), which is 60 days after the first date set for the meeting of creditors, unless before such time has expired the court for cause extends the time for the filing of such a motion. A motion filed after the expiration of the time period is presumptively invalid.

§707(b) motions, time limits for filing

Under the BAPCPA amendments to section 707(b), dismissal for abuse may be sought under either section 707(b)(1) or section 707(b)(2) of the Bankruptcy Code. If dismissal is sought under section 707(b)(1), the party seeking dismissal must affirmatively establish the presence of actual abuse by the debtor. If dismissal is sought under section 707(b)(2), the party seeking dismissal may rely on a presumption of abuse if such a presumption arises as a result of means testing, the particulars of which are described below.

dismissal for abuse, 707(b)(1) vs. 707(b)(2)

If dismissal is sought for actual abuse under section 707(b)(1), the court on its own initiative or, subject to the limitations on standing described in the next paragraph, on the motion of the U.S. trustee, the bankruptcy administrator (if one exists), the trustee serving in the case, or any party in interest (including a creditor), may dismiss the chapter 7 case of an individual debtor whose debts are primarily consumer debts if it finds that granting chapter 7 relief would be an abuse of the provisions of chapter 7. See 11 U.S.C. § 707(b)(1). It should be noted here that the degree of abuse required for dismissal under the amended section 707(b) does not have to be "substantial," as was required under prior law. See In re Masella, 373 B.R. 514 (ND OH, 2007).

dismissal for actual abuse

If dismissal is sought for presumptive abuse under section 707(b)(2), a means test is employed to determine whether a presumption of abuse arises. In addition, a means test is used to determine standing to seek dismissal under section 707(b). Taking the issue of standing first, if the current monthly income of the debtor multiplied by 12 is equal to or less than the median family income in the debtor's domicile state for a similar size family, only the court, the U.S. trustee, or the bankruptcy administrator (if one exists) has standing to seek dismissal for actual abuse under section 707(b)(1) and no one has standing to seek dismissal for presumptive abuse under section 707(b)(2). See 11 U.S.C. § 707(b)(6), (7)(A). In other words, if the debtor's current monthly income is less than the median family income described in the preceding sentence, the debtor is exempt from means testing and a presumption of abuse cannot arise because no one has standing to seek dismissal on that ground. Median family income is that calculated and reported by the U.S. Bureau of Census for the debtor's state and family size. See 11 U.S.C. § 101(39A).

dismissal for abuse, standing

Note that in computing a debtor's current monthly income for purposes of determining standing to seek dismissal for actual abuse under section 707(b)(1), the income of the debtor's spouse is counted only in a joint case. If the case is not a joint case, the income of the debtor's spouse is not counted. See 11 U.S.C. § 707(b)(6). The same rule is followed in determining current monthly income for presumptive abuse purposes under section 707(b)(2). See 11 U.S.C. § 101(10A). However, in determining standing to dismiss for presumptive abuse under section 707(b)(2), the income of the debtor's spouse is counted even if the case is not a joint case, unless the debtor and his or her spouse are separated or living apart and the debtor files a sworn statement to that effect. See 11 U.S.C. § 707(b)(7)(A), (B).

calculating correct monthly income, spousal income

If dismissal is sought for actual abuse under section 707(b)(1), (usually because a presumption of abuse either did not arise in the case or was successfully rebutted by the debtor), the court must consider whether the bankruptcy case was filed by the debtor in bad faith or whether under the totality of the debtor's financial circumstances abuse is demonstrated. In re Ng, 477 B.R. 118 (B.A.P. 9th Cir. 2012). In other words, if dismissal is sought for actual abuse under section 707(b)(1), dismissal may be granted by the court only if it is established either that the case was filed in bad faith or that the totality of the debtor's financial circumstances indicates the presence of abuse. (See 11 U.S.C. § 707(b)(3)(B)). A party seeking dismissal for actual abuse under section 707(b)(1) must affirmatively establish one of these grounds. Under the "totality of the circumstances" test for actual abuse under section 707(b)(3)(B) where the debtor's income is below the state median income, the debtor's actual and anticipated future income may be considered. See In re Pak, 343 B.R. 239 (ND CA, 2006).

dismissal for actual abuse, method of determining

means testing – presumption of abuse

In determining whether a presumption of abuse arises in a case, the basic rule is that a presumption of abuse arises if the debtor's current monthly disposable income (i.e., current monthly income less the permitted expenses described below) multiplied by 60 (the maximum length in months of a chapter 13 plan) is equal to or greater than the lesser of $10,950 or 25 percent of the debtor's nonpriority unsecured debts (the product of which is subject to a $6,575 minimum). In other words, under the minimum standard (i.e., a debtor with unsecured nonpriority debts of $26,300 or less), if the debtor's disposable monthly income is such that he or she is deemed to be able to pay $109.58 or more per month for 60 months to unsecured nonpriority creditors, then a presumption of abuse may arise in the case. Under the maximum standard (i.e., a debtor with unsecured nonpriority debts of $43,800 or more), if the debtor's monthly disposable income is such that he or she is deemed to be able to pay $182.50 or more per month for 60 months to unsecured nonpriority creditors, then a presumption of abuse will arise in the case. See 11 U.S.C. § 707(b)(2)(A)(i).

current monthly income, definition of

In computing a debtor's disposable monthly income for purposes of determining whether a presumption of abuse arises, the debtor's current monthly income must first be determined. A debtor's current monthly income is defined as the average monthly income from all sources that the debtor (or both debtors in a joint case) received during the 6-month period ending on the last day of the calendar month immediately preceding the filing of the bankruptcy case. For example, if the case was filed on May 10th, the 6-month period would end on April 30th. If the debtor fails to file a schedule of current income and expenditures, the 6-month period for determining his or her average income ends on the date on which the debtor's current monthly income is determined by the court. See 11 U.S.C. § 101(10A)(A). Both taxable and nontaxable income is counted. In In re Georgiu, 344 B.R. 47 (MD PA, 2006) the court stated that a debtor's monthly disability income of $9,000 is included as disposable income in a section 707(b) hearing. Also counted are any amounts paid by any entity other than debtor (or both debtors in a joint case) on a regular basis for the household expenses of the debtor(s) or their dependents. See In re Ellringer, 370 B.R. 905 (MN, 2007). However, social security benefits and payments to crime or terrorism victims are not counted. See 11 U.S.C. § 101(10A)(B). The court in In re Munger, 370 B.R. 21 (MA, 2007) ruled that unemployment compensation was a benefit received under the Social Security Act, and was therefore properly excluded from CMI calculation.

current monthly income, threshold amount

If the debtor's current monthly income multiplied by 60 is less than the lesser of $10,950 or 25 percent of the debtor's unsecured nonpriority debt (or $6,575 if the 25 percent figure is less than that amount), the debtor's monthly expenses need not be determined because in such a case a presumption of abuse cannot arise regardless of the amount of the expenses. See 11 U.S.C. § 707(b)(2)(A)(i). In other words, if the debtor's current monthly income does not meet the threshold amount described above, the debtor is not subject to means testing and a presumption of abuse cannot arise in the case.

If the debtor's current monthly income is such that he or she is subject to means testing to determine whether a presumption of abuse exists, the debtor's allowed monthly expenses (i.e., those expenses that may be deducted from the debtor's current monthly income) are as described in the following 11 paragraphs.

means testing – allowed monthly expenses

(1) The expenses currently established by the Internal Revenue Service for the area in which the debtor resides. These are national and local standard expenses for items such as housing, transportation, food, clothing, and other necessary expenses. These are standard expenses and are applicable regardless of what the debtor actually spends. However, these standard expenses cannot include debt payments, so if the debtor is making mortgage payments on a home or an automobile, these payments must be deducted from the IRS standard expenses. See 11 U.S.C. § 707(b)(2)(A)(ii)(I). See In re Guzman, 345 B.R. 640 (ED WI, 2006) (holding that section 707(b)(2) mandates the use of IRS guidelines for determining disposable income instead of schedules I and J); In re Barr, 341 B.R. 181 (MD NC, 2006). However, in In re Demonica, 245 B.R. 895 (ND IL, 2006), the court ruled that the "projected monthly income" on schedules I and J must be paid to a Chapter 13 plan, instead of the "disposable income" under the code formula. See In re Barraza, 346 B.R. 724 (ND TX, 2006) (holding that, as to a claim for ownership cost (as opposed to operating cost) of a vehicle, the IRS Collection Standards must be followed, and such standards do not permit an ownership expense where the car is paid for). However, see In re Scarafiotti, 375 B.R. 618 (CO, 2007), where the court allowed Chapter 7 debtors to claim vehicle ownership expense on 2 vehicles they owned free and clear, and allowed a modest increase in the local housing allowance because they had a son with special needs. The court in In re Lara, 347 B.R. 198 (ND TX, 2006) ruled that basic telephone service could not be deducted as an "other necessary expense" because it was already accounted for in "housing and utility". However, the cost of 2 cell phones, internet access and monthly life insurance premiums could be included in "other necessary expenses". In In re Delbecq, 368 B.R. 754 (SD IN, 2007) student loan payments did not constitute "other necessary expenses." But the court nonetheless found "special circumstances" existed and denied the trustee's motion to dismiss.

IRS standard expenses

(2) Reasonably necessary expenses incurred by the debtor for health insurance, disability insurance, and health savings accounts for the debtor and his or her spouse and dependents. See 11 U.S.C. § 707(b)(2)(A)(ii)(I).

health related expenses

(3) Reasonably necessary expenses incurred by the debtor to maintain the safety of the debtor and his or her family from family violence. See 11 U.S.C. § 707(b)(2)(A)(ii)(I).

expenses for family safety

additional allowance

(4) An additional food and clothing allowance of up to 5 percent of the amount specified in the IRS National Standards if the debtor establishes a necessity. See 11 U.S.C. § 707(b)(2)(A)(ii)(I).

payments incurred to care for another

(5) The continuation of actual expenses paid by the debtor that are reasonable and necessary for the care and support of an elderly, chronically ill, or disabled household member or member of the debtor's immediate family (including parents, grandparents, siblings, children and grandchildren of the debtor, the dependents of the debtor and the spouse of the debtor in a joint case who is not a dependent) who is unable to pay for such reasonable and necessary expenses. See 11 U.S.C. § 707(b)(2)(A)(ii)(II); In re Hicks, 370 B.R. 919 (ED MO, 2007) (disallowing a debtor's proposed deductions for payments to support her son under this section).

administrative expenses

(6) The actual administrative expenses of administering a chapter 13 plan (up to 10 percent of the total amount of projected plan payments), if the debtor is eligible for chapter 13. See 11 U.S.C. § 707(b)(2)(A)(ii)(III).

school expenses

(7) The actual expenses, not to exceed $1,650 per year per child, incurred by each dependent child of debtor to attend a private or public elementary or secondary school. See 11 U.S.C. § 707(b)(2)(A)(ii)(IV).

additional housing & utility expenses

(8) An additional allowance, beyond IRS standards, for housing and utilities, if reasonable and necessary and actually incurred and documented by the debtor. See 11 U.S.C. § 707(b)(2)(A)(ii)(V).

secured debt payments

(9) Secured debt payments equal to 1/60th of the total of all amounts scheduled as contractually due to the debtor's secured creditors during the 60 month period following the filing of the debtor's bankruptcy case, plus 1/60th of the total of any additional payments to secured creditors necessary under a chapter 13 plan, if filed by the debtor, to maintain possession of the debtor's primary residence, motor vehicle, or other property necessary for the support of the debtor and his or her dependents. See 11 U.S.C. § 707(b)(2)(A)(iii). In In re Sorrell, 359 B.R. 167 (SD OH, 2007) the court allowed Chapter 7 debtors to claim a secured debt expense on a vehicle they intended to surrender. In In re Mansella, 373 B.R. 514 (ND OH, 2007) a Chapter 7 debtor was allowed to deduct from CMI her mortgage payments on a residence she intended to surrender. In In re Thompson, 350 B.R. 770 (ND OH, 2006), the court ruled that payments made on a loan secured by the debtor's 401(k) are allowable deductions from current monthly income on Form 22A.

priority claims

(10) Priority claim payments equal to 1/60th of the sum of all priority claims (including priority claims for child support and alimony) owed by the debtor. See 11 U.S.C. § 707(b)(2)(A)(iv).

charitable expenses

(11) Continuing contributions made by the debtor to qualified religious or charitable entities. See 11 U.S.C. § 707(b)(1).

If, under the means test as described above, the debtor's disposable monthly income is such that a presumption of abuse exists, the presumption may be rebutted by the debtor only by showing that special circumstances exist, such as a serious medical condition or a call to active duty in the Armed Forces, and that the special circumstances justify additional expenses or adjustments of current monthly income for which there is no reasonable alternative. In order to establish special circumstances, the debtor must itemize each additional expense or income adjustment and provide documentation and a detailed explanation thereof under oath. Failure to submit documentation of extraordinary expenses to establish special circumstances will cause the court to deny any such claimed expenses. See In re Renicker, 342 B.R. 304 (WD MO, 2006). Even then, the presumption of abuse will be deemed rebutted only if the additional expenses or adjustments cause the debtor's current monthly income reduced by the allowed expenses listed above (i.e., the debtor's disposable monthly income) multiplied by 60 to be less than the lesser of 25 percent of the debtor's nonpriority unsecured claims (or $6,575 if that is greater), or $10,950. See 11 U.S.C. § 707(b)(2)(B).

presumption of abuse, rebuttal of

Courts are split on whether nondischargeable student loan payments are sufficiently "special circumstances" to rebut the means test presumption. See In re Harmon, 446 B.R. 721 (Bankr. E. D. Penn. 2011) (nondischargeable student loan payments not "special circumstances); In re Howell, 477 B.R. 314 (Bankr. W. D. N.Y. 2012) (student loans a "special circumstance"). In any event, the mere fact that the debtor passed the means test does not prevent an inquiry under the "totality of circumstances" test. See McGovern v. McDermott, 445 B.R. 821 (N.D. Ohio 2011); In re Ng, 477 B.R. 118 (B.A.P. 9th Cir. 2012).

If the debtor qualifies under Section 707(2)(D), the means test will not apply to his or her case, and the case will not be dismissed based upon any form of means testing. Section 707(2)(D) covers disabled veterans whose debts were incurred primarily when on active duty or performing a homeland defense activity as well as debtors who are on active duty or have been on active duty within 540 days of the petition date and National Guard and reserve members who are called to active duty.

means test, non-applicability

The "primarily consumer debts" requirement. Only the Chapter 7 case of an individual debtor whose debts are primarily consumer debts may be dismissed under Section 707(b). Therefore, if a debtor's debts are not primarily consumer debts, his or her Chapter 7 case may not be dismissed under Section 707(b) even if abuse exists. Two issues arise with respect to this requirement. The first issue is what does the word "primarily" mean with respect to consumer debts? The second issue is what constitutes a consumer debt? The "primarily consumer debt" defense is most likely to arise in Chapter 7 cases filed by debtors who are or have been engaged in business.

§707(b), primarily consumer debts requirement, issues

In In re Kelly, 841 F.2d 908 (9th Cir., 1988), the court held that "primarily" means "for the most part" and that a debtor's debts are primarily consumer debts when more than half of the dollar amount of the debts are consumer debts. See also In re Victoria, 389 B.R. 250 (MD AL, 2008). Therefore, even if the total number of consumer debts is greater than the total number of nonconsumer debts, if the total dollar amount of nonconsumer debts exceeds the total dollar amount of consumer debts, the debtor's debts are not primarily consumer debts and the case may not be dismissed under Section 707(b). See also In re Stewart, 175 F.3d 796 (10th Cir., 1999); In re Bell, 65 B.R. 575 (ED MI, 1986). While the above definition of "primarily" seems to be the majority rule, in In re Johnson, 115 B.R. 159 (SD IL, 1990), the court stated that the question of whether a Chapter 7 debtor's debts are primarily

"primarily consumer debts," definition of term

consumer debts for purposes of Section 707(b) should be evaluated in terms of both dollar amount and number of consumer debts. This approach was noted with approval in In re Booth, 858 F.2d 1051 (5th Cir., 1988).

The other issue in the "primarily consumer debt" defense is the issue of whether a particular debt is a consumer debt. A consumer debt is described in the Bankruptcy Code to mean a "debt incurred by an individual primarily for a personal, family, or household purpose." See 11 U.S.C. § 101(8). Under this definition a business-related debt is not a consumer debt. See In re Kelly, 841 F.2d 908 (9th Cir., 1988). Therefore, most debts in Chapter 7 consumer cases may be classified as either consumer debts or business debts.

consumer debt, definition of

In In re Booth, 858 F.2d 1051 (5th Cir., 1988), the court stated that the test for determining whether a debt should be classified as a business debt or a consumer debt for purposes of Section 707(b) is whether the debt was incurred with an eye toward profit. In that case the court held that a debt secured by the debtor's residence was a business debt because the proceeds of the loan that gave rise to the debt were used for business purposes. See also In re Palmer, 117 B.R. 443 (ND IA, 1990); In re Manning, 126 B.R. 984 (MD TN, 1991) (holding that a debt arising from a loan used to purchase a day care center and a limited partnership interest was not a consumer debt because the debtors derived income from the day care center and it was not used primarily for personal and family purposes and because the limited partnership interest was a business and not a personal investment). The debtor's activity as a professional off-road bicycle racer qualified as a business rather than a hobby in In re Fletcher, 248 B.R. 48 (VT, 2000), even though she made no profit from it. The debts arising from her racing were deemed to be business debts for purposes of Section 707(b).

business debt, what constitutes

In In re Marshalek, 158 B.R. 704 (ND OH, 1993), the court held that a judgment resulting from an automobile accident was not a consumer debt, and because that debt was over half of the dollar amount of the debtor's debts, dismissal under Section 707(b) was not permissible. In In re Traub, 140 B.R. 286 (NM, 1992), the court ruled that a credit card debt for money used in the debtor's business was not a consumer debt. However, the court in that case also ruled that a debt owed to the debtor's former spouse arising from a divorce settlement agreement was a consumer debt, as was a debt owed to the debtor's professional corporation for funds loaned to the debtor for household expenses. An obligation to pay a former spouse under a divorce decree is a consumer debt. See, e.g., In re Palmer, 117 B.R. 443 (ND IA, 1990); In re Stewart, 175 F.3d 796 (10th Cir., 1999). In In re Brashers, 216 B.R. 59 (ND OK, 1998), the debtor's state and federal tax debts were held not to be "consumer debts" for purposes of Section 707(b).

consumer debt, what constitutes

In In re Dickerson, 166 B.R. 480 (ND GA, 1993), since the determination of whether a particular debt is a consumer debt is governed by the purpose for which the debt is incurred, debts that were incurred for personal, family or household purposes were consumer debts even if they were secured by real property and were incurred to consolidate pre-existing mortgages and debts. In In re Berndt, 127 B.R. 222 (ND, 1991), unsecured debts derived from credit cards and checking account reserves that were used to purchase stock market investments was held to be consumer debts because the investments were made for personal rather than business reasons.

consumer debt, what constitutes

Debts for such items as personal credit cards, utilities, insurance, dental work, jewelry, magazines, and appliance repair are normally consumer debts, as are debts, including home mortgages, that are incurred to purchase, finance, or improve the debtor's home. See In re Palmer, 117 B.R. 443 (ND IA, 1990); In re Johnson, 115 B.R. 159 (SD IL, 1990). In addition, debts that a person would ordinarily expect to incur in the course of his or her daily affairs, other than business expenses, are consumer debts, such as expenses for movie rentals and dependent children payments. See In re Walton, 69 B.R. 150 (ED MO, 1986).

consumer debt, what constitutes

Factors considered in an actual abuse motion. Note that although the means test has received the bulk of the attention under Section 707(b), if the presumption arises but is sufficiently rebutted or does not apply at all in a case, the court will still consider whether the petition was filed in bad faith by the debtor.

bad faith standard for dismissal, applicability of

The good or bad faith of the debtor in filing the Chapter 7 case is a factor frequently considered by courts in deciding whether to dismiss a case for abuse under Section 707(b). The good faith of the debtor in filing the case works in favor of the debtor and can be the deciding factor in a close case. In In re Browne, 253 B.R. 854 (ND OH, 2000), the court refused to dismiss the case for abuse even though, counting the income of his nonfiling new wife, the debtor had a disposable income of nearly $500, where it was shown that the debtor had a modest lifestyle, worked two jobs, and his scheduled consumer debts indicated that he filed the Chapter 7 case in good faith. See also In re Bingham, 68 B.R. 933 (MD PA, 1987); In re Shepherd, 147 B.R. 422 (ND OH, 1992); In re Wegner, 91 B.R. 854 (MN, 1988); In re Wilkes, 114 B.R. 551 (WD TN, 1989). Good faith usually means that the debtor had a valid or unavoidable reason for filing the case and did not incur debts with the intention of discharging them in bankruptcy. See In re Butts, 148 B.R. 878 (ND IN, 1992).

abuse, effect of good faith

A finding of bad faith, on the other hand, can weigh heavily against the debtor in a Section 707(b) motion to dismiss. A debtor who, when faced with mounting debt, refuses to "tighten his belt" and control his spending, but instead seeks to impose his extravagance on his creditors is a likely candidate for a finding of bad faith and a Section 707(b) dismissal. See Tamecki v. Frank, 229 F.3d 205 (3d Cir., 2000); In re Goodson, 130 B.R. 897 (ND OK, 1991); In re Andrus, 94 B.R. 76 (WD PA, 1988). A debtor who files bankruptcy for the sole purposes of discharging the debts of a single creditor is also likely to be found to have filed the case in bad faith. See In re Shands, 63 B.R. 121 (ED MI, 1985) (case filed to "spite" ex-husband); In re Palmer, 117 B.R. 443 (ND IA, 1990) (case filed to circumvent order to pay $24,000 to ex-wife); In re Bruno, 68 B.R. 101 (WD MO, 1986) (case filed to discharge loans used for attorney fees and bond money in criminal prosecution against debtor for the murder of his wife). See also In re Sammons, 210 B.R. 197 (ND FL, 1997) (case filed by professional boxer to avoid promoter's contract so that the debtor could sign a more lucrative contract with another promoter).

abuse, effect of bad faith

Bibliography. For further reading on the issues discussed in this article, see the annotations and articles listed below.

Annotations:

Bankruptcy: When does filing of Chapter 7 petition constitute "substantial abuse" authorizing dismissal of petition under 11 U.S.C. § §707(b). 122 ALR Fed 141.

What are "primarily consumer debts," under 11 U.S.C. § §707(b), authorizing dismissal of Chapter 7 bankruptcy case if granting relief would be substantial abuse of Chapter's provision. 101 ALR Fed 771.

Articles:

Hon. Keith M. Lundin, Ten Principles of BAPCPA: Not What was Advertised, 24 AM. BANKR. INST. J. 1, 70 (Sept. 2005).

Erwin Chemerinsky, Constitutional Issues Posed in the Bankruptcy Abuse Prevention and Consumer Protection Act of 2005, 79 AM. BANKR. L.J. 571 (Summer 2005).

Sommer, Henry J., Trying To Make Sense Out of Nonsense: Representing Consumers Under the "Bankruptcy Abuse Prevention and Consumer Protection Act of 2005," 79 Am. Bank. L.J. 191 (Spring 2005).

Wedoff, Eugene R., Means Testing in the News §707(b), 79 Am. Bankr. L.J. 231 (Spring 2005).

Looking forward while looking back: Using debtors' post-petition financial changes to find bankruptcy abuse after BAPCPA. Note, 49 Wm. & Mary L. Rev. 335 (2007).

2.03 What is the extent of a debtor's right to redeem property under Section 722 of the Bankruptcy Code?

Text of statute. **Section 722 of the Bankruptcy Code (11 U.S.C. § 722) provides as follows:**

722. Redemption

> An individual debtor may, whether or not the debtor has waived the right to redeem under this section, redeem tangible personal property intended primarily for personal, family, or household use, from a lien securing a dischargeable consumer debt, if such property is exempted under section 522 of this title or has been abandoned under section 554 of this title, by paying the holder of such lien the amount of the allowed secured claim of such holder that is secured by such lien in full at the time of redemption. §722, text of

Introduction. **Section 722 was enacted with the Bankruptcy Reform Act of 1978 and was unamended from enactment until 2005, when the BAPCPA added the words "in full at the time of redemption" at the end of the section. The obvious purpose of the BAPCPA amendment is to prevent courts from allowing redemption payments to be made in installments or at a date subsequent to redemption. In practice, the BAPCPA amendment had little effect on section 722 redemptions because the courts have universally held that redemption payments must be made in a lump sum and not in installments, unless the creditor agrees otherwise.** §722, BAPCPA amendments to

According to its legislative history, the purpose of Section 722 is to enhance a debtor's postbankruptcy "fresh start" by permitting the debtor to retain possession at a modest cost of the type of secured personal property that is likely to be of considerable personal or practical value to the debtor and of relatively little value to the secured creditor. The legislative history of Section 722 and the inclusion in the statute of a nonwaivability provision indicates an intention by Congress to benefit Chapter 7 debtors and that Section 722 should be liberally construed for their benefit. Such an intent is also indicated by the fact that the redemption provisions of Section 722 are broader than the redemption provisions of the Uniform Commercial Code. See In re Taylor, 3 F.3d 1512 (11th Cir. 1993). §722, legislative history

Under the Bankruptcy Code there are two statutory methods by which a Chapter 7 debtor may retain possession of secured property. One method is by the reaffirmation of a debt under Section 524(c) of the Bankruptcy Code and the other is by the redemption of personal property under Section 722. See In re Pratt, 462 F.3d 14 (1st Cir., 2006) and Matter of Johnson, 89 F.3d 249 (5th Cir., 1996). Under either method the debtor may, under the sanction and protection of the Bankruptcy Code, retain possession of secured property during and after the bankruptcy case. A debtor who neither reaffirms the secured debt nor redeems the secured property may, after the close of the bankruptcy case and the expiration of the automatic stay, be unable to prevent the secured creditor from repossessing the property under a "default upon bankruptcy" clause in the security agreement. See In re Wilson, 97 B.R. 285 (WD VA, 1989); In re Pendlebury, 94 B.R. 120 (ED TN, 1988); In re Buck, 331 B.R. 322 (ND OH, 2005). §722 redemption vs. §524(c) reaffirmation "ride-through" after BAPCPA

What if the debtor is current on payments, yet does not reaffirm or redeem? Can the debtor simply continue to make payments and "ride through" the bankruptcy? The court in Coastal Federal Credit Union v. Hardiman, 398 B.R. 161 (ED NC, 2008) addressed this issue and stated that there remains a limited "ride through" option for Chapter 7 debtors to remain in possession of their motor vehicle, despite the bankruptcy court's refusal to approve their proposed reaffirmation agreement, simply by continuing to make their monthly payments to the lender. In In re Jones, 397 B.R. 775 (SD WV, 2008), the court stated that a post-BAPCPA ride through is not available to a debtor who does not file a statement of intention. The 9th Circuit likewise has eliminated the "ride through" option. See In re Dumont, 581 F.3d 1104 (9th Cir. 2009). The majority view seems to be that a "ride through" is generally unavailable, especially to those debtors who do not file a statement of intention. See In re Ward, 320 B.R. 760 (MD FL, 2005); In re Parker, 363 B.R. 621 (MD FL, 2007); In re Covel, 474 B.R. 702 (Bankr. W.D. Ark. 2012).

Section 722 permits an individual Chapter 7 debtor to redeem property from a secured creditor if the following conditions with respect to the property, the debt, and the redemption amount are satisfied:

§722 redemption, conditions of

(1) The property being redeemed must be
  (a) tangible personal property,
  (b) intended primarily for a personal, family or household use, and
  (c) either lawfully exempted by the debtor or abandoned by the trustee in the case.

(2) The debt secured by the creditor's lien must be
  (a) a consumer debt, and
  (b) a debt that is dischargeable in the case.

(3) Unless the creditor agrees otherwise, the redemption amount paid to the secured creditor must be
  (a) equal in amount to the amount of the creditor's allowed secured claim that is secured by the redeemed property, and
  (b) paid to the creditor in a lump sum.

§722 redemption, general requirements

An individual Chapter 7 debtor who timely satisfies each of the above conditions may redeem property under Section 722 whether or not the creditor consents to the redemption. It should be noted that Section 722 applies only to, and may only be used by, individual or joint Chapter 7 debtors. Section 722 may not be used by corporate or partnership debtors and may not be used by a debtor under any other chapter of the Bankruptcy Code, including Chapter 13. Each of the conditions listed above are discussed separately below. The procedure for redeeming property under Section 722 is also discussed below.

§722 redemption, property requirements

The property requirements for redemption. Only tangible personal property intended primarily for a personal, family or household use that is exempt to the debtor may be redeemed under Section 722. However, the debtor's right to redeem property under Section 722 extends to the whole of the property being redeemed and not just to the debtor's exempt interest in the property. See In re Herrera, 454 B.R. 559 (Bankr. E. D. N.Y. 2011); In re Fitzgerald, 20 B.R. 27 (ND NY, 1982). Thus, if a debtor has a $1,000 exempt equity in a $4,000 automobile, the debtor may redeem the entire interest in the automobile under Section 722 and not just the debtor's $1,000 exempt equity in the auto.

Because of the personal, family or household use requirement, business property may not be redeemed under Section 722. Therefore, motor vehicles and other personal property used by the debtor for business purposes may not be redeemed under Section 722, even if they are exempt to the debtor in the case. See Smith v. Household Auto. Fin. Corp., 313 B.R. 267 (ND IL, 2004); In re Brown, 37 B.R. 516 (ED MO, 1984). However, in many instances liens against exempt business property may be avoided by the debtor under Section 522(f) of the Bankruptcy Code. See article 1.05 of this handbook for a discussion of lien avoidance under Section 522(f).

§722, inapplicability to business property

While Section 722 contains no express requirement of this sort, generally in order to be redeemable under Section 722, the redemption must be for the benefit of the debtor and not for the benefit of another person. See In re Pipes, 78 B.R. 981 (WD MO, 1987) (holding in a joint case filed by spouses who were subsequently divorced prior to the redemption proceeding, that a pickup truck that was used solely by the ex-husband but which was owned by the ex-wife could not be redeemed by the ex-wife under Section 722 because the redemption was not for her benefit). Likewise, in In re Runski, 102 F.3d 744 (4th Cir., 1996), the court held that personal property may not be redeemed under Section 722 merely because it is exempt and titled in the debtor's name. The court stated that the property must also be intended primarily for a personal, family or household use and that therefore the medical and office equipment of a chiropractor could not be redeemed under Section 722. See In re Gonzalez, 376 B.R. 348 (SD FL, 2007), where the court said the debtor could not redeem from a creditor's security interest consumer goods that he previously purchased, but had gifted to his mother prior to the petition date.

§722 redemption, benefit of the debtor requirement

While it is clear that real property is not redeemable under Section 722, property that was personal property when acquired but which was later affixed to real property may be redeemed under Section 722. See In re Hall, 11 B.R. 3 (WD MO, 1980), where the court held that a fence installed at the debtor's home and intended to become a fixture to the realty was nevertheless tangible personal property within the meaning of Section 722 because the parties contemplated that in the event of default the fence would be removed for resale. In In re Walker, 173 B.R. 512 (MD NC, 1994), the court held that siding and trim attached to the debtor's home was tangible personal property for purposes of Section 722 and could be redeemed by the debtor after it was abandoned by the trustee, because the property, although affixed to realty, was treated as personal property by the parties.

§722 redemption, property affixed to realty

To be redeemable under Section 722, the property in question must also be either exempt to the debtor or abandoned by the trustee during the bankruptcy case. To be exempt to the debtor for purposes of Section 722 the property must be claimed as exempt by the debtor in the case and, if no objection to the exemption is timely filed, the claimed exemption must be allowed by the court. The exemption may be claimed by the debtor under either state or federal law, whichever is applicable to the debtor in the case. Further, the property may be claimed as exempt under any applicable exemption law, including a so-called wildcard exemption (i.e., an exemption applicable to any property chosen by the debtor).

§722 redemption, exempt property requirement

§722 redemption, equity in property, necessity of

Because Chapter 7 debtors seldom have prebankruptcy equities in property that is sought to be redeemed under Section 722, the existence of such an equity is not usually necessary for a Section 722 redemption. See In re Williams, 9 B.R. 83 (M.D. TN, 1981), where the court held that the debtor was entitled to redeem an automobile in which the debtor had no equity because if the debtor's Section 722 redemption rights were limited to property in which they have an exemptible equity, Section 722 would be meaningless because they could only redeem property by paying the secured debt in full, which right already existed under the Uniform Commercial Code prior to the enactment of Section 722. However, in In re Seguin, 76 B.R. 175 (CO, 1987) the court held that under Colorado law a Chapter 7 debtor who possessed no equity in an automobile covered by a perfected purchase money security interest was not entitled to an exemption in the property and therefore could not redeem it under Section 722 unless it was abandoned by the trustee. It would appear that this decision may be in conflict with the Supreme Court's holding in Owen v. Owen, 500 U.S. 305, 111 S. Ct. 1833 (1991), where the court held that in determining whether a lien impairs an exemption for purposes 11 U.S.C. § 522(f), the effect of the lien on the debtor's exemption should not be considered. See id. at 311.

§722 redemption, debt requirements

The debt requirements for redemption. The debt secured by the property being redeemed must be a dischargeable consumer debt. Therefore, if the underlying debt is nondischargeable for any reason, the property may not be redeemed under Section 722. Similarly, if the underlying debt is not a consumer debt, the property may not be redeemed under Section 722.

consumer debt, what constitutes

A consumer debt is defined in the Bankruptcy Code as a debt incurred by an individual primarily for a personal, family, or household purpose. See 11 U.S.C. § 101(8). A consumer debt is generally held to be any debt that a person would ordinarily expect to incur in his or her daily affairs, other than business expenses. See In re Walton, 69 B.R. 150 (ED MO, 1986); In re Kelly, 841 F.2d 908 (9th Cir., 1988). It is important, therefore, to ascertain whether the underlying debt was incurred for business purposes, because if it was the property securing the debt is not redeemable under Section 722. The mere fact that property is titled in the name of an individual debtor does not necessarily mean it is intended for personal, family, or household use. See In re Runski, 102 F.3d 744 (4th Cir., 1996). A debt incurred primarily to provide money or property for a business purpose is not a consumer debt and the property securing the debt is not redeemable under Section 722, even if the property is clearly personal to the debtor. For example, if a debtor mortgaged his or her personal automobile or household furniture primarily to raise money to operate a business, the automobile or furniture is not redeemable under Section 722.

consumer debt v. business debt, general rule

It is often difficult to ascertain whether a particular debt is a consumer debt or a business-related debt. The general rule is that whether a debt is a consumer debt is determined by the purpose for which the debt was incurred. See In re Dickerson, 166 B.R. 480 (ND GA, 1993); In re Booth, 858 F.2d 1051 (5th Cir., 1988) (holding that the test for determining whether a debt should be classified as a business debt or a consumer debt is whether the debt was incurred with an eye toward profit).

In In re Almendinger, 56 B.R. 97 (ND OH, 1985), the court held that a debt incurred by a stockbroker to cover stock market losses and for investment purposes was not a consumer debt because the losses and investments were business-related. However, in In re Berndt, 127 B.R. 222 (ND, 1991), a debt was a consumer debt even though the proceeds of the debt were used to purchase stock market investments because the investments were made for the personal purposes of the debtor. It would appear, then, that debts created for personal investments of the debtor are consumer debts while debts created for business-related investments are not consumer debts.

investment debts, consumer or business

Loans or other debts incurred primarily for such purposes as paying automobile accident judgments and business-related attorney's fees are not normally considered to be consumer debts. See In re White, 49 B.R. 869 (WD NC, 1985); In re Marshalek, 158 B.R. 704 (ND OH, 1993); In re Alvarez, 57 B.R. 65 (SD FL, 1985); In re Bernstein, 71 B.R. 259 (SD FL, 1987). On the other hand, loans or other debts incurred primarily for the purpose of paying alimony, maintenance or support obligations of the debtor are normally held to be consumer debts. See In re Traub, 140 B.R. 286 (NM, 1992); In re Walton, 69 B.R. 150 (ED MO, 1986). A debt incurred to pay attorney fees resulting from litigation concerning the debtor's home was held to be a consumer debt in In re Kelly, 841 F.2d 908 (9th Cir., 1988). In In re Boitnott, 4 B.R. 122 (WD VA, 1980) the consolidation of a consumer debt with other nonconsumer debts did not transform the consumer debt into a nonconsumer debt. See article 2.02 of this handbook for a discussion of what constitutes a consumer debt for purposes of Section 707(b) of the Bankruptcy Code.

consumer debts, what constitutes, cases

The payment requirements for redemption. There are two payment requirements applicable to Section 722 redemptions. The first requirement is that the debtor must pay to the holder of the lien (i.e., the secured creditor) the amount of the creditor's allowed secured claim secured by the lien. The second payment requirement is that the payment must be made in a lump sum and not in installments, unless the creditor agrees otherwise.

§722 redemption, payment requirements

The amount of a creditor's allowed secured claim must be determined in accordance with Section 506(a) of the Bankruptcy Code (11 U.S.C. § 506(a)), which provides as follows:

506. Determination of secured status

(a)(1) An allowed claim of a creditor secured by a lien on property in which the estate has an interest, or that is subject to setoff under section 553 of this title, is a secured claim to the extent of the value of such creditor's interest in the estate's interest in such property, or to the extent of the amount subject to setoff, as the case may be, and is an unsecured claim to the extent that the value of such creditor's interest or the amount so subject to setoff is less than the amount of such allowed claim. Such value shall be determined in light of the purpose of the valuation and of the proposed disposition or use of such property, and in conjunction with any hearing on such disposition or use or on a plan affecting such creditor's interest.

§506(a), text of

> (2) If the debtor is an individual in a case under chapter 7 or 13, such value with respect to personal property securing an allowed claim shall be determined based on the replacement value of such property as of the date of the filing of the petition without deduction for costs of sale or marketing. With respect to property acquired for personal, family, or household purposes, replacement value shall mean the price a retail merchant would charge for property of that kind considering the age and condition of the property at the time value is determined.

§722 redemption amount, how determined

Section 506(a) provides that an allowed claim is a secured claim to the extent of the value of the collateral and is an unsecured claim to the extent that the amount of the claim exceeds the value of the collateral. However, if the total amount of a creditor's allowed claim is less than the value of the collateral, the amount of the creditor's allowed secured claim is limited to the amount of the claim. Therefore, the redemption amount under Section 722 is the lesser of the value of the collateral or the amount owed to the creditor. See In re Breckinridge, 140 B.R. 642 (WD KY, 1992). Value for individual debtors will normally be determined based on replacement value

§722 redemption amount, when zero

If the property being redeemed is subject to two liens and if the amount of the first lien exceeds the value of the property, the second lien may be redeemable under Section 722 without payment because under Section 506(a) the value of the second lien holder's interest in the collateral is zero. In such a situation, however, it may be necessary to pay the second lien holder an amount equal to the filing and recording expenses of releasing its lien. See In re Lombardi, 195 B.R. 585 (WD NY, 1996); In re Altenburg, 6 BCD 331 (SD FL, 1980). If the Chapter 7 case is a converted Chapter 13 case and if the total payments made to the secured creditor in the Chapter 13 case prior to conversion were equal to or greater than the amount of the creditor's allowed secured claim in the Chapter 7 case, the property may also be redeemed without payment under Section 722. See In re Woodland, 325 B.R. 583 (WD TN, 2005); In re Cooke, 169 B.R. 662 (WD MO, 1994). It is clear that when the value of a secured claim is determined in a Chapter 13 case that is subsequently converted to Chapter 7, the debtor need only pay the remaining Chapter 13 claim balance in order to redeem the property under Section 722. See In re Rodgers, 273 B.R. 186 (CD IL, 2002); In re Dean, 281 B.R. 912 (WD TN, 2002); In re Archie, 240 B.R. 425 (SD AL, 1999).

§722 redemption amount, case converted from Chapter 13

valuation of collateral, general rules

As indicated above, the amount of a creditor's allowed secured claim is limited by the value of the collateral securing the claim. The debtor must present some evidence of the value of the property to be redeemed. See In re Miller, 394 B.R. 114 (SC, 2008). An important aspect of many Section 722 redemption proceedings, then, is that of valuing the collateral. Section 506(a) provides that collateral shall be valued in light of the proposed use of the property, which in a Section 722 proceeding means use by the debtor. Section 506(a)(2) makes it clear that for an individual in a chapter 7 or 13 case, value shall be determined based on the replacement value of the property sought to be redeemed. The addition of subsection (2) in 2005 was a significant change in the way valuations are undertaken in chapter 7 and 13 cases. The subsection has the effect of overturning previous opinions (including the U.S. Supreme Court ruling in Associates Commercial Corp. v. Rash, 520 U.S. 953, 117 S. Ct. 1879 (1997)) that permitted wholesale valuations of property. However, the age and condition of the property must still be taken into consideration.

Despite the addition of subsection (2) to Section 506(a), some courts still adhere to the rule of "redemption value = wholesale value". See In re Lloyd, 342 B.R. 301 (ED MO, 2006). In In re Lloyd the court adopted the wholesale value is stated in the NADA Guide as the valuation determinant of value, unless the vehicle is in poor condition.

determination of collateral value

The court in In re Ortiz used a "retail standard" approach to determine the redemption value of a debtor's vehicle. In Ortiz, the car was a 2005 model, yet required extensive repairs and maintenance. The court determined the retail value of the same make and model of the debtor's car, and then deducted the "retail," rather than the wholesale cost of repairs required to bring the debtor's car up to retail condition. The court then averaged the retail price figures submitted by both parties and subtracted the retail cost of repairs to determine a redemption value. See In re Ortiz, 20 FLW Fed. B 301 (SD FL, 2007). Note that in the Ortiz case neither the creditor or the debtor submitted an appraisal as of the petition date.

redemption valuation, "retail standard" test

The procedural requirements for redemption. A redemption under Section 722 may be either voluntary or involuntary. A voluntary redemption occurs when the debtor and the secured creditor agree on a redemption value and stipulate as to the redemption. Voluntary (or consensual) redemption agreements do not require court approval. See Sears, Roebuck & Co. v. Spivey, 265 B.R. 357 (ED NY, 2001). However, if court approval is sought the court must be provided with a basis for approving the agreement. See In re Ephraim, 249 B.R. 862 (ED MI, 2000). An involuntary redemption under Section 722, on the other hand, is a contested matter and requires the filing of a motion by the debtor for redemption under Bankruptcy Rule 6008. See In re Pendlebury, 94 B.R. 120 (ED TN, 1988).

§722 redemption, voluntary v. involuntary

Bankruptcy Rule 6008 provides that on the motion of the debtor, and after a hearing on notice, the court may authorize the redemption of property from a lien. An involuntary redemption of property under Section 722 is a contested matter under Bankruptcy Rule 9014 and requires the filing of a motion by the debtor in order to initiate the proceeding. The motion should be filed in accordance with Bankruptcy Rules 6008, 9013 and 9014. A Section 722 redemption proceeding is not an adversary proceeding and does not require the filing of a complaint under Part VII of the Bankruptcy Rules.

§722 redemption, procedure for

Section 722 contains no time requirements within which property may be redeemed. However, 11 U.S.C. § 521(2)(A) requires a Chapter 7 debtor to file a statement of the debtor's intention with respect to the retention or surrender of the debtor's property that secures consumer debts by the earlier of 30 days after the filing of the Chapter 7 petition or the date of the meeting of creditors, unless the court extends the period. 11 U.S.C. § 521(2)(B) requires a Chapter 7 debtor to perform his or her intention with respect to the secured property within 30 days after the first date set for the meeting of creditors under section 341(a) unless the court grants additional time.

§722 redemption, time requirements

statement of intention, effect of on §722 redemption rights

Note, however, that 11 U.S.C. § 521(2)(C) provides that nothing in 11 U.S.C. § 521(2)(A) or (B) shall alter the debtor's rights with respect to the secured property except as provided in section 362(h). Therefore, the time constraints set forth in 11 U.S.C. § 521(2)(A) and (B) are not necessarily binding on the debtor. See In re Cassar, 139 B.R. 253 (CO, 1992), where the court stated that the time limits set forth in 11 U.S.C. § 521 do not alter the debtor's substantive rights with respect to redemption and a failure to meet these deadlines does not impair the debtor's right to redeem property under Section 722. See also In re Eagle, 51 B.R. 959 (ND OH, 1985). See also In re Jewell, 232 B.R. 904 (ED TX, 1999) (ruling that the Bankruptcy Code does not confine the debtor to any time period for redeeming property under Section 722 and that therefore the debtor could file a motion to redeem prior to the deadline for filing objections to exemptions and complaints to except debts from discharge).

§722 redemption, time limitations

In In re Hawkins, 136 B.R. 649 (WD VA, 1991), the court held that the entry of a discharge order does not bar a motion by the debtor to redeem property under Section 722. The court stated that since the Bankruptcy Code was silent as to when debtors may exercise their right to redeem property under Section 722, and that since the concepts of redemption and reaffirmation were considered by Congress together, therefore the time frame for exercising one option should be equally applicable to the other. See also In re Bright, 18 FLW Fed. B. 192 (SD FL, 2005). However, the court in In re Buck ruled that a debtor lost his right to redeem after the automatic stay under 11 U.S.C. § 362(a) had been terminated. The court reasoned that, once the protections of the automatic stay are terminated, so are the rights of redemption. See In re Buck, 331 B.R. 322 (ND OH, 2005).

Bibliography. For further reading on the issues discussed in this article, see the annotations and articles listed below.

Annotations: None available.

Articles:

Beneath the Surface of BAPCPA – Rash and Ride Through Redux: The Terms for Holding on to Cars, Homes, and other Collateral Under the 2005 Act. Jean Braucler, 13 Am. Bankr. Inst. C. Rev. 457, 2005.

Redemption or reaffirmation: the debtor's exclusive means of retaining possession of collateral in Chapter 7. 56 Univ. of Pittsburgh L. Rev. 187, Fall 1994.

Property valuation and avoidance issues. 47 Consumer Fin. L.Q. Rep. 413, 1993.

Secured creditors and the eely character of bankruptcy valuations. 41 Am. Univ. L. Rev. 63, 1991.

CHAPTER THREE

CHAPTER 13 BANKRUPTCY ISSUES

The articles in this chapter deal with issues that arise under the provisions of Chapter 13 of the Bankruptcy Code. Therefore, these articles pertain only to Chapter 13 cases and are not applicable to Chapter 7 cases or cases under any other chapter of the Bankruptcy Code. scope of chapter

3.01 To what extent may defaults on secured obligations be cured and dealt with in Chapter 13 plans?

Text of statutes. **Sections 1322(b)(2), (3), (5), 1322(c), 1322(e), and 1325(a)(5) of the Bankruptcy Code (11 U.S.C. § 1322(b)(2), (3), (5), (c), (e), 1325(a)(5)) provide as follows:**

1322. Contents of plan

. . . .

(b) Subject to subsections (a) and (c) of this section, the plan may -

. . . .

Section 1322(b) (2), (3) & (5), text of

(2) modify the rights of holders of secured claims, other than a claim secured only by a security interest in real property that is the debtor's principal residence, or of holders of unsecured claims, or leave unaffected the rights of holders of any class of claims;

(3) provide for the curing or waiving of any default;

. . . .

(5) notwithstanding paragraph (2) of this subsection, provide for the curing of any default within a reasonable time and maintenance of payments while the case is pending on any unsecured claim or secured claim on which the last payment is due after the date on which the final payment under the plan is due;

. . . .

(c) Notwithstanding subsection (b)(2) and applicable nonbankruptcy law -

(1) a default with respect to, or that gave rise to, a lien on the debtor's principal residence may be cured under paragraph (3) or (5) of subsection (b) until such residence is sold at a foreclosure sale that is conducted in accordance with applicable nonbankruptcy law; and

Section 1322(c), text of

(2) in a case in which the last payment on the original payment schedule for a claim secured only by a security interest in real property that is the debtor's principal residence is due before the date on which the final payment under the plan is due, the plan may provide for the payment of the claim as modified pursuant to section 1325(a)(5) of this title.

. . . .

(e) Notwithstanding subsection (b)(2) of this section and sections 506(b) and 1325(a)(5) of this title, if it is proposed in a plan to cure a default, the amount necessary to cure the default, shall be determined in accordance with the underlying agreement and applicable nonbankruptcy law.

Section 1322(e), text of

1325. Confirmation of plan

Section 1325(a)(5), text of

(a) Except as provided in subsection (b), the court shall confirm a plan if -

* * * * * *

(5) with respect to each allowed secured claim provided for by the plan-

(A) the holder of such claim has accepted the plan;

(B)(i) the plan provides that –

(I) the holder of such claim retain the lien securing such claim until the earlier of –

(aa) the payment of the underlying debt determined under nonbankruptcy law;

or

(bb) discharge under section 1328; and

(II) if the case under this chapter is dismissed or converted without completion of the plan, such lien shall also be retained by such holder to the extent recognized by applicable nonbankruptcy law;

(ii) the value, as of the effective date of the plan, of property to be distributed under the plan on account of such claim is not less than the allowed amount of such claim; and

(iii) if –

(I) property to be distributed pursuant to this subsection is in the form of periodic payments, such payments shall be in equal monthly amounts; and

(II) the holder of the claim is secured by personal property, the amount of such payments shall not be less than an amount sufficient to provide to the holder of such claim adequate protection during the period of the plan; or

(C) the debtor surrenders the property securing such claim to such holder;

* * * * * *

Section 1325(a)(5) hanging paragraph, text of

For purposes of paragraph (5), section 506 shall not apply to a claim described in that paragraph if the creditor has a purchase money security interest securing the debt that is the subject of the claim, the debt was incurred within the 910-day preceding the date of the filing of the petition, and the collateral for that debt consists of a motor vehicle (as defined in section 30102 of title 49) acquired for the personal use of the debtor, or if collateral for that debt consists of any other thing of value, if the debt was incurred during the 1-year period preceding that filing.

curing defaults, general Chapter 13 provisions

Introduction. The curing of defaults on secured obligations in Chapter 13 plans generally involves the interaction of seven separate but related provisions of Chapter 13 of the Bankruptcy Code. Generally, Sections 1322(b)(3) and (5) provide for the curing of defaults in Chapter 13 plans, while Section 1322(b)(2) limits the debtor's right to cure defaults by prohibiting Chapter 13 plans from modifying the rights of creditors who are secured only by a security interest in real property that is the debtor's principal residence. Section 1322(c)(2) excepts obligations that mature prior to the close of the Chapter 13 plan from the Section 1322(b)(2) prohibition against modification. Section 1325(a)(5) further limits the debtor's right to cure defaults by requiring full payment of present value for all secured claims and prohibits cramdown against certain creditors, most notably holders of purchase money security interests in cars purchased for personal use by the debtor within 2 ½ years preceding bankruptcy. Finally, Sections 1322(c)(1) and 1322(e) deal with the debtor's right to cure defaults in foreclosure situations and the amounts necessary to cure defaults.

Sections 1322(b)(2), (3), (5) and 1325(a)(5) were enacted in the Bankruptcy Reform Act of 1978. Sections 1322(b)(2) and 1325(a) were amended slightly in 1984 by amendments that are not relevant to this subject. Sections 1322(c) and 1322(e) were enacted in the Bankruptcy Reform Act of 1994, and have remained unchanged since their enactment.

history of applicable statutes

The Bankruptcy Abuse Prevention and Consumer Protection Act of 2005 (the BAPCPA) did not amend sections 1322(b)(2), (3), (5), 1322(c) or 1322(e) of the Bankruptcy Code. However, the BAPCPA amended section 1325(a)(5) of the Bankruptcy Code and added 2 new sections to the Bankruptcy Code that affect a debtor's right to cure defaults on secured obligations. The amended Section 1325(c)(5) and the new Sections 1322(c)(4) and (f) are discussed below.

BAPCPA amendments & new sections

The BAPCPA amended subparagraph (B) of paragraph (5) in section 1325(a) and added the general paragraph (following subparagraph (5)(C) above) that now appears in the Bankruptcy Code at the end of section 1325(a) (commonly referred to as the "hanging paragraph").

BAPCPA amendments to §1325 (a)(5)(B)(i),

The amended section 1325(a)(5)(B)(i) provides that a secured creditor retains its lien until the earlier of the time of payment in full of its claim as determined under nonbankruptcy law or the time of the granting of the debtor's chapter 13 discharge. The effect of the BAPCPA amendment is to prevent a debtor from paying a creditor's secured claim in the manner provided for in the plan and obtaining a release of the creditor's lien prior to obtaining a chapter 13 discharge. What this means, of course, is that if the debtor is not granted a discharge in the case, the creditor's lien will remain valid and enforceable even if the creditor is paid the full amount provided for under the plan.

§1325 (a)(5)(B)(i), creditor lien retention

Section 1325(a)(5)(B)(iii) provides that a chapter 13 plan must provide for payments to secured creditors in equal monthly payments in amounts that are at least sufficient to provide adequate protection to the secured creditor. This means that each secured creditor who has not either accepted the plan or had its collateral surrendered by the debtor must be paid the full amount of its allowed secured claim in equal monthly installments. This also prevents the confirmation of plans that provide for the beginning of payments to some secured creditors prior to the beginning of payments to other secured creditors. Further, the requirement of adequate protection means that payments to each secured creditor must begin promptly after the filing of the chapter 13 case.

§1325 (a)(5)(B)(iii), creditor adequate protection & payments to

The general paragraph now appearing at the end of section 1325(a) provides that section 506 of the Bankruptcy Code does not apply to the secured claim of a creditor who has a purchase money security interest in a motor vehicle purchased by the debtor for his or her personal use within 910 days prior to bankruptcy or to a creditor who has a purchase money security interest in any other property of value that was purchased by the debtor within one year prior to bankruptcy. Section 506 is the section of the Bankruptcy Code that provides for the bifurcation of partially-secured claims into secured and unsecured portions. This BAPCPA amendment means that creditors with the types of purchase-money security interests described above must be paid the full amounts of their contract claims under the plan regardless of the value of their security and that their claims may not be bifurcated and stripped down under section 506, regardless of whether their claims are protected from modification under section 1322(b)(2). In other words, claims of this type are no longer subject to cramdown under section 1325(a).

In addition to the amendments to section 1325(a) described above, the 2005 BAPCPA added section 1322(a)(4) to the Bankruptcy Code:

1322. Contents of plan

(a) The plan shall –

§1322(a)(4), text of

* * * * * *

(4) notwithstanding any other provision of this section, a plan may provide for less than full payment of all amounts owed for a claim entitled to priority under section 507(a)(1)(B) only if the plan provides that all of the debtor's projected disposable income for a 5 year period beginning on the date that the first payment is due under the plan will be applied to make payments under the plan.

§1322(a)(4), effect of

Section 507(a)(1)(B) of the Bankruptcy Code refers to allowed unsecured priority claims for domestic support obligations that, prior to bankruptcy, were assigned to or owned directly by a governmental unit. This BAPCPA amendment means that priority domestic support obligation claims of governmental units may be paid less than the full amount of their claims under a chapter 13 plan if the plan provides that all of the debtor's projected disposable income for the entire 5 year period of the plan is to be applied to the making of payments under the plan. This, of course, is an exception to the general rule that a chapter 13 plan must provide for payment in full of all priority claims unless the holder of the claim agrees otherwise. It appears that a default in a domestic support obligation claim owed to a governmental unit may now be cured under the amended section 1322(a)(4) to the extent that the debtor is unable, under a 5 year plan, to pay the entire claim.

Section 1322(b)(2), provisions of

Section 1322(b)(2) states that except as otherwise provided in Section 1322(c), a Chapter 13 plan may modify the rights of any secured creditor except a creditor secured only by a security interest in real property that is the debtor's principal residence. In essence then, Section 1322(b)(2) prohibits a Chapter 13 plan from modifying the rights of a creditor who is secured only by a security interest in real property that is the debtor's principal residence, except as otherwise provided in Section 1322(c), which deals with the curing of defaults in the same type of property. See In re Shepherd, 381 B.R. 675 (ED TN, 2008).

Section 1322(b)(3) provides that a Chapter 13 plan may provide for the curing of any default except defaults in obligations that are protected from modification by Section 1322(b)(2). Section 1322(b)(5) deals with the curing of defaults in long-term obligations such as home mortgages. It provides that notwithstanding Section 1322(b)(2), obligations whose payments extend beyond the period of the plan may be cured within a reasonable time and permits the debtor to make contract payments on obligations of this type during the period of the plan. In essence, then, Section 1322(b)(5) permits the curing of defaults on long-term obligations secured only by a security interest in real property that is the debtor's principal residence. This means that defaults in most home mortgage obligations must be cured under Section 1322(b)(5) and not under Section 1322(b)(3).

Section 1322(b)(3), provisions of

Section 1322(b)(5), provisions of

Section 1322(c)(1) provides that defaults with respect to obligations secured by the debtor's principal residence may be cured under a Chapter 13 plan until such time as the residence is sold at a foreclosure sale conducted in accordance with state law. This section was enacted in 1994 to ensure that debtors are permitted to cure and reinstate home mortgages in Chapter 13 cases at least until the time of the foreclosure sale.

Section 1322(c)(1), provisions of

Section 1322(c)(2) provides that if the final payment on an obligation secured only by a security interest in real property that is the debtor's principal residence is due prior to the end of the period of a Chapter 13 plan, the obligation may be modified as long as the creditor receives full payment for the secured portion of its claim. In other words, Section 1322(c)(2) provides that the Section 1322(b)(2) prohibition against modification is not applicable to obligations where the final payment under the original agreement is due either prior to or during the plan period. It should be noted that short-term obligations of this type are not covered by Section 1322(b)(5) and they must therefore be cured under Section 1322(b)(3).

Section 1322(c)(2), provisions of

Section 1322(e) provides that the amount necessary to cure a default shall be determined in accordance with the underlying agreement and state law and not in accordance with bankruptcy law. The purpose of this section, as stated in the Congressional report set forth below in this article, is to eliminate the necessity imposed by the Supreme Court of paying interest on accrued interest and penalties in the curing of defaults.

Section 1322(e), provisions of

The 2005 BAPCPA also added section 1322(f) to the Bankruptcy Code. This section provides as follows:

1322. Contents of plan

* * * * * *

(f) A plan may not materially alter the terms of a loan described in section 362(b)(19) and any amounts required to repay such loan shall not constitute "disposable income" under section 1325.

§1322(f), text of

§1322(f), effect of

Section 362(b)(19) of the Bankruptcy Code, which was also added by 2005 BAPCPA, refers to loans owed by the debtor to pension, profit-sharing, stock bonus and other tax-sheltered employee benefit or retirement plans. Section 1322(f) prevents the alteration or cramdown of claims of this type, which means that defaults in obligations owed to creditors of this type must be cured in the manner provided for under nonbankruptcy law.

curing of defaults, types of obligations

Because of the importance of the provision in Section 1322(b)(2) prohibiting a Chapter 13 plan from modifying the rights of a creditor secured only by a security interest in real property that is the debtor's principal residence, the curing of defaults in secured obligations may be divided into two categories: (1) secured obligations that are protected from modification by Section 1322(b)(2) (which are usually home mortgages), and (2) secured obligations that are not so protected. Substantially different rules are applicable to the curing of defaults in obligations that are protected from modification by Section 1322(b)(2). For that reason it is important to determine initially whether an obligation is protected from modification by Section 1322(b)(2). Accordingly that subject will be discussed first below.

typical obligations protected by Section 1322(b)(2)

Determining whether an obligation is protected from modification by Section 1322(b)(2). The most common type of obligation that is protected from modification by Section 1322(b)(2) is the typical long-term home mortgage. Most home mortgage obligations are secured only by a security interest in real property that is the debtor's principal residence and are therefore protected from modification by Section 1322(b)(2). However, as will be explained in the paragraphs below, some types of home mortgage obligations are not protected from modification by Section 1322(b)(2).

other obligations protected by Section 1322(b)(2)

Secured obligations other than home mortgages may also be entitled to protection from modification by Section 1322(b)(2). In essence, any obligation secured only by a consentual lien on real estate that is the debtor's principal residence and that does not mature prior to the end of the Chapter 13 plan is protected from modification by Section 1322(b)(2). Such obligations as installment contracts for the purchase of real estate and second or third mortgages, including long-term home equity loans, may also be protected from modification by Section 1322(b)(2). See In re Fisher, 289 B.R. 544 (WD NY, 2003); In re Hayes, 101 B.R. 569 (ED AR, 1989); In re Guilbert, 176 B.R. 302 (RI, 1995); In re Johnson, 75 B.R. 927 (ND OH, 1987).

protection by Section 1322(b)(2), requirements

For an obligation to be protected from modification by Section 1322(b)(2), all of the requirements of that provision must be satisfied. This means that the obligation must be secured "only" by a "security interest" in "real property" that is the debtor's "principal residence." If even one of these requirements is not satisfied then the obligation is not protected from modification. Further, to be protected from modification by Section 1322(b)(2), the obligation must not be of a kind specified in Section 1322(c)(2), which means that it must mature after the close of the Chapter 13 plan.

Section 1322(c)(2) provides, in essence, that obligations whose final payment is due prior to the end of the Chapter 13 plan are not protected from modification by Section 1322(b)(2). This means that the rights of creditors secured only by a security interest in real property that is the debtor's principal residence may be modified in a Chapter 13 plan if the obligation matures either prior to or during the period of the plan. In essence, then, only long-term obligations that do not mature until after the close of the Chapter 13 plan are protected from modification by Section 1322(b)(2). Therefore, obligations secured only by the debtor's home that mature prior to the due date of the final payment under the plan are not protected from modification and are subject to cramdown. See In re Eason, 181 B.R. 127 (ND AL, 1995); In re Chang, 185 B.R. 50 (ND IL, 1995); In re Lobue, 189 B.R. 216 (SD FL, 1995); In re Young, 199 B.R. 643 (ED TN, 1996); Magnolia Mort., LLC v. Arnett, 278 B.R. 239 (SD AL, 2002).

Section 1322(c)(2), obligations subject to

Undersecured home mortgage obligations (i.e., obligations where the amount owed by the debtor under the obligation exceeds the value of the creditor's interest in the debtor's home), including junior home mortgage holders, are sometimes protected from modification by Section 1322(b)(2). However, several courts have held that creditors who are completely undersecured (i.e., where the value of the creditor's interest in the collateral is zero) are not entitled to modification protection under Section 1322(b)(2) because they are not secured creditors. This appears to be the majority view. See In re Pelosi, 382 B.R. 582 (MA, 2008); In re Somala, 295 B.R. 380 (NM, 2003); Zimmer v. PSB Lending Corp., 313 F.3d 1220 (9th Cir., 2002); Associates Fin. Servs. Corp. v. Purdue, 187 B.R. 188 (SD OH, 1995); Wright v. Commercial Credit Corp., 178 B.R. 703 (ED VA, 1995); Castellanos v. PNC Bank, N.A., 178 B.R. 393 (MD PA, 1994); Matter of Plouffe, 157 B.R. 198 (CT, 1993). Under this rule, the rights of a junior home mortgage holder may be modified if it is shown that the secured property is fully encumbered by senior liens or mortgages. See In re Vaillancourt, 197 B.R. 464 (MD PA, 1996); In re Sette, 164 B.R. 453 (ED NY, 1994); In re Woodhouse, 172 B.R. 1 (RI, 1994); In re Mitchell, 177 B.R. 900 (ED MO, 1994). However, if a junior creditor's claim is secured even in the slightest amount, modification of the obligation is prohibited. See In re Sullivan, 386 B.R. 355 (ND AL, 2008); In re Baez, 244 B.R. 480 (SD FL, 2000); Gelletich v. Household Realty Corp., 167 B.R. 370 (ED PA, 1994). Some courts prohibit home mortgage modification or lien stripping even if the creditor is completely unsecured. See In re Neverla, 194 B.R. 547 (WD NY, 1996); In re Enriquez, 244 B.R. 156 (SD CA, 2000); In re Barnes, 199 B.R. 256 (WD NY, 1996). These cases represent what appears to be the minority view on the issue.

completely undersecured creditors, status of under Section 1322(b)(2)

creditors with other security, status of under Section 1322(b)(2)

It is clear that a home mortgage obligation may be modified in a Chapter 13 plan if the obligation is not secured "only" by a security interest in real estate that is the debtor's principal residence. Therefore, if the creditor's security includes other real or personal property of the debtor or any property of another person, then modification is permitted. See Hammond v. Commonwealth Mortgage Corp. of Am., 27 F.3d 52 (3d Cir., 1994); In re Pedigo, 283 B.R. 493 (ED TN, 2002). The rights of a home mortgage holder may be modified in a Chapter 13 plan if the obligation in question is, on the bankruptcy filing date, also secured by such property as appliances, furniture, rents, bank accounts, motor vehicles, insurance proceeds or refunds, livestock, or other real property. See, e.g., Sapos v. Provident Instit. of Savings, 967 F.2d 918 (3d Cir., 1992); Johns v. Rousseau Mortgage Corp., 37 F.3d 1021 (3d Cir., 1994); In re Barrett, 188 B.R. 285 (OR, 1995). The additional collateral need not belong to the debtor to be additional security under Section 1322(b)(2). See, e.g., In re Beaudoin 160 B.R. 25 (ND NY, 1993).

creditors with other marginal security, status of under Section 1322(b)(2)

On the other hand, if the additional collateral is insignificant in value, many courts have held it does not constitute additional security for purposes of Section 1322(b)(2). In In re Davis, 989 F.2d 208 (6th Cir., 1993), a security interest in appurtenances, rents, royalties, profits and fixtures of the debtor's home did not constitute additional security for purposes of Section 1322(b)(2). Similarly, in In re Fountain, 197 B.R. 748 (NH, 1996), an assignment of rents granted a mortgagee in a standard mortgage clause that added little or no independent value to the mortgagee's security interest was not additional security for purposes of Section 1322(b)(2). In Brown v. Citicorp. Mortgage, 189 B.R. 3 (ED PA, 1995), a home mortgage that included a security interest in unaccrued rents was protected from modification by Section 1322(b)(2) because such collateral constituted reversionary realty under local law. See also Brown v. Master Finance, Inc., 311 B.R. 282 (MD FL, 2004). In In re Hernandez, 149 B.R. 441 (ED TX, 1993), it was held that a boilerplate mortgage provision assigning profits in oil, gas and mineral rights to the mortgagee did not constitute additional security under Section 1322(b)(2). In Matter of Washington, 967 F.2d 173 (5th Cir., 1992), the creditor's right to receive the proceeds of credit insurance voluntarily purchased by the debtor was not additional security for purposes of Section 1322(b)(2).

creditors with security interest in multiuse property, status of under Section 1322(b)(2)

The Section 1322(b)(2) prohibition against modification has also been held inapplicable to creditors with security interests in property used by the debtor for both residential and commercial purposes. See Litton Loan Servicing, LP v. Beamon, 298 B.R. 508 (ND NY, 2003); Lomas Mortgage v. Louis, 82 F.3d 1 (1st Cir., 1996) (where a creditor with a security interest in a 3 family home, one unit of which was used as a home by the debtor and the others rented out, was not protected from modification by Section 1322(b)(2)). See also In re Scarborough, 461 F.3d 406 (3d Cir., 2006); In re Del Valle, 186 B.R. 347 (CT, 1995) (similar rulings involving a 2 family dwelling in which the debtor resided in one unit and rented the other unit out); In re Moore, 441 B.R. 732 (Bankr. S. D. N.Y. 2010). In these cases Section 1322(b)(2) was not intended to preclude modification when the secured property was not used only as the debtor's residence. See also In re Lafata, 483 F.2d 13 (1st Cir. 2007 (antimodification does not apply when primary residence lies mostly on abutting lot); but see In re Macaluso, 254 B.R. 799 (WD NY, 2000) (protecting a creditor's mortgage from strip down even though the mortgage was secured by a piece of multi-use property which contained a tailor shop and two residential apartments, one of which the debtor resided in).

Note that it is the status of the creditor's security interest on the bankruptcy filing date and not on the date the mortgage was granted that determines the applicability of the Section 1322(b) prohibition against modification. See In re Lebrun, 185 B.R. 665 (MA, 1995). This also means that a creditor may not protect its claim from modification by releasing its security interest in other secured property after the Chapter 13 case has been filed. See Johns v. Rousseau Mortgage Corp., 37 F.3d 1021 (3d Cir., 1994).

status of security interest, when determined

The rule prohibiting modification is also not applicable if the debtor's residence does not constitute real property under local law. See In re Ennis, 558 F.3d 343 (4th Cir. 2009); In re Blevins, 152 B.R. 130 (ND TX, 1992) (where a creditor with a security interest in a mobile home used by the debtor as a residence was found not to be protected from modification by Section 1322(b)(2) because a mobile home did not constitute real property under local law). See also In re Herrin, 376 B.R. 316 (SD AL, 2007); In re Stratton, 248 B.R. 177 (MT, 2000); Nowlin v. Tammac Fin. Corp., 321 B.R. 678 (ED PA, 2005).

security interest in mobile home, status of

Section 1322(b)(2) modification protection is applicable only to creditors with consentual liens. It is not applicable to creditor's secured by statutory or judicial liens because such liens do not constitute security interests under the Bankruptcy Code (i.e. a "security interest" is defined as a lien created by an agreement in 11 U.S.C. § 101(51)). See In re Allard, 196 B.R. 402 (ND IL, 1996); In re Williams, 166 B.R. 615 (ED VA, 1994). A state tax lien is not a "security interest" for purposes of the Section 1322(b)(2) prohibition against modification. See, e.g., Rankin v. De Sarno, 89 F.3d 1123 (3d Cir., 1996).

creditors with judicial or statutory liens, status of

Curing defaults in secured obligations that are protected from modification by Section 1322(b)(2). Section 1322(b)(5) permits the curing of defaults in obligations that are protected from modification by Section 1322(b)(2). However, the Section 1322(b)(5) right to cure is tempered by the Section 1322(b)(2) protection against modification in that the cure must be effected in a manner so as not to modify the rights of the secured creditor. In essence, this means that undersecured obligations that are protected from modification by Section 1322(b)(2) or by the hanging paragraph of Section 1325(a)(5) are not subject to cramdown under Section 1325(a)(5)(B)(ii). This, in turn, means that undersecured claims of creditors protected by Section 1322(b)(2) or by the hanging paragraph of Section 1325(a)(5) may not be bifurcated under 11 U.S.C. § 506(a) and that liens of these creditors may not be "stripped down" under 11 U.S.C. § 506(d).

curing defaults in protected obligations, restrictions

In Nobleman v. American Savings Bank, 508 U.S. 324, 113 S.Ct. 2106 (1993), the Court held that Section 1322(b)(2) precludes a Chapter 13 plan from modifying either the secured or the unsecured portion of an undersecured claim secured only by a security interest in real property that is the debtor's principal residence. The court held that unlike other undersecured claims, an undersecured claim that is protected from modification by Section 1322(b)(2) may not be bifurcated under 11 U.S.C. § 506(a) into secured and unsecured portions for purposes of treatment in a Chapter 13 plan.

Nobleman case, holding of

Nobleman case, rule of, applicability

Before Nobleman most courts had permitted debtors to bifurcate undersecured home mortgage obligations into secured and unsecured claims and essentially pay little or nothing on the unsecured portion of the claim while curing only the secured portion. Most courts essentially held that the Section 1322(b)(2) prohibition against modification did not apply to the unsecured portion of an undersecured claim. Under Nobleman, however, neither the secured nor the unsecured portion of an undersecured obligation that qualifies for protection under Section 1322(b)(2) may be modified in a Chapter 13 plan in a way not permitted by Section 1322(b)(2). This fundamental rule must be adhered to in the curing of defaults in undersecured obligations that are protected from modification by Section 1322(b)(2).

Section 1322(b)(5), provisions of

long-term obligations, non-dischargeability of

Section 1322(b)(5) requires defaults to be cured within a reasonable time, whether or not the obligation is protected from modification under Section 1322(b)(2). Section 1322(b)(5) also permits the maintenance of payments on long-term obligations, such as home mortgage obligations, whose the last payment is due after the end of the plan period. Essentially, then, Section 1322(b)(5) permits a Chapter 13 debtor to maintain the contract payments on a long-term obligation during the period of the plan without acceleration by proposing in the plan to cure the default within a reasonable time. Note that the long-term obligations provided for in Section 1322(b)(5) are not dischargeable under either type of Chapter 13 discharge. See 11 U.S.C. § 1328(a)(1), 1328(c)(1).

acceleration clauses, effect of in cure of default

Most home mortgage obligations contain acceleration clauses whereby the lender can demand full payment of the obligation upon default by the borrower. It often happens that a home mortgage obligation becomes payable in full under an acceleration clause prior to the filing of a Chapter 13 case. It is clear that accelerated home mortgage obligations may be deaccelerated and cured under Section 1322(b)(5) in a timely-filed Chapter 13 case despite the Section 1322(b)(2) prohibition against modification. See In re Tewell, 355 B.R. 674 (ND IL, 2006); In re Soost, 290 B.R. 116 (MN, 2003); In re Taddeo, 685 F.2d 24 (2d Cir., 1982); Grubbs v. Houston First Am. Savings Assoc., 730 F.2d 236 (5th Cir., 1984); In re Glenn, 760 F.2d 1428 (6th Cir., 1985); Matter of Clark, 738 F.2d 869 (7th Cir., 1984). These cases hold that the deacceleration of a home mortgage obligation by permitting a reinstatement of installment payments under Section 1322(b)(5) does not constitute a modification of the creditor's rights under Section 1322(b)(2) as long as the other terms of the obligation are complied with in the curing of the default.

postpetition defaults, curing of

Both prepetition and postpetition defaults may be cured under Section 1322(b)(5). See In re Wilson, 321 B.R. 222 (ND IL, 2005); Green Tree Acceptance v. Hoggle, 12 F.3d 1008 (11th Cir., 1994). Therefore, a debtor who defaults on his or her mortgage payments during the period of the plan may modify the plan under Section 1322(b)(5) so as to cure the postpetition default over the remaining term of the plan. See In re Stafford, 123 B.R. 415 (ND AL, 1991); In re Gadlen, 110 B.R. 341 (WD TN, 1990).

defaults in matured obligations, curing of

However, Section 1322(b)(5) may not be used to cure defaults on obligations that mature, whether by virtue of a balloon payment or otherwise, prior to the end of the plan period. Such obligations must be cured under Section 1322(b)(3). Obligations of this type are also covered by Section 1322(c)(2), which means that they are not protected from modification by Section 1322(b)(2).

Section 1325(a)(5) deals with Chapter 13 plan confirmation requirements with respect to allowed secured claims. It provides that each secured creditor who does not agree otherwise and whose collateral is not returned must retain its lien and be paid an amount, equal to the present value of its allowed secured claim in equal monthly installments. This section is also the Chapter 13 "cramdown" provision whereby the claim of an undersecured creditor may be bifurcated into secured and unsecured portions under 11 U.S.C. § 506(a), with full present value paid only on the secured portion of the claim. However, because of the Supreme Court's ruling in Nobleman v. American Savings Bank, supra, cramdowns may not be implemented on undersecured creditors whose rights are protected from modification by Section 1322(b)(2). Additionally, the hanging paragraph of Section 1325(a)(5) now explicitly prohibits cramdown against holders of purchase money security interests in personal automobiles purchased by the debtor within 910 days prior to bankruptcy or in any other collateral if the debt was incurred within one year of filing. In effect, then, Section 1325(a)(5) requires present value to be paid on the full amount of undersecured obligations that are protected from modification by Section 1322(b)(2) or the Section 1325(a)(5) hanging paragraph.

Section 1325(a)(5), payment requirements for protected obligations

As indicated above, Section 1325(a)(5) requires full payment of present value for secured obligations that are protected from modification by Section 1322(b)(2) or the Section 1325(a)(5) hanging paragraph, regardless of whether the obligation is fully or partially secured. In order to cure a default in a protected long-term secured obligation, such as a home mortgage, that is not being completely paid off during the term of the plan, a Chapter 13 plan must provide for the following in order to meet the present value requirements of Section 1325(a)(5):

curing of defaults in long-term protected obligations, requirements

(1) maintenance of the regular contract payments on the obligation during the life of the plan, either by payments under the plan or outside the plan;
(2) payment of the arrearage caused by the default, either in a lump sum or in installment payments, within a reasonable period under the plan, and
(3) payment of preconfirmation and postconfirmation interest at a prescribed rate on the arrearage until it is paid off.

It is clear that Section 1322(b)(5) permits a Chapter 13 debtor to cure defaults in long-term home mortgage obligations that are protected from modification by Section 1322(b)(2) by reinstating the obligation and providing for the making of the contract payments to the creditor, either under the plan or outside plan, and curing the default under the plan in a manner that satisfies the present value requirements of Section 1325(a)(5). See In re Callahan, 158 B.R. 898 (WD NY, 1993); Rake v. Wade, 508 U.S. 464, 113 S.Ct. 2187 (1993). If a long-term obligation that is protected from modification by Section 1322(b)(2) is not cured in this manner, the present value of the entire balance of the obligation must be paid off during the period of the plan, regardless of the length of the original obligation. See In re Murphy, 175 B.R. 134 (MA, 1994).

curing defaults in home mortgages, requirements

payment of long-term mortgage installments outside of plan, when permitted

Note that several courts have held that reinstated long-term regular mortgage payments must be made under the plan and not outside the plan. See In re Foster, 670 F.2d 478 (5th Cir., 1982); In re Tartaglia, 61 B.R. 439 (RI, 1986); In re Weber, 114 B.R. 194 (NE, 1988). However, this practice is usually beneficial only to the trustee, who receives a percentage fee based on the payments. Such a practice is detrimental to both the debtor, who must pay a trustee's fee on what is essentially a nonadjusted but substantial debt, and the creditor, whose payment is typically delayed by this procedure. The result is that many courts now permit such payments to be made by the debtor outside the plan. See U.S. v. Donald, 170 B.R. 579 (SD MS, 1994); In re Delauder, 189 B.R. 639 (ED VA, 1995).

reasonable time for curing defaults, how determined

Section 1322(b)(5) also requires defaults in long-term obligations to be cured within a reasonable time. What constitutes a reasonable time for the curing of defaults in long-term obligations under Section 1322(b)(5) depends on the facts and circumstances of the case. See In re Martin, 156 B.R. 47 (B.A.P. 9th Cir., 1993). Such factors as the amount that the debtor can reasonably afford to pay, the amount of the arrearage, and the terms of the obligation are normally considered. See In re Randolph, 102 B.R. 902 (SD GA, 1989), and In re King, 23 B.R. 779 (B.A.P. 9th Cir., 1982). However, generally the cure must be completed within the plan period. See Sapos v. Provident Inst. of Savings, 967 F.2d 918 (3d Cir., 1992).

reasonable time for curing defaults, what constitutes

In In re Newton, 161 B.R. 207 (MN, 1993), the court held that 12 months was presumptively a reasonable period under Section 1322(b)(5). However, other courts have approved cure periods of up to 5 years. See Messenger v. Messenger, 331 B.R. 733 (ND OH, 2005); In re Masterson, 147 B.R. 295 (NH, 1992) (56 months approved as reasonable time); In re Harmon, 72 B.R. 458 (ED PA, 1987) (60 months approved as reasonable time); In re Randolph, 102 B.R. 902 (SD GA, 1989) (24 month period beginning 11 months after confirmation held reasonable and arbitrary 20 month limit held inappropriate); In re Chavez, 117 B.R. 733 (SD FL, 1990) (36 to 60 months may be approved as reasonable period); In re Capps, 836 F.2d 773 (3d Cir., 1987) (60 months approved as reasonable time). In PNC Mortgage Co. v. Dicks, 199 B.R. 674 (ND IN, 1996), the court held that the debtor could cure defaults by adding the arrearages to the remaining principal balance of the obligation for repayment over the 25 year term of the obligation.

curing defaults, interest rate on arrearage

As indicated above, interest must be paid on arrearage claims that result from the curing of defaults by the debtor on long-term obligations. Section 1322(e) provides that "the amount necessary to cure the default shall be determined in accordance with the underlying agreement and applicable nonbankruptcy law." Under Section 1322(e), then, the interest rates that are applied to arrearage claims must be determined from the underlying security agreement and applicable nonbankruptcy law. See In re Koster, 294 B.R. 737 (ED MO, 2003); In re Young, 310 B.R. 127 (ED WI, 2003); In re Trabal, 254 B.R. 99 (NJ, 2000) (stating the language in the mortgage agreement which identifies items to be considered part of the mortgage debt and specifies an interest rate should suffice to satisfy the requirements of Section 1322(e)).

What if the underlying agreement calls for the payment of attorneys' fees or other penalties in the event of a default under the agreement? Should these items be included determining the amount of the arrearage claim? In In re Lake, 245 B.R. 282 (ND OH, 2000), the court held that since there is nothing in Section 1322(e) to suggest that default charges should be limited to interest charges, attorneys' fees could be included in determining the amount necessary to cure the default if their inclusion is provided for in the security agreement and is not prohibited by state law. The court then found that under the facts of the case the inclusion of attorneys' fees in the arrearage claim was prohibited by state law and it therefore refused to include them. The general rule is to allow attorneys' fees in cure amounts. See In re Gagne, 378 B.R. 439 (NH, 2007). See also In re Hatala, 295 B.R. 62 (NJ, 2003) (capping the attorneys' fees recoverable by a creditor under Section 1322(c) to the amount allowed by the New Jersey Court Rules).

inclusion of attorney's fees in cure amount

An obviously important aspect of curing defaults in any type of secured obligation, including those protected from modification by Section 1322(b)(2), is that of determining whether the default in the obligation can legally be cured under a Chapter 13 plan. The issue usually is whether it is too late in the default process to cure the default. This issue is dealt with in Section 1322(c), which was enacted by Congress in the Bankruptcy Reform Act of 1994. Section 1322(c)(1) deals with home mortgage foreclosures and permits the curing of defaults in obligations secured by the debtor's residence until the residence is sold at a foreclosure sale conducted in accordance with state law. Section 1322(c)(2) deals with obligations protected from modification by Section 1322(b)(2) that mature during the period of the Chapter 13 plan or that have matured prior to the filing of the case. This section provides that if such an obligation becomes due prior to the end of the Chapter 13 plan, the plan may provide for the payment of the obligation under the plan in the manner provided under Section 1325(a)(5). In essence, then, obligations of this type are not protected from modification by Section 1322(b)(2) and are subject to cramdown under Section 1325(a)(5)(B)(ii).

curing of default, when permissible

Section 1322(c)(1), provisions of

Section 1322(c)(2), provisions of

curing of defaults after foreclosure sale, when permitted

Under Section 1322(c)(1) defaults can clearly be cured on covered obligations at least until the time of the foreclosure sale. Further, if, under local law, a default can be cured after that date, several courts have construed Section 1322(c)(1) so as to permit the curing of defaults after the foreclosure sale. See In re Rambo, 196 B.R. 181 (WD OK, 1996); In re Chang, 185 B.R. 50 (ND IL, 1995); In re Brown, 282 B.R. 880 (ED AR, 2002) (holding that under state law a judicial foreclosure sale was complete upon confirmation of the sale by the court, and that since the debtor had filed his bankruptcy petition on the day before the entry of the sale confirmation order, under Section 1322(c)(1) the debtor was not precluded from curing the default in a Chapter 13 plan). See also In re Spencer, 263 B.R. 227 (ND IL, 2001); In re Pellegrino, 284 B.R. 326 (CT, 2002). In In re Smith, 85 F.3d 1555 (11th Cir., 1996), the debtor was permitted to cure a default after the foreclosure sale but was not permitted to reinstate the obligation and was required to pay the obligation off in a lump sum within one year of foreclosure as required under Alabama law.

curing of default after foreclosure sale, when not permitted

However, in In re Mangano, 253 B.R. 339 (NJ, 2000), the court held that the phrase "sold at foreclosure sale" in Section 1322(c)(1) refers to the auction itself and that the debtor has no right thereafter to cure the default. In In re Bobo, 246 B.R. 453 (DC, 2000), the court held that under local law the foreclosure was complete "when the gavel falls" at the auction and therefore the default could not thereafter be cured. See also In re Townsville, 268 B.R. 95 (ED PA, 2001). See also Colon v. Option One Mortg. Corp., 319 F.3d 912 (7th Cir., 2003).

curing defaults in obligations, requirement of liability by debtor

A somewhat related question is under what circumstances, other than the lapse of too much time after default, is a Chapter 13 debtor precluded from curing a default in an obligation. First of all, the debtor must have standing or the legal right to cure the breach. That is, the breach sought to be cured must be that of the debtor or of someone in privity with the debtor so that a debtor-creditor relationship exists between the debtor and the creditor. In In re Threats, 159 B.R. 241 (ND IL, 1993), the court held that a Chapter 13 debtor who had purchased his home via a quitclaim deed in violation of a due-on-sale clause in the mortgage agreement secured by the property and who had not assumed the mortgage obligation and was therefore not personally liable and could not reinstate and cure defaults in the obligation because a debtor and creditor relationship did not exist between the parties. The court stated that while the Bankruptcy Code allows debtors to regain certain previously held property interests, it does not allow them to create new interests.

curing defaults in obligations for which debtor is not liable, when not permitted

In In re Martin, 176 B.R. 675 (CT, 1995), the debtor, as an unrelated, unauthorized transferee of mortgaged property, was not permitted to waive or cure a default arising from a due-on-sale clause in the mortgage contract. In In re Jones, 98 B.R. 757 (ND OH, 1989), the debtor was not permitted to cure a default in a mortgage obligation where the debtor had entered into an installment land contract with the mortgagee, had not assumed the mortgage, and had made no payments on the mortgage. In Washington v. GMAC, 137 B.R. 748 (ED AR, 1992), the debtor could not cure defaults in a motor vehicle purchase contract where the debtor's father had purchased the vehicle and obtained the financing only in his name.

However, if the default is that of the debtor or someone in privity with the debtor, then the default may be cured even if the debtor is not personally liable for the underlying obligation. In Johnson v. Home State Bank, 501 U.S. 78, 111 S.Ct. 2150 (1991), the Supreme Court held that a debtor who had previously discharged his personal liability to the mortgagee in a Chapter 7 case could still cure defaults in the mortgage obligation in a subsequent Chapter 13 case because the mortgagee still had a "claim" against the debtor's property that could be dealt with in a Chapter 13 plan. Other cases permitting debtors to cure defaults in obligations for which they had no personal liability include Downey S & L Assn. v. Metz, 820 F.2d 1495 (9th Cir., 1987); In re Saylors, 869 F.2d 1434 (11th Cir., 1989); In re Lumpkin, 144 B.R. 240 (CT, 1992) (permitting the debtor to cure defaults on a mortgage loan obtained by the debtor's mother, who later conveyed the property to the debtor, because the due-on-sale clause in the mortgage agreement was unenforceable). In In re Everhart, 87 B.R. 35 (ND OH, 1988), the mortgagee was held to be estopped from objecting to the cure of the mortgage obligation by the debtor, who was an unapproved transferee of the mortgaged property, because the mortgagee had accepted payments from the debtor and had issued the debtor a coupon book for making the mortgage payments.

curing defaults in obligations for which debtor is not liable, when permitted

Curing defaults in secured obligations that are not protected from modification by Section 1322(b)(2) or are not protected by Section 1325(a)(5) (hanging paragraph). Secured obligations that are not protected from modification by Section 1322(b)(2) are also not protected from cramdown under Section 1325(a)(5)(B). This means that undersecured obligations of this type are subject to cramdown under Section 1325(a)(5) and may be bifurcated under 11 U.S.C. § 506(a) into secured and unsecured portions and treated accordingly under the plan. Many courts have also held that liens securing unprotected obligations of this type may be "stripped down" under 11 U.S.C. § 506(d) to the amount of the allowed secured claim. Neither of these remedies are available against creditors whose rights are protected from modification by Section 1322(b)(2) or are otherwise protected by Section 1325(a)(9) (hanging paragraph). For the unfamiliar, the Chapter 13 cramdown procedures are described below in this article.

unprotected obligations, debtor's remedies against in plan

In the discussion below an "unprotected obligation" is a secured obligation that is not protected from modification by Section 1322(b)(2) or by Section 1325(a)(9) (hanging paragraph). In other words, an unprotected obligation is an obligation other than one that is secured by a security interest in real property that is the debtor's principal residence or a debt where the creditor has a purchase money security interest in the debtor's personal automobile that was obtained within 910 days of filing of the petition. In the discussion below a "long-term obligation" is an installment obligation that matures after the due date of the last payment under the debtor's Chapter 13 plan, while a "short-term obligation" is an obligation that matures prior to the due date of the last payment under the plan. The terms "unprotected obligation," "long-term obligation," and "short-term obligation" are used repeatedly in the discussion below.

unprotected obligation, what constitutes

long-term obligation, what constitutes

short-term obligation, what constitutes

unprotected obligations, categories of

For purposes of curing defaults, unprotected obligations may be divided into four categories: (1) long-term, fully-secured obligations, (2) long-term undersecured obligations, (3) short-term, fully secured obligations, and (4) short-term, undersecured obligations. The curing of defaults in each category of unprotected obligations is discussed separately below. It should be noted that while long-term obligations may be either protected or unprotected, all short-term obligations are unprotected because of Section 1322(c)(2).

unprotected obligations, types of

As indicated above, unprotected obligations are obligations which for any reason are excluded from protection under Section 1322(b) or Section 1325(a)(5) (hanging paragraph). Included are all obligations not secured by the debtor's residence and obligations secured by a PMSI in the debtor's car obtained within 2 ½ years of filing bankruptcy or by the debtor's residence that are excluded from Section 1322(b) protection for any of the reasons discussed above in this article (e.g., short-term obligations excluded by Section 1322(c)(2), obligations not secured "only" by the debtor's residence, obligations not secured by a "security interest" in the debtor's residence, and obligations secured by the debtor's residence that are completely undersecured). The curing of defaults in secured obligations of this type, whether long-term or short, is discussed under this heading.

defaults in unprotected obligations, curing of, applicable Code sections

Defaults in unprotected obligations may be cured under either Section 1322(b)(3) or Section 1322(b)(5), depending on the type of obligation. Defaults in long-term unprotected obligations which the debtor wishes to reinstate and cure must be cured under Section 1322(b)(5). Defaults in all other protected obligations must be cured under Section 1322(b)(3), which is applicable to unprotected obligations of any type, secured or unsecured, long-term or short. Short-term obligations secured only by a security interest in real property that is the debtor's principal residence may be cured under Section 1322(c)(2) as well as Section 1322(b)(3). Regardless of which section the defaults are cured under, however, the proposed cure must always satisfy the confirmation requirements of Section 1325(a)(5).

defaults in fully-secured long-term unprotected obligations, methods of curing

Defaults in fully-secured, long-term, unprotected obligations must be cured in essentially the same manner as defaults in protected obligations. This means that unprotected obligations of this type must be reinstated under Section 1322(b)(5) and the contract payments made, either under the plan or outside the plan, and the present value of the arrearage claim must be paid under the plan within a reasonable time. Under Section 1322(e), the interest paid on the arrearage claims must be determined in accordance with the underlying agreement and applicable nonbankruptcy law. However, if the obligation is oversecured and was entered into prior to the October 22, 1994 effective date of Section 1322(e), the interest paid on the arrearage claim must be determined in accordance with Rake v. Wade, supra.

Section 1322(b)(5) also permits the curing of defaults in long-term, unprotected obligations that are undersecured. See In re Smith, 179 B.R. 437 (ED PA, 1995). The curing of defaults in undersecured obligations of this type differs from the curing of defaults in fully-secured obligations of this type in that they are subject to cramdown under Section 1325(a)(5)(B). The Chapter 13 cramdown requirements and procedures are described below in this article.

undersecured long-term unprotected obligations, subject to cramdown

In curing defaults in long-term unprotected obligations, Section 1322(b)(5) requires that the arrearage claims be paid within a reasonable time and permits maintenance of the contract payments on the obligation by the debtor during the period of the plan. For obligations of this type that are undersecured, however, Section 1322(b)(5) permits maintenance of payments at the contract rate on only the secured portion of the original obligation. These payments must be continued only until such time as the secured portion of the original obligation is paid in full at the contract interest rate. See Brown v. Shorewood Fin., 175 B.R. 129 (MA, 1994); Homeowners Funding Co. v. Skinner, 129 B.R. 60 (ED NC, 1991). See also In re Koper, 284 B.R. 747 (CT, 2002) (holding that secured portion of a bifurcated undersecured claim must be paid off by the debtor during the plan period).

long-term undersecured unprotected obligations, cramdown requirements

The curing of defaults in long-term, undersecured, unprotected obligations requires three types of payments to be made by the debtor: (1) payment of the present value of the full amount of the arrearage claim under the plan; (2) maintenance of the installment payments in the contract amount until the secured portion of the original obligation is paid in full, either under the plan or outside the plan as may be required; and (3) payment of the unsecured portion of the original obligation under the plan as an unsecured, nonpriority claim in an amount that is not less than the amount that would be paid on the claim in a Chapter 7 liquidation of the debtor's estate. See In re Cruz, 152 B.R. 866 (SD NY, 1993); In re Murphy, 175 B.R. 134 (MA, 1994). If a long-term, undersecured, unprotected obligation is not cured in this manner, the present value of the full amount of the secured portion of the bifurcated claim must be paid by the debtor during the plan period. See Brown v. Shorewood Fin., 175 B.R. 129 (MA, 1994).

cramdowns of long-term undersecured unprotected obligations, payment requirements

Short-term secured obligations must be cured under Section 1322(b)(3), which means that reinstatement of the obligation is not permitted. Note that because of Section 1322(c)(2), all short-term secured obligations are unprotected and must be paid in the manner provided in Section 1325(a). This means that all short-term undersecured obligations are subject to cramdown under Section 1325(a)(5)(B) and that present value must be paid on the full amount of all fully-secured short-term obligations.

short-term obligations, payment requirements

As indicated above, in this discussion a short-term obligation is defined as an obligation whose last payment is due before the due date of the final payment under the debtor's plan. This definition is based on the provisions of Sections 1322(b)(5) and 1322(c)(2), which are geared not on the original term of an obligation, but on its maturity date. Under this definition, then, a 30 year obligation would be a short-term obligation if the obligation matures by its terms prior to the end of the debtor's plan.

short-term obligation, what constitutes

Section 1322(c)(2), effect on short-term obligations

It is clear that Section 1322(c)(2) permits a Chapter 13 plan to modify the rights of holders of obligations that mature prior to the end of the plan period, even if the obligation is secured only by a security interest in real property that is the debtor's principal residence. See In re Sturgill, 337 B.R. 599 (WD KY, 2006); In re Eason, 181 B.R. 127 (ND AL, 1995); In re Chang, 185 B.R. 50 (ND IL, 1995), In re Lobue, 189 B.R. 216 (SD FL, 1995); In re Young, 199 B.R. 643 (ED TN, 1996). Home mortgage obligations that mature during or prior to the plan period may be treated like any other short-term obligations. It should be noted that if a default is cured under Section 1322(c)(2), the cure payments must be completed within the period of the plan. See In re Javarone, 181 B.R. 151 (ND NY, 1995).

cramdown, origin of name

In the curing of defaults in short-term secured obligations, it is important to understand the procedures and requirements of cramdowns in Chapter 13 cases. The procedure described below is known as a "cramdown" because under Section 1325(a)(5)(B) it can be forced upon a secured creditor without the creditor's consent. See In re Laguna, 944 F.2d 542 (9th Cir., 1991).

Chapter 13 cramdown, requirements of

A Chapter 13 "cramdown" is a procedure whereby the debtor retains property in which a creditor has a security interest even if the creditor would prefer to repossess and liquidate the property and would have the right to do so in the absence of bankruptcy. In exchange for allowing the debtor to retain possession of the secured property, Section 1325(a)(5)(B) requires three things: (1) the secured creditor must retain its lien on the property, consistent with Section 1325(a)(5)(B)(I)(aa) or (bb); (2) the secured creditor must be paid a value which, as of the effective date of the plan, is not less than the amount of its allowed secured claim; and (3) payments are in equal monthly installments. This is the so-called "present value" requirement of Section 1325(a)(5).

allowed secured claim, amount of in cramdown

The amount of a creditor's allowed secured claim for purposes of Section 1325(a)(5)(B) is limited by the value of its collateral. If the creditor is undersecured, its claim may be bifurcated under 11 U.S.C. § 506(a) and divided into secured and unsecured portions. The secured portion of its claim is equal to the value, as determined by the court as of the effective date of the plan, of its interest in the secured property. This value constitutes the amount of its allowed secured claim for purposes of payment under Section 1325(a)(5). The balance of its claim (i.e., the unsecured portion) is treated as a nonpriority unsecured claim under Section 1325(a)(4). See generally, General Motors Acceptance Corp. v. Jones, 999 F.2d 63 (3d Cir., 1993).

present value of secured claim, what constitutes

In determining the "present value" of a secured claim for purposes of Section 1325(a)(5), the object is to put the secured creditor in the same financial position it would have been in had it been allowed to repossess and liquidate its collateral outside of bankruptcy. Therefore, if the debtor is unable to pay the secured claim in a lump sum and must pay the claim in installments under the plan, the secured creditor must be compensated for the delay in receiving its funds by the payment of interest on the claim. In essence, the amount of the debtor's installment payments is the amount which, if capitalized using the appropriate rate of interest over the period of the payments, will exactly equal the amount of the creditor's allowed secured claim.

As indicated above, interest must be paid on the secured portion of cramdown claims. It should be understood that "cramdown interest" is often calculated differently by the courts than "cure interest." This is because cure interest must be determined in accordance with Section 1322(e), which is not applicable to cramdown interest. Therefore, in determining cramdown interest the court is not required to determine the interest rate from the underlying agreement and applicable nonbankruptcy law. For example, in Household Auto. Fin. Corp. v. Burden, 315 F.3d 671 (6th Cir., 2003), the court held that for purposes of Section 1325(a)(5)(B), the proper interest rate to be applied in a Chapter 13 cramdown is the current conventional market rate used for similar loans in the region and not necessarily the contract rate. In In re Till, 301 F.3d 583 (7th Cir., 2002), the court held that the cramdown interest rate should be the rate the creditor could have obtained had it foreclosed and reinvested the proceeds in loans of equivalent duration and risk. This is commonly referred to as the "Till doctrine". See also In re Pledger, 275 B.R. 394 (ND AL, 2002); In re Senior, 255 B.R. 794 (MD FL, 2000); In re Gorham, 247 B.R. 272 (WD MO, 2000) In re Walkabout Creek Ltd. Dividend Housing Assoc. Ltd. Partnerhsip, 460 B.R. 567 (Bankr. D.C. 2011). As indicated above, different courts apply different theories in determining the interest rate to be paid on cramdown claims.

secured portion of cramdown claims, interest rate

The hanging paragraph of Section 1325(a)(5) created a new kind of debt under the code. It is commonly referred to as "910" debts, because of the time frame before filing bankruptcy within which a vehicle purchased with purchase money financing is protected from cramdown. Courts are split as to the exact treatment to give 910 debt in a chapter 13 plan. The majority of courts have held that 910 debts are to be treated as allowed secured claims and afforded the present value requirement under §1325(a)(5)(B)(ii). See In re Brown, 339 B.R. 818 (SD GA, 2006); In re Vega, 344 B.R. 616 (KS, 2006); In re Soards, 344 B.R. 829 (WD KY, 2006); In re Bufford, 343 B.R. 827 (ND TX, 2006); In re Brooks, 344 B.R. 417 (ED NC, 2006); In re Scruggs, 342 B.R. 571 (ED AR, 2006); In re Montgomery, 341 B.R. 843 (ED KY, 2006); In re Shaw, 341 B.R. 543 (MD NC, 2006); In re DeSardi, 340 B.R. 790 (SD TX, 2006); In re Montoya, 341 B.R. 41 (UT, 2006); In re Brown, 339 B.R. 818 (SD GA, 2006). Other courts have held that because the language of the hanging paragraph in section 1325(a)(5), providing that section 506, which ordinarily determines the secured status of a claim, does not apply to a PMSI debt falling within that paragraph, and therefore §506 does not apply. See In re Carver, 338 B.R. 521 (SD GA, 2006); In re Taranto, 344 B.R. 857 (ND OH, 2006); In re Wampler, 345 B.R. 730 (KS, 2006).

910 debts, secured status

After passage of the BAPCPA, the majority of courts still hold that interest on 910 debts should be calculated under the In re Till doctrine instead of paying interest at the contract rate when determining present value. See In re Lilly, 378 B.R. 232 (CD IL, 2007); In re Pryor 341 B.R. 648 (CD IL, 2006); In re DeSardi, 340 B.R. 790 (MD TX, 2006); In re Brown, 339 B.R. 822 (SD GA, 2006); In re Fleming, 339 B.R. 716 (ED MO, 2006); In re Wright, 338 B.R. 917 (MD AL, 2006); In re Robinson, 338 B.R. 70 (WD MO, 2006); In re Johnson, 337 B.R. 269 (MD NC, 2006) and In re Bufford, 343 B.R. 827 (ND TX, 2006). For cases holding that the Till doctrine is applicable, despite a lower contract interest rate than Till provides, see In re Pryor, 341 B.R. 648 (CD IL, 2006) and In re Soards, 344 B.R. 829 (WD KY, 2006).

910 debts, interest

910 debts, surrender of collateral

The new type of 910 debt also affects the situation where a debtor wishes to relinquish the collateral securing a 910 debt under the debtor's chapter 13 plan. How is this situation treated under the post-BAPCPA code? In In re Brown, 346 B.R. 868 (ND FL, 2006) a debtor proposed to surrender debtor's 910 motor vehicle subject to a PMSI in full satisfaction of the undersecured debt. The 910 creditor objected, arguing that it should also be entitled to unsecured creditor status for the balance of the claim above the value of the automobile. The court first held that despite language in the §1325(a) hanging paragraph, Code §506 does not apply to a PMSI debt, the debt is still a secured debt. The court then held that the hanging paragraph allows the debtor to surrender his vehicle in full satisfaction of the creditor's claim. This appears to be the majority view. See also In re Payne, 347 B.R. 278 (SD OH, 2006); In re Brown, 346 B.R. 868 (ND FL, 2006); In re Sparks, 346 B.R. 767 (SD OH, 2006); In re Ezell, 338 B.R. 330 (ED TN, 2006); In re Womble, 59 CBC 2d 674 (ED TN, 2008).

short-term fully secured claims, payment requirements

Defaults in short-term fully-secured obligations must be cured by providing in the plan the payment of the present value of the full amount of the secured claim, including the amount of any arrearage caused by the default, during the term of the plan.

types of defaults subject to cure

Note that defaults in short-term obligations other than payment defaults may be cured or waived in a Chapter 13 plan under Section 1322(b)(3). Defaults that trigger acceleration clauses or that occur by reason of due-on-sale clause violations, insurance-requirement clause violations, or violations of other contract requirements may be cured or waived under Section 1322(b)(3) in a Chapter 13 plan. See In re Bellinger, 179 B.R. 220 (ID, 1995); In re Lumpkin, 144 B.R. 240 (CT, 1992).

types of obligations subject to cure

Defaults in obligations other than loan or mortgage obligations may also be cured or waived under Section 1322(b)(3). For example, In re Dunlap, 143 B.R. 859 (MD TN, 1992), the debtor was permitted to cure a default in a pawn transaction as long as the property had not been sold by the pawnbroker, even though the redemption period under state law had expired. Defaults in installment land contracts may also be cured. See In re Hayes, 101 B.R. 569 (ED AR, 1989). In In re Brown, 82 B.R. 68 (WD AR, 1987), the debtor was permitted to cure defaults in a TV rental agreement (which was found to be a conditional sales contract) and in a cramdown force the creditor to accept payment of fair market value for the TV. However, In In re Unger, 95 B.R. 761 (Bankr. D. Or., 1989), a "rent-to-own" agreement was found to be a lease rather than a security agreement and therefore not subject to cure under Section 1322(b)(3). It should be noted that these cases were decided prior to the BAPCPA amendments to Section 1325(a)(5). After the BAPCPA amendments, these transactions would be protected from cramdown if they took place within one year prior to the debtor filing bankruptcy. Executory contracts and unexpired leases must be dealt with under Section 1322(b)(7) and 11 U.S.C. § 365.

lien stripping, importance of in Chapter 13 cases

When an undersecured, unprotected obligation is bifurcated and paid under a cramdown, it is important that the lien securing the obligation also be reduced, or "stripped down," to the amount of the allowed secured claim (i.e., to the amount of the secured portion of the original obligation). Otherwise, the unpaid portion of the lien will survive the bankruptcy and be enforceable by the creditor after the case to the extent permitted under local law even if the property is exempt. See 11 U.S.C. § 522(c)(2); Owen v. Owen, 500 U.S. 305, 308-309, 111 S.Ct. 1833 (1991).

11 U.S.C. § 506(d) provides that a lien is void to the extent that it secures a claim that is not an allowed secured claim. Under this provision a lien securing an undersecured claim could be reduced or "stripped down" to the amount of the allowed secured claim. However, in Dewsnup v. Timm, 502 U.S. 410, 112 S.Ct. 773 (1992), a Chapter 7 case that the lien of an undersecured creditor could not be "stripped down" under 11 U.S.C. § 506(d) to the amount of its allowed secured claim (i.e., to the amount of the value of its collateral) unless the claim was disallowed for other reasons. This means that in Chapter 7 cases, at least, the full unpaid amount of an unsecured creditor's lien survives the bankruptcy case and may be enforced after the case to the full extent permitted under local law even though the underlying claim is discharged. The question is whether Dewsnup v. Timm is applicable to Chapter 13 cases.

lien stripping, Dewsnup v. Timm, holding of

In Dewsnup v. Timm the Supreme Court expressly declined to rule on whether its holding applied to cases under other Chapters of the Bankruptcy Code. See 502 U.S. 410, 417. In Wade v. Bradford, 39 F.3d 1126 (10th Cir., 1994), the court limited Dewsnup v. Timm to its facts and did not prevent lien stripping under 11 U.S.C. § 506(d) in a Chapter 11 case. A legion of cases have held that because of the catastrophic effect on Chapter 13 plans of not permitting lien stripping under 11 U.S.C. § 506(d), Dewsnup v. Timm is not applicable to Chapter 13 cases. See also In re Pond, 252 F.3d 122 (2d Cir., 2001); Sapos v. Provident Instit. of Savings, 967 F.2d 918 (3d Cir., 1992); In re Lee, 162 B.R. 217 (MN, 1993); In re Hernandez, 175 B.R. 962 (ND IL, 1994); In re Hendrix, 179 B.R. 519, (ED KY, 1994); In re Butler, 139 B.R. 258 (ED OK, 1992); In re Young, 199 B.R. 643 (ED TN, 1996). Therefore, in most districts, if not all, a Chapter 13 debtor may, subject to the restrictions contained in Section 1325(a)(5) (hanging paragraph), include a provision in his or her plan avoiding the lien of an undersecured creditor upon completion of payments under the plan. See In re Castro, 285 B.R. 703 (AZ, 2002). Of course, if the payments under the plan are not completed, then the lien will not be avoided and the unpaid portion of the lien will survive the case, even if the debtor is granted a discharge under Section 1328(b). See In re Smith, 287 B.R. 882 (WD TX, 2002).

lien stripping in Chapter 13 cases, permissibility of

It is clear that liens securing fully secured obligations may not be stripped down under 11 U.S.C. § 506(d) because the entire obligation is an allowed secured claim for purposes of 11 U.S.C. § 506(d), unless the claim is not allowable for other reasons. It is also clear that undersecured, protected obligations may not be stripped down under 11 U.S.C. § 506(d), unless the claim is not allowable for other reasons. See Nobleman v. American Savings Bank, 508 U.S. 324, 113 S.Ct. 2106 (1993). However, because the full amount of the creditor's claim must be paid with respect to both fully-secured and protected obligations, the creditor's lien will be reduced to zero if all payments required by the plan are made by the debtor. Also, because no portion of a protected obligation is dischargeable under Chapter 13, whether or not the lien survives the case is not usually important. See 11 U.S.C. § 1328(a)(1), 1328(c)(1).

protected or fully secured obligations, necessity of lien stripping

Bibliography. **For further reading on the issues discussed in this article, see the annotations and articles listed below.**

Annotations:

Prohibition against modification in Chapter 13 bankruptcy proceeding as limited to long-term residential purchase-money mortgage. 110 ALR Fed 175.

Modification, in Chapter 13 proceeding, of undersecured portion of creditor's claim secured by debtor's principal residence under 11 USC §§506(a), 1322(b)(2). 104 ALR Fed 699.

Bankruptcy: Chapter 13 plan delaying payment of unaccelerated matured residential debt as improper modification of creditor's rights under 11 USC §1322(b)(2). 91 ALR Fed 512.

Determining amount of payments to secured creditor who is to receive, in installments, present value of property under Chapter 13 cram-down provision of Bankruptcy Code of 1978, 68 ALR Fed 537.

Right of debtor to deacceleration of residential mortgage indebtedness under Chapter 13 of Bankruptcy Code of 1978. 67 ALR Fed 217.

Reasonableness of Chapter 13 plan, under 1978 Bankruptcy Code, in terms of length of time proposed for cure of prepetition default in payments to creditor, 63 ALR Fed 309.

Effect of "Hanging" or "Anti-Cramdown" Paragraph Added to 11 U.S.C.A. § 1325(a) by Bankruptcy Abuse Prevention and Consumer Protection Act (BAPCPA). 19 ALR Fed 2d 157

Articles:

The 1994 Amendments to the Bankruptcy Code: Two Consumer Bankruptcy Issues From a Texas Creditor's Perspective. 59 Tex. B.J. 322 (April, 1996).

Bifurcation of undersecured claims in bankruptcy. 70 Am. Bankruptcy L.J. 1, Winter 1996.

Lien Stripping After Nobelman v. American Savings Bank: What Is "Additional Collateral". 32 Hous. L. Rev. 201 (Summer, 1995).

Entitlement to interest under the Bankruptcy Code. 12 Bankruptcy Dev. J. 149, 1995.

The death of the mortgage "cramdown" in Chapter 13: Nobleman v. American Savings Bank. 14 J. Law & Comm. 141, Fall 1994.

Nobleman v. American Savings Bank: bankruptcy, bifurcation, and residential mortgages - lender beware. 47 Ark. L. Rev. 907, 1994.

The Treatment of residential mortgages in Chapter 13 after Nobleman. 2 Am. Bankruptcy Instit. L. Rev. 147, Spring 1994.

The bifurcation of undersecured residential mortgages under §1322(b)(2) of the Bankruptcy Code: the final resolution. 67 Am Bankr L.J. 207, Spring, 1993.

3.02 To what extent may unsecured claims be treated unequally in a Chapter 13 plan?

Text of statutes. Sections 1322(a)(3), 1322(b)(1), 1322(b)(10), 1325(a)(4) and 1122 of the Bankruptcy Code (11 U.S.C. § 1322(a)(3), (b)(2), (b)(10), 1325(a)(4), 1122) are applicable to the subject discussed in this article. They provide as follows:

1322. Contents of plan

Section 1322(a)(3), text of

(a) The plan shall -

. . . .

(3) if the plan classifies claims, shall provide the same treatment for each claim within a particular class; and ...

Section 1322(b)(1), text of

(b) Subject to subsections (a) and (c) of this section, the plan may -

(1) designate a class or classes of unsecured claims, as provided in section 1122 of this title, but may not discriminate unfairly against any class so designated; however, such plan may treat claims for a consumer debt of the debtor if an individual is liable on such consumer debt with the debtor differently than other unsecured claims;

* * * * * *

Section 1322(b)(10), text of

(10) provide for the payment of interest accruing after the date of the filing of the petition on unsecured claims that are nondischargeable under section 1328(a), except that such interest may be paid only to the extent that the debtor has disposable income available to pay such interest after making provision for full payment of all allowed claims; and

1325. Confirmation of plan

Section 1325(a)(4), text of

(a) Except as provided in subsection (b), the court shall confirm a plan if -

. . . .

(4) the value, as of the effective date of the plan, of property to be distributed under the plan on account of each allowed unsecured claim is not less than the amount that would be paid on such claim if the estate of the debtor were liquidated under chapter 7 of this title on such date;

1122. Classification of claims or interests

Section 1122, text of

(a) Except as provided in subsection (b) of this section, a plan may place a claim or an interest in a particular class only if such claim or interest is substantially similar to the other claims or interests of such class.

(b) A plan may designate a separate class of claims consisting only of every unsecured claim that is less than or reduced to an amount that the court approves as reasonable and necessary for administrative convenience.

Introduction. The statutes shown above collectively govern the treatment of unsecured claims in Chapter 13 plans. Section 1322(b)(1) governs the relative treatment that must be accorded unsecured claims as amongst themselves. It provides, in essence, that unsecured claims may be treated unequally, provided that no claim is unfairly discriminated against. In order to treat unsecured claims unequally, however, they must first be divided into classes. Therefore, the first subject discussed in this article is the classification of unsecured claims. This is followed by a discussion of what constitutes unfair discrimination in the classification and treatment of unsecured claims. The article concludes with discussions of the classification and treatment requirements for the two types of claims most often dealt with in Chapter 13 plans: codebtor claims and student loan claims.

scope of article, subjects discussed in

All of these statutes were enacted in the Bankruptcy Reform Act of 1978. Section 1322(b)(1) was amended in 1984 by the addition of the proviso "however, such plan may treat claims for a consumer debt of the debtor if an individual is liable on such consumer debt with the debtor differently than other unsecured claims." No other changes have been made in these statutes since their enactment except for a BAPCPA amendment to Section 1322(b)(10) which permits a chapter 13 plan to pay interest that accrues during the period of the plan on one or more unsecured nondischargeable claims, whether or not interest is paid to the holders of other unsecured claims, provided that the plan provides for payment in full of all allowed claims, secured, and unsecured, and some technical corrections in 2010. Because of the payment in full of all other claims requirement, it is doubtful that this provision will be of much use to most chapter 13 debtors.

history of statutes

This article deals with unsecured nonpriority claims. In the discussions below, the term "unsecured claim" means nonpriority unsecured claim. Priority unsecured claims must be paid in full under a Chapter 13 plan unless the holder of the claim agrees otherwise. See 11 U.S.C. § 1322(a)(2). See 11 U.S.C. § 507(a) for a list of priority unsecured claims. Note that the claim of a spouse, former spouse, or child of the debtor for a domestic support obligation is a priority claim and must therefore be paid in full under the plan unless the holder of the claim agrees otherwise. See 11 U.S.C. § 507(a)(1). Priority unsecured claims may be classified, if desired, and discriminated against with respect to priority of payment under the plan, as long as the discrimination is not unfair. See In re Klaska, 152 B.R. 248 (CD IL, 1993).

unsecured claim, what constitutes

priority unsecured claims, payment requirements

unsecured claims, statutory classification and treatment requirements

The classification of unsecured claims. Section 1322(b)(1) permits a Chapter 13 plan to designate classes of unsecured claims, but prohibits a plan from unfairly discriminating against any class of unsecured claims. Section 1322(a)(3) requires a plan to provide the same treatment for each claim within a particular class. Section 1122, which is made applicable to Chapter 13 cases by Section 1322(b)(1), requires all claims within a particular class to be substantially similar, except that for administrative convenience a class of dissimilar small claims below an amount approved by the court may be created. Section 1325(a)(4) requires payment on each allowed unsecured claim in an amount that is not less than what would be paid on the claim in a Chapter 7 liquidation of the debtor's estate. Section 1322(b)(1) provides that a plan may treat unsecured claims for consumer debts that have been cosigned or guaranteed by other persons differently from other unsecured claims. Finally, Section 1322(b)(10) allows for the payment of interest on unsecured nondischargeable claims if full payment is made on all allowed claims.

classification and treatment of unsecured claims, applicable rules

The statutes described above create the following rules that are applicable to the classification and treatment of unsecured claims in a Chapter 13 plan:

(1) A plan may place unsecured claims in separate classes.
(2) All unsecured claims in a particular class must be substantially similar, except for one class of small claims.
(3) All substantially similar claims need not be placed in the same class.
(4) All claims in a class must receive the same treatment under the plan.
(5) Each unsecured claim in every class must be paid at least as much as it would have received had the debtor filed a Chapter 7 case.
(6) Unsecured claims for consumer debts that have been cosigned or guaranteed by another person may be treated differently than other unsecured claims.
(7) A plan may not unfairly discriminate against any class of unsecured claims.

unsecured claims, treatment of in plan, preliminary rules

Of the above rules, rules (6) and (7) are of most concern. The other rules are relatively easy to comply with. It is not difficult to comply with the rules requiring all claims in a class to receive the same treatment and be paid at least what they would receive in a Chapter 7 liquidation of the debtor's estate. It is also usually easy to comply with the rule permitting a Chapter 13 debtor to classify unsecured claims, provided that the claims within each class are substantially similar. In this regard, it should be noted that the payment of an unsecured claim by the debtor outside of the plan may constitute the creation of a separate class of claims. The requirements in rules (6) and (7) above dealing with codebtor claims and prohibiting unfair discrimination are discussed separately below in this article.

With respect to the preliminary rules discussed in the preceding paragraph, note that the requirement in Section 1122 that all claims within a class must be substantially similar does not mean that all substantially similar claims must be placed in the same class. If a valid reason exists for treating the claims differently, substantially similar claims may be placed in different classes. See In re Storberg, 94 B.R. 144 (MN, 1988); In re Leser, 939 F.2d 669 (8th Cir., 1991). The provision in Section 1322(b)(1) permitting codebtor claims to be treated differently implicitly permits codebtor claims to be classified. However, despite this provision, codebtor claims are subject to the rule prohibiting unfair discrimination. See In re Monroe, 281 B.R. 398 (ND GA, 2002). preliminary rules, construction of

Unfair discrimination in the classification and treatment of unsecured claims. Section 1322(b)(1) does not prohibit discrimination in the classification and treatment of unsecured claims, it prohibits only unfair discrimination. This means that one or more classes of unsecured claims may be discriminated against in a Chapter 13 plan as long as the discrimination is not unfair. The basic requirement in the classification and treatment of unsecured claims in a Chapter 13 plan, then, is one of overall fairness. In other words, the treatment accorded each class of claims under the plan relative to the treatment accorded other classes of unsecured claims must not be unfair. treatment of unsecured claims, basic requirement

Most courts employ a four part test in determining whether a proposed classification and treatment of unsecured claims that includes unequal treatment of one or more classes is unfair discrimination under Section 1322(b)(1). Under this test the following factors are considered: unfair discrimination, test for determining

(1) whether the proposed discrimination has a reasonable basis;
(2) whether it is feasible for the debtor to carry out the plan without the proposed discrimination;
(3) whether the discrimination is being proposed in good faith; and
(4) whether the degree of discrimination is directly related to the basis or rationale for the discrimination.

See In re Seatrain Corp., 2012 WL 524175 (Bankr. E.D. N.C., Oct. 23, 2012); In re Kruse, 406 B.R. 833 (ND IA, 2009); In re Webb, 370 B.R. 418 (ND GA, 2007); In re Carlson, 276 B.R. 653 (MT, 2002); In re Leser, 939 F.2d 669 (8th Cir., 1991); In re Davidson, 72 B.R. 384 (CO, 1987).

The burden of proof on the issue of unfair discrimination is on the debtor. See In re Groves, 39 F.3d 212 (8th Cir., 1994). If a proposed plan treats one class of unsecured claims more favorably than another class, the debtor must establish that the disparate treatment does not constitute unfair discrimination under Section 1322(b)(1). See In re Crawford v. Chatterton, 268 B.R. 832 (WD WI, 2001); In re Colley, 260 B.R. 532 (MD FL, 2000); In re Anderson, 173 B.R. 226 (CO, 1993). In In re Warner, 115 B.R. 233 (CD CA, 1989), the court stated that because ratable distribution among creditors is one of the strongest policies behind the bankruptcy laws, the court should act very cautiously in exercising its general equitable powers to favor one group of unsecured creditor at the expense of others. unfair discrimination, burden of proof

unfair discrimination, prospective viewed from

Most courts attempt to view the question from the perspective of both the debtor and the creditors. The question of unfair discrimination must be viewed from the prospective of creditors and not the debtor. See In re Eiland, 170 B.R. 370 (ND IL, 1994). However, in In re Lawson, 93 B.R. 979 (ND IL, 1988), the court held that the relevant interests in considering whether a classification is unfair discrimination should be the interests of the debtor and not the interests of particular creditors.

unfair discrimination, types of

Unfair discrimination under Section 1322(b)(1) can occur with respect to either the amounts paid to differing classes of claims or in the order or priority in which the differing classes of claims are paid under the plan. While the former is much more common than the latter, it is clear that the payment for no valid reason of one class of unsecured claims prior to the payment of other classes of similar claims can constitute unfair discrimination. See In re Foreman, 136 B.R. 532 (SD IA, 1992).

discrimination based on non-dischargeability of debt, general rule

As indicated in the four part test for unfair discrimination set forth on the previous page, in order for a proposed discrimination not to be unfair there must be a reasonable basis for the discrimination. A popular basis for discrimination is nondischargeability. It is obviously beneficial to debtors to provide for the full or substantial payment of their nondischargeable debts under a Chapter 13 plan so that they will not be burdened with these debts after the completion of the plan. This is probably the most common reason for filing under Chapter 13. Unfortunately for debtors, it is generally held that nondischargeability alone is not a reasonable basis for discriminatory treatment under a Chapter 13 plan. See Mc Donald v. Sperna, 173 B.R. 654 (B.A.P. 9th Cir., 1994); In re Groves, 39 F.3d 212 (8th Cir., 1994); In re Johnson, 69 B.R. 726 (WD NY, 1987); In re Cronk, 131 B.R. 710 (SD IA, 1990); In re Colfer, 159 B.R. 602 (ME, 1993).

non-dischargeability as basis for discrimination, general rule

However, in In re Whittaker, 113 B.R. 534 (MN, 1990), the court found that the debtor had a legitimate interest in not being burdened with a substantial nondischargeable debt upon the completion of the plan and permitted the classification and favorable treatment of a nondischargeable debt, in part at least, for that reason. See also In re Boggan, 125 B.R. 533 (ND IL, 1991); In re Tucker, 159 B.R. 325 (MT, 1993) (holding that the proposed discrimination had a reasonable basis in that it provided for the payment of a nondischargeable student loan).

necessity for continuation of business or livelihood as basis for discrimination

If the debtor is engaged in business, the necessity of paying a debt to ensure the continuation of the debtor's business may be a reasonable basis for discrimination in the classification and treatment of that debt. See In re Terry, 78 B.R. 171 (ED TN, 1987). In In re Sutherland, 3 B.R. 420 (WD AR, 1980), discrimination in favor of a bank from whom credit was necessary for the continued operation of the debtor's business was found not to be unfair. In In re Perskin, 9 B.R. 626 (ND TX, 1981), discrimination in favor of a credit card company whose card was necessary for the continuation of the debtor's livelihood as a traveling salesman was found not to be unfair.

Discrimination in favor of claims necessary for the continuation of the debtor's business or livelihood may also be justified under factor (2) above, because if the debtor's business or livelihood is not continued it usually will not be feasible for the debtor to carry out the plan. Plans approving special treatment for the claims of landlords, physicians, and attorneys have been approved, usually because it was shown that future services of the creditor were necessary in order for the debtor to carry out the plan and the services would not be provided if the creditor's claim was not paid. See In re Davis, 209 B.R. 893 (ND IL, 1997); In re Kovich, 4 B.R. 403 (WD MI, 1980); In re Hill, 4 B.R. 694 (KS, 1980).

necessity of discrimination for carrying out plan as basis for discrimination

Claims which, if not paid, may result in the imprisonment or punishment of the debtor may also be classified and treated preferentially if the likelihood of imprisonment or punishment is established. See In re Etheridge, 297 B.R. 810 (MD AL, 2003); In re Riggel, 142 B.R. 199 (SD OH, 1992); In re Stanley, 82 B.R. 858 (SD OH, 1987). However, in In re Hiner, 161 B.R. 688 (ID, 1993) a plan that discriminated in favor of creditors to whom the debtor had written short checks discriminated unfairly against other unsecured creditors.

punishment or imprisonment of debtor as basis for discrimination

With respect to factor (3) above, (i.e., whether the discrimination is being proposed in good faith), plans which for no justifiable reason pay substantial amounts to favorites of the debtor and little or nothing to other creditors are invariably disapproved, usually on this ground. See In re Warner, 115 B.R. 233 (CD CA, 1989) (where a plan that provided for a 100 percent payment on one claim and nothing on all other claims was disapproved because it unfairly discriminated against the other creditors); see also In re Edwards, 132 B.R. 400 (ED AR, 1991) (where a plan that provided for payment in full of a restitution debt and payment of only 3.2 percent of all other debts was not approved because of unfair discrimination).

favoring a creditor as unfair discrimination

Plans that provide for significant payments on all classes of claims except one are also likely to be disapproved as not being proposed in good faith. See In re Baker, 66 B.R. 253 (ND MS, 1986), where a plan that called for a 10 percent dividend to all unsecured creditors except one, who was to be paid nothing on a $23,000 claim, was disapproved because it unfairly discriminated against the omitted creditor.

penalizing a creditor as unfair discrimination

In In re Terry, 78 B.R. 171 (ED TN, 1987), the court stated that a Chapter 13 debtor may favor some unsecured claims over others, even where such favoritism is not necessary for the performance of the debtor's plan. Such favoritism, the court stated, is proper where it will facilitate the debtor's performance under the plan or improve the debtor's rehabilitation, provided that the favoritism is not unfair. Favoritism is fair, the court concluded, if the reasons for the proposed classification treatment justify treating the favored class in the proposed manner.

favoring creditor, when justifiable

payment of claim outside of plan as unfair discrimination

The payment by the debtor of an unsecured creditor outside the plan may be unfair discrimination if the outside creditor is paid more on its claim than similarly situated creditors under the plan. See In re Bradley, 705 F.2d 1409 (5th Cir., 1983), and In re Green, 70 B.R. 164 (WD AR, 1986). The payment of a partially secured creditor outside the plan can also be unfair discrimination under Section 1322(b)(1) if the creditor is paid more on the unsecured portion of its claim than other unsecured creditors. See In re Gunn, 37 B.R. 432 (OR, 1984). However, in In re Delauder, 189 B.R. 639 (ED VA, 1995), the payment of an undersecured automobile loan by the debtor outside the plan was approved, in part at least, because the last payment on the debt was due after the period of the plan, which meant that the loan payments could be maintained under Section 1322(b)(5) and that the debt was nondischargeable in the Chapter 13 case. See 11 U.S.C. § 1328(a)(1), (c)(1).

codebtor claims, right to classify

The classification and treatment of cosigned claims. In this discussion, the term "cosigned claim" includes claims based on consumer debts that have been cosigned or guaranteed by another individual or any other claim that is based on a consumer debt for which another individual is also liable. Section 1322(b)(1) expressly permits claims for consumer debts for which another individual is also liable to be treated differently than other unsecured claims. Because a claim cannot be treated differently unless it is classified, Section 1322(b)(1) implicitly permits Chapter 13 plans to classify claims for debts that have been cosigned or guaranteed by other individuals and treat them differently than other classes of unsecured claims. See In re Renteria, 470 B.R. 838 (B.A.P. 9th Cir. 2012); In re Monroe, 281 B.R. 398 (ND GA, 2002). The question is, to what degree may they be treated differently.

codebtor claims, classification requirements

If a debtor has more than one cosigned or guaranteed debt, all debts of this type must be treated equally under the plan unless there is a justifiable reason for not doing so. See In re Young, 102 B.R. 1022 (WD MO, 1989) (holding that while there is some latitude in the matter, one unsecured, cosigned consumer claim must normally be treated comparably to another unsecured, cosigned consumer claim).

Section 1322(b)(1) codebtor claim proviso, legislative history of

The proviso in Section 1322(b)(1) permitting different treatment for codebtor claims was enacted in 1984 to resolve a conflict in case law as to whether codebtor claims could be classified. The legislative history indicates that while there may be no theoretical difference between codebtor claims and other claims, there are important practical differences because codebtors are usually relatives or friends of the debtor whom the debtor feels a strong need to repay, even if repayment is not provided for in the debtor's plan. The report also indicates that because a debtor is required to devote all of his or her disposable income to the plan, the desire to repay a cosigned debt outside the plan may spell failure for the plan by leaving insufficient income to keep up the plan payments. As a practical matter, the report states, if a debtor is going to pay a codebtor claim, he or she should be permitted to separately classify the claim in the plan. See Senate Report No. 65, 98th Congress, First Session (1983) pp. 17-18.

Understood, however, that the proviso in Section 1322(b)(1) permitting different treatment for codebtor claims does not necessarily mean that the treatment given such claims is exempt from the unfair discrimination requirements of Section 1322(b)(1). Therefore, the treatment accorded a class of codebtor claims under a plan may not unfairly discriminate against any other class of unsecured claims. See In re Battista, 180 B.R. 355 (NH, 1995) (stating that the "however" clause in Section 1322(b)(1) does not provide an exception to the unfair discrimination test); but see In re Renteria, 470 B.R. 838 (B.A.P. 9th Cir. 2012).

codebtor claims, subject to unfair discrimination test

Because of the codebtor claim proviso in Section 1322(b)(1), most courts give more latitude to discriminate in favor of codebtor claims than in favor of most other types of unsecured claims. This does not mean, however, that a plan may, for no other reason, provide substantially better treatment for codebtor claims than for other unsecured claims. In In re Martin, 189 B.R. 619 (ED VA, 1995), a plan that proposed to pay 100 percent on two codebtor claims and only 6.5 percent on all other unsecured claims was disapproved for unfair discrimination in the absence of a valid reason for the discrimination other than the fact that the favored debts had cosigners. In Chacon v. Bracher, 202 F.3d 725 (5th Cir., 1999), a plan that proposed to pay a debt cosigned by the debtor's father in full with 12 percent interest prior to any distributions to general unsecured creditors was not confirmed. In Ramirez v. Bracher, 204 F.3d 595 (5th Cir., 2000), a plan that proposed to pay a debt cosigned by the debtor's sister in full with 12 percent interest prior to any distribution to general unsecured creditors was not confirmed because of unfair discrimination.

codebtor claims, degree of discrimination permitted

Even less latitude to discriminate is likely to be given if the codebtor is the debtor's nonfiling spouse. In In re Cheak, 171 B.R. 55 (SD IL, 1994), a plan that proposed to pay 100% of a debt that was cosigned by the debtor's nonfiling wife was found to discriminate unfairly against other creditors because the discrimination served no legitimate purpose. The court stated the identity of interests between the debtor and his cosigner distinguished the case from cases where the cosigner was a relative or friend of the debtor with a separate income and separate expenses. In In re Melendez, 145 B.R. 740 (PR, 1992), the court held that a note cosigned by the debtor's nonfiling spouse was not entitled to be classified separately from other unsecured claims because as the debtor's spouse the cosigner had benefitted from the loan.

spouse as codebtor, effect of on codebtor claim

A plan that proposed to pay 100% of a cosigned debt while only 10% to other general unsecured creditors was unfairly discriminatory in In re McNichols, 249 B.R. 160 (ND IL, 2000). In In re Easley, 72 B.R. 948 (MD TN, 1987), a plan that proposed to pay 100 percent of a cosigned claim and only 12 percent of another claim was unfairly discriminatory under Section 1322(b)(1) where the debtor offered no evidence justifying the proposed discrimination. In In re Whitelock, 122 B.R. 582 (UT, 1990), a 70 percent differential in amounts paid on a cosigned claim versus amounts paid on other unsecured claims was found to be unfairly discriminatory. In In re Birriel Gonzalez, 73 B.R. 259 (PR, 1987), a plan that called for payment in full of a separately classified codebtor claim was disapproved for unfair discrimination because it would result in other unsecured creditors getting less than what they would receive in a Chapter 7 liquidation.

treatment of codebtor claims as unfair discrimination

treatment of codebtor claim, when not unfair discrimination

If other reasons can be shown to justify discrimination in favor of a codebtor claim, the proposed discrimination is more likely to be approved. For example, in In re Ross, 161 B.R. 36 (CD IL, 1993), a plan that paid 100 percent of a claim guaranteed by the debtor's employer and only 9 percent on all other unsecured claims was approved as not being unfairly discriminatory because there was evidence showing that the debtor would lose his job if the guaranteed claim was not paid. In In re Monroe, 281 B.R. 398 (ND GA, 2002), a plan that proposed to pay an unsecured cosigned claim prior to the payment of secured claims was found confirmable.

student loan debts, non-dischargeability of

The classification and treatment of student loan claims. Generally, only nondischargeable student loan debts are dealt with in Chapter 13 plans. Dischargeable student loan debts are usually discharged by the debtor in a Chapter 7 case. Student loan debts are nondischargeable in both Chapter 7 and Chapter 13 cases unless not discharging the debt will impose an undue hardship on the debtor. See 11 U.S.C. § 523(a)(8), 1328(a)(2), (c)(2). See article 1.06 of this handbook for a discussion of the dischargeability of student loan debts.

student loan claims, right to classify

Generally student loan claims may be put into a separate class, provided that the classification does not result in unfair discrimination. See In re King, 460 B.R. 708 (Bankr. M. D. Tex. 2011); In re Gregg, 179 B.R. 828 (ED TX, 1995); In re Chapman, 146 B.R. 411 (ND IL, 1992). Therefore, the right to classify student loan claims is not usually an issue. The fact that the underlying debts are nondischargeable is a sufficient basis for the separate classification of student loan claims. It is the treatment accorded that class of claims that is of primary concern. See In re Keel, 143 B.R. 915 (NE, 1992).

student loan claim, non-dischargeability alone as basis for discriminatory treatment

As indicated earlier, generally nondischargeability alone is not a reasonable basis for according favorable discriminatory treatment to a student loan claim in a Chapter 13 plan. See In re Martellaro, 404 B.R. 548 (MT, 2008); In re Groves, 39 F.3d 212 (8th Cir., 1994); In re Bentley, 250 B.R. 475 (RI, 2000); In re Tucker, 130 B.R. 71 (SD IA, 1991). Accordingly, plans which, for no other reason than the nondischargeability of the underlying debt, provide substantially better treatment to nondischargeable student loan claims than to other unsecured claims are almost always found to discriminate unfairly against the other unsecured claims. See In re Carlson, 276 B.R. 653 (MT, 2002).

In In re Groves, 39 F.3d 212 (8th Cir., 1994), the court found a plan that called for full payment of student loan claims and payment of 10 to 40 percent on all other unsecured claims to be unfairly discriminatory. In In re Beauchamp, 283 B.R. 287 (MN, 2002), a plan that paid student loan claims in full and only pennies on the dollar to all other unsecured creditors was found to discriminate unfairly, especially since the debtors had cosigned the student loans for their children, who were primarily liable on the loans and the main benefactors. In Mc Cullough v. Brown, 162 B.R. 506 (ND IL, 1993), a plan that proposed to pay a 100 percent dividend on student loan claims and a 10 percent dividend on all other unsecured claims was found to be nonconfirmable because it discriminated unfairly against the other unsecured creditors. See also In re Thibodeau, 248 B.R. 699 (MA, 2000); In re Williams, 253 B.R. 220 (WD TN, 2000); In re Christophe, 151 B.R. 475 (ND IL, 1993); In re Smalberger, 157 B.R. 472 (OR, 1993); In re Colfer, 159 B.R. 602 (ME, 1993); In re Sullivan, 195 B.R. 649 (WD TX, 1996). Student loans whose defaults are cured under Section 1322(b)(5) must also pass the unfair discrimination muster. See In re Colley, 260 B.R. 532 (MD FL, 2000).

student loan claims, unfair discrimination, cases

On the other hand, in In re Tucker, 159 B.R. 325 (MT, 1993), a plan that paid a student loan claim in full and a 29 percent dividend on all other unsecured claims was approved as not being unfairly discriminatory with a notation by the court that the other unsecured creditors would have received nothing had the debtor filed under Chapter 7. The court found that the discrimination had a reasonable basis because it provided for the payment of a nondischargeable student loan and that the debtor could not carry out the plan without the proposed discrimination. In In re Furlow, 70 B.R. 973 (ED PA, 1987), a plan that proposed to pay 40 percent of a student loan claim and 10 percent of all other unsecured claims would be confirmed was not unfairly discriminatory if the debtor could prove that the discrimination was necessary to enable her to continue her education and retain her job as a school teacher. In In re Foreman, 136 B.R. 532 (SD IA, 1992), a plan that provided for the payment of 100 percent of all unsecured claims, but which provided for the payment of the debtor's student loan obligations first, was found not to unfairly discriminate against the other unsecured claims. See also, In re Pracht, 464 B.R. 486 (Bankr. M.D. Ga. 2012).

student loan claims, unfair discrimination not found, cases

If the final payment on a student loan obligation is payable after the due date of the final payment under the debtor's plan, Section 1322(b)(5) of the Bankruptcy Code permits maintenance of payments on the obligation during the pendency of the Chapter 13 case, either under or outside of the plan, and allows the debtor to cure defaults on the obligation under the plan. See In re Sullivan, 195 B.R. 649 (WD TX, 1996). By using Section 1322(b)(5), a debtor can prevent an acceleration of payments under the student loan obligation and thereby reduce the amount of the periodic payment necessary to keep the obligation current. By reducing the amount necessary to satisfy the student loan claim, this procedure permits the debtor to make larger payments to other unsecured creditors and thereby make the plan less discriminatory. See article 3.01 of this handbook for further reading on Section 1322(b)(5) and its usefulness in dealing with long-term obligations in Chapter 13 plans.

student loan claims, handling of under Section 1322(b)(5)

handling student loan claims under Section 1322(b)(5), case

Many courts are more likely to approve discriminatory treatment with respect to student loan claims if Section 1322(b)(5) can be used under the plan to prevent the loan from accelerating and becoming payable in full during the term of the plan. In In re Cox, 186 B.R. 744 (ND FL, 1995), the court held that a plan calling for the payment of 7 student loans according to their terms outside the plan was not unfairly discriminatory, even though their payment resulted in a 42 percent reduction in distribution to other unsecured creditors, because such treatment was specifically sanctioned by Section 1322(b)(5). See also In re Truss, 404 B.R. 329 (ED WI, 2009), where a dividend of between 60% - 79% paid on student loan debts which extended beyond the term of the plan was found to not be unfair to other unsecured creditors who would receive a 2.44% dividend.

handling student loan claims under Section 1322(b)(5), case

In In re Dodds, 140 B.R. 542 (MT, 1992), a plan providing for payment of a student loan according to its terms outside the plan over a period of 54 months, while paying other unsecured creditors 79 percent on their claims over the 36 month period of the plan, did not unfairly discriminate. The court stated that forcing the debtor into a 54 month plan could produce unfair results for the unsecured creditors, who were receiving more under the 36 month plan than they would in a Chapter 7 liquidation.

handling student loan claims under Section 1322(b)(5), factors considered

The factors or issues considered by the court in determining the question of unfair discrimination with respect to the treatment of student loan claims under Section 1322(b)(5) were summarized by the court in In re Eiland, 170 B.R. 370 (ND IL, 1994). The court, after stating that questions of unfair discrimination with respect to student loans should be viewed from the perspective of the other unsecured creditors, stated that the following circumstances should be considered:

(1) Whether the proposed plan will in fact harm or delay other unsecured creditors if it is not completed.

(2) Whether early repayment of the student loans is required to enable the debtor to complete school.

(3) Whether the last payment on the student loan is due after the due date of the last payment under the proposed plan (if so, the loan qualifies for treatment under Section 1322(b)(5)).

(4) Whether any arrearages exist under the student loan.

(5) Whether the student loan payments have been accelerated under the loan agreement.

(6) Whether the payout proposed by the plan would accelerate payments under the loan agreement.

(7) Whether the payments proposed by the plan are intended to cure any defaults.

Bibliography. For further reading on the issues discussed in this article, see the annotations and articles listed below.

Annotations:

Plan that Separately Classifies Student Loan Debt as Unfair Discriminatory Treatment of Class of Unsecured Claims Under § 1322(b)(1) of Bankruptcy Code. 6 ALR Fed. 2d 507.

Plan that Separately Classifies Alimony, Maintenance, or Support Debts as Unfair Discriminatory Treatment of Class of Unsecured Claims Under § 1322(b)(1) of Bankruptcy Code. 198 ALR Fed. 605.

Payments to partially secured creditors outside Chapter 13 plan as unfair discriminatory treatment of class of unsecured claims under Section 1322(b)(1) of Bankruptcy Code of 1978. 50 ALR Fed 694.

Articles:

Separate classification of student loans in Chapter 13. 73 Wash. Univ. L.Q. 269, Spring 1995.

Preferential classification in Chapter 13: how unfair discrimination has created a murky body of case law. 98 Comm. L.J. 486, Winter 1993.

Separate classification of child support arrearages in Chapter 13 bankruptcy plan: In re Leser, 25 Creighton L. Rev. 977, April 1992.

Classification of Claims and Interests in Chapter 11 and 13 cases. 75 Calif. L. Rev. 391, Jan. 1987.

3.03 What constitutes "good faith" in the proposal of a Chapter 13 plan?

Text of statute. Section 1325(a)(3) of the Bankruptcy Code (11 U.S.C. § 1325(a)(3)) provides as follows:

1325. Confirmation of plan

Section 1325(a)(3), text of

(a) Except as provided in subsection (b), the court shall confirm a plan if –

. . . .

(3) the plan has been proposed in good faith and not by any means forbidden by law;

filing plan in bad faith, penalty for

Introduction. Section 1325(a)(3) provides that in order to be confirmed, a Chapter 13 plan must be proposed by the debtor in good faith. The penalty for proposing a plan in bad faith is denial of confirmation, rather than dismissal of the case. See In re York, 282 B.R. 519 (MD GA, 2002); In re Love, 957 F.2d 1350 (7th Cir., 1992). It is, however, within the discretion of the court whether to simply refuse confirmation, or to dismiss the case. See In re Hall, 346 B.R. 420 (WD KY, 2006). Lack of good faith in proposing a plan should not be confused with lack of good faith in filing a bankruptcy petition. However, for a successful Chapter 13 case, good faith must exist both upon the filing of the petition and upon filing the debtor's plan. See In re Pearson, 354 B.R. 558 (MA, 2006); In re McFadden, 383 B.R. 386 (SC, 2008).

good faith, requirement of minimum payments to creditors

The Chapter 13 "good faith" requirement for confirmation has been the subject of both judicial and legislative concern since the enactment of Section 1325(a)(3) in the Bankruptcy Reform Act of 1978. Initially, a number of courts construed the good faith requirement in Section 1325(a)(3) as requiring a particular level of payments to unsecured creditors. Other courts rejected this approach and adopted an approach whereby good faith was determined by the totality of the debtor's circumstances with respect to the case. In 1984 Congress resolved the conflict by enacting Section 1325(b) of the Bankruptcy Code and inserting the clause "Except as provided in subsection (b)" in Section 1325(a).

Section 1325(b), requirements of

Section 1325(b) provides that to be confirmed a plan that does not provide for payment in full of all unsecured claims must provide that all of the debtor's projected disposable income for a three or five-year period will be applied to the making of payments under the plan unsecured creditors. On the level of payments issue, then, Section 1325(b) requires confirmation if the plan commits all of the debtor's projected disposable income to the plan for the applicable commitment period, regardless of the amount paid under the plan to unsecured creditors.

By adopting the "ability to pay" test, Section 1325(b) effectively overruled earlier case law requiring specified minimum payments to unsecured creditors in order to satisfy the good faith requirement of Section 1325(a)(3). As to good faith issues other than minimum payment requirements, most courts now apply the "totality of the circumstances" approach whereby a number of factors are considered in determining whether the plan was proposed in good faith. See In re Shafer, 393 B.R. 655 (WD WI, 2008); In re Smith, 328 B.R. 797 (WD MO, 2005); In re Etheridge, 297 B.R. 810 (MD AL, 2003); In re Le Maire, 898 F.2d 1346 (8th Cir., 1990); In re Rasmussen, 888 F.2d 703 (10th Cir., 1989); In re Barrett, 964 F.2d 588 (6th Cir., 1992); In re Tucker, 989 F.2d 328 (9th Cir., 1993). The "totality of the circumstances" approach is fact oriented, which means that a trial court's findings thereunder may be reviewed by an appellate court only on a "clearly erroneous" standard. See In re Porter, 371 B.R. 739 (ED PA, 2007); In re Rigales, 290 B.R. 401 (NM, 2003); In re Barrett, supra; In re Robinson, 987 F.2d 665 (10th Cir., 1993).

good faith, method of determining

Methods of determining good faith. While the Bankruptcy Code does not define the term "good faith," the courts have generally agreed that whether a plan is proposed in good faith involves inquiry into whether, under the circumstances of the case, there has been an abuse of the provisions, purpose, or spirit of the Bankruptcy Code in the plan or its proposal. In In re Norwood, 178 B.R. 683 (ED PA, 1995), the court also stated that in considering whether a Chapter 13 plan is proposed in good faith, the court should concentrate primarily on (1) whether the debtor has stated his debts and expenses accurately, (2) whether the debtor has made any fraudulent misrepresentations that mislead the court, and (3) whether the debtor has unfairly manipulated the Bankruptcy Code to the detriment of creditors. In In re Shafer, 393 B.R. 655 (WD WI, 2008), the court stated that the ultimate issue when determining good faith under Section 1325(a)(3) is whether the debtors are trying to pay their creditors or whether they are trying to thwart them.

good faith, what constitutes, generally

In In re Klevorn, 181 B.R. 8 (ND NY, 1995), the court stated that technical compliance with the provisions of the Bankruptcy Code alone is insufficient to establish good faith under Section 1325(a)(3), and that there must also be some assurance that a debtor who has invoked the provisions of Chapter 13 complies with the aims, objectives, and philosophy of Chapter 13 and the Bankruptcy Code. The determination of good faith in proposing a plan under Section 1325(a)(3) is made on a case-by-case basis with the court reviewing the totality of the circumstances. See In re Metz, 820 F.2d 1495 (9th Cir., 1987).

good faith, determination of, how made

In determining whether a Chapter 13 plan has been proposed in good faith under the totality of the circumstances approach, most courts consider the factors listed below, to the extent that they are material:

good faith, totality of circumstances approach, factors considered

(1) Whether the debtor has been accurate and truthful in disclosing his or her income and expenses and in applying disposable income to the plan.

(2) Whether the projected period of the plan is sufficiently long under the circumstances.

(3) Whether the debtor's prebankruptcy conduct renders the plan unjust or inequitable with respect to one or more creditors.

(4) Whether the debtor's motive in filing for relief is consistent with the spirit and intent of Chapter 13 and the Bankruptcy Code or whether the debtor is trying to manipulate the Bankruptcy Code at the expense of creditors.

(5) Whether any substantial debts dealt with in the case are nondischargeable under Chapter 7.

(6) Whether the debtor has sought bankruptcy relief in the past, and if so, when and how often.

(7) Whether any unsecured creditors are being preferred without justification in the debtor's plan.

(8) Whether the fee being paid to the debtor's attorney in the case is reasonable.

(9) Whether the debtor's earnings are likely to increase and/or fluctuate in the foreseeable future.

(10) Whether the debtor is subject to any special hardships, such as unusually high medical or family-related expenses.

(11) Whether the debtor has attempted to mislead the bankruptcy court or been guilty of fraudulent conduct in the case.

(12) Whether the administration of the debtor's plan will place an unfair burden on the trustee.

cases listing factors

See generally, In re Kirk, 465 B.R. 300 (Bankr. N. D. Ala. 2012); In re Welsh, 465 B.R. 843 (B.A.P. 9th Cir. 2012); In re Hall, 346 B.R. 420 (WD KY, 2006); In re Farber, 355 B.R. 362 (SD FL, 2006); In re Manthey, 262 B.R. 89 (ND CA, 2001); In re Soost, 290 B.R. 116 (MN, 2003); In re Cushman, 263 B.R. 293 (WD MO, 2001); In re Terry, 279 B.R. 240 (WD AR, 2002); In re Barrett, 964 F.2d 588 (6th Cir., 1992); In re Robinson, 987 F.2d 665 (10th Cir., 1993); Education Assistance Corp. v. Zellner, 827 F.2d 1222 (8th Cir., 1987); In re Caldwell, 851 F.2d 852 (6th Cir., 1988); In re Rose, 101 B.R. 934 (SD OH, 1989); In re Tobiason, 185 B.R. 59 (NE, 1995); In re Belt, 106 B.R. 553 (ND IN, 1989); In re Farley, 114 B.R. 711 (SD CA, 1990). No one factor within the group of factors cited above should be a dispositive indication of good or bad faith on the part of the debtor. See, e.g., In re Reymer, 403 B.R. 475 (ED MI, 2009).

totality of circumstances approach, rules applicable to

The application of the totality of the circumstances approach, it should be noted, is subject to two counter-balancing rules: (1) the statutorily-mandated rule that the Bankruptcy Code be construed liberally in favor of the debtor, and (2) the rule that the burden of proof to establish good faith under Section 1325(a)(3) is on the debtor. See In re Snipes, 314 B.R. 898 (SD GA, 2004), In re Barrett, 964 F.2d 588 (6th Cir., 1992); In re Warren, 89 B.R. 87 (B.A.P. 9th Cir., 1988).

Matters considered on the issue of good faith. As indicated above, Section 1325(b)(1)(B) requires a debtor who is not paying unsecured claims in full to apply all of his or her projected disposable income for the applicable commitment period to the making of payments to unsecured creditors under the plan. Section 1325(b)(2) defines "disposable income" as follows:

Section 1325(b), provisions of, effect on good faith requirement

> (2) For purposes of this subsection, the term "disposable income" means current monthly income received by the debtor (other than child support payments, foster care payments, or disability payments for a dependent child made in accordance with applicable nonbankruptcy law to the extent reasonably necessary to be expended for such child) less amounts reasonably necessary to be expended –
>
> (A)(i) for the maintenance or support of the debtor or a dependent of the debtor, or for a domestic support obligation, that first becomes payable after the date the petition is filed; and
>
> (ii) for charitable contributions (that meet the definition of "charitable contribution" under section 548(d)(3)) to a qualified religious or charitable entity or organization (as defined in section 548(d)(4)) in an amount not to exceed 15 percent of gross income of the debtor for the year in which the contributions are made; and
>
> (B) if the debtor is engaged in business, for the payment of expenditures necessary for the continuation, preservation, and operation of such business.

disposable income, definition of

Given the explicit wording of Section 1325(b), it is difficult to understand why matters related to the disclosure of income or expenses are considered under Section 1325(a)(3). If the debtor has failed to disclose income or has been dishonest or inaccurate with respect to necessary expenses, confirmation should be denied under Section 1325(b) and not under the good faith provisions of Section 1325(a)(3). Further, because Section 1325(b) requires the filing of an objection to confirmation by an unsecured creditor or the trustee to be invoked, if such an objection is not timely filed the court is without authority to even consider these matters. See In re Stiller, 323 B.R. 199 (WD MI, 2005); In re Fricker, 116 B.R. 431 (ED PA, 1990).

Nevertheless, many courts have considered the above-mentioned Section 1325(b) issues in determining good faith under Section 1325(a)(3). For example, in In re Farmer, 186 B.R. 781 (RI, 1995), confirmation of the debtor's plan was denied for lack of good faith under Section 1325(a)(3) in part at least because of the inclusion of an unexplained $150 miscellaneous item in the debtor's proposed monthly budget. In In re Kasun, 186 B.R. 62 (ED VA, 1995), confirmation was denied for lack of good faith under Section 1325(a)(3) because the debtor proposed to pay over $600 per month toward a luxury boat while paying unsecured creditors only 34.9 percent on their claims. In In re Clements, 185 B.R. 903 (MD FL, 1995), confirmation was denied for lack of good faith because the debtors, who proposed to pay only 2.9 percent of their unsecured debts, owned significant assets (house, automobile, life insurance, etc.) and were paying more to relatives who they were not legally obligated to support than they were to creditors to whom they were legally obligated. In In re Watson, 309 B.R. 652 (B.A.P. 1st Cir., 2004) private school tuition expenses were not reasonably necessary expenses where the debtors had not demonstrated any attempt to offset such expenses by eliminating or minimizing other expenses, and were proposing to pay unsecured creditors only 25% of the debt owed. See also In re Moroney, 330 B.R. 527 (ED VA, 2005) (where a proposed payment plan to unsecured creditors of 5.9% of the debt owed caused a chapter 13 plan to be dismissed). However, in In re Petty, 338 B.R. 805 (ED AR, 2006) good faith was found where a debtor proposed to tithe almost $15,000 over the course of a 3 year plan while paying unsecured creditors only $294 in monthly installments because the debtor was a deacon and had a long history of such tithing.

good faith, effect on of unnecessary expenses

On the other hand, in In re Hutcherson, 186 B.R. 546 (ND GA, 1995), the fact that the debtor's plan devoted all disposable income to the plan for a three-year period precluded creditors' allegations of bad faith based on the amounts being paid to them. In In re Belt, 106 B.R. 553 (ND IN, 1989), the court stated that unsecured creditors have the right to expect the debtor to commit all of his disposable income to the plan for 36 months and nothing more, including meaningful payments on their claims. See also In re Randall, 310 B.R. 830 (SD OH, 2004), In re Baker, 66 B.R. 253 (ND MS, 1986), and In re Hazel, 68 B.R. 287 (ED MI, 1986). Courts have stated that they cannot confirm a plan, unless, as of the effective date of the plan, it provides for all of the debtor's "projected disposable income" to be committed to paying unsecured creditors. See In re Van Bodegon Smith, 383 B.R. 441 (ED WI, 2008).

good faith, effect on of plan payments

Payment of minimal or no dividends to unsecured creditors does not, without more, constitute bad faith. See In re Warren, 89 B.R. 87 (B.A.P. 9th Cir., 1988); In re Ashton, 85 B.R. 766 (SD OH, 1988); In re Sutliff, 79 B.R. 151 (ND NY, 1987); In re Tobiason, 185 B.R. 59 (NE, 1995). The attitude of most courts is summarized in In re Porter, 102 B.R. 773 (B.A.P. 9th Cir., 1989), where the court stated that even though there is no substantial repayment requirement under Section 1325(a)(3), the court should pay particular scrutiny to a debtor's good faith when a plan proposes nominal repayment and a nondischargeable debt is present. See also In re Todd, 65 B.R. 249 (ND IL, 1986); In re Konowicz, 470 B.R. 725 (Bankr. N. J. 2012) (single debtor's plan to stay in 6,100 square foot five bedroom house not good faith).

good faith, effect on of payments to creditors

The debtor's prebankruptcy conduct can have an effect on good faith determinations in Chapter 13 cases. If the debt was incurred in a manner that makes discharging the debt without making significant payments to the creditor appear unjust or inequitable, the court is likely to find that the plan was not proposed in good faith. See In re Dicey, 312 B.R. 456 (NH, 2004); In re White, 255 B.R. 737 (WD MO, 2000). In In re Le Maire, 898 F.2d 1346 (8th Cir., 1990), although prefiling conduct was not in itself determinative of the good faith issue under Section 1325(a)(3), it was relevant. The court then reversed as clearly erroneous the bankruptcy court's finding that the plan was proposed in good faith in a case where the debtor had shot the principal creditor, even though the debtor had already served a prison sentence for the shooting and had committed all disposable income to the plan for a five-year period. In In re Norwood, 178 B.R. 683 (ED PA, 1995), a plan which proposed no payments to a primary creditor whose claim was based on a sexual assault judgment was found not to have been proposed in good faith. See also In re Lancaster, 280 B.R. 468 (WD MO, 2002); In re Rose, 101 B.R. 934 (SD OH, 1989). See also In re Derryberry, 367 B.R. 616 (ED TN, 2007) (where good faith was not found in a debtor's plan that proposed to repay only a portion owed to a creditor whose business was a damaged by a fire set by the debtor).

prebankruptcy criminal conduct, effect of on good faith

Conduct other than criminal conduct may also be considered on the issue of good faith. In In re Robertson, 84 B.R. 109 (SD OH, 1988), a debtor who made a personal $1,000 loan to a friend shortly before filing his Chapter 13 petition while neglecting to pay his creditors and who allowed his copartner uncle to divert $33,000 from their business to his tax-exempt ministry, was found to have proposed his plan in bad faith. In In re Crayton, 169 B.R. 243 (SD GA, 1994), the debtor's failure to file income tax returns for several years prior to filing his Chapter 13 petition, coupled with his postpetition failure to bring himself into compliance with the federal tax laws, was bad faith under Section 1325(a)(3). In In re Altmann, 256 B.R. 468 (SD MS, 2000), the debtor's plan was

noncriminal conduct, effect of on good faith

not proposed in good faith where the debtor had taken money from his grandmother and was using Chapter 13 to avoid paying a state court judgment that his grandmother had obtained against him.

On the other hand, in In re Belt, 106 B.R. 553 (ND IN, 1989), the court held that a Chapter 13 plan may be confirmed even in the face of egregious prefiling conduct by the debtor if other factors suggest that the plan represents a good-faith effort by the debtor to satisfy his creditors' claims. The court held that the fact the debtor's plan provided only nominal payments on a large claim for damages resulting from the debtor's drunken driving, which was nondischargeable under Chapter 7, did not preclude a finding of good faith because, although the debtor's prefiling conduct was negligent and reckless, his acts were not intentional or consensual. See also In re Tobiason, 185 B.R. 59 (NE, 1995). In In re Baez, 106 B.R. 16 (PR, 1989), a plan was proposed in good faith despite a creditor's allegation of bad faith for failing to make any payments on a conditional automobile sales contract, which acts had previously been found to constitute sufficient bad faith to warrant the granting of relief from the automatic stay. See also, in re Keach, 243 B.R. 851 (B.A.P. 1st Cir., 2000) (stating that the debtor's prefiling conduct is not relevant to the issue of good faith); In re Lapin, 302 B.R. 184 (SD TX, 2003) (holding that a debtor's pre-bankruptcy mindset is only relevant if the debtor intended to seek Chapter 13 protection at the time of committing any alleged fraud, otherwise, only post-petition intent should be considered when determining good faith); In re Jongsma, 402 B.R. 858 (ND IN, 2009).

prefiling conduct, effect of on good faith

Even though Section 1325(a)(3) deals with the good faith of the debtor in proposing a plan, the courts often consider the debtor's motive in filing the Chapter 13 petition when ruling on the issue of good faith under Section 1325(a)(3). In determining whether the debtor's motive in filing under Chapter 13 is consistent with the spirit of Chapter 13, courts often consider the related issues of whether the debtor has substantial debts that are dischargeable under Chapter 13 but not under Chapter 7 and whether the debtor has sought bankruptcy relief in the recent past. In essence, many bankruptcy courts question the good faith of debtors who appear to be using Chapter 13 as a subterfuge to inexpensively rid themselves of nondischargeable debts or who appear to be using Chapter 13 only to unfairly frustrate a particular creditor. Neither of these motives are consistent with the spirit and intent of Chapter 13. See In re Rasmussen, 888 F.2d 703 (10th Cir., 1989); In re Breon, 94 B.R. 576 (MN, 1988); In re Hazel, 68 B.R. 287 (ED MI, 1986); In re Smith, 328 B.R. 797 (WD MO, 2005); In re Russell, 348 B.R. 441 (SD TX, 2006).

good faith, effect on of debtor's motive in filing under Chapter 13

The intent of Chapter 13 is designed to encourage debtors to make a sincere effort to repay as much of their prepetition debts as they can reasonably afford from their future income. In re Warner, 115 B.R. 233 (CD CA, 1989). The broader discharge available to Chapter 13 debtors who successfully complete a plan is generally viewed as the debtor's reward for making a good faith effort to repay as much of his or her unsecured debts as is feasible over a three to five year period.

Chapter 13, intent and purpose of

case filed to deal with non-dischargeable debts, effect of on good faith

Many Chapter 13 cases are filed for the purpose of dealing with debts that are nondischargeable under Chapter 7. The general rule is that the mere fact that a debt dealt with in the debtor's plan is nondischargeable under Chapter 7 and dischargeable under Chapter 13, while relevant on the issue of good faith, is not alone sufficient to warrant a finding of bad faith under Section 1325(a)(3). See In re Smith, 848 F.2d 813 (7th Cir., 1988), and In re Manthey, 262 B.R. 89 (ND CA, 2001). A plan whose primary purpose is to discharge all or most of a nondischargeable debt is not per se proposed in bad faith under Section 1325(a)(3). See In re Schaitz, 913 F.2d 452 (7th Cir., 1990). However, Chapter 13 plans which propose to repay only a small portion of a debt that would be nondischargeable under Chapter 7 are given particular scrutiny under Section 1325(a)(3). See In re Caldwell, 895 F.2d 1123 (6th Cir., 1990) (stating that bankruptcy courts should not approve Chapter 13 plans which are nothing but "veiled" Chapter 7 plans (i.e., plans which pay little or nothing to unsecured creditors and whose primary purpose is to discharge debts)); see also, In re Larson, 245 B.R. 609 (MN, 2000).

good faith, existence of in cases filed to discharge debts

In In re Rasmussen, 888 F.2d 703 (10th Cir., 1989), the court held that a Chapter 13 filing was not made in good faith under Section 1325(a)(3) because the filing was found to be a manipulation of the Bankruptcy Code designed to obtain the discharge, for a minimal payment under a Chapter 13 plan, of a debt that was nondischargeable under Chapter 7. See also, In re Newberry, 84 B.R. 681 (ED CA, 1988), where the court held that for purposes of establishing good faith under Section 1325(a)(3), the burden is on the debtor to prove that the principal purpose of his or her plan is consistent with the spirit and intent of Chapter 13, which is rehabilitation and repayment, and is not proposed primarily to obtain the discharge of a debt that would be nondischargeable in a Chapter 7 case.

Section 109(g), effect of on repetitive filings

Repetitive bankruptcy filings by the debtor are also viewed by many courts as a bad faith attempt to manipulate the Bankruptcy Code to the detriment of creditors. In this regard it should be noted that the enactment of 11 U.S.C. § 109(g) in 1984 was clearly an attempt by Congress to deal with the issue of repetitive bankruptcy filings. It can be argued, therefore, that because Congress chose to deal with the issue of repetitive filings in Section 109(g), the intent of Congress was that this matter should not be an issue in determining good faith under Section 1325(a)(3). See Johnson v. Home State Bank, 501 U.S. 78, 87, 77, 111 S. Ct. 2150 (1991). See article 1.01 of this handbook for a discussion of Section 109(g).

repetitive filings, types of

Chapter 20 filing, what constitutes

Repetitive or serial bankruptcy filings may consist of a series of Chapter 13 cases or a Chapter 7 case followed by one or more Chapter 13 cases. Note that it is not uncommon for a debtor to file a Chapter 7 case to obtain the discharge of his or her dischargeable debts and then file a Chapter 13 case for the purpose of dealing with the nondischargeable debts. Serial cases of this sort are often referred to as "Chapter 20" filings. See In re Bridges, 326 B.R. 345 (DC SC, 2005).

In Johnson v. Home State Bank, 501 U.S. 78, 111 S. Ct. 2150 (1991), the Supreme Court held that a claim arising from a mortgage lien could be dealt with in a Chapter 13 plan even though the debtor's personal liability for the underlying debt had previously been discharged in a Chapter 7 case. In that case the court held that by expressly prohibiting various forms of serial filings in Section 109(g) and by not prohibiting the filing of a Chapter 13 case by a Chapter 7 debtor, Congress indicated that it did not intend to prevent such filings. The court also implied that the issue of the debtor's good faith in the filing of the subsequent Chapter 13 case could be considered by the court under Section 1325(a)(3). See 501 U.S. 78, 87.

Johnson v. Home State Bank, holding of case

The rule after Johnson v. Home State Bank, supra, appears to be that "Chapter 20" filings are not prohibited by the Bankruptcy Code but the motive of the debtor in filing the subsequent Chapter 13 case may be considered by the court in ruling on the issue of whether the debtor's plan was proposed in good faith. See In re Bridges, 326 B.R. 345 (DC SC, 2005); In re Pickering, 195 B.R. 759 (MT, 1996); In re Hodurski, 156 B.R. 353 (MA, 1993); In re Sunderland, 157 B.R. 39 (MD FL, 1993). If the debtor's circumstances have changed since the Chapter 7 filing or if the Chapter 13 case is filed primarily to obtain more time in which to pay off claims that were nondischargeable in the Chapter 7 case, then a finding of good faith is likely to be made. See In re Harlan, 179 B.R. 133 (WD AR, 1995); In re Metz, 820 F.2d 1495 (9th Cir., 1987). In In re Keach, 243 B.R. 851 (B.A.P. 1st Cir., 2000), filing a Chapter 13 case after a Chapter 7 case is not relevant to the issue of good faith in the Chapter 13 case. See also In re Bowen, 349 B.R. 814 (ID, 2006); but see In re Renz, 476 B.R. 382 (Bankr. E. D. N.Y. 2012) (Chapter 13 case filed in bad faith soon after receiving a discharge under Chapter 7).

Chapter 20 filings, permissibility of, cases

It is not uncommon to file a Chapter 13 case for the purpose of stopping a foreclosure or preventing the enforcement of a judgment against the debtor. It is clear that the filing of a Chapter 13 case for the purpose of stopping a foreclosure does not, without more, constitute bad faith under Section 1325(a)(3). See In re Vivado, 94 B.R. 785 (DC, 1989). It is also clear that filing a Chapter 13 case on the eve of a trial or immediately after the entry of judgment against the debtor does not, without more, constitute bad faith for purposes of Section 1325(a)(3). See In re Poole, 383 B.R. 308 (SC, 2007); Noreen v. Slattengren, 974 F.2d 75 (8th Cir., 1992); In re Robinson, 987 F.2d 665 (10th Cir., 1993); In re Smith, 848 F.2d 813 (7th Cir., 1988); In re March, 83 B.R. 270 (ED PA, 1988). However, the timing of such filings is relevant on the issue of good faith. See In re Smith, 848 F.2d 813 (7th Cir., 1988); In re Oliver, 186 B.R. 403 (ED VA, 1995).

case filed to stop creditor action, effect of on good faith

It is not bad faith per se to file a Chapter 13 case for the primary purpose of dealing with a single creditor. See In re Keenan, 364 B.R. 786 (NM, 2007), and Brown v. Davis, 172 B.R. 696 (SD GA, 1993). However, if the Chapter 13 case is filed merely as a litigating tactic to gain leverage in a state court action, then a finding of bad faith is likely to be entered in the Chapter 13 case. See In re Hawes, 73 B.R. 584 (ED WI, 1987). See also In re Scotten, 281 B.R. 147 (MA, 2002), In re Banks, 248 B.R. 799 (B.A.P. 8th Cir., 2000), and In re Virden, 279 B.R. 401 (MA, 2002), where good faith was found lacking in a Chapter 13 case that dealt with a single creditor.

case filed to deal with single creditor, effect of on good faith repetitive cases, effect of on good faith

Multiple or successive bankruptcy filings may, but do not alone, constitute bad faith under Section 1325(a). See In re Ford, 345 B.R. 713 (CO, 2006). If a debtor files repetitive bankruptcy cases which have had the cumulative effect of forestalling a foreclosure or frustrating the collection of a nondischargeable debt, then the court may infer that the cases were filed primarily for that purpose and deny confirmation of the debtor's plan because of bad faith. See In re Huerta, 137 B.R. 356 (CD CA, 1992). However, if the debtor's circumstances have changed between filings, it is more likely the court will find good faith. See In re Barrett, 964 F.2d 588 (6th Cir., 1992). See also, In re Oglesby, 161 B.R. 917 (ED PA, 1993); In re Corino, 191 B.R. 283 (ND NY, 1995) (good faith found despite the fact that the current Chapter 13 case was the debtor's fourth bankruptcy case). In In re Bates, 243 B.R. 466 (ND AL, 1999), the debtor's plan was found to have been proposed in good faith under the totality of the circumstances despite the fact that it was the debtor's sixth bankruptcy filing.

unfair discrimination, effect of on good faith

While it was obviously the intent of Congress that issues related to the unequal treatment of unsecured creditors be resolved under the unfair discrimination provisions of Section 1322(b)(1) of the Bankruptcy Code, many courts refer to this issue in their good faith rulings under Section 1325(a)(3). See In re Namic, 395 B.R. 594 (SC, 2008). For example, in In re Reyes, 106 B.R. 155 (ND IL, 1989), a finding of bad faith was made in part because the debtor proposed to pay 100 percent of an unsecured claim that was cosigned by his father and only 10 percent of other unsecured claims. See also, In re Whitelock, 122 B.R. 582 (UT, 1990); In re Cordes, 147 B.R. 498 (MN, 1992) (where a plan proposing full payment of a claim secured by the debtor's recreational boat prior to the payment of unsecured creditors, who would receive only 46 percent of their claims, not proposed in good faith). See also In re Leone, 292 B.R. 243 (WD PA, 2003). See article 3.02 of this handbook for further reading on the unfair discrimination requirements of Section 1322(b)(1).

debtor's attorney's fee, effect of on good faith

The court clearly has the authority to regulate and establish the amount paid to the debtor's attorney in a Chapter 13 case. See 11 U.S.C. §§ 329 & 330; Bankruptcy Rule 2017. This being the case, it is again difficult to see how the amount that is proposed in a plan to be paid to the debtor's attorney can be a good faith issue under Section 1325(a)(3) when the amount of the fee is governed by other statutes and can be summarily reduced by the court to a reasonable amount. In In re Belt, 106 B.R. 553 (ND IN, 1989), the court held that the fact that the debtor's plan proposed to pay the debtor's attorney $2,000 while paying unsecured creditors a total of only $2,900 was not indicative of bad faith under Section 1325(a)(3) because the attorney's fee was not unreasonable based on the services rendered in the case.

A showing that the debtor's earnings are likely to increase in the future is indicative of bad faith because it implies that the debtor is seeking to rid himself of his debts before his income increases. See In re Stoodt, 302 B.R. 549 (ND OH, 2003); In re Porter, 102 B.R. 773 (B.A.P. 9th Cir., 1989). An attempt by the debtor to mislead the bankruptcy court or evidence of fraudulent conduct by the debtor during the case is clearly indicative of bad faith by the debtor. See In re York, 282 B.R. 519 (MD GA, 2002); In re Murrell, 160 B.R. 128 (WD MO, 1993); In re Sitarz, 150 B.R. 710 (MN, 1993); Beard v. U.S. Trustee, 188 B.R. 220 (WD LA, 1995). On the other hand, a showing that the debtor is subject to special physical or financial hardships is normally indicative of good faith because it establishes a justifiable reason for the debtor's financial situation. See In re Corino, 191 B.R. 283 (ND NY, 1995); In re Owens, 82 B.R. 960 (ND IL, 1988); In re Oglesby, 161 B.R. 917 (ED PA, 1993).

increase in income, effect of on good faith

fraud or misleading of court, effect of on good faith

special hardship, effect of on good faith

Bibliography. For further reading on the issues discussed in this article, see the annotations and articles listed below.

Annotations:

Effect on good-faith requirement of Section 1325(a)(3) of Bankruptcy Code of 1978 for confirmation of Chapter 13 plan of debtor's offer of less than full repayment to unsecured creditors. 73 ALR Fed 10.

Articles:

Chapter 20 cases: an appropriate debtor tool? 4 J. Bankruptcy L. & Pract. 53, Nov.-Dec. 1994.

Chapter 20's: creative lawyering or manipulation of the Bankruptcy Code? 4 Hofstra Prop. L.J. 265, Spring 1992.

Honor thy creditors: The religious debtor's constitutional conflict with Section 1325(b). 98 Comm. L.J. 257, Summer 1993.

Chapter 13 good faith: a change in the law. 29 Tenn. B.J. 28, Mar.-Apr. 1993.

Individual consumer "Chapter 20" cases after Johnson v. Home State Bank: an introduction to nonbusiness serial filings under Chapter 7 and Chapter 13 of the Bankruptcy Code. 9 Bankruptcy Dev. J. 357, 1992.

Johnson v. Home State Bank and the Chapter 20 dilemma. 25 Conn. L. Rev. 173, Fall 1992.

Johnson v. Home State Bank: seven plus thirteen can equal twenty. 43 Mercer L. Rev. 1291, Summer 1992.

The bankruptcy good faith issue. 47 Consumer Fin. L.Q. Report 402, 1993.

SUBJECT INDEX

SUBJECT INDEX

SUBJECT INDEX

SUBJECT INDEX

SUBJECT INDEX

SUBJECT INDEX

www.ingramcontent.com/pod-product-compliance
Lightning Source LLC
LaVergne TN
LVHW080020210926
848481LV00011B/3069